Praise for Learning iPad Programming

"This amazing, thorough book takes an interesting approach by working through the design and development of a simple, yet realistic iPad app from start to finish. It is refreshing to see a technical book that explains how and why without inundating you with endless toy examples or throwing you into a sea of mind-numbing details. Particularly amazing is that it does this without assuming a large amount of experience at first. Yet it covers advanced topics at sufficient depth and in a logical order for all developers to get plenty of valuable information and insight. Kirby and Tom know this material and have done a great job of introducing the various frameworks and the reasoning behind how, why, and when you would use them. I highly recommend *Learning iPad Programming* to anyone interested in developing for this amazing platform."

—Julio Barros
   E-String.com

"This is a great introduction to iPad programming with a well-done sample project built throughout. It's great for beginners as well as those familiar with iPhone development looking to learn the differences in developing for the larger screen."

—Patrick Burleson
   Owner, BitBQ LLC (http://bitbq.com)

"Kirby Turner and Tom Harrington's *Learning iPad Programming* provides a comprehensive introduction to one of today's hottest topics. It's a great read for the aspiring iPad programmer."

—Robert Clair
   Author, *Learning Objective-C 2.0*

"*Learning iPad Programming* is now my go-to reference when developing apps for the iPad. This book is an absolute treasure trove of useful information and tips for developing on the iPad. While it's easy to think of the iPad as just a bigger iPhone, there are specific topics that need to be treated differently on the iPad, such as making best use of the larger display. *Learning iPad Programming* provides an incredible amount of depth on all areas of iPad programming and takes you from design to fully functioning application—which for me is a killer feature of the book. This should be in everyone's reference library."

—Mike Daley
   Author, *Learning iOS Game Programming*
   Cofounder, 71Squared.com

Learning iPad Programming

Learning iPad Programming

A Hands-On Guide to Building iPad Apps with iOS 5

Kirby Turner

Tom Harrington

✦✦Addison-Wesley

Upper Saddle River, NJ • Boston • Indianapolis • San Francisco
New York • Toronto • Montreal • London • Munich • Paris • Madrid
Capetown • Sydney • Tokyo • Singapore • Mexico City

The publisher offers excellent discounts on this book when ordered in quantity for bulk purchases or special sales, which may include electronic versions and/or custom covers and content particular to your business, training goals, marketing focus, and branding interests. For more information, please contact:

U.S. Corporate and Government Sales
(800) 382-3419
corpsales@pearsontechgroup.com

For sales outside the United States, please contact:

International Sales
international@pearson.com

Visit us on the Web: informit.com/aw

Library of Congress Cataloging-in-Publication Data

Turner, Kirby, 1966–
  Learning iPad programming : a hands-on guide to building iPad apps with iOS 5 / Kirby Turner, Tom Harrington.
        p.   cm.
  Includes index.
  ISBN 978-0-321-75040-2 (pbk. : alk. paper)
1. iPad (Computer)—Programming. 2. Application software—Development. 3. Mobile computing. 4. Laptop computers. 5. Macintosh (Computer) 6. iOS (Electronic resource) I. Harrington, Tom. II. Title.
  QA76.8.I863T87 2012
  005.258—dc23
                                2011042203

ISBN-13: 978-0-321-75040-2
ISBN-10:   0-321-75040-3
Text printed in the United States on recycled paper at Edwards Brothers in Ann Arbor, Michigan.
First printing, December 2011

Editor-in-Chief
Mark Taub

Senior Acquisitions Editor
Chuck Toporek

Development Editor
Chuck Toporek

Managing Editor
John Fuller

Project Editor
Anna Popick

Copy Editor
Barbara Wood

Indexer
Ted Laux

Proofreader
Linda Begley

Technical Reviewers
Patrick Burleson
Matt Martel
Erik Price
Mike Shields

Publishing Coordinator
Olivia Basegio

Cover Designer
Chuti Prasertsith

Compositor
Rob Mauhar

❖

To Steve Jobs, who saw further than most.
— Kirby Turner and Tom Harrington

To Melanie and Rowan, for their continuous love and support.
And to my mom, the person who made me who I am today.
—Kirby Turner

To Carey, who gave me the courage to pursue my dreams.
—Tom Harrington

❖

Contents at a Glance

Contents

Foreword

Aren't books great?

Anyone who's known me for any amount of time knows I'm a total bookworm. I love books. Well-written books are one of the cheapest and fastest tools for self-education. I can remember a number of books that were hugely significant in my personal and professional development—books like *Object Oriented Software Construction* by Bertrand Meyer; Scott Knaster and Stephen Chernicoff's early Mac programming books; Dave Mark's C programming books; Robert C. Martin's horribly titled (but wonderfully full of aha! moments) *Designing Object Oriented C++ Applications Using the Booch Method*; and of course the late W. Richard Stevens's UNIX and network programming books. I remember lessons learned from these tomes, even those I read over 25 years ago.

Unfortunately not all books are created equal. I've seen some real stinkers in my time. When I first made the transition from Mac programming to iPhone programming, some of the books I got were great. And some were terrible. Really terrible, almost as if someone had filed the serial numbers off of *Instant Visual Basic Programming Guide for Complete Dummies in 24 Hours* and pasted on pictures of iPhones. There was one early iPad book that literally had an error on every page I skimmed at the bookstore. Some were just typos. Some were subtle errors, understandable if you haven't already lived in the Cocoa universe for a couple of years. Some of it was downright bad advice, obviously from someone who did not know what he or she was doing. There is a certain expectation of trust when you drop your hard-earned currency on a book, and violating that trust is unforgivable.

So, this book, *Learning iPad Programming*. Is it worth the price? Does it fall into my first category of books (awesome) or the second (unequivocally lame)? Good question. Glad you asked.

First, a good book needs to cover its topic, and cover it well. *Learning iPad Programming*, just by judging its heft, contains a lot of material. Well, assuming you've got the print version in hand. *War and Peace* weighs the same as *The Little Prince* in ebook form, so it's hard to tell. Just skim through the table of contents and you can see that it covers a lot of stuff. A metric freakload of stuff. And it's all relevant stuff. It covers the basics like installing the development tools. Model-View-Controller. Master-Detail. Table views. `UIViewController`. Navigation views. Handling device rotation. There are also more advanced topics such as consuming Web services, the media library, touch gestures, data persistence, and the raw unpleasantness that is Apple's device provisioning. And there's some cutting-edge stuff, such as storyboards, AirPrint, AirPlay, iCloud, and Core Image. Kirby and Tom have suffered the arrows in their backs dealing with months of flaky prerelease software so that you don't have to.

Very good books are timely but not exploitative. I saw the first iPad programming book about three months after the device was announced. There was no way this book could convey the iPad gestalt to the reader because nobody had had a device in hand for that long. It was pumped out as fast as possible to hit the market, and it showed. The core of *Learning iPad Programming* has been in development for well over a year as I write this. Good books take time to achieve high levels of awesomeness.

Great books transcend their subject matter. This book is called *Learning iPad Programming*. It would be easy to assume that it just covers introductory iPad programming in a simplistic manner. "Views are cool!" "Yay! Tapping a button!" But it's more. Not many books have a single project that lives and evolves through the entire narrative. The reason not many books do this is because it is difficult to do well. Important toolkit features get shoehorned into weird places because the author didn't do enough up-front design. This book, though, takes you from design, to a throwaway prototype, to the Real Deal.

And then it goes further. Not many books talk about the inner game of design. This one does. Even fewer books talk about the inner game of debugging. Debugging is a fundamental part of the day-to-day life of a programmer, and few books devote more than a paragraph or two to it. *Learning iPad Programming* has an entire chapter on the topic, and it's much more than how to single-step with the debugger. As I was reading preproduction versions of the chapters so that I could sound halfway intelligent in this foreword, I emitted an audible "SQUEE" when I hit Chapter 25. I love debugging, and love seeing such an important topic covered in detail in what is ostensibly a beginner's book. And as you can tell, I love learning stuff. I learned some stuff from Chapter 25.

Finally, those who *create* the great books transcend the ordinary. The Mac and iPhone community is pretty small and well connected. You tend to learn quickly who the trusted players are. Many of the lame books I alluded to earlier are by individuals I had never heard of before, and never heard from again. No blogs, no appearances at conferences, no footprint on the community. Get in, crank out something, and get out.

Kirby and Tom are different. They're known entities. They have blogs. Tom has his name on a Core Data book. They've shipped products. They have happy customers. They answer questions online. They organize and speak at conferences. They organize CocoaHeads chapters. They have invested a great deal of their time into the betterment of the community. It is why I am honored and humbled that they asked me to write this foreword.

As you can probably tell, I'm pretty excited about this book. There are many excellent introductory iOS programming books. I recommend reading all of them (at least the good ones) because iOS is such a huge topic that even Kirby and Tom can't cover everything you need to know in one volume. But if you're specifically targeting the iPad, this one is the one to get. I have the feeling it's destined to become one of those influential books for some of you out there.

—Mark Dalrymple
    Cofounder of CocoaHeads, the international Mac and iPhone programmer community
    Author of *Advanced Mac OS X Programming: The Big Nerd Ranch Guide*
    November 12, 2011

Preface

In October 2011, Apple CEO Tim Cook shared some interesting facts about the iPad, including

- Ninety-two percent of Fortune 500 companies are testing or deploying iPads.
- Over 80 percent of U.S.-based hospitals are testing or piloting the iPad.
- Every state in the United States has some type of iPad deployment program in place or in pilot.

And the news about the iPad doesn't stop there. The FAA has approved the use of the iPad instead of paper charts for on-duty airline pilots. Without a doubt, the iPad is changing the way people think about (and use) computers today. And it continues to get better with the release of iOS 5, the latest operating system for iPad and iPhone devices.

Make no mistake, the iPad packs a punch. With its patented multi-touch interface, an onboard graphics chip, the powerful A5 processor, and 3G and/or WiFi networking, the iPad is the benchmark in a post-PC world. More important, though, is how the iPad 2 fits into the Mac/iOS ecosystem. Mac OS X Lion and iOS 5 users can use FaceTime for video chat from desktop to device. What's more, iOS 5's iMessage enables users to text from their iPad with other iPad and iPhone users. The iPad is a unique marriage of hardware and technology, and it is the Gold Standard for tablets.

This book is written with iOS 5 in mind and is aimed at new developers who want to build apps for the iPad. The book will also appeal to iPhone developers who want to learn more about how to make their apps sing on the iPad. While some people look at the iPad as just a bigger iPhone, it really isn't. There is a lot more that you as a developer can do with the iPad from a user interface perspective that you just can't do on the iPhone.

While the book will include brief discussions of iPhone programming where appropriate, the primary focus of the book is the iPad. The book highlights those areas of the iOS 5 SDK that are unique to the iPad, and it isn't a rehash of similar books targeting the iPhone. Additionally, the book covers new features in iOS 5, such as container view controllers, iCloud, and Core Image, as well as some of the great new features in Xcode 4.2, such as storyboarding. Apple has gone to great lengths to make it easier for you to develop for iOS and OS X, and the plan for this book is to make it even easier for you to get there.

What Will I Learn?

This book will teach you how to build apps specifically for the iPad, taking you step by step through the process of making a real app that is freely available in the App Store right now! The app you'll build in this book is called PhotoWheel.

> **Download the App!**
>
> You can download PhotoWheel from the App Store: **itunes.apple.com/app/photowheel/ id424927196&mt=8**. The app is freely available, so go ahead—download PhotoWheel, and start playing around with it.

PhotoWheel is a spin on the Photos app that comes on every iPad (pun intended). With PhotoWheel you can organize your favorite photos into albums, share photos with family and friends over email, and view them on your TV wirelessly using Air-Play. But more important than the app is what you will learn as you build the app.

You will learn how to take advantage of the latest features in iOS 5 and Xcode, including storyboarding, Automatic Reference Counting, iCloud, and Core Image. You will learn how to leverage other iOS features such as AirPrint, AirPlay, and Grand Central Dispatch (GCD). And you will learn how to extend the boundaries of your app by communicating with Web services hosted on the Internet.

Think of this book as an epic-length tutorial, showing you how you can make a real iPad app from start to finish. You'll be coding along with the book, and we'll explain things step by step. By the time you have finished reading and working through this book, you'll have a fully functional version of PhotoWheel that you can proudly show off to friends and family (you can even share it with them, too). Best of all, you'll have confidence and the knowledge of what it takes to design, program, and distribute iPad apps of your own.

What Makes the iPad So Different?

While the iPad runs the same version of iOS that runs on the iPhone, iPod touch, and Apple TV, the iPad is significantly different from those other iOS-based devices. Each device is used differently, and iOS brings certain things to the table for each of them. For example, the version of iOS that runs in your Apple TV doesn't yet offer the same touch interface; in fact, the interface is totally different. Apple TV's UI runs as a layer on top of iOS, providing a completely different user experience.

But the iPad is so different. It is not something you can hold in the palm of your hand, like the iPhone and iPod touch. You use both hands. You swipe. You touch. You interact with it more than with most iPhone apps. It's easy to dismiss the iPad as "just a large iPhone," but it really isn't.

While the physical size is the obvious difference between the iPad and iPhone, the real difference, the difference that sets the iPad apart from the iPhone, is conceptual. The conceptual differences stem from how an iPad application is designed and how the user interacts with the application. And the conceptual differences start with the bigger display.

Bigger Display

The iPad's bigger screen provides more than double the screen real estate found on the iPhone. This means that your application can display more information, giving you more space to work with for your user interface. A good example of this is WeatherBug.

WeatherBug HD has been designed to take full advantage of the iPad's larger screen. As you can see in Figure P.1, the iPad version of WeatherBug displays much more weather-related information on a single screen than you can get on the iPhone

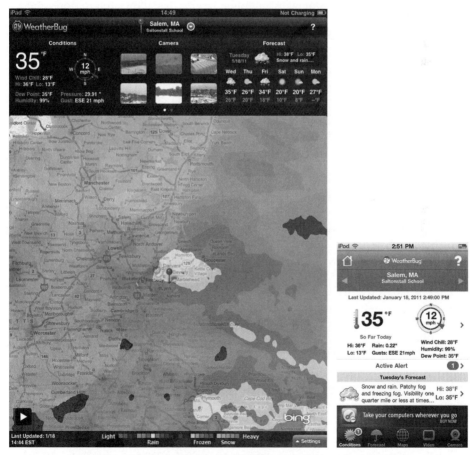

Figure P.1   On the left is the WeatherBug app displayed on the iPad. The screen shot on the right is the same WeatherBug app running on the iPhone. (Used with permission of Earth Networks.)

version. Instead of your having to touch and swipe (and sometimes pray) to find additional weather information, WeatherBug HD on the iPad gives you everything you need to know right on the main screen. No additional touching or swiping needed. Of course, additional detail is still available at a touch.

Less Hierarchical

Because of the smaller screen, many iPhone applications tend to sport a hierarchical navigation system. You see this throughout many iPhone apps. The user taps an item and a new screen slides into view. Tap another item and another view slides in. To navigate back, you tap a back button, usually found in the upper left corner of the screen.

The Dropbox app illustrates the hierarchical navigation system quite well. Dropbox, for those who may not know, is an online service that allows you to store your data files, documents, and images in the cloud. Stored files are then synced across all of your computers and devices that run the Dropbox client software. Say, for example, you are working on a text document from your laptop. You save the text document to your Dropbox folder. Later you need to review the text document, so you open the same text document on your iPhone. Dropbox makes this possible.

When you use the Dropbox app on your iPhone, you see a list of files and folders sorted alphabetically. Tapping a file or folder will open it, causing the new screen to slide into view. If you open a file, you see the contents of the file. If, however, you open a folder, you see a new list of files and folders. Continue tapping folders to navigate further down the hierarchy.

To move back up the hierarchy, tap the back button in the upper left corner. The text label for this button can vary. Usually it displays the name of the previous item on the stack, but sometimes it displays the word *Back*. While the text label may vary, the style of the back button does not. The back button has a pointy left side. This almost arrowlike style conveys a sense of moving backward through the screens.

The forward and backward navigation through the hierarchy is illustrated in Figure P.2.

Dropbox is also available for the iPad. So how did the developers redesign an app that obviously requires hierarchical navigation to make it feel flatter, less hierarchical? They took advantage of an iOS object available only to the iPad called `UISplitViewController`, shown in Figure P.3.

The split view controller is a nonvisual object that controls the display of two side-by-side views. When you hold your iPad in landscape mode, the two views are displayed side by side. Rotate your iPad to portrait and the left-side view disappears. This allows the user to focus his attention on the main content displayed on the right side.

> **Note**
>
> You get hands-on writing a split-view-based application in Chapter 8, "Creating a Master-Detail App."

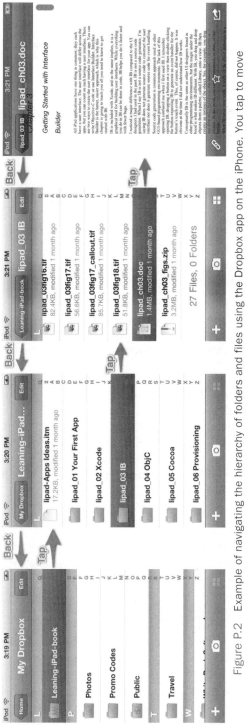

Figure P.2 Example of navigating the hierarchy of folders and files using the Dropbox app on the iPhone. You tap to move forward, or drill down, to more content, and you tap the back button to move backward.

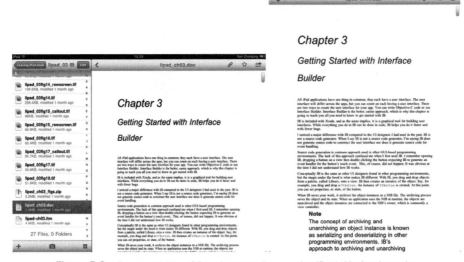

Figure P.3   Screen shots of Dropbox running on the iPad. Notice how the navigation is displayed in the left-side view when the device is held in a landscape orientation and is hidden when the iPad is rotated to portrait.

This view pattern is often called "master-detail," where the master view is displayed on the left side and the detail view is displayed on the right side. The master view is used to navigate the hierarchy of data, or in the case of Dropbox, the master view is used to navigate the list of files and folders. When you find the file you want to view, tap it in the master view and the file contents are displayed on the right in the detail view. Rotate your iPad to a portrait position to focus your attention on the file's content, hiding the master view.

Orientation Matters

Most iPhone applications support only a single orientation. Many iPhone games are played in landscape mode, while many other iPhone apps are displayed in portrait. Like the iPad, the iPhone does support rotation and orientation, but the small size of the device makes supporting different orientations unnecessary. Most users hold their iPhones in portrait mode with the Home button at the bottom when using applications, rotating to landscape only to play a game.

The iPad is different. With the iPad, users grab the device and turn it on without regard to a certain orientation. This is even truer when the iPad is not in a case. Try this little experiment...

Place your iPhone, or iPod touch, on your desk or table with the Home button pointing at 10 o'clock. Walk away or turn around. Come back to the device and pick it up. Take a look at the device as you hold it in your hand. There's a good chance that as you picked up the device, you rotated it so that the Home button is at the bottom. You did this rotation even before turning on the device. It is an almost natural instinct to hold your iPhone with the Home button at the bottom.

Now try the same experiment, but this time use your iPad. Place it on your desk or table. Make sure the Home button is positioned away from you, say, at 10 o'clock, then walk away. Come back and pick up your iPad. Chances are good you did not rotate the device. Instead, you are likely holding your iPad in the same orientation it was in before you picked it up.

Multi-Touch Amped Up

Did you know that the iPad and iPhone support the same multi-touch interface? They do. As a matter of fact, the iOS multi-touch interface supports up to 11 simultaneous touches. This means that you can use all your fingers—and maybe one or two more if you have a friend nearby—to interact with an application.

The iPad with its larger screen makes multi-touch more feasible. While two-handed gestures have limited use on the iPhone, they can become a natural part of interacting with an iPad application. Take, for example, Apple's own Keynote app for the iPad. It takes advantage of the multi-touch interface to provide features once reserved for the point-and-click world of the desktop. Selecting multiple slides and moving them is just one example of how Keynote on the iPad maximizes the user experience with multi-touch.

So you already know that the multi-touch interface supports up to 11 simultaneous touches, but how can you confirm this? Write an iPad app that counts the number of simultaneous touches. That is exactly what Matt Legend Gemmell did. He wrote a really neat iPad app, shown in Figure P.4, that shows the number of simultaneous touches. But Matt went beyond just showing the touch count. He made the app sci-fi-looking, which also makes it fun to play with.

You can read more about Matt's iPad multi-touch sample and download the source code from his blog posting (**mattgemmell.com/2010/05/09/ipad-multi-touch**).

Another way to explore the iPad multi-touch interface is to play with Uzu for iPad, only $1.99 in the App Store (**bit.ly/learnipadprog-UzuApp**). Uzu is a "kinetic multi-touch particle visualizer" and it's highly addicting. (Figure P.5 doesn't do the app justice; you should really download and play around with Uzu if you want to see some clever use of multi-touch.)

The iPad Bridges the Gap between the Phone and the Computer

So, everyone agrees that the iPad is not an oversize iPhone. Great, glad to have you on the same page here. Now on to the larger question: Is the iPad a replacement for a laptop or desktop? No, not yet, but it's pretty darn close.

For many, the iPad represents a mobile device bridging the gap between the smartphone and a full-fledged computer, whether a laptop or desktop computer. While many individuals use the iPad for content consumption, the iPad is also used

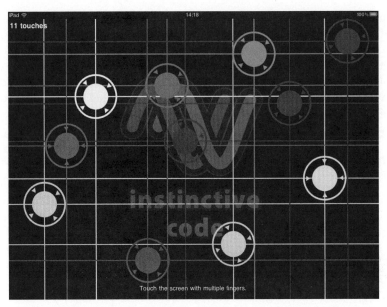

Figure P.4   Matt Legend Gemmell's multi-touch sample app for the iPad
illustrating 11 touches

Figure P.5   Uzu, the particle visualizer for the iPad

to perform a good number of tasks previously left to the desktop or laptop computer. This causes iOS developers to rethink how to implement software concepts that have been around for eons. Word-processing software is one such concept that is seeing new life on the iPad.

The iPad opens the door to a wide range of applications not feasible on the small form factor of the iPhone. Word processing, again, is one such application that comes to mind.

While the iPhone is great for capturing quick notes, it is not ideal for writing lengthy documents. And while it is technically possible to implement a full-featured word processor on the iPhone, why would you? The screen is too small, and even in landscape mode, typing two-thumbed on a tiny screen would be less than productive. The iPhone is ideal for performing simple, quick tasks—writing a note, scheduling an event, marking a to-do item as complete—but it is less than ideal for lengthier tasks such as writing a book.

Enter the iPad

The iPad provides an experience similar to a small laptop. And when combined with a wireless keyboard, your iPad becomes a nice setup for writing long documents. I'm speaking from experience. A lot of the text in this book was originally written on an iPad. I can't imagine what writing a book on an iPhone would be like, but I know what it is like on the iPad, and it is a joy. Best of all, the iPad allows you to concentrate on a single task. This eliminates distractions and gives you better focus on the task at hand.

Organization of This Book

This book provides you with a hands-on guide for, as the book's title states, learning iPad programming. It walks you through every stage of the process, from downloading and installing the iOS SDK to submitting the first application to Apple for review.

There are 27 chapters and one appendix in the book, as follows:

- Part I, "Getting Started"

    Part I introduces you to the tools of the trade. Here you learn about developer tools such as Xcode and Interface Builder. You learn how to write code using Objective-C and the Cocoa framework. And you learn what it takes to provision your iPad as a development device.

    - Chapter 1, "Your First App"

        This chapter immediately immerses you in creating your first application. The chapter provides a step-by-step guide to creating a simple, but functional, iPad application that runs in the iPad Simulator. You'll use Xcode to create the application, which means there is also some light coding to be done, but knowledge of Objective-C is not required at this point in the book. The goal of this chapter is for you to immediately get your hands on the tools and the code you'll use to create iPad apps.

- Chapter 2, "Getting Started with Xcode"

Xcode is the developer's IDE (Integrated Development Environment) used to write Objective-C code for iPad applications. This chapter highlights key features of Xcode, including recommended preference settings, commonly used shortcut keys, and descriptions of the various windows you will see when using Xcode.

- Chapter 3, "Getting Started with Interface Builder"

In this chapter, you explore Interface Builder (IB). Interface Builder is the tool used to create an application user interface (UI) with no programming required. This chapter explains how to use IB and many of its useful features. In addition, the chapter warns you about common mistakes made when using IB, such as forgetting to associate an event to an IBAction.

- Chapter 4, "Getting Started with Objective-C"

This chapter introduces you to Objective-C with a brief overview of the programming language of choice for iPad programming. The goal for this chapter is not to be a comprehensive review of the programming language but instead to provide enough information to get you started writing your first real iPad app.

- Chapter 5, "Getting Started with Cocoa"

A programming language is only as powerful as the frameworks that support it, and Cocoa provides an impressive stack of frameworks and a library that make it possible for you to build your iPad app in less time.

- Chapter 6, "Provisioning Your iPad"

Walking down the yellow brick road to the wonderful world of iPad development can have its own set of scary moments. One of the scariest is dealing with provisioning profiles, certificates, and registering a device for testing. Xcode 4 provides improvements in this area, but it is still far from perfect. This chapter guides you through the scary forest of provisioning profiles, certificates, and device registration.

- Chapter 7, "App Design"

You can't build an app if you don't know what you're building. This chapter shares tips on designing an application before the first line of code is ever written.

- Part II, "Building PhotoWheel"

Part II is the heart of the book. This is where you get hands-on building a real iPad app. The app you build is no simple Hello World app. It is PhotoWheel, a full-featured photo app. In Part II, you learn everything from custom animations for view transitions to iCloud syncing to viewing your photos on TV.

- Chapter 8, "Creating a Master-Detail App"

  You start building PhotoWheel by first building a prototype of it. While building the prototype you get a chance to learn about the split-view controller used in master-detail apps.

- Chapter 9, "Using Table Views"

  In this chapter, you learn the basics of displaying data using table views. You also learn how to reorder, delete, and even edit data displayed in a table view.

- Chapter 10, "Working with Views"

  In this chapter, you dive into the world of views. Here you learn how to create a custom wheel view for displaying photos.

- Chapter 11, "Using Touch Gestures"

  In this chapter, you learn how to take advantage of the iPad's multi-touch screen. You learn to use touch gestures so that users can interact with your app.

- Chapter 12, "Adding Photos"

  PhotoWheel is about photos, so it is only natural that you need to learn how to add photos to the app. In this chapter, you learn how to retrieve photos from the Photos app library and how to take new photos using the built-in camera.

- Chapter 13, "Data Persistence"

  PhotoWheel won't be very useful if people can't save their work. There are numerous methods for storing and retrieving app data. In this chapter, you explore two of them, and you learn to use Core Data.

- Chapter 14, "Storyboarding in Xcode"

  A storyboard is an exciting new way for designing an app's user interface. In this chapter, you get hands-on with storyboarding, and you learn how you can do more with less code using Interface Builder.

- Chapter 15, "Doing More with View Controllers"

  A storyboard can take you only so far. At some point in time, you must write code to make your app really shine. In this chapter, you learn how to take advantage of view controllers to do more.

- Chapter 16, "Building the Main Screen"

  In this chapter, you dive into PhotoWheel. Prototyping is over and you have the basic UI in place with a storyboard. Now it's time to build the main screen, and that's exactly what you do in this chapter. You also learn how to use container view controllers, and you build a custom grid view that can be used in other projects.

- Chapter 17, "Creating a Photo Browser"

  In this chapter, you learn how to use a scroll view to create a full-screen photo browser. You also learn how to use a pinch gesture to zoom in and out on a photo.

- Chapter 18, "Supporting Device Rotation"

  Users expect iPad apps to display properly regardless of how the device is being held. A user may hold his iPad with the Home button on the left or right, or maybe on the top or bottom. And it is your job to ensure that your app displays properly regardless. That is what you learn in this chapter: how to support device rotation.

- Chapter 19, "Printing with AirPrint"

  This chapter gets straight to the point and teaches you how to print from your app using AirPrint.

- Chapter 20, "Sending Email"

  Virtually everyone has an email account these days, and everyone loves looking at photos. So it only makes sense that PhotoWheel users want to share photos with family and friends using email. In this chapter, you learn how to send email from your app.

- Chapter 21, "Web Services"

  Adding photos already found on your iPad to PhotoWheel is a nice exercise, but many people keep their photos stored elsewhere. In this chapter, you learn how to communicate between an iPad app and a Web server to search for and download photos from Flickr.

- Chapter 22, "Syncing with iCloud"

  Many people have multiple iOS devices, and it would be great if they could use PhotoWheel with the same data on all of them. Syncing can be hard, but with iCloud it is a lot easier than it could be. In this chapter, we add online syncing of photos and albums.

- Chapter 23, "Producing a Slideshow with AirPlay"

  The iPad has a great screen, but you might want to show photos to a group, and it's awkward to gather everyone around a hand-held device. In this chapter, you see how to make use of external wireless displays—a large TV set, maybe—from an iPad app. And you do it using AirPlay, so you don't need to run cables across the room.

- Chapter 24, "Visual Effects with Core Image"

  Core Image is an amazingly cool framework for analyzing and changing images. As if color effects and automatic photo enhancement weren't enough, you can also use Core Data Image to locate the faces of any people in the picture. You add all of this to PhotoWheel in a convenient user interface that allows people to preview effects before committing to them.

- Part III, "The Finishing Touches"

  In the final part of the book, you learn tips on debugging your app. But more important, you learn how to distribute your app to others.

- Chapter 25, "Debugging"

  At this point you know how to create an iPad application, but what happens when a problem occurs? This chapter is devoted to application debugging. It introduces you to the GDB and shows you how to turn on and off break-points, and how to use sounds to debug. The chapter also introduces you to more advanced debugging techniques such as using Instruments to track down memory leaks.

- Chapter 26, "Distributing Your App"

  The application is written. It has been debugged and tested. The next step is getting the application into the hands of users. This chapter explores the options for distributing iPad applications, focusing on the two most commonly used distribution methods: Ad Hoc and App Store.

- Chapter 27, "The Final Word"

  The book ends with some final words of encouragement for the new iPad programmer.

- Appendix A, "Installing the Developer Tools"

  This appendix walks you through the steps needed to start programming for the iPad. This includes setting up an iOS developer account, downloading the iOS SDK, and installing the developer tools on your Mac.

Learning iPad Programming takes you from app design to the App Store. Along the way you learn about the developer tools, the programming language, and the frameworks. But more important, you learn how to build a full-featured iPad app that you can show off to family and friends.

Audience for This Book

This book is intended for programmers who are new to the iOS platform and want to learn how to write applications that target the iPad. The book assumes that you are new to iPad programming and have little to no experience with Xcode and the Objective-C programming language. However, the book assumes that you have some prior programming experience with other tools and programming languages. It is not intended for individuals with absolutely no prior programming experience.

This book is targeted to programmers who want to learn how to develop sophisticated applications for the iPad using iOS 5. You are expected to have a Mac on which you can program using Xcode and Interface Builder, as well as an iOS developer account and an iPad. Some programming experience is helpful, particularly knowledge of C, although there is a chapter on object-oriented programming with Objective-C to give you a head start.

The book will also appeal to experienced iOS developers, people who have programmed and have shipped apps to the App Store for the iPhone and iPod touch. If you are an experienced reader, you can skip over the basics, if you so choose, and quickly get to work on the example projects used throughout the book.

Getting the Source Code for PhotoWheel

The source code from each chapter as well as the source code for PhotoWheel as presented in this book is available from the book's Web site (**learnipadprogramming .com/source-code/**). Work on PhotoWheel doesn't stop at the end of this book either. There is so much more to do with the app and so much more to learn. The most up-to-date source code is available on github (**github.com/kirbyt/PhotoWheel**).

You will also find more how-to articles and tips for improving PhotoWheel at the book's blog site (**learnipadprogramming.com/blog/**).

And should you have additional questions, or want to report a bug or contribute a new feature to PhotoWheel, feel free to send email to kirby@whitepeaksoftware.com or tph@atomicbird.com, or send a message to @kirbyt or @atomicbird on Twitter.

There is plenty of code to review throughout the book along with exercises for you to try, so it is assumed that you have access to the Apple developer tools such as Xcode and the iOS SDK. Both of these can be downloaded from the Apple iOS Dev Center.[1]

Artwork Provided by

Matt McCray is the swell guy who provided the artwork in PhotoWheel. Reach out to Matt if you're looking for a designer for your next app. He can be reached at matt@elucidata.net and his Web site is at **www.elucidata.net**.

---

1. Apple's iOS Dev Center: **developer.apple.com/ios.**

Acknowledgments

As for any book that gets written, there's an entire cast and crew who remain hidden from the limelight; please take a moment to hear us out as we thank the supporting cast...

Acknowledgments from Kirby Turner

I want to first thank my wife, Melanie, and my son, Rowan, for their support and patience while I focused on completing this book. I want to thank Tom for agreeing to be coauthor during the final stages of this book, which would have been delayed even more if not for his help. I want to give a huge THANKS to Chuck Toporek for giving me this opportunity to write a book. And, of course, I want to say thanks to the technical reviewers and the production team for all their hard work in a short amount of time.

I want to send an extra thanks to Daft Punk for the *TRON: Legacy* album. It was the soundtrack for most of this book.

I want to thank Steve Jobs and the amazing Apple engineers for bringing the fun back to programming for me. Last, I want to thank the Mac and iOS developer community. None of this would be possible if not for the passion and spirit of this unique community.

Acknowledgments from Tom Harrington

I'd like to thank Kirby for inviting me to be part of this book. I'd especially like to thank Chuck Toporek, our technical reviewers, and the rest of the production team for all their hard work making me look good in print. Kirby and I wrote this book while iOS 5 was still in beta testing, and we often found it necessary to make revisions before we were finished, just to keep up with the pace of change in iOS and the developer tools. Everyone involved has done a great job dealing with the challenges of writing a book on a topic that's constantly in flux.

On a closely related note, thanks to everyone at Apple for their hard work on iOS 5 and the iPad. Without them we wouldn't have such a cool topic to write about.

Finally, as of this writing we've only just learned that Steve Jobs has passed away after a long and highly successful tenure as CEO of Apple. I got started writing software nearly 30 years ago on an Apple II, and it set the tone for my future career. Thanks for all you've done over the years, Steve.

About the Authors

This book is brought to you by...

Kirby Turner

Kirby Turner is an independent software developer and business owner focusing on Mac and iOS programming. Kirby has been programming since the early 1980s. He sells his own apps through his company, White Peak Software, and he does contract programming when time allows.

When Kirby is not sitting behind the keyboard, he can be found hanging out with his wife, Melanie, and son, Rowan, hiking the mountains of New England, kayaking the waters in and around Salem, Massachusetts, and snowboarding down mountains in search of perfect powder.

Tom Harrington

Tom Harrington switched from writing software for embedded systems and Linux to Mac OS X in 2002 when he started Atomic Bird, LLC. After six years of developing highly regarded Mac software, he moved to iPhone in 2008. He now develops iOS software on a contract basis for a variety of clients. In addition to this book, Tom is coauthor of *Core Data for iOS*. Tom also organizes iOS developer events in Colorado. When not writing software, he can often be found on his mountain bike. You can find Tom on Twitter as @atomicbird.

Part I

Getting Started

1

Your First App

There is no better way to learn than by actually doing something, so let's dive in by writing a really simple iPad app. The first application you will write is a Hello World app. Yes, the Hello World sample application is overdone, but don't worry. You will be building more sophisticated applications later in this book. For now, it's important to get your hands dirty with some code and the tools.

The goal for this chapter is to give you a sneak peek at the tools you will be using to build your iPad applications. If you are already familiar with Xcode, you may wish to skip ahead to Chapter 4, "Getting Started with Objective-C," or Chapter 6, "Provisioning Your iPad." If you are new to Xcode, please continue reading.

The rest of this chapter will guide you through the steps needed to create your first iPad application. The chapter does not go into detail about Xcode; those details are covered in the following chapters: Chapter 2, "Getting Started with Xcode," and Chapter 3, "Getting Started with Interface Builder."

Note

Before you begin, you must have Xcode and the iOS SDK installed on your Mac computer. If you do not have these installed, jump to Appendix A, *Installing the Developer Tools*, for instructions on how to set up your Mac for iPad programming. And yes, a Mac computer is required.

Creating the Hello World Project

Let's begin by launching Xcode. Xcode is available in Launchpad, shown in Figure 1.1, if you installed it from the Mac App Store; otherwise it is on the Dock. Click the Xcode icon to launch it.

Note

If Xcode is not available in Launchpad or on the Dock, you should add it. Xcode can be found (assuming a default install) on your hard drive in the directory */Developer/Applications/*. To add Xcode to the Dock, launch it. While Xcode is running, right-click (or **Control-click**) on the Xcode icon that appears in the Dock and select **Options > Keep in Dock**. This will keep the Xcode icon in the Dock even when the program is not running, making it easier to launch Xcode the next time you need it.

Figure 1.1   The Xcode icon as seen in Launchpad. The Mac App Store
Xcode Installer puts Xcode in the Developer group.

The first window you see after launching Xcode is the Welcome to Xcode screen, shown in Figure 1.2. You can do a number of things from this window. You can create a new project, connect to a source code repository, go to the *Xcode 4 User Guide* (a tutorial on using Xcode), or visit Apple's developer site (**developer.apple.com**). If you have created or opened Xcode projects in the past, you will also see a list of recent projects to the right. You can open a recent project by selecting one from the list and clicking **Open**.

Tucked away in the lower left corner is the **Open Other...** button. You can click this button to open an existing Xcode project found on your hard drive. Next to this button is a check box indicating whether the Welcome to Xcode window is displayed when Xcode launches.

> **Note**
>
> If you are new to Xcode, you should take the time to read through the *Xcode 4 User Guide*. The *User Guide* provides complete coverage of the entire Xcode tool set. You will learn about Xcode in this book; however, reading the official guides from Apple is always a good thing.

You want to create a new iPad application, so click **Create a new Xcode project**. This opens the new project window, as shown in Figure 1.3. Let's explore this

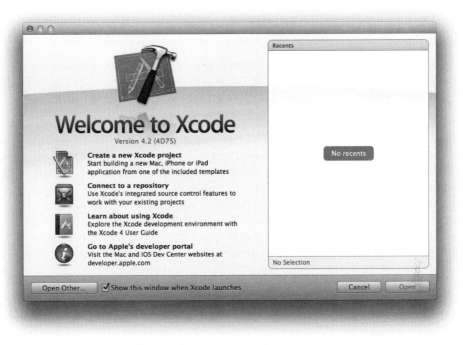

Figure 1.2   Welcome to Xcode window

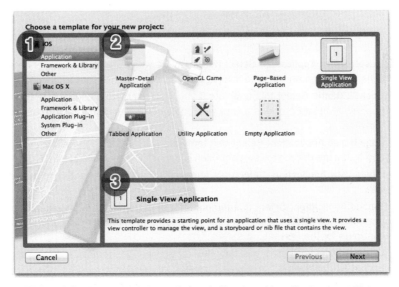

Figure 1.3   The new project window in Xcode, with callouts on sections
of Xcode's user interface (1: target type; 2: project template;
3: template detail)

window for a moment before continuing. As you can see in the figure, the new project has three main sections:

1. Target type
2. Project template
3. Template detail

In section 1, you select the target type, iOS or Mac OS X. iPad applications run on iOS, so you can ignore the Mac OS X target type for now. Under iOS you can build two types of targets: Application and Framework & Library. The Application type is exactly what the name implies; you use it to build iPhone and iPad applications. The Library target type is for building reusable static libraries, which you can also ignore for now.

The Hello World application you are building is just that, an application. So in section 1 under iOS, select **Application**. When you do this, you'll notice that the contents in section 2 change. Section 2 now displays the list of available templates for the selected target type. A template is used to generate the initial files needed for an Xcode project.

If you have spent time playing with your iPad, you may have noticed that there are some common application types, or styles. The templates listed in section 2 help speed the process of creating an application of a particular style. For example, if you wanted to create an application that looks similar to the Mail app on the iPad, you would select **Master–Detail Application**.

Application Templates

The application templates you'll encounter in Xcode after selecting iOS as your target include the following types:

- **Master-Detail Application:** Select this template when you have a master-detail-style application and wish to leverage the split view controller for display.
- **OpenGL Game:** Select this template if you wish to create a game using OpenGL ES. This template provides a view with an OpenGL scene and timer to animate the view.
- **Page-Based Application:** Select this template to create a book- or magazine-style app that uses the page view controller.
- **Single View Application:** Select this template for applications that use a single view.
- **Tabbed Application:** Select this template for applications that have separate areas defined by tabs. This template provides a tab bar controller and a view controller for the first tab.
- **Utility Application:** Select this template for applications that have a main view and an alternate view.
- **Empty Application:** This template provides a starting point for any type of application. Select this template when you want to start with a bare-bones project shell.

The Hello World application will consist of a single view, so select Single View Application from the list of templates. When you do this, notice that the contents of the template detail section change. This section shows a brief description of the template selected in the project template section.

Clicking the **Next** button takes you to the project options screen, shown in Figure 1.4. Project options vary slightly based on the template. Each template has options for the Product Name, Company Identifier, Bundler Identifier (which is completed for you based on the Company Identifier), and the Device Family. Additional options that may be found on an application template include Use Storyboard, Use Automatic Reference Counting, Use Core Data, and Include Unit Tests.

For the Hello World app you are building, enter "Hello World" for the Product Name. For the Company Identifier, enter your name or company name using the reverse domain name format. (For example, com.kirbyturner is my individual name and com.whitepeaksoftware is my company name.) Chapter 6, "Provisioning Your iPad," explains the relationship between the company and bundle identifiers and how they are used to form the App ID.

Next, select iPad as the Device Family. There are three device family types in iOS: iPad, iPhone, and Universal. The device family iPad indicates that the app is designed for and runs on the iPad only. The iPhone device family indicates that the app is designed for the iPhone, and Universal says that the app is designed for and runs on both the iPad and the iPhone.

You do not need storyboard and unit tests in this Hello World app, so leave those options unselected. But do select the Use Automatic Reference Counting option.

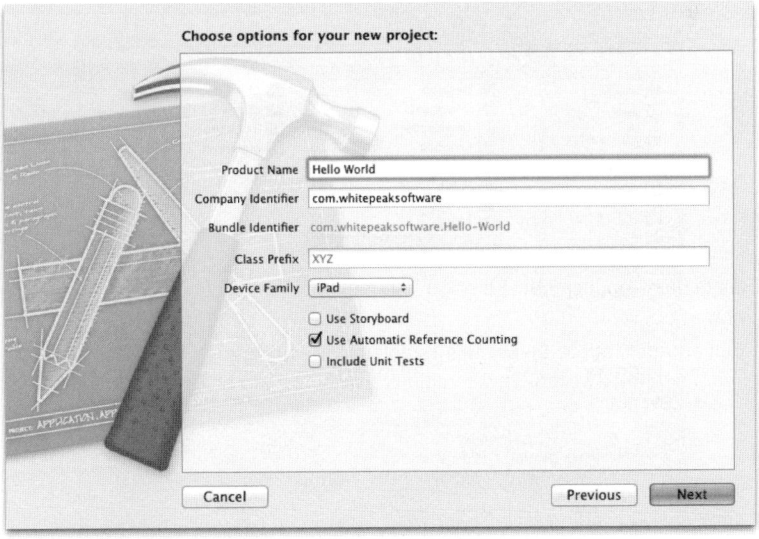

Figure 1.4   Project options for the Single View Application template

This option is explained in the Memory Management section of Chapter 4, "Getting Started with Objective-C." Click the **Next** button, choose a location to store the Xcode project, and click the **Create** button (shown in Figure 1.5).

Universal App

iPhone apps can run on the iPad, but they run in an iPhone emulator. They do not take advantage of the iPad's full screen. This leads to a less than ideal user experience. A universal app, on the other hand, is designed to take full advantage of the screen real estate provided by both the iPhone and the iPad. When a universal app is run on an iPhone, it looks as if it was designed for the iPhone. And when a universal app is run on an iPad, it looks like an iPad app, not an iPhone app.

A universal app gives the user the best of both worlds, a single app that looks great on both devices. However, this comes at a cost to you, the developer. Developing a universal app, in many ways, is like developing two separate apps, one for the iPad and one for the iPhone, and packaging them into a single app binary.

Universal apps are designed to target both the iPad and the iPhone. The focus of this book, however, is on writing iPad applications. To keep you focused, and to avoid the additional complexities of writing universal apps as you start your journey toward becoming an iOS developer, universal apps are not covered in this book.

Note

Storyboard is a concept, introduced in iOS 5, for visually designing user interfaces in iOS apps. Storyboarding is covered in Chapter 14, "Storyboarding in Xcode."

Figure 1.5   Choose the location where your Xcode project is stored.

Note

I like to keep all my source code together in a single location, so I created a *Source* directory within my home directory. I place all my Xcode projects under *Source* so I can easily locate them in the future.

Congratulations! You just created your first iPad application. You don't believe it? Click the **Run** button (shown in Figure 1.6), or type ⌘-**R**. Be sure that the active schema is set to the iPad Simulator. If it is not, click it and change it to the simulator.

When you click **Run**, Xcode compiles the project, builds an application package, installs the application on the iPad Simulator, and finally launches the application inside the simulator. As you can see in Figure 1.7, the application is nothing more than a white screen. Guess what? You just built your first flashlight app for the iPad!

Note

Sometimes you will notice a delay between the time the simulator is launched and the time your app launches within the simulator. When this delay happens, you see nothing but a black screen within the simulator. This is normal, and it usually happens only the first time you launch your app in the simulator.

You can take your newly created flashlight application and submit it to Apple for review. However, there is a high level of certainty that Apple will reject the

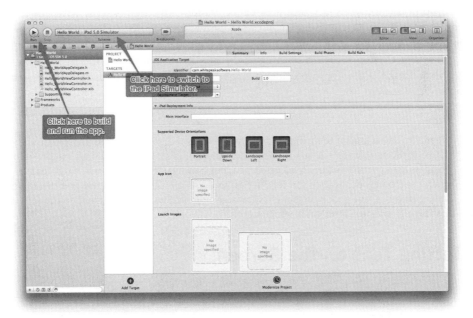

Figure 1.6   Xcode project window for the Hello World app

Figure 1.7   A "blank" single view app running in the iPad Simulator

application because of its lack of functionality. Besides, you are not done with this app. You want to build a Hello World application, and as you can see, "Hello World" does not appear when this application is run. So let's continue working on it.

First, stop the app, which is running in the simulator. You can do this by clicking the **Stop** button at the upper left side of Xcode or type ⌘-.. Now you're ready to start modifying the app.

> **Note**
>
> When you use a project template, Xcode gives you a valid, runnable iPad application without your having to write a single line of code. Maybe it is because I still have memories of being a teenager building apps 30 years ago, but I always get a little warm, fuzzy feeling when I see a new application run for the first time. As a matter of fact, the first thing I do when I create a new Xcode project is to build and run it. Seeing the application run for the first time gives me a little jolt of excitement.

Getting Text on the Screen

This is a Hello World app, so it should display "Hello World" somewhere on the screen. This can be accomplished by writing some code, but the easiest approach is to use Interface Builder. Interface Builder, or IB as it is often called, is the visual user interface designer that is built into Xcode. You'll learn more about IB in Chapter 3, "Getting Started with Interface Builder," but for now steps are provided to guide you through turning this blank application into a not so useful Hello World app.

To add "Hello World" to the display, you'll edit the file *ViewController.xib*. A *.xib* file, pronounced "zib," is an XML representation of a NIB file. A NIB file, or *.nib*, is the binary predecessor to the *.xib* file. Being text-based, a *.xib* file has the benefit of working better with version control systems when compared to the earlier binary *.nib* version. That said, *.xib* files are still compiled down to *.nib* files when you build the application.

What is a NIB file? A NIB file is a file created by Interface Builder to archive interface objects and their relationships. Put another way, a NIB represents the objects that make up the visual display of a screen. You create and edit NIB files using IB, and your application uses the NIB files at run time to display the user interface of the app.

Note

It's common for iOS developers to refer to a *.xib* file as a NIB file because it is, after all, just a text-based representation of a NIB file.

History

The *N* in NIB is a carryover from the NeXTSTEP days when it was used to indicate the NeXT-style property list file. And the *IB* indicates that the file is an Interface Builder file.

Begin by opening the file *ViewController.xib*, available in the Project navigator. This changes the contents of the Editor area. It displays the NIB file using the IB designer, as shown in Figure 1.8.

Note

Chapter 3, "Getting Started with Interface Builder," covers all the utilities available with IB.

IB has a set of available utilities for working with a NIB file. Type **Control-Option-⌘-3** to display the Object library. The Object library contains a list of visual and nonvisual components that are used to construct the user interface. In the filter bar at the bottom type "Label" without the quotes. This will filter the object list, displaying only label-type objects.

Drag and drop the label object onto the view's canvas area. This creates a new `UILabel` instance, which is the type of object representing a label. Next, open the Attributes inspector (**Option-⌘-4**). At the top of the Attributes inspector is a property named Text. Change the default value "Label" to "Hello World." Xcode should now look similar to the screen shot in Figure 1.8.

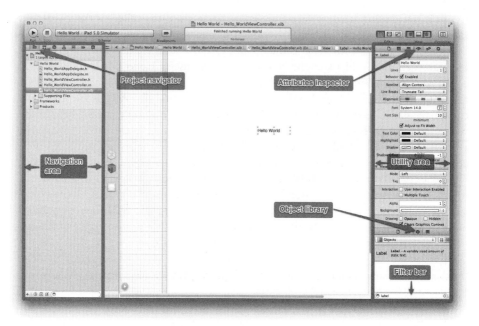

Figure 1.8   Adding "Hello World" to the main view of the app

Note

You may need to resize the label to view the entire "Hello World" content. To resize, move the mouse cursor to the right edge of the label object. The cursor will change to the resize indicator. Click and drag the mouse to the right to increase the width of the label.

Build and run the app in the iPad Simulator. Congratulations! You have written your first Hello World app for the iPad.

Note

Don't worry if none of this is making sense yet. Remember that the goal of this chapter is to give you a sneak peak into iPad programming by way of a step-by-step guide. This will give you a sense of what it is like to program for the iPad. Later chapters will explain all you need to know in detail, and before you know it, the steps for creating iPad applications will be second nature to you.

Say Hello

Now that the excitement of creating your first application for the iPad has worn off, let's extend the application by adding some functionality to it. Instead having it always display "Hello World," let's change the app to ask for a name, then display "Hello" to the name entered. This exercise is more involved and requires you to write some

Objective-C code. Do not worry if you have never seen Objective-C code before. You will be told exactly what to type, and you will explore Objective-C in more detail in Chapter 4, "Getting Started with Objective-C."

In life there is often more than one way to accomplish a task. The beauty of iPad programming is that there are many more ways than just one to do something. It is this flexibility in the development tools that makes many programmers prefer Xcode to other development tools. But it does take time to learn all the ins and outs, which can be frustrating for programmers new to Xcode.

One of the goals of this book is to show you the different ways a task can be accomplished. Armed with this knowledge, you can decide what approaches work best for you. For example, it is possible to use IB to generate Objective-C code that declares objects and actions defined in a *.xib* file. However, this discussion is saved for a later chapter. Instead, you're going to write the Objective-C code yourself to extend functionality in the Hello World app.

Two screen elements are needed, one that accepts user input for the name and the other to display "Hello." A third element, a button, is also needed to tell the app when to display the hello message. The NIB file defines the objects that make up the user interface, but there is no automatic connection between the objects and the source code. Instead, you must make the connection.

Start by opening the file *ViewController.h*. You can find this file in the Project navigator. When you click it, the Editor area will display the contents of the file. Modify the file's contents so that the source code looks exactly as it does in Listing 1.1.

Listing 1.1   **Modified Version of** *ViewController.h*

```
#import <UIKit/UIKit.h>

@interface ViewController : UIViewController

@property (nonatomic, strong) IBOutlet UILabel *helloLabel;
@property (nonatomic, strong) IBOutlet UITextField *nameField;

- (IBAction)displayHelloName:(id)sender;

@end
```

Next, open the file *ViewController.m*. Replace the generated source code found in the file with the source code in Listing 1.2.

Listing 1.2   **Modified Version of** *ViewController.m*

```
#import "ViewController.h"

@implementation ViewController

@synthesize helloLabel;
@synthesize nameField;
```

```
- (IBAction)displayHelloName:(id)sender
{
    NSString *hello = [NSString stringWithFormat:@"Hello %@", [nameField text]];
    [helloLabel setText:hello];
}

@end
```

The code in Listing 1.1 does a number of things. First, two properties are added to the class ViewController. These properties are marked with IBOutlet, which is a hint to IB that the class contains a reference to an object. Next, the method display-HelloName: is declared. It is marked with IBAction, another hint to IB, this time telling IB that an action exists in the class definition. At this point, the interface for the class ViewController has been defined.

What Are IBOutlet **and** IBAction?

IBOutlet and IBAction are special indicators for Interface Builder, hence the IB prefix. Interface Builder uses these indicators to connect objects and actions to elements in the user interface.

An IBOutlet is used to connect an object reference defined in Objective-C code to the object instance used in Interface Builder. For example, earlier in this chapter you placed a label on the view. That label is actually a UILabel. (UILabel is the class name for the label.) To access the label in code you must have a reference to the instance of the UILabel. You will see later in this chapter how you connect the reference declared in code to the instance displayed in IB.

An IBAction is used to connect an event sent by an object to a method defined in code. For example, a button has an event that is fired when a user lifts her finger. This action can be connected to the IBAction defined in the Objective-C class.

The code in Listing 1.2 represents the implementation for the class View-Controller. The implementation begins by synthesizing the properties declared in the class interface, helloLabel and nameField. Property synthesis is an Objective-C compiler feature that generates the accessor methods for these properties at compile time. More on this in Chapter 4, "Getting Started with Objective-C."

This is followed by the implementation for the method displayHelloName:. This method is the action that is called when the user interacts with the app, specifically when the user taps a button, which you will provide momentarily. The implementation of this method creates a local string variable containing the name entered by the user with the prefix "Hello." This string is then displayed on the screen as the text value for the helloLabel.

If you were to run the app at this point, you would see no difference from the earlier version. While the code has been updated to do what you want it to do, the user interface has not been updated and the connections for the outlets and actions have not been made.

> **Note**
>
> This decoupling of the source code, in this particular case the controller, and the user interface, aka the view, is representative of the Model-View-Controller design pattern, which is discussed in Chapter 5, "Getting Started with Cocoa."

To complete the app, you need to update the user interface and connect the UI objects to the properties defined in the controller class. Once again, open the file *ViewController.xib*. Double-click the Hello World label and change its text value to "What is your name?" Resize the label as needed to display the entire text.

Search through the Object library in the Utilities area for the Text Field object. Alternatively you can filter the object list by typing "text field" in the filter bar. Drag and drop a text field to the right of the "What is your name?" label.

Now search through the Object library for the Round Rect Button. Drag and drop an instance of the button to the right of the text field. In the Attributes inspector, change the Title property to "Say Hello."

Finally, search the Object library for Label, and drag and drop a new label onto the canvas, placing it under the other objects. Be sure to increase the width of the label to accommodate the string value created in the method `displayHelloName:`. The view should look similar to the screen shot in Figure 1.9.

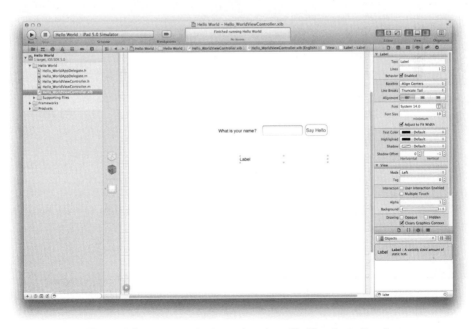

Figure 1.9   The modified user interface file *ViewController.xib*

Now it's time to connect the objects and events defined in the NIB with the outlets and actions defined in the view controller source code. One way to connect objects to outlets and actions is to **Control–Click** an object, then drag the mouse cursor to another object. When the mouse button is released, IB will display a Heads-Up Display (HUD) of the connection options. For example, when you **Control–Click** the File's Owner object (the translucent cube displayed in the left-side bar in the Editor area) and drag to the text field (shown in Figure 1.10), a HUD is displayed allowing you to connect the text field to the properties `nameField` and `view`. Select `name-Field` to connect the text field to the property defined in *ViewController.h*.

Do the same thing to connect the label to the property `helloLabel`. **Control–Click** the File's Owner cube and drag to the label where the output of the `display-HelloName:` will be displayed.

To connect the action to the **Say Hello** button, you **Control–Click** the button and drag to the File's Owner cube. This will assign the action `displayHelloName:` to the button event Touch Up Inside.

With the connections in place, the Hello World app is now functional. Build and run the app in the simulator. Tap the name field in the simulator to enter a value. Then tap the **Say Hello** button to display the hello message. The final app should look similar to the screen shot in Figure 1.11.

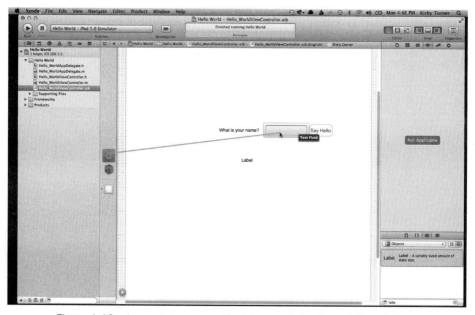

Figure 1.10   Connect the `nameField` property to the text field defined in the NIB file.

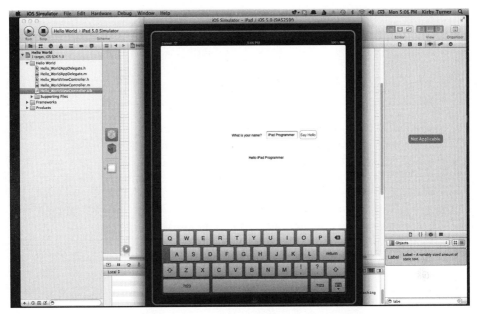

Figure 1.11   The new and improved Hello World app

You may be wondering how IB is able to identify the correct Objective-C header file. It's simple: The file's owner is defined as being of type `ViewController`. This tells IB which source file to look at for outlets and actions. You can see this by clicking the File's Owner cube, then typing **Option-⌘-3**. The class name is set to `View-Controller`. This is how an object defined in IB knows it type.

> **Note**
>
> A common mistake made in Interface Builder is forgetting to associate your outlets and actions. If you run the application and notice that the display does not update after the **Say Hello** button is touched, chances are good the Touch Up Inside event for the `UIButton` is not associated to the `displayName:` action.

Summary

Congratulations! You have completed your first iPad application. And you just got a sneak peak into iPad programming. This chapter should leave you itching to learn more. Before you dive into the meat of iPad programming, you need to learn more about the tools and programming language you will use. Let's begin by taking a closer look at Xcode in the next chapter.

2

Getting Started with Xcode

In Chapter 1, "Your First App," you used Xcode to create your first iPad application, but what is Xcode exactly?

Xcode is the combination of an Integrated Development Environment (IDE) and a collection of stand-alone development tools forming a complete developer tool set for Mac and iOS software development.

Xcode is the world you live in as you create and build your iPad apps. Xcode will become your friend. There will be times when the two of you get along nicely, but there will also be times when you disagree. You may even become annoyed with your new friend from time to time, but there's good news. As you spend more time together, you will get to know each other much better, and your friendship will grow. Who knows? You may even become BFFs (metaphorically speaking, of course).

Over more years than I care to count, I have used many different IDEs. When I first encountered Xcode—version 3 at the time—I thought I was stepping back in time. I thought, "It's a glorified text editor with some handy menu items and shortcuts for compiling projects." My opinion changed over time as I grew more accustomed to using Xcode day in and day out (and sometimes all night long). And with Xcode 4, things have only gotten better.

Xcode is simple, fast, and powerful, just like the applications created with it for the Mac, iPhone, and iPad. Each appears simple on the surface, allowing the power to be exposed as you become better acquainted with the software. Xcode is no different. As you become more familiar with Xcode, you'll start seeing its power and how it is more than just a glorified text editor.

This chapter helps jump-start your friendship with Xcode and helps you become better acquainted with it. So let's get started.

The IDE

Xcode is the developer tool most often used to create and build applications for the iPad. It's a complete IDE that you use to write Objective-C code, manage project files and settings, and make builds of your iPad applications. You also debug your apps using Xcode, and you can even unit test your code with it. Xcode does all this and more.

Disclaimer

Obviously there is no way to talk about all things Xcode in a single chapter. Some topics are discussed in later chapters (such as debugging in Chapter 25, "Debugging"), while other more advanced topics (such as refactoring) are left out completely. The point of this chapter is to be not a complete guide to Xcode but rather a starting point for getting familiar with it.

The programming language of choice for most iPad applications is Objective-C, so it is only natural that Xcode provides outstanding support for Objective-C. But Xcode also supports other programming languages. After all, Xcode is used for programming duties other than writing iPad apps.

Xcode supports the C, C++, Objective-C, Objective-C++, Python, Ruby, Apple-Script, and Java programming languages. Xcode also supports, with the help of third parties, GNU Pascal, Free Pascal, Ada, C#, Perl, and a list of other languages. And it does a reasonable job of supporting HTML and JavaScript.

Note

Despite Xcode's support for a number of programming languages, you are limited to C, C++, and most commonly Objective-C for writing iPad applications in Xcode. You cannot use the other languages such as Java or Perl for writing iPad applications. That doesn't mean you will not have a need for the other programming languages in Xcode. Many iPad developers use programming languages such as Python or Ruby to write scripts that aid in producing iPad applications. I, for one, use Python scripts to make Ad Hoc and App Store distribution builds of my applications.

Workspace Window

Xcode can open a project or workspace. A workspace is an Xcode file type that stores references to one or more projects that are typically related to one another, though a relationship is not required. When you open a project or workspace in Xcode, it is displayed in a workspace window.

The workspace window has five distinct areas, shown in Figure 2.1. These areas are

1. Toolbar

2. Navigation area

3. Editor area

4. Utilities area

5. Debug area

Toolbar Area

The toolbar is displayed at the top of the workspace window (Figure 2.2). It provides quick access to run and stop the app defined by the active scheme, change the active scheme and set the run destination (a device or the simulator), turn on and off all

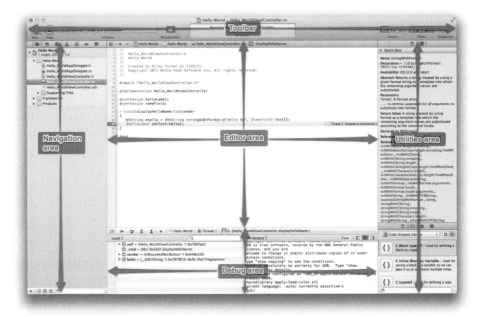

Figure 2.1   The workspace window and its areas

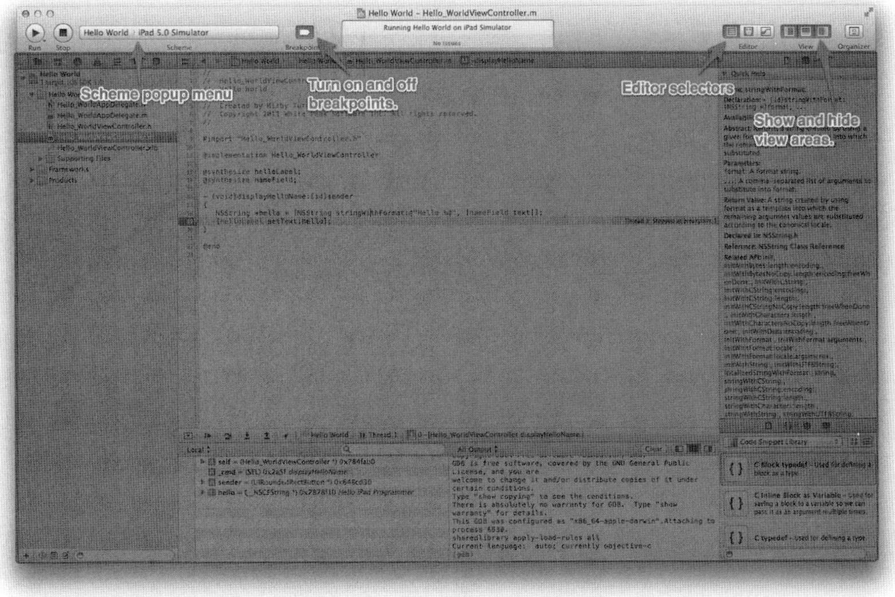

Figure 2.2   The workspace window toolbar

breakpoints, change editors, show and hide the other areas (Navigation, Utility, and Debug), and display Organizer. The center of the toolbar displays the current status of the project (is running, finished running, build succeeded, etc.).

Navigation Area

The Navigation area is where you navigate through a project. The area has a mini toolbar at the top that gives you access to seven different navigators (see Figure 2.3):

1. **Project navigator**: Displays the project files in a hierarchical tree. Use this navigator to open files within the project.

2. **Symbol navigator**: Provides a way to quickly navigate a project using local symbols such as classes and protocols that make up the application.

3. **Search navigator**: Performs project-wide find-and-replace queries.

4. **Issue navigator**: Shows compiler warnings and errors as well as live issues found as you edit code.

5. **Debug navigator**: Shows debug information by thread and queue, helpful with writing a multithreaded application.

6. **Breakpoint navigator**: Shows the breakpoints defined within the project. You can also manage (edit, enable/disable, delete, and so on) breakpoints from here.

7. **Log navigator**: Shows logs from current and past debug and build sessions.

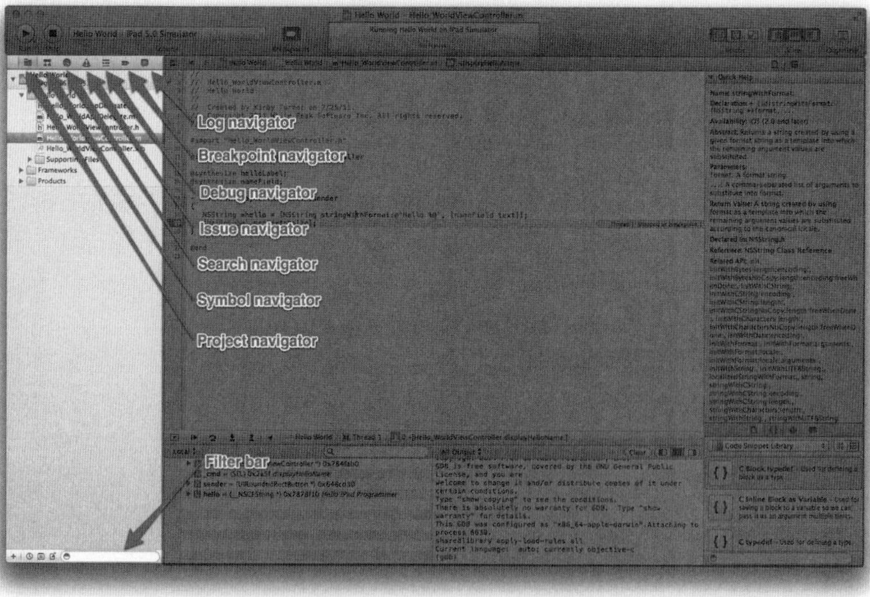

Figure 2.3   The workspace window Navigation area

You switch between the navigators using the mini toolbar found at the top of the Navigation area, or you can use **View > Navigators** from the menu. Shortcut keys are also available. Use **⌘-1** for the Project navigator, **⌘-2** for the Symbol, **⌘-3** for the Search, and so forth through **⌘-7**, which shows the Log navigator. You can also show and hide the Navigation area with **⌘-0**.

At the bottom of the Navigation area is the filter bar. Use it to limit the scope of the items displayed within the navigator.

Editor Area

The Editor area, which is always visible, is where file editing occurs (see Figure 2.4). The editor changes based on the file type. When you select, for example, a source code file (a *.h* or *.m*), the standard text editor is displayed. Select the project file, and you'll see the project editor. Select a NIB, and you'll see the UI designer Interface Builder.

At the top of the Editor area is a mini toolbar. The first button of the mini toolbar displays a popup menu of recently opened files and unsaved files. The next two buttons, go back (**Control-⌘-Right**) and go forward (**Control-⌘-Left**), enable you to navigate through your browsing history. Those are followed by the jump bar. The jump bar provides a quick way to jump between files and locations within the current file. Just click any part of the jump bar to display files and locations within files that you can jump to.

Figure 2.4   The workspace window Editor area

Utility Area

The Utilities area, which you can show and hide using **Option-⌘-0**, displays different inspectors and libraries (see Figure 2.5). The available inspectors will vary based on the file type, but every file type has at least two inspectors, the File and Quick Help inspectors. You can switch between inspectors by clicking the icons in the mini toolbar displayed at the top of the Utilities area.

Below the Inspector area is the Library area. There are four different libraries available for use:

1. File Template library

2. Code Snippet library

3. Object library

4. Media library

The File Template library is used to create and add new files to the project. Drag and drop a file template into the project to create a new file based on the template.

The Code Snippet library contains a set of code snippets that can help speed up development. To use a code snippet, drag and drop it into the text editor. You can also create your own code snippets by dragging and dropping a block of code from the text editor into the Code Snippet library. To view the contents of a code snippet, click the

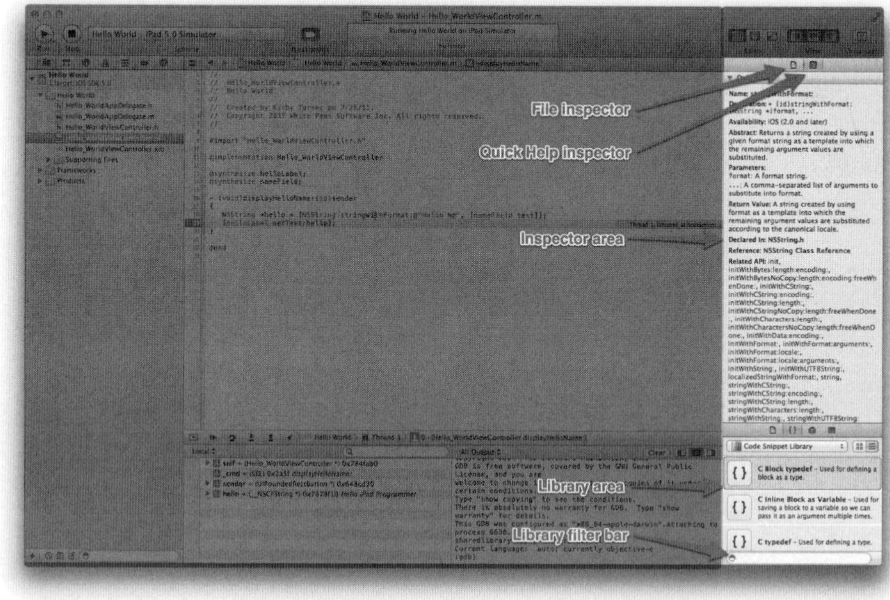

Figure 2.5   The workspace window Utilities area

snippet and wait a second or two. A popover will display showing the snippet's content. You can also edit snippets that you create from the popover.

The Object library is used by Interface Builder. It contains objects used to construct the user interface of your app. Depending on the object, you will drag and drop the object to the designer canvas, to the canvas of another object such as a view, or to the IB dock. (Using IB to create user interfaces is discussed in Chapter 3, "Getting Started with Interface Builder.")

The Media library displays the list of media (images and sounds) available in the project. This library is used by Interface Builder. In IB, you can drag and drop an image into your user interface. This will create a view to display the image. And you can drag and drop an image on an object that can contain an image, such as a `UIButton`, to have that object display the image. Sounds work the same way. Drop a sound on a `UIButton` to assign the sound to the button.

At the bottom of the Utilities area is a filter bar. The filter bar is used to limit the displayed items in the selected library.

Debug Area

The Debug area (**Shift-⌘-Y** to show and hide it) is used when debugging your app (Figure 2.6). As with the other areas, it too has a mini toolbar at the top, which allows you to control the debugging session. From here you can pause the running app, step

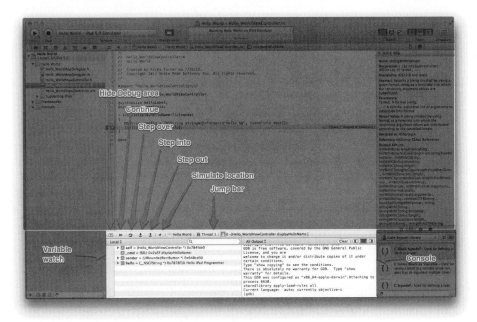

Figure 2.6   The workspace window Debug area

over a line of code, step into a line of code, and step out from a call. Below the mini toolbar is the watch area for variables, and next to that is the console window.

> **Note**
>
> More information on the Debug area, as well as tips and how-to instructions for debugging, is provided in Chapter 25, "Debugging."

Preferences

Xcode can be customized to your liking. The Xcode Preferences (**Xcode > Preferences** or **⌘-,**) has a long list of options that you set to fine-tune the appearance and behavior of Xcode. Developers new to Xcode will find the default preference settings suitable for day-to-day work. The exception, however, might be the display of the text editor. Programmers are a picky bunch, who tend to prefer a certain look and feel to the text editors they use, so it should be no surprise that you can customize the look of the text editor used in Xcode.

Fonts and Colors

For starters, you can change the fonts and colors used by the text editor (Figure 2.7). Xcode provides a list of predefined themes that you can select from, or you can add

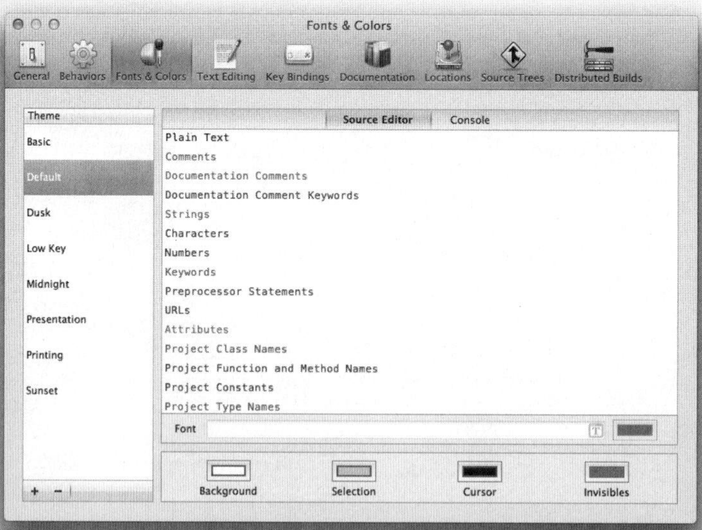

Figure 2.7   Fonts & Colors preferences

your own theme by duplicating an existing theme or creating a new theme from one of the available templates.

> **Note**
>
> Xcode includes the Presentation theme in Fonts & Colors. This theme uses a larger font size that is ideal for display on a projector. If you ever find yourself giving a presentation at a meeting or a conference and you need to show off some code, you definitely want to use the Presentation theme. It will help ensure that everyone in the room, including those sitting in the back, can see your source code.

Text Editing

Fonts and colors are not the only changes you can make to the text editor. Additional customizations for the text editor are available under Text Editing. Select **Editing** in the Text Editing preferences (shown in Figure 2.8) to show or hide line numbers, set the page guide column position, and turn on and off the code folding ribbon (also known as the focus ribbon). An example of what the text editor looks like with these settings turned on is shown in Figure 2.9. You can also change code completion behavior and configure how the text editor will handle things such as end of line and file encoding.

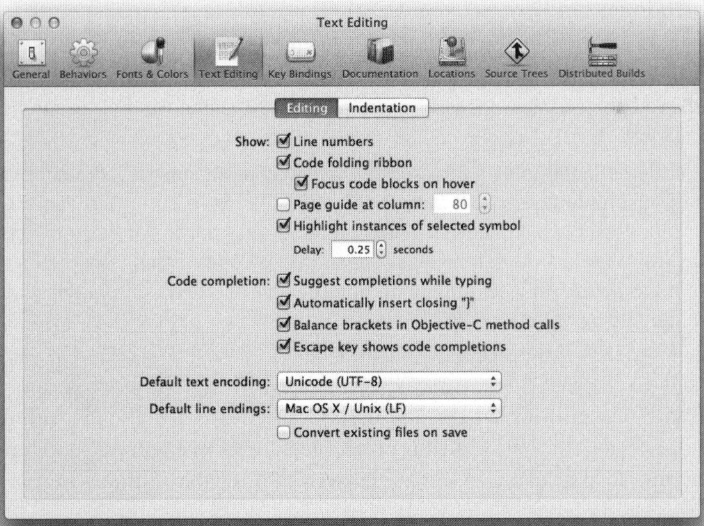

Figure 2.8   Text Editing preferences

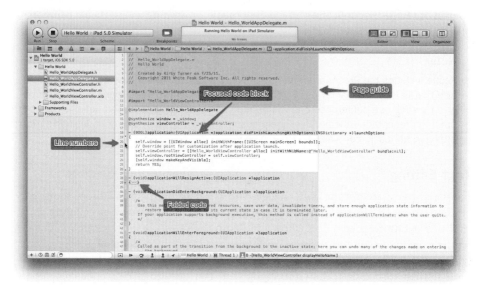

Figure 2.9   Text editor with features turned on

What Is Code Folding?

Code folding is a feature that allows you to selectively show and hide blocks of code. It's a handy way to manage large source code files. You can think of code folding as a way to expand and collapse blocks of code in much the same way you expand and collapse an outline.

The introduction of code folding into Xcode 3 allowed the Xcode development team to include other useful features built around the code folding feature. One such useful feature is code focus, which shows the scope depth of a particular block of code. A high-level view of the scope depth can be seen in the code folding (aka focus) ribbon displayed in the gutter. To view the scope depth within the text editor, simply mouse over the code folding ribbon.

The fun with text editor changes doesn't end here. There is also an **Indentation** preferences option for the Text Editing preferences, seen in Figure 2.10. Here you can control behaviors such as using spaces in place of tabs, enabling line wrapping, and using syntax–aware indenting.

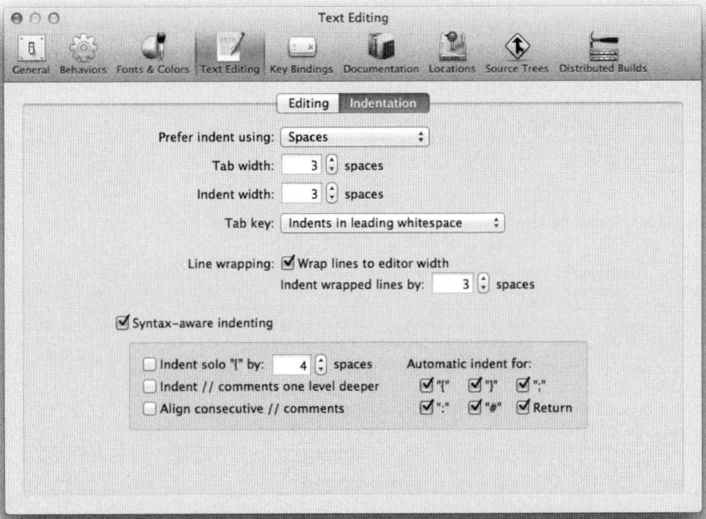

Figure 2.10   Text Editing **Indentation** preferences

Note

Having the tab key insert spaces is one of the first settings I make with any text editor, so it's no surprise that I do the same with Xcode. I prefer spaces over tabs for the simple reason that with spaces you know how indented code looks regardless of the program used to display it. While Xcode allows you to specify the tab width, not all applications do, and in many applications the tab width defaults to eight spaces. This can make your code look ugly when a tab character is used instead of spaces and the source code is displayed in another application, such as a Web browser or an email message.

Line Wrapping

Line wrapping is an interesting setting. I originally did not use this setting, which is turned off by default, because I assumed it worked the same way as word wrapping in other text editors. A friend encouraged me to turn it on, and I haven't turned it off since.

Xcode's wrapping doesn't wrap the line to the first column of the next line. Instead, the wrapped line is indented under the starting line, as seen in Figure 2.11. And the number of spaces for wrapped line indention is configurable in the Text Editing preferences. Using line wrapping with indentions keeps the structure and readability of your code intact, which is something I like.

```
16    @synthesize viewController = _viewController;
17
18    - (BOOL)application:(UIApplication *)application didFinishLaunchingWithOptions:(NSDictionary *)
         launchOptions
19    {
20        self.window = [[UIWindow alloc] initWithFrame:[[UIScreen mainScreen] bounds]];
21        // Override point for customization after application launch.
22        self.viewController = [[Hello_WorldViewController alloc] initWithNibName:
             @"Hello_WorldViewController" bundle:nil];
23        self.window.rootViewController = self.viewController;
24        [self.window makeKeyAndVisible];
25        return YES;
26    }
27
28    - (void)applicationWillResignActive:(UIApplication *)application
29    {
30        /*
31        Sent when the application is about to move from active to inactive state. This can occur for
             certain types of temporary interruptions (such as an incoming phone call or SMS message) or
             when the user quits the application and it begins the transition to the background state.
32        Use this method to pause ongoing tasks, disable timers, and throttle down OpenGL ES frame rates
             . Games should use this method to pause the game.
33        */
34    }
35
36    - (void)applicationDidEnterBackground:(UIApplication *)application
37    {
```

Figure 2.11   Example of line wrapping. Lines 18, 22, 31, and 32
are wrapped.

Coding Styles

When you start changing the behavior of a text editor with settings such as spaces instead of tabs, indentions of three characters instead of four, and so on, you start forming your own coding style. Sticking to a coding style can be important, especially if you work on a team with other developers. There is nothing more annoying than seeing multiple coding styles within a project. A standard, consistent coding style within a project makes the code easier to read and maintain.

Selecting a coding style is often a matter of personal preference. A developer who often works alone will have his own style. Convincing that developer to change styles can be a tough battle. And there may be times when you are the developer who must change to conform to the coding style of the team.

If you are reading this book, you are likely to be new to iPad and Objective-C programming; if so, now is a good time to learn a coding style. You can start by bringing over elements of style from past experience, or you can learn from the coding styles of others. Here are three guidelines for coding styles that you may find helpful:

- *Google Objective-C Style Guide*, available at **google-styleguide.googlecode.com/svn/trunk/objcguide.xml**
- *Zarra Studios Coding Style Guide*, available at **www.cimgf.com/zds-code-style-guide/**
- *WebKit Coding Style Guidelines*, available at **www.webkit.org/coding/coding-style.html**

Key Bindings Preferences

Now that you have configured Xcode to your liking, it's time to get more productive with Xcode by using shortcut keys. Shortcut keys save you time by allowing you to execute some action by simply typing a combination of keys. For instance, typing **⌘-S** to save changes to a file is faster than moving your hand to the mouse, moving the mouse cursor to the menu bar, clicking the **File** menu item, followed by clicking the **Save** menu item.

Xcode comes with a long list of shortcut keys, which Xcode calls *key bindings*. As you might expect, Xcode allows you to select from a list of predefined key bindings, change existing key bindings, and create new key bindings of your own. All of this is available in the Key Bindings preferences, shown in Figure 2.12.

The hardest part about becoming more productive using shortcut keys is remembering the long list of key combinations. One technique that can help is to learn at least one new shortcut key per week. When you realize you are repeating the same action, take a look at the Key Bindings preferences to see if a shortcut key exists. If there is no shortcut key, add one. Make a point to use the shortcut key throughout the week until it is ingrained in your brain. It's not a perfect process, and you will find yourself relearning and re-remembering the same useful but less frequently used shortcut keys all the time. Still, the more shortcut keys you can learn, the more productive you will be using Xcode.

Table 2.1 shows some of the commonly used shortcut keys.

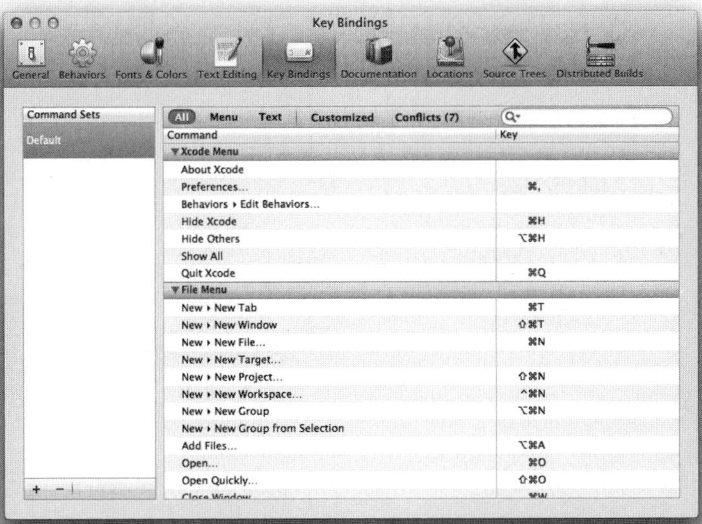

Figure 2.12   Key Bindings preferences

Table 2.1   **Essential Keyboard Shortcuts for Xcode**

Shortcut	Description
Control-⌘-Up and Control-⌘-Down	Switches between the *.h* and *.m* files
Control-⌘-Left	Moves to the previous file in the File History
Control-⌘-Right	Moves to the next file in the File History
Escape	Displays the list of available code completions
⌘-/	Inserts comments and comment/uncomment blocks of selected lines
⌘-0	Shows and hides the Navigation area
Option-⌘-0	Shows and hides the Utilities area
Shift-⌘-Y	Shows and hides the Debug area
⌘-[	Indents the current line or selected lines
⌘-]	Unindents the current line or selected lines
Control-i	Formats the selected block of code
Option-⌘-Left	Folds code
Option-⌘-Right	Unfolds code
⌘-S	Saves the current file
Option-⌘-S	Saves all modified files
⌘-B	Builds the project
Shift-⌘-k	Cleans the project
⌘-R	Runs the app (and builds if needed)
⌘-`	Switches between different Xcode project windows

Colin Wheeler's Xcode Shortcut List

Colin Wheeler, aka Cocoa Samurai (**www.cocoasamurai.com**), has compiled a list of Xcode shortcut keys and published it in a free PDF document. Sure, you can view the same list in Xcode's Key Bindings preferences, but it's a pain compared to Colin's outstanding list.

He publishes two versions, one in color and the other in black and white. I highly recommend downloading Colin's shortcut list. Then print it out and tape it somewhere near your monitor for quick and easy reference. I keep a copy taped on the wall between my MacBook Pro and my 20-inch external monitor.

The shortcut list covering Xcode 4 is available at **cocoasamurai.blogspot.com/2011/03/xcode-4-keyboard-shortcuts-now.html**.

Code Completion

Code completion is a standard feature in any modern-day IDE. Code completion helps speed development by displaying a popup list of possible code to insert into your source code. Xcode's code completion determines the possible code after you type only a couple of characters and wait briefly. You can also display the popup list by pressing **Escape** or **Control-.**. Press the **Enter** key to select the completion code from the list.

> **Note**
>
> Preference settings for code completion can be found under the **Editing** section of the Text Editing preferences.

A really cool feature of code completion is placeholders. Placeholders are inserted for the parameters on a method call, as shown in Figure 2.13. The placeholder displays the data type and parameter name, making it easier to determine what is needed to satisfy the call. And to help speed up the development process, type **Control-/** to move from one placeholder to another or type **Tab** to move to the next placeholder and **Shift-Tab** to move to the previous one.

More Ways to Be Really Productive

Shortcut keys and code completion aren't the only options for being more productive in Xcode. There are third-party add-ons that extend and enhance productivity. Here are two very popular tools:

- Code Pilot (**codepilot.cc**) is a favorite of many Xcoders. Code Pilot makes project navigation easier. If you are a keyboard junkie like me, you owe it to yourself to try out Code Pilot.

- Accessorizer (**www.kevincallahan.org/software/accessorizer.html**) is my personal favorite. Accessorizer saves you time by generating boilerplate code for you. For instance, you can use Accessorizer to generate the @synthesize code for declared properties and to generate accessor methods using a number of different design approaches. This is just a sample of what Accessorizer can do for you. If you are looking to save time writing code in Xcode, there is no better add-on tool than Accessorizer.

```
20  self.window = [[UIWindow alloc] initWithFrame:[[UIScreen mainScreen] bounds]];
21  // Override point for customization after application launch.
22  self.viewController = [[Hello_WorldViewController alloc] initWithNibName:(NSString *) bundle:(NSBundle *)
23  self.window.rootViewController = self.viewController;
24  [self.window makeKeyAndVisible];
25  return YES;
```

Figure 2.13   Placeholders for the `initWithNibName:bundle:` method on line 22

Developer Documentation

Apple provides a great deal of really useful documentation with Xcode. The developer documentation, available from the menu bar by selecting **Help > Documentation and API Reference**, includes all the information you need to do iPad programming, from well-written programming guides, to API documentation, to sample source code. About the only negative mark on the documentation is its size. The amount of documentation is enormous, containing tens of thousands of pages. For instance, the UIKit Framework document has nearly 1,100 pages devoted to it, and it is only one of the many frameworks used for application development. Combine the documentation for various frameworks, how-to guides, code samples, and other general and overview documentation included in the developer documentation, and you can easily become overwhelmed. It's not hard to imagine, based on the sheer size of the documentation, that it can sometimes be hard to find the information you are looking for. That's where books like this one help, by consolidating the wealth of knowledge from Apple into a condensed guide.

Xcode does a great job of helping you find the documentation you need. For instance, you can **Option-Click** a class or method name to display a Quick Help popup, as seen in Figure 2.14. Click the book icon in the popup to view the Help page in the developer documentation, or click the *.h* icon to view the header file containing the element's declaration. You can also view the Help by opening the Quick Help inspector (**Option-⌘-2**).

Figure 2.14   Example of the Quick Help popup and Quick Help inspector

Editors

Xcode provides three different editors. They are not really editors per se, but rather modes of an editor. They are

1. Standard editor

2. Assistant editor

3. Version editor

The Standard editor is your main editor (Figure 2.15). This is where you edit source code, design a user interface, or create a data model. The editor changes based on the file type of the selected file. For instance, when you are editing source code, the Standard editor displays the text editor. Interface Builder is displayed when you are editing a user interface file (NIB or storyboard). And if you select the project file in the Project navigator, the Standard editor displays the project editor.

The Assistant editor provides a split view editor (Figure 2.16). This allows you to view and edit different parts of the same file or different files at the same time. The Assistant editor is a handy way to view the *.h* and *.m* files of a class side by side. In fact, the Assistant editor will automatically display the counterpart file for you. When you have the Assistant editor open and you select a *.h* file, the Assistant will automatically display the corresponding *.m* file in the second editor window. You can also manually open another file in the Assistant editor by using the jump bar at the top of the editor window. You can also open more than one Assistant editor to view more than two files at the same time. Just click the **+** button on the Assistant editor's mini toolbar.

Figure 2.15   The Standard editor displaying the text editor

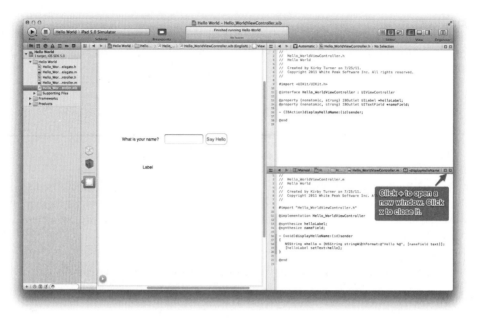

Figure 2.16   The Assistant editor displaying IB in one window and a text
editor in another two

The third editor mode is the Version editor (Figure 2.17). This editor lets you
compare a revision to another for the same file. You can use Xcode's snapshot feature
to keep a history of changes, but a better approach is to use a source code repository.
Xcode supports Git and Subversion. Using a source code repository makes the Version
editor even more useful, allowing you not only to compare revisions, but also to view
the blame and log for the file.

Project Settings

Select the project file in the Project navigator and you'll see the project settings editor
(Figure 2.18). Here you can set various options for the project and targets belonging to
the project.

There are two types of settings for a project: Info and Build Settings. Info lets you
set basic preferences for the project. This includes the iOS deployment target, base
configuration files for the build types (debug, release, and so on), and the default build
configuration for command-line builds.

The other type of settings is Build Settings. Build Settings make it possible for you
to fine-tune the build process. The number of Build Settings options is too large to
cover in this chapter or even in this book. Luckily, the default settings work for most
iOS projects, so covering them here is not necessary.

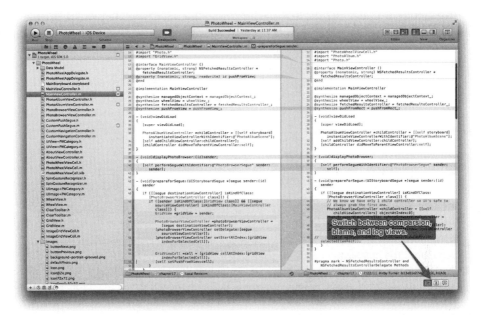

Figure 2.17   The Version editor

Figure 2.18   The project settings editor

Project settings represent the base settings for each target created by the project. A target is the artifact created by a build process. For example, the iPad app created when you build a project is a target. A project has one or more targets, and each target has its own set of settings. The target settings are derived from the project settings. That is to say, the project settings represent the base, or default, settings across all targets, and target settings contain nondefault settings that are unique to the particular target.

As someone new to Xcode and iPad programming, you do not need to worry about project and target settings yet. The default settings are fine for the sample apps presented in this book and most apps that you initially create. You'll start making changes to the settings only when you want to do more advanced work, such as supporting earlier versions of iOS or using a different compiler.

Setting the Organization Name

There is one particular project setting that is not in the project settings: the organization name. The organization name is used as part of the copyright notice generated in the top comment block when you create a new source file, as shown in Figure 2.19. If you find you are working on different projects for different companies (as a freelancer, contractor, or consultant), you may want to use a different organization name for each project.

Perform these steps to change the organization name for a project:

1. Select the project file in the Project navigator.

2. Open the File inspector in the Utilities area (**Option-⌘-1**).

3. Type in the name in the Organization field found in the Project Document section (Figure 2.19).

Figure 2.19   Set the organization name in the File inspector for the project file.

That's it.

The new organization name will be used when you create new source files. Changing the organization name does not change the name used in the commented copyright notice found in previously created source files. You must manually change those or use Find and Replace.

Schemes

A scheme is a collection of settings specifying targets to build, build configurations to use, unit tests to execute, and run destinations to use when a target is launched. Xcode creates a default scheme for you when a new project is created. For iOS projects, the default scheme has two run destinations: devices and simulator.

You can create as many schemes as you want, or edit and delete existing schemes from the manage schemes screen (**Product > Manage Schemes...**), shown in Figure 2.20. Note that when a scheme is created, it is intended for personal use only. If you are working on a project as part of a team, other team members will not see the schemes you create. Only shared schemes can be used by all team members. To share a scheme, mark the Shared check box for the scheme in the manage schemes window.

You can change the active scheme and run destination by using the Scheme popup found in the upper left corner of the project window (see Figure 2.21). You can also edit the scheme, create a new one, and manage all the schemes from the popup menu.

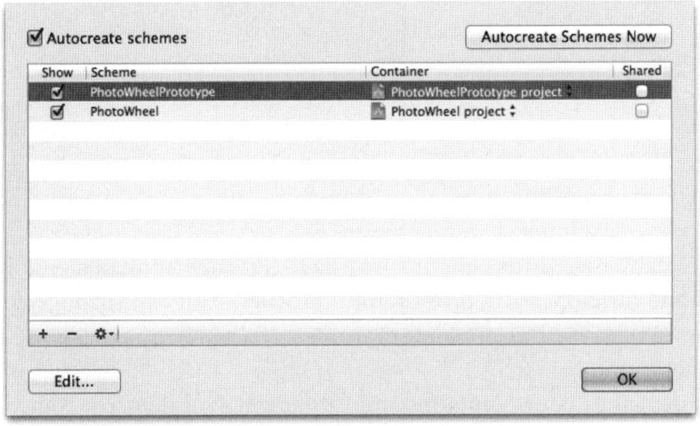

Figure 2.20   The manage schemes window

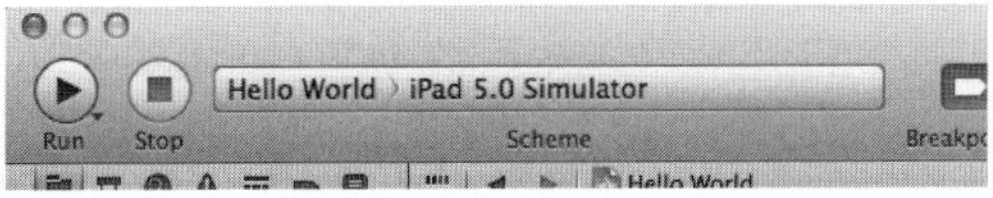

Figure 2.21   The Scheme popup menu found in the workspace window toolbar

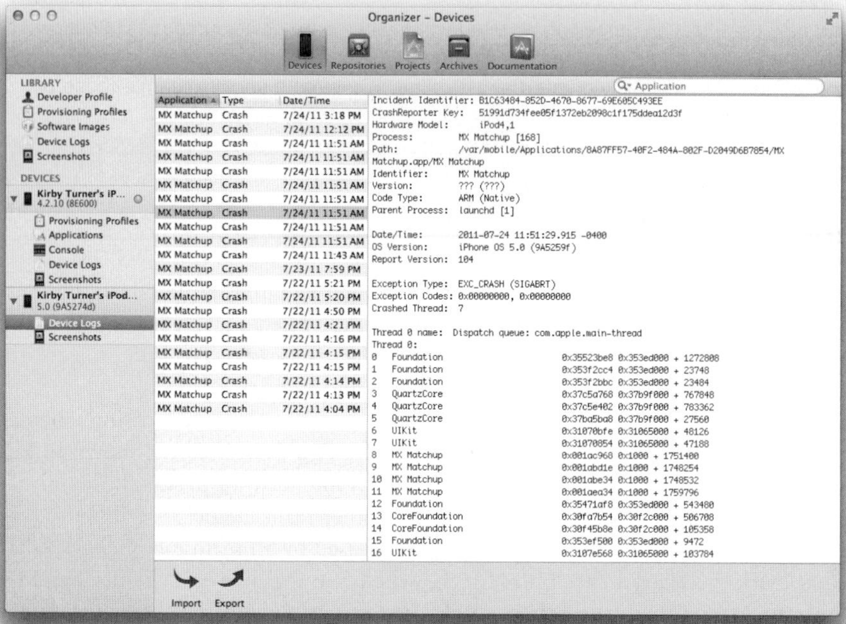

Figure 2.22   Organizer

Organizer

Organizer, shown in Figure 2.22, is a project-independent window available in Xcode (**Shift-⌘-2** or **Window > Organizer**). It is used to manage your devices, add and remove source code repositories, view project cache areas and snapshots, access product archives, and view developer documentation.

One of the really nice things about Organizer is its device management. Here you can view and add developer and provisioning profiles. You can manage copies of earlier iOS software releases. But the feature most useful to many is viewing crash logs found on devices.

Connect a device to your computer and Organizer will detect it. Once the device is connected, you can view the crash logs stored on your device (found under Device Logs). Not only can you see the crash logs for your app, but you can view the logs from any app on the device. This can be helpful if you want to report a crash to a fellow iOS developer. You can also view, using Organizer, the console for an attached device. This too is helpful when troubleshooting an app that is running on the device.

Other Xcode Tools

As mentioned earlier, Xcode is not just an IDE. It is also a collection of developer tools provided by Apple. So far we have talked only about Xcode the IDE, but what are some of the other developer tools included in Xcode?

The iPad Simulator, which you used in Chapter 1, "Your First App," is one of the Xcode tools that you will use frequently. The iPad Simulator allows you to test your iPad application from your computer without a physical iPad device. While there is no substitute for running your application on a real device, there is no faster way to debug your app than with the iPad Simulator.

Note

The iPad Simulator does an incredible job of simulating the iPad device, but at the end of the day you still need to test your application on a real device. The iPad Simulator, as good as it is, is just that, a *simulator*. And there are times when it will behave differently from a real device. There are also limitations on what you can test using the simulator. For example, you can't test the accelerometer in the iPad Simulator; for that you need a real device. The same goes for testing OpenGL ES code, which tends to run faster on your desktop or laptop (thanks to a faster processor and loads more RAM) than in the simulator.

As a general rule of thumb: **Always** test your application on a real device before submitting it to Apple or distributing it to users.

Instruments (found in */Developer/Applications*) is another invaluable tool included with Xcode. With Instruments you profile your application to find memory leaks, determine memory usage, monitor activity, and take CPU samples. You will learn more about Instruments in Chapter 25, "Debugging."

Note

Apple's *iOS Development Guide* has a must-read section on tuning applications.[1] This section gives you more information on using Instruments to tune your iPhone and iPad applications.

Summary

By now you see that Xcode is more than a fancy text editor. It is a collection of developer tools that you use to build applications for the Mac, iPhone, and of course the iPad. Some of the tools are built into Xcode's IDE (i.e., text editing, Interface Builder, project file management, build, and debugging), while other tools are separate,

---

1. iOS Development Guide, section on performance tuning: **developer.apple.com/ iphone/library/documentation/Xcode/Conceptual/iphone_development/ 140-Tunning_Applications/tunning_applications.html**.

stand-alone applications (i.e., Instruments). It's this combination of developer tools that gives Xcode its power.

This chapter highlighted the areas of Xcode that are most useful to new iPad programmers. A lot of detail is missing, as are advanced features, such as refactoring. To cover everything provided by Xcode would take an entire book. That's why it is strongly recommended that you read through the *Xcode User Guide* (**Help > Xcode User Guide** from the Xcode menu bar), which covers Xcode in more detail.

Meanwhile, do not worry if you are not using all of the features of Xcode on day one. Learning a new development environment takes time.

That said, there is one particular tool of Xcode that deserves more attention. It's Interface Builder, the built-in user interface design tool, and it has its own chapter, Chapter 3, "Getting Started with Interface Builder."

Getting Started with Interface Builder

All iPad applications have one thing in common: Each has a user interface. The user interface will differ across the apps, but you can count on each app having one. There are two ways to create the user interface for your app: You can write Objective-C code or use Interface Builder. Interface Builder is the better, easier approach, which is why this chapter teaches you all you need to know to get started with IB.

Interface Builder

IB is built into Xcode, and as the name implies, it is a graphical tool for building user interfaces. While everything you do in IB can be done in code, IB helps you do it faster and with fewer bugs.

You may find IB different from the UI designers that you have used in the past, the biggest difference being that IB is not a source code generator. It does not generate source code to construct the user interface, nor does it generate source code for event handling.

Source code generation is a common approach used in other GUI-based programming environments. The lack of this approach can be confusing at first. For instance, say you want to display a button on a screen and have that button perform some action. With other UI designers, you drop a button into a design canvas, then double-click the button to jump to the event handler for the button. The designer generates the event handler shell code when you double-click the button. This, of course, does not happen with IB.

> **Note**
>
> I say IB doesn't generate code, but that's not exactly true. You will learn later in this chapter that there are now ways to have Xcode generate code for you using IB with the Assistant editor.

Conceptually IB is the same as other UI designers found in other programming environments, but the magic under the hood is what makes IB different. With IB, you drag and drop objects from a palette, called Library, onto a canvas such as a view. IB then creates an instance of the object. Say, for example, you drag and drop a `UIButton`. An instance of `UIButton` is created. At this point, you can set the properties, or state, of the button.

When IB saves your work, it archives the object instances to a NIB file. The archiving process saves the object and its state. When an application uses the NIB at run time, the object is unarchived and the object instances are connected to the NIB's owner, which is commonly a view controller.

Note

The concept of archiving and unarchiving an object instance is known as serializing and deserializing in other programming environments. IB's approach to archiving and unarchiving UI objects might seem familiar to those coming from Delphi and C++ Builder as those programming environments use a similar approach. Think of a *.xib* file as being the same as a *.dfm* file.

How Does IB Work?

Understanding how IB works is one of the biggest challenges new iOS developers face. I know because I went through countless frustrating hours trying to design user interfaces that behaved the way I wanted, only to abandon IB in favor of doing it all in code. What I didn't realize at the time was how much harder I was making it for myself. I also ended up writing more code than necessary, which I had to support. Simple changes to the UI were no longer simple because I had to dig through lines of Objective-C code instead of applying the changes in IB.

How does IB work? For starters, IB stores information about the user interface and its supporting objects in a file called a NIB file. The name NIB is a carryover from the NeXT days. Older versions of IB stored the user interface data in a binary-formatted file with the *.nib* extension, but this has since changed. Today IB stores the data in an XML-formatted file. Because the data format has changed, Apple decided to change the file extension for NIB files. The new extension is *.xib*.

When IB saves a NIB file, it archives the objects contained in the NIB. All state for the objects is saved when they are archived. When an application loads the NIB file, the objects are unarchived and object instances are connected to your code. In Objective-C code, you give IB hints on how to connect the object instance to your code. These hints are `IBOutlet` and `IBAction`. `IBOutlet` connects an ivar or declared property defined in your code to an object instance in the NIB, and `IBAction` connects a method defined in your class code to events called by objects in the NIB.

> **Note**
>
> *Ivar* is short for "instance variable." An instance variable is a variable defined as part of an Objective-C class and is available to instances of the class. See Chapter 4, "Getting Started with Objective-C," for more.

Admittedly, this can become confusing. You define a property in your class, say, a `UILabel`, to display some text message. You create an instance of `UILabel` in IB, then set the position, font, text color, and other state. You then connect the `UILabel` to the declared property using IB. This seems counterproductive, even error-prone, but it is faster in practice than it sounds. Also, Apple is constantly improving Xcode and IB, and the process is getting better all the time.

> **Note**
>
> You may be surprised to learn that Interface Builder has been around since 1988, and it was one of the first applications of its kind to allow interface objects such as buttons, labels, menus, and windows to be drawn in an interface using a mouse. Check out the Interface Builder page at Wikipedia to learn more about the history of IB.[1]

Getting Hands-On with IB

IB has many useful features. The best way to explore these features is hands-on. Let's begin by creating a new iPad project in Xcode. This time around the steps are provided for creating a new project but not as many screen shots. Revisit Chapter 1, "Your First App," if you want to see screen shots of each step.

Okay, let's get started.

1. Launch Xcode.
2. Create a new project (**File > New Project** or **Shift-⌘-N**).
3. Select the Single View Application template (Figure 3.1).
4. Click the **Next** button.
5. Enter "IBPlayground" as the product name and class prefix.
6. Select iPad for the device family.
7. Uncheck Use Storyboard.
8. Click the **Next** button.
9. Save the project to the source directory of your choosing.
10. Build and run (**⌘-R**) the app. You will see a blank application running in the iPad Simulator.
11. Exit the app and return to Xcode.

---

1. Brief history of Interface Builder: **en.wikipedia.org/wiki/Interface_Builder**.

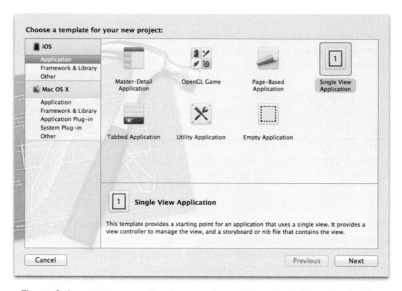

Figure 3.1   Create a new Xcode project using the Single View Application
template for the iPad.

Now have some fun playing with IB. In the Project navigator, find and select the
file *IBPlaygroundViewController.xib*. This will open and display the file in IB, which is
displayed in the Standard editor, as shown in Figure 3.2.

To help you focus on IB, type **⌘-0** to hide the Navigation area and type
Option-⌘-0 to show the Utilities area. Finally, type **Control-Option-⌘-3** to show
the Object library. The workspace window should look like the screen shot in Figure
3.3. You already know about the Utilities area, which is covered in Chapter 2, "Getting Started with Xcode," but you may not be as familiar with IB as it is displayed in
the Standard editor.

To the far left is the IB dock. The dock shows icons for the objects that make
up the user interface. The main content area is the design canvas. Grid lines deco-
rate the designer canvas. The canvas has one visible object in it, a view, which is of
type UIView. Toward the lower left corner is a round disclosure indicator. Click this
to switch between the IB dock and the Document Outline area, shown in Figure
3.4. You can also switch between the two by selecting the **Editor > Show (Hide)
Document Outline** menu item.

The NIB should now be open in IB. Add two labels to the view so that you have
something to play with. To accomplish this, scroll through the list of objects in the
Object library and look for the label object. If scrolling isn't your thing, you can use
the filter box to find the label for you. The filter box is at the bottom of the Library
area. Keyboard junkies can type **Option-⌘-L** to jump to the filter box.

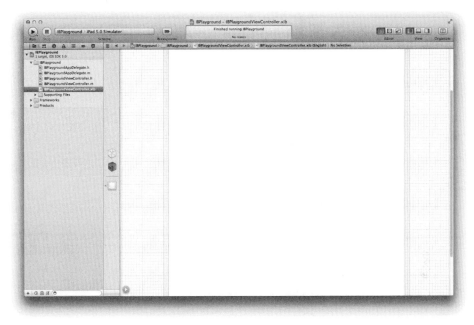

Figure 3.2   Select the file *IBPlaygroundViewController.xib* to display it in
IB under the Standard editor.

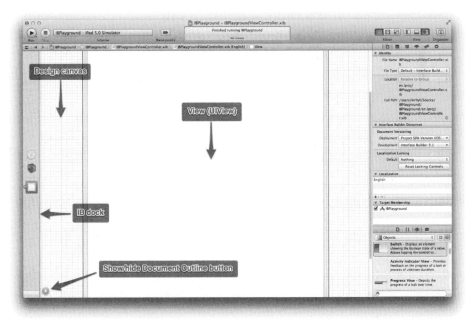

Figure 3.3   Interface Builder displayed in the Standard editor

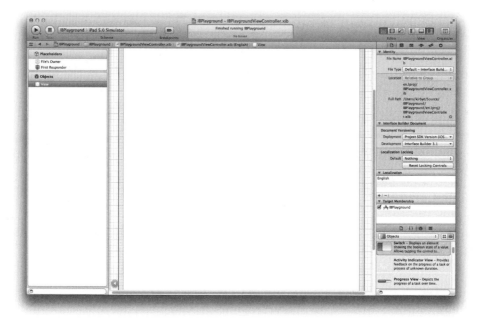

Figure 3.4   The workspace window with the document outline showing
instead of the IB dock

Type the word *label* to filter the list of available objects. You can also filter the list by entering the class name, which is `UILabel`. Now drag and drop a label object from the Library window to the view window. While you are at it, go ahead and drag a second label object so that the view looks similar to Figure 3.5.

Selecting and Copying Objects

Dragging and dropping two labels from the Library window isn't the only way to get the two on the view. You can copy an object in the view by clicking and dragging the object while holding down the **Option** key. This creates a copy of the selected object.

> **Note**
>
> To delete an object from a view, select the object and press the **Delete** key.

You can use this trick to copy more than one object as well. Simply select multiple objects within the view, **Option-Click** and drag, and now you have copies of the selected objects. To select multiple objects, use your mouse, click and drag on the view—this draws a box on the screen—then box off the objects to select. Or you can mouse-click an object to select it, then mouse-click the additional objects while holding down ⌘.

Neat trick, eh? It gets better.

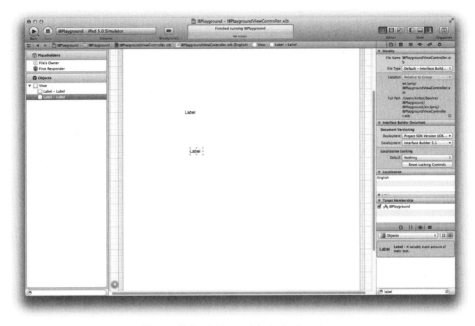

Figure 3.5   Add two labels to the view.

Aligning Objects

Click and drag a label, moving it to the right of another label. IB displays alignment guides for you. Use the vertical and horizontal guides to get the desired alignment. You can also align two or more objects by selecting **Editor > Align** and choosing from the list of available alignment options (Figure 3.6).

For additional help with aligning and positioning objects, add one or more vertical (**Editor > Add Vertical Guide**, or ⌘-|) and horizontal (**Editor > Add Horizontal Guide**, or ⌘-_) guides, seen in Figure 3.7. You place these guides at specific locations within the view by sliding the guide up and down or left and right using the mouse. To do this, place the mouse cursor over the guide. When the mouse cursor changes to the resize cursor, mouse-click the guide and move the mouse up and down for horizontal guides and left and right for vertical guides.

As you move a guide, you will notice two numbers displayed. These numbers represent the distance between the guide and the edge of the view. For instance, a horizontal guide displays the distance between the guide and the top edge of the view as the top number. The distance to the bottom of the view is displayed as the bottom number. This helps provide more precise placement of the guide.

To remove a guide, drag the guide off the view. Poof! A smoke cloud.

A favorite alignment feature is the positioning guides. This feature helps you get precise positioning of objects on the screen. Here's how to do it. Select an object in

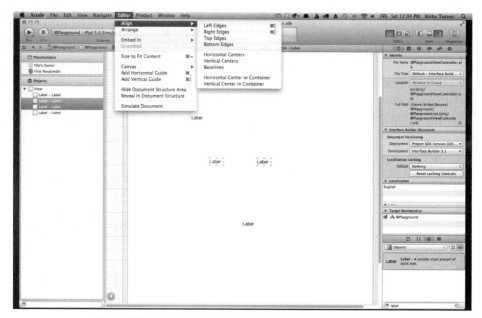

Figure 3.6   **Editor > Align** lists additional alignment options.

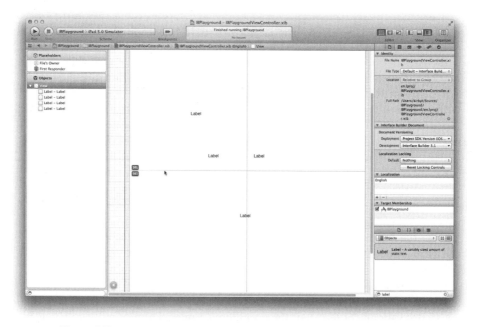

Figure 3.7   Example of the horizontal and vertical guides. Note the point
location of the horizontal guide. This is displayed as you move the guide.

the view. Now hold down the **Option** key, making sure the mouse cursor is not over the selected object. This displays the frame size of the selected object and the distances between the object's frame and the top, left, right, and bottom edges of the container view, as seen in Figure 3.8. Use the arrow keys to move the object up, down, left, and right. You'll notice that the distances to the edge change as the object moves.

This, however, is not the only reason positioning guides are a favorite alignment feature.

Continue to hold down the **Option** key and move the mouse cursor over another object in the view. The guide changes to show you the distance between the selected object and the object under the mouse cursor (Figure 3.9). And yes, you can use the arrow keys to move the selected object while displaying the distance between the two objects. How awesome is that!

Ever had a request to place two buttons on the screen 10 pixels apart? Select one of the buttons, place the mouse cursor over the other button, and hold down the **Option** key. Now use the arrow keys to move the selected button 10 pixels from the other button. It doesn't get much easier, and that's why this is a favorite alignment feature in IB.

> **Note**
>
> You do not need to hold down the **Option** key when using the arrow keys to move a selected object or group of selected objects. Holding down the **Option** key, however, will display the really useful guides and positioning information.

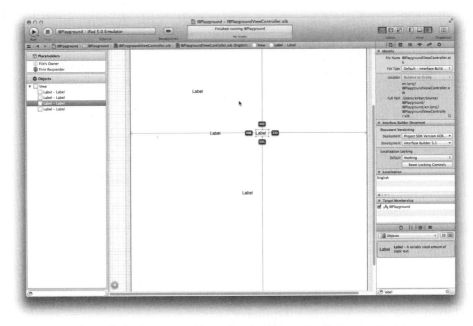

Figure 3.8   Select an object, then hold down the **Option** key to get position information about the object.

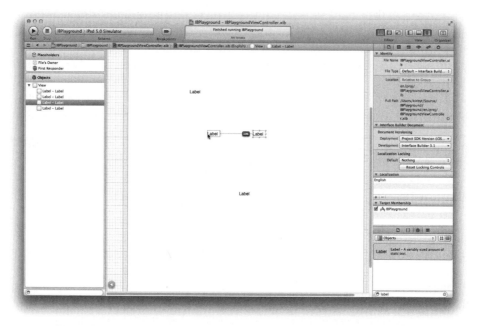

Figure 3.9   Select an object, then mouse over another object. Hold down
the **Option** key to see the distance between the two objects.

Layout Rectangle

While playing with the position guides, did you notice that the selected object is
enclosed in a rectangle? This rectangle is handy for seeing the layout of an object,
especially for objects that do not have visual borders. You can turn this feature on for
all objects by selecting **Editor > Canvas > Show Layout Rectangles** from the
menu, as seen in Figure 3.10. This feature is really useful when you want to make sure
one object does not overlap another object.

> **Note**
>
> You can also show the bounds rectangle (**Editor > Canvas > Show Bounds Rectangles**) if
> all you want to see is the size of an object.

Changing State

The size and position of an object can also be changed in the Inspector area within the
Utilities area. You may remember from Chapter 2, "Getting Started with Xcode," that
the Inspector area has the File and Quick Help inspectors. Well, when using IB, there
are four additional inspectors: Identity (**Option-⌘-3**), Attributes (**Option-⌘-4**), Size
(**Option-⌘-5**), and Connection (**Option-⌘-6**).

The Identity inspector, shown in Figure 3.11, is where you specify the class name
for the object. The class name is one of the classes from the Cocoa Touch Framework

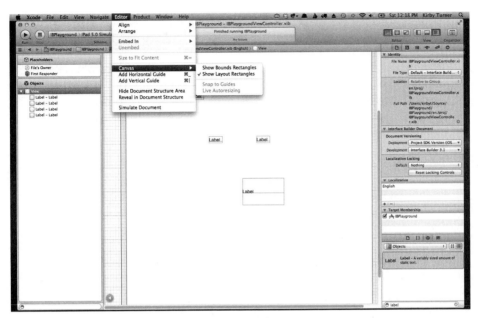

Figure 3.10   Layout Rectangles enabled. Notice that one of the labels
has a larger frame than the others. You would not be able to see this with
Layout Rectangles turned off.

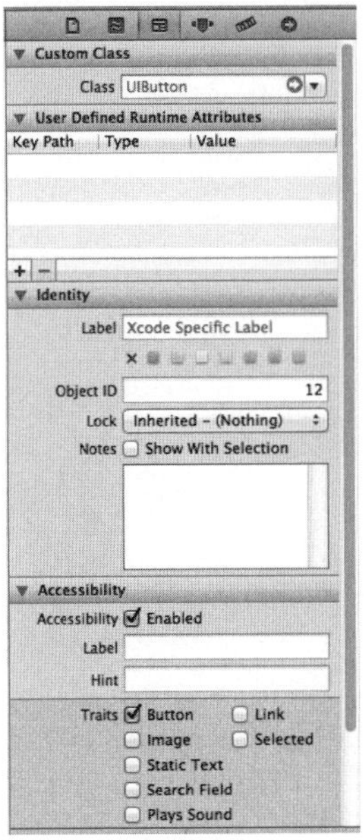

Figure 3.11   The Identity inspector for a `UIButton` object

or a custom class created within your Xcode project. You also set the accessibility settings for the object in the Identity inspector. Accessibility makes it possible for visually impaired individuals to use your application.

The Attributes inspector is where you set the property values, or attribute values, for the selected object (Figure 3.12). The list of attributes will vary based on the object type. Examples of attributes include content mode, alpha setting, background color, tag value, and drawing settings. Setting an attribute value is a simple matter of entering a new value, selecting from a list of possible values, or ticking and unticking a check box.

The Size inspector, shown in Figure 3.13, enables you to set the size and position of the selected object without having to size and move the object with the mouse. This is a faster way to size and position an object when you know the exact dimensions and position. Also within this inspector, you can specify the autosizing setting for the object.

Autosizing lets you specify whether the object's width, height, top, left, right, and bottom positions are fixed or flexible. By using a combination of these settings, you control how the object is sized and positioned when the container view is resized. Autosizing also shows an animated view of how the settings will affect the object's size and positioning.

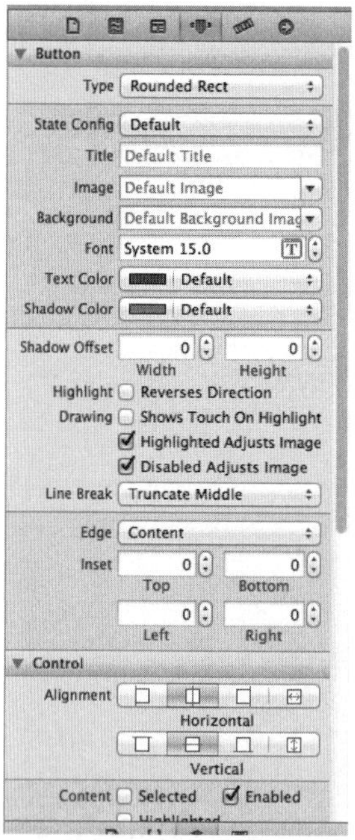

Figure 3.12   The list of attributes, or properties, for a UIButton as
seen in the Attributes inspector

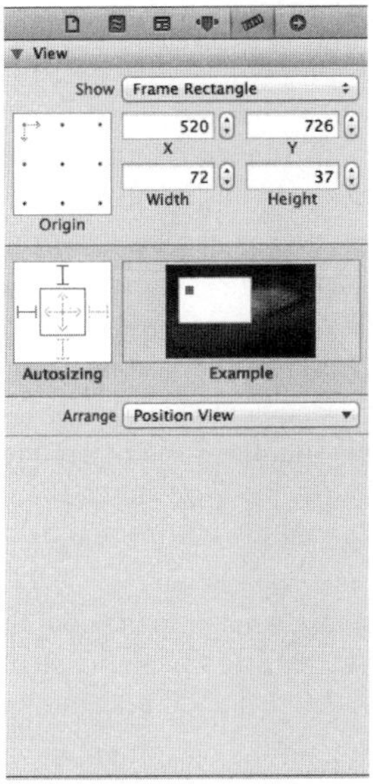

Figure 3.13   The Size inspector

The Connections inspector shows the connections between the selected object and some other object. You can also make new connections within this area. Take a look at Figure 3.14. Notice the small circles to the right of the events and outlets references. If you were to move the mouse cursor over one of the empty circles, it would change

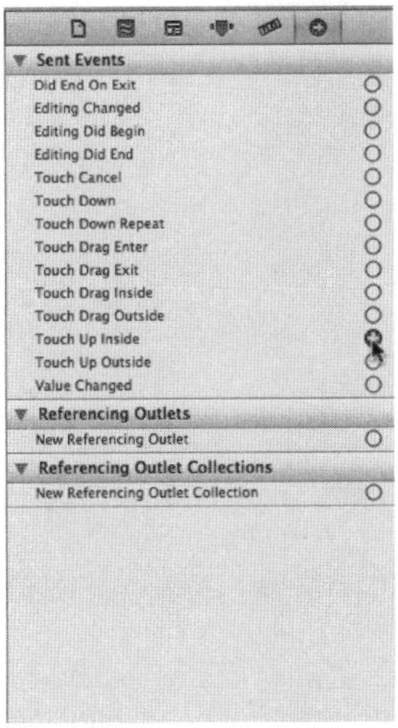

Figure 3.14   List of events and outlets references for a `UIButton` as seen in the Connections inspector

to a circle with a plus sign in it. Clicking and dragging the plus sign draws a line on the screen. When the plus sign is moved around, objects that support the connection will be highlighted. Objects that do not support the connection will not be highlighted. When you find the desired object, drop the plus sign on the object to connect it. This will pop up a list of actions or outlets that can be used for the connection. Select the appropriate action or outlet to make the connection.

What Is the File's Owner?

When looking at the IB dock or Document Outline area, you may notice an object named File's Owner. File's Owner identifies the object that owns the NIB when it is loaded at run time. A placeholder object represents the File's Owner. A placeholder object is a reference to an object that is not created by the NIB. Other names for placeholder include proxy and external object, as it is called in the Object library.

The File's Owner placeholder object is used to indicate the type of object that owns the NIB once loaded. The object type, or class name, is displayed in the Identity inspector, and it can be changed in the same inspector, as shown in Figure 3.15.

The File's Owner type is the name of the class that is responsible for managing objects at run time that are defined in the NIB. The File's Owner type is typically the

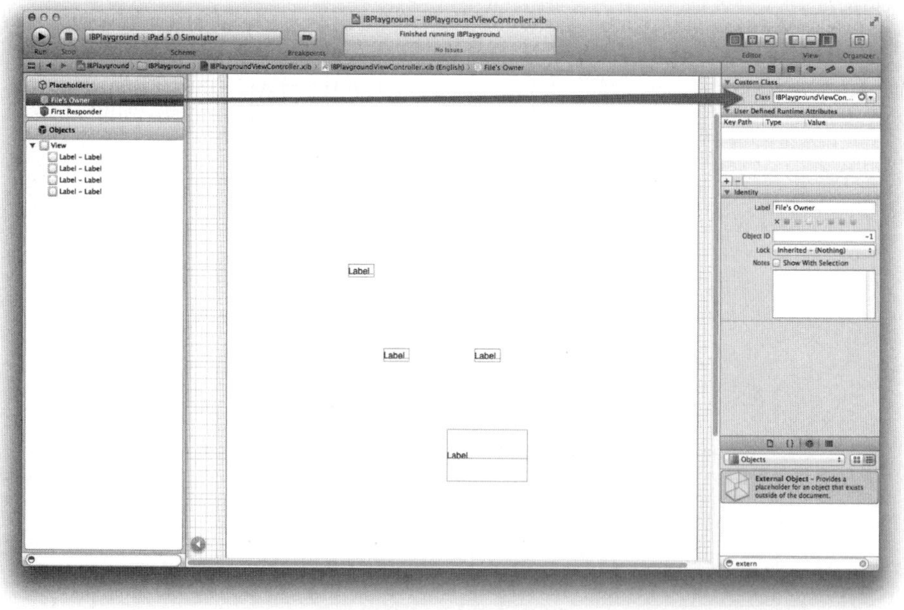

Figure 3.15   The File's Owner is a placeholder object. Its type is the class name set in the Identity inspector.

view controller class, but it does not have to be a view controller. Likewise, you can have other placeholder objects defined in the NIB that are not the File's Owner.

IB uses the class type to determine which header file to read when it's looking for outlets and actions. We'll see this in action momentarily.

Connecting Your NIB to Your Code

The objects created in a NIB are connected to classes defined in source code by way of two IB hints, IBOutlet and IBAction. These are special macros that resolve to nothing and void respectively, but Interface Builder uses them as a way to identify references for outlets and actions defined in source code. From the point of view of the source code as well as the compiled application, these macros do nothing. They are useless. IB, however, uses them as hints for finding and connecting outlets and actions to objects defined in the NIB.

So what are outlets and action? An outlet is a reference to an object, and an action is a reference to a method implemented by a class.

For the moment, think of a view as a representation of the screen the user sees in your application. The view displays a label object with some text and a button object. A controller class manages interaction with the view. The controller has a reference to the label defined in the view. The label reference is the outlet since it is a reference to an object. If the controller needs a reference to the button, another outlet can be defined referencing the button object.

Now let's assume that when the user taps the button, text in the label changes. The button has a touch event that calls a method. The method is implemented in the controller class and is responsible for changing the label's text. This method represents the action.

An object reference defined in a class interface is decorated with IBOutlet and a method declaration is decorated with IBAction when each is to be connected to objects and events defined in a NIB. IB looks for these macros to find the available outlets and actions defined within a class. This is how objects created in a NIB are connected to the source code that powers your application.

> **Note**
>
> If you are familiar with the design pattern Model-View-Controller, some of what was just said should make sense. iOS applications use MVC throughout. The MVC pattern is covered in Chapter 5, "Getting Started with Cocoa."

To connect an object created in the NIB to an object reference or an object's event to a method, the outlet and action must be defined in your code. Two approaches can be used to accomplish this: You can add the code manually to the class interface, or you can use the IB with the Assistant editor.

Defining an Outlet in Code

For many iOS programmers, adding an outlet or action declaration manually to a class interface is a more natural workflow. Manually adding outlets and actions gives you the opportunity to focus on the class interface and implementation without concerning yourself with the look of the user interface.

To see how this works, go back to the previous scenario where you have a view containing a label and a button. When the user taps the button, the label's text changes to display "Hello from iOS." To implement this feature, your source code needs a reference to the UILabel, which is the outlet, and a reference to a method, which is the action that executes the code needed to update the label text.

Now, to make this so...

Show the Project navigator (⌘-0) and select the file *IBPlaygroundViewController.h*. Update the class interface to include the code in Listing 3.1.

Listing 3.1   Code to Be Added to *IBPlaygroundViewController.h*

```
@interface IBPlaygroundViewController : UIViewController

// Add the following code:

@property (nonatomic, strong) IBOutlet UILabel *label;

- (IBAction)buttonTapped:(id)sender;

// End of code to add.

@end
```

What's going on here? First, a declared property is added. @property is special Objective-C sauce instructing the compiler to define an instance variable name label that stores a reference to an instance of UILabel. IBOutlet is the hint given to IB so that a connection to the instance of UILabel defined in the NIB can be made to the declared property found in the class interface. Second, a forward declaration for the method buttonTapped: is defined. Note that the return type is set to IBAction. This tells IB that this method is an action.

If you try compiling the project, you will receive a build error. The build fails because the implementations for the declared property and method have not been provided. So open the file *IBPlaygroundViewController.m* (**Control-⌘-Up** or **Control-⌘-Down** while in the counterpart *.h* file) and add the implementation code shown in Listing 3.2.

Listing 3.2   Updated *IBPlaygroundViewController.m*

```
#import "IBPlaygroundViewController.h"

@implementation IBPlaygroundViewController
```

```
// ----
// Add the following code:

@synthesize label;

- (IBAction)buttonTapped:(id)sender
{
    NSLog(@"button was tapped.");
    [label setText:@"Hello from iOS."];
}

// End of new code.


// Other code provided by the template is not presented here.

@end
```

For the moment it is assumed that you have little to no Objective-C experience. Therefore, this code may seen strange, especially the @synthesize statement. @synthesize is more special sauce from Objective-C that tells the compiler to create getter and setter methods for the declared property. In the case of this code, @synthesize creates the getter and setter methods for the declared property label. You can write the getter and setter methods, but why bother when the compiler can do it for you?

> **Note**
>
> For the moment, do not worry about the details of @property and @synthesize. All will be revealed in Chapter 4, "Getting Started with Objective-C."

Following the synthesizing of the declared property is the implementation for the method buttonTapped:. This method accepts a single parameter named sender. sender is a reference to the object calling the method. In our current scenario sender is the button found in the view.

The method has two lines of code. The first statement calls NSLog(). NSLog() is a C function that sends output to the console. The output, of course, is the string parameter to the NSLog() call. The second line of code sets the text property for the object reference label. This is where the source code actually uses the IBOutlet.

What's Really Going On?

As I mentioned, IB looks for IBOutlet, and IBAction has hints to the available outlets and actions. But how does IB know what files to look at? The answer is the File's Owner. The File's Owner is of type IBPlaygroundViewController. This tells IB to read and parse the header file *IBPlaygroundViewController.h* for any IBOutlet and IBAction hints.

With IBOutlet and IBAction defined in the class interface, it's time to update the user interface. Select the file *IBPlaygroundViewController.xib* in the Project navigator to open the NIB in IB. Add a new button (UIButton) to the view defined in the NIB. It's assumed there is at least one label in the view from the earlier playtime. If not, add a label to the view as well.

Right-click the button found in the view. This shows a list of events triggered by the object. Click and drag the circle for the Touch Up Inside event and drop it on the File's Owner (see Figure 3.16). IB displays the list of available actions; button-Tapped: should be the only action available at this time. Click the buttonTapped: action to connect the button's Touch Up Inside event to the buttonTapped: action method.

Note

Another way to connect the button to the action is to **Control-Click** the button and drag the mouse cursor to the File's Owner. This will connect the buttonTapped: action to the Touch Up Inside event of the button.

The label should be connected as well; otherwise the app will not behave the way you want. In the Document Outline area right-click the File's Owner, then drag and drop the circled plus sign onto a UILabel instance found in the view. This connects the label to the declared property outlet label.

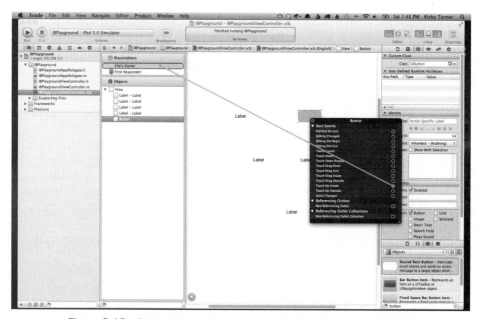

Figure 3.16   Right-click the button to see the list of events. Click and drag an event to connect it to an action defined in another object.

> **Note**
>
> Here again you can **Control-Click** the File's Owner and drag the mouse cursor to the label to make the connection.

Think this through for a moment. In the header file there is an outlet referencing a `UILabel` and a method declaration representing an action. Nowhere in code do you find the instantiation of the `label` object, nor do you see a reference of any sort identifying the button that calls the method `buttonTapped:`. This is because the objects for the label and button are defined in the NIB as are the connections to `IBOutlet` `label` and `IBAction buttonTapped:`. The Cocoa Framework performs the magic for you, creating the object instances and making the connections. The real beauty here is that you did not have to write code, and IB did not generate source code, to create the object instances and connect the event callbacks.

At this point, you should be able to build and run (**⌘-R**) the app without errors. Run it and see what happens. When you tap the button, does the label's text change? If not, the most likely cause is that either the `IBOutlet` or the `IBAction` connection was not made. Double-check the connections.

A point to be aware of: When a connection is not made, the compiler does not warn you and typically your app will not crash. All that happens is, well, nothing. Nothing at all happens, which means you have to play detective and find the cause of the nothingness. Did you forget to make the connections, or did you forget to implement the method, as might be the case for `IBAction`?

If you are like many other iOS programmers who are just starting out, you will likely forget to make the connections. It's one of the most common mistakes, which is why you should always check the connections first when nothing happens. This bears repeating: Whenever nothingness happens, check the connections in IB. Chances are the connections are not there.

> **Note**
>
> While nothingness is the common behavior, there are situations where exceptions are thrown that cause your app to crash because the proper connections have not been made. Most notable is when you define a view controller as the File's Owner and you do not connect the view outlet to a view. I often make this mistake, so much so that when my app crashes after adding a new NIB, I know with almost 100% certainty that I forgot to connect the view outlet.

Using the Assistant Editor

The other way to connect outlets and actions is to use the Assistant editor. With the Assistant editor, it's possible to drag objects from IB into the class interface and have Xcode create the necessary source code for you.

To see this in action, add another label and button to the view. This gives you new objects to connect without having to go back and delete the other code. Next, show the Assistant editor (**Option-⌘-Return**). Things might be a little crowded, so you may want to hide the Navigation (**⌘-0**) and Utilities (**Option-0**) areas. Notice that when you show the Assistant editor, it automatically displays the *IBPlaygroundViewController.h* file. Xcode knows this is the counterpart file for the NIB. Figure 3.17 shows an example of the workspace window with IB and the Assistant editor open.

> **Note**
>
> If for some reason *IBPlaygroundViewController.h* is not open in the Assistant, use the jump bar to open it.

To declare the outlet for the label in the class interface while at the same time making the connection, **Control-Click** the label and drag the mouse cursor to the class interface in the Assistant window. When you release the mouse, a popover is displayed, prompting you for the name of the outlet (see Figure 3.18). Call it "label2" and click the **Connect** button. This creates the declared property decorated with IBOutlet and makes the connection with the object defined in the NIB.

> **Note**
>
> You can place the outlet declaration anywhere you like so long as it is between the @interface and @end statements for the class.

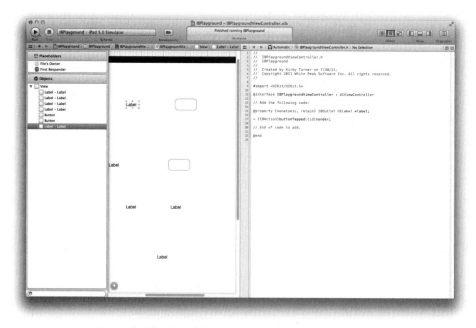

Figure 3.17   IB and the Assistant editor working together

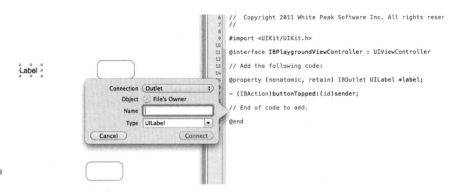

Figure 3.18   Popover displayed when connecting an outlet using the
Assistant editor

You do the same thing to declare the action and connect the button. **Control-Click** the button and drag the mouse cursor to the class interface. This time when the popover is presented, change the connection from Outlet to Action and name the action "button2Tapped." The popover should look like the screen shot in Figure 3.19. Finally, click the **Connect** button to create the action.

When you add an action using the Assistant, it not only creates the declaration in the class interface but it also adds the method shell to the implementation. Open *IBPlaygroundViewController.m* and scroll to the bottom to see the method shell for `button2Tapped:`.

Storyboards

One of the options you may see when creating a new Xcode project is Use Storyboard. So far in this book, you have been told not to check this option. But what is a storyboard?

A storyboard, or storyboarding, is a way of designing the user interface for your application. It has the benefit of showing all the screens, at the same time, that make

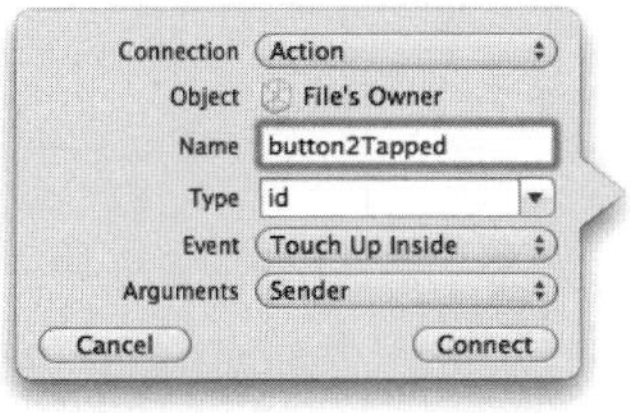

Figure 3.19   Popover displayed when connecting an action using the
Assistant editor

up the application. This feature is built on top of Interface Builder, so everything you learned in this chapter about using IB with a NIB applies to storyboards. The primary difference, however, is that a storyboard can display multiple screens, or NIBs if you will, at the same time. This gives you a complete, single picture of the application's user interface and the relationships between the screens.

You begin using storyboards in Chapter 14, "Storyboarding in Xcode."

Summary

This concludes our tour of Interface Builder. We hope you enjoyed your flight and will consider using IB for future UI designs.

Kidding aside, you now have the basic knowledge needed to use Interface Builder. It may seem daunting in the beginning, but it will become easier over time. The key point to remember is to always make the connections for outlets and actions. If you created a super-nice UI but it is not displaying content or actions are not invoked on touch, chances are good the connections are missing.

4

Getting Started with Objective-C

Objective-C is the programming language used in this book, so it only makes sense to include a chapter on this mighty fine programming language. Besides, Objective-C is the programming language you will use as you learn iPad programming. It is not the only programming language used for iPad programming, but it is by far the most popular. And Apple recommends Objective-C for iOS programming. That's why it is used for all of the source code provided in this book.

All things Objective-C is simply too large a topic to be covered in a single chapter, and it is beyond the scope of this book. There are, however, some excellent books devoted to Objective-C, including

- *Learning Objective-C 2.0: A Hands-On Guide to Objective-C for Mac and iOS Developers by Robert Clair (Addison-Wesley Professional, 2010)*
- *Programming in Objective-C 2.0, Third Edition, by Stephen G. Kochan (Addison-Wesley Professional, 2011)*
- *Objective-C Programming: The Big Nerd Ranch Guide by Aaron Hillegass (Big Nerd Ranch, Inc., 2012)*

These are outstanding books that dive deep into the Objective-C programming language. Meanwhile, this chapter covers the basics of Objective-C, giving you the jump start needed to write your first iPad app. Once you finish this book, you can read one of the recommended Objective-C books to gain a deeper understanding of the language.

What Is Objective-C?

Objective-C is an extension to the C programming language that turns C into an object-oriented programming language. But unlike C++, which is derived from C, Objective-C is a set of extensions added to the C programming language.

To make this happen, a small set of new syntax is added to the language. The compiler converts the Objective-C syntax to C as part of the compile process. Objective-C also relies on a runtime environment, which gives Objective-C its dynamic nature.

Objective-C is modeled after Smalltalk, one of the first object-oriented programming languages to come onto the scene. Like Smalltalk, Objective-C sends a message to a receiver. The receiver, which is an object, then invokes a method based on the message it receives. This allows apps written in Objective-C to construct a message at run time that is sent to an object, which in turn invokes a method. This is different from other programming languages such as C++, which bind method calls at compile time.

The dynamic behavior of Objective-C makes it an ideal programming language for frameworks and SDKs, which might be one of the reasons Apple uses it in its own frameworks, SDKs, and operating systems.

> **Note**
>
> Objective-C extends the C programming language, turning it into an object-oriented programming language. If you already know C, learning Objective-C will be a snap. But don't worry if you have never written a line of C code. You can learn Objective-C without any prior C knowledge.

Hands-On with Objective-C

The best way to learn Objective-C is to use it, and that's what you will do now. You are going to create a simple coin toss application that runs in the Terminal window. Writing this app will help you gain insight into Objective-C.

Let's begin by launching Xcode. Next, create a new Command Line Tool app. You can select either the "Create a new Xcode project" option on the Welcome to Xcode screen, shown in Figure 4.1, or you can select **File > New > New Project** (**Shift-⌘-N**) from the menu bar.

You want to create a console app. A console app runs from the command line in the Terminal window. iOS does not support command-line applications, so you want to select the Command Line Tool project template found under the Mac OS X group, shown in Figure 4.2. Select this template, then click the **Next** button.

Name the project "CoinToss." Select Foundation as the Type (Figure 4.3). This creates a console application that links to the Foundation framework. You will learn more about this and other frameworks in Chapter 5, "Getting Started with Cocoa." Be sure that the Use Automatic Reference Counting option is turned on. This option is described later in this chapter. Click **Next** to continue.

Save the project to your source directory. If you do not have a source directory yet, create one.

You may have noticed the option to create a local Git repository at the bottom of the screen shown in Figure 4.4. Git is a popular distributed version control system. Xcode has built-in support for both Git and Subversion, another popular version control system. Unless you are already familiar with Git, leave this option unmarked. The sample code in this book does not require the use of a version control system.

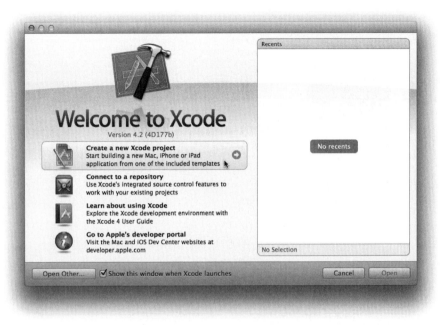

Figure 4.1   Welcome to Xcode window

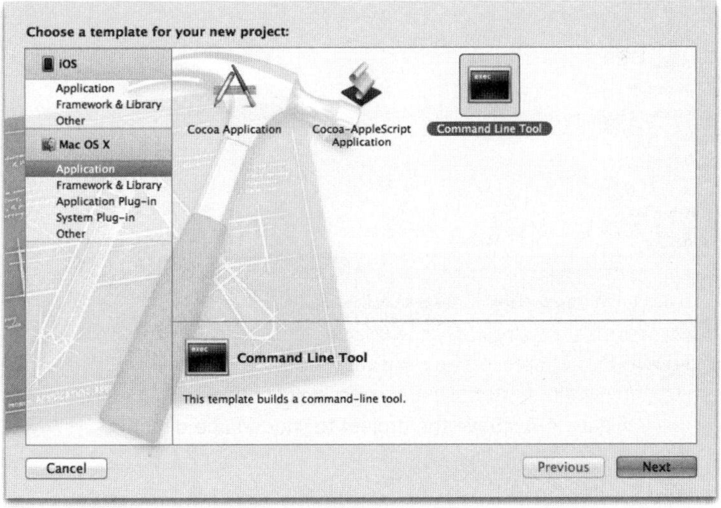

Figure 4.2   Select the Command Line Tool template.

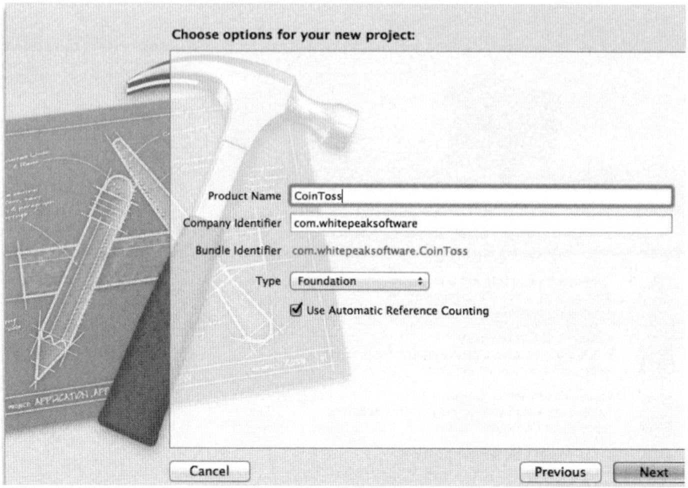

Figure 4.3   Project options

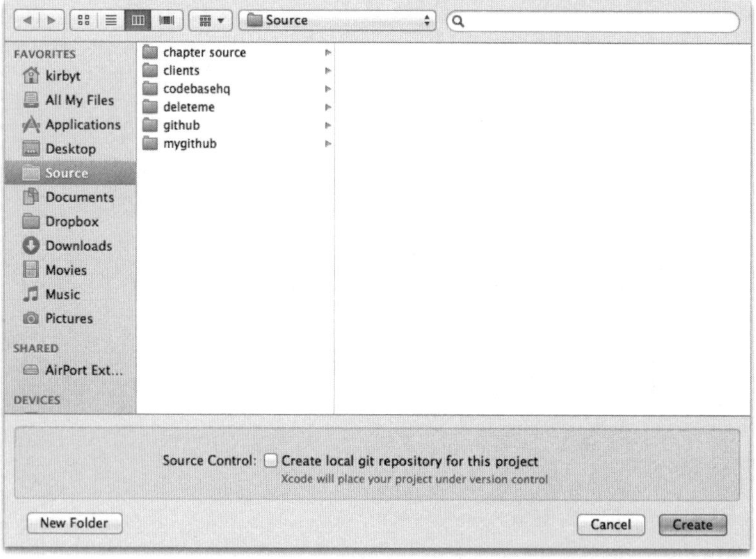

Figure 4.4   Save the project to your source directory.

Make sure the project was properly created by doing a build (⌘-**B**), then run
(⌘-**R**). This will build and run the app, which displays "Hello, World!" to the console window, as seen in Figure 4.5. Because the app is a command-line application,
you will not see the output unless you have the output window open in the Debug
area. You can open the output window by typing **Shift-⌘-C**.

```
All Output ▾                                    ( Clear ) ▢ ▦ ▢
GNU gdb 6.3.50-20050815 (Apple version gdb-1708) (Mon Aug  8 20:32:45 UTC 2011)
Copyright 2004 Free Software Foundation, Inc.
GDB is free software, covered by the GNU General Public License, and you are
welcome to change it and/or distribute copies of it under certain conditions.
Type "show copying" to see the conditions.
There is absolutely no warranty for GDB.  Type "show warranty" for details.
This GDB was configured as "x86_64-apple-darwin".tty /dev/ttys001
[Switching to process 2266 thread 0x0]
2011-09-07 13:09:25.635 CoinToss[2266:707] Hello, World!
Program ended with exit code: 0|
```

Figure 4.5   Output window displaying "Hello, World!" from the console app

Let's Write Some Code

With the project in place, it's time to write some code. In the Project navigator, open the file *main.m*. C programs always start with a `main()` function, which is found in the *main.m* file. However, the *main.m* file is your first hint that you are using Objective-C. C language source files have *.c* as the file extension. Objective-C source files use *.m* as the file extension.

Find and delete the line of code that reads `NSLog(@"Hello world!")` and add the following code in its place:

```
int randomValue = (arc4random()%10) + 1; // Returns an int between 1 and 10.
if (randomValue % 2) {
   NSLog(@"Heads");
} else {
   NSLog(@"Tails");
}
```

The source code for *main.m* should now look like Listing 4.1.

Listing 4.1   **Simple Coin Toss Algorithm in** *main.m*

```
#import <Foundation/Foundation.h>

int main (int argc, const char * argv[])
{

   @autoreleasepool {

       int randomValue = (arc4random()%10) + 1; // Returns an int between 1 and 10.
       if (randomValue % 2) {
          NSLog(@"Heads");
       } else {
          NSLog(@"Tails");
       }

   }
    return 0;
}
```

This code retrieves a random integer value from the function arc4random(). It then does a check to see if the random value is an even or odd number. An odd number logs "Heads" to the console, and an even number logs "Tails."

> **Note**
>
> NSLog is a C function that displays output to the standard console. It is the Objective-C equivalent of the printf function found in the C programming language. NSLog is commonly used to send output to the console when debugging an application. You can find out more about using NSLog in Chapter 5, "Getting Started with Cocoa."

Build and run (**⌘-R**) the application. As you can see in the output window (**Shift-⌘-C**), this is not a very exciting app. It only does a single coin toss. To do more coin tosses, you must run the app again and again. Let's make the app a bit more interesting by changing the source code to loop through ten times to see how random the coin tosses actually are. To accomplish this, add the following code:

```
for (int index=0; index < 10; index++) {
    int randomValue = (arc4random()%10) + 1; // Returns an int between 1 and 10.
    if (randomValue % 2) {
        NSLog(@"Heads");
    } else {
        NSLog(@"Tails");
    }
}
```

The app is slightly more interesting now, but what's more interesting is that up to now you haven't written any Objective-C code. Let's change that by creating a CoinTosser object.

Object

What is an object? In the software world, an object is a programming unit that contains attributes and behavior. That is, the object contains data and code where data represents the attributes (also known as properties) and code represents the behavior of the object (methods performed by the object). The object's data and code are related in that the code performs some action using the data contained within the object.

An object encapsulates related data and code into a single unit, making it easier to reuse the unit in other parts of the application. Many times an object models a real-world concept. If, for example, you were writing a payroll application, Employee would likely be one of the objects found within the application.

CoinToss is not a complex or large application, but it can still benefit from using objects. Instead of including the coin toss logic in the for loop of the main function, the app can use a CoinTosser object. CoinTosser becomes responsible for flipping the coin. This means that as the app grows and becomes more complex, the logic for flipping the coin does not have to be copied throughout the app. Instead, the app can use the CoinTosser object when it wants to flip a coin.

The new `CoinTosser` object can have some intelligence, too. It doesn't have to be solely a worker bee flipping coins all day. It can keep track of the number of times a coin has been flipped, and it can track the number of times the coin lands on heads and tails. This "intelligence" can be used for reporting the statistics of a set of coin tosses.

Class

An object is used by an application when it is running, but before the object can be used, it must be defined. A class defines an object. A class describes the attributes and behaviors supported by the object. In more practical terms, the class is what you create in source code that defines the object. The object is an instance of the class created at run time.

To use a `CoinTosser` object in the CoinToss app, you must first define the class for the object. To accomplish this you need to create a new file (**File > New > New File** or **⌘-N**). Select the Objective-C class template found under **Mac OS X > Cocoa**, seen in Figure 4.6.

Click the **Next** button. Xcode asks you for the class name and the subclass. Enter "CoinTosser" for the class name, and make it a subclass of `NSObject`. Don't worry if subclass doesn't make sense. It will be explained later in the chapter.

Click the **Next** button, and then click the **Create** button (Figure 4.7) to create and add the new class file to the project.

Let's talk for a moment about what just happened.

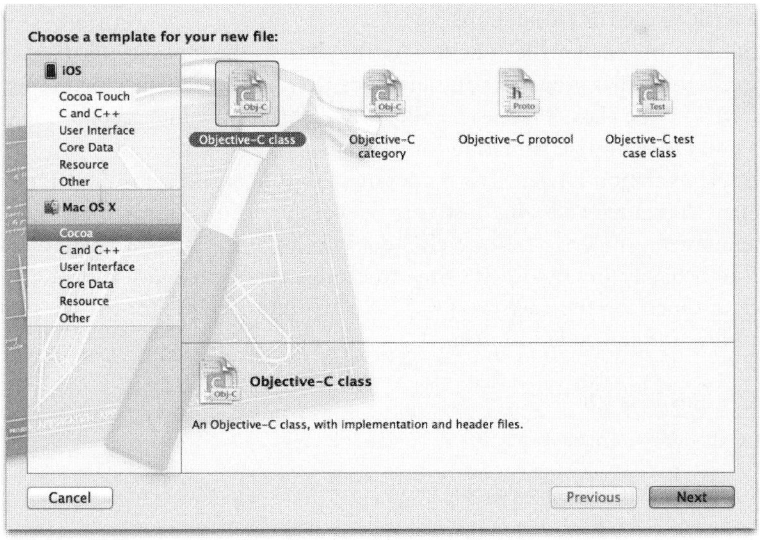

Figure 4.6   Select the Objective-C class template.

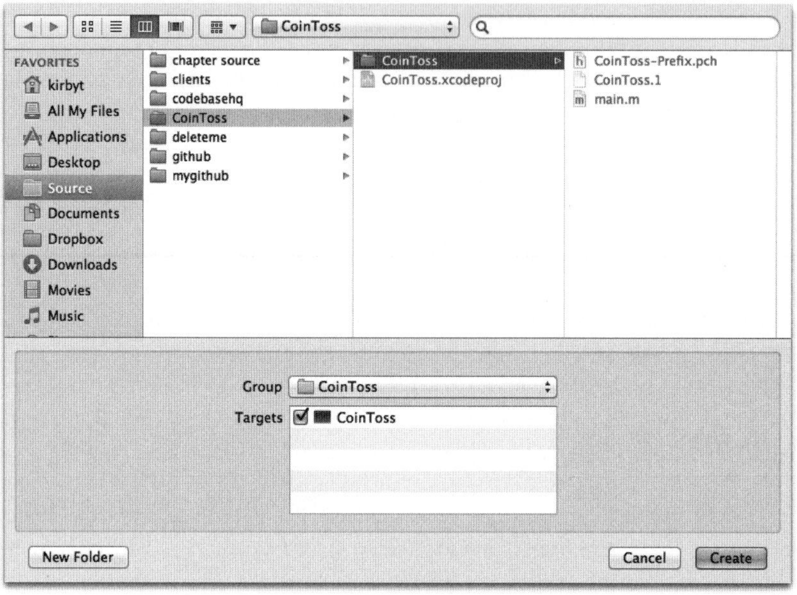

Figure 4.7   Save the class to the project by clicking the **Create** button.

When you created the new CoinTosser class, two files were added to the project, *CoinTosser.h* and *CoinTosser.m*. Objective-C, like C, uses two files to represent a source module. This is different from other programming languages such as C# and Java in which one file is used as a source module.

The *.h* file is the header file. The header file defines the interface for the class. The interface tells you what properties and methods (attributes and behaviors respectively) are supported by the class. The header file only describes the interface for the class. It does not provide the implementation for the class.

The implementation for the class is contained in the *.m* file. This implementation file is where the source code that instructs the computer to do something goes.

At the moment, the CoinTosser class does nothing. It has no attributes (properties) and no behavior (methods). It's time to change that. Start with the interface for the class. Open the file *CoinTosser.h*. This is the interface file for the class Coin-Tosser. Now add the code in Listing 4.2.

Listing 4.2   *CoinTosser.h*

```
#import <Foundation/Foundation.h>

@interface CoinTosser : NSObject

@property (nonatomic, assign) int headsCount;
@property (nonatomic, assign) int tailsCount;
```

```
@property (nonatomic, strong) NSString *lastResult;

- (void)flip;

@end
```

The first line is `#import <Foundation/Foundation.h>`. *Foundation.h* is another header file that defines the references for all functions and classes found in the Foundation framework. For the C programmers reading this, `#import` is similar to `#include`. However, `#import` ensures that the file is included only once, avoiding the problem of recursive includes.

The angled brackets surrounding `Foundation/Foundation.h` indicate that the header file is a system header file. System header files are stored outside of the project and are provided by the development environment and SDK. The system header files needed for iPad programming are added to your computer when you install Xcode and the iOS SDK.

If you want to import a header file that is part of the project, you enclose the header file name with quote characters, for example, `#import "CoinTosser.h"`. An example of this can be found in the *CoinTosser.m* implementation file.

Foundation is imported into the `CoinTosser` class so that it can reference other classes defined within the Foundation framework. The next line of code, for example, includes a reference to `NSObject`. `NSObject` is a Foundation object. In other words, it is defined in the Foundation framework.

NSObject

`NSObject` is the root object for all Objective-C objects (with only a few exceptions). `NSObject` provides the foundation for the class `CoinTosser` to be an object. `NSObject` provides the base properties and methods for all objects so that other objects do not have to reimplement the same code. This is a key advantage to using objects. An object can inherit properties and methods from another object. When a class inherits from another, it is called a subclass. `CoinTosser` is a subclass of `NSObject`. `NSObject` is the superclass to `CoinTosser`.

Because `CoinTosser` inherits from `NSObject`, it is able to do anything `NSObject` can do. The same is not true for the superclass. `NSObject` cannot do the same things `CoinTosser` can. This is because `NSObject` does not inherit properties and methods from `CoinTosser`. `CoinTosser`, on the other hand, does inherit properties and methods from `NSObject`.

Objective-C, like Java, C#, and Object Pascal, supports single class inheritance. Other programming languages such as C++, Perl, and Python support multiple class inheritance. Ambiguities can occur with multiple inheritance, which is why languages such as Objective-C follow the single inheritance model.

Interface

To define a class you use @interface. In Listing 4.2, the CoinTosser class definition starts with the line @interface CoinTosser : NSObject. @interface
is Objective-C syntax that tells the compiler that what follows is a class definition.
CoinTosser is the name of the class. The colon character separates the class name
from the name of the superclass. The new class inherits properties and methods from
the superclass.

The class definition starts with @interface and ends at the first occurrence of
@end. This tells the compiler it has reached the end of the class definition.

A class interface has three distinct sections. Local variables called instance variables, or ivars for short, are declared between the curly braces. Declared properties and
methods are defined after the curly braces. The order of the declared properties and
methods does not matter, but Objective-C convention is to declare properties after
ivars and declare methods after properties.

Now you may notice that there are no curly braces in Listing 4.2. The curly braces
are not included because there are no ivars defined for this class. Back in the day,
ivars were required to store data within the class instance (i.e., the object). However,
the convention today is to use what is called a declared property to store data in the
object. There was a time when Objective-C required each declared property to have
an explicitly declared ivar, but that is no longer the case. The compiler implicitly
declares the ivar for a declared property for you.

What does all this mean? Let's take a closer look, starting with instance variables.

Instance Variables

An instance variable is a variable that is created by and made available to the class
instance, which is an object. Instance variables, or ivars as Objective-C programmers more commonly call them, are used to store data needed within the object. Ivars
can be C data types such as int, float, or double, or Objective-C classes such as
NSString, NSArray, or NSDictionary.

When you define an ivar of an Objective-C class type, what you are actually doing
is defining a pointer to the object. Pointers are denoted in C and Objective-C with
the asterisk character (*).

Take a look at the ivars defined for the old-style version of the CoinTosser class
shown in Listing 4.3. There are three ivars. Two are defined as C int types. The int
data type is a primitive C data type. Primitive data types are not pointers, hence the
lack of the asterisk. The third ivar is of type NSString. NSString is an Objective-C
object defined in Foundation. Because it is an object, the ivar is declared as a pointer.
So NSString *lastResult says that the ivar lastResult is a pointer to an instance
of class NSString.

Listing 4.3   **Old-Style Version of the** `CoinTosser` **Interface**

```
#import <Foundation/Foundation.h>


@interface CoinTosser : NSObject
{
@private
   int headsCount;
   int tailsCount;
   NSString *lastResult;
}

@property (nonatomic, assign) int headsCount;
@property (nonatomic, assign) int tailsCount;
@property (nonatomic, copy) NSString *lastResult;

- (void)flip;

@end
```

Listing 4.3 shows the old style for defining a class. The old style used ivars to provide a storage location for declared properties. The declared properties are those items in the listing that start with `@property`. This style of coding is no longer common in Objective-C thanks to improvements in the compiler and Objective-C runtime. The common style today is to not explicitly declare the ivars and instead let the compiler take care of them for you. But even though explicitly declaring ivars is becoming a thing of the past, understanding the role ivars play is important, especially when you are talking about declared properties.

Declared Properties

The general convention followed in most object-oriented programming languages is to never directly get or set an ivar from outside the object that defines it. The standard convention, instead, is to use getter and setter accessor methods. These methods hide the details of the data storage from the outside world, where the "outside world" is any code using the object. The concept of information hiding is a key concept in object orientation called encapsulation.

An object encapsulates the data to protect the rest of the application from changes that might occur within the object. When accessor methods are used, changes can be made to the data inside that object without impacting the rest of the application. For example, let's say you have a `Person` object, and this object has an ivar called `name`. The application using this object gets and sets a person's name as needed. Sometime later it's determined that you need to have `firstName` and `lastName`. `name` becomes the concatenation of first and last name. If you are using getter and setter accessor methods for `name` instead of accessing the ivar directly, the implementation details for the accessor methods can change without impacting the rest of the application.

The problem with getter and setter access methods is that you have to declare each as part of the interface. This means that for every ivar value that is exposed to the outside world, you need to declare two methods. The code for the `Person` interface looks like this:

```
@interface Person : NSObject {
@private
    NSString *name_;
}
- (NSString *)name;
- (void)setName:(NSString *)newName;
@end
```

> **Note**
>
> The Objective-C convention for getter methods is to use only the name. Other object-oriented programming languages prefix the method with `get` (e.g., `getName`).

In addition to the getter and setter accessor methods being declared in the interface, each method must be implemented in the implementation file. This means writing a lot of boilerplate code just to get and set a property value. Luckily, Objective-C 2.0 introduced the concept of declared properties.

A declared property is a compiler directive that generates the accessor methods for you. This means that you do not need to declare the accessor methods in the interface. Thus the `Person` class interface becomes this:

```
@interface Person : NSObject {
@private
    NSString *name_;
}
@property (strong) NSString *name;
@end
```

To make things even easier, with the release of the iOS 4.0 SDK, explicit declarations for ivars are no longer required. This means that the `Person` class interface becomes this:

```
@interface Person : NSObject
@property (strong) NSString *name;
@end
```

Using declared properties is more convenient now that ivars are no longer required. But before you use a declared property, you need to understand how to define one.

A declared property is defined with the compiler directive `@property`. This tells the compiler that what follows is a declared property. The declared property definition ends at the first semicolon (;) character following the `@property` directive.

A number of attributes are available to the `@property` directive. These attributes include `nonatomic`, `assign`, `copy`, `retain`, `readwrite`, and `readonly`. These attributes are enclosed with parentheses found after `@property`. You can use a combination of the settings, but not all settings can be combined. Combining `readwrite` with `readonly`, for example, makes no sense.

> **Note**
>
> Two additional declared property attributes, `strong` and `weak`, are available when Automatic Reference Counting is enabled. These are covered later in this chapter.

Declared properties are, by default, considered atomic. There is no attribute keyword to denote atomic. The lack of `nonatomic` indicates that the property is atomic.

An atomic property is thread safe. The property value retrieved by the getter or set by the setter can be performed safely in a multithreaded application regardless of other concurrently executing threads. This thread safety does introduce a slight overhead in the accessor methods, but it is well worth it if multiple threads access the object at the same time.

`nonatomic` is not thread safe, which means that if two threads running concurrently attempt to get and set the property value at the same time, unexpected results can occur.

`assign`, `copy`, and `retain` control how memory is managed within the setter method for the declared property. `assign` simply assigns the new value to the ivar. (Remember, an ivar is still used even when you do not explicitly declare it.) You always want to use `assign` when declaring a property of a primitive data type such as `int`, `float`, `double`, and `BOOL`. `copy` and `retain` are used for Objective-C objects. These two attributes extend the lifetime of the object. `assign` is also used with objects, but it does not extend the object's lifetime.

In addition to `assign`, `copy`, and `retain`, two other attributes are available for use when Automatic Reference Counting is turned on. These two attributes are `strong` and `weak`, and they too control how memory is managed. Details on memory management of objects are covered in the Memory Management section found later in this chapter. For now, just know that these attributes control how memory is managed.

`readonly` and `readwrite` attributes do exactly as their names imply. `readonly` makes the declared property read-only. This means that the property does not have a setter method and users of the object cannot change its value. `readwrite` tells the compiler to generate both the getter and setter methods. The default is `readwrite` when neither is explicitly declared.

There are two additional attributes that come in handy from time to time: `getter` and `setter`. These two attributes allow you to rename the getter and setter access methods. The `getter` attribute is commonly used with property values of Boolean (`BOOL`) type. The Objective-C convention for naming Booleans is to leave off the `is` prefix. For instance, instead of having a property named `isVisible`, the convention is to name the property `visible`. However, to make the code more readable, the getter accessor method is renamed `isVisible`. You define this property like this:

```
@property (assign, getter = isVisible) BOOL visible;
```

> **Note**
>
> BOOL is the Objective-C type equivalent of `bool` found in C. While you can use `bool` in Objective-C code, it is recommended that you stick with BOOL since all of Apple's Objective-C frameworks use it. This keeps your code compatible with Apple should it ever decide to change the BOOL type. Also, YES and NO (not `true` and `false`) are the preferred Objective-C values for setting and testing BOOL values.

Methods

Take another look at the `CoinToss` class interface. Following the declared properties is the declaration for a method named –flip. The method declaration looks like this:

```
- (void)flip;
```

A method performs an action on behalf of the object. The action typically involves using data that is associated with the object. The method –flip, for example, executes the code needed to flip a coin. It then stores the results in the declared properties for the object.

A method can have a return value and zero, one, or more parameters. The data type for the return value is specified in parentheses before the method name. A method with no return value uses void as the data type. Parameters are included as part of the method name. Objective-C does not use named parameters. Instead, the colon character is used to indicate the presence of a parameter. This tends to make Objective-C more verbose, but more readable, than other programming languages. Here is an example of a method declaration with parameters:

```
- (int)incrementValue:(int)value bySomeValue:(int)someValue;
```

Methods come in two flavors: class method and instance method. A class method is denoted with a + character at the beginning. A class method is executed from the class, not an object (which is an instance of the class). Class methods are commonly provided by a class as a matter of convenience. For instance, many of the Foundation classes provide class methods that return an instance of the class. Using [NSArray array] is much more convenient than using [[[NSArray alloc] init] autorelease].

The other method type is called an instance method. An instance method is a method available only to an instance of the class (i.e., the object). Instance methods are denoted with a – character at the beginning. The –flip method defined for the CoinToss class is an instance method.

Implementation

A class is made up of two pieces: an interface and an implementation. The interface defines what the class looks like—its properties and methods. The implementation is where code that is executed at run time lives. In Objective-C, the implementation file uses the *.m* file extension. Why *.m*? Well, according to a thread on StackOverflow, the creator of Objective-C, Brad Cox, said that *m* is used "because .o and .c were taken. Simple as that."[1] Others believe *.m* stands for "messages" or "methods." Regardless, the implementation of an Objective-C class is in the *.m* file.

Let's take a look at the implementation file for the `CoinTosser` class. The implementation is shown in Listing 4.4. Be sure to open the file *CoinTosser.m* and add this code to your `CoinTosser` class.

Listing 4.4 `CoinTosser` **Class Implementation**

```
#import "CoinTosser.h"

@implementation CoinTosser

@synthesize headsCount = _headsCount;
@synthesize tailsCount = _tailsCount;
@synthesize lastResult = _lastResult;

- (id)init
{
   self = [super init];
   if (self) {
      [self setLastResult:@""];
   }

   return self;
}

- (void)flip
{
   int randomValue = (arc4random()%10) + 1; // Returns an int between 1 and 10.
   if (randomValue % 2) {
      [self setLastResult:@"Heads"];
      [self setHeadsCount:[self headsCount] + 1];
   } else {
      [self setLastResult:@"Tails"];
      [self setTailsCount:[self tailsCount] + 1];
   }

}

@end
```

The implementation of a class starts with the compiler directive `@implementation`. The `@implementation` section ends with the first occurrence of the `@end` compiler directive. The implementation is the code or actions performed by the class. It consists of methods that are defined as part of the class interface as well as methods not defined

---

1. **stackoverflow.com/questions/652186/why-do-objective-c-files-use-the-m-extension/652266#652266.**

by the interface. Methods not defined by the class interface are private and can be used only within the class itself.

Synthesize

The first block of code typically found in the implementation is the @synthesize statement for each declared property. The @synthesize statement is responsible for telling the compiler that it needs to provide the accessor methods for the declared properties. The @synthesize directive is followed by the name of the property to synthesize. For instance, @synthesize headsCount will generate the required accessor methods for the declared property headsCount.

By default, a synthesized property will use an ivar that has the exact same name as the property. This means that the statement @synthesize headsCount will implicitly declare an ivar named headsCount. You can change the ivar name by setting the synthesized property name equal to another name, for example:

```
@synthesize headsCount = _headsCount;
```

This line of code synthesizes the declared property headsCount. It generates the accessor methods for the property, and it implicitly declares the ivar _headsCount. The underscore is just a naming convention. It has no special meaning. The ivar could be called headsCount_ or even bob.

Why would you want to rename the ivar to something other than the property name? One of the best reasons to rename the ivar is to avoid conflicts with parameter names used in method declarations. If the parameter name for a method matches the ivar name, the compiler will produce a warning that the local variable hides the ivar.

As a real-world example, consider a view controller that contains a table view. The declared property for the table view is named tableView. In the implementation, the tableView property is synthesized and the ivar is not renamed. It remains tableView. You declare the delegate methods for the table view delegate object, and each of these methods has a parameter named tableView. This now hides the ivar from the method's implementation, producing a warning message from the compiler.

The example just described likely sounds foreign to you, but it will make sense later after you spend time writing your first iPad app. For now, just know that renaming the ivar for a declared property is a good thing.

init

Following the @synthesize statements is the method named -init. This method is defined in the NSObject class, which is why you do not see it in the CoinTosser interface. The method -init is called when an object is created. In Objective-C, you commonly see the following pattern:

```
MyClass *myObject = [[MyClass alloc] init];
```

The method +alloc is a class method. It is responsible for allocating a new object as an instance of the class. The instance method -init is called to initialize the object.

The –init method is where you typically place code responsible for initializing the object. For instance, the –init method for `CoinTosser` sets the `lastResult` property to a zero-length string.

The –init method for the `CoinTosser` class makes references to the variable `self`. The `self` variable is a special variable that references the current instance of the class. It is used within the methods of a class to access properties and methods defined by the class. The line of code `[self setLastResult:@""]` is saying to call the `-setLastResult:` (this is the setter method for the declared property `lastResult`) method on this instance of the class.

> **Note**
>
> Other object-oriented programming languages use `self`, `this`, and `me` to reference the current instance of a class.

super

The first line of code in the –init method from Listing 4.4 is `self = [super init]`. The keyword `super` instructs the code to call the method from the superclass. You often call `super` when you override a method defined in the superclass. This ensures that behavior from the superclass is executed as part of the implementation for the overridden method.

flip

The final method defined in the `CoinTosser` implementation is `-flip`. This method is an instance method, which means it can be called only on an instance of the `CoinTosser` class. The `-flip` method uses the same algorithm used earlier in the C version of the app. It generates a random number and checks to see if the number is even or odd. The difference, however, is that the results of the flip are no longer reported via the `NSLog` function. Instead, the declared property `lastResult` is set to either "Heads" or "Tails," and the heads and tails counts are incremented.

This code may look a bit odd at first. You may be wondering about the brackets enclosing some of the lines of code, and the string literal that has an @ symbol at the beginning. What you are seeing here is Objective-C code. In fact, when you look at the implementation for the –flip method, you see a mix of C and Objective-C code. `int randomValue = (arc4random()%10) + 1` and `if (randomValue % 2)` are C statements. The statements enclosed with brackets are Objective-C statements.

A quick way to identify Objective-C statements is to look for the brackets, though this is not always true, as you will see in a moment.

The string literals `@"Heads"` and `@"Tails"` are Unicode strings used by Objective-C. The @ signals to the compiler that the string literal is for Objective-C. An Objective-C string literal is actually shorthand syntax to define a pointer to an Objective-C string object. If the @ symbol is missing, the compiler assumes that the string literal is a C string literal, which is generally not used in Objective-C. A C string literal is a pointer to a `char` data type and not an object.

Let's take another look at a snippet of the Objective-C code from the -flip method. The code is

```
[self setLastResult:@"Heads"];
[self setHeadsCount:[self headsCount] + 1];
```

What exactly is going on here? The first line of code is of course Objective-C code. The brackets tell you (and the compiler) that. self is the object and the receiver of the message setLastResult:. Message, not method? Yes, message.

The Objective-C runtime environment is a dynamic environment. It is a message-based environment similar to Smalltalk. So while it looks as if the code is calling the method setLastResult:, it is in fact sending a message to the object self. self is the receiver, and the message it receives is setLastResult:. The message is then mapped to the method -setLastResult:, implemented in the class that defines the object. So while it looks as if the code is calling the method -setLastResult:, under the Objective-C hood a message is being sent to the receiver self. And this all happens at run time.

Why is this important? It is important because it means that the method (or message) is not required to be known at compile time. It can be determined at run time.

Selector

A method is the implementation of some functionality within a class. At run time, a message is sent to a receiver (object) that in turn invokes the method. The message is called a selector, and a selector is another data type in Objective-C. The SEL type defines a selector. In code, you can create a reference to a selector by using the @selector compiler directive. For example:

```
SEL selector = @selector(flip);
```

This line of code assigns a selector for the message flip to the variable selector. The selector can then be invoked by calling -performSelector:, which is available on NSObject. This means that the Objective-C code you write can determine at run time what selector (or method) to invoke. An example of this is shown in Chapter 16, "Building the Main Screen."

Dynamically invoking methods isn't the only thing you can do with selectors. You can use selectors to determine if an object implements a particular method. This means that you can query an object at run time to determine if it supports a particular method. If the method is supported, it is called; otherwise a different course of action is taken. Examples of this are found throughout this book, starting with Chapter 15, "Doing More with View Controllers."

Let's return to the code snippet:

```
[self setLastResult:@"Heads"];
[self setHeadsCount:[self headsCount] + 1];
```

So self is the object that receives the message. self is also considered the receiver, and the message is the selector. In the first line of code, the message is setLast-Result:. This message corresponds to a method defined in the class for self. self is an instance of the class CoinTosser, so the message corresponds to the method -setLastResult: defined in the class CoinTosser. But this method is not defined anywhere in the class. Why?

The method -setLastResult: is a setter method for the declared property lastResult. The @synthesize statement for lastResult generates the -set-LastResult: method at compile time, which is why it is not explicitly declared in the class implementation.

The same is true for the line of code that follows. headsCount is a property. It is synthesized, making the setter method setHeadsCount: available in the object. But the second line of code includes the statement [self headsCount]. This is the getter method for the declared property. So what you see here are two lines of Objective-C code accessing declared properties using the accessor methods for the properties.

Now you can, if you want, access the property values directly by using the ivar for each property. The code looks like this:

```
lastResult_ = @"Heads";
headsCount_ = headsCount_ + 1;
```

The problem, however, is that you should never (except under very rare circumstances) directly access the ivar. Accessing the ivar is not good object-oriented programming. A declared property does more than just wrap access to the ivar. It manages the memory associated with the ivar.

In the case of lastResult, directly setting the ivar lastResult_ can result in a memory leak. In fact, the line of code lastResult_ = @"Heads" can cause a memory leak. The ivar may have been pointing to another NSString object. By directly setting the ivar and bypassing the memory management provided by declared properties, you have orphaned the other NSString object, leaving it in memory until the app quits. Leaking memory from one NSString object is not going to crash your app, but leaking hundreds, even thousands, will potentially crash your app and annoy your users.

So the general rule of thumb is never to access ivars directly. Always use accessor methods to get and set property values.

But you say, "Okay, I'll only use the accessor methods. But isn't there a way to simplify the code and avoid the brackets?" Why, yes, there is, but...

Dot Syntax

Objective-C supports dot syntax. Dot syntax is a shortcut way for writing code that accesses properties. Here is the same code snippet, this time using dot syntax:

```
self.lastResult = @"Heads";
self.headsCount = self.headsCount + 1;
```

Each line of code still states the object (or receiver) and the method (or message and selector). But the brackets have been eliminated to make the code easier to read.

While dot syntax simplifies the code, its use in Objective-C has sparred a religious war of sorts. Some Objective-C developers like using dot syntax anywhere and everywhere, while others are completely opposed to its use. Both groups have good arguments favoring their beliefs. You can do a Google search on the phrase "Objective-C use dot syntax or not" to read arguments from both sides.

This book does not take a stance on the use, or lack of use, of dot syntax. However, most of the code in this book uses the messaging-style format instead of dot syntax. Why? For many newcomers to Objective-C, using the messaging style is easier to grok.

Using the `CoinTosser` **Class**

Let's get back to the CoinToss app. You have created the class `CoinTosser` and added it to the project. If you have not, go back to the Class and Implementation sections and copy the code from the listings.

Now open the file *main.m* and update it with the code from Listing 4.5.

Listing 4.5   **Updated** *main.m* **File**

```
#import <Foundation/Foundation.h>
#import "CoinTosser.h"                                        // 1

int main (int argc, const char * argv[])
{

    @autoreleasepool {

        CoinTosser *tosser = [[CoinTosser alloc] init];       // 2
        for (int index = 0; index < 10; index++ ) {           // 3
            [tosser flip];                                    // 4
            NSLog(@"%@", [tosser lastResult]);                // 5
        }
        NSLog(@"Tally: heads %i tails %i", [tosser headsCount],
            [tosser tailsCount]);                             // 6

    }
    return 0;
}
```

Now let's walk through the code changes:

1. The first change is the addition of the #import "CoinTosser.h" header file. The code in *main.m* uses the CoinTosser class, so the header file must be imported.

2. A local variable named `tosser` is created. It is a pointer to an instance of the class `CoinTosser`. The class method `+alloc` is called to create the object, and the instance method `-init` is called to initialize the object.

3. A `for` loop is created that loops ten times. This `for` loop is standard C code.

4. The instance method `-flip` is called. Under the hood, Objective-C is sending the message `flip` to the receiving object `tosser`, which in turns invokes the method `-flip`. But to keep things simple, let's just say the method `-flip` is called.

5. The function `NSLog` is called. It sends the current string value for the declared `lastResult` to the output window.

6. After the `for` loop completes, an additional `NSLog` is called to show the total number of times the coin lands on heads and lands on tails.

After you make the changes to *main.m*, run the app (**⌘-R**) and see how many times the coin lands on heads and tails.

Memory Management

One aspect of programming for iOS that is a pain point for newcomers is memory management. The iOS platform is designed for mobile devices, which have limited available memory. Apple does not publish information about the amount of available RAM on the iPad, but it's believed that the first-generation iPad has only 256MB and the iPad 2 has 512MB of memory. Compare this to the MacBook Air, which starts with 2GB of memory and can go up to 4GB, or the MacBook Pro, which starts with 4GB and supports up to 8GB. The iPad, by today's standard, doesn't have much memory.

The iOS platform is finely tuned for these low-memory mobile devices, which means some technology trade-offs had to be made to ensure high performance and great battery life. One such trade-off is the lack of garbage collection, a technology that many of today's programmers take for granted. Without garbage collection, you, the programmer, are responsible for memory management within your application. But what does this mean exactly?

Each time you allocate an object, you are responsible for releasing it. If you fail to release the object, the object leaks. This means that the memory used by the object remains allocated with no way of releasing it. A memory leak is one of the most common errors found in iOS apps today, and it leads to low-memory conditions on the device, which can ultimately crash the app. And no one likes a crasher.

Memory leaks are caused by sloppy programming where a programmer is not following the retain-and-release pattern. When you allocate (or copy) an object, you take ownership of the object. It's like saying, "You retain ownership of this object." As the owner of the object, it is your job to release (or free) the object when it is no longer needed. If the object is not released, it sits in memory until the app quits. Hence retain and release. If you retain an object, you must release it. No *ifs*, *ands*, or *buts*.

Garbage collection frees the programmer from having to worry about memory management. The garbage collector monitors the object and memory usage, and it automatically releases the object when it knows the object is no longer needed. Garbage collection, however, is not available on iOS. It is available for the Mac desktop, which also has a lot more available RAM than an iOS device. But you're not here to learn about Mac programming. You're here to learn about iOS programming, and you have to accept the fact that no garbage collection is available for iOS.

But fear not, soon-to-be-skilled iOS programmer, because Apple engineers have come up with a way to relieve you from the burden of memory management while at the same time keeping iOS a finely tuned mobile OS without garbage collection.

Automatic Reference Counting

Automatic Reference Counting, or ARC for short, is a compiler-level feature that simplifies the memory management of an object. It's like garbage collection, but better for mobile devices.

Objects in Objective-C are reference counted. Each time you retain an object, the reference count for the object increments. When you release the object, the reference count for the object decrements. When the reference count reaches zero, the object is de-allocated. This frees the memory used by the object, giving the memory back to the operating system so that it can be allocated for another purpose at another time.

With ARC, your code is analyzed during compile time, and the appropriate management of the lifetime for an object is injected into the compiled binary. This means that you never need to release an object. It is done automatically. Prior to ARC, you had to explicitly call release on each object that you retained. This is no longer required. In fact, calling release is no longer possible. Attempting to call release on an object while using ARC will result in a compile error.

What does ARC mean for you, the newcomer to iPad programming? It means you don't have to worry (as much) about the lifetime (i.e., memory management) of an object. You allocate an object when it is needed, and it is released automatically. This means less code for you to write, making your code easier to read and less likely to ever cause a memory leak.

ARC also introduces two new property attributes for declared properties: weak and strong. These two keywords control the memory management aspects of the property. The keyword strong is used in place of retain. A strong property is claiming "ownership," and its object is automatically released when the object is no longer referenced.

A weak property does not extend the lifetime of the object. In other words, it does not assume ownership, so it is possible that the object is released while the property has a reference to it. However, weak properties are automatically set to nil when the object is released. This is a huge benefit to the iOS programmer. Before ARC, when an object was released, the reference to the de-allocated object still pointed to the memory address for the object. If you attempted to make a call to the released object, it would crash your app.

With ARC, when the object pointed to by a weak property is released, the reference is automatically set to `nil`. And in Objective-C, sending a message to a `nil` object does absolutely nothing. This means that your app will not crash. It does not mean that your app will function properly, but at least the crasher has been eliminated.

When you create a new iOS project, one of the project options is "Use Automatic Reference Counting." In general, you should always turn on this feature.

Note

ARC is available for iOS 4 and above.

Summary

As stated at the beginning, this chapter is a brief overview of Objective-C. The goal is to arm you with enough knowledge that you can work your way though this book. You will learn more as you read along, but there is so much more to Objective-C than what is covered here.

If you want to learn more about Objective-C, or you're not yet comfortable with Objective-C, read one of the books listed at the beginning of the chapter. Or read the *Objective-C Programming Language*[2] and *Object-Oriented Programming with Objective-C*[3] documents published by Apple and available for free online at **developer.apple.com** and in the iBookstore.

---

2. **developer.apple.com/library/prerelease/ios/#documentation/Cocoa/Conceptual/ ObjectiveC/Introduction/introObjectiveC.html**.
3. **developer.apple.com/library/prerelease/ios/#documentation/Cocoa/Conceptual/ OOP_ObjC/Introduction/Introduction.html**.

Getting Started with Cocoa

Objective-C is the preferred programming language for writing iOS applications. The ability to use Objective-C for writing iOS applications would be limited, however, if not for the support of a solid, well-designed application framework called Cocoa. It is the combination of Objective-C with Cocoa that makes it possible for you to write iOS applications.

Cocoa is an application framework—written mostly in Objective-C—that makes it possible to rapidly write robust, full-featured applications for iOS. Cocoa provides frameworks, libraries, and APIs for virtually every conceivable development necessity imaginable. Without Cocoa there would not be hundreds of thousands of iOS applications available in the App Store today.

This chapter introduces you to the Cocoa stack, two of its key frameworks (Foundation and UIKit), and common design patterns found in Cocoa. These frameworks and patterns are fundamental to iOS programming and require a general understanding before you continue beyond this chapter.

This chapter is split into four sections. The first introduces you to the Cocoa architectural stack. A quick reference to many of the more frequently used classes found in the Foundation framework follows this. UIKit, the framework responsible for providing objects that create and manage the user interface for the applications you will create, is covered after Foundation. And finally, the chapter wraps up with a review of common design patterns found in Cocoa and in the sample code for the book.

Let's get started by talking more about the Cocoa stack.

The Cocoa Stack

Cocoa is the application environment for iOS. Its collection of frameworks, libraries, and APIs provides the building blocks for creating awesome iOS applications. The breadth and richness of the Cocoa stack are truly amazing.

Cocoa's architectural stack for iOS applications consists of four key layers, as seen in Figure 5.1.

- **Cocoa Touch**: Supports iOS applications. It includes frameworks such as UIKit, GameKit, iAd, and Map Kit.

Figure 5.1   Cocoa's architectural stack for iOS. Note the two key frameworks, UIKit and Foundation.

- **Media**: Provides graphical and multimedia support to the Cocoa Touch layer, and it depends on Core Services. It includes frameworks such as Core Animation, Core Audio, AVFoundation, Core Graphics, OpenGL ES, and Core Text.

- **Core Services**: As the layer name implies, the Core Services layer provides core services such as string management, collections classes, networking, URL utilities, and preferences. It also provides frameworks for hardware-based services such as GPS, compass, accelerometer, and the gyroscope on iPhone 4, and it provides services and frameworks for data persistence. Some of the key frameworks found in the Core Services layer include Core Data, Foundation, Core Foundation, Core Location, and System Configuration.

- **Core OS**: At Cocoa's foundation is Core OS. This layer abstracts the rest of Cocoa from the actual operating system. It provides the kernel, the file system, networking infrastructure, security, power management, and device drivers.

Cocoa is also available on Mac OS X where it is the predominant application environment for building Mac applications. Most but not all of the frameworks provided in Cocoa for iOS are available on Mac OS X, excluding Cocoa Touch, of course. This means you can achieve a certain amount of code reuse when developing applications for both iOS and Mac OS X.

As you read this book, you will get hands-on experience with different Cocoa frameworks, but you need to be aware of two key frameworks before continuing: Foundation and UIKit. Much of what you do with Cocoa centers on these two frameworks, so much so that a brief overview is warranted.

Note

When I learn a new programming environment, the first thing I like to do is get an overview of what features are available. I don't need to know the intimate details. I just need a quick reference for what's available so that my mind can start relating features of the new environment to environments I've worked with in the past. That's the purpose of the remainder of this chapter: to give you an overview of Cocoa's two key frameworks.

If you have been reading since Chapter 1, "Your First App"—and you probably have—you have already used both Foundation and UIKit. So what are these two frameworks?

Foundation is a library of Objective-C classes providing

- A set of useful primitive data classes
- Small utility classes
- Support for Unicode strings
- Support for object persistence

Foundation also provides a level of OS independence. It is this OS independence that allows you to reuse the same code between iOS and Mac OS X.

UIKit is a library of user interface objects for constructing and managing an application's user interface. Unlike Foundation, UIKit is tied directly to iOS. This means you cannot use UIKit-related code for Mac OS X applications.

Note

Mac developers use a similar user interface framework called AppKit.

Let's look at some of the more frequently used classes in these two frameworks, starting with Foundation.

Foundation

Foundation, as the name implies, provides the foundation for many primitive data type classes, utility classes, Unicode string support, and object persistence for iOS applications. Much of Foundation is, just to reiterate, available on iOS and Mac OS X, so code you write using Foundation can be used in applications built for both platforms.

This chapter does not cover every class in Foundation—there are simply too many classes to cover each one—but it does cover the ones you will see most often, especially throughout this book.

Foundation versus Core Foundation

It's not uncommon for developers to think that Foundation and Core Foundation are the same, but in truth the two frameworks are different. Core Foundation is a library found further down the Cocoa stack. It provides types and interfaces implemented in C, not Objective-C. Foundation, on the other hand, is an object layer that sits on top of Core Foundation, providing Objective-C objects for Foundation types and services.

A quick way to know if you are working with a Foundation type versus a Core Foundation type is to look at the prefix in the type's name. Foundation types are prefixed with NS, and Core Foundation types are prefixed with CF. For example, NSString resides in the Foundation framework and CFString resides in Core Foundation. The same goes for other types such as NSDate and CFDate, NSArray and CFArray, NSDictionary and CFDictionary, and NSNumber and CFNumber.

Most Core Foundation types have counterparts in the Foundation framework. This close relationship between types means that Foundation types can be used in place of Core Foundation types. This is called "toll-free bridging."

Toll-free bridging makes it possible to use the types interchangeably with a simple cast. For example, Foundation's NSDate is toll-free bridged with CFDate found in Core Foundation. This means you can use an NSDate instance on API calls expecting CFDate as a parameter.

Data Type

As you learned in Chapter 4, "Getting Started with Objective-C," you can use the primitive C data types in your applications. But Foundation also provides a set of classes for primitive data types that help simplify your code.

> **Note**
>
> Some of the Foundation types are Objective-C classes and others are structure types defined in C. The only way to tell the difference is to look at the documentation or the header file where the type is defined.

Some Foundation classes come in two flavors: immutable and mutable. An immutable type cannot have its value changed once it has been initialized. Immutable types are, in a sense, static. Their values cannot change. A mutable type, on the other hard, can have its value changed over and over during the life of the object.

So why have both immutable and mutable classes? Immutable classes tend to be more efficient because immutable objects do not have to worry about data changes. Mutable classes, on the other hand, are more flexible in that the data managed by a mutable object can change during the life span of the object. The general rule of thumb is that unless you have a need to change an object's value, you will want to use immutable types whenever possible.

> **Note**
>
> A mutable type has the word *mutable* in its name, for example, NSMutableString, NSMutableArray, and NSMutableDictionary. Immutable types do not, for example, NSString, NSArray, and NSDictionary.

NSData **and** NSMutableData

NSData provides an object interface for a byte buffer. NSData is used to store a stream of bytes in memory. It includes methods for retrieving the bytes, retrieving subsets of bytes, and determining the length of the byte buffer, as well as methods for writing the bytes to a file. NSMutableData is the mutable version of NSData, which means its data can change. See Listing 5.1 for an example of using NSData, and see Listing 5.17 for an example of using NSMutableData.

Listing 5.1   New NSData **Instance Loaded with Bytes from the Image File** *home.png*

```
NSString *path = [[NSBundle mainBundle] pathForResource:@"home" ofType:@"png"];
NSData *data = [NSData dataWithContentsOfFile:path];
```

NSCalendar

NSCalendar is an object representing a system of time in which beginning, length, and subdivisions of the year are defined. NSCalendar is often used when performing date arithmetic with NSDate. Use the class method currentCalendar to return the logical calendar for the user. This calendar is created from the user's system locale and custom settings from System Preferences. You can also specify the calendar by calling initWithCalendarIdentifier: and passing in one of the NSLocale calendar keys, shown in Listing 5.2. See Listing 5.3 for sample code using NSCalendar.

Listing 5.2   NSLocale **Calendar Keys**

```
NSString * const NSGregorianCalendar;
NSString * const NSBuddhistCalendar;
NSString * const NSChineseCalendar;
NSString * const NSHebrewCalendar;
NSString * const NSIslamicCalendar;
NSString * const NSIslamicCivilCalendar;
NSString * const NSJapaneseCalendar;
NSString * const NSRepublicOfChinaCalendar;
NSString * const NSPersianCalendar;
NSString * const NSIndianCalendar;
NSString * const NSISO8601Calendar;
```

NSDate

NSDate is an object representing a single point in time. It provides methods for creating dates, comparing dates, calculating time intervals, and other date-related functionality. NSDate is toll-free bridged with CFDate. See Listing 5.3 for sample code using NSDate.

NSDateComponents

NSDateComponents is used to create a date object from the parts of a date and time: month, day, year, hour, minute, and second. You can also use NSDateComponents to retrieve the parts of the date and time. See Listing 5.3 for sample code using NSDateComponents.

Listing 5.3   **Sample Code Calculating My Son Rowan's Age Based on His Birth Date**

```
NSCalendar *calendar = [NSCalendar currentCalendar];
NSDate *now = [NSDate date];

NSDateComponents *components = [[NSDateComponents alloc] init];
[components setDay:29];
[components setMonth:3];
[components setYear:2008];
[components setCalendar:calendar];      // New as of iOS 4.0
NSDate *birthdate = [components date]; // New as of iOS 4.0

// Alternative approach used prior to iOS 4.0
// and still perfectly valid today.
//NSDate *birthdate = [calendar dateFromComponents:components];

// Flag determining which components of the date we want.
NSUInteger unitFlags = NSYearCalendarUnit|NSMonthCalendarUnit|NSDayCalendarUnit;

NSDateComponents *age = [calendar components:unitFlags
                                     fromDate:birthdate
                                       toDate:now
                                      options:0];

NSLog(@"Rowan is %i years %i months %i days old.",
      [age year], [age month], [age day]);
```

NSDecimalNumber

NSDecimalNumber is an object wrapper for decimal numbers derived from
NSNumber. According to Apple's developer documentation, NSDecimalNumber can
represent any number that can be "expressed as mantissa x $10^{exponent}$ where mantissa is a decimal integer up to 38 digits long, and exponent is an integer from -128
through 127." An example of using NSDecimalNumber is provided in Listing 5.4.

> **Note**
>
> NSDecimalNumber isn't the easiest object to work with, but Marcus Zarra makes a
> darn good argument as to why you should use it, especially if you are dealing with currency. Read his blog posting and don't be lazy with NSDecimalNumber.[1]

---

1. **www.cimgf.com/2008/04/23/cocoa-tutorial-dont-be-lazy-with-nsdecimalnumber-like-me/.**

Listing 5.4   **Rounding Example Using** NSDecimalNumber

```
NSDecimalNumber *number = [NSDecimalNumber decimalNumberWithMantissa:1445
                                                            exponent:-3
                                                          isNegative:NO];

NSDecimalNumberHandler *behavior =
   [NSDecimalNumberHandler decimalNumberHandlerWithRoundingMode:NSRoundPlain
                                                          scale:2
                                                raiseOnExactness:NO
                                                 raiseOnOverflow:NO
                                                raiseOnUnderflow:NO
                                             raiseOnDivideByZero:NO];

NSDecimalNumber *result =
   [number decimalNumberByRoundingAccordingToBehavior:behavior];

NSLog(@"%@ rounds to %@", number, result);
```

NSInteger **and** NSUInteger

NSInteger is a C typedef to describe an integer. NSInteger is a 32-bit integer in 32-bit applications and a 64-bit integer in 64-bit applications. NSUInteger is an unsigned NSInteger. Examples of using the integer types are shown in Listing 5.5.

Listing 5.5   **Examples of Initializing** NSInteger **and** NSUInteger

```
NSInteger x = 5;
NSInteger y = -20;
NSUInteger z = 12;
```

> **Note**
>
> NSInteger and NSUInteger provide architecturally safe data types for the corresponding C scalar types. This can be helpful when sharing code between iOS and Mac OS X. However, there may be times when you want to use the C scalar type. For instance, the use of NSInteger could cause unnecessary memory bloat to your application. A 4-bit integer uses half as much memory as an 8-bit integer. If your application is storing millions of short integers in memory, using the C scalar type may make more sense. However, generally speaking, using the Foundation types is fine for most applications where the number of these values stored in memory at one time is relatively small and the lifetime of the value is short-lived, that is, a local function variable.

NSNumber

NSNumber is an immutable object representing any C scalar (numeric) type. It provides methods for getting and setting signed and unsigned C scalar types char, short int, int, long int, long long int, float, double, and bool. NSNumber also includes a `compare:` method to compare values from two `NSNumber` instances. List-ing 5.6 shows examples of using the `NSNumber` object.

Listing 5.6   **Examples of Using** `NSNumber` **to Initialize and Retrieve Values**

```
NSNumber *number;
number = [NSNumber numberWithFloat:1.5];
float aFloat = [number floatValue];
number = [NSNumber numberWithBool:YES];
BOOL aBool = [number boolValue];
```

NSNull

`NSNull` is a singleton object used to represent `NULL` in a collection object, such as `NSArray` and `NSDictionary`, where `nil` is not allowed. An example of using the `NSNull` object in an `NSArray` is shown in Listing 5.7.

Listing 5.7   **Example of Using** `NSNull` **to Add a** `NULL` **Placeholder Object to an Array**

```
// [NSNull null] places a null object in the array.
// nil ends the array.
NSArray *items = [NSArray arrayWithObjects:
                  @"one", @"two", [NSNull null], @"four", nil];
NSLog(@"items = %@", items);
```

NSObject

`NSObject` is the root class for most Objective-C classes. Any class you create that does not derive from an existing class higher up the object hierarchy should derive from `NSObject`. Listing 5.8 shows an example of a class that is a subclass of `NSObject`.

Listing 5.8   **Example of a Class Derived from** `NSObject`

```
@interface MyClass : NSObject
{

}

@end
```

NSString **and** NSMutableString

`NSString` is an object representation of a text string. It provides methods for deter-mining the length of the string, retrieving characters at a particular position within the string, and text string comparisons.

The text string is stored as an array of Unicode characters. Unicode string literals are enclosed with double quotation marks and prefixed with the @ symbol. C string literals, on the other hand, are enclosed with only double quotation marks, no prefix. You will receive a compile error if you try to set an NSString to a C string literal. Listing 5.9 shows an example of creating a new NSString instance with a string literal.

Listing 5.9   **Creating a New** NSString **Instance from a String Literal**

```
// Create a new NSString instance with a string literal.
NSString *aString = @"This is a string literal";
```

Use NSMutableString when you need to update the string value after it has been initialized, as shown in Listing 5.10.

Listing 5.10   **Simple Sample of Appending New Strings to an** NSMutableString

```
NSMutableString *string = [[NSMutableString alloc] init];
for (int i=0; i < 10; i++) {
    [string appendFormat:@"Item %i\n", i];
}
NSLog(@"%@", string);
```

Collection Classes

NSArray **and** NSMutableArray

NSArray manages an ordered collection of objects. NSArray creates a static array, and NSMutableArray creates a dynamic array. An object added to the array receives a retain message. When the object is removed, which is possible only with NSMutable-Array, the object receives a release message. And when the array is released, all objects contained by the array receive a release message. An example of using NSArray is shown in Listing 5.11.

Listing 5.11   **Example of Using** NSArray **and** NSMutableArray

```
NSArray *staticArray = [NSArray arrayWithObjects:
                        @"one", @"two", @"three", @"four", nil];
NSLog(@"%@", staticArray);

NSMutableArray *dynamicArray = [[NSMutableArray alloc] init];
[dynamicArray addObject:@"one"];
[dynamicArray addObject:@"two"];
[dynamicArray addObject:@"three"];
[dynamicArray addObject:@"four"];
NSLog(@"%@", dynamicArray);
[dynamicArray release];
```

NSDictionary **and** NSMutableDictionary

NSDictionary manages a static collection of objects associated by key-value pairs. NSMutableDictionary manages a dynamic collection of objects. The key identifies the object and the value is the object. As with NSArray and NSMutableArray, an object added to a dictionary receives a retain message. The object receives a release message when removed from the dictionary. And all objects contained in the dictionary receive a release message when the dictionary is released. Examples of using dictionaries are shown in Listing 5.12.

Listing 5.12 **Examples of** NSDictionary **and** NSMutableDictionary

```
NSDictionary *dict = [NSDictionary dictionaryWithObjectsAndKeys:
                        @"John Doe", @"name",
                        @"Seattle", @"city",
                        @"WA", @"state",
                        nil];
NSMutableDictionary *mutableDict =
    [NSMutableDictionary dictionaryWithDictionary:dict];
[mutableDict setObject:@"555-1212" forKey:@"phone"];
[mutableDict setObject:@"john.doe@domain.com" forKey:@"email"];
```

NSSet, NSMutableSet, **and** NSCountedSet

NSSet, NSMutableSet, and NSCountedSet manage a collection of unordered objects. You use a set in place of an array when order is not important and you need to check if the set contains the object.

> **Note**
>
> Checking for the existence of an object in an array is not as fast as checking a set. So if order is not important and you need to determine if an object already exists in some collection, use one of the set objects.

NSSet creates a static set of distinct objects. Objects cannot be added or removed after the set is initialized. You can, however, change the object contained in a static set. In other words, you can change the properties of an object contained in an NSSet, but you cannot remove the object reference from the static set.

NSMutableSet creates a dynamic set of distinct objects. Objects can be added and removed even after the set has been initialized.

NSCountedSet is a mutable set of indistinct objects. Whereas NSSet and NSMutableSet contain at most one reference to an object, NSCountedSet can contain any number of references to the same object. NSCountedSet keeps track of the number of times an object is added to and removed from the set. To completely remove an object from NSCountedSet, the object must be removed the same number of times it is added. Examples of using sets are shown in Listing 5.13.

> **Note**
>
> NSCountedSet is also known as a bag.

Listing 5.13 Examples of Using NSSet, NSMutableSet, **and** NSCountedSet

```
NSString *peter = @"Peter";
NSString *mary = @"Mary";
NSString *paul = @"Paul";


NSSet *set = [NSSet setWithObjects:paul, mary, nil];
NSLog(@"%@", set);


NSMutableSet *mutableSet = [NSMutableSet setWithSet:set];
[mutableSet addObject:peter];
NSLog(@"%@", mutableSet);


NSCountedSet *countedSet = [NSCountedSet setWithObjects:
                                 peter, paul, mary, peter, nil];
NSLog(@"%@", countedSet);
```

Utility Classes and Functions

NSLog

NSLog sends a message to the Apple System Log facility. The message can be viewed in the console. When calling NSLog, you first pass the format string followed by a variable number of arguments displayed as part of the output message. Table 5.1 lists some of the more common format specifiers supported by format strings. For a complete list, read the "String Format Specifiers"[2] article in the developer documentation.

NSBundle

NSBundle is an object representing a location on the file system containing the code and resources used by the application. In iOS, NSBundle is used to find the path to

Table 5.1 Commonly Used String Format Specifiers

Specifier	Description
%@	Objective-C object; displays the string returned by descriptionWithLocale: (if available) or description
%%	"%" literal character
%d, %D, %i	Signed integer
%u, %U	Unsigned integer
%f	Floating-point number
%s	Null-terminated char array (8-bit, C language string)
%S	Null-terminated Unicode char array (16-bit)
%p	Pointer address displayed in hex

---

2. **developer.apple.com/library/ios/#documentation/Cocoa/Conceptual/Strings/Articles/formatSpecifiers.html**.

resources such as images and *plist* files included in your application. An example of using the NSBundle object is shown in Listing 5.14.

Listing 5.14   Example of Retrieving the Path to the Application's Icon Image File Using NSBundle

```
NSString *path = [[NSBundle mainBundle] pathForResource:@"icon" ofType:@"png"];
```

> **Note**
>
> A bundle can be one of three types: Application, Framework, or plug-in. However, under iOS you can create a bundle only of type Application. iOS third-party developers cannot create Framework and plug-in bundles.

NSFileManager

NSFileManager is a class wrapper for performing generic file system operations such as copying, or moving, a file from one path to another, determining if a file exists, creating a new directory path, and so on.

> **Note**
>
> NSFileManager provides a singleton reference by calling the class method defaultManager. However, it is recommended that you use [[NSFileManager alloc] init] instead of the singleton object to ensure thread safety.

NSDateFormatter

NSDateFormatter creates a string representation of an NSDate and can convert string representations of a date to NSDate. You can specify the date and time format or use predefined date and time styles. Using a style is preferred since it takes into account the user's localization settings for the date and time formatting in the System Preferences.

NSNumberFormatter

NSNumberFormatter is used to convert a string representation of a number into an NSNumber and convert an NSNumber to a string.

NSPredicate

NSPredicate is used to create logical conditions for searching and filtering data. Predicates are created using a format string that looks similar to SQL syntax. Predicates are used to search and filter fetched data, as with Core Data, and for in-memory searching and filtering. An example of using NSPredicate is shown in Listing 5.15.

Listing 5.15   Example of Filtering an Array of Names Using NSPredicate

```
NSArray *names = [NSArray arrayWithObjects:@"Peter", @"Paul", @"Mary", nil];
NSPredicate *predicate =
   [NSPredicate predicateWithFormat:@"SELF BEGINSWITH[cd] 'P'"];
NSArray *namesBeginningWithP = [names filteredArrayUsingPredicate:predicate];
NSLog(@"%@", namesBeginningWithP);
```

NSRegularExpression

NSRegularExpression is a utility class for creating and applying regular expressions to strings.

NSTimer

NSTimer is used to create a timer object. A timer object waits until some time interval has elapsed, then calls the desired action on a target. A timer is not a real-time mechanism. Instead, a timer is fired when the associated run loop determines that the time interval has passed. Timers are good for performing actions after a period of time has passed and the time interval does not have to be exact. For instance, timers are useful when you want to update the display after some time interval. An example of using a timer is shown in Listing 5.16.

Listing 5.16   Example of Setting Up a Timer That Fires Every 5 Seconds

```
NSTimer *timer = [NSTimer scheduledTimerWithTimeInterval:5.0
                                      target:self
                                      selector:@selector(timerFired:)
                                      userInfo:nil
                                      repeats:YES];
```

NSXMLParser

NSXMLParser is a forward-only, event-based SAX parser for XML. The parser notifies your code as it walks through the XML tree. Your code is responsible for maintaining the state and creating objects for data you want to track as the XML is parsed. Your application receives the notifications by implementing methods defined by the NSXMLParserDelegate protocol.

Other XML Parsers

While NSXMLParser is the only XML parser provided by Cocoa, it is not the only parser available to you. There are a number of open source alternatives available for consuming and producing XML. Some of the more popular parsers include libxml2, TouchXML, and KissXML.

Ray Wenderlich has an outstanding blog post on choosing the best XML parser for your iOS project.[3] His blog post includes an overview of the most popular XML parsers available to iOS developers, and he has included a sample app for testing XML parser performance. If you plan to consume XML in your application, Ray's blog posting is a must-read for you.

---

3. **www.raywenderlich.com/553/how-to-chose-the-best-xml-parser-for-your-iphone-project**.

NSURLRequest

NSURLRequest represents a URL load request in a protocol- and URL-schema-independent manner. See Listing 5.17 for an example of using NSURLRequest.

NSURLConnection

NSURLConnecton performs the request as defined by an NSURLRequest instance. See Listing 5.17 for an example of using NSURLConnection.

Listing 5.17   **Example of Downloading Data from the Web Using** NSURLRequest, NSURLConnection, **and** NSMutableData

```
// ---- SimpleDownloader.h ----

@interface SimpleDownloader : NSObject

- (void)downloadWithURL:(NSURL *)url;

@end


// ---- SimpleDownloader.m ----

#import "SimpleDownloader.h"

@interface SimpleDownloader ()
@property (nonatomic, strong) NSMutableData *receivedData;
@end

@implementation SimpleDownloader

@synthesize receivedData = _receivedData;

- (id)init
{
    self = [super init];
    if (self) {
        [self setReceivedData:[[NSMutableData alloc] init]];
    }
    return self;
}

- (void)downloadWithURL:(NSURL *)url
{
    NSURLRequest *request = [[NSURLRequest alloc] initWithURL:url];
    NSURLConnection *connection = [[NSURLConnection alloc] initWithRequest:request
                                                        delegate:self
                                                        startImmediately:NO];
```

```
    [connection scheduleInRunLoop:[NSRunLoop currentRunLoop]
                        forMode:NSRunLoopCommonModes];
    [connection start];
}

- (void)connection:(NSURLConnection *)connection
didReceiveResponse:(NSURLResponse *)response
{
    [[self receivedData] setLength:0];
}

- (void)connection:(NSURLConnection *)connection didReceiveData:(NSData *)data
{
    [[self receivedData] appendData:data];
}

- (void)connectionDidFinishLoading:(NSURLConnection *)connection
{
    NSLog(@"%@", [self receivedData]);
}


@end
```

Now that you have an understanding of commonly used Foundation classes, let's move up the Cocoa stack to UIKit and explore what is available for constructing really useful user interfaces.

UIKit

UIKit provides a set of objects for creating and managing the user interface for your application. These objects display text, accept input from the user, display lists of data, and provide pick lists for the user and touchable buttons to request that your application perform some action. While UIKit is not required for building application user interfaces—there are plenty of apps available in the App Store, mostly games, that use other frameworks, such as OpenGL ES, for UI creation and management—it is the most common way to create user interfaces for iOS applications.

> **Note**
>
> Unlike Foundation, UIKit is available only on iOS. This means you cannot use UIKit-related code for Mac applications.

UIApplication

UIApplication is a singleton object providing control for applications running on iOS. Each application has only one UIApplication, or subclass of UIApplication,

instance. You can access the application object by calling the class method
`[UIApplication sharedApplication]`.

UIWindow

`UIWindow` objects manage the windows of your application. A window is the root
view in a view hierarchy. It is responsible for sending events to the views contained
within the window. iOS applications typically have only one window. There are,
however, good reasons for having multiple windows. For instance, if your application
supports video out to a secondary display, your app will have at least two windows, a
primary window for display on the device and a secondary window for display on the
external monitor or device.

UIScreen

`UIScreen` objects contain information about a device's entire screen. This information
is typically used when setting up a window in your application.

UIView

`UIView` defines a display area on the screen. It manages the content in that area and is
responsible for rendering any content contained within the view.

UIViewController

`UIViewController` is the controller for a `UIView`. The controller coordinates interactions between the model and the view.

UIWebView

`UIWebView` is a view for displaying HTML content. It supports rendering of HTML
and execution of JavaScript. You can track and change behavior as the Web content
is loaded by setting the `delegate` property to an object conforming to the `UIWeb-
ViewDelegate` protocol.

UILabel

`UILabel` displays read-only text. You have control over the visual aspects of the
object by setting properties such as the font family type, size, color, justification,
shadow effects, and more. `UILabel` can display a single line of text or multiple lines.

UITextField

`UITextField` displays a single line of editable text (Figure 5.2). You can set the
various visual aspects such as the font type, size, and color. `UITextField` includes a
`placeholder` property for display of default text when the text field value is empty.

Figure 5.2 UITextField with the placeholder property set to
"Placeholder text"

UITextField is ideal when your application needs to capture a small amount of text from the user.

UITextView

UITextView displays multiple lines of editable text in a scrollable view. You would typically use UITextView to display large amounts of text or to allow the user to enter and edit multiple lines of text.

> **Note**
>
> A property missing from UITextView is placeholder. UITextField has a placeholder property, which is used to display default text to the user, but this property is not available on a text view. Default text is typically used to give the user an indication of how to use the UITextField, what type of input the object expects, or the purpose of the field. It is unfortunate that UITextView doesn't have the same property.
>
> To get around this problem, I wrote a subclass to UITextView that provides a placeholder property. You can read more about this and download the source code from my blog site.[4]

UIButton

UIButton is the base class for button display (Figure 5.3). Use UIButton to provide an area on the screen that when touched will tell your application to perform an action. UIButton supports a number of touch events, but typically your application should respond to the touchUpInside: event. Why? A button should typically tell the app to perform the action when the user lifts her finger, which is touching the button, from the device.

UIButton also supports different display styles when rounded rectangle is the default. The custom style is commonly used to display an image as a button. One style sadly missing from UIButton is a gradient button style.

Figure 5.3 Round rectangle UIButton

---

4. **blog.whitepeaksoftware.com/2010/12/08/adding-placeholder-text-to-uitextview/**.

How to Make a Gradient Button

Many developers new to iOS are surprised to learn that `UIButton` does not include a gradient button style. What makes this surprising is the fact that most of Apple's own applications display gradient buttons, and many views managed by the iOS SDK, such as an action sheet, display gradient buttons. Fortunately, the iOS development community has stepped up to fill this void in the iOS SDK.

One way to display a gradient button is to place a gradient image on the button's background. But how do you make the background image look like the gradient buttons displayed by parts of the iOS SDK and other Apple applications? ButtonMaker is one option.

ButtonMaker is an iPhone application designed to run in the simulator only. It uses private APIs to create really nice gradient images for your buttons. ButtonMaker is open source and available on github.[5]

Another option, and the one I tend to prefer, is to use the gradient button class created by Jeff LaMarche. The class makes it possible to display a gradient button without relying on a background image.

Jeff's gradient button class is open source and licensed under the MIT License, which means you can use the code in your application even if it's a commercial app. The original source code is hosted in a Google Code project[6] with improved versions available on github.

`UITableView` **and** `UITableViewCell`

`UITableView` is used to display a scrollable list of data (Figure 5.4). A table view has only one column, but you can customize the table view cell to give the appearance of multiple columns. Each row of the table view contains a `UITableViewCell`. `UITableViewCell` defines the look of the cell within the table view. The table view cell supports a number of predefined cell display styles, or you can customize the cell's look by using a custom view.

California

Brea

Burlingame

Canoga Park

Carlsbad

Section Footer

Figure 5.4 `UITableView`

---

5. **github.com/dermdaly/ButtonMaker**.
6. **code.google.com/p/iphonegradientbuttons/**.

UIScrollView

`UIScrollView` provides a scrollable view. You use a scroll view to display content that is larger that the display area on the screen. The user uses swiping gestures to scroll through the content. The scroll view can also let the user zoom in and out on the content using pinching gestures.

UIPageControl

`UIPageControl` displays a set of dots (Figure 5.5). Each dot represents a page within some context. The page control is often used with a `UIScrollView` to indicate the number of pages and current page for the scrollable content.

UIPickerView

`UIPickerView` is a base class for providing a pick list of values (Figure 5.6). The picker displays the list of values using a spinning wheel or slot-machine-style metaphor. The user uses flick gestures to spin the wheel of values up and down.

UIDatePicker

`UIDatePicker` is a specialized `UIPickerView` class providing a pick list of date and time values (Figure 5.7). The date picker can also be used to display time intervals for a countdown timer.

Figure 5.5   `UIPageControl` indicating five pages total with the second page as the current page

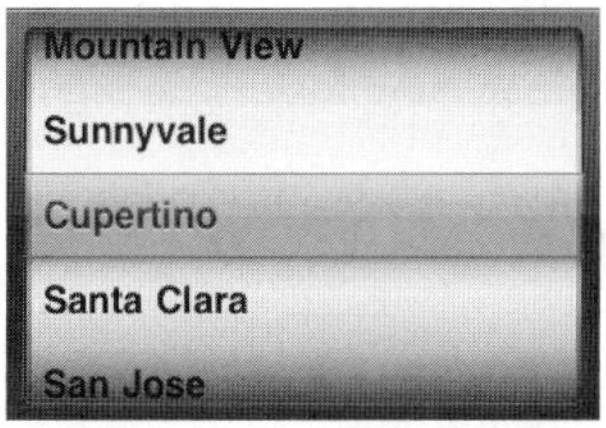

Figure 5.6   `UIPickerView`

Figure 5.7   `UIDatePicker`

Figure 5.8   `UISwitch`

UISwitch

`UISwitch` displays an **On/Off** button (Figure 5.8).

UISlider

`UISlider` displays a horizontal bar representing a continuous set of values (Figure 5.9). An indicator, or thumb, is displayed on the horizontal bar indicating the current value. A user slides the thumb left and right to change the value.

UIMenuController **and** UIMenuItem

`UIMenuController` is a singleton object for displaying a menu for the **Cut**, **Copy**, **Paste**, **Replace**, **Select**, **Select All**, and **Delete** commands (Figure 5.10). You can add your own menu items by adding instances of `UIMenuItem` to the `menuItems` property.

UIImage

`UIImage` is a wrapper class for holding the bytes of an image. A complete list of image types supported by `UIImage` is shown in Table 5.2. You can use `UIImage` to convert an image from one type to another, though you most commonly use it to provide an image to `UIImageView`.

UIImageView

`UIImageView` provides a container view for displaying a single image (Figure 5.11) or an animated set of images.

Figure 5.9   `UISlider`

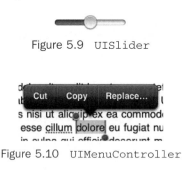

Figure 5.10   `UIMenuController`

Table 5.2   **Image Formats Supported by** UIImage

Format	File Name Extension
Tagged Image File Format (TIFF)	*.tiff, .tif*
Joint Photographic Experts Group (JPEG)	*.jpg, .jpeg*
Graphic Interchange Format (GIF)	*.gif*
Portable Network Graphic (PNG)	*.png*
Windows Bitmap Format (DIB)	*.bmp, .BMPf*
Windows Icon Format	*.ico*
Windows Cursor	*.cur*
XWindow bitmap	*.xbm*

Figure 5.11   UIImageView displaying a UIImage

UINavigationBar

UINavigationBar is a bar used to navigate a hierarchy of data (Figure 5.12). The bar, typically displayed at the top of a screen, has buttons for navigating up and down within the data hierarchy. The navigation bar has three primary properties: a left button for moving back (up) through the data, a title displayed in the center of the bar, and an optional right button. You can also use custom views for these properties to provide a customized look.

Figure 5.12 `UINavigationBar` created by a
`UINavigationController`

> **Note**
> You will often use a `UINavigationController`, which creates and manages a `UINavigationBar`, instead of creating and managing the navigation bar yourself.

UINavigationController

`UINavigationController` is a specialized view controller that manages the navigation of hierarchical data. It creates and manages a `UINavigationBar`, and it manages view controllers using a navigation stack. The bottom item on the navigation stack is the root view controller, and the top stack item is the view controller currently displayed. You add view controllers to the stack by pushing a view controller onto the stack. Pushing the view controller will cause its view to display since it is the top view controller on the stack. When you pop a view controller from the stack, the topmost view controller is removed and the new topmost view controller is displayed. You can programmatically pop view controllers from the stack, or `UINavigationController` will do it for you when the user taps the left (back) button on the navigation bar.

UIToolbar

`UIToolbar` displays a bar of buttons (Figure 5.13). Typically the toolbar is displayed at the bottom of the screen in iPhone apps and at the top of the screen in iPad applications. Each button displayed in the toolbar is a `UIBarButtonItem`.

UITabBar

`UITabBar` displays a set of buttons used to navigate to particular areas of your application (Figure 5.14). The buttons act like a set of radio buttons in that one button is always in a selected state. `UITabBar` can display only a limited number of buttons on the screen at one time. If the tab bar is configured with more buttons than can be displayed on the screen, a **More** button is displayed as the last button.

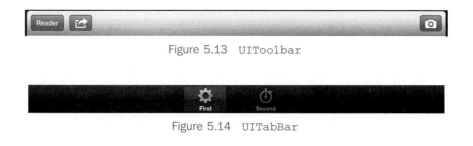

Figure 5.13 `UIToolbar`

Figure 5.14 `UITabBar`

The **More** button displays a list of all available buttons. The user can select a button from the list to navigate to the particular area of the application. The user can also select which buttons to display in the tab bar from the More screen.

UIBarButtonItem

UIBarButtonItem is a specialized button for display on a UINavigationBar and UIToolbar. The bar button item has a style property that you set to control the display of the item. The plain style will make the button glow when tapped. The border style gives the item a rounded-corner rectangle look. The done style gives the item a highlighted background color. You typically use the done style to indicate that the bar button item will complete some action, such as saving data, then return to the previous view. You can also display a custom view for additional display control.

The iOS SDK provides a set of system-supplied bar button items for common purposes. Some examples include **Done**, **Cancel**, **Edit**, **Save**, **Add**, **Reply**, **Action**, **Camera**, **Trash**, **Play**, **Pause**, **Rewind**, and **Fast Forward**. Using a system-supplied bar button item gives your application a consistent look that users will find familiar.

There are two special-case system-supplied bar button items: flexible space and fixed space. You use these invisible bar button items to control the spacing and positioning of visible bar button items. A flexible space bar button item will fill the area between two bar button items, or the edges of the bar, with spaces. Fixed space will fill the area between two bar button items, or the edges of the bar, with a fixed amount of space.

UISegmentedControl

UISegmentedControl displays a horizontal group of segments, with each segment acting as a button (Figure 5.15). As for the UITabBar, only one segment is selected at a time. UISegmentedControl is typically used within a screen to display related information.

> **Note**
>
> UIToolbar, UITabBar, and UISegmentedControl are similar yet different. The primary purpose of each is what differentiates these controls. You use UIToolbar to display a set of buttons that typically perform some type of action. UITabBar displays a set of buttons that, when tapped, navigate the user to new screens, or areas, of the application. UISegmentedControl displays a set of buttons that group content displayed on the screen. However, unlike UITabBar, UISegmentedControl does not navigate the user to a new screen. Instead, it displays a new grouping within the current screen.

Figure 5.15   UISegmentedControl

That completes the tour of Cocoa on iOS and its two key frameworks, Foundation and UIKit. Now let's turn our attention to design patterns commonly found in Cocoa.

Common Design Patterns in Cocoa

In Cocoa, as with other application environments and programming languages, common design patterns have emerged to become the de facto standard for constructing applications. To cover them all would fill a book, but two patterns are so commonly used in iOS app development (and throughout the sample code in this book) that they deserve special mention: Model-View-Controller and Target-Action.

> **Note**
>
> To learn more about these two design patterns and 26 other commonly used patterns in Cocoa, read the book *Cocoa Design Patterns* by Erik M. Buck and Donald A. Yacktman (Addison-Wesley, 2009).

Model-View-Controller

Model-View-Controller (MVC) is central to iOS development. Its use is not only encouraged but enforced by development tools. Views created in Interface Builder are expected to have a view controller, and this enforcement is even more obvious when using storyboards. But what is MVC?

> **Note**
>
> Storyboards are discussed in Chapter 14, "Storyboarding in Xcode."

To understand MVC, you must understand each component that makes up the design pattern.

The model is an object representing data and state used by the application. The model responds to requests about the data, and it responds to requests to change the state (or data) managed by the object. The model also defines business rules and relationships between objects.

The view is a visual representation of the model, and it provides user interaction with the visually rendered model data. It is the user interface element, such as a text field, or collection of elements (labels, text fields, selection boxes, etc.) that make up the screen presented to the user.

The controller mediates the interactions (requests and responses) between the view and the model. It receives the user input from the view and instructs the model object to perform a particular action or change state based on the user input. It also updates the view based on responses from the model.

The decoupling of the view and model increases the flexibility and maintainability of the code. As a result, MVC has become a commonly used pattern not only in Objective-C but in other programming frameworks, including Web frameworks such as Ruby on Rails and Django.

> **Note**
>
> For an entertaining lesson on MVC, watch the video of James Dempsey singing his MVC song at WWDC 2003 (**www.youtube.com/watch?v=YYvOGPMLVDo**).

Target-Action

Target-Action is a pattern whereby a dynamic relationship is formed between two objects such that one object holds information needed to send a message to the other object when an event occurs. You can think of Target-Action as a callback mechanism for objects where one object calls a method (the action) on the other object (the target) when an event occurs.

> **Note**
>
> Read more about Target-Action in the "Cocoa Application Competencies for iOS" document provided by Apple (**developer.apple.com/library/ios/#documentation/general/ conceptual/Devpedia-CocoaApp/TargetAction.html**).

Target-Action is commonly used with UI elements (such as `UIButton`) where the target and action are specified for a particular event (such as Touch Up Inside). You can set the target and action on an object in code or by using Interface Builder.

Summary

In this chapter you took a closer look at Cocoa, the application framework used with Objective-C that makes it possible to rapidly create great iOS applications. You reviewed a list of commonly used classes and objects from Cocoa's two key frameworks, Foundation and UIKit. And you got an overview of common design patterns used throughout Cocoa.

Provisioning Your iPad

Before you ship the next killer app, you must test it on an iPad. Using the iPad Simulator to test and debug your application will only get you so far. That's why it's important to always test your app on the real thing. But before your app will run on a real device, you must set up your iPad as a development device. This is where provisioning comes in, and that's exactly what you will do in this chapter: provision your iPad for development purposes.

The steps involved are tedious. Fortunately you do not have to repeat them often, only a few times a year. And Apple is continuously improving the provisioning process. Provisioning a device today using Xcode is easy-peasy compared to what one had to do back in the day ... the dark days of 2008.

About the iOS Provisioning Portal

The iOS Provisioning Portal is the Web site, shown in Figure 6.1, used to request and download certificates, register device IDs, create App IDs, and create and download provisioning profiles. The Web site and all of its features are not available to everyone. You have access to the portal if you are one of the following:

- An individual registered as a paid member of the iOS Developer Program. You can be registered as an individual or a company.

- An individual registered as a team member for a company that is a paid member of the iOS Developer Program. Depending on your team member role, your access to the Provisioning Portal may be limited. There is no cost to the individual team member, and team members have access to all of the same developer resources that a paid member has, courtesy of the paid company membership.

If you are not a paid member or a team member of a company, you will not have access to the iOS Provisioning Portal. Without access, you will not be able to provision your device.

Note

You can read more about joining the iOS Developer Program in Appendix A, *Installing the Developer Tools*.

Figure 6.1   iOS Provisioning Portal home page

iOS Developer Program Team Roles

When you join the iOS Developer Program as a paid member, you have the option to join as an individual or a company. The main difference between the two is that a company can include team members and an individual cannot. As a company, you can invite other developers to join your team and assign roles to them. The roles are as follows:

- **Team Agent**: A Team Agent is the individual who originally enrolled in the iOS Developer Program. A Team Agent has full access to the iOS Provisioning Portal, privileges not available to others. A Team Agent can invite others to be Team Admins or Team Members. A Team Agent can also approve certificate requests, register devices, create App IDs, create Push Notification Service SSL certificates, enable In App Purchase, retrieve the distribution certificate, and create development and distribution provisioning profiles.

- **Team Admin**: A Team Admin can invite new Team Admins and Team Members to joint the team. The Team Admin can also approve certificate requests, register devices, and create development provisioning profiles.

- **Team Member**: A Team Member can request and download a development certificate and download development provisioning profiles.

- **No Access**: No Access is a role given to developers to prevent them from accessing the iOS Provisioning Portal. This role is used when the company is enrolled in multiple Apple developer programs, that is, the iOS Developer Program and Mac Developer Program.

The Provisioning Process: A Brief Overview

Provisioning a new device is not difficult in and of itself, but there are a number of steps that must be performed first. You must be a paid member of the iOS Developer Program or be a team member of a company that is a paid member. You must request and install a development certificate on your development machine. You must register your device ID. You must create an App ID. You must create and install a development provisioning profile. All of this must be done before you can provision your iPad and run your application on it.

Note

It should go without saying, but you really should have an iPad if you plan to write iPad applications. You can learn iPad programming without an iPad, but you will be limited in what you can test. It's my opinion that having a physical device is a necessity for anyone serious about iPad programming.

Luckily you do not have to perform each of these steps often. Some of the steps, such as requesting and installing a development certificate, need to be done only once a year, and Xcode performs other steps for you as needed. Still, knowing about each step helps when a problem does come up, and yes, you will encounter a problem with the process at some point in your iOS career. It's just the nature of writing apps for mobile devices.

Note

A development certificate is valid for one year. You must request a new development certificate when the old one expires.

You've had a number of new terms thrown your way, such as device ID, App ID, and provisioning profile, but what exactly are these?

What Is a Device ID?

A device ID, also known as the Unique Device Identifier or UDID for short, is a 40-character string that uniquely identifies the device. The UDID is tied to a single device; no two devices will ever share the same device ID. The device ID is added to a provisioning profile. This restricts applications built with the provisioning profile to run on only the devices associated to the profile.

You register devices in the iOS Provisioning Portal. You can register up to 100 devices per year. The devices you register are for development and testing purposes only. You do not register the devices of your customers who download and install your application through the App Store.

Registering a device counts toward your yearly limit even if you remove the device. Say you register your iPad, then delete it from the list of registered devices. It still counts toward your annual limit of registered devices. If after deleting your iPad UDID from the list you decide to add it back, it will count again toward your yearly limit. Put another way, deleting a device does not reduce the number of registered devices for the year.

What Is an App ID?

The App ID is used during the development and provisioning processes to share Keychain data among a suite of applications, and it is used for document sharing, syncing, and configuration of iCloud. The App ID also allows the application to communicate with the Push Notification Service and external hardware accessories.

The App ID is the combination of a Bundle Seed ID and a Bundle Identifier. The Bundle Seed ID is a universally unique, ten-character, alphanumeric string. Its value is generated by Apple within the iOS Provisioning Portal. The Bundle Identifier is a string value you add to your application bundle. The Bundle Identifier is used by the operating system to identify your application for tasks such as applying application updates.

The common naming convention for the Bundle Identifier is the reverse domain name style. If your company name is Acme and your application name is Awesome App, you would define the Bundle Identifier as com.acme.awesomeApp.

The Bundle Identifier portion of the App ID can contain the wildcard character (*). The wildcard character, if used, must be the last character of the Bundle Identifier, for example, com.acme.*. Using the wildcard character allows the App ID, and its associated provisioning profiles, to be used with multiple applications.

> **Note**
>
> The Bundle Identifier portion of the App ID can be a wildcard only. In other words, the Bundle Identifier value can be a single asterisk character. As you will learn momentarily, the wildcard App ID created by Xcode's Organizer window is a single asterisk character.

A wildcard App ID is convenient because it can be used for multiple applications. Xcode's Organizer window creates a wildcard App ID that can be used by any application. The App ID looks like the last example in Table 6.1.

> **Note**
>
> When creating an App ID in the Provisioning Portal, you add a description of the purpose of the App ID. The App ID created by Organizer has the description "Xcode: Wildcard AppID."

Table 6.1   **App ID Examples**

App ID	Remarks
ABCDE12345.com.acme.awesomeApp	An explicit App ID for Acme's Awesome App
ABCDE12345.com.acme.*	A wildcard App ID for Acme applications
ABCDE12345.*	A wildcard App ID for all applications

You can also create an explicit App ID. An explicit App ID restricts the provisioning profile to a single application. Certain Apple services such as Push Notification and In App Purchase require an explicit App ID. If you plan to use an Apple service, you must use an explicit App ID.

Changing from a Wildcard to an Explicit App ID

You can change from a wildcard App ID to an explicit ID. You may find that you need to do this if, for example, you decide to add Game Center support to your application after it has been released. While you will be changing the App ID, you must not change the Bundle ID as defined in your application's *info.plist*. The Bundle ID defined in the app is used to identify your application for new releases, that is, updates to your application. Changing this breaks the app update process, and Apple will reject your app update submission if the Bundle ID changes.

Changing the Bundle ID suffix in the App ID is not the same as changing the Bundle ID in the application. This is why you can safely switch from a wildcard App ID to an explicit App ID. Changing the App ID's Bundle ID suffix does not change the application's real Bundle ID.

To change from a wildcard App ID, you must create a new App ID. You can use the same Bundle Seed ID or generate a new one. For the Bundle ID suffix, enter the bundle ID exactly as it is defined in your application's *info.plist*.

Because you now have a new App ID, you need to create a new provisioning profile that uses the new App ID.

Note

If your existing application uses the Keychain, select the same Bundle Seed ID for the new App ID. If you use a different Bundle Seed ID, your application will not be able to access any existing Keychain data.

What Is a Development Provisioning Profile?

A development provisioning profile ties developers, devices, and App IDs to a development team. A provisioning profile makes it possible for the developer to install and run the application on a device for the purpose of debugging and testing. To make this possible, the development provisioning profile must be installed on the device. A device, however, can contain more than one development provisioning profile.

Note

There is a second type of provisioning profile, the distribution provisioning profile. A distribution provisioning profile is used for Ad Hoc distribution—distribution to registered devices for the purpose of testing an application—and App Store distribution. More information on the distribution provisioning profile is included in Chapter 26, "Distributing Your App."

Now that you understand the pieces, let's get your development computer and device ready.

Do I Need a Dedicated Development Device?

A common question asked by new iOS developers is whether a dedicated development device is needed or not. The answer to this question depends entirely on you. Many iOS developers own only one device, but many other developers own multiple devices.

I have seven devices at the time of this writing: two iPads, three iPod touches (a first gen, a second gen, and a fourth generation), one iPhone 3GS, and one iPhone 4 CDMA. I use the older iPod touches to test my applications on older versions of iOS. I use the fourth-gen iPod touch to test on the latest version of iOS and to test retina display images. I usually keep one iPad up-to-date with the latest public release of iOS, and I use the other iPad, which is my primary iPad development device, to run beta versions of iOS. And I use my iPhone 3GS for testing on a phone, which can behave differently from an iPod touch, receiving incoming phone calls and SMS messages, for example.

I write a number of client apps, and my clients have different requirements, which is why I have multiple devices—and that number is growing every few months as I continue to buy new devices. It's doubtful that the average iOS developer needs this many devices. You can produce your application using only one device. However, there are advantages to having a dedicated development device.

I find I often need to reset my device to factory-install state, or I want to test my app on the latest beta release of iOS. You can still do this while owning only one device, but it does mean your device is constantly changing. That game you bought last night and got halfway through gets deleted when you reset your device, or your favorite app crashes on the new iOS beta release. This can be frustrating if your development device is your only device and you use the device for personal reasons.

Because of this, it is helpful—and it saves you time—to own devices dedicated to development purposes. Owning multiple devices, however, can get expensive, especially for the iPad. That's why I typically buy used devices for development. The Apple Refurbish Store is a good place to shop for used devices at an affordable price. Also, ask family and friends what they plan to do with their old devices if they are upgrading to newer hardware. This might be an opportunity to score a development device for free or close to free.

Setting Up Your Development Machine

The first thing you must do is set up your Mac development machine for code signing. Coding signing your application serves two purposes: It confirms the app author, and it guarantees that the app has not been altered since it was signed. iOS requires each application to be digitally signed before the app can run on a device. Code signing is never a joy, but it is a necessity, ensuring that the application comes from a trusted source.

To code sign your app, you must have a public and private key pair and a digital certificate. When your application is in development, you use a development certificate to code sign the application. This allows you to run and test your app on your own device. When you are ready to deploy your application to other devices, whether through the App Store or through Ad Hoc and enterprise distribution, you use a distribution certificate to code sign the app.

> **Note**
>
> Chapter 26, "Distributing Your App," covers distribution of your application. Therefore, I do not cover the distribution certificate in this chapter. Steps to request and install the distribution certificate are covered in Chapter 26.

Requesting a Development Certificate

To prepare your development Mac for code signing, you must first request a development certificate. To request a development certificate you need to generate a Certificate Signing Request (CSR). You use the Mac desktop application Keychain Access to generate the CSR. As Keychain Access creates your CSR, it also generates a public and private key pair for you and stores the pair in the login Keychain. The key pair identifies you as an iOS developer and is associated to the development certificate.

The Keychain Access application is available in the **Applications > Utilities** folder. Alternatively, you can launch the app using Spotlight. Press ⌘-**Space** and start typing "Keychain," without the quotes, in the Spotlight box. Spotlight will find the Keychain Access application for you. All you need to do then is press the **Enter** key to launch the application.

The first thing you need to do in Keychain Access is select **Preferences** from the menu (or type ⌘-,). Click **Certificates** and turn off Online Certificate Status Protocol (OCSP) and Certificate Revocation List (CRL) as shown in Figure 6.2.

Close the Preferences window, then select **Keychain Access > Certificate Assistant > Request a Certificate from a Certificate Authority** from the menu bar. At this point, you are ready to enter the certificate information, as seen in Figure 6.3. Enter your email address in the User Email Address field. This must be the same email address you submitted when registering as an iOS Developer.

Enter your name in the Common Name field. The name must match the name submitted when you registered as an iOS Developer. Leave the CA Email Address field blank. Mark the options "Saved to disk" and "Let me specify key pair information."

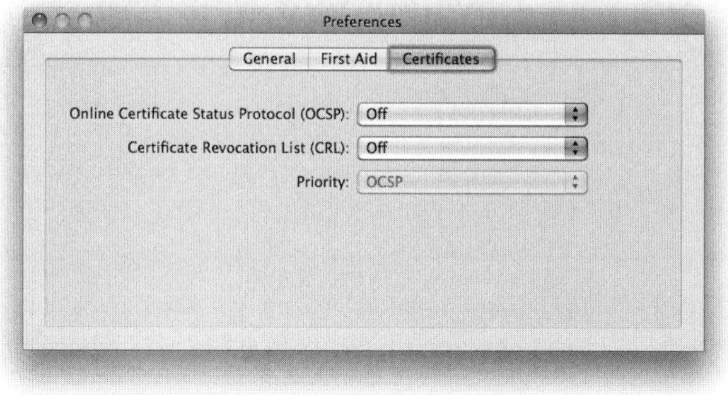

Figure 6.2   Turn off the OCSP and CRL settings in the **Preferences > Certificates** screen.

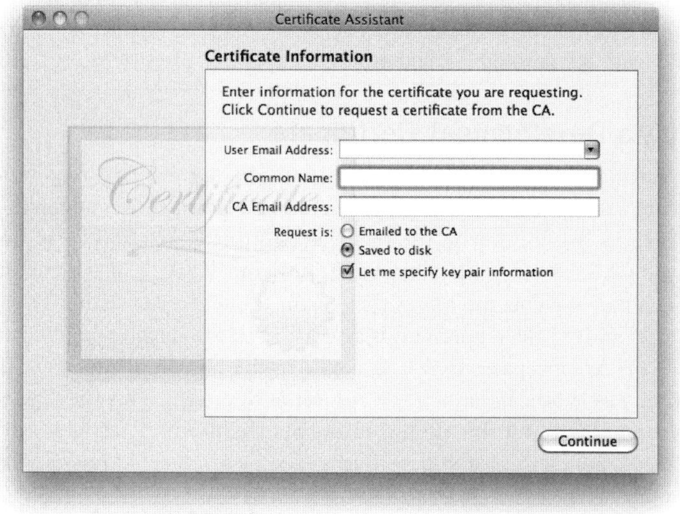

Figure 6.3   Certificate Assistant window in Keychain Access

When you have finished, click the **Continue** button. The Assistant will ask where to save the CSR. Your desktop is as good a place as any, so save the CSR to your desktop.

Make sure you selected the "Let me specify key pair information" option in the Certificate Information window (Figure 6.3). This tells the Certificate Assistant to display the Key Pair Information window, shown in Figure 6.4. Here you set the options for generating the key pair. Select 2048 bits for the Key Size and RSA for the Algorithm. Click **Continue**.

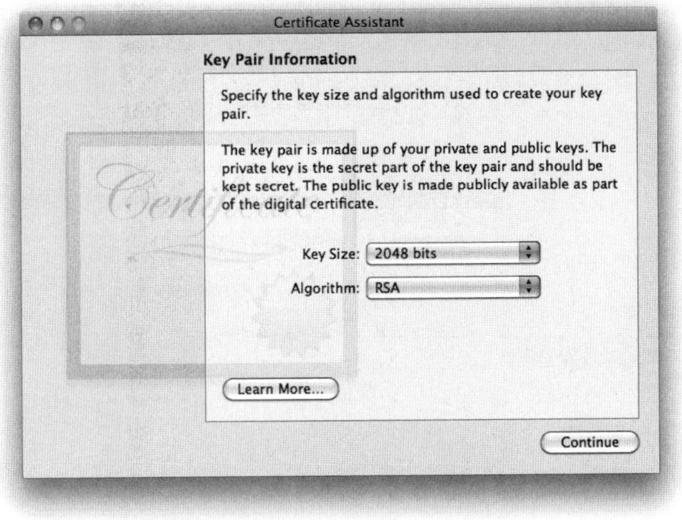

Figure 6.4   Key Pair Information window

Note

Your certificate request will be rejected if you do not specify the Key Size as 2048 bits and the Algorithm as RSA.

The Certificate Assistant will generate the CSR and save it to your desktop. A public and private key pair is also generated for you and stored in the login Keychain. The key pair can be viewed in the Keychain Access application under the Keys category as seen in Figure 6.5.

Note

If you are doing development from more than one Mac, you must copy the private key to each development machine. You will not be able to sign your application and test on your iPad without your private key. Use Keychain Access to export your private key and import it to your other development machines.

For a step-by-step guide on exporting your private key, visit **developer.apple.com/ios/ manage/certificates/team/howto.action**, scroll to the bottom of the Web page, and read the information under the "Saving your Private Key and Transferring to other Systems" section.

Click **Done** to close the Certificate Assistant. The generated CSR file is on your desktop. Your next step is to submit the CSR for approval.

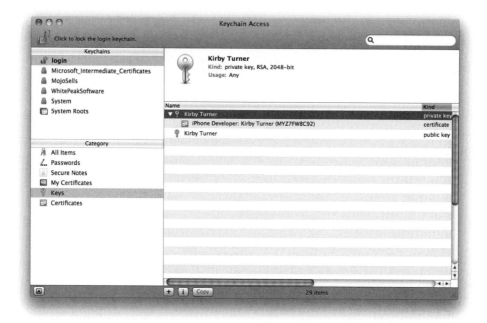

Figure 6.5   Public and private key pairs stored in the login Keychain

Getting More Help

The iOS Provisioning Portal requires you to perform a number of steps before you can test your application on your iPad and prepare your applications for distribution. A set of helpful resources is available in the Portal Resources.

The Portal Resources include a detailed user guide and how-to videos for requesting and installing your development certificate, assigning devices, creating App IDs, and creating provisioning profiles. If you need additional help with the iOS Provisioning Portal or you prefer seeing the steps performed, you should check out the Portal Resources.

The Portal Resources are available on the iOS Provisioning Portal home page under the section Portal Resources, found on the upper right side of the page, as seen in Figure 6.6.

Submit Your CSR for Approval

The next step is submitting your CSR for approval, and it is less involved than the previous step. A Team Agent or Admin approves or rejects your CSR. You will receive an email notifying you of your certificate status. If your request is approved, you download your digital certificate from the Provisioning Portal and install it on your development machine.

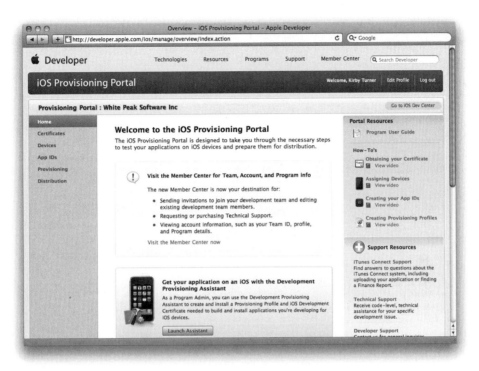

Figure 6.6   Portal Resources containing a user guide and how-to videos

> **Note**
>
> All certificate requests must be approved through the iOS Provisioning Portal. If you are the Team Agent or Team Admin, you still must approve your own certificate request.

To submit your CSR, sign in to the iOS Provisioning Portal. If you have trouble remembering the URL of the iOS Provisioning Portal, sign in to the iOS Dev Center (**developer.apple.com/ios**). Toward the upper right side of the iOS Dev Center home page there is a section titled iOS Developer Program, shown in Figure 6.7. This section includes links for the iOS Provisioning Portal, iTunes Connect, Apple Developer Forums, and the Developer Support Center. Click the **iOS Provisioning Portal** link to be transported to the portal Web site.

From the iOS Provisioning Portal home page, click the **Certificates** link found in the left-side menu bar. Next click the **Development** tab, then the **Add Certificate** button. Scroll down to find the **Choose file** button. Click the button and select the CSR file that you saved to the desktop. Click the **Submit** button to upload your CSR. If you are unable to submit your CSR through the Web site, email the CSR file to the Team Agent.

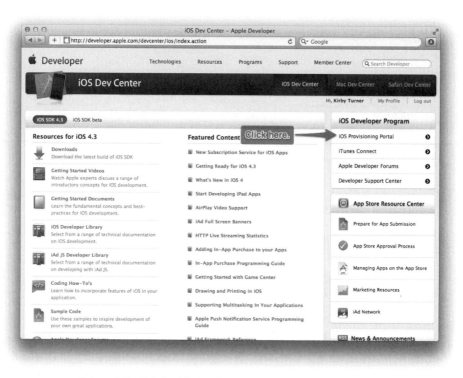

Figure 6.7   iOS Dev Center home page with a link to the iOS
Provisioning Portal

Download and Install Your Certificate

The Team Admin will be notified by email after your submitted CSR has been
received. Once the Admin approves or rejects your request, you will receive a notification email with your certificate status. When it has been approved, you sign in to
the Provisioning Portal again, then click **Certificates > Development**. You'll see
your approved certificate listed at the top. Click the **Download** button under the
Action column to save the certificate to your development machine.

> **Note**
>
> If this is your first time setting up your development machine, you need to download
> and install the WWDR intermediate certificate. Click the download link and save the
> *AppleWWDRCA.cer* file to your development machine. Use Finder to navigate to the saved
> *AppleWWDRCA.cer* file, and double-click the file to launch Keychain Access; this installs
> the certificate on your machine.

On your development machine, use Finder to locate the saved *.cer* file. Double-
click the *.cer* file to launch Keychain Access and to install your certificate. Save the

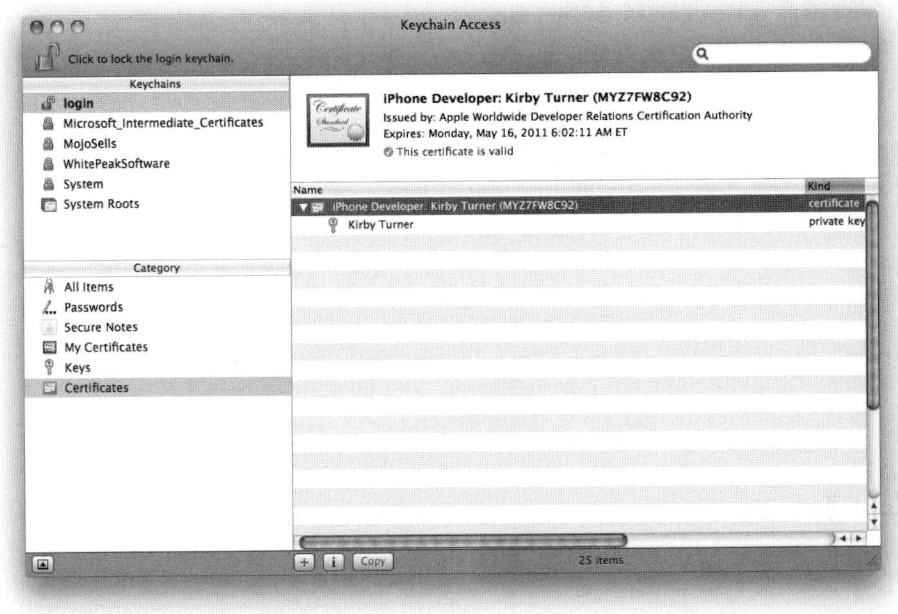

Figure 6.8   You can view your certificate in the Certificates category.

certificate to your login Keychain. Once it is installed, you can view the certificate by selecting the Certificates category for the login Keychain in Keychain Access (Figure 6.8). Your certificate name will be "iPhone Developer: Your Name."

While still in Keychain Access, click the Keys category for the login Keychain. Here you will see your public and private keys generated by the Certificate Assistant. Expand the private key by clicking the disclosure triangle. You will see that the certificate has been associated to your private key. Apple never receives your private key when you submit the CSR. Your private key is available only to you. This is why it is important that you not lose it.

Note

Make sure you have a backup of your key pair. If you do not have a backup and you lose the private key, you must go through the certificate request process all over again. I use Time Machine to make hourly backups of my primary development machine. I also use SuperDuper! to make complete system backups weekly. This provides a suitable backup of my public-private key pair. You should do something similar.

Your development machine is now set up to code sign builds of your application, but you cannot run your app on your iPad yet. You still have a few more steps to follow. Next up is setting up your device.

Setting Up Your Device

Now that your development machine is set up, it's time to set up your iPad for development. Here's what needs to happen:

1. You need to register your device ID.
2. You need to create an App ID.
3. You need to create a development provisioning profile.
4. You need to download and install the development provisioning profile.

These steps can be performed in one of two ways: by using the Xcode Organizer window or the iOS Provisioning Portal. Using Organizer is by far the easier way to set up your iPad for development. It performs the steps automatically for you. This approach is, however, not without its limits.

Organizer creates a wildcard App ID, and as you may recall, a wildcard App ID cannot be used if you plan to use Apple services like Game Center, In App Purchase, and Push Notification. That said, you should still let Xcode do its magic. While you may not use a wildcard App ID for your next awesome iPad app, it can be used to build and run sample apps and to test proofs of concept and prototype applications on your iPad.

Use for Development

The steps to set up your iPad for development are quite easy using Xcode. Tether your iPad to your development computer. Launch Xcode and open the Organizer window (**Windows > Organizer** or **Shift-⌘-2**). Organizer shows the list of registered and attached iOS devices. Attached devices have a status icon displayed to the right of the device name. A white status icon means the device is not ready for development. A green status icon means the device is ready for development. A yellow status icon means the device is busy.

Click the name of your iPad in the Devices list. You should see a screen similar to the one shown in Figure 6.9. Click the **Use for Development** button. Xcode will prompt you for your iOS Provisioning Portal credentials. Enter your Apple ID and password used for your iOS Developer account.

Xcode automatically sets up your device for development. It registers your device with the iOS Provisioning Portal, creates a wildcard App ID and development provisioning profile, if needed, and last downloads and installs the provisioning profile.

> **Note**
>
> Figure 6.9 shows a new iPod touch. The setup instructions are the same regardless of the device type. I chose to use an iPod touch to capture the screen shot because my development iPad was in use at the time.

The process can take a few minutes. While the process is running, the status icon is yellow. Do not disconnect your iPad from your computer while the process is

Figure 6.9   Organizer window with a new Apple device attached to
the computer

running. Once the process is compete, the status icon changes to green and you will
see a screen similar to the one in Figure 6.10.

You are now ready to build and run iOS applications on your iPad. To test that
everything has been set up correctly, create a new project in Xcode. You can select
any iOS application template; it does not matter which one. Make sure you select your
iPad as the device for the active scheme (seen in Figure 6.11). Build and run (⌘-R)
the project. Assuming your development machine and iPad are set up correctly, you
will see the sample app running on your iPad.

> **Note**
>
> Sign in to the iOS Provisioning Portal to see the App ID and development provisioning
> profile created by Xcode. The App ID has the description "Xcode: Wildcard AppID," and the
> development provisioning profile has the name "Team Provisioning Profile: *." The status
> for the profile will also show "Managed by Xcode."

As you just learned, using Xcode is the easiest way to set up a new device. But what
happens if there is a problem? And what if you plan to use Apple services like iCloud,
Game Center, or In App Purchase, which require an explicit App ID? You need to use
the iOS Provisioning Portal to manually perform the steps.

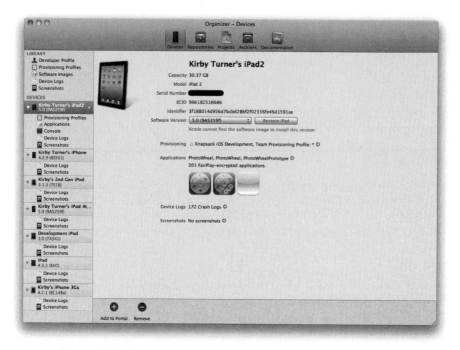

Figure 6.10   Organizer window with an attached Apple device ready
for development

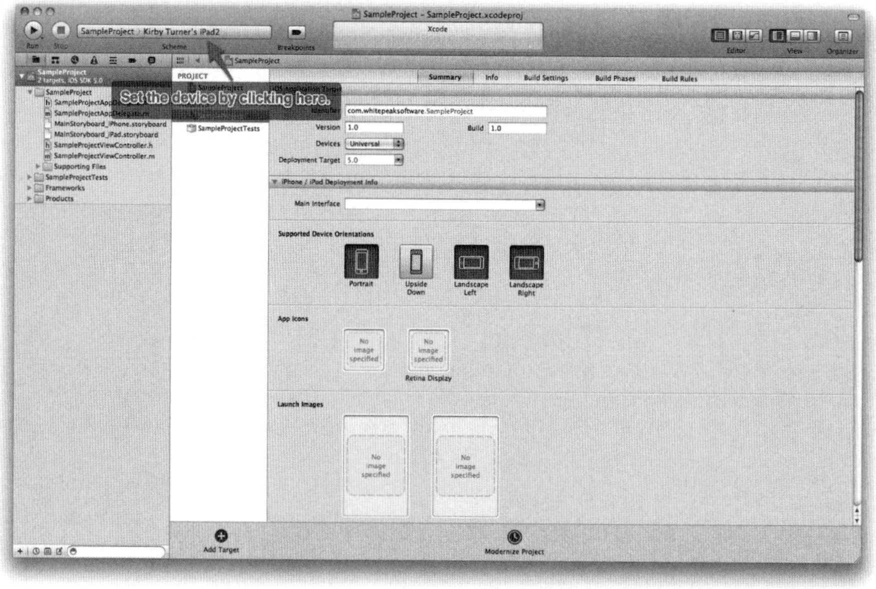

Figure 6.11   Use the scheme popup menu to set the run destination.

Using the iOS Provisioning Portal

As you already know, the iOS Provisioning Portal is used to request and download developer certificates, to register devices, to create App IDs, and to create and download provisioning profiles. You have already gone through the steps for requesting and downloading the developer certificate; the rest of this chapter will focus on the other areas of the Provisioning Portal.

Adding a Device ID

You can add a device ID individually, or you can upload a batch of device IDs in a *.deviceids* file generated by the iOS Configuration Utility. The iOS Configuration Utility is available to enterprise members only, so it is not covered here. Instead, the following walks you through adding an individual device ID.

Start by signing into the iOS Provisioning Portal Web site (**developer.apple.com/ios/manage/overview/index.action**), then click Devices in the left-side menu bar. Click the **Add Devices** button found on the right side of the Devices Web page. Enter a device name followed by the 40-character device ID, as seen in Figure 6.12. (I tend to be descriptive with the device name, adding the device owner's name and device type, for example, "Kirby Turner's iPad2.") Click the plus sign (**+**) button to

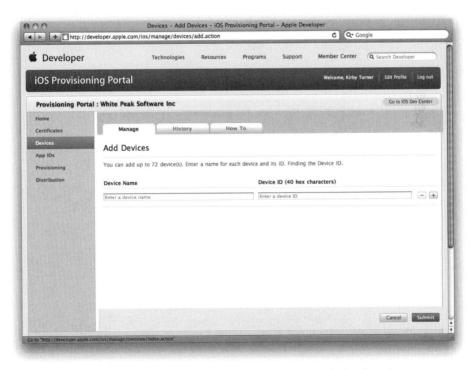

Figure 6.12   Add Devices page in the iOS Provisioning Portal

enter another device. When you have entered all the devices, click the **Submit** button. That's it. The device IDs are now registered.

Note

Only the Team Agent and Team Admin can register a device ID. A Team Member must send his device ID to the agent or admin to be registered.

You can edit the name of a registered device, but you cannot change the device ID. If a device ID is no longer valid—for example, you no longer own the device—you can remove the device from the list by marking the check box next to the device name, then clicking the **Remove Selected** button at the bottom of the registered device list.

How to Find the UDID for a Device

Finding the UDID for a device is not hard if you know where to look. There are different ways to find the ID of a device. The easiest for developers is to use Xcode's Organizer window. Open the Organizer window (**Shift-⌘-2**) and select the device. The device ID is displayed in the Identifier field as shown in Figure 6.13.

Another way to find the ID, albeit more obscure, is to use iTunes. Connect your device to your computer, then launch iTunes. In iTunes, select the device to see the device information screen, shown in Figure 6.14. Click the serial number. This will display the

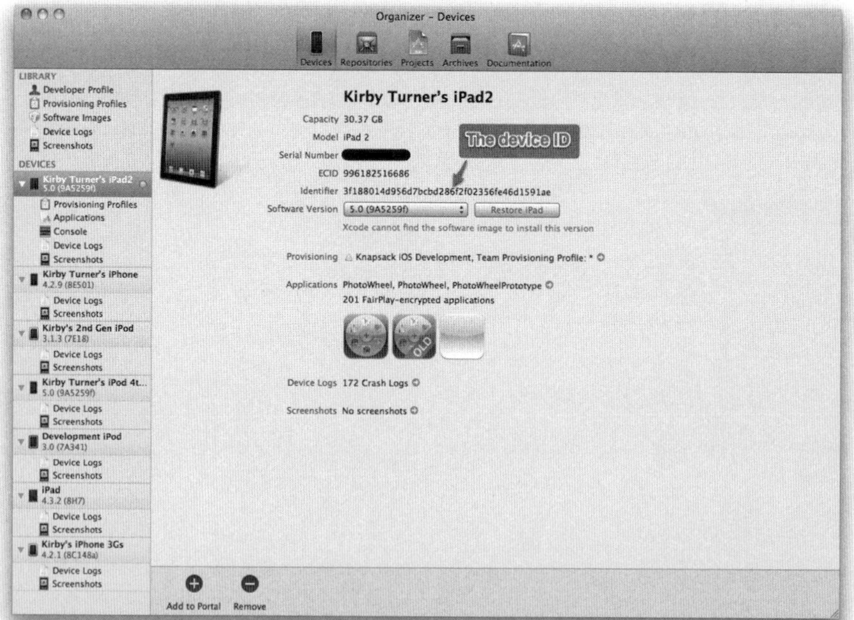

Figure 6.13   Device information displayed in the Organizer window

Figure 6.14   Device information displayed in iTunes

UDID in place of the serial number. Once the UDID is showing, type ⌘-C to copy it to the clipboard. Click the field again to return to the serial number.

> **Note**
> You can also click the software version to see the build number.

Another common way to retrieve the UDID is to use one of the many free UDID apps available in the App Store. These apps not only retrieve the UDID from the device but also provide options to copy the ID to the clipboard and to email the device ID to the recipient of your choosing. Using a UDID app is the easiest way for nondevelopers to send you their device IDs.

To download a UDID app, go to the App Store and search on "UDID." Select the app that appeals to you the most.

Adding an App ID

Adding an App ID is almost as easy as registering a device ID. Once again, sign in to the iOS Provisioning Portal. Click the App IDs menu item in the left-side menu bar, then click the **New App ID** button found on the right side of the page, shown in Figure 6.15. This takes you to the Create App ID page.

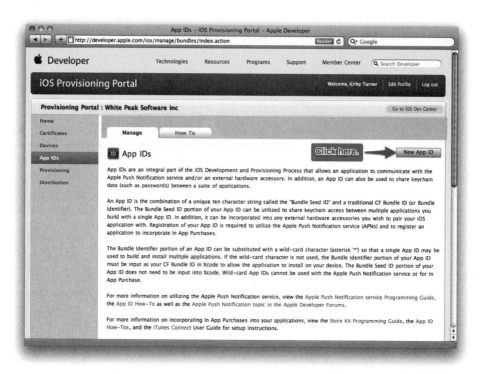

Figure 6.15   Click the **New App** button found on the App IDs page in the iOS Provisioning Portal.

> **Note**
>
> The Team Agent is the only team member who can add a new App ID.

On the Create App ID page, seen in Figure 6.16, enter the description for the App ID. Use a name or description that makes sense to you. For instance, you might use the name of your application when creating an explicit App ID. The description you enter is used throughout the portal, so enter a name or description that will help you identify the App ID.

Next, set the Bundle Seed ID, aka the App ID prefix. You can have the portal generate a new seed for you, or you can select from a seed that you previously generated. If you plan to share Keychain data access among multiple applications, you need to use the same Bundle Seed ID for each application's App ID.

Last, enter the Bundle Identifier, aka the App ID suffix. Remember to use the reverse domain name naming convention. Include an asterisk (*) as the last character if you wish to create a wildcard App ID.

Click the **Submit** button to save the App ID. Clicking the button returns you to the App IDs page. Scroll down the page to see the newly created App ID in the list of App IDs.

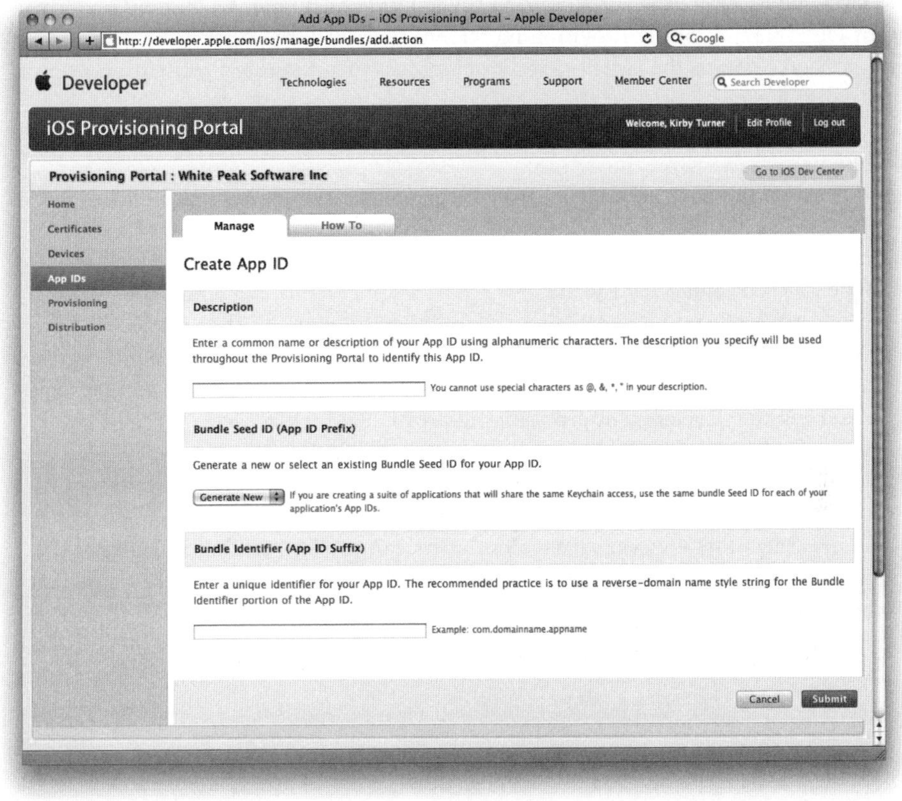

Figure 6.16   The Create App ID page

In the list of App IDs, you can choose between two actions: Details and Configure. The Details action is available only for wildcard App IDs. Click the action to see the details of the wildcard App ID.

The Configure action is available only for explicit App IDs. Click the action to configure the App ID for Push Notification. You do not need to configure the explicit App ID for In App Purchase and Game Center services as these services are enabled by default for explicit App IDs.

> **Note**
> You cannot delete an App ID once it has been created.

Creating a Development Provisioning Profile

The development provisioning profile brings you (the developer), your device, and your App ID together so that you can run and test your application on your iPad. To create a new development provisioning profile, log in to the iOS Provisioning Portal and click the Provisioning link found in the left-side menu bar. Click the **Development** tab at the top of the Provisioning screen, then click the **New Profile** button. This will take you to the Create iOS Development Provisioning Profile page, seen in Figure 6.17.

> **Note**
>
> Only Team Agent and Team Admin members can create development provisioning profiles.

Enter a name for the provisioning profile. (I like to use descriptive names, for example, "Hey Peanut Dev Profile.")

Select the development certificates that will be associated to the provisioning profile. This identifies the development certificates used to code sign the application for development. You should select the developer certificate for each team member who will be using the development provisioning profile.

Select the App ID for the profile. Each profile can have only one App ID. You can use a wildcard App ID if you wish to use the same development provisioning profile for more than one application.

Finally, select the devices that the developers can use for running and testing the application on a device. Then click the **Submit** button to generate the development provisioning profile.

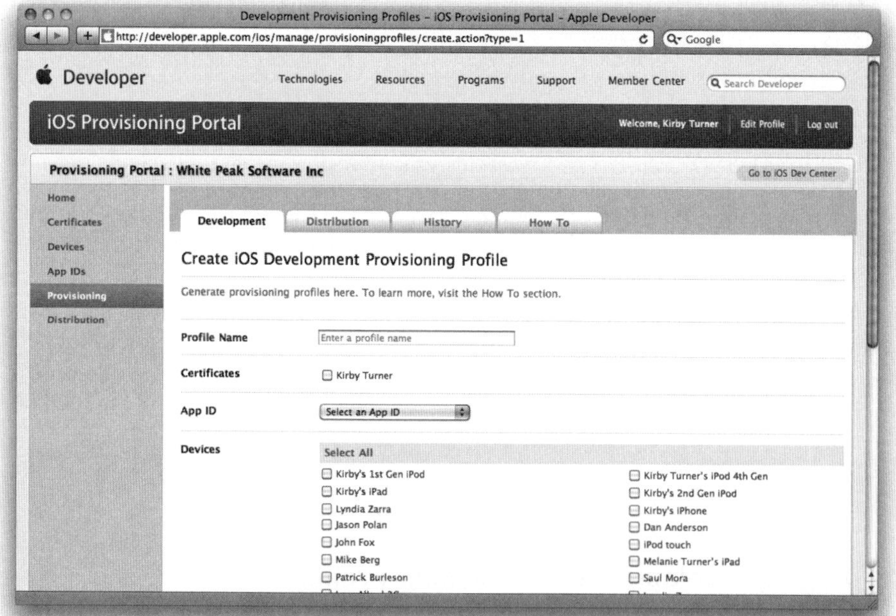

Figure 6.17   Create iOS Development Provisioning Profile page

Downloading a Development Provisioning Profile

Once a development provisioning profile has been generated, team members can download and install the profile. To download the development provisioning profile, log in to the iOS Provisioning Profile, click the **Provisioning** menu item, then click the **Development** tab on the Provisioning page. You will see a list of development provisioning profiles, as shown in Figure 6.18. Click the **Download** button for the profile you wish to install.

Now you are ready to install the provisioning profile.

Installing a Development Provisioning Profile

There are a few ways to install a development provisioning profile. You can copy the profile file to *~/Library/MobileDevice/Provisioning Profile*, but the most common way is to use the Organizer window in Xcode. This will ensure that the profile is stored in the proper directory, and it will create the directory if it does not already exist.

> **Note**
>
> The development provisioning profile you download has the file extension *.mobileprovision*.

To install using Organizer, launch Xcode and open the Organizer window (**Shift-⌘-2**). Select a device on which to install the provisioning profile, then click the

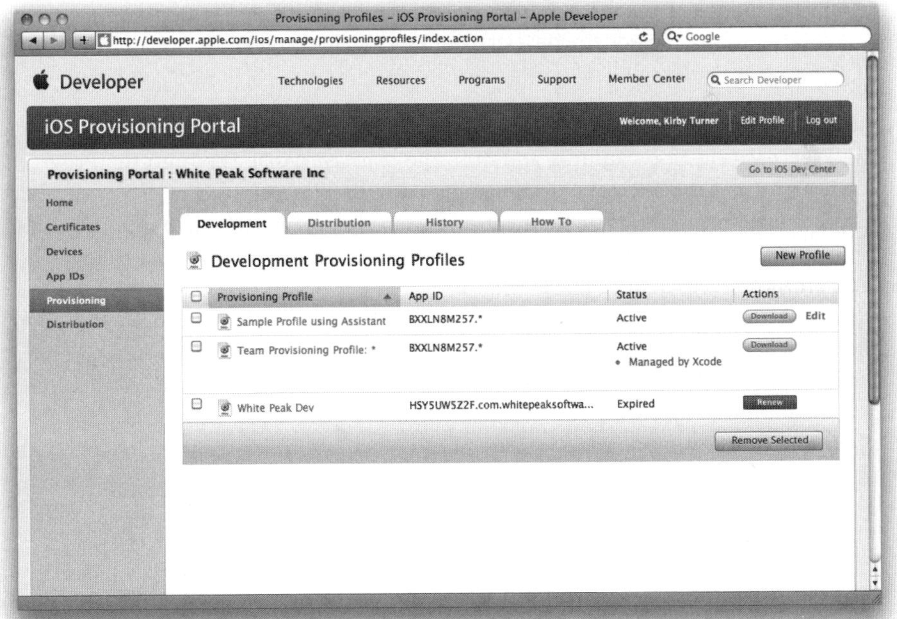

Figure 6.18   List of development provisioning profiles

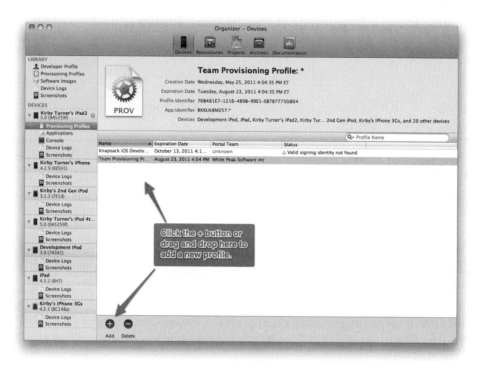

Figure 6.19   Click the + button or drag and drop the *.mobileprovision* file
to add the development provisioning profile.

+ button to select the *.mobileprovision* file you downloaded from the iOS Provisioning
Portal. Alternatively, you can drag and drop the *.mobileprovision* file onto the Provisioning list in the Organizer window; see Figure 6.19.

Another way to install a development provisioning profile is to drag and drop the file onto the iTunes icon in the dock. Note, however, that this will fail if the provisioning profile directory does not exist.

You can also copy the *.mobileprovision* file directly to the ~/*Library/MobileDevice/Provisioning Profiles* directory. To make it easier, add a shortcut for the directory to Finder. When you need to install a new provisioning profile, simply drag and drop the downloaded file onto this shortcut; see Figure 6.20.

A third option is to drag and drop the provisioning file onto the Xcode icon in the Dock. This will copy the provisioning profile to the appropriate directory and to your iPad device if connected.

That's it for installing a development provisioning profile.

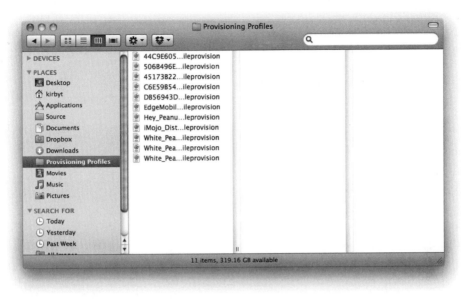

Figure 6.20   Finder window with a shortcut folder to the provisioning
profile directory

Summary

At this point, your development machine should be set up for code signing iOS applications, and your iPad should be ready for development. You're now ready to write
iPad applications that you can run on your own device. But first, let's talk a bit about
app design as it relates to the iPad.

7

App Design

Before you can write the next killer app, you have to know what it is you are creating. You need to spend time up front coming up with the app design. App design, in the context of this chapter, doesn't mean making your app look pretty, though that is an important part of the process. You need to know what it is you are building. You need to know whom you are building it for. And you need to know how it will work.

The app design represents the blueprint for your application. It tells you what, who, and how before you write a single line of code. Without it you are likely to lose focus, and this will come across in your final product.

Good app designs consist of two main parts: an App Charter and UI mockups. The App Charter defines your app. It tells the "what" and "who" about your app. The UI mockups tell the "how"—how the app will work.

Let's talk about these two parts in more detail.

Defining Your App

The first thing you need to do when designing your app is to understand what it is you want to create. You need to define your application, what it will do, and whom it is for. A good place to start is with the App Charter.

The App Charter describes your app, providing the basis for creating the blueprint for the product you're building. Creating the App Charter forces you to think about your app before you spend time and money writing code. This up-front time will either leave you excited about the app idea or tell you that you have a dud. Either way, you have gained a better understanding of your app idea without spending a ton of time or money.

The App Charter is also a good way to share your idea with others. You may think that keeping your app concept a secret is a good idea, but it isn't. You need to share the idea with others to get their feedback. Often the feedback you receive will help you improve on what you believe is already an awesome concept, but other times the feedback will tell you it's time to jump ship and focus on another app idea. Either way, feedback from others at the early stage is invaluable.

What goes into the App Charter? The list of items included in the App Charter is short. In fact, you really only need the following:

- **App name**: The actual app name or a tentative name
- **App summary**: A short description of your application and its differentiator
- **Feature list**: A list of features that will someday be included in the app
- **Target audience**: The ideal user of your application
- **Competing products**: A list of other apps competing against yours

Let's take a closer look at each of these items.

App Name

Every app has a name, but coming up with a great name can sometimes be more challenging than building the app itself. In fact, there are Madison Avenue–type agencies that specialize in coming up with *über*-cool names. Of course, these companies charge thousands of dollars, which is something most iOS developers don't have, so it's up to you to name your app.

You don't need to spend a lot of time thinking of the app name. Often a good name comes to you later as you are developing the app, so it's okay to use a tentative app name in the beginning.

Using a tentative app name is common practice in the software development world, so common, in fact, that many software shops always use code names when referring to apps that are in development. A code name is nothing more than a tentative name you give your app while it is in development.

Using a theme for code names is also common practice. For instance, Apple uses cat names for major releases of OS X, and Microsoft uses names of mountains and cities for different flavors of Windows OS. You can use whatever code name you like, but following a theme can be fun. (I'm a snowboarder, so I like to use the names of ski trails from my favorite resorts as code names.)

Of course, you don't have to use a code name. Maybe you already have the perfect name, which is great. But if you don't have that perfect name yet, use a code name for now and move on with your app design. Who knows? You may decide to use the code name as the app name. The point is to give your app a name while it is in development. You can always change it later.

App Summary

The app summary is a brief description of your application. It should be about a paragraph long, no more than three or four sentences. It should give the reader a general understanding of your application, and it should include what makes your application unique. This is called the differentiator or "unique value proposition." The unique value proposition is what makes your application different from all the rest. It's the added value your app provides its users that other similar apps do not provide.

Let's look at an example. Here is the app summary for a fictitious app called Ovation.

"Ovation is a Twitter client for the iPad that focuses on finding conversations about your company and products. It searches Twitter's public timeline for you and streamlines the processing of responses to comments made about your organization."

There are many Twitter clients available for the iPad. Ovation is different in that its primary function is to find mentions of your company and products within the public timeline on Twitter. Ovation's primary function is its unique value proposition, its differentiator. It's what makes this application different from the rest.

The app summary not only describes your app but also helps you decide what features to include in the app. When deciding what features to include, you should ask, "Does this feature fit within the app summary?" If it's not a fit, chances are good that the feature does not belong in the app.

This brings us to the next piece of the App Charter, the feature list.

Feature List

An app is nothing without features. Features are the tasks the application performs. A feature list tells what your application can and will do. You need to come up with the feature list for your app, but how do you get started? Brainstorming feature ideas is a wonderful way to get started.

What Is Brainstorming?

Brainstorming is a technique by which you capture all ideas, suggestions, and creative solutions to a problem or topic. There are no bad ideas when you're brainstorming. Every idea is welcome even if it seems unrealistic or far-fetched. The goal of brainstorming is to capture as many ideas as possible.

Brainstorming works best when you have at least one other person participating, but it is still an outstanding approach for the one-person team.

To brainstorm, get yourself in front of a whiteboard, grab some paper or a stack of Post-It Notes, then start capturing every idea that comes to mind. Mind mapping on the iPad works well when brainstorming solo, as shown in Figure 7.1. What you use to capture the ideas doesn't matter. All that matters is that you capture each and every idea.

> **Note**
>
> Post-It Notes and index cards are useful in brainstorming sessions because you can move them around, group them by release schedule or priority, and so on. Try different ways of capturing ideas during brainstorming sessions. Eventually you will find what works best for you and your team.

My Big Fat Feature List

Have a brainstorming session to create your feature list. Capture every conceivable feature that comes to mind, even the far-fetched ones. Remember, you are brainstorming here, so there are no wacky or unrealistic features. It's doesn't matter how outlandish a feature may seem; it belongs on the list.

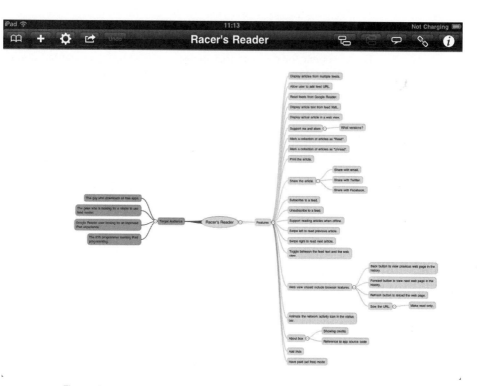

Figure 7.1   Mind map of features and target audience for the make-believe app Racer's Reader

You may be thinking to yourself, "I will end up with a big list of features," and you are right. You will end up with a big list of features. That is the goal, to produce a big fat feature list. Not to worry. You'll trim the list soon enough.

The big list gives you something to work with when it's time to decide exactly what goes into the application. It also gives you insight into the potential of your application. For instance, that wacky feature you came up with might turn into the differentiator for your application.

Target Audience

With your big feature list complete, start thinking about the target audience for your app. Think about every possible user, from the individual who will see your app once for only 30 seconds to the power user who will do things with your app you never dreamed possible. Within this range is your ideal user.

Start thinking about the ideal user for your app and list the characteristics of this user. Is the user male or female, a teenager or a retired senior? Is the user someone who travels often? A soccer mom? Does she love snowboarding but doesn't get to the slopes as often as she would like? Capture every conceivable characteristic of the ideal user.

As you think about your ideal user, think about the conditions the user might be facing at the time she is using your app. Add this to your list of characteristics. Will the user be under a lot of stress at the moment she is using your application? Is the user likely to be in a rush? These types of characteristics should be captured as well, as they can have a direct impact on the features and usability of your application.

Once you determine the characteristics of your ideal user, you know who your target audience is. Armed with this knowledge, you can start trimming down your feature list to include only those features that complement the characteristics of your target audience.

> **Note**
>
> Often you will think of new features as you think about the target audience. When this happens, be sure to add the new features to your big feature list.

Revisit Your Feature List

Creating the App Charter is an iterative process. You don't make one pass defining the aspects of your app; you make multiple passes, constantly refining the definition based on new knowledge. As you list the characteristics of the ideal user, for instance, new features will likely come to mind. Those features should be added to the big feature list.

At some point, however, you must decide what actually goes into your application. A good time to start trimming down the feature list is after you understand who the target audience is. Then you trim down the big list of features into the list of features that appeal to the target audience.

As you trim down the feature list, make sure you consider the device. A particular feature may or may not make sense on the iPad. If the feature is inappropriate for the device, strike it from the list.

The trimmed-down version of the feature list is what you include in the App Charter. This list represents all the features that you would like to see in your app over its lifetime. Don't assume this list represents version 1.0 of your app. Version 1.0 will most likely include only a small subset of the feature list.

Competing Products

Knowing your competition is important. It helps you decide what makes your app different. It also tells you if a market exists for your application. If there is zero competition for your app, your idea is beyond anything ever conceived before, which is unlikely; or there is no market for your app, which is the more likely scenario.

If you think Google or Yahoo! invented the search engine, think again. Before these search engines existed there was Archie (see **www.searchenginehistory.com** for more on search engine history). Google and Yahoo! simply found better ways of indexing and searching ... and to beat out the competition.

To beat the competition, you must know who the competition is, and this should be included in the App Charter. Including the competition in the App Charter forces you to acknowledge that competition exists. It also forces you to learn who your competition is and to determine if there is a market for your app.

What you capture about your competition is up to you, but at a minimum you want the name of the app, the vendor's name, the URL to the app's Web site, and any notes or remarks you have about the competing app.

A Sample App Charter

In Part II of this book you will build an iPad app. Before you begin, you need to know what the app is and whom it is for—you need its App Charter. Following is the App Charter for the app you will build in the next part of this book.

> **Note**
>
> The app summary section shown here is not that of a top 100 app in the App Store, but it does convey the primary intention of the app, to teach programmers how to write iPad applications. This differentiator will not result in millions of downloads, but it does provide focus as you write the application. The app is not attempting to be the best photo library app in the App Store. It is a means to an end, where the end is you becoming a competent iPad programmer.

Target Audience for PhotoWheel

The target audience in the PhotoWheel App Charter might seem a bit odd. It's not your typical ideal user for an app, but PhotoWheel is not your typical app. When I thought about the target audience for PhotoWheel, four types of users came to mind:

- The individual who downloads all available free apps
- The individual looking for another way to store photos
- The individual looking to store favorite photos from Flickr
- The iOS programmer learning iPad programming

The first user type is not someone PhotoWheel cares about. This person will likely download the app, use it for 10 seconds, then post a 1-star rating saying the free app costs too much.

The second and third user types are good ideal users for PhotoWheel, but they don't fit the application summary.

Why make this distinction? PhotoWheel is intended to help you learn iPad programming. It says so in the app summary. Its goal is not to support photo editing and other photo sites such as SmugMug.com. These user types, however, will expect full support, which is beyond the scope of the app you are building. This could change over time, but for now these two user types are not PhotoWheel's ideal users.

The fourth user type, the programmer learning iPad programming, is the ideal user. This user is you, and your goal at the moment is not to write a top 100 photo app. Your goal is to learn how to write iPad apps. This user type fits nicely within the app summary, and for these reasons this is PhotoWheel's target audience.

App Name

PhotoWheel

App Summary

PhotoWheel puts a spin on personal photo libraries. Collect your favorite photos in one or more photo albums. Print and email photos, apply special effects, and display them on your TV using AirPlay.

PhotoWheel is a personal photo library app for the iPad written as the companion app to the book *Learning iPad Programming: A Hands-on Guide to Building Apps for the iPad*, which teaches programmers how to build iPad applications.

Feature List (in no particular order)

- Display photos from one or more photo albums.
- Add, edit, and remove photo albums.
- Rename photo albums.
- Add and remove photos from photo albums.
- Import photos from the Photos app library.
- Import photos from Flickr.
- Print one or more photos.
- Email one or more photos.
- View slideshows of photos.
- Display slideshows over AirPlay.
- Sync photo albums among multiple devices.

Target Audience

The iOS programmer who is reading *Learning iPad Programming*.

Competing Products

Flickpad HD

Vendor: Shacked Software LLC

Price: $2.99

Rating: 4.0 stars

Last update: July 2, 2011

Web site: **flickpadapp.com/**

iTunes: **itunes.apple.com/us/app/flickpad-hd-for-facebook-flickr/id358635466?mt=8**

Photo Stack

Vendor: Seong Hun Lim

Price: Free (pro version $0.99)

Rating: 4.0 stars

Last update: May 27, 2011

Web site: iTunes: **itunes.apple.com/us/app/photo-stack/id427552502?mt=8**

UI Design Considerations

You have completed your App Charter. You know what you want to build and for whom, but you don't know how your app will work. Your next step is to come up with the UI design. But before you start sketching a UI for your app, there are a few things you need to consider and do.

Read the HIG

A must-read for all iOS developers is the *iOS Human Interface Guidelines* (**bit.ly/ learnipadprod-HIG**), more commonly referred to as just "the HIG." This guideline, published by Apple, provides a general overview of what you should and should not do in an iOS application. Apple publishes updates to the HIG whenever it issues a new build of the iOS SDK, which means you should reread it from time to time.

> **Note**
>
> The iOS HIG is also available in the iBookstore. Search for "Apple Developer Publications" or "Human Interface Guidelines" to find it.

Much of what is covered in the HIG is based on Apple's usability research for iOS devices and apps, and Apple shares this information with you. You are doing a disservice to yourself, your app, and your users if you don't read the HIG before designing your app's UI.

Make Your App "Tapworthy"

Another invaluable resource for the nondesigner type of programmer is Josh Clark's book *Tapworthy: Designing Great iPhone Apps*. While *Tapworthy*'s focus is on iPhone app design, many of the principles apply to iPad app design. For example, the ideal hit target for an on-screen object is 44 pixels. Why 44 pixels? Well, that's about the size of a fingertip. Make the hit target smaller, and people will have trouble tapping it.

Design for the Device

When designing your iPad app, keep in mind that you are designing for a touch environment, not a point-and-click environment. The rules for the iPad are different from those for the desktop or even a Web site. Touches and mouse clicks, for example, are different, yet sometimes designers, programmers, and even users compare them as if they were the same and required the same amount of effort. But this is not true. A touch is not the same as a mouse click.

Mouse clicks are often considered expensive. Designers are always trying to find the best design that requires the fewest number of clicks. This is why you see a lot of Web sites that cram a ton of content onto the home page. While mouse clicks are considered expensive, the same is not necessarily true for touches.

A touch is not as involved as moving a mouse, aligning the mouse cursor to the correct screen location, then clicking the mouse button. With a touch, you see the object you wish to see. You move your finger and tap the object. That's it.

Touching is so simple that an 18-month-old can do it. There's even a YouTube video (**bit.ly/SmuleCatPlay**) of a cat playing with Smule's Magic Piano (**bit.ly/learnipadprog-SmuleMagicPiano**). The point here is that, by nature, humans are a tactile lot, and that's why the iPad has taken off so quickly. It's much easier to launch an app, touch or swipe something, and get it to quickly do what you want. Compare that to Microsoft Word with all its toolbars, menus, and palettes. If all you want to do is type a letter to someone, Word is overkill; in fact, it's like a death sentence (no pun intended).

Keep this in mind while designing your application. Don't just assume that because a particular design practice is commonplace in the point-and-click world it will translate to the touch world. (I can't imagine trying to use a touch-based version of Word, but give me Pages for iPad—**bit.ly/learnipadprog-Pages**—and I can tear things up.)

People Use iOS Devices Differently from the Web or Desktop

When designing your iPad app, keep in mind that people do not use iOS devices in the same way they use the Web or desktop. This should be reflected in the design of your application. Web site designs, for example, try to display as much information as possible at the top half of the page. This is called "above the fold," a term that comes from the newspaper world. This is the section of a newspaper that is literally above the fold, where the paper is folded in half. It is where newspapers print the biggest headlines and other attention-grabbing information.

On the Web, the concept of above the fold refers to everything you see before scrolling down. Web site designers try to display the most important, eye-catching content above the fold, at the top half of the Web page, to get the reader's attention. The rationale is that the user is unlikely to scroll down a Web page to view additional content. This is one of the reasons SEO (Search Engine Optimization) experts say you want your Web site to appear above the fold when a user does a search. Those first four or five matches are the ones the user is most likely to click. Matches falling below the fold, those that are hidden until the reader scrolls down, are less likely to be clicked.

This is not true on iOS devices. Scrolling is a natural behavior, whether it's flicking up and down or left and right. This means you do not need to cram a ton of information on the screen at one time. Instead, you want to provide a balanced amount of information in a visually pleasing manner and allow the user to use touch gestures to scroll and pop over for additional information.

Wear Your Industrial Designer Hat

App design for iPad is a bit more involved than app design for the point-and-click world. With the iPad the user interacts directly with the objects on the screen by touching them. This leads to a different set of sensations compared to the indirect interaction of using a mouse. This also means your app design must consider user interaction within the app from an industrial design point of view.

Industrial design considers the aesthetics, ergonomics, and usability of a product. The iPad has no physical buttons interacting with your application—even the keyboard is virtual—so it's up to you to include on-screen objects with which the user interacts. The placement of these objects is important to the usability and the ergonomics of your application. Left-handed users, for example, will find certain object placement more ideal than right-handed users. This is more noticeable on the iPhone than on the iPad, but it's still important to consider when designing your iPad app.

Apple has made some recommendations in the iOS HIG that fall into the industrial design realm. Toolbars should be displayed at the top of the screen on the iPad. This is a change from the recommendation for the iPhone, where toolbars are displayed at the bottom of the screen. This difference is because the user interacts with the devices differently. An iPhone user often interacts with toolbar buttons using a thumb. Placing the toolbar at the bottom of the screen makes it easier for the user to thumb tap the buttons. Meanwhile, an iPad user is likely to hold the device in one hand, freeing the other hand to tap the screen. With the toolbar at the top, the user is made more aware of its presence, and she can easily tap the desired button with her free hand.

Metaphors

iOS has a complete set of UI objects that you can use to construct your app's user interface. These standard controls make it easier for users to use your application because the UI looks familiar, but the standard controls look rather bland. And using the standard controls will not make your app stand out. It will look like all the other apps in the App Store that use the same standard controls.

One way to stand out in the crowded App Store is to provide a real-world-like experience to the user. You accomplish this by making use of various metaphors that loosely mimic the real world. The user interacts with the iPad using touch gestures, which mimic behaviors in the real world, for instance, turning a page in a book. This is a much more engaging experience compared to the point-and-click world of the personal computer.

Proper use of metaphors will not only give the user a sense of interacting with real objects; it provides a user interface that is familiar to the user and is easier to learn.

Metaphors should be subtle, not overdone. iBooks (**bit.ly/learningipadprog-iBooksApp**) is a good example of an iPad application that pushes the limits of real-world metaphors without going overboard. Your books are displayed on a wood-grain bookcase, as shown in Figure 7.2. Tap a book cover to open it. Flick your finger left and right to turn pages. This experience is similar to picking a physical book from a bookshelf and reading it. The trick, however, is not to go too far with metaphors. Metaphors should be subtle.

Figure 7.2   An iBooks library

How could iBooks take the real-world metaphor too far? For starters, if the iBooks bookcase looked anything like many real-world bookcases, the books would be two or three levels deep. Books would be crammed into every possible space, sitting on top of one another, turned so the book title is hidden, and sitting at different angles. And there would be a slight bend in the shelves caused by the weight of all the books.

Luckily, Apple did not take the bookcase metaphor this far. If it had, iBooks would not be the beautiful, useful app it is today. Instead, it would cause the same frustrations you might experience in the real world when looking for a particular book.

Learn from Apple: Keep the metaphors simple and don't go overboard.

Sound Effects

Another way to give your application that real-world feel is to provide audio feedback with sound effects. But just as with visual metaphors, don't go over the top with them.

The virtual keyboard provided by iOS is a good example of appropriate audio feedback. As you type on the keyboard, you hear soft clicking sounds. This sound effect resonates with users, taking advantage of hearing to give a sense of typing on a real keyboard.

You should do the same with your users—tap into their sense of hearing by providing subtle sound effects within your application. Say, for example, your app displays a light switch that the user flicks on and off. Adding a soft click as the user flicks the switch will give your app a real-world sensation.

Your goal when using sounds effects is to tap into the users' senses, not to annoy them. Don't go overboard with sound effects. Keep them subtle. And remember, users can use device controls that affect sounds. They can switch the device to silent with the Silent switch, and they can turn the volume up and down with the volume controls. Users can even listen to music from the iPod player while they use your app. Be mindful of this when adding sound effects to your app.

> **Note**
>
> The HIG has a lengthy section on using sounds in apps, but you already know this because you have read the HIG. You *have* read the HIG, right?

Customize Existing Controls

A common pitfall programmers new to iOS fall into is reinventing the wheel. The programmer wants to implement a real-world metaphor, say, a three-way switch. The initial thought is to write this UI control from scratch because there is no three-way switch in the list of standard controls. But that would be a waste of time. A better approach is to reexamine the standard controls and find one that provides the basic behavior you are looking for. When you find the right standard control, customize its look and behavior.

This is exactly what the team at Raizlabs did with their app Clock Radio (**bit.ly/learnipadprog-ClockRadioApp**), shown in Figure 7.3.

At the bottom of Clock Radio's screen is a three-way switch. You can slide the switch to the On, Off, and Alarm positions. This action of sliding the switch is similar to using UISlider.

UISlider is a horizontal bar that allows the user to select a value from a continuous range of values. This is the same behavior found in the On/Off/Alarm switch in Clock Radio. The slider is configured to support three values representing On, Off, and Alarm. The switch slides along a horizontal bar, which again is a behavior found in UISlider. So to implement the three-way switch in Clock Radio, Raizlabs customized the UISlider control. They didn't have to reinvent the wheel. They took an existing wheel and gave it a new look.

Before you start down the path of creating your own custom control, take a look at the standard controls provided by iOS. Chances are very good that the behavior you are looking for has already been implemented in one of the standard controls. All you need to do is give the control a new look.

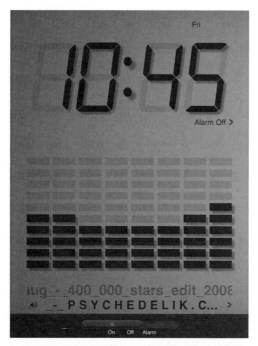

Figure 7.3 Clock Radio from Raizlabs. Notice the On/Off/Alarm switch at the bottom of the screen. This is the standard control `UISlider` with a new look.

Hire a Designer

Unless you are a master of Photoshop and have an eye for design, your best option for creating an awesome-looking application is to hire a designer. If you happen to be one of those rare (and lucky) programmers who possess both programming and design skills, you might be able to avoid hiring a designer. But for the everyday programmer, hiring a designer is the best way to have an amazing-looking app.

A designer can help you in many different areas. Your budget will determine how you can best leverage the skills of a designer. At a minimum, you should have a designer create your app icon. The app icon is the first visual impression potential users will have of your application when deciding whether to download it or not. If you stick an ugly icon on your app, you run the risk of losing customers before they even load your app's profile page in iTunes. Remember, first impressions can mean a lot, and if you've got some cheap, cheesy graphic as an app icon, chances are your app won't sail to the top of the charts, no matter how great and useful it is.

If you can afford it, get a professional designer involved in the design of your app, specifically the UI design. This could save you time down the road when you're polishing your app, in other words, making it look pretty.

You have defined your app. You have read the HIG. You are starting to visualize what your app might look like and the metaphors it will use. You may even have hired a designer to help out. Now it's time to start sketching UI designs for your app.

Mockups

One of the fastest ways to validate your app design is with mockups. Mockups make it possible to get a sense of how your app looks and flows between screens. Mockups also help reduce software development cost in that they help identify major flaws within the app design prior to your writing a single line of code.

What Is a Mockup?

A mockup is a static rendering of a visual design—"static" because a mockup is rendered in a format that does not allow user interaction the way a real application does. Mockups are used to show a visual design concept and give a basic sense of what the app screen will look like when finished.

> ### Note
> Mockups are used for a variety of visual designs. In the software development world, mockups are used for everything visual from artwork to screen design. For brevity's sake, this section focuses on mockups for screen design.

A mockup can come in many different forms. It can be a hand-drawn sketch, as seen in Figure 7.4, or it can look exactly like the real application. A mockup can even be as basic as a wireframe produced in Keynote or some other drawing app. Regardless of the form, a mockup serves the same purpose: to convey the look and feel of a visual design.

Wireframes are the easiest kind of mockup to create. A wireframe is nothing more than boxes and simple objects sketched to show the general layout of the application screen. What makes wireframes easy is that you can sketch them with nothing more than pencil and paper, and no artistic skills are required.

A mockup can be made to look like the real application screen. This is a bit more involved and requires more than pencil and paper. A realistic-looking mockup is great when you are pitching an app concept to a potential client because it shows exactly how the application will look. Wireframes, on the other hand, require the people reviewing them to use a bit of imagination, but this is not a bad thing.

As awesome-looking and impressive as realistic mockups can be, they are not without their own set of problems. First of all, it requires more time to create realistic-looking mockups. Second, showing realistic mockups can mislead clients and others into thinking the app is nearly complete even though a single line of code has not been written. People who do not understand software development see a realistic-looking screen mockup and think all you now need to do is sprinkle in some code and the app is done. As a programmer, you know better.

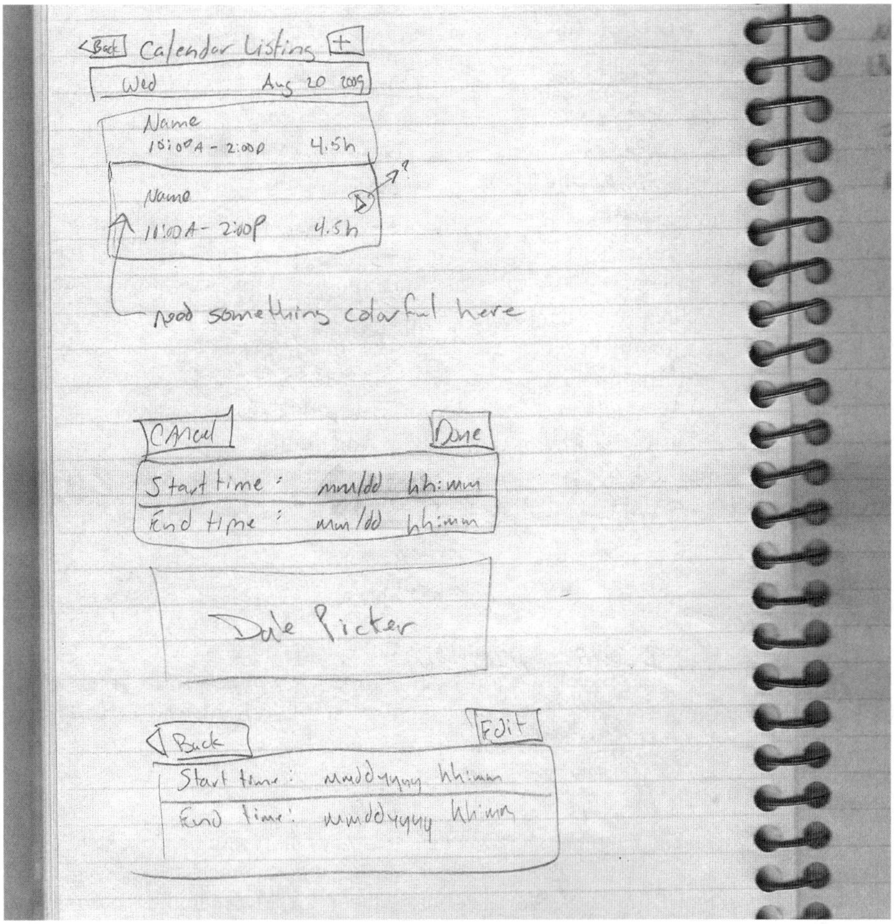

Figure 7.4   A set of wireframes sketched by hand

Note

This has happened to me on more than one occasion. I present a set of mockups to the client. Each mockup looks like a real screen shot. The client knows little about the software development process and upon seeing the realistic-looking mockups jumps to the conclusion that the app is nearly finished—this despite my explaining that what is being reviewed is only a mockup, a static rendering of a screen design. I'm now of the opinion that it is best to avoid creating realistic-looking mockups unless you know that the person reviewing them understands that they were drawn and not created from snapshots of a functioning app.

What to Mock Up

What to mock up really depends on the circumstances. You can mock up as little or as much of the application as you feel is necessary. Remember, the goal of mockups is to convey the basic look and feel of the application, including the flow of the app. It need not be perfect or contain every possible detail. It just needs to include enough details for everyone to understand the UI design and workflow of the app.

It's not always necessary to create a mockup of each and every screen. If a mockup has done its job conveying the app design, you can assume that the additional screens not included in the mockups follow the same look and feel. However, if the app you are building is for a client, the client might expect, and prefer, mockups for every screen. Use your best judgment when deciding how much or how little to mock up.

Keep in mind that using mockups is not just about designing screens for your application. Mockups are also really useful for designing artwork that is included in your application. Figure 7.5 shows some of the mockups for the Labor Mate app icon.

There are no limits to what you can mock up. The more mockups you create, the better off your design. And best of all, creating mockups is a great way to get the creative juices flowing.

Tools to Use

How you create a mockup can vary as much as the details you include in the mockup. You may find that drawing sketches with paper and pencil works best for you. Or you may find that a combination of hand-drawn sketches and wireframes created in Keynote is best. Find what works best for you and run with it.

> **Note**
>
> My approach varies based on the project. I tend to always start with paper sketches. Once I'm comfortable with the design, I may or may not redo the mockups in Keynote or iMockups. If the mockup is for a client, I will more times than not redo the mockups in an app. This gives them a more professional appearance when I present the UI designs to clients.

To find what works best for you, you need to know what tools are available for creating mockups. Let's go over some of the more popular ones.

Figure 7.5   Example mockups for the Labor Mate app icon, starting with hand-drawn sketches and ending with the final app icon

Paper and Pencil

Paper and pencil is by far the most commonly used mechanism for creating mockups. A paper mockup is quick and simple, and it doesn't require a learning curve. You just start drawing. Best of all, artistic skills are not required. Your sketch doesn't have to look great. It simply needs to covey a sense of how the screen looks and behaves within the app.

Hand-drawn sketches are no longer limited to paper. The iPad has become an excellent device for sketching. Apps such as Penultimate (**bit.ly/learnipadprog-PenultimateApp**) make drawing sketches as much fun as finger painting. However, using a finger can be somewhat troublesome, especially if you are doing a large number of sketches. This is why a number of folks use a capacitive stylus for drawing on the iPad. Whether you use your finger or a stylus, the iPad is a good alternative to paper.

> **Note**
>
> I reviewed the Pogo Sketch and Boxwave Capacitive Stylus on my blog site (**blog.whitepeaksoftware.com/2010/08/29/ipad-stylus-review/**). Check it out if you want more details on capacitive styluses for the iPad.

Photoshop

Another option for creating mockups is Adobe Photoshop. This is a popular choice with designers who have designed Web sites for years using Photoshop.

Doing mockups in Photoshop has a few advantages over paper. First of all, you can create a mockup that looks exactly like the real thing. Photoshop is an excellent choice when you want to create realistic-looking mockups. Second, Photoshop makes it easy to slice out custom artwork that will be included in your app.

The downside to using Photoshop is the time it takes to learn. Many designers already know how to use Photoshop and can produce mockups in a short amount of time. But for some folks, using Photoshop to create a good-looking mockup is about as realistic as your mom, who has never programmed before, writing a good iOS application in a short amount of time. Not that it can't be done; just that it is difficult to do in a reasonable amount of time.

All is not lost should you still want to create realistic mockups using Photoshop. There are a number of templates available that help get you started. One template that looks particularly good is the iPad GUI PSD (**www.teehanlax.com/blog/2010/02/01/ipad-gui-psd/**). This PSD includes most, if not all, of the standard elements you need to create really useful, realistic-looking mockups using Photoshop.

> **Note**
>
> A trick you can use to suggest a real app using nothing more than mockups is to save each screen mockup as a *.png* or *.jpg* image. Copy the images to your iPad and view the images using the Photos app. While the screen elements are not functional, you can still flip through the screens to get a sense of how the application will look and feel on the device.

Keynote

Keynote may seem like an odd choice for creating mockups, but it's a really useful way to create nice-looking mockups for the nondesigner type who struggles with Photoshop. Keynote, and PowerPoint for those who prefer it, makes it possible to create realistic-looking iPad screen mockups with very little effort. And Keynote does an outstanding job of drawing boxes, making wireframe mockups a snap to create.

As with Photoshop, starting with a template can save you time. One free template is MockApp (**mockapp.com**). MockApp is designed for creating iPhone mockups, but since many of the screen elements are the same, it can also be used to create iPad screen mockups.

MockApp has a template for Keynote and PowerPoint. The templates are available as "tweetware." This means that, while the templates are free to use, the author asks that you send a tweet about using MockApp to help spread the word about it.

Another Keynote template for creating iPad wireframes is Keynote Wireframe Toolkit (**keynotekungfu.com**). You won't be creating realistic-looking iPad mockups with Keynote Wireframe Toolkit, but remember, that's not necessarily a bad thing. The toolkit makes it easy to create good-looking wireframes for iPad applications. It also includes a really nice feature that allows you to link wireframes to one another. A screen element can be made clickable, sending you to another wireframe screen. This is a great way to prototype the application workflow in a low-cost, efficient manner.

Keynote Wireframe Toolkit comes with support for Keynote and PowerPoint, and the cost is only $12.

Icon Sets

Creating realistic-looking screen mockups means including artwork for icons. Creating original artwork will ensure that your application has a unique look, but sometimes there just is not enough time. What you can do in these situations is to use stock icons within your mockups and the real application.

There are a number of free and paid icon sets available on the Internet. One of the most popular is Glyphish (**glyphish.com**), which includes over 200 stylish icons designed for iPhone and iPad.

One additional note: While stock icon sets are great for in-app displays on buttons, toolbars, and tab bars, they don't make for great app icons. Your app icon should be original artwork. If you are not a designer, hire one to create your app icon. Remember, the app icon is the first visual impression potential users will have of your app. This impression should be a good one, not a bad one, so spend the extra money to have your app icon professionally designed.

Mockup Apps

Another option you have for creating screen mockups is to use an app devoted to creating wireframes. Mockup apps have all the features you need for creating screen mockups. However, these apps focus on creating wireframe mockups, not realistic-looking ones. Don't view this as a limitation. Remember, realistic mockups can lead to confusion. Wireframes, on the other hand, allow you to focus on the screen layout and screen flow without worrying about pixel-perfect display.

One useful app available on the iPad is iMockups (**bit.ly/learnipadprog-iMockupsApp**), shown in Figure 7.6. iMockups makes it possible to create UI mockups for iPad, iPhone, and Web apps. It includes page linking so that you can prototype your app's workflow, and it supports VGA out for presenting your mockups on an overhead projector. iMockups includes a library for every screen widget you need, and you can export mockups. iMockups is the perfect iPad app for creating professional-looking wireframe mockups of your app.

OmniGraffle from OmniGroup (**bit.ly/learnipadprog-OmniGraffleApp**), shown in Figure 7.7, is another popular application for creating wireframe mockups. OmniGraffle is available for the Mac desktop and iPad. OmniGraffle works by using stencils of different object types and shapes. The wide array of stencils, provided by OmniGroup and the user community, makes it possible to create virtually any type of diagram you need, from flowcharts to wireframes. OmniGraffle on the iPad also has a freehand mode in which you can draw your mockups using your finger or a stylus.

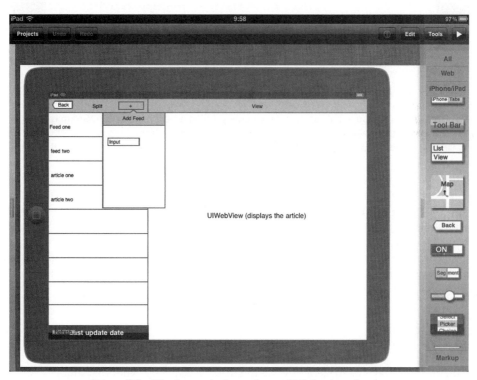

Figure 7.6   iMockups wireframe for an RSS feed reader app

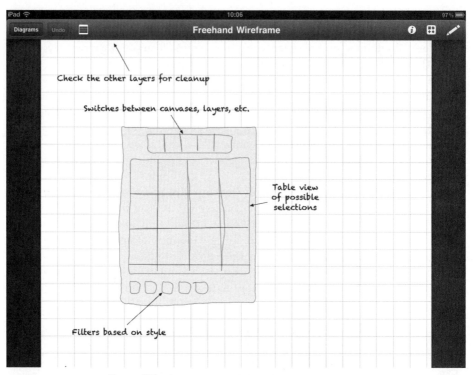

Figure 7.7   Screen shot of OmniGraffle for the iPad

> **Note**
>
> OmniGraffle for iPad's $50 price tag may give you sticker shock, but OmniGroup does
> offer a unique money-back guarantee. If you are unhappy with the iPad version of Omni-
> Graffle for any reason, send OmniGroup a copy of your iTunes receipt and they will issue
> you a refund. Now that's customer service.

One other app that is popular for creating wireframes and mockups is Balsamiq
Mockups (**balsamiq.com**), shown in Figure 7.8. Balsamiq is a cross-platform desktop
app for sketching mockups. It is also available as a plug-in for Confluence, JIRA, Fog-
Bugz, and XWiki, and a Web version is in the works. In addition to including all the
features you would expect from a mockup and wireframing app, the folks at Balsamiq
have released an online collaboration solution called myBalsamiq. myBalsamiq makes
it possible for remote teams to work together on UI design and mockups.

Prototyping

A mockup is a good way to validate your UI design, and tools like iMockups,
Balsamiq, and Keynote make it possible to create clickable mockups that simulate the
workflow of your app. But sometimes this is not enough.

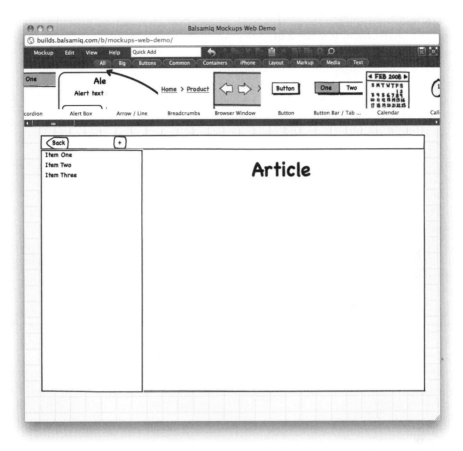

Figure 7.8   Wireframing a sample iPad app using Balsamiq

Maybe you need to see the animation between screen transitions, or maybe you want to verify that data can be retrieved from a Web service. These types of validations are not possible in a static mockup. What you need to do is to prototype the concept in a functional app.

What Is a Prototype?

In the realm of software development, a prototype is a sample application written to validate a design concept or group of concepts. A prototype app is a quick-and-dirty version of a sample application intended to be a throwaway. As with mockups, the goal of a prototype is to validate a design concept or decision. But unlike mockups, a prototype is a functioning application. This means that you can interact with it, add and retrieve data, perform calculations, and more.

The primary purpose of a prototype is to validate a concept or show how something might be accomplished. This goes a step further than a mockup in that a prototype is a real application written with source code. However, a prototype is not a complete application. It is not an app that someone would use on a regular basis to accomplish a task.

A prototype should be limited to validating a design concept or proving that an approach is feasible. Often a prototype is buggy, contains no error handling (unless you are prototyping how to handle errors), and is ugly. A prototype is quick and dirty. It is not something you share with the world.

You should not spend a lot of time on a prototype. There is no reason a prototype should look and behave like the real application. You should treat a prototype as a throwaway. This last point is very important and deserves repeating: You should treat a prototype as a throwaway.

Often programmers will turn a prototype into the real application. This is a huge mistake. A production app—that is to say, the real app, the one you share with the world—should be far more robust than a quick-and-dirty prototype.

When writing a prototype, it's likely you will not follow good coding styles and conventions. After all, you're writing something quick and dirty. You end up taking shortcuts that you would never do in a real application. Turning this same code into a real application makes your application less stable, uncaught bugs are more likely, and enhancing and maintaining the app written from prototype code is a nightmare. In the long run, you end up wasting more time with a prototype app turned into a production app than you would had you thrown out the prototype and written the real app from scratch.

Throwing out the prototype app might seem like a waste, but it is not. Remember, the primary goal of the prototype is to validate one or more concepts. In the course of creating the prototype app you gain knowledge about which techniques work and which ones do not. Armed with this knowledge, you are able to write better code for the real app in less time.

How to Create a Prototype

Of course you can use a clickable mockup for creating your prototype. This is fast and efficient, but you are limited to prototyping the workflow of your app. To go beyond this, you need to create a prototype app.

A prototype app is like any other app. The only difference is that your prototype app will not be shared with the world, and the world will not use your prototype to solve real-world problems. Instead, your prototype app will be used by you and maybe a small, select group of interested individuals for a short period of time to validate that the concept indeed works. For example, say you are writing a streaming radio app. The first thing you might do is to write a prototype app that proves you can play back streaming audio from the Internet. The user interface for this app will be ugly, or there may be no UI at all. And the URL to the radio station is hard-coded in the prototype app.

This is not the type of app you share with the world. It's not the type of app Apple approves for the App Store. But this app does serve a purpose. It proves that you know how to stream audio from the Internet, and that is very important knowledge to have if you're planning to write a streaming radio app.

Often the fastest way to write a prototype app is to use one of the application templates provided in Xcode. The application templates provide a jump start to a working app. With this in place, you are free to hack away with your prototype code. It doesn't matter which application template you use. Pick the one that best matches the purpose of your prototype app.

> **Note**
>
> A short description of each application template is available in the "Application Templates" sidebar found in Chapter 1, "Your First App."

Summary

App design is a very important part of creating iPad applications. You need to spend the time up front thinking about and designing your app before you write a single line of code. Create an App Charter to define the "what" and "who" of your application. Have brainstorming sessions to come up with a big list of app features, then trim down that list once you know who your target audience is.

Take advantage of visual and audio metaphors within your application, but don't go overboard. The metaphors should enhance the user experience, not distract from it. And look for ways to customize the standard UI controls instead of writing a new control from scratch.

Don't forget to consider the ergonomics and aesthetics of your application. Take a step back and look at your app design with the eyes of an industrial designer.

Hire a professional designer. Enough said. Unless you have design skills, you're better off letting a designer give your application a polished look.

When it's time to figure out the "how" of your app, use mockups and prototypes. Creating mockups and prototypes is a cost-effective way of validating your app design before writing code for the real application. Remember, mockups are great for validating visual designs, and prototypes are great for validating designs that can be tested only in code. Use both throughout your software development process to save time and build better apps.

And last, read the *iOS Human Interface Guidelines*, the HIG. Then read it again in a few months. Then read it again, and again, and again. Apple has spent an extraordinary amount of time researching and performing usability testing for iOS. Your app can only benefit from the advice provided in the HIG.

Part II

Building PhotoWheel

8

Creating a Master-Detail App

In Part I you learned about the tools, programming language, and frameworks used to build iPad apps. Now it's time to use what you have learned to build a real app. This is no simple app you are building. It's not yet another flashlight app. No, it's a real-world app that uses most if not all of the most commonly used elements of iOS. You will be building an app that displays photos, has animation, persists data in a local database, and calls Web services over the Internet.

What's the app? It's PhotoWheel, and the App Charter was presented in Chapter 7, "App Design."

Just to recap: PhotoWheel is a photo app that allows you to store your favorite photos in one or more albums. It gets its name from the spinning wheel, or disc, of photo albums. You use your finger to rotate through the set of photo albums displayed in the wheel.

It's a good idea to read Part II with your computer nearby so that you can work on the app as you read. This hands-on approach will help you learn faster. If you are the type who prefers to know what's going on first, feel free to read the chapter and then return to the beginning to work on the app.

Let's get started building PhotoWheel.

Building a Prototype App

As you learned in Chapter 7, "App Design," a common technique for building a new application is to start with mockups followed by a prototype app. The mockups for PhotoWheel have already been done for you. Figure 8.1 shows the mockup for the prototype app. The prototype app is used to prove core concepts of the app you are building. It is a throwaway, and it will look nothing like the final app. The mockup of the final PhotoWheel app is shown in Figure 8.2.

Note
You will find the complete set of mockups, including hand-drawn mockups, in the mockups directory included with the source code.

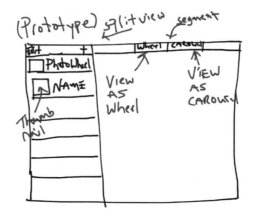

Figure 8.1   Early mockup drawing of the PhotoWheel prototype app

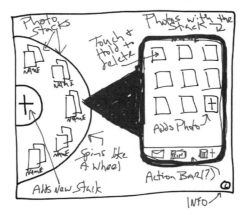

Figure 8.2   A mockup drawing for the final version of the PhotoWheel app

A quick way to build a prototype app is to use one of the application templates provided by Xcode. PhotoWheel will contain a collection of photo albums, and each photo album will contain one or more photos. This is the classic Master-Detail pattern, where the photo album represents the master data and the photos within the album represent the detail. The Master-Detail Application template is perfect for this type of app, so let's use it for the prototype app. But first...

What Is the Split View Controller?

The iPad application created from the Master-Detail Application template uses a split view controller to display master and detail information. The split view controller—or more specifically `UISplitViewController`, which is the class name—is a nonvisual controller that manages the display for two view controllers, a master view controller and a detail view controller. When the iPad orientation is landscape, the split view controller displays the views for both view controllers at the same time. The master view is displayed on the left side of the screen and the detail view is displayed on the right side.

When the device is rotated to the portrait orientation, only the detail view is displayed. The master is hidden to allow the user to focus on the content presented in the detail view. The master view is still available to the user as a button on the toolbar, but its view is hidden.

The Mail app included on the iPad uses `UISplitViewController`, as seen in Figure 8.3. When you hold the iPad so that the **Home** button is on the left or right (called landscape orientation), you see the list of inboxes, accounts, and emails on the left side of the screen. Tap an email on the left side to view its contents on the right side. Now rotate the iPad so that the **Home** button is at either the top or the bottom (called the portrait orientation). Only the email's contents are displayed. If you need to navigate the list of emails, inboxes, and accounts while in portrait, tap the button in the upper left corner. This will reveal the view managed by the master view controller.

Now that you know what the split view controller is and what it does, let's create a new master-detail app to serve as the PhotoWheel prototype.

Figure 8.3   A screen shot of the Mail app in action on the iPad

Create a New Project

To begin, you need to create a new project in Xcode. Start by launching Xcode. Next, select **File > New > New Project (Shift-⌘-N)**. Choose **Master-Detail Application** from the list of application templates, then click the **Next** button, shown in Figure 8.4.

Enter "PhotoWheelPrototype" as the product name. Accept the default Company Identifier value or edit it to reflect the identifier you prefer to use. Refer back to Chapter 6, "Provisioning Your iPad," to learn more about the Company Identifier value.

Leave the Class Prefix field blank. Select iPad for the Device Family, and uncheck the options Use Storyboard, Use Core Data, and Include Unit Tests. These options are not needed for the prototype and will be covered in later chapters. Finally, select the option Use Automatic Reference Counting. Your settings for the project should look like those in Figure 8.5.

Click the **Next** button, then select a folder in which to store the project. Finally, click the **Create** button.

> **Note**
>
> If you are a Git user and you wish to use it, select "Create local git repository for this project." For the purpose of this book, Git is not required and will not be discussed.

You now have a master-detail app project. Build and run (**⌘-R**) the app to see the generated app in action. Be sure to select the simulator in the scheme list, shown in Figure 8.6, to run the app in the simulator; otherwise the app will run on your iPad, assuming it is tethered to your computer.

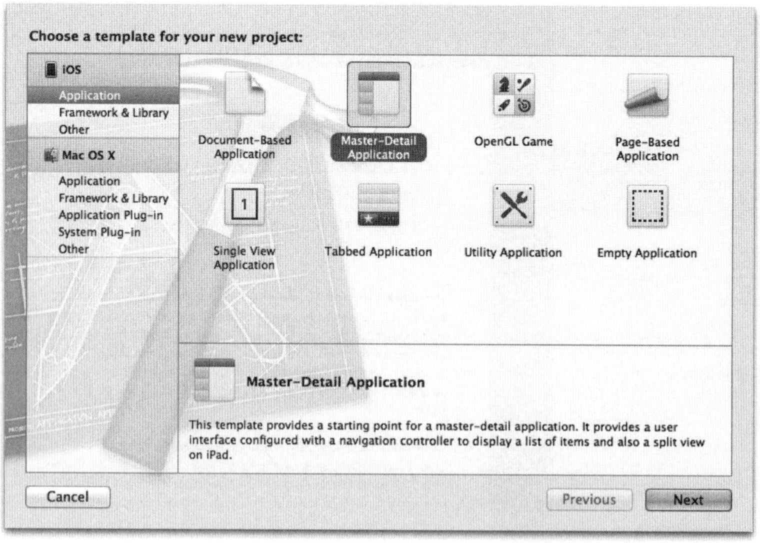

Figure 8.4   List of the iOS application templates available in Xcode

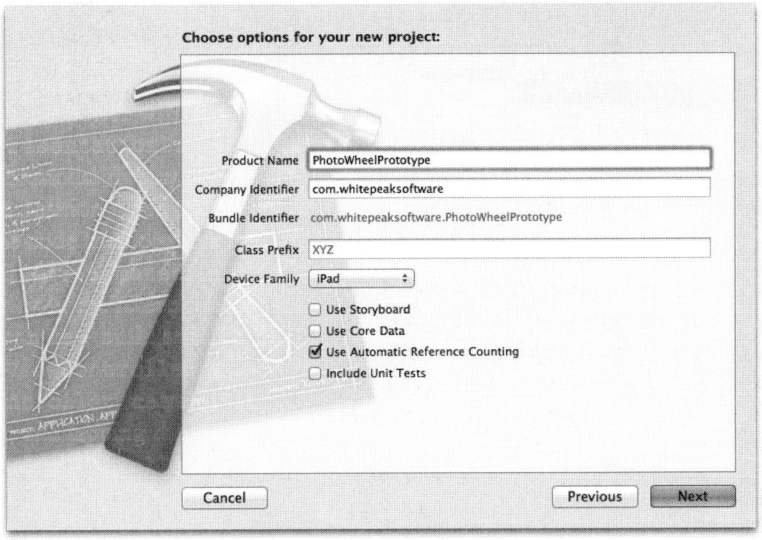

Figure 8.5   Project options for the Master-Detail Application template

Figure 8.6   Select the scheme from the list found near the upper left
corner of the Xcode project window.

Using the Simulator

Using the iPad Simulator is a fast and easy way to test your app. By default, the simulator launches with the device orientation in portrait mode. You rotate the device
using **⌘-Left Arrow** and **⌘-Right Arrow** (or **Hardware > Rotate Left** and
Hardware > Rotate Right from the menu bar).

Also by default, the device size is displayed at 50%. You make it larger by selecting
Window > Scale > 100% (⌘-1) or **Window > Scale > 75% (⌘-2)**. **Window >
Scale > 50% (⌘-3)** returns the simulator to a 50% scale.

Take a look under the **Hardware** menu item for more juicy goodness. You can
have the simulator simulate the shake gesture, tap the **Home** button, and lock the
screen. There are also options to call up the keyboard, simulate low memory warnings, and simulate an external display with **TV Out**.

PhotoWheelPrototype is a master-detail application, which means it uses the split
view controller. To see it completely, you need to rotate the iPad Simulator to the
landscape orientation. Type **⌘-Left** (or **⌘-Right**) to rotate the simulated device. You
should now see the app as shown in Figure 8.7.

Figure 8.7   Master-detail application using the
`UISplitViewController` running in the iPad Simulator

How to Quit Your App

You may have noticed that when you run your app from Xcode, whether in the simulator or on the iPad, and you touch the **Home** button to exit the app, the app doesn't actually quit. Xcode shows that the app is still running.

What's going on here?

iOS has a service called multitasking. Multitasking allows one or more apps to run at the same time when the active app is in the foreground and all other running apps are in the background. When you launch an app, it becomes the foreground app. When you tap the **Home** button or fast swap to another app, the foreground app transitions to the background. When you return to the app, it transitions from the background to the foreground. Your app receives messages such as `applicationDidBecomeActive:` and `applicationDidEnterBackground:` as it transitions from the foreground and background so that the app can act accordingly based on the new state.

This is an overly simplified explanation of multitasking on iOS. For a more complete explanation, read the "Multitasking" section of *The Core Application Design* document provided by Apple (**developer.apple.com/library/ios/#documentation/iPhone/Conceptual/iPhoneOSProgrammingGuide/CoreApplication/CoreApplication.html**). But until you do, all you need to know is that when you touch the **Home** button, your app doesn't actually quit; it simply moves to the background. This is why Xcode shows that your app is still running.

There is a logical reason for this behavior. It allows you to debug your app while it runs in the background. If Xcode automatically terminated the app when you touched the **Home** button, there would be no way to debug apps running in the background.

So what do you do when you want to quit or terminate your app? There are a couple of options available to you. Every time you finish a debugging session, you can click the **Stop** button or use the shortcut ⌘-. in Xcode. This will terminate your app. The other option is to quit the simulator, which is as simple as typing ⌘-**Q**. I tend to use ⌘-**Q** to quit the simulator most often.

A Closer Look

When you ran the app, you may have noticed that the application template did a number of things for you. First and most important, it created a functional master-detail app. Granted, the app isn't useful, but it does have basic functionality commonly found in master-detail apps.

You can rotate the device to change from the master-detail view to the detail-only view. A toolbar button is added that displays the master view in a popover when the device orientation is portrait. And tapping an item in the master view will update the details display. The template has set up a functional project structure that can be used to build a really useful app.

Project Structure

The application template creates the project structure shown in Figure 8.8. The project contains the following files:

- *AppDelegate.h* **and** *.m*: This is the application delegate. It derives from `NSObject` and conforms to the `UIApplicationDelegate` protocol.

- *MasterViewController.h* **and** *.m*: This is the view controller for the master view. It derives from the `UITableViewController`.

- *DetailViewController.h* **and** *.m*: This is the view controller for the detail view—the view displayed on the right side of the screen when the iPad orientation is landscape. This class derives from `UIViewController` and conforms to the `UISplitViewControllerDelegate` protocol.

- *MasterViewController.xib*: This is the user interface NIB file for the root view. It contains a table view, and it is controlled by `MasterViewController`.

- *DetailViewController.xib*: This is the user interface NIB file for the detail view. It contains a toolbar and a display label, and it is controlled by `DetailViewController`.

These files represent the primary source code to your app, and these are the files you will work with most often. There are, however, a few more files created by the

Figure 8.8   Project navigator for the PhotoWheelPrototype project

application template that are worth mentioning. Click the disclosure indicator next to the Supporting Files group to open it. You'll see the following files:

- **PhotoWheelPrototype-Info.plist**: This is the *info.plist* file for your application. It contains additional metadata about the application used by the build process. Settings in the *info.plist* are used to define various characteristics about the app such as supported interface orientation, main NIB file or storyboard, version number, and icon files.

- **PhotoWheelPrototype-Prefix.pch**: This is the precompile header file. It is used by the compiler to improve compile-time performance and typically contains references to other frequently used header files.

- **main.m**: This source file contains the `main()` function needed by all programs created in the C programming language. It calls the function `UIApplication-Main()`, which in turn loads the main NIB file if defined in the *info.plist* file, causing the app delegate class to be instantiated.

App Delegate

From the iOS developer's point of view, the app delegate is the launch point of the application. The class `AppDelegate` defines the app delegate for the PhotoWheelPrototype app. Let's examine this class a bit more. Open the *AppDelegate.h* file in Xcode. You accomplish this by clicking the file name in the Project navigator. You will see the code in Xcode's text editor as shown in Listing 8.1.

Listing 8.1   **Source Code from the** *AppDelegate.h* **File**

```
#import <UIKit/UIKit.h>

@interface AppDelegate : UIResponder <UIApplicationDelegate>
```

```
@property (strong, nonatomic) UIWindow *window;

@property (strong, nonatomic) UISplitViewController *splitViewController;

@end
```

The first line of code is `#import <UIKit/UIKit.h>`. This tells the compiler to include the UIKit header file, which contains declarations for the objects found in the UIKit framework.

The next line of code begins with the compiler directive `@interface`. This indicates the start of the interface declaration for the class `AppDelegate`. You see from this line of code that `AppDelegate` derives from the class `UIResponder` as indicated by `: UIResponder`. `AppDelegate` also conforms to the protocol `UIApplicationDelegate` as indicated by `<UIApplicationDelegate>`.

> **Note**
>
> In Objective-C a class can be derived from one and only one class. This is called single inheritance. While an Objective-C class can inherit behaviors and features from only one class, it can conform to more than one protocol. To indicate that a class conforms to more than one protocol, separate each protocol listed between the < and > symbols with a comma, for example, `<UITableViewDataSource, UITableViewDelegate>`.

Next you find a set of declared property declarations. There are two declared properties in Listing 8.1: `window` of type `UIWindow` and `splitViewController` of type `UISplitViewController`.

> **Note**
>
> As you learned in Chapter 4, "Getting Started with Objective-C," the `@property` compiler directive indicates a declared property. Following the `@property` is the list of settings for each declared property. The asterisk in front of each of the property names tells the compiler that the property is a pointer. A pointer is a reference to an object or data stored in memory. Refer back to Chapter 4 for a refresher on declared properties.

The class definition ends with the `@end` compiler directive. This concludes the interface declaration for the class `AppDelegate`.

You now have an idea of what the class `AppDelegate` looks like, but you still don't know how it is implemented. To see the implementation, open the file *AppDelegate.m*. A portion of the implementation file is shown in Listing 8.2.

> **Note**
>
> A quick way to navigate between the *.h* and *.m* files is to use the **Control-⌘-Up** and **Control-⌘-Down** shortcut keys.

Let's step through Listing 8.2 so that you have a better understanding of what is happening.

Listing 8.2 *AppDelegate.m*

```objc
#import "AppDelegate.h"
#import "MasterViewController.h"
#import "DetailViewController.h"

@implementation AppDelegate

@synthesize window = _window;
@synthesize splitViewController = _splitViewController;

- (BOOL)application:(UIApplication *)application
didFinishLaunchingWithOptions:(NSDictionary *)launchOptions
{
    self.window = [[UIWindow alloc] initWithFrame:[[UIScreen mainScreen] bounds]];
    // Override point for customization after application launch.

    MasterViewController *masterViewController =
        [[MasterViewController alloc] initWithNibName:@"MasterViewController"
                                               bundle:nil];
    UINavigationController *masterNavigationController =
        [[UINavigationController alloc]
          initWithRootViewController:masterViewController];

    DetailViewController *detailViewController =
        [[DetailViewController alloc] initWithNibName:@"DetailViewController"
                                               bundle:nil];
    UINavigationController *detailNavigationController =
        [[UINavigationController alloc]
          initWithRootViewController:detailViewController];

    self.splitViewController = [[UISplitViewController alloc] init];
    self.splitViewController.delegate = detailViewController;
    self.splitViewController.viewControllers = [NSArray arrayWithObjects:
                                                masterNavigationController,
                                                detailNavigationController,
                                                nil];
    self.window.rootViewController = self.splitViewController;
    [self.window makeKeyAndVisible];
    return YES;
}

@end
```

> **Note**
>
> If you are looking at the implementation file in Xcode, you'll notice that the application template generates much more code than what is shown in Listing 8.2. The additional code is not used at the moment. For the sake of brevity, Listing 8.2 shows only the parts of the implementation file that are of interest now.

The first things you see in Listing 8.2 are three `#import` statements. The first imports the header file for the `AppDelegate` class. This is followed by imports of `MasterViewController` and `DetailViewController` header files. The header files for these two classes are imported so that the classes can be used within the code in this file.

Following the `#import` statements is the `@implementation` compiler directive. This is the companion to the `@interface` compiler directive found in the *AppDelegate.h* file. `@implementation` tells the compiler that what follows is the implementation for the class `AppDelegate`.

Following `@implementation` is a set of `@synthesize` compiler directives. As you may recall from Chapter 4, "Getting Started with Objective-C," each declared property must have accessor methods (getter and setter methods). `@synthesize` generates the needed accessor methods for you during compile time. This reduces the amount of code you must write.

Each `@synthesize` directive is followed by the property name. This name matches the names defined in the *.h* file. Following the property name is an equal sign followed by the property name with an underscore character as a prefix. This allows you to map a declared property to an ivar of a different name.

By default `@synthesize` assumes that the ivar name for a declared property is the same as the property name. For example, the code `@synthesize myProperty` tells the compiler to generate the accessor methods for `myProperty` and use the ivar `myProperty`. You can override this by setting the property name equal to a new ivar name, for example, `@synthesize myProperty = _myProperty`. This does the same as the first example except the ivar name is now `_myProperty`.

Why use an ivar name that is different from the property name? To help maintain your sanity. Often programmers new to Objective-C will confuse a property with an ivar. Take, for example, the code snippet in Listing 8.3.

Listing 8.3   **A Simple** `Person` **Class**

```
@interface Person : NSObject
{

}
@property (nonatomic, copy) NSString *name;
@end

@implementation Person
```

```
@synthesize name;

- (void)foo
{
    NSLog(@"name: %@", [self name]);
}

- (void)bar
{
    NSLog(@"name: %@", name);
}

@end
```

In Listing 8.3 the class `Person` is defined. It has a declared property called `name`. `name` is synthesized to generate the accessor methods and the ivar, which is also called `name`. The implementation includes two methods, `foo` and `bar`. Both produce the same output, but `foo` uses the accessor method for the declared property while `bar` uses the ivar.

> **Note**
>
> `NSLog()` is a C function that outputs a string to the console. It is similar to the C function `printf` in that it takes a format string followed by a list of arguments. However, `NSLog` differs in that it can handle Objective-C objects. Refer back to Chapter 5, "Getting Started with Cocoa," for more information on `NSLog`.

There are a few problems with the code snippet. First of all, and most important, you should always avoid directly accessing ivars. Accessing ivars directly is not good OO programming. Instead, you should always go through the accessor methods for the declared property. This ensures that any side effects implemented by the accessor methods are taken into account. For example, the property name could have an accessor method that actually concatenates two strings, first and last names, to form the `name` string.

Second, using the declared property with `@synthesize` ensures that proper memory management is used. iOS does not support garbage collection, so your code must manage memory, and any help you can get from the compiler is a good thing.

For someone new to Objective-C the difference between the methods `foo` and `bar` might not be obvious. But if you rename the ivar something different from the property name, there is no mistaking how you are accessing the data. This underscore prefix in the modified version of `bar`, shown in Listing 8.4, stands out more than it did in Listing 8.3.

Listing 8.4 **Modified Version of** bar

```
- (void)bar
{
   NSLog(@"name: %@", _name);
}
```

Using an underscore as a prefix (or suffix) to your ivar names makes it easy to scan your code for references to ivars. If you find code that references an ivar, that code is likely wrong. It should be changed to use the accessor methods instead.

> **Note**
>
> The code in Listing 8.4 accesses the ivar directly. It is done to illustrate the point that an ivar with an underscore at the beginning or end of the name is easy to find. The code sample in Listing 8.4 should not be viewed as good programming style as direct access to the ivar is not recommended.

Let's return to Listing 8.2 and take a look at the next line of code, which is the method declaration for -application:didFinishLaunchingWithOptions.

Launch Options

The appropriately named UIApplicationDelegate method application:did-FinishLaunchingWithOptions: is called when the OS finishes launching the app. This is the first time, under normal circumstances, that your code has an opportunity to do something useful. This is when your code initializes the app and its delegate for use.

A master-detail application first creates an instance of a UIWindow. This is the main window displayed by the application. Next, an instance of MasterViewController is created and used to initialize a new UINavigationController instance. An instance of DetailViewController is created next, and it too is used to initialize a new UINavigationController instance. This is followed by the creation of the UISplit-ViewController. The DetailViewController instance is made the delegate for the split view controller, and the navigation controllers, one containing the MasterView-Controller instance and the other containing the DetailViewController instance, are added to the split view controller. The navigation controller masterNavigation-Controller represents the "master" and the other navigation controller, detail-NavigationController, represents the "detail."

The steps for initialization can and will differ between apps. You just saw, for example, the steps needed to prepare a split view controller with master and detail controllers. Other application templates would follow different steps, but a few steps are common among all apps. Those steps include

- Setting the rootViewController property for the window
- Making the window visible by calling makeKeyAndVisible on the window
- Returning YES

Setting the `rootViewController` for the window assigns the view managed by the root view controller as the content view for the window. `makeKeyAndVisible`, as the name implies, makes the window the key—a key window is the active window—and makes it visible.

The concept of a key window comes from the OS X world where an application often has more than one window. Unlike the desktop, however, an iPad app has only one window. The exception to this is when the iPad is connected to an external display. At this time the iPad app can create a second window that is used to display content on the secondary screen. But even with a secondary screen the iPad app has only one key window, and that is the window displayed on the device itself.

Last, `application:didFinishLaunchingWithOptions:` returns YES. If it were to return NO, the app would not launch. Your app will almost always return YES for this method, but there are times when NO is the appropriate return value, for instance, when the app is unable to handle the launch options. Here's why.

`application:didFinishLaunchingWithOptions:` has two input parameters: `application` and `launchOptions`. `application` is a reference to the `UIApplication` instance for the running app. `launchOptions` is a key-value pair dictionary indicating the reasons for launching the application.

`launchOptions` are used when your application is launched by some means other than the user tapping the app icon from the Home screen. For instance, say your app supports a particular file type and the user received an email attachment of that file type. The user has the option to open the file type in a different app from within the Mail app. When the user does this, your app is launched from the Mail app and the `launchOptions` dictionary contains the URL to the file attachment. Your app can now open the file attachment and process its contents.

If the app is able to process the incoming file attachment successfully, the return value for `application:didFinishLaunchingWithOptions:` is YES. But if the file attachment cannot be processed, say it's a bad file format, NO is the appropriate return value. Returning NO tells the operating system that your app will not continue the launch process.

Other `UIApplicationDelegate` Methods

`application:didFinishLaunchingWithOptions:` is not the only method implemented by the app delegate. There are others, although they are not as frequently implemented. The other commonly implemented `UIApplicationDelegate` methods are the following:

- **`applicationWillResignActive:`**: This method is called when the application is about to change from an active state to an inactive state. This can happen for a number of reasons: an incoming phone call, SMS message, or push notification, or when the user has quit the app by tapping the **Home** button. You typically pause your app when this method is called. This could mean disabling timers, pausing long-running operations, or, if your app is a game, pausing game play.

- **applicationDidBecomeActive:**: This method is called when the app is about to change from an inactive state to an active one. This is when your app would restart those things previously paused in `applicationWillResignActive:`.

- **applicationDidEnterBackground:**: This method is called when the user leaves your app. This is a good place to save data and release shared resources used by your app. This method is also called if your application supports multitasking; otherwise, `applicationWillTerminate:` is called.

- **applicationWillEnterForeground:**: This method is the opposite of `applicationDidEnterBackground:`. It is called when your application becomes active, but only if your app supports multitasking.

- **applicationWillTerminate:**: This method is called just prior to the operating system terminating your app. This is a good place to save any unsaved data changes within your app. Because termination of your app is controlled by the operating system, your code has only a few seconds to complete any remaining tasks before termination. This means that code you implement in this method should do its job quickly and efficiently. This is not the place for a long-running task such as updating data to a Web service as there is no guarantee that the OS will let the task complete before the app is terminated.

A Tour of `UISplitViewController`

As you have already learned, `UISplitViewController` is a nonvisual controller that manages the display of two view controllers, a master and a detail. `UISplitViewController` has two properties, shown in Listing 8.5.

Listing 8.5   `UISplitViewController` **Interface**

```
@property(nonatomic, copy) NSArray *viewControllers;
@property(nonatomic, assign) id <UISplitViewControllerDelegate> delegate;
```

`viewControllers` is an array consisting of two elements. The first element, `objectAtIndex:0`, is the master controller and the second element, `objectAtIndex:1`, is the detail controller.

> **Note**
> `objectAtIndex:` is a method on `NSArray`, which is the data type for the `viewControllers` property. It is important to note that arrays in C and Objective-C are zero-based, not one-based.

`UISplitViewController`'s other property is `delegate`. This is a reference to an object that conforms to the `UISplitViewControllerDelegate` protocol. The methods from this protocol are shown in Listing 8.6, which is taken from the *UISplitViewController.h* header file. Let's take a closer look.

Listing 8.6 `UISplitViewControllerDelegate` **Definition**

```
@protocol UISplitViewControllerDelegate

@optional

// Called when a button should be added to a toolbar for a hidden view controller
- (void)splitViewController: (UISplitViewController*)svc
     willHideViewController:(UIViewController *)aViewController
          withBarButtonItem:(UIBarButtonItem*)barButtonItem
       forPopoverController: (UIPopoverController*)pc;

// Called when the view is shown again in the split view, invalidating the
// button and popover controller
- (void)splitViewController: (UISplitViewController*)svc
     willShowViewController:(UIViewController *)aViewController
  invalidatingBarButtonItem:(UIBarButtonItem *)barButtonItem;

// Called when the view controller is shown in a popover so the delegate can
// take action such as hiding other popovers.
- (void)splitViewController: (UISplitViewController*)svc
          popoverController: (UIPopoverController*)pc
  willPresentViewController:(UIViewController *)aViewController;

@end
```

UISplitViewControllerDelegate has three methods that tell the delegate when the master view controller is about to hide, when it is about to show, and when the master view is about to show in a popover as the result of the user tapping the bar button item.

The delegate method `splitViewController:willHideViewController:withBarButtonItem:forPopoverController:` is called when the master view controller is about to be hidden. This happens when the device orientation changes from landscape to portrait. This allows the user to focus attention on the detail view. As a convenience, this method also provides the `UIBarButtonItem` and `UIPopoverController`.

You should add the bar button item to the toolbar or navigation bar displayed in the detail view. This provides the user with a way to view the contents of the master view controller without rotating the device back to the landscape orientation.

The `UIPopoverController` passed in this method call is a reference to the popover controller that displays the master view when the bar button item is tapped. You can store the reference within your view controller or ignore it, depending on your needs.

When the user taps the bar button item, the `splitViewController:popoverController:willPresentViewController:` method is called. This gives your code a chance to perform some action prior to the display of the master view within the popover control. For example, if the app is already displaying a popover, this is a good time to close it before displaying the master view popover.

The third and final method is `splitViewController:willShowViewControl ler:invalidatingBarButtonItem:`. This method is called when the user rotates the device back to the landscape orientation. The bar button item added to the toolbar during the hide method is no longer needed. This is because the master view will now be displayed on the left side of the screen. Therefore, you should remove the bar button item from the toolbar.

Viewing Header Files

When implementing a class that conforms to a particular protocol, often you want to copy and paste the method declarations. This saves you the time of typing the sometimes lengthy declaration statements. There are two ways to copy the method declaration:

1. Copy from the SDK documentation.
2. Copy from the header file.

For many programmers new to Xcode, copying a method declaration from the SDK documentation is the popular choice. You launch the documentation view in Organizer, search for the protocol, then copy the desired methods from the documentation page.

A quick way to get to the documentation page for a protocol is to **Option-Click** the protocol name in Xcode's text editor. When you do this, a preview Help popover is displayed. From here you can click the documentation icon in the upper right corner (Figure 8.9). This will load the Help page into the document view within the Organizer window.

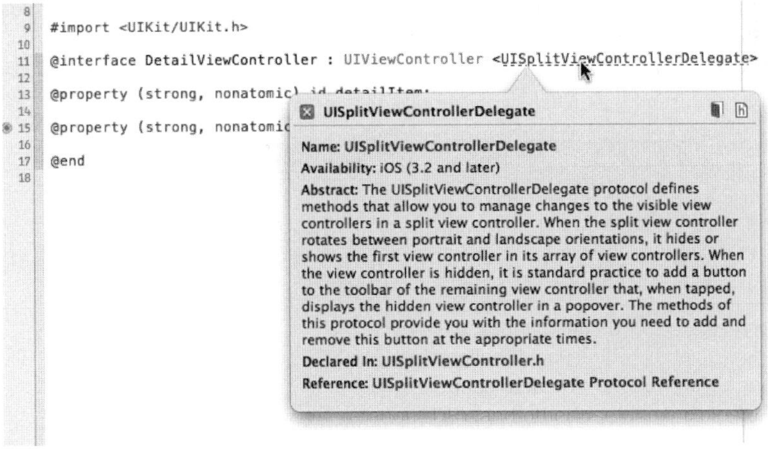

Figure 8.9   **Option-Click** for a popover view of the documentation.

While it is common for new Xcode programmers to copy delegate methods from the documentation, this is not the fastest way. Also, you are limited to copying only one method at a time. If you need to implement more than one method, which is common for many protocols, bouncing back and forth between the documentation and the text editor can be less than efficient. A better approach is to copy the method declarations from the header.

There are two quick ways to open a header file. The first is to select **File > Open Quickly...** (**Shift-⌘-O**) from the menu bar. This approach works well when you know the name of the header file you wish to open. However, a better, faster way is to use the Xcode feature Jump to Definition, which works from within the text editor and doesn't require knowing the name of the header file.

To open the header file for a protocol in the text editor, **⌘-Click** the protocol name. This will jump you to the header file containing the protocol definition. You can also place the text editor cursor on the protocol name and type **Control-⌘-D** (or select **Navigate > Jump to Definition** from the menu bar) to jump to the header file containing the protocol definition.

From the header file you can see all the methods defined for the protocol and copy one or more to include in your app. I tend to copy all the methods, paste them into my app, then remove the ones I don't need.

The best part of this trick is that Jump to Definition is not limited to protocols defined in the SDK. You can jump to definitions found in your own code. And the item doesn't have to be a protocol. It can be a class name, a variable, a declared property, and more. In fact, a common pattern you see in Objective-C code is to separate blocks of code with a `#pragma mark` – statement.

`#pragma mark` – allows you to include a brief remark following the dash character that describes the block of code. This is commonly used to denote a block of delegate methods. A common practice is to include the name of the protocol for the delegate methods in the `#pragma mark` – statement, as seen in Figure 8.10. Doing so makes it easy for you (and other devs who might have to support your code down the road) to jump to the protocol definition.

Figure 8.10   You can **Option-Click** the name even if it is part of a comment or #pragma mark.

Assigning the Split View Controller Delegate

As you saw in Listing 8.2, the split view controller delegate is set to an instance of the `DetailViewController`. If you take a look at the source file *DetailViewController.h*, you will see that the interface declaration shows that the class conforms to the `UISplit-ViewControllerDelegate` protocol. And if you look at *DetailViewController.m*, you will see the implementation of each `UISplitViewControllerDelegate` method, courtesy of the application template. The generated code is also given in Listing 8.7.

Listing 8.7   Implementation of `UISplitViewControllerDelegate` Methods in
DetailViewController.m

```
#pragma mark - UISplitViewControllerDelegate

- (void)splitViewController:(UISplitViewController *)svc
      willHideViewController:(UIViewController *)aViewController
           withBarButtonItem:(UIBarButtonItem *)barButtonItem
       forPopoverController: (UIPopoverController *)pc
{
   barButtonItem.title = NSLocalizedString(@"Master", @"Master");
   [self.navigationItem setLeftBarButtonItem:barButtonItem animated:YES];
   self.masterPopoverController = popoverController;
}


- (void)splitViewController:(UISplitViewController *)svc
      willShowViewController:(UIViewController *)aViewController
   invalidatingBarButtonItem:(UIBarButtonItem *)barButtonItem
{
   // Called when the view is shown again in the split view, invalidating
   // the button and popover controller.
   [self.navigationItem setLeftBarButtonItem:nil animated:YES];
   self.masterPopoverController = nil;
}
```

As you can see, the application template provides implementations for both the hide and show delegate methods. In the hide method, the button title is set to the string literal "Master" and the button is added to the navigation bar. In the show method, the button is removed from the navigation bar. You can see this code in action by running the project (⌘-R) and rotating the device (or simulator) between landscape and portrait orientations.

Detail View Controller

The `DetailViewController` is not only the delegate for the `UISplitView-Controller`; it is also the controller for the detail view displayed on the right side of the screen when the device orientation is landscape or full-screen when the orientation is portrait. This view is defined in the *DetailViewController.xib* file, shown in Figure 8.11.

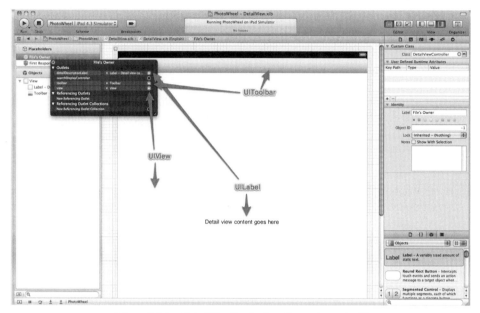

Figure 8.11   *DetailViewController.xib* as shown in IB

The view has a label (UILabel) displayed in the center of the screen. The view and label are connected to outlets defined as declared properties in the DetailView-Controller class.

Master View Controller

There is one other view controller class in the project that hasn't been discussed: MasterViewController. You may be thinking to yourself that the MasterView-Controller is the controller for the master view, and you would be almost right. But only almost.

The MasterViewController is used, but it's not the controller assigned to the first element of the UISplitViewController's viewControllers array. Instead, an instance of UINavigationController is the master view controller, as shown in Listing 8.2.

UINavigationController is a specialized controller that manages a stack of view controllers. It provides methods for pushing and popping view controllers on and off the stack, and it can display a navigation bar with a back button, making it possible for the user to return to a previous view with the tap of a finger.

The UINavigationController assigned as the master view controller for the split view controller contains an instance of MasterViewController as the first controller in its stack. This means that the view managed by the MasterViewController instance is displayed when the app loads, making it seem as if the MasterView-Controller is the master view controller.

MasterViewController derives from the class named UITableViewController. UITableViewController is a specialized view controller that simplifies the display and management of a UITableView. The UITableView is one of the most used views in UIKit. Many apps, especially on the iPhone, use UITableView to display data. You will work with UITableView in Chapter 9, "Using Table Views," so no further details are given here.

Why use a navigation controller? As you will see in the next chapter, additional view controllers will be displayed within the master area of the split view controller. Using a navigation controller gives the user a way to navigate back through the stack of view controllers.

Summary

This chapter talked a lot about the Xcode project and project files generated by the Master-Detail Application template. While the focus has been on one particular application template, most of what is covered in this chapter applies to the other iOS application templates.

Each template has its own unique characteristics. The Master-Detail Application template creates a shell project that uses the split view controller for the iPad. The Single View Application template creates a shell app that uses a single view. And so on. The key takeaway, however, is that other than their unique characteristics, each application template performs pretty much the same duties.

Each template creates an Xcode project with an app delegate, an *info.plist* for the project, and so on. So while the walk-through in this chapter focused on the Master-Detail Application template, most of what you learned applies to the other application templates as well.

Note
Refer back to Chapter 1, "Your First App," for a detailed list of iOS application templates.

Exercises

1. Change the title for the bar button item to display "Photo Album" instead of "Master."

2. Change the font for the "Detail view content goes here" label displayed in the detail view controller to bold.

3. Change the font color for the same label to red.

4. Create a project for each iOS application template. Build and run the projects and compare the app types. Identify which templates are for iPad, iPhone, and both (called universal).

9

Using Table Views

In the last chapter you created a master-detail app using the application template provided by Xcode. While the app is functional, it is not very useful. In this chapter you will start making the app more useful by adding the ability to add, edit, and remove photo albums. You'll learn how to work with a table view and its data source and how to delegate protocols, create a new view with a controller, and communicate between view controllers.

First Things First

When the app runs and the device orientation is landscape, the word *Master* is displayed at the top of the master view. The table view represents a list of photo albums, so naming this list "Master" doesn't really make sense. Changing it is simple: You set the title for the `MasterViewController`. That's it. The `UINavigationController` does the work of actually displaying the title for you.

A good place to set the title is in the `-initWithNibName:bundle:` or `-viewDidLoad` method. The template-generated code sets the title in the former, but the latter is preferable. Setting the title in the `-initWithNibName:bundle:` method will work only when that method is called. If, for example, the `MasterViewController` is loaded without a NIB, the title will not be set. On the other hand, `-viewDidLoad` is always called, regardless of whether the controller is created with a NIB or not.

Update the code in *MasterViewController.m* to set the title in `-viewDidLoad` by copying the line of code that sets the title in `-initWithNibName:bundle:` and pasting it to the `-viewDidLoad` method, then change "Master" to "Photo Album." Listing 9.1 shows the changes that need to be made.

Listing 9.1   **Set the Title for** `MasterViewController`

```
- (id)initWithNibName:(NSString *)nibNameOrNil bundle:(NSBundle *)nibBundleOrNil
{
    self = [super initWithNibName:nibNameOrNil bundle:nibBundleOrNil];
    if (self) {
        self.clearsSelectionOnViewWillAppear = NO;
        self.contentSizeForViewInPopover = CGSizeMake(320.0, 600.0);
    }
```

```
    return self;
}


- (void)viewDidLoad
{
    [super viewDidLoad];
    // Do any additional setup after loading the view, typically from a nib.
    [self.tableView selectRowAtIndexPath:[NSIndexPath indexPathForRow:0
                                                       inSection:0]
                        animated:NO
                    scrollPosition:UITableViewScrollPositionMiddle];

    self.title = NSLocalizedString(@"Photo Albums", @"Photo albums title");
}
```

> **Note**
>
> The code that sets the title calls the C function NSLocalizedString(). This func-
> tion is used to retrieve the localized version of a string. The first parameter is the key,
> and the second parameter is the comment. The key is used to look up the localized string
> resource. The key value is used if the string resource for the key does not exist. The com-
> ment is included in the localized string resource file and is used to provide context to
> the string or relay a message to the language translator. The comment is never displayed
> within your app.
>
> I'm of the opinion that developers should always use NSLocalizedString() even if
> there are no initial plans to support other languages. By preparing your code at the onset,
> you save time down the road should those plans change. That said, for brevity's sake,
> NSLocalizedString() is not used in the sample code for the book.
>
> More information on internationalizing your app is available in the *Introduction to Inter-
> nationalization Programming Topics* provided by Apple (**developer.apple.com/library/
> ios/#documentation/MacOSX/Conceptual/BPInternational/BPInternational.html**).

The -initWithNibName:bundle: method has a couple of lines of code worth
discussing. The first, self.clearsSelectionOnViewWillAppear = NO, sets
the property found on UITableViewController, the superclass for MasterView-
Controller. This property determines whether or not the object should clear the
selection within the table view just before the view appears to the user.

Following that line is self.contentSizeForViewInPopover = CGSize-
Make(320.0, 600.0). contentSizeForViewInPopover is a property on UIView-
Controller, which is the superclass to UITableViewController. This property
tells the popover control, if any, the preferred content size for the view. This property
doesn't guarantee that the popover will resize. It does, however, state that the popover
should be at least this size.

> **Note**
>
> `contentSizeForViewInPopover` is used when a view managed by the view controller is displayed within a popover, such as when the `MasterViewController` view is displayed after the toolbar button is tapped when the iPad orientation is portrait. This property provides a hint to the popover controller of the initial size for the popover's content area. It doesn't actually control the size of the popover. Say, for example, you have two views displayed within a popover controller. The controller for the first view sets the `contentSizeForViewInPopover` to 320 x 600. The controller for the second view sets the property to 320 x 400. You might think that the content area for the popover will resize itself to the smaller size when the second view is displayed, but that will not happen. The popover's content area only grows larger, not smaller.
>
> To force the content size to a smaller size you much explicitly set the size on the `UIPopoverController`. This is accomplished by setting the `popoverContent-Size` property on `UIPopoverController`.

Run the app and test your change. With the device orientation in landscape, the navigation bar in the master view now reads "Photo Albums," as shown in Figure 9.1. Now rotate the device to portrait. The button added to the toolbar reads "Master." Not exactly what we're going for. It should read "Photo Albums" to be consistent with the `MasterViewController` title. Change the text to read "Photo Albums." Remember, it's the `DetailViewController` that is responsible for displaying the

Figure 9.1   Screen shot of the PhotoWheelPrototype app in landscape

button on the toolbar, not the `MasterViewController`. Therefore, you make the change in *DetailViewController.m*.

Here are the steps you want to follow:

1. Open the file *DetailViewController.m*.

2. Scroll down to the method `-splitViewController:willHideViewController:withBarButtonItem:forPopoverController:`.

3. Change the string literal "Master" to "Photo Albums."

4. Save your changes (**⌘-S**).

Once you have made these changes, build and run (**⌘-R**) the app and verify that the changes are complete. The detail view for PhotoWheelPrototype should look like the screen shot in Figure 9.2. Check your work if it does not.

With that out of the way, let's now turn our attention to table views.

Figure 9.2   Screen shot of the PhotoWheelPrototype app in portrait

A Closer Look

The table view is a visual control for displaying a list of information. It is widely used on iPhone and has its place on iPad as well. The table view implements common features needed when displaying a list of data, including scrolling up and down, item selection, and highlighting. It has two styles, grouped and plain, and has different built-in layouts for data display. It also allows you to completely customize the look.

UITableView

A table view is an instance of the class `UITableView`. `UITableView` derives from `UIScrollView`, which gives the table view its scrolling behavior. But unlike `UIScrollView`, which supports scrolling horizontally and vertically, `UITableView` supports only vertical scrolling.

One of the more surprising aspects of `UITableView` is that it supports only a single column of data. This design choice was made to support the small screen of iOS devices. While `UITableView` supports only one column, it is possible to customize the look of the table view to give it the appearance of multiple columns.

`UITableView` supports two styles, which must be specified when creating the instance of the table: plain and grouped. The style cannot be changed after the table instance is created. A plain table displays a single list of data. A grouped table allows rows to be visually separated into individual sections. `UITableView` can also display a header and footer, and it can display section headers and footers. Figure 9.3 shows examples of each table style.

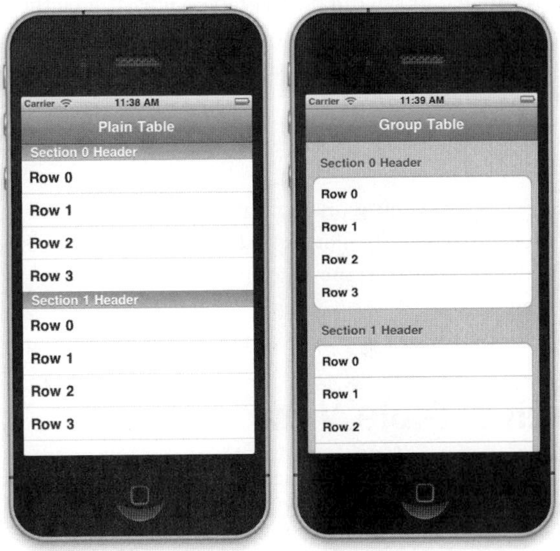

Figure 9.3   On the left is a sample of a plain table, and a grouped table is shown on the right.

UITableViewCell

Each row of the UITableView is called a cell. The cell is an instance of UITableView-Cell or a subclass of the same. A cell's position within the table view is determined by the NSIndexPath. The NSIndexPath has two properties that are used to determine the cell's location within the table view: section and row. The section is the section index within the table, and the row is the row index within the section.

UITableView contains properties for accessing cells and sections using an index path. There are also methods for scrolling to a particular row based on the index path.

UITableViewDelegate

In addition to configuring a UITableView through its properties, a delegate object conforming to the protocol UITableViewDelegate is used to do things such as set the height of rows and return the views for section headers and footers. Also included in the UITableViewDelegate protocol are methods that manage the row selections, editing, and reordering.

UITableView interacts with your application by way of the UITableViewDelegate to configure and manage rows of the table, but a different protocol is used to populate the table view with data. This protocol is UITableViewDataSource, and as the name implies, it defines methods for providing data to the table view.

UITableViewDataSource

The UITableView property dataSource references an object that conforms to the UITableViewDataSource protocol. The dataSource provides information about the data needed to construct and maintain the table view. It tells the table view how many sections are in the table and how many rows are in each section. It provides the title for each section header and footer and the cell for each row. The dataSource also has methods to determine if rows can be added, removed, and reordered.

UITableViewController

One other class that is useful when working with a table view is UITableView-Controller. This specialized controller provides common management tasks for working with a table view, reducing the amount of code you must write to display and work with a table view.

With the introductions out of the way, it's time to work hands-on with table views.

Working with a Table View

To use a table view, a few things must happen first. First and foremost, an instance of UITableView must be created. This is handled for you in MasterViewController's NIB file. MasterViewController is a subclass of UITableViewController, and as previously mentioned, UITableViewController is a specialized controller for displaying a UITableView.

Also needed are the table view's `delegate` and `dataSource`. The `MasterView-Controller` will play the role of both by conforming to the protocols `UITable-ViewDelegate` and `UITableViewDataSource`.

A Simple Model

Before the table view can display data, the data must be defined and stored in a model. The data needed for the table view in the PhotoWheelPrototype app is the photo album. At the moment, the only attribute needed from a photo album is `name`. You could create a custom class called `PhotoAlbum` that has a single property called `name`, but that's overkill. After all, you're still in the prototyping stage of the app.

So what data structure should be used as the model for the photo albums? An array of strings works nicely. Each string in the array is the name of a different photo album. But iOS 5 introduces a new collection type called `NSOrderedSet`. `NSOrderedSet` manages a collection of objects that are stored in sequential order, just like `NSArray`. But unlike `NSArray`, `NSOrderedSet` contains a particular object once and only once. `NSArray` allows the same object to be added to the array at multiple indexes. For the PhotoWheelPrototype, you want only one instance of each photo album to exist in the collection, so `NSOrderedSet` is the better data structure for your needs.

To create the model data, you need to create an ordered set. The user should be able to add photo albums to the app, so the set needs to be mutable. This means the data type needed is `NSMutableOrderedSet`. Also, the `MasterViewController` is the controller most interested in the list of photo albums, so you'll add the mutable set to `MasterViewController`.

Start by opening *MasterViewController.h*. Add a declared property called `data` of type `NSMutableOrderedSet`. The modified interface for `MasterViewController` should now look like the code in Listing 9.2.

Listing 9.2   `MasterViewController` **Interface Modified to Include the** `data`
          Property

```
#import <UIKit/UIKit.h>

@class DetailViewController;

@interface MasterViewController : UITableViewController

@property (strong, nonatomic) DetailViewController *detailViewController;
@property (strong, nonatomic) NSMutableOrderedSet *data;

@end
```

Note

The property `detailViewController` was added by the Xcode template when the master-detail project was created.

Before the declared property data can be used, the accessor methods—the getter and setter methods—must be created. Let the compiler do this for you by using the @synthesize compiler directive.

Here are the steps to follow:

1. Open the file *MasterViewController.m*.

2. After the line of code @implement MasterViewController add the following: @synthesize data = _data;.

3. Save your changes (⌘-S).

Before you can use data it must be instantiated. A good place to create the instance is in the -viewDidLoad event. This method is called after the content view managed by the view controller has been loaded. While you are at it, go ahead and add a couple of entries to the order set.

To accomplish this, follow these steps:

1. Open the file *MasterViewController.m*.

2. Scroll to the -viewDidLoad method.

3. At the bottom of -viewDidLoad add the following code:

```
[self setData:[[NSMutableOrderedSet alloc] init]];
[[self data] addObject:@"A Sample Photo Album"];
[[self data] addObject:@"Another Photo Album"];
```

4. Save your changes.

The -viewDidLoad method should now look like the code in Listing 9.3.

Listing 9.3 Instantiate data and Add Two Sample Photo Albums

```
- (void)viewDidLoad
{
    [super viewDidLoad];
    // Do any additional setup after loading the view, typically from a nib.
    [self.tableView selectRowAtIndexPath:[NSIndexPath indexPathForRow:0
                                                           inSection:0]
                    animated:NO
              scrollPosition:UITableViewScrollPositionMiddle];

    self.title = NSLocalizedString(@"Photo Albums", @"Photo albums title");

    [self setData:[[NSMutableOrderedSet alloc] init]];
    [[self data] addObject:@"A Sample Photo Album"];
    [[self data] addObject:@"Another Photo Album"];

}
```

> **Note**
>
> The source code in Listing 9.3 mixes the use of dot syntax with the messaging style. The Xcode template generated the dot syntax code in the listing. In a real-world project, you would clean up this code to use one style consistently throughout the project.

You may have noticed that -viewDidLoad already had two lines of code in it before you made your changes. The first line, [super viewDidLoad], tells the object instance to invoke the -viewDidLoad method implemented in the superclass. The implementation in MasterViewController overrides the method in the super-class UITableViewController. It is unknown if the superclass's implementation performs any important tasks. Calling the super's implementation ensures that important tasks, if any, are executed prior to exiting the code in the local implementation.

The next line of code autoselects the first row in the UITableView. At the moment, the DetailViewController is not attached to the MasterViewController, so selecting the first row in the table doesn't do anything other than to highlight the row in the table view. This will change once you tell the MasterViewController how to communicate to the DetailViewController.

Display Data

MasterViewController now has model data to display, and the collection set representing the model data has two items in it representing the photo albums, "A Sample Photo Album" and "Another Photo Album." However, when you run the app, these photo album names do not appear in the table view within the MasterView-Controller. This is because you haven't told the table view what to display.

To tell a UITableView about data, your code must provide a data source object that conforms to, that is to say, implements, the methods of the protocol UITableViewDataSource. MasterViewController is a subclass of UITableView-Controller, so by default the dataSource property for the UITableView is set to the MasterViewController instance. This can be done explicitly in the code by saying [[self tableView] setDataSource:self], but this is not necessary when using an instance of UITableViewController unless the data source is an object instance other than the controller itself.

That's right, a data source does not have to be the view controller. However, it is usually convenient to have the view controller serve as the data source for a UITableView. In fact, the application template used to create the PhotoWheelPrototype project has already generated method stubs for responding to UITableViewData-Source calls. But these calls do not know about the ordered set data. Therefore, it is up to you to tell the UITableView about the data by way of the UITableView-DataSource methods. Listing 9.4 shows the changes you need to make before the table view can display data.

Listing 9.4   `UITableViewDataSource` **Method Implementations in**
           MasterViewController.m

```
#pragma mark - UITableViewDelegate and UITableViewDataSource methods

// Customize the number of sections in the table view.
- (NSInteger)numberOfSectionsInTableView:(UITableView *)tableView
{
    return 1;
}


- (NSInteger)tableView:(UITableView *)tableView
 numberOfRowsInSection:(NSInteger)section
{
    NSInteger count =[[self data] count];
    return count;
}


// Customize the appearance of table view cells.
- (UITableViewCell *)tableView:(UITableView *)tableView
         cellForRowAtIndexPath:(NSIndexPath *)indexPath
{
    static NSString *CellIdentifier = @"Cell";

    UITableViewCell *cell =
       [tableView dequeueReusableCellWithIdentifier:CellIdentifier];
    if (cell == nil) {
       cell = [[UITableViewCell alloc] initWithStyle:UITableViewCellStyleDefault
                                    reuseIdentifier:CellIdentifier];
    }

    // Configure the cell.
    NSString *text = [[self data] objectAtIndex:[indexPath row]];
    [[cell textLabel] setText:text];
    return cell;
}
```

Let's walk through the code in Listing 9.4.

The first method is -numberOfSectionsInTableView:. This method returns the number of sections within a table view. Sections are a way to group related data within the table view. The table view for this app has only one section, so the return value is always 1.

The next method implemented is -tableView:numberOfRowsInSection:. This method is called for each section, where the number of sections is determined by -numberOfSectionsInTableView:. PhotoWheel has only one section, so -tableView:numberOfRowsInSection: is called only once to load the table. The number of rows is determined by the number of elements in the data array. This means the return value is the count of `data`.

> **Note**
>
> You may be wondering why I chose to implement `-tableView:numberOfRowsIn-Section:` as two lines of code, setting the count to a local variable, then returning the count stored in the local variable. I use this pattern to make the code easier to debug. The method could have been implemented with a single line of code, `return [[self data] count]`. While this is perfectly valid, it makes it harder to see the count when debugging the app. By setting a local variable to the count, I'm able to see the value during a debug session, which lists the local variables in scope at the point where the program is stopped. You'll learn more about debugging an app in Chapter 25, "Debugging."

The last method implemented from the `UITableViewDataSource` protocol is `-tableView:cellForRowAtIndexPath:`. The index path is of type `NSIndexPath`, and it consists of two properties of interest, `section` and `row`. The `section` property returns the index of the current section. Because this app has only one section, the `section` value will always be 0. `row` is the index of the current row within the section. For this app, `row` is equal to the index identifying the element from `data` to be displayed. Plainly put, the parameter variable `indexPath` tells the code which element in `data` to retrieve. But before the app can display the name of the photo album, it needs a `UITableViewCell` instance.

You may recall from the previous section that `UITableViewCell` is used to display content within a `UITableView`. The method `-tableView:cellForRowAtIndex-Path:` is called by the table view to request the cell for display. `UITableViewCell` is a subclass of `UIView`, meaning that the cell is really nothing more than a view. But `UITableViewCell` comes with a set of standard display styles. The styles for `UITableViewCell` are

- **UITableViewCellStyleDefault**: Displays a basic cell with a text label and an optional image view
- **UITableViewCellStyleValue1**: Displays a left-aligned label on the left side of the cell and a right-aligned label with blue text on the right side
- **UITableViewCellStyleValue2**: Displays a right-aligned label with blue text on the left side and a left-aligned label on the right side
- **UITableViewCellStyleSubtitle**: Displays a right-aligned label at the top of the cell and a left-aligned label with gray text at the bottom

More complex views can be displayed by customizing the cell. This can be accomplished by adding subviews to the cell's `contentView` hierarchy. PhotoWheel's needs are simple at the moment, so the default style `UITableViewCellStyleDefault` will work nicely.

To return a `UITableViewCell` in the method `-tableView:cellForRowAtIndex-Path:` the code must create an instance of `UITableViewCell`. Creating a new cell for each row, especially when there are many rows, can hurt the scroll performance of the table view. A better approach is to create a new instance of UITableViewCell only when absolutely necessary. Luckily for you, the Apple engineers already thought of this problem and have provided a solution.

A table view may contain more rows than are visible at a given point in time. Keeping cells for nonvisible rows needlessly consumes system resources. To reduce memory overhead, nonvisible cells can be disposed of. However, this is wasteful too, given that once a nonvisible row becomes visible, a new cell instance must be created. But, as has already been mentioned, creating a new cell instance each time hurts performance as the user scrolls through the list of rows.

The solution the Apple engineers came up with is to cache, or queue, unneeded UITableViewCells. As a cell goes from a visible state to a nonvisible state, the cell is placed in a queue to be reused. When the table view requests a cell for a particular indexPath, a call is made to the table view asking to dequeue a previously used table cell. If no queued cells are available, your code must create a new instance, but if a queued cell is available, it is recycled and used as the return value for -tableView: cellForRowAtIndexPath:. This means that at any given time, the total number of table view cells in memory is equal to the number of visible rows plus a small number of additional, queued cells. This approach reduces memory overhead and improves performance.

> **Note**
>
> In Chapter 16, "Building the Main Screen," you will learn to build a custom grid view that is based on the same pattern used by UITableView. This will give you a much better understanding of, and appreciation for, what is happening under the hood of UITableView.

That explains how to create and return a UITableViewCell. Let's now see how this is accomplished in code. Refer back to Listing 9.4 and look at the implementation for the UITableViewDataSource delegate method -tableView:cellForRowAtIndexPath:.

The first line sets a local variable to the string literal "Cell." This value is used to identify the cell within the queue. If, for example, the table view consists of cells with different formats, a different identifier is used. This allows the table view to queue cells of different formats, or styles. Your code uses the identifier to dequeue the cell of the appropriate format. This is exactly what is happening in the next line of code; a local variable called cell is created and is set to a dequeued, reusable cell with the specified identifier.

When the -dequeueReusableCellWithIdentifier: method is called, the table view returns a reference to an instance of a cell with the specified identifier. If there is no available cell, nil is returned. The nil return value means it's up to your code to create a new cell instance as seen in the if (cell == nil) statement.

Within the if block is the code needed to create an instance of UITableViewCell. You see the standard alloc init pattern used here.

Once a cell instance is retrieved, either by dequeuing or with `alloc init`, it is configured with the data to display. Following the `if` block is `NSString *text = [[self data] objectAtIndex:[indexPath row]]`. This statement retrieves the object for the current row from the `data` array. `NSMutableOrderedSet` can contain objects of any type, but we know our set contains only strings, so it is safe to set a local string variable to the object.

The table cell was init'd with the style `UITableViewCellStyleDefault`. The default style has a text label. The property name of the text label is `textLabel`. `textLabel` is of type `UILabel`, which has a `text` property. So to set the display text you set the `text` property of the `textLabel` of the cell as shown in the statement `[[cell textLabel] setText:text]`.

> **Note**
>
> Other cell styles display secondary text. The property for the secondary text is called `detailTextLabel`.

At this point the table view has the information it needs to display photo album names contained in the `data` set. Now build and run the app to make sure the changed code works.

As you can see in Figure 9.4, the app crashes with an uncaught exception. What's going on here? If you look at the code in the `-viewDidLoad` method, you see that the first row of the table is selected. But the table contains no data at the time this line of code executes. You need to move the line of code that selects the first row of the table to the end of `-viewDidLoad`, as shown in Listing 9.5.

Listing 9.5 **Updated** `-viewDidLoad` **Method Preventing the Crash**

```
- (void)viewDidLoad
{
    [super viewDidLoad];
    // Do any additional setup after loading the view, typically from a nib.

    self.title = NSLocalizedString(@"Photo Albums", @"Photo albums title");

    [self setData:[[NSMutableOrderedSet alloc] init]];
    [[self data] addObject:@"A Sample Photo Album"];
    [[self data] addObject:@"Another Photo Album"];


    [self.tableView selectRowAtIndexPath:[NSIndexPath indexPathForRow:0
                                                            inSection:0]
                                animated:NO
                          scrollPosition:UITableViewScrollPositionMiddle];
}
```

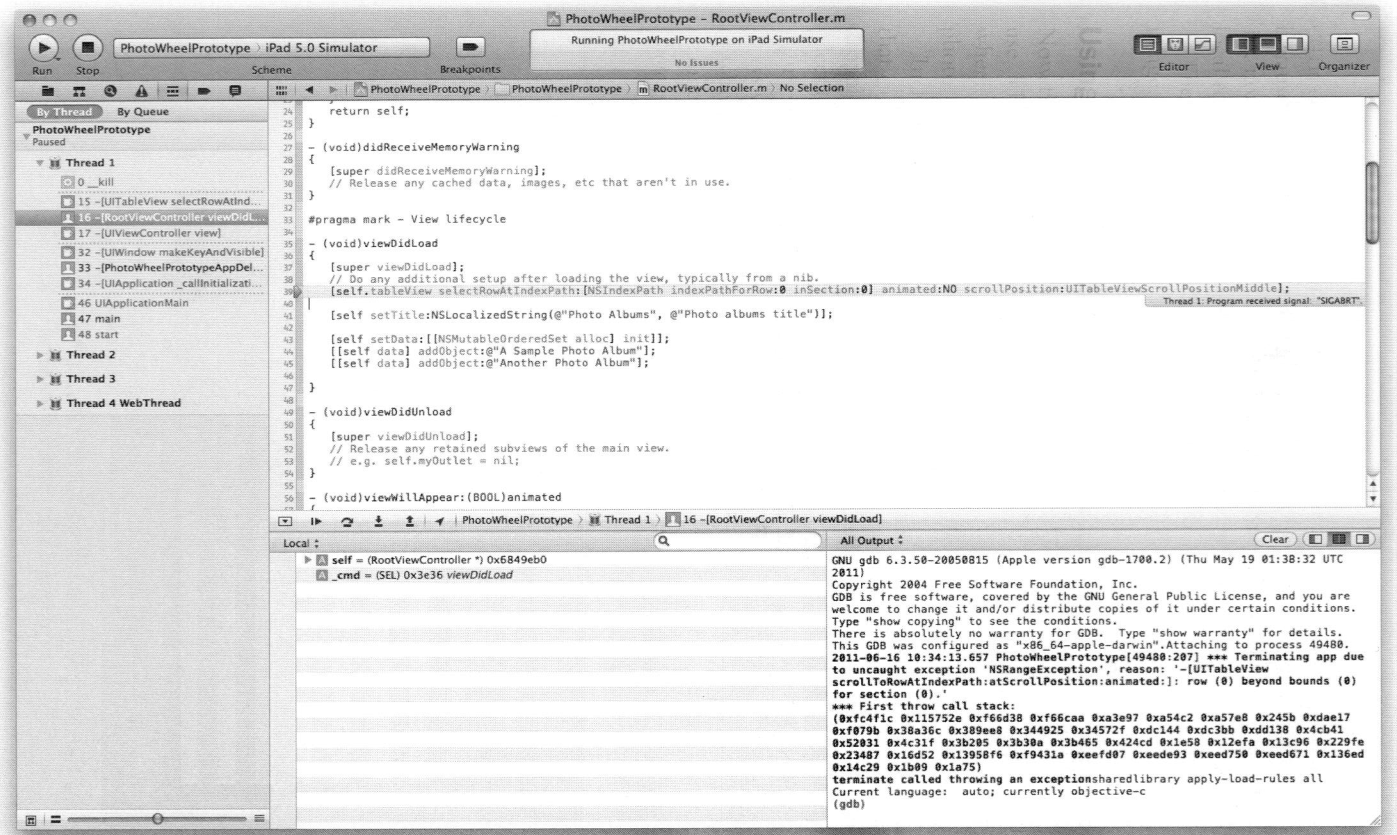

Figure 9.4 Xcode reporting the uncaught exception. Note that the line of code where the exception occurs is highlighted, and the output window in the lower right corner shows the exception message.

Figure 9.5   Screen shot of the PhotoWheelPrototype app with sample
photo albums

Make the needed code change shown in Listing 9.5, then build and run the app. This time around the app will run, and you will see the two photo albums listed in the Photo Albums table view, as shown in Figure 9.5. Check your work if you do not see the sample results.

Add Data

You have the table view displaying the list of photo albums in data, but there is no way for the user to add new photo albums. Let's change that right now.

A good way to accomplish this is to have an add button displayed on the navigation bar. iOS provides a built-in add button that displays **+** as the button text. When the user taps the **+** button, a new view is displayed, allowing the user to enter the name of the photo album. Let's get started by setting up the plumbing. Once that's in place, we can add the photo album name editor.

Here are the steps to perform:

1. Open *MasterViewController.m*.

2. In the -viewDidLoad method, add an "add"-style UIBarButtonItem to the navigation bar.

3. Add the -add: action method to MasterViewController.

4. Save your changes.

The code changes are shown in Listing 9.6. Make these changes to your project, then return to the book for a walk-through of the code.

Listing 9.6   Adding an "Add" Feature to `MasterViewController`

```
- (void)viewDidLoad
{
    [super viewDidLoad];
    // Do any additional setup after loading the view, typically from a nib.

    self.title = NSLocalizedString(@"Photo Albums", @"Photo albums title");

    [self setData:[[NSMutableOrderedSet alloc] init]];
    [[self data] addObject:@"A Sample Photo Album"];
    [[self data] addObject:@"Another Photo Album"];


    [self.tableView selectRowAtIndexPath:[NSIndexPath indexPathForRow:0
                                                           inSection:0]
                                animated:NO
                          scrollPosition:UITableViewScrollPositionMiddle];

    UIBarButtonItem *addButton = [[UIBarButtonItem alloc]
            initWithBarButtonSystemItem:UIBarButtonSystemItemAdd
                                 target:self
                                 action:@selector(add:)];
    [[self navigationItem] setRightBarButtonItem:addButton];
}

- (void)add:(id)sender
{
    NSLog(@"%s", __PRETTY_FUNCTION__);
}
```

Let's walk through the code changes; first up, the changes to -viewDidLoad. The + button, or add button as it is often called, is an instance of UIBarButtonItem. The button is added to the navigation bar displayed at the top of the MasterView-Controller content area. To add it, you first create an instance of UIBarButtonItem. This object has a custom init method called initWithBarButtonSystemItem: target:action. iOS has a list of predefined system bar buttons that you can use. The system button needed for the PhotoWheel app is UIBarButtonSystemItemAdd. This displays the + button.

The init method takes two additional methods, target and action. Target-Action is a common design pattern used throughout Cocoa. target is the receiver of an action, and action is the message sent to the target. Refer to Chapter 5, "Getting Started with Cocoa," if you need a refresher on the Target-Action pattern.

Next you add the button instance to the navigation bar, but you do not add it to the UINavigationBar itself. Instead, UIViewController has a property called navigationItem. A navigationItem, or, as it is defined in UIKit, UINavigation-Item, represents the navigational items available within the scope of the current view controller. In other words, it manages the display of navigation items for the view controller.

Note

You use the navigationItem property only when your view controller is part of a navigation stack managed by a UINavigationController.

To display a button on the left side of the navigation bar, you set the leftBar-ButtonItem property of the navigation item. The code in Listing 9.6, however, places the button on the right side of the navigation bar by calling [[self navigation-Item] setRightBarButtonItem:addButton].

When you created the UIBarButtonItem addButton, you specified a target and an action. These represent the object (the target) and the method (the action) that is called when the user taps the button. You can think of this as the on-tap event or a callback from the addButton. The target for addButton is self, which is the MasterViewController. The action is the method -add:, which follows the -viewDidLoad method in Listing 9.6.

Note

The compiler directive @selector is used to create a reference to add:. It's important that the colon character follow add; otherwise -add: is not called by addButton. In other words, the methods add and add: have different signatures and are, therefore, different methods.

The method -add: takes a single parameter, (id) sender. The sender is a reference to the UIBarButtonItem. Having this reference can be handy when you need to perform some action with the object sending the message, for example, displaying a popover. For now, we don't know what the implementation of -add: will look like, so an NSLog statement is used. This allows you to test that the addButton is added to the navigation bar of the navigationItem and that the target and action are properly set.

What you haven't seen before is __PRETTY_FUNCTION__, which is a macro that returns the name of the current class and method as a C string. The %s format is used to display the C string as part of the output. When you run the app and tap the + button, you should see the statement [MasterViewController add:] in the debug output window, shown in Figure 9.6. This tells you that the add button has been properly set up to call the -add: method defined in the MasterViewController. If you do not see this message, check your work.

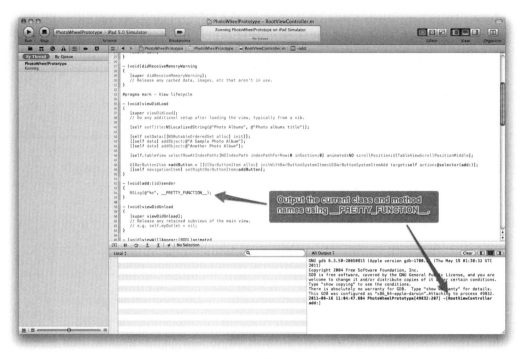

Figure 9.6   Example of __PRETTY_FUNCTION__ output

At this point, your app has a data model for content display, and it has a way for the user to add to the model using the add button. But the app needs to go one step further to allow the user to add the name of the new photo album. To enable this you'll create a new `NameEditorViewController` that allows the user to enter the name of the new photo album. Here are the steps to follow:

1. Select **File > New > New File** or type ⌘-N.

2. Under **iOS > Cocoa Touch**, select the UIViewController subclass file template (shown in Figure 9.7).

3. Click the **Next** button.

4. Type `NameEditorViewController` for the class name.

5. Leave the Subclass of as `UIViewController`.

6. Do not select the Targeted for iPad check box. The name editor will be smaller than a normal iPad view.

7. Select the "With XIB for user interface" check box. This will create a companion *.xib* file for the view controller.

8. Click the **Next** button.

9. Last, click the **Create** button. This will save the class files to the project directory.

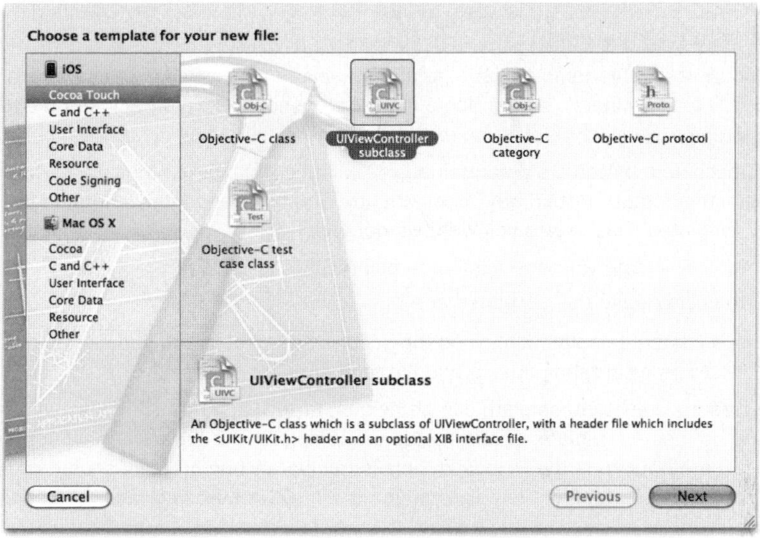

Figure 9.7   Select the UIViewController subclass file template

This creates three new files and adds them to the Xcode project, as seen in Figure 9.8. The class `NameEditorViewController` is defined in the *NameEditorViewController.h* interface file, and its implementation is in the *NameEditorViewController.m* file. The view for this controller is defined in the NIB file *NameEditorViewController.xib*. These three files contain the basic setup of a view controller and its view. Your next step will be to modify these files to display the name editor for a new photo album.

Figure 9.8 `NameEditorViewController` added to the project

An Alternative Approach

Xcode project and file templates are great time-savers for many iOS programmers (especially for beginners), but for some more experienced iOS programmers the templates are not overly useful. Let me explain.

As you become a better iOS programmer, you will find that you do things a certain way, and sometimes that "certain way" does not jibe with code and files generated by the Xcode templates. This leaves you with two options:

1. You can create your own custom templates.
2. You cannot use the templates at all.

Creating a custom template is beyond the scope of this book. You can search the Internet for tips on creating project and file templates for Xcode.

While creating a custom template can be helpful, I have found that what works best for me is to not use a template, or rather, use the template with the fewest side effects. For me, that template is the Objective-C class template when creating source code and the Empty user interface file template, found under **iOS > User Interface**, when creating a new NIB file.

I have found that when I use a template I spend more time deleting generated code and renaming files than if I were to create the files from scratch. But the speed with which to write code using a minimum template comes with experience, and even I learned by using the Xcode-provided templates. Only after a great deal of time did I discover the style that works best for me. For example, my own personal version of the steps for creating the `NameEditorViewController` are as follows:

1. Type ⌘-N.
2. Select **iOS > Cocoa Touch > Objective-C class**.
3. Click the **Next** button.
4. Type "`NameEditorViewController`" for the class name.
5. Set the Subclass to `UIViewController`.
6. Click the **Next** button.
7. Click the **Create** button.

This creates two files, *NameEditorViewController.h* and *.m*. Other than the `@inter-face` and `@implementation` stubs, the files are essentially empty. After implementing my view controller, I create the user interface with the following steps:

1. Type ⌘-N.
2. Select **iOS > User Interface > Empty** and click the **Next** button.
3. Select the Device Family iPhone and click the **Next** button.
4. Save the file as *NameEditorView* and click the **Create** button.

The biggest difference in this approach, other than doing the steps manually, is that the NIB file is named *NameEditorView.xib*, not *NameEditorViewController.xib*. The NIB represents a view, not a controller, and it has always bugged me that Xcode adds *Controller* to the NIB file name when it is created with the view controller.

Another similar approach is to follow the original steps of selecting the UIView-Controller subclass template and turning off the "With XIB for user interface" option. This gives you the generated stubs common to most view controllers without the *.xib* file. You can then manually create the NIB file yourself using the empty, view, or one of the other user interface NIB templates.

The key takeaway here is to explore the options provided by Xcode and find the approach that works best for you.

The photo album name editor is really simple. All it needs to do is allow the user to type in a name that is used as the photo album name. Xcode created the shell view controller and NIB needed for the name editor, but it is up to you to complete the implementation. To do so, however, you need to know the requirements.

The name editor will allow the user to edit a name, which is nothing more than free-form text (i.e., a string). This means that the controller needs to expose a name property of type NSString. But the UI also needs a text field that the user can type into. UITextField is perfect for this, and because it stores the current text, it can be used to retrieve the photo album name.

You also want to make the user interface as friendly as possible. If the user accidentally taps the add button, the name editor should provide a way for the user to cancel. And the UI needs a way for the user to indicate he is finished editing the name of the new photo album. The cancel and done features can be provided as buttons displayed at the top of the name editor.

All that is left with regard to defining the requirements for the name editor is a mechanism for communicating back to the calling view controller. This communication is needed to inform the calling view controller of the user's desire to cancel or save the photo album. For this, you'll define a protocol that allows callbacks to the calling view controller.

Now that you understand the requirements, let's make the needed changes.

Open the interface file *NameEditorViewController.h* and add a declared property of UITextField with the name nameTextField. Note that this property will be connected to an instance of UITextField defined in the NIB, so make sure that UITextField is also defined as an IBOutlet. Take a look at Listing 9.7 to see an example.

The requirements also call for two actions, cancel and done, so add two methods for these actions to NameEditorViewController's interface. These methods will be connected to buttons defined in the NIB, so be sure to set the return type for each action to IBAction. This helps IB find the action methods. Also, as you saw earlier with the UIBarButtonItem, include the (id)sender parameter to the actions. While the sender is not required, it's good to explicitly state it because you never know when you will need it.

One last piece is needed for the NameEditorViewController interface: a delegate that is told when the user cancels or is done with the name editor. The delegate is an instance of an object, also called a receiver in this context, that receives one or more messages based on some action or condition. A protocol is defined to ensure that the delegate implements the appropriate methods. The delegate must then conform to the protocol if it wishes to receive the messages.

> **Note**
>
> If you're coming from another language such as Java or C#, you can think of the protocol as an interface that is implemented by some other object. Read Chapter 4, "Getting Started with Objective-C," if you need a refresher on protocols."

As a convention, the delegate protocol name for a view controller is often the name of the view controller followed by the suffix Delegate. You have already seen this convention used with the protocol UITableViewDelegate. Following the same convention, the protocol for NameEditorViewController will be called NameEditorViewControllerDelegate. Since this protocol is always used in conjunction with the NameEditorViewController, it is perfectly okay to include the protocol declaration in the same *.h* interface file as the view controller. This means that the declaration for NameEditorViewControllerDelegate is added to *NameEditorViewController.h*.

Defining the protocol is only part of the step. The NameEditorViewController must have a declared property that references the delegate object. This means that you need to add another property to NameEditorViewController called delegate. Because the object can be of any type, the delegate property is declared as type id. To assist the compiler, the protocol name is included with the type id. This tells the compiler to verify that the delegate conforms to the protocol. The declared property looks like this:

```
@property (nonatomic, strong) id<NameEditorViewControllerDelegate> delegate;
```

This introduces an interesting problem in the *NameEditorViewController.h* file. The interface NameEditorViewController has a property that uses the NameEditorViewControllerDelegate protocol, but the protocol has not been defined. And as you will see shortly, the protocol uses the class name NameEditorViewController for the data type of one of the method parameters. This means that either the class or the protocol must have a forward declaration in the *NameEditorViewController.h* file. A common convention is to forward declare the protocol with an @protocol statement, then define the protocol after the class definition. This is the approach used in Listing 9.7.

The protocol NameEditorViewControllerDelegate supports two optional methods: -nameEditorViewControllerDidFinish: and -nameEditorViewControllerDidCancel:. The delegate object is not required to implement these methods because they are declared as optional. To make the methods required, use the compiler directive @required.

You might be thinking that the names of these two methods are a bit wordy, and you would be right. The method names could be didFinish: and didCancel:, but those method names are not very descriptive. Imagine if you had other view controller delegate protocols that had the same names as didFinish: and didCancel:. It would be difficult to distinguish the protocol implementations. By prefixing the protocol method names with the name of the primary sender—that is, the view controller name—you make your code much more readable.

This raises another point, or rather points, about another convention. Similar to action methods, which include a sender parameter, it is common for delegate protocol methods to include a parameter referencing the object that is sending the message. However, it is not called sender. Instead, a more meaningful parameter name is used. For instance, only an instance of NameEditorViewController will ever send a NameEditorViewControllerDelegate message, so the parameter name representing the sender is called controller.

This is a lot to chew on for someone new to iOS programming. Don't worry. The changes needed to *NameEditorViewController.h* are shown in Listing 9.7. Go ahead and make these changes to your project.

Listing 9.7 *NameEditorViewController.h* **after Making the Needed Code Changes**

```
#import <UIKit/UIKit.h>

@protocol NameEditorViewControllerDelegate;

@interface NameEditorViewController : UIViewController

@property (strong, nonatomic) IBOutlet UITextField *nameTextField;
@property (strong, nonatomic) id<NameEditorViewControllerDelegate> delegate;

- (IBAction)cancel:(id)sender;
- (IBAction)done:(id)sender;

- (id)initWithDefaultNib;

@end


@protocol NameEditorViewControllerDelegate <NSObject>
@optional
- (void)nameEditorViewControllerDidFinish:(NameEditorViewController *)controller;
- (void)nameEditorViewControllerDidCancel:(NameEditorViewController *)controller;
@end
```

With the interface defined, it's now time to update the implementation. Implementation for NameEditorViewController is fairly straightforward. The first thing you want to do is synthesize the declared properties using the @synthesize compiler directive. And you need to implement methods for the two actions, -cancel: and

-done:. The code for these changes is given in Listing 9.8. There are, however, a few additions worth discussing.

Listing 9.8   *NameEditorViewController.m* **after Making the Needed Code Changes**

```objc
#import "NameEditorViewController.h"

@implementation NameEditorViewController

@synthesize nameTextField = _nameTextField;
@synthesize delegate = _delegate;

- (id)initWithDefaultNib
{
   self = [super initWithNibName:@"NameEditorViewController" bundle:nil];
   if (self) {
      // Custom initialization.
   }
   return self;
}

- (void)viewDidUnload
{
   [self setNameTextField:nil];
   [super viewDidUnload];
}

- (BOOL)shouldAutorotateToInterfaceOrientation:
(UIInterfaceOrientation)interfaceOrientation
{
   return YES;
}

#pragma mark - Actions methods

- (IBAction)cancel:(id)sender
{
   id<NameEditorViewControllerDelegate> delegate = [self delegate];
   if (delegate &&
       [delegate respondsToSelector:@selector(nameEditorViewControllerDidCan
cel:)])
   {
      [delegate nameEditorViewControllerDidCancel:self];
   }
   [self dismissModalViewControllerAnimated:YES];
}
```

```
- (IBAction)done:(id)sender
{
    id<NameEditorViewControllerDelegate> delegate = [self delegate];
    if (delegate &&
          [delegate respondsToSelector:@selector(nameEditorViewControllerDidFin
ish:)])
    {
    [delegate nameEditorViewControllerDidFinish:self];
    }
    [self dismissModalViewControllerAnimated:YES];
}

@end
```

> **Note**
>
> Much of the code provided by the Xcode file template has been changed or removed. This
> is done for brevity's sake, but also, as explained in the "An Alternative Approach" sidebar,
> it's my style to clean up the code.

Let's first talk about the -initWithDefaultNib. This is jumping ahead, but...
A new view controller that has a companion NIB is instantiated in code with the
-initWithNibName:bundle: method. This init method makes it possible for different NIBs to be used with the same controller. However, in most iOS applications,
a view controller works with one and only one NIB file. Therefore, it is handy to
include the custom init method -initWithDefaultNib that loads the NIB file for
you. Its implementation knows which NIB file to load, which means the NIB file
name does not have to be scattered through your application if the view controller is
used in multiple places.

> **Note**
>
> Because -initWithDefaultNib is used outside NameEditorViewController,
> it must be included in the controller's interface, as shown in Listing 9.7.

The method -viewDidUnload is called when the view managed by a view controller is unloaded from memory. When this method is called, the view is no longer
valid. Holding on to the IBOutlet references is a waste of memory. iOS devices have
limited memory capacity, so releasing memory when it is no longer needed is a wise
thing to do. By setting the IBOutlet property to nil, the app is telling the operating system that the memory is no longer needed by this controller and to release it as
it sees fit. It also sets the local ivar reference to nil to avoid potential problems with
accessing an invalid pointer. Even if this makes no sense to you (yet), you should make
it a habit to always set IBOutlets to nil in the -viewDidUnload method of the
view controller.

Following -viewDidUnload is the -shouldAutorotateToInterface-
Orientation: method. This is called when the view controller is loaded, and it gives
the view controller an opportunity to tell the system what orientations are supported
when the device is rotated. PhotoWheelPrototype supports all orientations, so for now
this method always returns YES for this and any other view controllers.

The last two methods implement the functionality needed for the **Cancel** and **Done**
buttons. Both implementations are similar with only slight differences. -cancel:
calls the -nameEditorViewControllerDidCancel: method on the delegate, and
-done: calls the -nameEditorViewControllerDidFinish: method.

The first line in each of these methods sets a local variable to the delegate. This is
done so that [self delegate] does not have to be used throughout the method.
Having [self delegate] all over the place can make the code messy and harder to
read. The ivar _delegate could also have been used, but direct access to ivars is not
good OO programming. This is why a local variable is used.

The if statement performs two checks. It first checks to see that delegate points
to an object. If delegate is nil, the if statement short-circuits and the method
returns control to the caller. If delegate is not nil, a check is made to ensure that
delegate has an implementation for the particular selector, -nameEditorView-
ControllerDidCancel: for the -cancel: method and -nameEditorView-
ControllerDidFinish: for the -done: method. This is one of Objective-C's
strengths, the ability to query an object to determine what it does and does not
implement. If the delegate does not implement the method, the program flow control does not enter the if block; otherwise the if block is entered and the delegate
method is called.

It is always a good idea to check that an object implements a particular method when
a protocol method is defined as @optional. Calling a missing optional method is a
surefire way to crash your app. The check is not needed if the method is @required.
However, it can still be a good thing to perform the -respondsToSelector: check
on required methods. This protects your code should you (or someone else) change the
method from required to optional in the future.

> **Note**
>
> In Objective-C, sending a message to a nil object does nothing. This means that the if
> statement could have been written as if ([delegate respondsToSelector:
> @selector(nameEditorViewControllerDidFinish:)]). The first check to
> test whether delegate is nil or not is not needed. However, after years of program-
> ming in various other programming languages, this old dog finds that eliminating tests for
> nil in Objective-C is a hard habit to break.

The view controller NameEditorViewController is ready to go. Its interface
has been defined, a protocol has been created to call back to a delegate object, and the
NameEditorViewController implementation is complete. All that remains before
the app can use this view controller is to complete the user interface (i.e., the view).

The view will display a toolbar at the top. The toolbar will have two buttons, a **Cancel** button displayed on the left and a **Done** button displayed on the right. Below the toolbar in the view area will be a UITextField. This is the text input box that the user uses to enter a new name. The UITextField will be connected to the IBOutlet nameTextField. The **Cancel** button will connect to the cancel: IBAction method, and the **Done** button will connect to the done: IBAction method. Here are the steps to follow:

> **Note**
>
> Read Chapter 3, "Getting Started with Interface Builder," if you have problems with these steps.

1. Open the file *NameEditorViewController.xib*.

2. Drag and drop a toolbar (UIToolbar) from the Library to the view. Place the toolbar at the top of the view.

3. Select and delete the **Item** button displayed in the toolbar.

4. Open the Size inspector and set up the toolbar autosize to anchor to the top. See Figure 9.9.

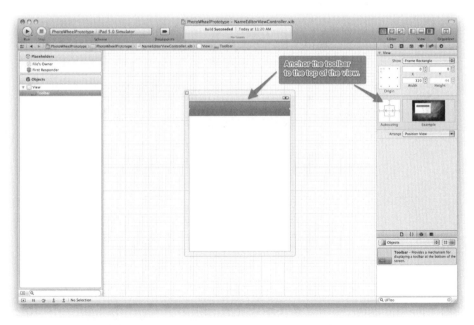

Figure 9.9   Anchor the toolbar to the top of the view by setting the autosizing property.

1. Drag and drop a bar button item (`UIBarButtonItem`) on the toolbar.

2. Drag and drop a flexible space bar button item (`UIBarButtonItem`) on the toolbar, placed to the right of the other bar button item.

3. Drag and drop a bar button item (`UIBarButtonItem`) on the toolbar, placed to the right of the flexible space bar button item.

4. Change the title for the bar button item on the left to "Cancel."

5. Change the title for the bar button item on the right to "Done."

6. While the **Done** button is still selected, open the Attributes inspector (**Option-⌘-4**) and set the style to Done.

7. Drag and drop a text field (`UITextField`) on the view and place it just below the toolbar. Size the text field to fill most of the width of the view. Set the auto-sizing to a flexible width (see Figure 9.10).

8. In the Attributes inspector for the text field, set the Placeholder property to "Enter the photo album name".

At this point your view should look like the one shown in Figure 9.11. Make any needed adjustments if it does not. Once that is done, move on to connecting the `IBActions` and `IBOutlets`.

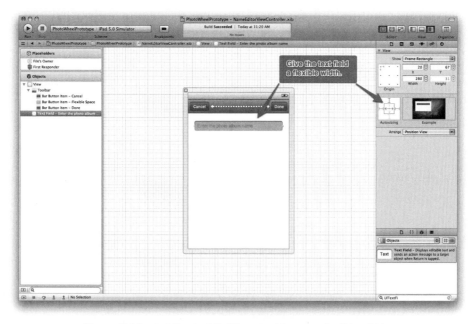

Figure 9.10   Set the text field's autosizing to a flexible width.

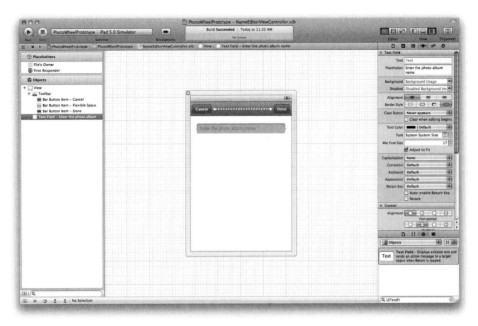

Figure 9.11   Screen shot of the `NameEditorView` NIB file

1. **Control-Click** (or right-click) the File's Owner placeholder object. Note that the Xcode file template already assigned File's Owner to the class `NameEditorViewController`.

2. Connect the `nameTextField` outlet to the text field in the view.

3. Connect the `cancel:` action to the **Cancel** button.

4. Connect the `done:` action to the **Done** button.

5. Save your changes (⌘-**S**).

That's it. The view is now ready. All that remains is modifying `MasterView-Controller` so that it can use the new `NameEditorViewController`. Start by adding `#import "NameEditorViewController.h"` to the top of *MasterViewController.h*. Next add `<NameEditorViewControllerDelegate>` to the `@interface` declaration for `MasterViewController`. The interface file should look like the code in Listing 9.9.

Listing 9.9   **Updated** *MasterViewController.h*

```
#import <UIKit/UIKit.h>
#import "NameEditorViewController.h"

@class DetailViewController;
```

```
@interface MasterViewController : UITableViewController
<NameEditorViewControllerDelegate>

@property (strong, nonatomic) DetailViewController *detailViewController;
@property (strong, nonatomic) NSMutableOrderedSet *data;

@end
```

Now for the implementation. At the bottom of *MasterViewController.m*, add the implementations for the `NameEditorViewControllerDelegate` methods. You also need to modify the `-add:` method in *MasterViewController.m* to create an instance of `NameEditorViewController`, set the `delegate`, and display the view. The code changes are given in Listing 9.10. For brevity's sake, only the changes are included in the listing, not the complete code source.

Listing 9.10   **Modifications Needed in** *MasterViewController.m*

```
@implementation MasterViewController

/* ... */

- (void)add:(id)sender
{
   NameEditorViewController *newController =
      [[NameEditorViewController alloc] initWithDefaultNib];
   [newController setDelegate:self];
   [newController setModalPresentationStyle:UIModalPresentationFormSheet];
   [self presentModalViewController:newController animated:YES];
}

#pragma mark - NameEditorViewControllerDelegate

- (void)nameEditorViewControllerDidFinish:(NameEditorViewController *)controller
{
   NSLog(@"%s", __PRETTY_FUNCTION__);
}

- (void)nameEditorViewControllerDidCancel:(NameEditorViewController *)controller
{
   NSLog(@"%s", __PRETTY_FUNCTION__);
}

@end
```

Take a look at the modified version of the `-add:` method. Before it was a single `NSLog` statement, but now it has real functionality. It creates an instance of the

`NameEditorViewController` using the custom `init` method `-initWithDefault-Nib`. It sets the delegate to `self`, which is the current instance of `MasterView-Controller`, which conforms to the `NameEditorViewControllerDelegate`.

The name editor will display modally. To ensure a good look, the controller's `modalPresentationStyle` is set to `UIModalPresentationFormSheet`. This will center the modal display on the screen, graying out the background view. It will also adjust its position when the virtual keyboard is displayed. After the presentation style is set, the code then displays the new controller modally using `presentModalView-Controller:animated:`. This causes the new controller to slide up from the bottom and display in the screen's center.

You can now build and run the app. When you tap the **+** button, the new `Name-EditorViewController` is displayed. Tapping the **Cancel** button displays `[Master-ViewController nameEditorViewControllerDidCancel:]` in the debug output window, and tapping the **Done** button displays `[MasterViewController name-EditorViewControllerDidFinish:]`. The finished version should look like the screen shot in Figure 9.12.

Before returning focus to the `UITableView`, there are a few loose ends that must be tied up. The **Done** button should add a new entry into the data array, so replace the `MasterViewController`'s implementation for `-nameEditorViewController-DidFinish:` with the code in Listing 9.11.

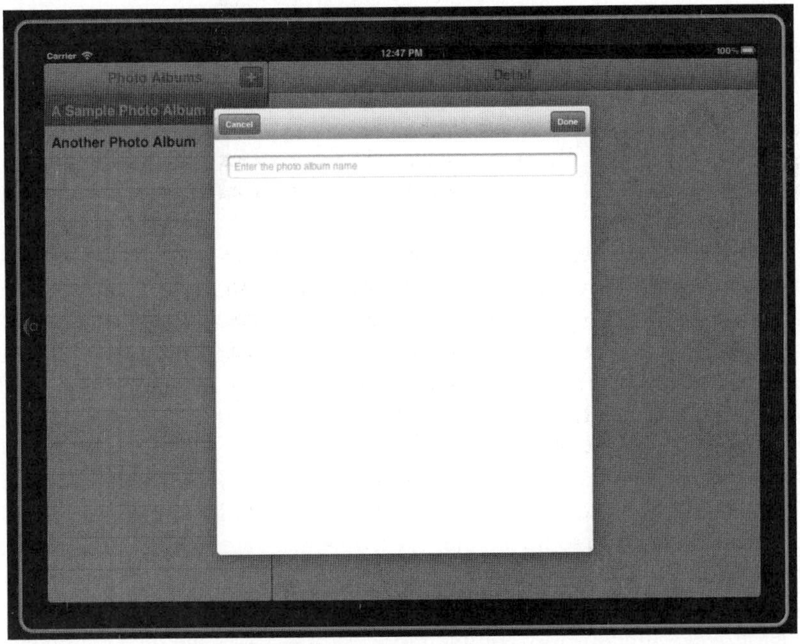

Figure 9.12   Screen shot of the name editor

Listing 9.11   **Updated** -nameEditorViewControllerDidFinish: **in**
MasterViewController.m

```
- (void)nameEditorViewControllerDidFinish:(NameEditorViewController *)controller
{
    NSString *newName = [[controller nameTextField] text];
    if (newName && [newName length] > 0) {
        [[self data] addObject:newName];
        [[self tableView] reloadData];
    }
}
```

Let's walk through the code. In -nameEditorViewControllerDidFinish: a
local variable, newName, is set to the string returned by the text field displayed in
NameEditorViewController. If the newName is not nil and the string length is
greater than zero, the new name is added to the data array as a new photo album and
tableView is told to reload the data.

That's it. The user can now add a new photo album to the table view.

> **Note**
>
> Calling reloadData on a table view is a quick and easy way to update the display.
> However, the table view will go through the process of rebuilding and displaying the cells
> for the table. If you want to avoid this extra processing, use the UITableViewData-
> Source protocol methods for inserting and deleting table rows (-tableView:
> commitEditingStyle:forRowAtIndexPath: and -tableView:
> canEditRowAtIndexPath:).

Edit Data

What good is adding data if the user can't edit it? Let's add an edit feature that allows
the user to change the name of an existing photo album. To save time, you'll reuse the
name editor, this time to edit an existing name.

You need a way to allow the user to edit an existing item. Luckily, UITableView
already supports the concept of editing. When a UITableView is in edit mode, the
table cells are indented, a red circle is added to allow deleting, and rows in the table
can be reordered. To put the table in edit mode, we need an **Edit** button. A good
place for the **Edit** button is on the left side of the navigation bar for the MasterView-
Controller, our master view.

To add a new button, all you need to do is create a new UIBarButtonItem and
add it to the left side of the navigation bar. This code is similar to the code you already
wrote in the -viewDidLoad method for MasterViewController that adds the
+ button to the navigation bar. But wait! There's another way.

As mentioned earlier, a benefit of using UITableViewController is that the
controller provides functionality common to UITableView. One such common

functionality is an **Edit** button. Without `UITableViewController` you would be responsible for creating a new edit bar button item and implementing the action that puts the table view into edit mode. You would also have to change the **Edit** button to a **Done** button and toggle back to normal mode when the user taps it. You get this functionality for free with `UITableViewController`, which conveniently is the superclass for `MasterViewController`.

To add the **Edit** button to the navigation controller, add the code in Listing 9.12 to the bottom of the `-viewDidLoad` method in *MasterViewController.m*. The property `editButtonItem` returns a reference to a bar button item configured as an **Edit** button for the table view.

Listing 9.12   Adding an *Edit* Button to the Navigation Bar

```
- (void)viewDidLoad
{
    [super viewDidLoad];

    /* ... */

    [[self navigationItem] setLeftBarButtonItem:[self editButtonItem]];
}
```

Build and run the app. The app now has an **Edit** button that toggles the table view between normal and edit modes. But you're still not able to edit the row. To actually enable editing an item, a bit more code is needed. First, a detail disclosure button should be displayed to indicate to the user that the row can be edited. Next, code must be added to handle the selection of the item to edit. When the item is selected, the name editor must be displayed. And when the user taps the **Done** button on the name editor, the data and table must be updated to reflect the new name.

The `NameEditorViewController` must also be modified to support edit mode. `UIViewController` already has an editing property that can be used to tell the controller it is in edit mode. But the controller needs to know more, such as the index path to the row that is being edited.

Let's start with updating `MasterViewController`. The code changes are shown in Listing 9.13. The first change is to set the accessory type for the table cell when the table is in edit mode. The next change adds an implementation for the `UITableViewDelegate` method `-tableView:accessoryButtonTappedForRowWithIndexPath:`. This method is called when the user taps the detail disclosure button on a cell. The implementation creates an instance of the name editor, prepares it for editing, then displays it. Last, the `-nameEditorViewControllerDidFinish:` method is changed to support editing. Add the changes in Listing 9.13 to your project.

Listing 9.13   **Modifications to** *MasterViewController.m* **to Support Editing a Photo Album**
Name

```
- (UITableViewCell *)tableView:(UITableView *)tableView
        cellForRowAtIndexPath:(NSIndexPath *)indexPath
{
    static NSString *CellIdentifier = @"Cell";

    UITableViewCell *cell = [tableView dequeueReusableCellWithIdentifier:CellIdenti
fier];
    if (cell == nil) {
        cell = [[UITableViewCell alloc] initWithStyle:UITableViewCellStyleDefault
                                        reuseIdentifier:CellIdentifier];

        // Display the detail disclosure button when the table is
        // in edit mode. This is the line you must add:
        [cell setEditingAccessoryType:UITableViewCellAccessoryDetailDisclosureButton];
    }

    // Configure the cell.
    NSString *text = [[self data] objectAtIndex:[indexPath row]];
    [[cell textLabel] setText:text];

    return cell;
}


- (void)tableView:(UITableView *)tableView
accessoryButtonTappedForRowWithIndexPath:(NSIndexPath *)indexPath
{
    NameEditorViewController *newController = [[NameEditorViewController alloc]
                                        initWithDefaultNib];
    [newController setDelegate:self];
    [newController setEditing:YES];
    [newController setIndexPath:indexPath];
    NSString *name = [[self data] objectAtIndex:[indexPath row]];
    [[newController nameTextField] setText:name];
    [newController setModalPresentationStyle:UIModalPresentationFormSheet];
    [self presentModalViewController:newController animated:YES];
}


- (void)nameEditorViewControllerDidFinish:(NameEditorViewController *)controller
{
    NSString *newName = [[controller nameTextField] text];
    if (newName && [newName length] > 0) {
        if ([controller isEditing]) {
            [[self data] replaceObjectAtIndex:[[controller indexPath] row]
                                withObject:newName];
        } else {
```

```
            [[self data] addObject:newName];
        }
        [[self tableView] reloadData];
    }
}
```

> **Note**
>
> As before, only the changes are shown in Listing 9.13. The full version of
> *MasterViewController.m* is not displayed to save the trees.

For the moment, the project will not cleanly compile. The changes to Name-
EditorViewController are missing. A new declared property called indexPath
of type NSIndexPath must be added. The property must also be synthesized and
released in the NameEditorViewController implementation. The changes are listed
in Listing 9.14.

Listing 9.14 Changes to *NameEditorViewController.h* and *.m*

```
@interface NameEditorViewController : UIViewController

/* Other code purposely left out for brevity's sake. */

@property (strong, nonatomic) NSIndexPath *indexPath;

@end




@implementation NameEditorViewController

@synthesize nameTextField = _nameTextField;
@synthesize delegate = _delegate;
@synthesize indexPath = _indexPath;

/* Other code purposely left out for brevity's sake. */

@end
```

Once the changes are complete, run the project and see what happens. Be sure to
test the new edit feature. Did you notice anything funny going on? The name editor
does not display the original photo album name when in edit mode, this despite setting
the nameTextField's text property prior to displaying the view. What's going on?

nameTextField is a UITextField that is instantiated by the NIB when the NIB
is loaded. The MasterViewController calls [[newController nameTextField]
setText:name] to set the text value, but the text field has not been created and

initialized yet. And when it does finally initialize, it uses an empty string for the text value. This is why the photo album name is not displayed. How do you get around this problem?

The solution involves two steps:

1. Add a declared property to NameEditorViewController called default-NameText of type NSString.

2. During the -viewDidLoad method, set the text property of the nameTextField.

This works because -viewDidLoad is not called until the view has been loaded and its subviews have been initialized.

The code changes to NameEditorViewController are shown in Listing 9.15. Be sure to synthesize and release the new declared property in the implementation.

Listing 9.15   **Changes Needed to** *NameEditorViewController.h* **and** *.m*

```
@interface NameEditorViewController : UIViewController

/* Other code purposely left out for brevity's sake. */

@property (nonatomic, copy) NSString *defaultNameText;

@end



@implementation NameEditorViewController

@synthesize nameTextField = _nameTextField;
@synthesize delegate = _delegate;
@synthesize indexPath = _indexPath;

// Add this line:
@synthesize defaultNameText = _defaultNameText;

- (void)viewDidLoad
{
    [super viewDidLoad];
    if ([self isEditing]) {
        [[self nameTextField] setText:[self defaultNameText]];
    }
}

/* Other code purposely left out for brevity's sake. */

@end
```

And the final change: Replace the [[newController nameTextField] setText:name] call in *MasterViewController.m* with [newController setDefaultNameText:name] as shown in Listing 9.16.

Listing 9.16   Changes to *MasterViewController.m* Needed to Set the Default Name Text

```
- (void)tableView:(UITableView *)tableView
accessoryButtonTappedForRowWithIndexPath:(NSIndexPath *)indexPath
{
   NameEditorViewController *newController =
      [[NameEditorViewController alloc] initWithDefaultNib];
   [newController setDelegate:self];
   [newController setEditing:YES];
   [newController setIndexPath:indexPath];
   NSString *name = [[self data] objectAtIndex:[indexPath row]];

   // Replace [[newController nameTextField] setText:name]; with
   // the following:
   [newController setDefaultNameText:name];

   [newController setModalPresentationStyle:UIModalPresentationFormSheet];
   [self presentModalViewController:newController animated:YES];
}
```

Delete Data

Let's not stop with adding and editing data. Let's also allow the user to delete data. The structure is already in place to support deleting a row. The user can tap the **Edit** button, then tap the red circle. This causes the table view to display a **Delete** button for the cell. And when the user swipes his finger across the row, when the table is not in edit mode, the **Delete** button for the cell is displayed. A little more plumbing is needed in MasterViewController to provide full delete capabilities.

To allow deleting, you need to implement two additional methods from the UITableViewDataSource delegate: -tableView:canEditRowAtIndexPath: and -tableView:commitEditingStyle:forRowAtIndexPath:. The first method allows the app to control whether a particular row in the table is editable or not. For the purposes of this project, the method always returns YES, but you may have apps in the future that return YES for some rows and NO for others.

The next method is -tableView:commitEditingStyle:forRowAtIndexPath:. In previous code, when a new row is added or an existing one is edited, the code calls [tableView reloadData]. Here a different approach is used. Instead of reloading the data, which works, the existing row is removed from the table view. This provides a better user experience in that the removal of the row is animated and the table view is not completely redrawn. In this particular case, UITableViewRowAnimationFade is used to fade out the row being deleted.

The implementation for these two methods is shown in Listing 9.17. Be sure to add this code to your project.

Listing 9.17   **Two** `UITableViewDataSource` **Methods to Add Delete Support to** *MasterViewController.m*

```
- (BOOL)tableView:(UITableView *)tableView
canEditRowAtIndexPath:(NSIndexPath *)indexPath
{
    return YES;
}


- (void)tableView:(UITableView *)tableView
commitEditingStyle:(UITableViewCellEditingStyle)editingStyle
forRowAtIndexPath:(NSIndexPath *)indexPath
{
    if (editingStyle == UITableViewCellEditingStyleDelete) {
        [[self data] removeObjectAtIndex:[indexPath row]];
        [tableView deleteRowsAtIndexPaths:[NSArray arrayWithObject:indexPath]
                    withRowAnimation:UITableViewRowAnimationFade];
    }
}
```

Reorder Data

There is another nifty feature of `UITableView`. It is reordering data. `UITableView` allows the user to move rows up or down to change the sequence. Adding support for reordering is a simple two-step process:

1. Configure the cell to display the reorder control.

2. Implement the `UITableViewDataSource` delegate method `-tableView:` `moveRowAtIndexPath:toIndexPath:`.

The code changes for *MasterViewController.m* are shown in Listing 9.18. Make and save the changes to your project, then run the app to test reordering.

Listing 9.18   **Changes in** *MasterViewController.m* **Needed to Support Reordering of Table Rows**

```
- (UITableViewCell *)tableView:(UITableView *)tableView
cellForRowAtIndexPath:(NSIndexPath *)indexPath
{
    static NSString *CellIdentifier = @"Cell";

    UITableViewCell *cell =
        [tableView dequeueReusableCellWithIdentifier:CellIdentifier];
    if (cell == nil) {
```

```
    cell = [[UITableViewCell alloc] initWithStyle:UITableViewCellStyleDefault
                            reuseIdentifier:CellIdentifier];
    [cell setEditingAccessoryType:UITableViewCellAccessoryDetailDisclosureButton];

        // Add this line:
        [cell setShowsReorderControl:YES];
    }

    // Configure the cell.
    NSString *text = [[self data] objectAtIndex:[indexPath row]];
    [[cell textLabel] setText:text];

    return cell;
}

- (void)tableView:(UITableView *)tableView
moveRowAtIndexPath:(NSIndexPath *)fromIndexPath
        toIndexPath:(NSIndexPath *)toIndexPath
{
    [[self data] exchangeObjectAtIndex:[fromIndexPath row]
                     withObjectAtIndex:[toIndexPath row]];
}
```

As with editing a row, the UITableViewDataSource protocol includes a method named –tableView:canMoveRowAtIndexPath: that allows your code to determine if a row can be moved or not. Return YES to allow the row to be moved, and return NO to prevent moving the row. This method is not implemented in Listing 9.18 so that the user will be able to move all of the rows.

Select Data

There is one last feature you need to implement before closing the chapter on table views. When a user taps a row in the table view, the detail view controller—Remember that fella? It's been a while since we spoke of him—needs to be told which item was selected. This works similarly to editing a row. UITableViewDelegate includes the method –tableView:didSelectRowAtIndexPath:, which is called when the user taps the row. However, the MasterViewController knows nothing about the DetailViewController, so let's fix that first.

MasterViewController needs a declared property of type DetailView-Controller, and the property must be synthesized in the MasterViewController's implementation. Go ahead and make those changes now. This has been done for you by the master-detail template used to create the project. Let's take a closer look at that, which is shown in Listing 9.19.

Listing 9.19   `detailViewController` **as a Declared Property to**
              `MasterViewController`

```
#import <UIKit/UIKit.h>
#import "NameEditorViewController.h"

@class DetailViewController;

@interface MasterViewController : UITableViewController
<NameEditorViewControllerDelegate>

@property (strong, nonatomic) DetailViewController *detailViewController;
@property (strong, nonatomic) NSMutableOrderedSet *data;

@end


#import "MasterViewController.h"
#import " DetailViewController.h"

@implementation MasterViewController

@synthesize detailViewController = _detailViewController;
@synthesize data = _data;

/* Other code purposely left out for brevity's sake. */

@end
```

In Listing 9.19, the directive `@class` is used to inform the compiler that the class
name is available, but the interface file for the class is not imported in the header
file. The compiler does not need to know the interface for the class until the class
is actually used, for example, when creating a new instance of the class or sending a
message to a class instance. It is only when the class is used that its interface must be
imported. Plainly put, if you use the class in your implementation, you must include
the `#import` for the class header in your *.m* file. However, the `#import` is not needed
in the interface's *.h* file when `@class` is used.

The exception to this rule is when the header declares an interface that extends
another class or conforms to a protocol. You need to include the `#import` in the
header file when this happens.

> **Note**
>
> The approach of telling the compiler that something exists without providing the details is
> called a forward declaration. Forward declarations are common in the C programming lan-
> guage and therefore are common in Objective-C. The compiler directive `@class` is

a forward declaration of a class name, but forward declarations are not limited to class names. Forward declarations are used throughout C and Objective-C to inform the compiler about protocols, methods, and functions that are yet to be defined.

The method -tableView:didSelectRowAtIndexPath: can now be implemented. The implementation of this method should look familiar to you. You use the indexPath to retrieve the photo album name from the data array. Then you pass the value to the detail view controller. This is similar to the approach used to edit a row. The biggest difference is that the detail view controller has already been created, so there is no need to create a new instance. Let's take a look at the code shown in Listing 9.20, which replaces the code generated by the Xcode template.

Listing 9.20   **Code Added to** *MasterViewController.m* **to Display the Photo Album Name in the Detail View Controller**

```
- (void)tableView:(UITableView *)tableView
didSelectRowAtIndexPath:(NSIndexPath *)indexPath
{
    NSString *name = [[self data] objectAtIndex:[indexPath row]];
    [[self detailViewController] setDetailItem:name];
}
```

The final step is to set the property detailViewController on the MasterViewController instance to the instance of DetailViewController created in the app delegate. Open *AppDelegate.m* and assign the DetailViewController instance to the detailViewController property on the MasterViewController. Listing 9.21 shows the final code.

Listing 9.21   **Assigning the** DetailViewController **Instance to the** detailViewController **Property**

```
- (BOOL)application:(UIApplication *)application
didFinishLaunchingWithOptions:(NSDictionary *)launchOptions
{
    self.window = [[UIWindow alloc] initWithFrame:[[UIScreen mainScreen] bounds]];
    // Override point for customization after application launch.

    MasterViewController *masterViewController =
        [[MasterViewController alloc] initWithNibName:@"MasterViewController"
                                         bundle:nil];
    UINavigationController *masterNavigationController =
        [[UINavigationController alloc]
          initWithRootViewController:masterViewController];

    DetailViewController *detailViewController =
        [[DetailViewController alloc] initWithNibName:@"DetailViewController"
                                         bundle:nil];
```

```
UINavigationController *detailNavigationController =
    [[UINavigationController alloc]
        initWithRootViewController:detailViewController];

// Add this line. It tells the master view controller which
// detail view controller to use.
[masterViewController setDetailViewController:detailViewController];

self.splitViewController = [[UISplitViewController alloc] init];
self.splitViewController.delegate = detailViewController;
self.splitViewController.viewControllers = [NSArray arrayWithObjects:
                                            masterNavigationController,
                                            detailNavigationController,
                                            nil];
self.window.rootViewController = self.splitViewController;
[self.window makeKeyAndVisible];
return YES;
}
```

That's it. Build and run the app. When you tap a photo album in the table view, its name should appear in the detail view. Check your work if you see different behavior.

Summary

This chapter focused on `UITableView` and its supporting protocols and classes, but you were also introduced to other essential concepts, including creating and displaying view controllers, communicating between view controllers using delegates, and using the Target-Action pattern. It's a lot of information to take in at once. Don't worry, though. You'll be repeating the essential concepts again and again as you progress through the book.

Exercises

1. Open the header file for `UITableViewDelegate` and `UITableViewData-Source`. Review the list of delegate methods provided by these protocols. (Refer back to Chapter 8, "Creating a Master-Detail App," for tips on opening header files.)

2. Move the **Edit** button to the right side and the **+** button to the left. When you are done, move the buttons back.

3. Change the bar button item style for the **+** button to other styles and note the visual difference.

4. Modify the app to prevent the first table view row from being edited.

5. Modify the app to prevent the user from moving the last row.

10

Working with Views

In the last chapter you learned about using view controllers and communicating between them. In this chapter you will learn how to create your own custom view. The concept of a photo album has already been introduced. Now it's time to display photos, and a custom view is just what the doctor ordered.

Custom Views

UIKit provides an outstanding set of views that make it easier and faster to create iPad apps. However, there are times when your app's UI needs more than what is provided by the SDK. This is where custom views come in. Creating a custom view is not difficult. In fact, it's as easy as creating a new `UIView` subclass.

Why would you ever need to create a custom view? There are many reasons. The most common reason is to simplify the code in your app. Let's say, for example, that the app must present the same set of visual controls—for instance, a `UILabel` followed by a `UITextField`—to display a label followed by a text input box. Now say the display of these controls is repeated over and over throughout the app. The constant repeat violates the DRY principle, making your code harder to maintain. You can simplify the app's code base by creating a new view that is responsible for displaying the label and text field. Then, instead of repeating the label and text field combo throughout the app, only the view that contains the label and text field is repeated. Should you need to make a change, such as reversing the order of the two controls, the change is made in one place and propagated throughout the app.

> **Note**
>
> DRY, short for "Don't Repeat Yourself," is a fundamental software engineering principle whose goal is to reduce redundancy. When it is applied, blocks of code, logic, sets of UI elements, and so forth exist only once and are reused instead of being copied and pasted throughout an application. To learn more about DRY and other useful principles of programming, read *The Pragmatic Programmer: From Journeyman to Master* (Addison-Wesley, 1999).

View Controller Not

Creating a custom view is simple. The challenge comes when deciding whether a user interface element is better implemented as a custom view or as part of a view controller. It's not uncommon to implement a view controller to display some part of the UI only to discover later that the code can be made more reusable if implemented as a view. And not only is the view easier to reuse as opposed to the view controller, but you can create specializations of the custom view, extending its appearance and behavior.

Take, for example, a set of photos displayed in a circular formation. An initial solution for implementing the UI is to write a view controller that manages the layout of the photos. But once you do this, you'll realize that a good amount of controller code is devoted to the layout of the photos. It's the implementation of the layout code that is ideal for a custom view, not a view controller.

Let the view controller mediate data between the view and the model. Let the view manage the visual layout of the data provided by the controller.

A good example of this is a wheel view. Looking at the sketch of the prototype app, shown in Figure 10.1, you see a wheel of photos. The photo wheel is nothing more than a set of photos laid out to form a circle. While this can be implemented within the `DetailViewController`, a better approach is to create a new custom view that manages the layout of photos. Let's take a look at how a wheel view can be implemented as a custom view.

> **Note**
>
> The original inspiration for PhotoWheel came from the View-Master (**en.wikipedia.org/wiki/View_Master**). The View-Master, a device for viewing 3D pictures, was introduced in 1939 and has since become a popular children's toy. It uses a disk containing 14 images and pairs the images, giving the viewer 7 pictures to view in stunning 3D.

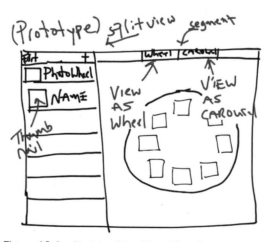

Figure 10.1   Sketch of the PhotoWheelPrototype app

A Wheel View

The wheel view displays a set of subviews laid out in a circle. Why a set of subviews and not a set of photos? There's no good reason to limit the wheel view to photos only. A UIView, or some subclass of it such as UIImageView, is all that is needed to display a photo. The wheel view doesn't care what type of subview it is given so long as it is at least a view of some sort. This means that the wheel view doesn't have to be limited to the display of photos. It can be used to display any view you see fit to display.

How does the wheel view know about the subviews to display? One option is to pass in an array or set of views, but this means the views must be created in memory before ever being referenced by the wheel view. This can waste valuable system resources (i.e., memory) on a mobile device. Instead, a better approach is to have the wheel view ask some source for each subview as it needs it.

This pattern should sound familiar to you. It's the same pattern used by UITableView. UITableView has no intimate knowledge of the cell displayed in each row. It instead relies on a UITableViewDataSource object to provide each cell when needed. The wheel view you create will do the same.

To start, you need to create a new class. Call the new class WheelView. Follow these steps to accomplish this:

1. Type ⌘-N.
2. Select **iOS > Cocoa Touch > Objective-C class**.
3. Click the **Next** button.
4. Set the Class to WheelView.
5. Set the "Subclass of" to UIView.
6. Click the **Next** button.
7. Click the **Create** button.

Open the interface file *WheelView.h* and add the code in Listing 10.1.

Listing 10.1   **Source Code for *WheelView.h***

```
#import <UIKit/UIKit.h>

@protocol WheelViewDataSource;
@class WheelViewCell;

@interface WheelView : UIView

@property (nonatomic, strong) IBOutlet id<WheelViewDataSource> dataSource;

@end
```

```
@protocol WheelViewDataSource <NSObject>
@required
- (NSInteger)wheelViewNumberOfCells:(WheelView *)wheelView;
- (WheelViewCell *)wheelView:(WheelView *)wheelView cellAtIndex:(NSInteger)index;
@end


@interface WheelViewCell : UIView
@end
```

Walking through the code, you first see the #import statement for *UIKit.h*. This allows the WheelView class to reference classes within UIKit. Following this are two forward declarations, one for the protocol WheelViewDataSource and one for the class WheelViewCell. The forward declarations tell the compiler about the types when it encounters a reference to the protocol or class prior to the actual declaration of each.

Next up is the interface declaration for WheelView. The class derives from UIView, and it has one declared property called dataSource. dataSource can be any Objective-C object regardless of the kind of class, so the id data type is used as the property's data type. To assist the compiler with syntax checking, the protocol Wheel-ViewDataSource is added to the id data type. This tells the compiler that the object referenced by dataSource must conform to the WheelViewDataSource protocol.

Note that dataSource is also marked as an outlet. This allows you to set the property reference within IB, which you will see momentarily.

Following the interface declaration for WheelView is the protocol declaration for WheelViewDataSource. WheelView needs to know two things about the data it will be displaying:

1. The number of cells to display

2. The cell for a particular index

So, two required methods are added to the WheelViewDataSource protocol. Any object that conforms to this protocol must provide implementations for these methods.

Last, in the source code you see the declaration for WheelViewCell, which is a subclass of UIView. We have said that WheelView does not care about the type of view displayed in the wheel, but this could change down the road. There might come a time when WheelView needs to store internal information on the object. By declaring a generalized class now, you prepare the code for possible changes down the road. And since this class type is used in the methods for the WheelViewDataSource protocol, you reduce the impact of change on the app should WheelView need to store internal data within the view cell.

> **Note**
>
> You may be wondering why `WheelView`, `WheelViewDataSource`, and `Wheel-`
> `ViewCell` are all defined in the same interface file. Each could have been defined
> in its own interface file, but I elected to keep them together because each is tightly
> coupled with the others, and it's easier to reuse `WheelView` in other projects by copying
> *WheelView.h* and *.m* files instead of copying *WheelView.h* and *.m*, *WheelViewDataSource.h*,
> and *WheelViewCell.h* and *.m*.

Now open *WheelView.m* and replace the template-generated code with the code
presented in Listing 10.2.

Listing 10.2   `WheelView`'s **Implementation**

```
#import "WheelView.h"


@implementation WheelView

@synthesize dataSource = _dataSource;

- (void)setAngle:(CGFloat)angle
{
    // The following code is inspired by the carousel example at
    // http://stackoverflow.com/questions/5243614/3d-carousel-effect-on-the-ipad

    CGPoint center = CGPointMake(CGRectGetMidX([self bounds]),
                                 CGRectGetMidY([self bounds]));
    CGFloat radiusX = MIN([self bounds].size.width,
                          [self bounds].size.height) * 0.35;
    CGFloat radiusY = radiusX;

    NSInteger cellCount = [[self dataSource] wheelViewNumberOfCells:self];
    float angleToAdd = 360.0f / cellCount;

    for (NSInteger index = 0; index < cellCount; index++)
    {
        WheelViewCell *cell = [[self dataSource] wheelView:self cellAtIndex:index];
        if ([cell superview] == nil) {
            [self addSubview:cell];
        }

        float angleInRadians = (angle + 180.0) * M_PI / 180.0f;

        // Get a position based on the angle
        float xPosition = center.x + (radiusX * sinf(angleInRadians))
            - (CGRectGetWidth([cell frame]) / 2);
        float yPosition = center.y + (radiusY * cosf(angleInRadians))
            - (CGRectGetHeight([cell frame]) / 2);
```

```
    [cell setTransform:CGAffineTransformMakeTranslation(xPosition, yPosition)];

    // Work out what the next angle is going to be
    angle += angleToAdd;
  }
}

- (void)layoutSubviews
{
   [self setAngle:0];
}

@end


@implementation WheelViewCell

@end
```

Online Help

Did you notice the comment in Listing 10.2 that mentions the origin of the algorithm used to lay out the subviews? The algorithm comes from a posting on **stackoverflow. com**, and kudos to "Tommy" for providing a nice solution.

Programming today is far different from what it was like 30 years ago. Back in the 1980s, I needed to implement the YMODEM file transport protocol for a system I was working on. I found out that sample code was available in a past issue of *Dr. Dobb's Journal*, so I went to the library at the local university to look at a copy of the magazine.

Unfortunately, the issue wasn't available. I had to request the microfilm of the magazine, which took a few days to arrive. When it did, I had to return to the university's library to view the microfilm on its reader. I found the article I needed, read through it multiple times until I was confident I understood it, and I wrote, by hand on paper, the sample source code. If I remember correctly, the entire process, from research to implementation, took almost two weeks before I had a working version of the transfer protocol.

Today, many programming problems can be solved in minutes, not days or weeks. Thanks to the Internet, **Google.com** and online developer communities and forums such as **stackoverflow.com** and Apple's own **devforums.apple.com** make programming today much, much easier. Definitely make a habit of checking online resources such as these Web sites when faced with a programming challenge or when you just want to see how others might implement solutions to the same problems. And be a good developer community citizen by giving back with postings of your answers and solutions to questions from others.

WheelView is now ready to be used within the app. The wheel view will be displayed in the DetailView. IB doesn't know about WheelView, so you must tell IB about it. This is accomplished by changing the class name in the Identity inspector from UIView to WheelView. Once IB knows that the view is of type WheelView, the File's Owner can be set as the data source to the wheel view. Here are the steps to follow:

1. Open *DetailView.xib*.

2. Delete the UILabel "Detail view content goes here."

3. Add a new UIView instance to the main container view.

4. Open the Size inspector (**Option-⌘-5**) and set the Width and Height to 768.

5. Center the UIView within the screen. You can do this in the Size inspector by setting X to 0 and Y to 138.

6. Turn on flexible top, bottom, left, right, width, and height in Autoresizing (see Figure 10.2).

7. Open the Identity inspector (**Option-⌘-3**).

8. Change the class name from UIView to WheelView.

9. **Control-Click** the WheelView and connect the dataSource outlet to the File's Owner (see Figure 10.3).

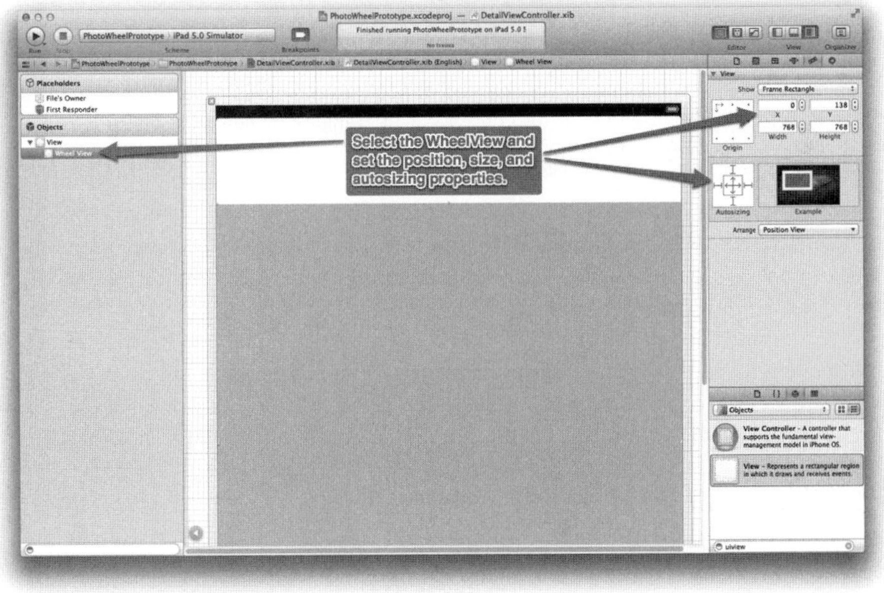

Figure 10.2   Set the WheelView position, size, and autosize properties in the Size inspector.

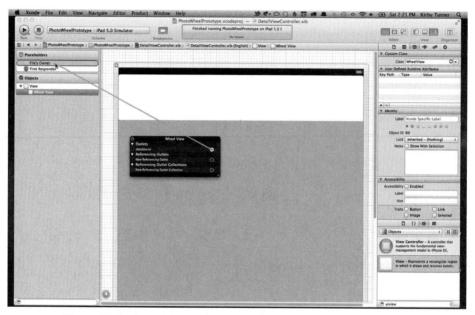

Figure 10.3   Connect the WheelView's dataSource outlet to the
File's Owner.

Note

Seeing a UIView within a UIView can be difficult if both views have the same background color. To get around this, turn on Layout Rectangles by selecting **Editor > Canvas > Show Layout Rectangles** from the menu bar.

Finally, the DetailViewController must be updated with implementations for the WheelViewDataSource protocol methods. This is necessary because Detail-ViewController is the File's Owner, and the File's Owner has been set as the data source for the wheel view.

To accomplish this, start by opening *DetailViewController.h* and add WheelView-DataSource to the list of protocols implemented by the class. Note that you will also need to import *WheelView.h*, which contains the declaration for WheelViewData-Source. Once modified, the header file should contain the code found in Listing 10.3.

Listing 10.3   **Modified Version of** *DetailViewController.h*

```
#import <UIKit/UIKit.h>
#import "WheelView.h"

@interface DetailViewController : UIViewController
<UISplitViewControllerDelegate, WheelViewDataSource>
```

```
@property (strong, nonatomic) id detailItem;
@property (strong, nonatomic) IBOutlet UILabel *detailDescriptionLabel;

@end
```

Before you can implement the `WheelViewDataSource` methods within `Detail-ViewController`, the app needs a collection of views to display. A good place to create this data is in the `-viewDidLoad` event of the `DetailViewController`. A private data property is needed to store the collection of views. The code changes are shown in Listing 10.4.

Listing 10.4   Initializing an Array of Views in *DetailViewController.m*

```
@interface DetailViewController ()
@property (strong, nonatomic) NSArray *data;
// Other code left out for brevity's sake.
@end

@implementation DetailViewController

@synthesize data = _data;

// Other code left out for brevity's sake.

- (void)viewDidLoad
{
    [super viewDidLoad];

    CGRect cellFrame = CGRectMake(0, 0, 75, 75);
    NSInteger count = 10;
    NSMutableArray *newArray = [[NSMutableArray alloc] initWithCapacity:count];
    for (NSInteger index = 0; index < count; index++) {
        WheelViewCell *cell = [[WheelViewCell alloc] initWithFrame:cellFrame];
        [cell setBackgroundColor:[UIColor blueColor]];
        [newArray addObject:cell];
    }
    [self setData:[newArray copy]];
}

// Other code left out for brevity's sake.

@end
```

`DetailViewController` is the data source, and it contains the private property data, which contains the array of views to display in the `WheelView`. All that remains is implementing the `WheelViewDataSource` protocol methods. Add the code in

Listing 10.5 to the bottom of the DetailViewController implementation (but
before the @end statement).

Listing 10.5   **Updated** *DetailViewController.m*

```
#pragma mark - WheelViewDataSource methods

- (NSInteger)wheelViewNumberOfCells:(WheelView *)wheelView
{
    NSInteger count = [[self data] count];
    return count;
}

- (WheelViewCell *)wheelView:(WheelView *)wheelView cellAtIndex:(NSInteger)index
{
    WheelViewCell *cell = [[self data] objectAtIndex:index];
    return cell;
}
```

Build and run the app. The detail view within the app now displays a circle of blue
square views, as shown in Figure 10.4.

A Carousel View

The wheel view looks nice, but a carousel view might look better. You won't know
until you try it. The wheel can be turned into a carousel with some minor tweaking

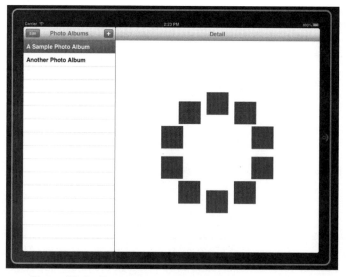

Figure 10.4   The prototype app with a wheel of squares.

of the algorithm used to lay out the wheel view cells. This is a perfect time to experiment. After all, this is a prototype app, and there is no better place to experiment with concepts.

Making the carousel is as simple as turning the wheel on its side, but which way looks better? A good way to compare is to add a feature to the prototype app that enables the user to switch between the two display styles.

To make it so, open *WheelView.h* and add a new declared property called style. To make the code more readable, use an enumeration type to define the list of display styles. Your code should look like the code in Listing 10.6.

Listing 10.6   Modified Version of *WheelView.h*

```
#import <UIKit/UIKit.h>

@protocol WheelViewDataSource;
@class WheelViewCell;

typedef enum   {
   WheelViewStyleWheel,
   WheelViewStyleCarousel,
} WheelViewStyle;


@interface WheelView : UIView

@property (nonatomic, strong) IBOutlet id<WheelViewDataSource> dataSource;
@property (nonatomic, assign) WheelViewStyle style;

@end


@protocol WheelViewDataSource <NSObject>
@required
- (NSInteger)wheelViewNumberOfCells:(WheelView *)wheelView;
- (WheelViewCell *)wheelView:(WheelView *)wheelView cellAtIndex:(NSInteger)index;
@end


@interface WheelViewCell : UIView
@end
```

> **Note**
>
> The declared property style uses the property setting assign. This is used instead of strong because style's data type is an enumeration, which is a C type, not an Objective-C object.

Now it's time to add carousel support to the `WheelView` class. Open *WheelView.m* and synthesize the new `style` property. When this property is set, the layout of the view must change. Therefore, you need to add an implementation for the `style`'s setter method. The code changes are given in Listing 10.7.

Listing 10.7   **Synthesizing the `style` Property and Implementing a Custom Setting Method in *WheelView.m***

```
@implementation WheelView

@synthesize dataSource = _dataSource;
@synthesize style = _style;

// Other source code not shown for brevity's sake.

// Add to the bottom of the WheelView implementation.
- (void)setStyle:(WheelViewStyle)newStyle
{
if (_style != newStyle) {
    _style = newStyle;

    [UIView beginAnimations:@"WheelViewStyleChange" context:nil];
    [self setAngle:0];
    [UIView commitAnimations];
    }
}

@end
```

Let's take a closer look at the setter method -`setStyle:`.

It checks to see if the new style is different from the current style. If it is, the current style is set to the new style. This part of the code should be obvious to you, but not so obvious is the rest of the code in the `if` block.

A call is made to `setAngle:` to force `WheelView` to redraw. At the moment, the app always passes in 0 for the angle. In the next chapter, Chapter 11, "Using Touch Gestures," you'll change the app to use different angle values, but 0 works for the current needs of the app.

Stranger than always passing in 0 is the code above and below `[self setAngle:0]`. This is your first look at using Core Animation. What this bit of code does is wrap the drawing of the wheel from one style to another in an animation block. The +`beginAnimation:context:` and +`commitAnimations` methods on `UIView` indicate to the Core Animation framework the start and end points of the animation sequence. -`setAngle:` will draw the view based on the new style, and Core Animation calculates and renders the visual aspects needed to animate the transition from one style to another.

> **Note**
>
> Core Animation is an extremely powerful framework for producing animations within iOS applications, and it is used throughout iOS. The bounce effect you see when scrolling through the app icons on the Home screen, the animation effect you see when launching and quitting apps, the pushing and popping of view controllers from a navigation controller—these are all examples of where Core Animation is used.
>
> To learn more about Core Animation, read Marcus Zarra and Matt Long's book *Core Animation: Simplified Animation Techniques for Mac and iPhone Development* (Addison-Wesley, 2009), and Bill Dudney's *Core Animation for Mac OS X and the iPhone: Creating Compelling Dynamic User Interfaces* (Pragmatic Programmers, 2008).

Now you need to tweak the display algorithm in the -setAngle: method. To give the wheel a carousel look, the circle needs to look more like an oval. Also, the views displayed in the back of the carousel should be smaller than those in the front and slightly faded. This gives an effect of visual depth to the carousel. The updated code is shown in Listing 10.8.

Listing 10.8 Updated -setAngle: Method Supporting the Carousel as a Display Style

```
#import "WheelView.h"
#import <QuartzCore/QuartzCore.h>


@implementation WheelView

// Other source code not shown for brevity's sake.

- (void)setAngle:(CGFloat)angle
{
   // The following code is inspired by the carousel example at
   // http://stackoverflow.com/questions/5243614/3d-carousel-effect-on-the-ipad

   CGPoint center = CGPointMake(CGRectGetMidX([self bounds]),
                                CGRectGetMidY([self bounds]));
   CGFloat radiusX = MIN([self bounds].size.width,
                         [self bounds].size.height) * 0.35;
   CGFloat radiusY = radiusX;
   if ([self style] == WheelViewStyleCarousel) {
      radiusY = radiusX * 0.30;
   }

   NSInteger cellCount = [[self dataSource] wheelViewNumberOfCells:self];
   float angleToAdd = 360.0f / cellCount;

   for (NSInteger index = 0; index < cellCount; index++)
   {
      WheelViewCell *cell = [[self dataSource] wheelView:self cellAtIndex:index];
```

```
      if ([cell superview] == nil) {
        [self addSubview:cell];
      }

      float angleInRadians = (angle + 180.0) * M_PI / 180.0f;

      // Get a position based on the angle
      float xPosition = center.x + (radiusX * sinf(angleInRadians))
      - (CGRectGetWidth([cell frame]) / 2);
      float yPosition = center.y + (radiusY * cosf(angleInRadians))
      - (CGRectGetHeight([cell frame]) / 2);

      float scale = 0.75f + 0.25f * (cosf(angleInRadians) + 1.0);

      // Apply location and scale
      if ([self style] == WheelViewStyleCarousel) {
        [cell setTransform:CGAffineTransformScale(
                CGAffineTransformMakeTranslation(xPosition, yPosition),
                scale,
                scale)];
        // Tweak alpha using the same system as applied for scale,
        // this time with 0.3 as the minimum and a semicircle range
        // of 0.5
        [cell setAlpha:(0.3f + 0.5f * (cosf(angleInRadians) + 1.0))];

      } else {
        [cell setTransform:CGAffineTransformMakeTranslation(xPosition,
                                                       yPosition)];
        [cell setAlpha:1.0];
      }

      [[cell layer] setZPosition:scale];

      // Work out what the next angle is going to be
      angle += angleToAdd;
    }
}

// Other source code not shown for brevity's sake.

@end
```

The code has now been modified to support two different display styles: wheel and carousel. To produce the carousel effect, the Y-axis is adjusted to be 30% of the X-axis. Also, the scale and alpha for each cell are set based on the position within the circle. The last change is the setting of the Z-position for the layer. This effectively mimics setting the draw order of the views without having to actually reorder the list views.

> **Note**
>
> If Xcode is reporting a warning message on the line of code [[cell layer]
> setZPosition:scale], you likely forgot to include the #import <QuartzCore/
> QuartzCore.h> statement at the top of the *WheelView.m* file. Add the import state-
> ment and the warning will go away.

Now that WheelView is ready, it's time to update the app so that the user can switch between the two display styles. A segmented control in the DetailView's navigation bar is a good way for the user to do this. But first, the DetailView-Controller needs a new outlet that references the wheel view so that the style can be changed programmatically. Open *DetailViewController.h* and add the new outlet for the WheelView. The source code is shown in Listing 10.9.

Listing 10.9   New Outlet Added to DetailViewController

```
#import <UIKit/UIKit.h>
#import "WheelView.h"

@interface DetailViewController : UIViewController
<UISplitViewControllerDelegate, WheelViewDataSource>

// Other source code not shown for brevity's sake.

@property (strong, nonatomic) IBOutlet WheelView *wheelView;

@end
```

Next, synthesize the wheelView property in the *DetailViewController* implementa-tion file. The @synthesize statement is shown in Listing 10.10.

Listing 10.10   Updated Implementation for the DetailViewController

```
@implementation DetailViewController

// Other source code not shown for brevity's sake.

@synthesize wheelView = _wheelView;

// Other source code not shown for brevity's sake.

@end
```

Now open *DetailView.xib* and connect the WheelView instance to the wheelView outlet, as shown in Figure 10.5.

Next you need to add a segmented control to the navigation bar. The navigation bar is managed by the UINavigationController containing the DetailViewController

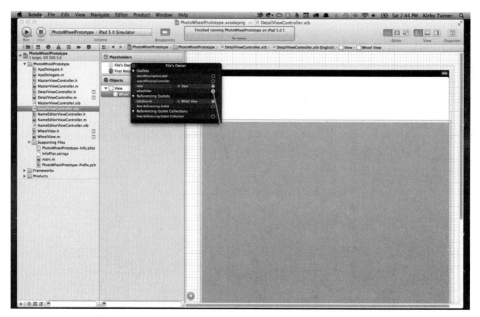

Figure 10.5　Connecting the outlet

instance. The navigation controller displays a label that contains the view controller's title in the middle of the navigation bar. In the prototype app you are working on, the view controller's title is set to "Detail" in the `-initWithNibName:bundle:` method found in the *DetailViewController.m* file.

The navigation controller can also display a custom view in place of the title label in the middle of the navigation bar. To do this, set the `titleView` property of the view controller's navigation item.

You want to display a `UISegmentedControl` instead of the default title view in the navigation bar. To do this, you must create a new instance of `UISegmented-Control` and set the `titleView` property on the navigation item for the `Detail-ViewController` instance. You also need to define a new action that is called when the user taps a segment. The action's implementation will set the `wheelView` style based on the selected segment index. The code to accomplish this is shown in Listing 10.11. Add the same code to your project.

Listing 10.11　**Update to** *DetailViewController.m*

```
- (void)viewDidLoad
{
    // Other source code not shown for brevity's sake.

    NSArray *segmentedItems = [NSArray arrayWithObjects:
                        @"Wheel", @"Carousel", nil];
```

```
    UISegmentedControl *segmentedControl = [[UISegmentedControl alloc]
                                    initWithItems:segmentedItems];
    [segmentedControl addTarget:self
                    action:@selector(segmentedControlValueChanged:)
            forControlEvents:UIControlEventValueChanged];
    [segmentedControl setSegmentedControlStyle:UISegmentedControlStyleBar];
    [segmentedControl setSelectedSegmentIndex:0];
    [[self navigationItem] setTitleView:segmentedControl];
}


- (void)segmentedControlValueChanged:(id)sender
{
    NSInteger index = [sender selectedSegmentIndex];
    if (index == 0) {
        [[self wheelView] setStyle:WheelViewStyleWheel];
    } else {
        [[self wheelView] setStyle:WheelViewStyleCarousel];
    }
}
```

That's it. Save the changes, then build and run the app. Test the new feature by tapping **Wheel** and **Carousel** in the navigation bar. The carousel should look like the one in Figure 10.6.

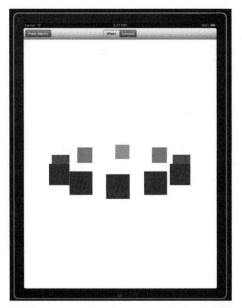

Figure 10.6   Screen shot of the new carousel display style

A Photo Wheel View Cell

You now have a generic, reusable view that displays a wheel or carousel of subviews, but the specific needs of the app call for the display of photos. What is needed now is a specialized type of WheelViewCell. This subclass of WheelViewCell will display an image.

The easiest way to display an image is to use UIImageView. To use UIImageView, simply create an instance of it, then add it to the view hierarchy. Next, set the image view's image property to an image.

This is not the only way to display an image. You can also set content for the layer that backs the view. (It sounds complicated but it's not.)

In iOS, all UIViews are backed by a CALayer. This means that each UIView has a CALayer. This makes it possible to take advantage of Core Animation effects on your UIView. You can think of a layer as something that sits behind or within the view that stores additional information for drawing and animating views.

> **Note**
>
> Views on Mac OS X are not CALayer-backed by default. Instead, you must explicitly turn on backing if you need a CALayer-backed view.

Placing an image on a CALayer is a common practice when you need to display a large number of images. Its use is overkill for the prototype app, but let's use it anyway so you can see how it's done. Also, while you're at it, draw a border and shadow around the image to enhance the visual display.

Here are the steps to follow. Note that the steps are purposely brief, as you should now be familiar with creating new classes.

1. Create a new Objective-C class.
2. Name the new class PhotoWheelViewCell.
3. Specify WheelViewCell as the subclass for the new class.

PhotoWheelViewCell needs a way to set the current image. This can be implemented as a declared property, but the cell view has no need to hang on to the image. The image will, instead, be added to the contents of the view's layer. So instead of adding a new property to the class, all that is needed is a single method, -setImage:, that will add an image to the layer's contents. The header file for PhotoWheelViewCell is shown in Listing 10.12, and the implementation is shown in Listing 10.13.

Listing 10.12 **Header File for** *PhotoWheelViewCell.h*

```
#import "WheelView.h"

@interface PhotoWheelViewCell : WheelViewCell

- (void)setImage:(UIImage *)newImage;

@end
```

Listing 10.13   **Implementation for** *PhotoWheelViewCell.m*

```
#import "PhotoWheelViewCell.h"
#import <QuartzCore/QuartzCore.h>

@implementation PhotoWheelViewCell

- (void)setImage:(UIImage *)newImage
{
   // Add the image to the layer's contents.
   CALayer *layer = [self layer];
   id imageRef = (__bridge id)[newImage CGImage];
   [layer setContents:imageRef];

   // Add border and shadow.
   [layer setBorderColor:[UIColor colorWithWhite:1.0 alpha:1.0].CGColor];
   [layer setBorderWidth:5.0];
   [layer setShadowOffset:CGSizeMake(0, 3)];
   [layer setShadowOpacity:0.7];
   [layer setShouldRasterize:YES];
}

@end
```

The implementation starts by importing *PhotoWheelViewCell.h* and *QuartzCore.h*. The QuartzCore header is needed because the code uses an object of type CALayer.

The implementation of -setImage: is straightforward. It grabs a local reference to [self layer] to make the code more readable. Next, the CGImageRef from the given image is stored in a local variable. Okay, so maybe the code here is not that straightforward. Here's what is going on.

To display an image in the contents of a layer, you must set the contents to a CGImageRef. CGImageRef is a C structure that contains bitmap information about the image. It is a Core Foundation–style object, and its lifetime is not automatically managed by ARC.

Note
Revisit Chapter 4, "Getting Started with Objective-C," if you need a refresher on ARC.

contents, on the other hand, is an Objective-C object of type id. id is a general object type for any kind of Objective-C object regardless of the class. To set contents to a CGImageRef the image ref must be casted to id. This is true anytime you need to cast between an Objective-C type and a Core Foundation–style object.

To cast between the types you must use the __bridge syntax. (__bridge type) performs a noop cast. (__bridge_transfer type) releases the reference being cast. (__bridge_retain type) adds a count to the retain count. For PhotoWheel-ViewCell, only a noop cast is needed. The CGImageRef returned by [newImage

CGImage] is casted to id. Once casted, it can be passed to the layer's contents. And because __bridge syntax is used, ARC will not attempt to manage the memory for id, nor will the compiler complain about not knowing the memory ownership for the local reference.

The rest of the code is used to draw the border and shadow effect around the image. Feel free to play with these settings to see what other effects you can create.

Using PhotoWheelViewCell

Now that PhotoWheelViewCell has been implemented, it's time to put it to good use. The prototype app doesn't yet have the ability to add new photos to a photo wheel, so let's add a default photo to the app that is displayed until the user adds a photo.

Included with the sample source code for this chapter is *defaultPhoto.png*, an image that can be used as the default photo. Add this file to your project by dragging and dropping it from Finder to the Xcode Project navigator for your project. Be sure to select the option "Copy items into destination group's folder (if needed)," as shown in Figure 10.7. This will ensure that the file is copied to the project directory.

As you may recall, DetailViewController is responsible for creating the array of wheel view cells. It does this in its -viewDidLoad method. The code must be changed to create instances of PhotoWheelViewCell and to set the image to *default-Photo.png*. The code changes are given in Listing 10.14.

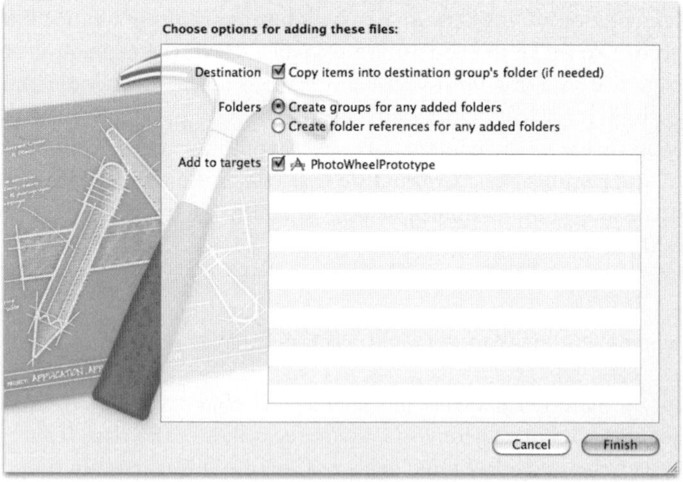

Figure 10.7 Select "Copy items into destination group's folder" when adding the image to the project.

Listing 10.14   **Modified** `DetailViewController` **to Use** `PhotoWheelViewCell`
             Instead of `WheelViewCell`

```
#import "DetailViewController.h"
#import "PhotoWheelViewCell.h"

// Other source code not shown for brevity's sake.

@implementation DetailViewController

// Other source code not shown for brevity's sake.

- (void)viewDidLoad
{
   [super viewDidLoad];

   UIImage *defaultPhoto = [UIImage imageNamed:@"defaultPhoto.png"];
   CGRect cellFrame = CGRectMake(0, 0, 75, 75);
   NSInteger count = 10;
   NSMutableArray *newArray = [[NSMutableArray alloc] initWithCapacity:count];
   for (NSInteger index = 0; index < count; index++) {
      PhotoWheelViewCell *cell =
         [[PhotoWheelViewCell alloc] initWithFrame:cellFrame];
      [cell setImage:defaultPhoto];
      [newArray addObject:cell];
   }
   [self setData:[newArray copy]];

   // Other source code not shown for brevity's sake.
}

// Other source code not shown for brevity's sake.

@end
```

The default photo image is loaded into memory by calling `[UIImage image-`
`Named:]`. This returns a reference to the image that is passed to the `PhotoWheel-`
`ViewCell`. Within the `for` loop, the code that created instances of `WheelViewCell`
and set the background color to blue is replaced with `PhotoWheelViewCell` and setting the image to `defaultPhoto`.

With these changes, your `PhotoWheelViewCell` class is now used to display an
image as the wheel cell instead of the boring blue box. Build and run the app, and you
will see the new display as shown in Figure 10.8.

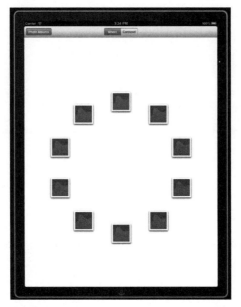

Figure 10.8   A photo wheel with stylish cells

Summary

In this chapter, you learned how to create and use custom views to enhance the look of the app. You learned how to create a reusable wheel view that supports different display styles, and you learned how to use a delegate pattern to decouple the view from the data that it displays. And you learned how to create a specialized class for a view to extend the visual display even further.

You may have already noticed a recurring theme over the last couple of chapters. The wheel view you created in this chapter loosely follows the same design pattern used by UITableView. The patterns of reusable views, delegates and data sources, and custom views to extend the appearance of apps are common in iOS.

Exercises

1. Play with the math used in the wheel and carousel algorithm to change the display effects. Some changes to try include changing the Y-axis percentage and changing the scale size of the background views.

2. Change the border color and size of the photo wheel view cell. Change the shadow effect of the cell.

3. Add more cells to the photo wheel. Display fewer photos in the wheel.

4. Comment out the animation used in the WheelView -setStyle: setter method. Make note of how it differs from the animated version of the code.

11

Using Touch Gestures

The wheel view you built in the last chapter looks nice, especially when you use the photo wheel view cell. And the transitions between wheel and carousel are smooth thanks to Core Animation. But there's still something missing. The user cannot interact with the photo wheel. That changes in this chapter as you learn about touch handling and gesture recognizers.

Touch Gestures Explained

Prior to iOS, most touch interfaces on mobile devices simply replaced the mouse with a finger. Users used a finger to move the mouse cursor around the screen, tapped to simulate a mouse click, and double-tapped to simulate a double click. Needless to say, this was a less than ideal user experience. Mouse-driven operating systems expect the mouse cursor to be much more precise than what can be achieved with a normal-size human finger (remember the rule of 44 mentioned in Chapter 7, "App Design"). iOS changed all of this.

iOS was built from the start with multi-touch as the central feature of the platform. It was not an attempt to implement a multi-touch interface on top of a desktop OS. Instead, iOS has introduced a whole new way for users to interact with software using nothing more than a finger.

There are two ways your application can handle and respond to touch events. One is to respond to touch events sent by the operating system. These touch events are forwarded to your app by way of the `UIResponder` class.

The Apple documentation says, "The `UIResponder` class defines an interface for objects that respond to and handle events." `UIView` is a subclass of `UIResponder`. This means that any `UIView` can respond to and handle events. But what events?

There are two types of events that pass through `UIResponder`: touch and motion. The primary touch events are `touchesBegan:withEvent:`, `touchesMoved:withEvent:`, `touchesEnded:withEvent:`, and `touchesCancelled:withEvent:`. The primary motion events include `motionBegan:withEvent:`, `motionEnded:withEvent:`, and `motionCancelled:withEvent:`. All a view must do to respond to and handle any of these events is to override one or more of these methods. If, for example, you want `PhotoWheelViewCell` to respond to a single or double tap, override the `touchesBegan:withEvent:` and `touchesEnded:withEvent:` methods in the `PhotoWheelViewCell` class.

The problem with this approach is that code for commonly used touch gestures is copied through your view classes, and you must subclass `UIView` to override the touch handling events. If two different view classes must respond to a double tap, each class must implement the logic needed to detect the double-tap gesture. This violates the DRY principle discussed in Chapter 10, "Working with Views". To get around this problem, Apple engineers created the `UIGestureRecognizer` class.

The `UIGestureRecognizer` class was introduced in iOS 3.2, the first iOS version for the iPad. The class is an abstract base class used to create concrete gesture recognizers. Concrete gesture recognizers are then added to views that need to respond to and handle specific touch gestures. This approach to handling gestures means that logic for a touch gesture is implemented only once, as opposed to the "old way" that required the logic to be reimplemented in each view that needed to respond to a particular gesture.

Predefined Touch Gestures

When Apple introduced gesture recognizers to the SDK, it also provided implementation, or concrete, classes for a number of common touch gestures. Here is the list of gestures provided by the SDK:

- **UITapGestureRecognizer**: Detects one or more taps from one or more fingers
- **UIPinchGestureRecognizer**: Detects the two-finger pinch gesture
- **UIRotationGestureRecognizer**: Detects the two-finger rotation gesture
- **UISwipeGestureRecognizer**: Detects a swipe gesture in one or more directions
- **UIPanGestureRecognizer**: Detects the panning, or dragging, gesture
- **UILongPressGestureRecognizer**: Detects long presses of one or more fingers touching a view for a minimum amount of time

Gesture Types

Gestures are broken down into two types: discrete and continuous. A discrete gesture calls the action once for the touch sequence. `UITapGestureRecognizer` and `UISwipeGestureRecognizer` are examples of discrete gesture recognizers. The action is called once each time the gesture is detected.

A continuous recognizer calls the action message at each incremental change until the sequence has completed. `UIPinchGestureRecognizer`, `UIRotationGesture-Recognizer`, `UIPanGestureRecognizer`, and `UILongPressGestureRecognizer` are all continuous gesture recognizers.

How to Use Gesture Recognizers

Using a gesture recognizer is as easy as creating an instance of the recognizer and adding it to the view that will receive the touch events. Each recognizer has its own set of properties that enable you to fine-tune the behavior of the gesture recognizer. For instance, `UITapGestureRecognizer` has two tap-specific properties: `numberOf-TapsRequired` and `numberOfTouchesRequired`.

The property `numberOfTapsRequired` specifies the number of taps required. The default is 1. If you wish to detect a double tap, you would change this value to 2. A triple tap would be, of course, 3, and so on.

The property `numberOfTouchesRequired` tells the recognizer how many fingers are required to detect the gesture. Again, the default value is 1. If you want to detect a tap with two fingers, you would set the property to 2. Here is an example of using a tap gesture recognizer to detect a double tap with two fingers:

```
UITapGestureRecognizer *twoFingerDoubleTap =
   [[UITapGestureRecognizer alloc] initWithTarget:self
   action:@selector(twoFingerDoubleTapped:)];
[twoFingerDoubleTap setNumberOfTapsRequired:2];
[twoFingerDoubleTap setNumberOfTouchesRequired:2];
```

You can also extend the behavior of a recognizer by setting the `delegate` property and implementing the methods defined in the `UIGestureRecognizerDelegate` protocol. This allows the app to extend the behaviors of the recognizer without having to subclass `UIGestureRecognizer`.

To get a better understanding of how to use gesture recognizers, let's modify the PhotoWheelPrototype app and have it use a gesture recognizer or two. First, you'll add a single-tap recognizer to each cell of the photo wheel and have the action implementation do nothing more than log the class and method name. (Hint: Use `NSLog(@"%s", __PRETTY_FUNCTION__)`.) Next, you'll add a double-tap recognizer to each cell and log the class and method name in the action implementation. Let's get started.

Note

The real implementation for the tap action will come in Chapter 12, "Adding Photos," where a single tap is used to add a photo to a cell.

To add the tap gesture recognizer to the cell, open *DetailViewController.m* and add a new instance of `UITapGestureRecognizer` to each cell. The recognizer could be added to the `PhotoWheelViewCell` class, but that would reduce the reusability of the cell class. The tap action is specific to this app, which means the view controller is the more appropriate place for the action.

The code change is shown in Listing 11.1.

Listing 11.1   **Tap Gesture Recognizer Added to Each Photo Wheel View Cell**

```
@implementation DetailViewController

// Other code left out for brevity's sake.

- (void)viewDidLoad
{
    [super viewDidLoad];

    UIImage *defaultPhoto = [UIImage imageNamed:@"defaultPhoto.png"];
    CGRect cellFrame = CGRectMake(0, 0, 75, 75);
    NSInteger count = 10;
    NSMutableArray *newArray = [[NSMutableArray alloc] initWithCapacity:count];
    for (NSInteger index = 0; index < count; index++) {
        PhotoWheelViewCell *cell =
            [[PhotoWheelViewCell alloc] initWithFrame:cellFrame];
        [cell setImage:defaultPhoto];

        // Add single-tap gesture to the cell.
        UITapGestureRecognizer *tap = [[UITapGestureRecognizer alloc]
                                       initWithTarget:self
                                       action:@selector(cellTapped:)];
        [cell addGestureRecognizer:tap];

        [newArray addObject:cell];
    }
    [self setData:[newArray copy]];

    // Other code left out for brevity's sake.

}

// Other code left out for brevity's sake.

- (void)cellTapped:(UIGestureRecognizer *)recognizer
{
    NSLog(@"%s", __PRETTY_FUNCTION__);
}

@end
```

That's it. Two lines of code, and now the app can detect taps on each photo wheel view cell. The -cellTapped: method outputs the class and method name to the console window. Obviously a real application will do more than this.

Next, add a double-tap gesture to each cell. This gets slightly more complicated because the cell already has the tap recognizer. Trying to decide when the user is performing single taps versus double taps can be a challenge. Luckily, gesture recognizers make it easy to handle this scenario with the -requireGestureRecognizer-ToFail: method. This method says that a gesture is not recognized unless another gesture recognizer fails. In the case of tap and double tap, we want a tap to be recognized only after it has been determined that the user isn't attempting a double tap.

Listing 11.2 shows the updated code that adds the double tap.

Listing 11.2   **Adding a Double Tap to the Cell**

```objc
- (void)viewDidLoad
{
   [super viewDidLoad];

   UIImage *defaultPhoto = [UIImage imageNamed:@"defaultPhoto.png"];
   CGRect cellFrame = CGRectMake(0, 0, 75, 75);
   NSInteger count = 10;
   NSMutableArray *newArray = [[NSMutableArray alloc] initWithCapacity:count];
   for (NSInteger index = 0; index < count; index++) {
      PhotoWheelViewCell *cell =
         [[PhotoWheelViewCell alloc] initWithFrame:cellFrame];
      [cell setImage:defaultPhoto];

      // Add a double-tap gesture to the cell.
      UITapGestureRecognizer *doubleTap;
      doubleTap = [[UITapGestureRecognizer alloc]
                  initWithTarget:self
                  action:@selector(cellDoubleTapped:)];

      [doubleTap setNumberOfTapsRequired:2];
      [cell addGestureRecognizer:doubleTap];

      // Add a single-tap gesture to the cell.
      UITapGestureRecognizer *tap = [[UITapGestureRecognizer alloc]
                                    initWithTarget:self
                                    action:@selector(cellTapped:)];
      [tap requireGestureRecognizerToFail:doubleTap];
      [cell addGestureRecognizer:tap];

      [newArray addObject:cell];
   }
   [self setData:[newArray copy]];

   // Other code left out for brevity's sake.
}

// Other code left out for brevity's sake.
```

```
- (void)cellDoubleTapped:(UIGestureRecognizer *)recognizer
{
    NSLog(@"%s", __PRETTY_FUNCTION__);
}
```

Notice that even though the `doubleTap` gesture recognizer was added to the cell first, the order in which the recognizers are added doesn't matter. The order does not determine if tap or double tap is detected first. It is the `-requireGesture-RecognizerToFail:` call on the tap gesture that determines when a single tap is detected and when a double tap is detected.

> **Note**
>
> To learn more about gesture recognizers, how to use them, and how they work, watch the WWDC 2010 video *Session 120—Simplifying Touch Event Handling with Gesture Recognizers*. This video is free to all registered members of the iOS Developer Program (**developer.apple.com/videos/wwdc/2010/**).

Custom Touch Gestures

Most iPad apps will only ever need to use the predefined gesture recognizers. If, however, you find that you need to track a gesture that is not provided by the SDK, you can create your own subclass of `UIGestureRecognizer`.

A subclass of `UIGestureRecognizer` will respond to one or more touch handling events: `touchesBegan:withEvent:`, `touchesMoved:withEvent:`, `touchesEnded:withEvent:`, and `touchesCancelled:withEvent:`. Gesture recognizers operate on a state machine. As incoming touch events are received, the gesture recognizer transitions between states.

All recognizers start in the *possible* state (`UIGestureRecognizerStatePossible`). Discrete recognizers transition to either a *recognized* state (`UIGestureRecognizerStateRecognized`) or a *failed* state (`UIGestureRecognizerStateFailed`). The action message associated with the recognizer is sent to the target when the recognizer enters the *recognized* state.

Continuous recognizers transition from the *possible* state to a *began* state (`UIGestureRecognizerStateBegan`), then to the *changed* state (`UIGestureRecognizerStateChanged`) as touch events occur, then finally to either the *end* state (`UIGestureRecognizerStateEnd`) or the *cancelled* state (`UIGestureRecognizerStateCancelled`). The *changed* state is optional, and it may occur multiple times during a touch sequence. The action message is sent to the target each time there is a state transition.

When you subclass `UIGestureRecognizer`, you must import *UIGestureRecognizerSubclass.h*. This header file declares the methods and properties that a subclass must override or set. For example, the property `state` is read-only on the abstract base class `UIGestureRecognizer`, but including *UIGestureRecognizerSubclass.h* in your concrete class makes the `state` property a read-write property for use within the subclass implementation only. Users of your concrete gesture recognizer class will still have read-only access to the `state` property.

That's a brief overview of what you need to know when subclassing `UIGesture-Recognizer`. Now let's create one.

Creating a Spin Gesture Recognizer

The prototype app has a nice-looking wheel view. How cool would it be if users could spin the wheel? Very cool, that's how cool.

Spinning the wheel view is as easy as rotating the wheel view as the user touches it. And it just so happens that iOS provides the gesture recognizer `UIRotation-GestureRecognizer`. The problem with this recognizer is that it requires two fingers to perform the rotation. A spinning gesture is more natural using only one finger, so `UIRotationGestureRecognizer` does not satisfy the app's particular need for spinning. Instead, you need to create a new concrete gesture recognizer to spin a view.

Start by creating a new Objective-C class named `SpinGestureRecognizer` that is a subclass of `UIGestureRecognizer`. The class will have one declared property named `rotation` that is of type `CGFloat`. This will report the rotation of the gesture in radians since its last change. The source code *SpinGestureRecognizer.h* is shown in Listing 11.3.

Listing 11.3 *SpinGestureRecognizer.h*

```
#import <UIKit/UIKit.h>

@interface SpinGestureRecognizer : UIGestureRecognizer

/**
 The rotation of the gesture in radians since its last change.
 */
@property (nonatomic, assign) CGFloat rotation;

@end
```

The implementation for `SpinGestureRecognizer` must import *UIGestureRecognizerSubclass.h*. This header file is needed so that the subclass can change the `state` property value and override the touch handling events. The implementation must also synthesize the rotation property.

The recognizer should work with only one finger. Two or more simultaneous touches will not be allowed, so `touchesBegan:withEvent:` will check the touch count. With anything greater than 1 the gesture recognizer will fail.

The touch handling events `touchesEnd:withEvent:` and `touchesCancelled:withEvent:` will transition the recognizer's state machine to the *end* state and *cancelled* state respectively. This leaves `touchesMoved:withEvent:`.

This is where the bulk of the work is performed, which will be explained momentarily. The implementation source code is shown in Listing 11.4.

Listing 11.4   *SpinGestureRecognizer.m*

```objc
#import "SpinGestureRecognizer.h"
#import <UIKit/UIGestureRecognizerSubclass.h>

@implementation SpinGestureRecognizer

@synthesize rotation = _rotation;

- (void)touchesBegan:(NSSet *)touches withEvent:(UIEvent *)event
{
   // Fail when more than 1 finger detected.
   if ([[event touchesForGestureRecognizer:self] count] > 1) {
      [self setState:UIGestureRecognizerStateFailed];
   }
}

- (void)touchesEnded:(NSSet *)touches withEvent:(UIEvent *)event
{
   [self setState:UIGestureRecognizerStateEnded];
}

- (void)touchesCancelled:(NSSet *)touches withEvent:(UIEvent *)event
{
   [self setState:UIGestureRecognizerStateFailed];
}

- (void)touchesMoved:(NSSet *)touches withEvent:(UIEvent *)event
{
   if ([self state] == UIGestureRecognizerStatePossible) {
      [self setState:UIGestureRecognizerStateBegan];
   } else {
      [self setState:UIGestureRecognizerStateChanged];
   }

   // We can look at any touch object since we know we
   // have only 1. If there were more than 1,
   // touchesBegan:withEvent: would have failed the recognizer.
   UITouch *touch = [touches anyObject];

   // To rotate with one finger, we simulate a second finger.
   // The second finger is on the opposite side of the virtual
   // circle that represents the rotation gesture.
```

```
    UIView *view = [self view];
    CGPoint center = CGPointMake(CGRectGetMidX([view bounds]),
                                 CGRectGetMidY([view bounds]));
    CGPoint currentTouchPoint = [touch locationInView:view];
    CGPoint previousTouchPoint = [touch previousLocationInView:view];

    CGPoint line2Start = currentTouchPoint;
    CGPoint line1Start = previousTouchPoint;
    CGPoint line2End = CGPointMake(center.x + (center.x - line2Start.x),
                                   center.y + (center.y - line2Start.y));
    CGPoint line1End = CGPointMake(center.x + (center.x - line1Start.x),
                                   center.y + (center.y - line1Start.y));

    //////
    // Calculate the angle in radians.
    // From http://bit.ly/oJ9UHY
    CGFloat a = line1End.x - line1Start.x;
    CGFloat b = line1End.y - line1Start.y;
    CGFloat c = line2End.x - line2Start.x;
    CGFloat d = line2End.y - line2Start.y;

    CGFloat line1Slope = (line1End.y - line1Start.y) / (line1End.x - line1Start.x);
    CGFloat line2Slope = (line2End.y - line2Start.y) / (line2End.x - line2Start.x);

    CGFloat degs =
        acosf(((a*c) + (b*d)) / ((sqrt(a*a + b*b)) * (sqrt(c*c + d*d))));

    CGFloat angleInRadians = (line2Slope > line1Slope) ? degs : -degs;
    //////

    [self setRotation:angleInRadians];
}

@end
```

Let's walk through the code for touchesMoved:withEvent: to see what is going on.

The moment the recognizer detects movement, the state transitions from the *possible* state to the *began* state. Any additional movement will trigger the transition to the *changed* state. The recognizer does not immediately go from the *possible* state to the *changed* state because a tap could have caused the movement. A tap can have slight movement, so the recognizer transitions first to the *began* state. If it turns out that the touch gesture is a tap, it will immediately end with a call to touchesEnded:withEvent:. If the touch is not a tap and additional movement is detected, the state transitions to *changed* and the action message is sent to the target.

Once the state transition has been set, the work of calculating the rotation of the spin is performed. The calculation uses the current and previous touch points within the view attached to the gesture recognizer to calculate the current angle of the rotation. It uses an artificial second finger to perform the calculation as if two fingers were rotating around a single center point. This, in essence, causes the spin gesture recognizer to track finger movement around a central point where the central point is the center of the view.

> **Note**
>
> I often say, "Math is hard." And it is ... for me, that is. Thanks to Jeff LaMarche for providing the math used to calculate the angle of the rotation in his blog post about a better two-finger rotation (**iphonedevelopment.blogspot.com/2009/12/better-two-finger-rotate-gesture.html**).

Using the Spin Gesture Recognizer

To see your work in action, you must add the spin gesture recognizer to the wheel view. The recognizer is added to the wheel view instead of the detail view controller in order to make the spinning wheel a feature of the view. `WheelView` must also be updated to support the new spinning behavior. The updated *WheelView.m* is shown in Listing 11.5.

Listing 11.5 Updated *WheelView.m* with Spinning View Support

```
#import "WheelView.h"
#import <QuartzCore/QuartzCore.h>
#import "SpinGestureRecognizer.h"

@interface WheelView ()
@property (nonatomic, assign) CGFloat currentAngle;
@end

@implementation WheelView

@synthesize dataSource = _dataSource;
@synthesize style = _style;
@synthesize currentAngle = _currentAngle;

- (void)commonInit
{
    [self setCurrentAngle:0.0];

    SpinGestureRecognizer *spin = [[SpinGestureRecognizer alloc]
                             initWithTarget:self
                             action:@selector(spin:)];
    [self addGestureRecognizer:spin];
}
```

```objc
- (id)init
{
   self = [super init];
   if (self) {
      [self commonInit];
   }
   return self;
}

- (id)initWithCoder:(NSCoder *)aDecoder
{
   self = [super initWithCoder:aDecoder];
   if (self) {
      [self commonInit];
   }
   return self;
}

- (id)initWithFrame:(CGRect)frame
{
   self = [super initWithFrame:frame];
   if (self) {
      [self commonInit];
   }
   return self;
}

- (void)setAngle:(CGFloat)angle
{
   // The following code is inspired by the carousel example at
   // http://stackoverflow.com/questions/5243614/3d-carousel-effect-on-the-ipad

   CGPoint center = CGPointMake(CGRectGetMidX([self bounds]),
                                CGRectGetMidY([self bounds]));
   CGFloat radiusX = MIN([self bounds].size.width,
                         [self bounds].size.height) * 0.35;
   CGFloat radiusY = radiusX;
   if ([self style] == WheelViewStyleCarousel) {
      radiusY = radiusX * 0.30;
   }

   NSInteger cellCount = [[self dataSource] wheelViewNumberOfCells:self];
   float angleToAdd = 360.0f / cellCount;

   for (NSInteger index = 0; index < cellCount; index++)
   {
      WheelViewCell *cell = [[self dataSource] wheelView:self cellAtIndex:index];
```

```objc
    if ([cell superview] == nil) {
        [self addSubview:cell];
    }

    float angleInRadians = (angle + 180.0) * M_PI / 180.0f;

    // Get a position based on the angle
    float xPosition = center.x + (radiusX * sinf(angleInRadians))
    - (CGRectGetWidth([cell frame]) / 2);
    float yPosition = center.y + (radiusY * cosf(angleInRadians))
    - (CGRectGetHeight([cell frame]) / 2);

    float scale = 0.75f + 0.25f * (cosf(angleInRadians) + 1.0);

    // Apply location and scale
    if ([self style] == WheelViewStyleCarousel) {
        [cell setTransform:CGAffineTransformScale(
                CGAffineTransformMakeTranslation(xPosition, yPosition),
                scale, scale)];
        // Tweak alpha using the same system as applied for scale, this time
        // with 0.3 as the minimum and a semicircle range of 0.5
        [cell setAlpha:(0.3f + 0.5f * (cosf(angleInRadians) + 1.0))];

    } else {
        [cell setTransform:CGAffineTransformMakeTranslation(xPosition,
                                                            yPosition)];
        [cell setAlpha:1.0];
    }

    [[cell layer] setZPosition:scale];

    // Work out what the next angle is going to be
    angle += angleToAdd;
    }
}

- (void)layoutSubviews
{
    [self setAngle:[self currentAngle]];
}

- (void)setStyle:(WheelViewStyle)newStyle
{
    if (_style != newStyle) {
        _style = newStyle;

        [UIView beginAnimations:@"WheelViewStyleChange" context:nil];
        [self setAngle:[self currentAngle]];
```

```
        [UIView commitAnimations];
    }
}

- (void)spin:(SpinGestureRecognizer *)recognizer
{
    CGFloat angleInRadians = -[recognizer rotation];
    CGFloat degrees = 180.0 * angleInRadians / M_PI;   // radians to degrees
    [self setCurrentAngle:[self currentAngle] + degrees];
    [self setAngle:[self currentAngle]];
}

@end


@implementation WheelViewCell

@end
```

What exactly changed? Let's take a look.

First, the *SpinGestureRecognizer.h* header file is imported. This, of course, is needed since the wheel view class now uses a SpinGestureRecognizer object.

Following the import, a new private declared property, currentAngle, is added. This property is made private by using an Objective-C feature called class extensions. A class extension is similar to a category but with exceptions:

- A class extension is declared just like a category, but without a name.

- A class extension's properties and methods must be implemented in the main @implementation block for the class.

- A class extension allows you to declare required methods and properties for the class in a location other than the main @interface block for the class.

Class extensions are a handy way to declare private methods and properties on the class that are used within the class. As you can see in Listing 11.5, a class extension is created for WheelView that declares the private property currentAngle. This tells the compiler that the property exists on the class, but it is intended for internal use only.

Note

To learn more about class extensions, read the outstanding post from Bill Bumgarner entitled *Class Extensions Explained* (**www.friday.com/bbum/2009/09/11/class-extensions-explained/**).

Continuing the walk-through of code changes in Listing 11.5, you see the @synthesize statement for the private property currentAngle. Even though the property is declared in the class extension, it must still follow the same rules as publicly declared properties.

The next block of changes includes the new methods `commonInit`, `init`, `initWithCoder:`, and `initWithFrame:`. The three `init` methods are needed to allow the view class to be instantiated by conventions common to iOS. `init` and `initWithFrame:` are commonly used when programmatically creating the class instance. `initWithCoder:` is the `init` method called when the class instance is created as the result of unarchiving the object. Put simply, this is the method called when the class instance is created during the load of a NIB file.

Each `init` method calls `commonInit`. This follows the DRY principle and eliminates the need to copy and paste the same initialization code to each `init` method. `commonInit` performs the steps needed to initialize the class instance. It sets `currentAngle` to 0.0, but more important, it creates an instance of `SpinGestureRecognizer` and adds it to the wheel view. This enables the wheel view to detect the spin gesture.

Following the `init` methods is `setAngle:`. Nothing has changed in this method. Its implementation remains the same as it was before the changes in Listing 11.5.

`layoutSubviews` and `setStyle:` have one change each. Instead of calling `[self setAngle:0.0]`, both methods were modified to call `[self setAngle:[self currentAngle]]`. This tells `setAngle:` to use to the most recent angle when drawing the wheel view.

Last but not least is `spin:`. This is the action method assigned to the `SpinGestureRecognizer` instance created in `commonInit`. This method is called each time the gesture recognizer state changes. When this method is called, it grabs the rotation angle in radians from the provided `SpinGestureRecognizer`. Note that the rotation value is negated. The math in `setAngle:` assumes that degree 0 of the wheel is at the bottom, but the spin gesture recognizer assumes that degree 0 is at the top. By negating the rotation value, the code makes the adjustment for the location of degree 0 within the wheel.

Next, `spin:` converts the rotation angle from radians to degrees. This conversion could have been avoided by not converting the degrees to radians within `SpinGestureRecognizer`. However, `UIRotationGestureRecognizer` uses radians for its rotation property value. `SpinGestureRecognizer` does the same to remain consistent with `UIRotationGestureRecognizer`.

Last, `spin:` increments the `currentAngle` with the current change in degrees, then tells the class to draw the wheel with the new angle setting by calling `setAngle:`. And with that, you now have a wheel that you can spin with a finger. Build and run the app, and test the new touch gesture.

Summary

This chapter was all about touch and how gesture recognizers make it much easier to detect different multi-touch gestures without copying and pasting touch handling code throughout your app. Typically, your apps will use the predefined touch gestures the majority of the time, but you now also know how to create your own concrete gesture recognizer should your app need to support some other touch gesture.

Exercises

1. Remove the negation of the rotation value in `spin:` and observe the effect it has on spinning the wheel.

2. Remove the need to convert degrees to radians in `SpinGestureRecognizer` and make the needed change to `-spin:` to ensure that spinning still works as expected.

3. In addition to the rotation property, `UIRotationGestureRecognizer` has the property velocity. Add velocity to `SpinGestureRecognizer` and implement the appropriate math needed so that the property returns the correct velocity for the rotation.

12

Adding Photos

The photo wheel view you created in Chapter 10, "Working with Views," is ready to display photos, but the prototype app does not yet have a way to add photos. It's time to change that. In this chapter, you will learn how to access photos managed by the Photos app, which is available on all iPads and iPhones. And you will add support for adding photos to the prototype app you have been building since Chapter 8, "Creating a Master-Detail App."

Two Approaches

The iOS SDK provides two different approaches for third-party apps to retrieve photos and videos from the Photos app. The first is to use the Assets Library framework. The second is to use the image picker controller (`UIImagePickerController`). Which approach an app uses depends largely on the needs of the app.

Assets Library

The Assets Library framework provides classes used to access photos and videos managed by the Photos app. Not only does it give third-party apps access to photos and videos, but it also provides access to metadata associated with each asset. The metadata includes information such as the type of asset, duration if the asset is a video, orientation, creation date, representation (for example, RAW and JPEG), and location information, which is available only if Location Services has been turned on for the app. Third-party applications can also store and retrieve application-specific metadata on an asset.

To access photos and videos using the Assets Library framework, you create an instance of `ALAssetsLibrary`. You can retrieve a specific asset using the method `-assetForURL:resultBlock:failureBlock:`, and you can retrieve a group of assets using `-enumerateGroupsWithTypes:usingBlock:failureBlock:`.

An asset, that is, a photo or video from the Photos app, is represented by an instance of the class `ALAsset`. The class has methods and properties for accessing metadata on the asset, making changes to the asset, retrieving the representation (of which there could be more than one), and retrieving the thumbnail of the asset.

Using the Assets Library framework is ideal when your application needs direct access to assets managed by the Photos application. But it does have one odd requirement. To retrieve a group of assets, using the `-enumerateGroupsWithTypes:using Block:failureBlock:` method, or to retrieve saved location information on an asset, Location Services must be enabled.

The Location Services requirement is odd because it leads to a confusing user experience, which is not something for which Apple is known. Imagine, if you will, that you want to create an app that displays photos and videos managed by the Photos app. Your app wants only to display the photos and videos, nothing else. It doesn't care about any of the metadata on the asset. To enumerate and display the list of available photos and videos, the user of your app must enable Location Services.

The first time the application attempts to access the assets the user is presented with a message box asking for permission to use Location Services, shown in Figure 12.1. As the message says, "This allows access to location information in photos and videos." The user of the app wants only to display photos and videos; she doesn't care about location information. She may think the same thing: "I only want to see the photos. There's no reason this app needs access to location information." So she taps **Don't Allow**.

Now it may seem that as a result of the user's action, all that has happened is that location information is not available to the app. After all, the message did say, "This allows access to location information in the photos and videos." However, as it turns out, the app will not have access to any information, including the asset itself. Yes, that's right. When Location Services is turned off, the app is not granted access to the

Figure 12.1   The Location Services prompt displayed when an app uses the Assets Library framework for the first time

photos and videos. In other words, Location Services must be turned on for any app to find and display photos and videos managed by the Photos application using the Assets Library framework. Thankfully, there is another option for third-party developers.

> **Note**
>
> My gripe with the Location Services requirement is twofold. One, Location Services should be required only if the application needs to access location information. And even then it seems odd. The location information on an asset isn't necessarily the current location of the user. It's where the user was at the time the asset was created. Still, it's my opinion that Location Services should be required only to access the location information. It should not be required to access the asset and other non-location-specific metadata found on the asset.
>
> My second gripe is with the message displayed by iOS. It is not clear. It says that Location Services is needed to allow access to location information, but in fact Location Services is required to allow access to the assets themselves. A user may not want an app to have access to location information but still have access to the photos and videos, and the message from the iOS gives the impression that this is possible, which it is not. This leads to a confusing user experience.

Image Picker Controller

The image picker controller (`UIImagePickerController`) is a specialized navigation controller that displays photos and videos managed by the Photos app. The controller allows the user to select a photo or video that is returned to the calling app. And the image picker controller allows the user to take a photo or record a video that is also returned to the calling app. Best of all, the image picker controller does not require Location Services to be turned on.

The image picker controller is ideal for apps that use the iOS-supplied user interface for taking photos and videos and choosing saved photos and videos for use within the app. The downside to using the image picker controller is that the user can take only one photo or video, or select only one photo or video, at a time. This is usually not an issue for most apps. And you can get around this limitation by leaving the image picker controller open and visible to the user. If, however, you have a need to import more than one photo or video at a time, your best option is to use the Assets Library framework, though you will be required to create your own UI.

For the PhotoWheel prototype, selecting one photo at a time is perfectly acceptable. This means that `UIImagePickerController` will work nicely. It also means that you do not have to create your own user interface for selecting photos. With the image picker controller, the UI is provided for you.

Using the Image Picker Controller

Like so many other objects in Cocoa Touch, using the image picker controller is simple and straightforward. You create an instance of `UIImagePickerController` and present it to the user. User interaction with the views presented by the image picker are managed by the controller, and the results of those interactions are reported back to your app courtesy of a delegate object that conforms to the UIImagePicker-ControllerDelegate protocol.

In Chapter 11, "Using Touch Gestures," you added a tap gesture to each photo wheel cell. Let's modify that code so that a tap on the cell will display the image picker or camera. When the user selects a photo or takes a new photo, the cell's image will be updated to display the returned photo.

While the image picker controller is simple to use, a number of changes are still needed on the DetailViewController class. For starters, when a photo wheel cell is tapped, the cell must be saved as the selected photo wheel cell. Other methods in the view controller need to know what cell is the selected one. Also, if the device has a camera, the app should ask the user from where to retrieve the photo. Does the user want to add an existing photo managed by the Photos app, or does she want to take a new photo using the camera? Once the user has selected the photo to add, the app adds it to the selected cell. That should be it for the needed changes.

Start making changes by opening *DetailViewController.m* and adding a new private declared property named selectedPhotoWheelViewCell. Its data type is a pointer to PhotoWheelViewCell. Next, modify the -cellTapped: method to save off the selected cell to the selectedPhotoWheelViewCell property. The code changes are given in Listing 12.1.

Listing 12.1   Adding the selectedPhotoWheelViewCell **Property to** DetailViewController.m

```
@interface DetailViewController ()

// Other code left out for brevity's sake.

@property (strong, nonatomic) PhotoWheelViewCell *selectedPhotoWheelViewCell;

// Other code left out for brevity's sake.

@end

@implementation DetailViewController

// Other code left out for brevity's sake.

@synthesize selectedPhotoWheelViewCell = _selectedPhotoWheelViewCell;

// Other code left out for brevity's sake.

- (void)cellTapped:(UIGestureRecognizer *)recognizer
{
    [self setSelectedPhotoWheelViewCell:(PhotoWheelViewCell *)[recognizer view]];
}
```

```
// Other code left out for brevity's sake.
```

```
@end
```

DetailViewController now knows what photo wheel cell has been selected. Next, the app should check to see if the device supports a camera or not. UIImagePickerController can help. It has the method +isSourceTypeAvailable: that is used to determine if a particular photo or video source is available.

> **Note**
>
> UIImagePickerController also has the method +isCameraDeviceAvailable:, which one might think is the correct method to call when determining if the device supports a camera. However, +isCameraDeviceAvailable: is used to determine if a camera is available on the front or rear of the device. This method can be used to determine if a camera device, regardless of location, is available, but it involves performing two checks, once for the presence of the rear camera and once for the front camera. +isSourceTypeAvailable: does this for us with a single call, which is why it's used here.

If the device has a camera, the app needs to give the user the option of taking a photo or choosing from the library managed by the Photos app. Modify the -cellTapped: method to perform this check. If the camera is available, the app will display a popup menu of choices (or actions); otherwise the app should display the image picker. For now, write stub methods for presenting the menu and image picker. The code changes are given in Listing 12.2.

Listing 12.2   Checking for a Camera on the Device

```
- (void)presentPhotoLibrary
{
    NSLog(@"%s", __PRETTY_FUNCTION__);
}


- (void)presentPhotoPickerMenu
{
    NSLog(@"%s", __PRETTY_FUNCTION__);
}


- (void)cellTapped:(UIGestureRecognizer *)recognizer
{
    [self setSelectedPhotoWheelViewCell:(PhotoWheelViewCell *)[recognizer view]];

    BOOL hasCamera =
        [UIImagePickerController
         isSourceTypeAvailable:UIImagePickerControllerSourceTypeCamera];
    if (hasCamera) {
        [self presentPhotoPickerMenu];
```

```
    } else {
       [self presentPhotoLibrary];
    }
}
```

Build and run the app, first from the iPad Simulator. Tap a photo wheel cell and take a look at the output window. You should see that -presentPhotoLibrary is called, as shown in Figure 12.2. Now run the app on a real iPad. You will see that -presentPhotoPickerMenu is called.

Using Action Sheets

Next, you need to provide the real implementation for the stubbed methods. Start with -presentPhotoPickerMenu. It will display a popup menu giving the user the choice of taking a photo or choosing an existing one from the Photos library. This means that the app needs to present a list of actions for the user to choose from, and UIActionSheet is the perfect object for the task.

UIActionSheet is used to display a list of options or actions to a user. An action sheet has an optional title and one or more buttons. Each button represents an action. An action sheet is often used to allow the user to request a specific action such as send email or print. It can also be used to ask the user for confirmation of some action such as deleting data.

On the iPhone, an action sheet typically slides up from the bottom of the screen. The action sheet is dismissed when the user taps a button, and a cancel button is usually provided so that the user can dismiss the action sheet without requesting an action.

The display of an action sheet on the iPad is different. An action sheet is displayed in a popover that appears in the center of the screen or is anchored to the view with which the user interacted to request the action sheet (for example, a button on a toolbar). A cancel button is not provided on the iPad. Instead, the user taps outside of the popover to dismiss the action sheet.

Change the implementation in -presentPhotoPickerMenu to display an action sheet. The action sheet will display two options: **Take Photo** and **Choose from Library**. DetailViewController must also be made the delegate to the action sheet. This will inform the view controller which button (or action) the user selected. The code changes are given in Listing 12.3.

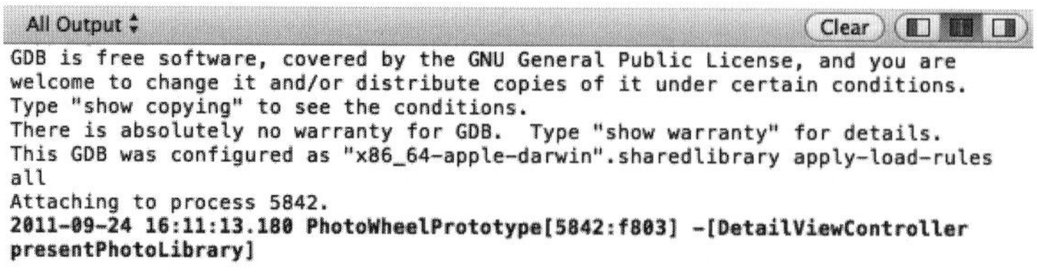

```
All Output ▾                                    ( Clear )  ▣ ▦ ▢
GDB is free software, covered by the GNU General Public License, and you are
welcome to change it and/or distribute copies of it under certain conditions.
Type "show copying" to see the conditions.
There is absolutely no warranty for GDB.  Type "show warranty" for details.
This GDB was configured as "x86_64-apple-darwin".sharedlibrary apply-load-rules
all
Attaching to process 5842.
2011-09-24 16:11:13.180 PhotoWheelPrototype[5842:f803] -[DetailViewController
presentPhotoLibrary]
```

Figure 12.2   Logged output to the output window

Listing 12.3   Adding an Action Sheet to the `DetailViewController`

```
/////////////
// DetailViewController.h

#import <UIKit/UIKit.h>
#import "WheelView.h"

@interface DetailViewController : UIViewController
<UISplitViewControllerDelegate, WheelViewDataSource, UIActionSheetDelegate>

// Other code left out for brevity's sake.

@end


/////////////
// DetailViewController.m

#import "DetailViewController.h"
#import "PhotoWheelViewCell.h"

@interface DetailViewController ()

// Other code left out for brevity's sake.

@property (strong, nonatomic) UIActionSheet *actionSheet;

// Other code left out for brevity's sake.
@end

@implementation DetailViewController

// Other code left out for brevity's sake.

@synthesize actionSheet = _actionSheet;

// Other code left out for brevity's sake.

- (void)willRotateToInterfaceOrientation:(UIInterfaceOrientation)
toInterfaceOrientation duration:(NSTimeInterval)duration
{
    if ([self actionSheet]) {
        [[self actionSheet] dismissWithClickedButtonIndex:-1 animated:YES];
    }
}
```

```objc
// Other code left out for brevity's sake.

- (void)presentCamera
{
    NSLog(@"%s", __PRETTY_FUNCTION__);
}


- (void)presentPhotoPickerMenu
{
    UIActionSheet *actionSheet = [[UIActionSheet alloc] init];
    [actionSheet setDelegate:self];
    [actionSheet addButtonWithTitle:@"Take Photo"];
    [actionSheet addButtonWithTitle:@"Choose from Library"];

    UIView *view = [self selectedPhotoWheelViewCell];
    CGRect rect = [view bounds];
    [actionSheet showFromRect:rect inView:view animated:YES];

    [self setActionSheet:actionSheet];
}

// Other code left out for brevity's sake.

#pragma mark - UIActionSheetDelegate methods

- (void)actionSheet:(UIActionSheet *)actionSheet
clickedButtonAtIndex:(NSInteger)buttonIndex
{
    switch (buttonIndex) {
        case 0:
            [self presentCamera];
            break;
        case 1:
            [self presentPhotoLibrary];
            break;
    }
}

- (void)actionSheet:(UIActionSheet *)actionSheet
didDismissWithButtonIndex:(NSInteger)buttonIndex
{
    [self setActionSheet:nil];
}

@end
```

As you can see in Listing 12.3, `UIActionSheetDelegate` is added to the list of conforming protocols for `DetailViewController`. The implementation for the `UIActionSheetDelegate` protocol methods `-actionSheet:clickedButton-AtIndex:` and `-actionSheet:didDismissWithButtonIndex:` are found in the *DetailViewController.m* implementation file. The first method, `-actionSheet:clicked-ButtonAtIndex:`, checks the `buttonIndex` value. If it is 0, the user has requested to take a photo. If it is 1, the user has requested to pick a photo from the library. This method is called each time the user taps a button in the action sheet.

Note

The `buttonIndex` value is determined based on the order in which the buttons are added to the action sheet. The first button is index 0. The second button is index 1. And so on.

The second method, `-actionSheet:didDismissWithButtonIndex:`, is called every time the action sheet is dismissed regardless of how it is dismissed (the user taps a button, the user taps outside the popover, or the action sheet is dismissed programmatically). Here the private declared property for the action sheet is set to `nil` as the reference is no longer needed.

At the top of the implementation section in Listing 12.3, you see the declaration for the private property `actionSheet` and the `@synthesize` statement. This is followed by a method that has not been discussed yet, `-willRotateToInterfaceOrientation:duration:`. This method is called when the device is rotated. The HIG recommends dismissing popovers when the device is rotated, and that is what the implementation for this method does. It checks to see if the view controller has a reference to the action sheet, and if so, it then programmatically dismisses the action sheet.

Note

Rotation support is covered in detail in Chapter 18, "Supporting Device Rotation."

The meat of the code change in Listing 12.3 is the implementation for the method `-presentPhotoPickerMenu`. This is where the action sheet is created and displayed. The method first creates a new instance of `UIActionSheet`. It sets the delegate to `self`, which is the `DetailViewController` instance. Next, two buttons are added, **Take Photo** and **Choose from Library**. Then the action sheet is displayed, and last the `actionSheet` property is set to the newly created action sheet.

`UIActionSheet` has a number of methods for displaying the action sheet. The methods, as defined in *UIActionSheet.h*, are as follows:

```
- (void)showFromToolbar:(UIToolbar *)view;
- (void)showFromTabBar:(UITabBar *)view;
- (void)showFromBarButtonItem:(UIBarButtonItem *)item
animated:(BOOL)animated __OSX_AVAILABLE_STARTING(__MAC_NA, __IPHONE_3_2);
- (void)showFromRect:(CGRect)rect inView:(UIView *)view
```

```
animated:(BOOL)animated __OSX_AVAILABLE_STARTING(__MAC_NA, __IPHONE_3_2);
- (void)showInView:(UIView *)view;
```

These methods allow the app to anchor the action sheet to specific views within the view hierarchy. To anchor the action sheet to the selected photo wheel cell, `-showFromRect:inView:animated:` is used. The `rect` is the bounds of the selected photo wheel cell, the `view` is the cell itself, and the animated flag is set to `YES` to animate the display of the action sheet.

Build and run the app, making sure to run it on your iPad; otherwise you will not see the action sheet. The action sheet, as you know, is displayed only when a camera is available, and the iPad Simulator does not have a camera. Your app should look similar to the screen shot in Figure 12.3.

Using `UIImagePickerController`

Finally, the app needs to use `UIImagePickerController` so that the user can add a photo to the photo wheel. Stub methods already exist to display the photo library and camera, `-presentPhotoLibrary` and `-presentCamera`. Let's start by adding a private property to the `DetailViewController` named `imagePickerController` that is a pointer to the type `UIImagePickerController`. Instantiate the image picker in the `initWithNibName:bundle:` method, as shown in Listing 12.4. This gives the detail view controller an image picker controller to work with.

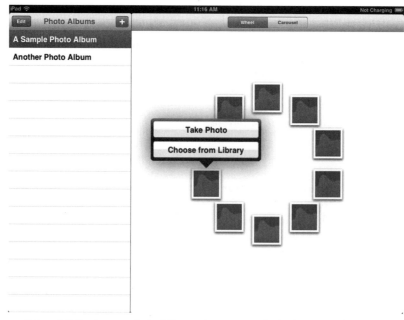

Figure 12.3   Screen shot of the prototype app displaying an action sheet

It is important to note that the UIImagePickerController delegate property expects the object to conform to two protocols: UINavigationController-Delegate and UIImagePickerControllerDelegate. DetailViewController is derived from UIView. Therefore, you must add both of these protocols to the list of protocols to which DetailViewController conforms, as shown in Listing 12.4.

Listing 12.4 **Adding** imagePickerController **to** DetailViewController

```
/////////////
// DetailViewController.h

@interface DetailViewController : UIViewController
<UISplitViewControllerDelegate, WheelViewDataSource, UIActionSheetDelegate,
UINavigationControllerDelegate, UIImagePickerControllerDelegate>

// Other code left out for brevity's sake.

@end


/////////////
// DetailViewController.m

@interface DetailViewController ()

// Other code left out for brevity's sake.

@property (strong, nonatomic) UIImagePickerController *imagePickerController;

// Other code left out for brevity's sake.

@end

@implementation DetailViewController

// Other code left out for brevity's sake.

@synthesize imagePickerController = _imagePickerController;

- (id)initWithNibName:(NSString *)nibNameOrNil bundle:(NSBundle *)nibBundleOrNil
{
    self = [super initWithNibName:nibNameOrNil bundle:nibBundleOrNil];
    if (self) {
        self.title = NSLocalizedString(@"Detail", @"Detail");

        [self setImagePickerController:[[UIImagePickerController alloc] init]];
        [[self imagePickerController] setDelegate:self];
    }
```

```
    return self;
}

// Other code left out for brevity's sake.

@end
```

Next, update the implementation for the stub methods –presentCamera and –presentPhotoLibrary. The first method displays a full-screen camera, and the second method displays the image picker in a popover controller. The property popoverController already exists for DetailViewController. It was added at the start of the project to support the display of the master view when the device orientation is portrait. The new implementations for –presentCamera and –present-PhotoLibrary are shown in Listing 12.5.

Listing 12.5 –presentCamera **and** –presentPhotoLibrary **Implementations in** *DetailViewController.m*

```
- (void)presentCamera
{
   // Display the camera.
   [[self imagePickerController]
    setSourceType:UIImagePickerControllerSourceTypeCamera];
   [self presentModalViewController:[self imagePickerController] animated:YES];
}

- (void)presentPhotoLibrary
{
   // Display assets from the Photos library only.
   [[self imagePickerController]
    setSourceType:UIImagePickerControllerSourceTypePhotoLibrary];

   UIView *view = [self selectedPhotoWheelViewCell];
   CGRect rect = [view bounds];

   UIPopoverController *newPopoverController =
      [[UIPopoverController alloc]
        initWithContentViewController:[self imagePickerController]];
   [newPopoverController presentPopoverFromRect:rect inView:view
                      permittedArrowDirections:UIPopoverArrowDirectionAny
                                        animated:YES];
   [self setMasterPopoverController:newPopoverController];
}
```

To display the camera, the image picker controller's source type is set to UIImage-PickerControllerSourceTypeCamera. To display the camera full-screen, the image picker controller is presented as a modal view controller, which by default displays full-screen.

The code for displaying the Photos library isn't much different from other code you have seen. The image picker controller's source type is set to UIImagePicker-ControllerSourceTypePhotoLibrary. Local variable references to the selected photo wheel view cell and its bounds rect are created and are used to anchor the popover to the cell, much as the action sheet was anchored earlier in the code. A new popover controller is created and presented to the user. And last, the popover controller reference is stored in the popoverController property on the DetailViewController.

The detail view controller needs to do one last thing. It must respond to the UIImagePickerControllerDelegate method -imagePickerController:didFinishPickingMediaWithInfo:, as shown in Listing 12.6. This method is called after the user selects a new photo from the camera or from the Photos library. It receives an NSDictionary object named info, which contains the selected image, among other things. The image reference is retrieved from the dictionary and sent to the selected photo wheel view cell for display.

> **Note**
>
> To see the entire contents of the NSDictionary info, set a breakpoint in the -imagePickerController:didFinishPickingMediaWithInfo: method and type "po info" in the output console window. For more debugging tricks, read Chapter 25, "Debugging."

Listing 12.6 Responding to the UIImagePickerController Delegate Method

```
#pragma mark - UIImagePickerControllerDelegate methods

- (void)imagePickerController:(UIImagePickerController *)picker
didFinishPickingMediaWithInfo:(NSDictionary *)info
{
    // Dismiss the popover controller if available;
    // otherwise dismiss the camera view.
    if ([self masterPopoverController]) {
        [[self masterPopoverController] dismissPopoverAnimated:YES];
        [self setMasterPopoverController:nil];
    } else {
        [self dismissModalViewControllerAnimated:YES];
    }

    // Retrieve and display the image.
    UIImage *image = [info objectForKey:UIImagePickerControllerOriginalImage];
    [[self selectedPhotoWheelViewCell] setImage:image];
}
```

Figure 12.4   Screen shot of the PhotoWheelPrototype app with the image
picker controller

Build and run the app to see the image picker in action, shown in Figure 12.4. You should run it on both an iPad and in the iPad Simulator. Remember that the action sheet is not displayed when the app is run on the simulator because the simulator does not have a camera device. You can choose the camera or Photos library only when the app is run on a real iPad.

Congratulations! Your prototype app now supports adding photos.

> **Note**
>
> You may notice that some photos look a little funny when scaled down to thumbnail size in the photo wheel. A better approach for scaling images is covered in Chapter 13, "Data Persistence."

> **Note**
>
> A quick and easy way to save photos to the Photos app used in the iPad Simulator is to drag and drop images from your desktop environment onto Mobile Safari running in the simulator. Then touch and hold (click and hold since you are using the simulator) the image displayed in Safari until the popup menu is displayed. This menu has an option to **Save Image**. Select this option to save the photo to the Photos app library.

Saving to the Camera Roll

When the camera is used to take a photo, the photo is not automatically saved to the Photos app's camera roll. It's up to the app to save the photo. Your app can save a photo to the camera roll by calling the function `UIImageWriteToSavedPhotosAlbum()`.

```
void UIImageWriteToSavedPhotosAlbum (
    UIImage  *image,
    id       completionTarget,
    SEL      completionSelector,
    void     *contextInfo
);
```

The four parameters are

- **image**: The image to save to the camera roll
- **completionTarget (optional)**: The object whose selector is called after the image has been saved to the camera roll
- **completionSelector (optional)**: The selector called on the completion-Target after the image has been saved to the camera roll
- **contextInfo (optional)**: A pointer to any context data you wish to pass to the completion selector

Note

`UIImageWriteToSavedPhotosAlbum()` will save the photo to the Photo Stream if Photo Streaming has been enabled on the device.

Go ahead and modify `imagePickerController:didFinishPickingMedia-WithInfo:` to use the `UIImageWriteToSavedPhotosAlbum` function and save new photos captured with the camera to the camera roll. The updated source code is given in Listing 12.7.

Listing 12.7   Modification to Save the Photo to the Camera Roll

```
- (void)imagePickerController:(UIImagePickerController *)picker
didFinishPickingMediaWithInfo:(NSDictionary *)info{
    // If the popover controller is available,
    // assume the photo is selected from the library
    // and not from the camera.
    BOOL takenWithCamera = ([self popoverController] == nil);

    // Dismiss the popover controller if available;
    // otherwise dismiss the camera view.
    if ([self popoverController]) {
        [[self popoverController] dismissPopoverAnimated:YES];
        [self setPopoverController:nil];
```

```
  } else {
    [self dismissModalViewControllerAnimated:YES];
  }

  // Retrieve and display the image.
  UIImage *image = [info objectForKey:UIImagePickerControllerOriginalImage];
  [[self selectedPhotoWheelViewCell] setImage:image];

  if (takenWithCamera) {
    UIImageWriteToSavedPhotosAlbum(image, nil, nil, nil);
  }
}
```

Build and run the app. Test the change and make sure that photos captured with the camera are saved to the camera roll.

Summary

The prototype app now supports adding photos to a photo wheel, and you have hands-on experience with the image picker controller. You also learned about action sheets and how to use them. And you got a glimpse of rotation handling.

The prototype app has proven itself useful, allowing you to explore different iOS concepts that will be used in the final PhotoWheel app. But there is one last concept that must be explored before you are ready to write the "real" app. That concept is data persistence, which is covered in the next chapter.

Exercises

1. Add more action items to the action sheet. Create stub methods that call NSLog() to handle each new action you add.

2. Remove the rotation handling code. Observe the side effects when the action sheet is displayed and the device is rotated.

13

Data Persistence

In the preceding chapter we added the ability for the prototype app to take photos with the device cameras. Now that photos are coming into the app, it's time to develop a system for saving and managing them. In this chapter we'll discuss what kind of data the app will deal with and how to manage and save it effectively. This chapter will implement the Model part of the Model-View-Controller design pattern.

The Data Model

In order to effectively build the data model, you need to have a clear idea of what kind of data you'll be working with and how the various types of data relate to each other. For this app there are two types of data: photos and photo albums.

Photos

Since this app arranges photos in albums, the most obvious data item is the original photo itself, straight from the device camera. You'll save and display the original photo, so the photo will be part of the data model.

But think about how the photos will actually be used in the app. When the user is viewing an album, many photos could be on the screen at the same time. Original photos on iPad can be fairly large data objects, even when compressed as JPEGs. To avoid running out of memory, you'll probably want to use thumbnail-size versions of the photo in album views. You might need to have other sizes in other situations. When planning the model, plan for multiple photo sizes, including the original and one or more scaled versions.

You probably want to store some metadata with each photo, too—the date the photo was taken, for example, or the location.

Finally, each photo will belong to a photo album. The photo data in the model needs to include a reference or relationship of some kind to the album that contains the photo, so that when working with a photo you can find other photos in the album.

Photo Albums

The primary requirement for the photo album is that it must track the photos that the album contains. This is the reverse of the relationship described for photos. Each photo album has a relationship to some number of photos that are the contents of the album. The photo album should also have a thumbnail property or relationship to a separate photo thumbnail object that can be used when displaying a collection of albums.

Albums will have metadata of their own, such as the album name and the date the album was created.

Thinking Ahead

PhotoWheelPrototype has a simple data model. But apps have a way of growing in unexpected ways, both before the initial release and in features added in later updates. When planning your data model, it's important to plan ahead, to design a model that can be adapted and improved as new requirements develop. Initially it's tempting to design the simplest possible model that works. But doing this can constrain future development if the model isn't flexible or robust enough to be adapted to new requirements. This chapter will cover two different approaches, one relatively simple but limited, and one that is not quite so simple but offers much more power and flexibility.

Building the Model with Property Lists

Based on what we have covered so far, it seems that a simple way to handle the data model would be to manage and store the data in a property list. Basic data types such as strings and arrays cover the requirements, so it is a convenient approach at this stage.

As you read this section, keep in mind that although we are discussing property list techniques, we won't be using this technique in later chapters in the book. It is useful to know how to deal with property lists and to see more than one approach to dealing with data management. If you're building the app as you read the book, you may want to just read this section and continue building the app later on in the section Building the Model with Core Data. Both this section and the later one build on code from the previous chapter, so if you want to work through both, consider making a second copy of the code you have so far.

What Is a Property List?

Property lists are generic data structures often used in Cocoa Touch. A property list is any instance of NSString, NSData, NSNumber, NSDate, or any collection of those objects into an NSArray or NSDictionary. Arrays and dictionaries can recursively contain other arrays or dictionaries to whatever depth is needed. An extra requirement is that if any NSDictionary objects appear, the dictionary keys must be NSStrings. It is possible to use NSDictionary with nonstring keys, but those dictionaries wouldn't meet the definition of a property list.

The advantage of property lists is that they are very easy to read from and write to files. NSDictionary, NSArray, NSString, and NSData all define convenience methods that can initialize an instance from a file or write one to a file in a single line of code.

When property lists are saved, they are written in an undocumented binary format. There are a couple of other property list file formats, one using XML and one using a text format that is almost but not quite the same as JSON. You can use any of these formats when instantiating property list objects.

Setting Up the Data Model

You don't need any special model classes to use property lists. You can't read and write custom classes to property list files anyway. The model flows directly from the definitions in the model requirements. Main storage will be an array of photo albums, each album will be an array of photos and an album name, and each photo will be a dictionary of properties for a specific photo.

What would be useful are defined keys for use in the dictionaries. Since you will need to use these in multiple places in the app, they will go in a new file that can be imported wherever it is needed. Create a new class in Xcode, using the Objective-C class template, and name it GlobalPhotoKeys. Xcode will create a header file and an implementation file. This isn't really going to be a class, but using that template is an easy way to create both header and implementation files in one step. Delete the contents of both files, but keep the files.

Add the key declarations from Listing 13.1 to *GlobalPhotoKeys.h*. These declare dictionary keys for both the photo albums and the photos in the albums, as well as the file name where the photo album will be stored. They are declared extern, which means the definitions will appear elsewhere.

Listing 13.1   Key Declarations for *GlobalPhotoKeys.h*

```
// Keys for photo albums
extern NSString *kPhotoAlbumNameKey;
extern NSString *kPhotoAlbumDateAddedKey;
extern NSString *kPhotoAlbumPhotosKey;

// File name where the photo album is stored
extern NSString *kPhotoAlbumFilename;

// Keys for individual photos
extern NSString *kPhotoDataKey;
extern NSString *kPhotoDateAddedKey;
extern NSString *kPhotoFilenameKey;

// Notification that a new photo has been added and the album needs to be saved
extern NSString *kPhotoAlbumSaveNotification;
```

The definitions of these keys will go in *GlobalPhotoKeys.m* (Listing 13.2). All declarations from the header file are mirrored here with their defined values.

Listing 13.2   **Definitions in** *GlobalPhotoKeys.m*

```
// Keys for photo albums
const NSString *kPhotoAlbumNameKey = @"name";
const NSString *kPhotoAlbumDateAddedKey = @"dateAdded";
const NSString *kPhotoAlbumPhotosKey = @"photos";

// File name where the photo album is stored
const NSString *kPhotoAlbumFilename = @"photoAlbums.plist";

// Keys for individual photos
const NSString *kPhotoDataKey = @"photoData";
const NSString *kPhotoDateAddedKey = @"dateAdded";
const NSString *kPhotoFilenameKey = @"filename";

const NSString *kPhotoAlbumSaveNotification = @"save albums notification";
```

Reading and Saving Photo Albums

Now you're ready to start working with photo albums. You'll do this in `Master-ViewController`. First, edit *MasterViewController.h* and change the type of the `data` property from `NSMutableOrderedSet` to `NSMutableArray`. These classes work similarly, but `NSMutableOrderedSet` is not a property list type so it can't be used here. Also, remove the code in `-viewDidLoad` that initializes `data`. You'll add code later on to initialize it in a different way.

Now add the code from Listing 13.3 to the top of *MasterViewController.m*.

Listing 13.3   **Top-Level Code to Add to** *MasterViewController.m*

```
#import "GlobalPhotoKeys.h"

@interface MasterViewController ()
@property (readwrite, assign) NSUInteger currentAlbumIndex;
@end
```

The first line just imports the keys we declared earlier. The following code uses a class extension to declare `currentAlbumIndex`. This property will be used to keep track of the album being displayed in the detail view, so that `MasterView-Controller` can show the user which one is currently selected. Make sure to add a `@synthesize` statement for `currentAlbumIndex`.

Next come several new methods for reading and writing photo albums. Add the code from Listing 13.4 to *MasterViewController.m*. Make sure to put this code before `-viewDidLoad` in the file, or else add method declarations to the class extension. Otherwise the compiler won't know about them when you call them.

Listing 13.4   **Methods to Manage Photo Albums in** *MasterViewController.m*

```objc
#pragma mark - Read and save photo albums
- (NSURL *)photoAlbumPath
{
   NSURL *documentsDirectory = [[[NSFileManager defaultManager]
         URLsForDirectory:NSDocumentDirectory
         inDomains:NSUserDomainMask]
      lastObject];
   NSURL *photoAlbumPath = [documentsDirectory
      URLByAppendingPathComponent:(NSString *)kPhotoAlbumFilename];
   return photoAlbumPath;
}


- (NSMutableDictionary *)newPhotoAlbumWithName:(NSString *)albumName
{
   NSMutableDictionary *newAlbum = [NSMutableDictionary dictionary];
   [newAlbum setObject:albumName forKey:kPhotoAlbumNameKey];
   [newAlbum setObject:[NSDate date] forKey:kPhotoAlbumDateAddedKey];
   NSMutableArray *photos = [NSMutableArray array];
   for (NSUInteger index=0; index<10; index++) {
       [photos addObject:[NSDictionary dictionary]];
   }
   [newAlbum setObject:photos forKey:kPhotoAlbumPhotosKey];
   return newAlbum;
}


- (void)savePhotoAlbum
{
   [[self data] writeToURL:[self photoAlbumPath] atomically:YES];
}


- (void)readSavedPhotoAlbums
{
   NSMutableArray *savedAlbums = nil;

   NSData *photoAlbumData = [NSData dataWithContentsOfURL:[self photoAlbumPath]];
   if (photoAlbumData != nil) {
      NSMutableArray *albums = [NSPropertyListSerialization
         propertyListWithData:photoAlbumData
         options:NSPropertyListMutableContainers
         format:nil
         error:nil];
      [self setData:albums];
   } else {
      savedAlbums = [NSMutableArray array];
      // Create an initial album
      [savedAlbums addObject:[self newPhotoAlbumWithName:@"First album"]];
```

```
        [self setData:savedAlbums];
        [self savePhotoAlbum];
    }
}

- (void)photoAlbumSaveNeeded:(NSNotification *)notification
{
    [self savePhotoAlbum];
}
```

The first of these methods, photoAlbumPath, is a convenience method to provide the full path to the photo album property list file as a file URL. It does this by looking up the app's documents directory and appending the album file name (declared earlier in *GlobalPhotoKeys.h*). This method doesn't do anything with albums directly, but it is used by other methods that do.

The next method, newPhotoAlbumWithName, is a convenience method for creating a new photo album. The code creates a mutable dictionary to hold the album and sets the creation date using kPhotoAlbumNameKey. It also sets the album's name to the value of the incoming albumName argument. The for loop creates an array of empty photo entries. This is where photo information will go once the user starts adding photos. The code creates these placeholders so that photos can be added at any index instead of starting at index 0 and growing from there.

The next two methods handle the actual reading and writing of photo albums. The first, savePhotoAlbums, is pretty simple. Photo albums will be kept in Master-ViewController's data property. To save a photo album, it looks up the location using the photoAlbumPath method and then writes the property list from memory to that file.

Reading photo albums may be more complex than you had expected. The first line of readSavedPhotoAlbums just reverses the save process, reading the property list from the save location. But it is stored as an instance of NSData instead of NSMutableData. Why is this? When Cocoa reads property lists from files, it always creates immutable data structures. You might save an NSMutableDictionary, but what comes back when you read the file is an NSDictionary. But photo albums need to be editable so that new photos can be added, and the list of albums also needs to be editable. That means that mutable dictionaries and arrays are needed so that entries can be added and replaced as needed.

To manage this, the code makes use of NSPropertyListSerialization. This class provides several utility methods that are useful when dealing with property lists. In this case the code uses it to convert the immutable data structure read from the photo album file into one with mutable container objects. The NSPropertyList-MutableContainers option flag means that the returned data structure will have mutable arrays instead of immutable ones.

If no albums exist yet, readSavedPhotoAlbums creates an empty album so that an album will be available the first time the app runs.

Finally, the method `photoAlbumSaveNeeded` is set up to receive notifications that a new photo has been added to an album, indicating that the current photo album needs to be saved. This notification is configured in `viewDidLoad`. Listing 13.5 shows the new version of `viewDidLoad`.

Listing 13.5   New Version of `MasterViewController`'s `viewDidLoad`

```
- (void)viewDidLoad
{
    [super viewDidLoad];
    // Do any additional setup after loading the view, typically from a nib.

    self.title = NSLocalizedString(@"Photo Albums", @"Photo albums title");

    UIBarButtonItem *addButton = [[UIBarButtonItem alloc]
            initWithBarButtonSystemItem:UIBarButtonSystemItemAdd
                                 target:self
                                 action:@selector(add:)];
    [[self navigationItem] setRightBarButtonItem:addButton];
    [[self navigationItem] setLeftBarButtonItem:[self editButtonItem]];

    [self readSavedPhotoAlbums];

    [[self detailViewController] setPhotoAlbum:[[self data] objectAtIndex:0]];

    [[NSNotificationCenter defaultCenter] addObserver:self
        selector:@selector(photoAlbumSaveNeeded:)
        name:kPhotoAlbumSaveNotification
        object:[self detailViewController]];
}
```

The first of the highlighted lines calls the `readSavedPhotoAlbums` method we set up earlier. The next line tells the detail view controller which album is currently displayed. You haven't added anything to `DetailViewController` to handle this yet, but you will. When the app starts up, the code always passes the first album found in the property list file to the detail view controller.

The last line configures an `NSNotification` observer. `NSNotifications` are a convenient way for one part of an app to send a global signal of some kind, which may be received by one or more observers. The four arguments configure a notification observer as follows:

If [self detailViewController] posts a notification

...and that notification is named kPhotoAlbumSaveNotification

...then call a method named photoAlbumSaveNeeded:

...and call this method on self.

If you compare the previous chapter's version of `viewDidLoad` to the implementation of `newPhotoAlbumWithName:`, you'll notice that the structure of the `data` array has changed. Instead of just storing a list of names, it now stores a list of dictionaries, with the name stored as one of the dictionary keys. Because of this a few other changes are needed so that the album list table view will work. In `-tableView:cellForRowAtIndexPath:`, change the cell configuration code to look like Listing 13.6. This change looks up the album dictionary in `[self data]`, gets the value for its `kPhotoAlbumNameKey` key, and uses that in the table. It also uses the value of `currentAlbumIndex` to display a check mark next to the currently selected album.

Listing 13.6   **Updated Table Cell Code in** *MasterViewController.m*

```
// Configure the cell.
NSDictionary *album = [[self data] objectAtIndex:[indexPath row]];
[[cell textLabel] setText:[album objectForKey:kPhotoAlbumNameKey]];

if ([indexPath row] == [self currentAlbumIndex]) {
   [cell setAccessoryType:UITableViewCellAccessoryCheckmark];
} else {
   [cell setAccessoryType:UITableViewCellAccessoryNone];
}
```

Make a similar change in `-tableView:accessoryButtonTappedForRowWithIndexPath:`, so that instead of looking up the album name directly in the data array, you look up the name in the album's dictionary.

When the user selects a new photo album in the album list, the app needs to tell the detail view controller about the change so that it can update its display. This is handled by adding a single line to the `-tableView:didSelectRowAtIndexPath:` method:

```
[[self detailViewController]
   setPhotoAlbum:[[self data] objectAtIndex:[indexPath row]]];
```

Finally, the callback from `NameEditorViewController` needs some changes to handle the property list format. Make the method look like Listing 13.7.

Listing 13.7   **Photo Album Name Editor Callback**

```
- (void)nameEditorViewControllerDidFinish:(NameEditorViewController *)controller
{
   NSString *newName = [[controller nameTextField] text];
   if (newName && [newName length] > 0) {
      if ([controller isEditing]) {
         NSMutableDictionary *photoAlbum = [[self data]
            objectAtIndex:[[controller indexPath] row]];
         [photoAlbum setObject:newName forKey:kPhotoAlbumNameKey];
      } else {
         [[self data] addObject:[self newPhotoAlbumWithName:newName]];
      }
```

```
        [self savePhotoAlbum];
        [[self tableView] reloadData];
    }
}
```

If the controller is editing an album name, the new code looks up the dictionary for the album and replaces the value for its kPhotoAlbumNameKey. If the controller is not editing an album name, the new code creates a new album using the requested name, using the -newPhotoAlbumWithName: method declared earlier. In either case the code calls savePhotoAlbum to write the changes to the property list file.

Adding New Photos to an Album

Now that you're managing photo albums, it's time to get some pictures into those albums. Albums will be displayed by DetailViewController, which will also handle the process of taking new photos. So the first thing you need to do is add a way for DetailViewController to know what album is selected. First, add a new property to DetailViewController to store a reference to the album. Add this to *DetailViewController.h*:

```
@property (strong, nonatomic) NSMutableDictionary *photoAlbum;
```

Also add a @synthesize statement for this property in *DetailViewController.m*.

Now DetailViewController can keep a reference to a photo album. You set that reference earlier in Listing 13.5, on the line that calls -setPhotoAlbum:.

Next, fill in MasterViewController's implementation of -tableView:did-SelectRowAtIndexPath: so that when the user taps on a new album, DetailView-Controller will know that the selected album has changed (Listing 13.8).

Listing 13.8 **Changing the Selected Album**

```
- (void)tableView:(UITableView *)tableView
didSelectRowAtIndexPath:(NSIndexPath *)indexPath
{
    NSIndexPath *oldCurrentAlbumIndexPath =
        [NSIndexPath indexPathForRow:[self currentAlbumIndex] inSection:0];
    [self setCurrentAlbumIndex:[indexPath row]];
    [tableView reloadRowsAtIndexPaths:
        [NSArray arrayWithObjects:indexPath, oldCurrentAlbumIndexPath, nil]
        withRowAnimation:UITableViewRowAnimationNone];

    [[self detailViewController]
        setPhotoAlbum:[[self data] objectAtIndex:[indexPath row]]];
}
```

The first part of this code handles updating the current album index and reloading data in the table view to show the new selection. It saves the old selected index in an

NSIndexPath and then updates the selection by setting a new value for current-AlbumIndex. Then the method tells the table view to reload data at both the previous and new selection values. This will lead to calls to -tableView:cellForRowAt-IndexPath: for both of those index paths, and that will remove the check mark at the old selected row and add one at the new selection. Finally, the code tells detail-ViewController about the new selection, so that it can update its display.

Getting new photos from the camera or the device library works as in earlier chapters. What is new here is that the incoming photo will be added to the current album at an index corresponding to the cell tapped by the user. To track the tapped cell you'll add a property in DetailViewController called selectedWheelViewCellIndex. It is just an integer that saves the index of the thumbnail view the user tapped on. Add the declaration in the class extension at the top of *DetailViewController.m*:

```
@property (assign, nonatomic) NSUInteger selectedWheelViewCellIndex;
```

Also add a @synthesize statement for this property. In the cellTapped method, add a line to set the value of this property to the index of the tapped cell (Listing 13.9).

Listing 13.9   Updated Version of *DetailViewController.m*'s cellTapped: **Method**

```
- (void)cellTapped:(UIGestureRecognizer *)recognizer
{
    [self setSelectedPhotoWheelViewCell:
        (PhotoWheelViewCell *)[recognizer view]];
    [self setSelectedWheelViewCellIndex:
        [[self data] indexOfObject:[self selectedPhotoWheelViewCell]]];

    BOOL hasCamera =
    [UIImagePickerController
     isSourceTypeAvailable:UIImagePickerControllerSourceTypeCamera];
    if (hasCamera) {
        [self presentPhotoPickerMenu];
    } else {
        [self presentPhotoLibrary];
    }
}
```

The highlighted line looks up the index of the selected cell view in the data array and saves that value for later use.

When the user selects a photo, the app will receive it in a UIIpagePicker-Controller delegate callback, just as before. You'll need to add the incoming picture to the current album. The new implementation of this method is shown in Listing 13.10. This method makes use of keys declared in *GlobalPhotoKeys.h*, so make sure to import that header file at the top of *DetailViewController.m*.

Listing 13.10   **Adding New Photos to the Photo Album**

```
- (void)imagePickerController:(UIImagePickerController *)picker
    didFinishPickingMediaWithInfo:(NSDictionary *)info
{
    // If the popover controller is available,
    // assume the photo is selected from the library
    // and not from the camera.
    BOOL takenWithCamera = ([self popoverController] == nil);

    // Dismiss the popover controller if available,
    // otherwise dismiss the camera view.
    if ([self masterPopoverController]) {
        [[self masterPopoverController] dismissPopoverAnimated:YES];
        [self setMasterPopoverController:nil];
    } else {
        [self dismissModalViewControllerAnimated:YES];
    }

    UIImage *image = [info objectForKey:UIImagePickerControllerOriginalImage];
    [self.selectedPhotoWheelViewCell setImage:image];

    NSData *photoData = UIImageJPEGRepresentation(image, 0.8);

    NSString *photoFilename = [[self uuidString]
        stringByAppendingPathExtension:@"jpg"];
    [photoData writeToURL:
            [[self documentsDirectory]
                URLByAppendingPathComponent:photoFilename]
        atomically:YES];

    NSMutableDictionary *newPhotoEntry = [NSMutableDictionary dictionary];
    [newPhotoEntry setObject:[NSDate date] forKey:kPhotoDateAddedKey];
    [newPhotoEntry setObject:photoFilename forKey:kPhotoFilenameKey];

    NSMutableArray *photos = [[self photoAlbum]
        objectForKey:kPhotoAlbumPhotosKey];
    [photos replaceObjectAtIndex:[self selectedWheelViewCellIndex]
        withObject:newPhotoEntry];

    [[NSNotificationCenter defaultCenter]
        postNotificationName:kPhotoAlbumSaveNotification
        object:self];

    if (takenWithCamera) {
        UIImageWriteToSavedPhotosAlbum(image, nil, nil, nil);
    }
}
```

Some of this is unchanged from what you have seen before. The new code is shown in boldface text.

To save the image, the new code converts the incoming UIImage object to a JPEG using the utility method UIImageJPEGRepresentation. There is a similar method to convert a UIImage to PNG format, but JPEG is usually better for photos. The first argument to this function is a UIImage containing the new photo, and the second is the JPEG compression factor. Compression ranges from 1.0 for best quality to 0.0 for worst. This gives you an NSData object containing the JPEG data.

The code saves the photo data to a file rather than keeping it in the property list. That is better for memory management, since the entire property list is in memory. Writing the photo data to a file means it won't get loaded except when it is actually needed instead of staying in memory all the time. It doesn't actually matter what the file name is so long as it is something unique that the app can keep track of. In this case the file name is a UUID, a universally unique ID. The UUID is obtained using the uuidString method, which returns a string that is guaranteed to be unique. The image data is saved in a file named from the UUID, in the app's documents directory. The code finds the documents directory using a utility method called -documents-Directory. The code for these two methods is shown in Listing 13.11. You need to add this code to the file *DetailViewController.m*.

Listing 13.11   Helper Methods Used When Saving a Photo to the File System

```
- (NSString *)uuidString
{
   CFUUIDRef uuid = CFUUIDCreate(kCFAllocatorDefault);
   CFStringRef uuidCFString = CFUUIDCreateString(kCFAllocatorDefault, uuid);
   NSString *uuidString = [(__bridge NSString *)uuidCFString copy];
   CFRelease(uuid);
   CFRelease(uuidCFString);
   return uuidString;
}


- (NSURL *)documentsDirectory
{
   NSFileManager *fm = [NSFileManager defaultManager];
   NSArray *urls = [fm URLsForDirectory:NSDocumentDirectory
                               inDomains:NSUserDomainMask];
   return [urls lastObject];
}
```

Next, the code creates a new dictionary entry to store the new photo. Two values are stored in the dictionary, one with the current time and date to record when the photo was added, and one containing the image file name just created. Once this new dictionary has been created, it is inserted into the current photo album at the selected cell index you saved previously. Finally, the code posts the kPhotoAlbumDidSaveNotification, so that `MasterViewController` will know that a new photo has been added and can save the new information.

Displaying Photos in an Album

Now that you have photo albums that actually contain photos, how are you going to get them onto the wheel view so that the user can see them? When new photos are added, they are displayed immediately by the `UIImagePickerController` delegate method discussed with Listing 13.10. What about when the user selects a new album?

`DetailViewController` needs to update the wheel contents anytime a new photo album is selected, so it makes sense to create a custom setter method for the photo album and perform this update there. That way the update happens immediately when the new album is chosen. Add this setter method to `DetailViewController` (Listing 13.12).

Listing 13.12   **Updating the Wheel View When a New Photo Album Is Selected**

```
- (void)setPhotoAlbum:(NSMutableDictionary *)photoAlbum
{
   photoAlbum_ = photoAlbum;

   UIImage *defaultPhoto = [UIImage imageNamed:@"defaultPhoto.png"];
   for (NSUInteger index=0; index<10; index++) {
      PhotoWheelViewCell *nub = [[self data] objectAtIndex:index];
      NSDictionary *photoInfo = [[[self photoAlbum]
            objectForKey:kPhotoAlbumPhotosKey]
         objectAtIndex:index];
      NSString *photoFilename = [photoInfo objectForKey:kPhotoFilenameKey];
      NSData *imageData;
      if (photoFilename != nil) {
         imageData = [NSData dataWithContentsOfURL:
            [[self documentsDirectory]
               URLByAppendingPathComponent:photoFilename]];
      } else {
         imageData = nil;
      }
      if (imageData != nil) {
         [nub setImage:[UIImage imageWithData:imageData]];
      } else {
         [nub setImage:defaultPhoto];
      }
   }
}
```

The first line in this method handles the actual setting needed by this setter method by assigning the incoming object to an instance variable. The rest of the code runs through the album one item at a time and updates the wheel view for each entry in the album. In the `for` loop the code finds both the cell view and the entry in the photo album corresponding to the index, and then it tries to find a photo file from the album entry. If it finds a photo file, the code loads the JPEG data into `imageData`. Otherwise it sets `imageData` to `nil` to indicate that no image was found.

In the bottom part of the loop the code checks to see if any image data was found. If so, it creates a `UIImage` for the photo and displays that in the cell. If not, it uses a default placeholder image indicating that no photo exists for that cell.

With these changes the app is now ready for use, at least as a prototype. Users can create and delete albums and add photos to albums. There are some improvements that would be nice to make, though.

At this point the photo album doesn't have a "key" photo that could be used when displaying a collection of albums. There are a couple of ways to add that. One would be to create a separate entry in the album dictionary and duplicate the photo informa-tion. Duplicating data like that is always kind of ugly. Also, the app would need to be careful about maintaining the key photo if the user were to delete or replace that photo. It would be necessary to check the duplicate entry and update or replace it. A different approach would be to add a "key" Boolean attribute to each photo and run through the list of photos to locate the key photo. That is also undesirable, since it means traversing a list to locate an item instead of just looking it up directly.

The property list approach is limited in other areas. In a future version of the app you might decide to implement undo behavior, or to give users the option to sort pho-tos by date instead of keeping them in the same order. These improvements are cer-tainly possible with property lists, but the apparent simplicity of this data model will quickly be erased by the challenges posed by sorting, undo, and other new features. Property lists are simple to begin but often become brittle and awkward in anything but the simplest of applications.

Building the Model with Core Data

Saving application data in property lists is certainly convenient, but as an applica-tion's data gets larger or more complex, it can become awkward. Things like keeping memory use under control and managing relationships get increasingly difficult as the data set grows. There are many ways of dealing with this, and many developers have devised their own schemes. Apple provides a framework called Core Data which is designed to handle these tasks and many others for you. Core Data can seem daunt-ing at first, but its principles and the techniques for using it are easy to learn and well worth the effort of doing so.

> **Note**
>
> This chapter provides a basic introduction to Core Data. For more detailed information, see *Core Data for iOS* by Tim Isted and Tom Harrington (Addison-Wesley, 2011).

What Is Core Data?

Core Data is designed to be an object store for your model object. Using Core Data, you read and write model objects directly, without needing to translate between your model objects and the file format. The purpose of Core Data is to provide a persistent data store that can handle whatever type of objects your app uses.

Details of how the objects are stored are mostly irrelevant, leaving you to focus on using those objects in your app. You may have heard that Core Data can use SQLite to store data, but that is an implementation detail. Core Data is not simply an Objective-C wrapper on SQLite, and although it scales to very large data sets, it is not designed to be used as a database. Core Data can also use other, nondatabase formats to store data. This is why the term *data store* is intentionally vague. It refers to the means used to store data in a persistent manner, but Core Data isn't tied to a specific means. You can even create your own if you need to.

Core Data has the following advantages:

- It can reduce memory usage. Core Data loads only the objects you request. If your data set contains millions of objects but you need to work with only a few, only those few will be loaded into memory. This makes it possible to deal with data sets that are larger than available memory.
- Relationships are managed automatically. If two objects have a relationship, you define this using the same syntax as you would to set a property value.
- Core Data provides a rich system of predicates that can be used to search your data set for objects of interest.
- Objects can be automatically sorted when you look them up.
- It has optional data validation, to enforce rules defining acceptable values for properties.
- It has automatic undo management.

Managed Objects and Entity Descriptions

When using Core Data, you'll be using managed objects as your model. A managed object is an instance of `NSManagedObject` or of a custom subclass of `NSManaged-Object`. It contains your model data. Core Data manages it, which means that Core Data handles creating it, maintaining relationships with other objects, saving changed property values, and other important tasks. Managed objects are read from and saved to data stores. Normally your model objects would subclass `NSObject` or some other Foundation class like `NSDictionary`, but with Core Data you must use `NSManagedObject`.

A managed object makes use of a related object called its entity description object. An entity description is an instance of `NSEntityDescription`. Entity descriptions contain definitions of all of the properties and relationships of a managed object, as well as optional extra details such as default values and validation rules. An entity description is roughly comparable to a table definition in a database, while a managed object is roughly comparable to a single entry in the table. Entity descriptions are configured in the managed object model, which defines all the entities available in the data store. You don't usually use entity description objects directly in code; instead, you create them in Xcode.

When using Core Data, you'll start by creating entity descriptions for any model objects you need. Xcode provides a handy graph-based utility for doing this. Once you have an entity description, you can start creating managed objects defined by it.

You can work with instances of NSManagedObject, but it is usually more convenient to use custom subclasses that correspond to your model objects. The advantage is that these subclasses can add methods to implement any model-specific behaviors you might need and can provide accessor methods for your model properties. A plain NSManagedObject won't have custom accessor methods, so instead you must use key-value coding (KVC) to access property values. For example, if you have an Employee entity with a name property, you would set and retrieve the employee name on an NSManagedObject instance like this:

```
NSManagedObject *newEmployee = // Defined elsewhere
[newEmployee setValue:@"John Smith" forKey:@"name"];
NSString *employeeName = [newEmployee valueForKey:@"name"];
```

That's fine and it works, but it doesn't let the compiler provide type checking to make sure that you are actually assigning a string value for the name property. It also can't verify that you spelled "name" correctly. What's more, since newEmployee is declared as an instance of a generic class, it may not be immediately obvious what entity it is intended to use.

If you instead had an Employee class that subclassed NSManagedObject and provided custom accessor methods, the preceding code could be replaced with

```
Employee *newEmployee = // Defined elsewhere
[newEmployee setName:@"John Smith"];
NSString *employeeName = [newEmployee name];
```

That's a lot clearer and less error-prone.

Xcode can automatically generate NSManagedObject subclasses with property-specific accessor methods based on entity definitions.

When you load an NSManagedObject from a data store, it is normally created as a *fault* object. Fault objects are placeholders, which have the identity of a specific managed object but none of its data. The properties are loaded—or, in Core Data terminology, the fault fires—on demand when you access a property. That means that they use hardly any memory at all until you directly access their properties.

Managed Object Contexts

Your main access point for getting and saving managed objects is the managed object context, an instance of NSManagedObjectContext. When you need to get your model objects, you'll ask the managed object context. When you need to save changes to model objects, you'll ask the managed object context to save them. The managed object context does most of the actual managing of managed objects.

You get managed objects from the data store by requesting them from the managed object context with a fetch request. Fetch requests specify, at a minimum, what kind of entity you want. They can also include a predicate that determines which instances of that entity are returned and a set of sort descriptors that determine how the resulting objects are sorted. Following the previous `Employee` example, the following code would find all employees currently in the data store:

```
NSManagedObjectContext *context = // Defined and configured elsewhere
NSFetchRequest *request = [[NSFetchRequest alloc] initWithEntityName:@"Employee"];
NSError *fetchError = nil;
NSArray *allEmployees = [context executeFetchRequest:request error:&fetchError];
```

When you need to create a new managed object, you'll normally do so by way of the managed object context. The following line finds an entity named `Employee` in the managed object context, creates a new managed object based on that entity, inserts it in the managed object context, and returns it:

```
Employee *newEmployee = [NSEntityDescription
     insertNewObjectForEntityForName:@"Employee"
     inManagedObjectContext:context];
```

It is common for entities to have the same name as the `NSManagedObject` subclass that uses them, but this is not required.

After the user has worked with the app for a while, there will probably be changes that need to be saved. Saving goes through the `NSManagedObjectContext`, which will save any outstanding changes on any objects loaded from or added to the context:

```
NSError *saveError = nil;
[context save:&saveError];
```

Persistent Stores and Persistent Store Coordinators

The managed object context doesn't actually save objects itself—it makes use of another object that handles the file-level interaction necessary for this. Core Data saves objects to a persistent data store. The data store itself is managed by a persistent store coordinator, an instance of `NSPersistentStoreCoordinator`. This is where managed objects finally become SQLite records, or part of a binary file, or are converted to some other format suitable for saving to a file. You'll never work directly with the persistent store coordinator except when you create it. After that, all interaction goes through the managed object context.

Why keep the persistent store separate? It is possible to use more than one persistent store simultaneously. The `NSPersistentStoreCoordinator`, as its name suggests, is responsible for coordinating the persistent stores. You may use only one data store in an app, but the Core Data stack doesn't restrict you to just one.

Adding Core Data to PhotoWheelPrototype

When you create a new project in Xcode, one of the options is to have Xcode automatically add code and files related to Core Data. That is convenient, but Xcode's template Core Data code is not always what you want. Also, sometimes you may need to add Core Data to a project that didn't previously use it. PhotoWheelPrototype doesn't have Core Data yet, so in this section we'll go through adding Core Data to the project.

This section builds on code from the previous chapter, so it starts without any of the property list code developed earlier in this chapter.

Adding the Core Data Framework

Before you can write any code using Core Data classes, you need to add the Core Data framework to the project. The framework contains the header files and implementations for Core Data classes. Until the framework is added, the compiler and linker won't know about Core Data.

To see the frameworks used in PhotoWheelPrototype, click on the project entry in the file navigator and then on the app target in the editor pane (Figure 13.1). In the Editor area, the **Build Phases** tab has a section named Link Binary With Libraries that lists the current frameworks.

To add a framework, click the **+** button at the bottom of the framework list. Xcode will present a list of known frameworks available for the project (Figure 13.2). Select

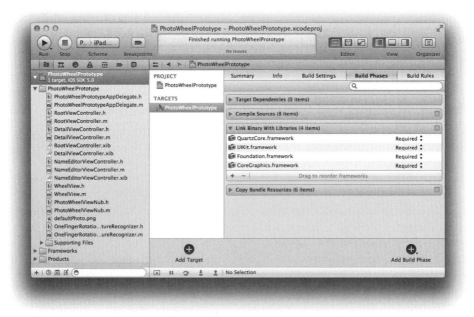

Figure 13.1   Xcode view of frameworks used in an app

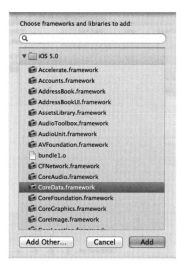

Figure 13.2   Adding the Core Data framework

CoreData.framework from the list and click the **Add** button. Xcode will then add Core Data to the project.

Adding the framework allows the linker to link Core Data classes. Next, you need to make sure that the compiler knows about the class declarations so that it can compile the code. You'll be using Core Data in a variety of places in the app, so the best place to do this is in the prefix header file *PhotoWheelPrototype-Prefix.pch*. This file already imports headers for UIKit and Foundation. Edit the file and add *CoreData.h* (Listing 13.13).

Listing 13.13   **Adding Core Data to the Prefix Header File**

```
#ifdef __OBJC__
    #import <UIKit/UIKit.h>
    #import <Foundation/Foundation.h>
    #import <CoreData/CoreData.h>
#endif
```

Setting Up the Core Data Stack

The set of objects necessary to use Core Data is often referred to as a stack. The managed object context depends on the persistent store coordinator, which in turn depends on the managed object model. The model is at the bottom of the stack, so you'll start there and build upward.

First you'll create the file that will contain the managed object model. Create a new file in Xcode. In the category list on the left of the new file window there is a section

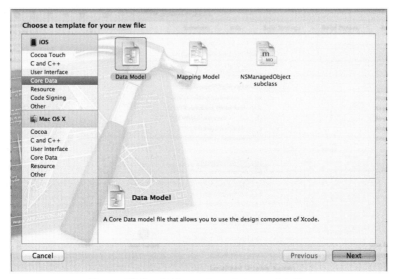

Figure 13.3   Adding a Core Data model file

labeled Core Data, and in that section there's a file type called Data Model (Figure 13.3). Use this file type and create a file named *PhotoWheelPrototype.xcdatamodeld* (Xcode will add the *.xcdatamodeld* extension). You'll create Core Data entities in this file. The *.xcdatamodeld* is the normal extension for an uncompiled model file. When you build the app, it will be compiled into a *.momd* file.

Next, you need to add code to load the data model file and configure the Core Data stack. In this case you'll add the setup methods to the application delegate. That's convenient when you have one data store that you use throughout the app, but it is not always ideal. In many cases it makes sense to set up Core Data in a dedicated model manager class or in one of the view controllers. In this case, though, you'll put it in the app delegate.

Edit *AppDelegate.h* and add the code shown in Listing 13.14. This code creates properties for the Core Data stack objects. It also declares a utility method called `save-Context` that will save any outstanding changes in the managed object context.

Listing 13.14   **Core Data Code for** *PhotoWheelPrototypeAppDelegate.h*

```
@property (readonly, strong, nonatomic) NSManagedObjectContext
*managedObjectContext;
@property (readonly, strong, nonatomic) NSManagedObjectModel *managedObjectModel;
@property (readonly, strong, nonatomic) NSPersistentStoreCoordinator
*persistentStoreCoordinator;
```

In *AppDelegate.m*, start by synthesizing the properties you just added in the header (Listing 13.15).

Listing 13.15   **Synthesize Statements for Core Data Stack Objects**

```
@synthesize managedObjectContext = __managedObjectContext;
@synthesize managedObjectModel = __managedObjectModel;
@synthesize persistentStoreCoordinator = __persistentStoreCoordinator;
```

Next, add the method to create the managed object model file (Listing 13.16). This method loads the compiled *.momd* file that corresponds to the uncompiled *.xcdatamodeld* file you created earlier. The code looks for the model file in the app's bundle and allocates an *NSManagedObjectModel* file with its contents.

Listing 13.16   **Creating the Managed Object Model Instance**

```
- (NSManagedObjectModel *)managedObjectModel
{
    if (__managedObjectModel != nil)
    {
        return __managedObjectModel;
    }
    NSURL *modelURL = [[NSBundle mainBundle]
        URLForResource:@"PhotoWheelPrototype"
        withExtension:@"momd"];
    __managedObjectModel =
        [[NSManagedObjectModel alloc] initWithContentsOfURL:modelURL];
    return __managedObjectModel;
}
```

Now add code for the persistent store coordinator (Listing 13.17). This method creates the persistent store coordinator using the managed object model created earlier. It then adds a data store to the coordinator. If the data store exists, it must contain only entities defined in the data model, and the definitions must match. If the data store doesn't exist yet, the method creates an empty one. This version creates a SQLite-backed data store, indicated by NSSQLiteStoreType.

Listing 13.17   **Creating the Persistent Store Coordinator**

```
- (NSPersistentStoreCoordinator *)persistentStoreCoordinator
{
    if (__persistentStoreCoordinator != nil)
    {
        return __persistentStoreCoordinator;
    }

    NSURL *applicationDocumentsDirectory = [[[NSFileManager defaultManager]
            URLsForDirectory:NSDocumentDirectory
            inDomains:NSUserDomainMask]
        lastObject];
```

```
    NSURL *storeURL = [applicationDocumentsDirectory
        URLByAppendingPathComponent:@"PhotoWheelPrototype.sqlite"];

    NSError *error = nil;
    __persistentStoreCoordinator = [[NSPersistentStoreCoordinator alloc]
        initWithManagedObjectModel:[self managedObjectModel]];
    if (![__persistentStoreCoordinator
        addPersistentStoreWithType:NSSQLiteStoreType
        configuration:nil
        URL:storeURL
        options:nil
        error:&error])
    {
        NSLog(@"Unresolved error %@, %@", error, [error userInfo]);
        abort();
    }

    return __persistentStoreCoordinator;
}
```

The last part of the Core Data stack is the managed object context (Listing 13.18).
The code that creates the context makes use of the persistent store coordinator method
in Listing 13.17, which in turn uses the managed object model created in Listing 13.16.
These three objects together form the Core Data "stack."

Listing 13.18 Creating the Managed Object Context

```
- (NSManagedObjectContext *)managedObjectContext
{
    if (__managedObjectContext != nil)
    {
        return __managedObjectContext;
    }

    NSPersistentStoreCoordinator *coordinator = [self persistentStoreCoordinator];
    if (coordinator != nil)
    {
        __managedObjectContext = [[NSManagedObjectContext alloc] init];
        [__managedObjectContext setPersistentStoreCoordinator:coordinator];
    }
    return __managedObjectContext;
}
```

Finally, you need to pass a reference to this managed object context to the Master-
ViewController so that it can make use of the data store when reading and writing
photos and albums. First, of course, MasterViewController needs to be able to hold

a reference to the managed object context. Add a new managed object property to
MasterViewController.h:

```
@property (strong, nonatomic) NSManagedObjectContext *managedObjectContext;
```

Also add a corresponding @synthesize to *MasterViewController.m*.

Once that is done, add a line to set a value for that new property in *AppDelegate.m*,
in the -application:didFinishLaunchingWithOptions: method. Add this just
after the call to -setDetailViewController:.

```
[masterViewController setManagedObjectContext:
   [self managedObjectContext]];
```

Now MasterViewController has access to the managed object context.

Using Core Data in PhotoWheel

Now it's time to use Core Data to implement the model classes described earlier in the
chapter.

The Core Data Model Editor

In Xcode find the file named *PhotoWheelPrototype.xcdatamodeld* that you created earlier.
Click on it to bring up the model editor, shown in Figure 13.4. The model editor lists
the entities in the model with their attributes, relationships, and fetched properties.

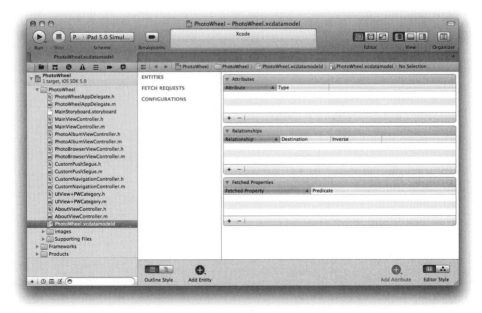

Figure 13.4 The Xcode Core Data model editor

The toggle at the bottom right corner of the editor switches between a table-style view and a graph style similar to an entity-relationship diagram. As with other Xcode editors, you can click the Editor toggle at the top of the window to show or hide the utility section of the window on the right. Make sure it is showing, because you'll need it to configure the entities.

There is not much to see, since you haven't created any entities yet.

Adding the Entities

To create the Photo entity:

1. Click the **Add Entity** button at the bottom of the window. You'll see a new entity appear in the editor. Set its name to Photo.

2. In the Inspector, set the Class to be Photo as well. This tells Core Data that instances of the Photo entity should be instances of a subclass of NSManaged-Object that is also named Photo. The entity and the class aren't required to have the same name, but it is convenient to make them the same. So far you don't have a Photo class, but you can still configure the class name here.

3. In the Attributes section of the editor, click the **+** button to create a new attribute. Set its name to dateAdded, and use the popup menu under Type to set the attribute type to Date.

4. Create another new attribute and name it originalImageData. This will save the original image data received from the camera. Set the Attribute Type to Binary Data.

5. Select the originalImageData attribute. In the Inspector pane on the right, find a check box labeled Allows External Storage. Check this box (Figure 13.5).

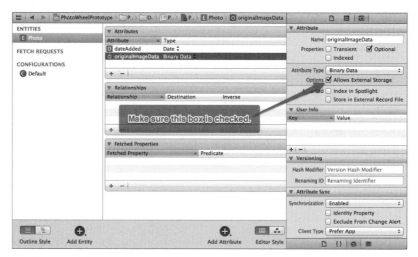

Figure 13.5 The Inspector pane showing the originalImageData attribute on the Photo entity

This setting tells Core Data that the image data should not be kept directly in the data store but should be automatically saved in an external file. This will prevent excessive memory use when loading `Photo` entities.

6. Repeat the previous step for properties named `thumbnailImageData` and `largeImageData`.

To create the `PhotoAlbum` entity:

1. Click the **Add Entity** button at the bottom of the window. Name the new entity `PhotoAlbum`.

2. Set the Class for the `PhotoAlbum` entity to be a class named `PhotoAlbum`.

3. Add an attribute named `name` and set its Type to String.

4. Add an attribute named `dateAdded` and set its Type to Date.

Now that the entities exist, click the Editor style toggle on the bottom to switch to the graph view. You'll see both entities with their attributes listed below them. You can drag them around in the graph view and arrange them as you like. You can work in either the model editor's table view or the graph view. The following steps describe using the graph view.

Now, you need to add the relationship between the `Photo` entity and the `Photo-Album` entity. This will be a one-to-many relationship from `PhotoAlbum` to `Photo`, since each album can contain multiple photos but each photo can belong to only one album.

1. Click once on the `PhotoAlbum` entity to select it.

2. Click and hold the **Add Attribute** button. A menu of options appears. Click on **Add Relationship** to add a relationship from the `PhotoAlbum` entity. Notice that the button's label changes to read **Add Relationship**. The button's label changes to reflect the most recently used choice from the popup menu.

3. Double-click on the new relationship to make its name editable, and set its name to `photos`.

4. In the Inspector, click on the popup menu labeled Destination and select `Photo` as the destination entity.

5. Check the box in the Inspector labeled To-Many Relationship. Also be sure to check the one labeled Ordered, so that the order will be maintained on the relationship. Without this the relationship would be unordered, and you'll be adding code soon that needs to know the order.

6. Click on the popup menu labeled Delete Rule and select Cascade. This setting will mean that deleting a `PhotoAlbum` will cascade to related `Photos` and delete them as well. At this point the model should look like Figure 13.6.

7. Now click once on the `Photo` entity to select it.

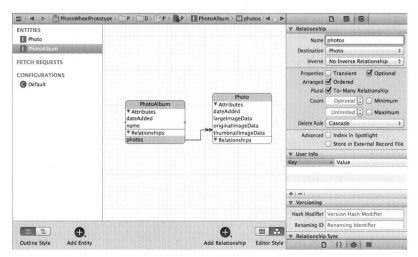

Figure 13.6   Model editor after adding the `photos` relationship to the
`PhotoAlbum` entity

8. Click and hold the **Add Relationship** button (the one that earlier read **Add Relationship)**.

9. Double-click on the new relationship to make its name editable, and set its name to `photoAlbum`.

10. In the Inspector, click on the popup menu labeled Destination and select `Photo-Album` as the destination entity.

11. In the Inspector, click on the popup menu labeled Inverse and select `photos` as the inverse relationship. This tells Core Data that `PhotoAlbum`'s `photos` relationship and `Photo`'s `photoAlbum` relationship are at opposite ends of the same relationship.

12. In the Inspector, uncheck the box marked Optional. Since photos must belong to an album, this relationship is mandatory. Contrast that with `PhotoAlbum`'s `photos` relationship. It was left as optional, because a photo album may be empty.

13. Leave the Delete Rule for this relationship set to Nullify. This tells Core Data that when a `Photo` is deleted, incoming relationships should be set to `nil`. At the same time the deletion should not cascade to the `PhotoAlbum`.

At this point the model should look like Figure 13.7.

Creating `NSManagedObject` **Subclasses**

Now that you have created the model entities, you can have Xcode create custom `NSManagedObject` subclasses that match the entities. When Xcode creates the class

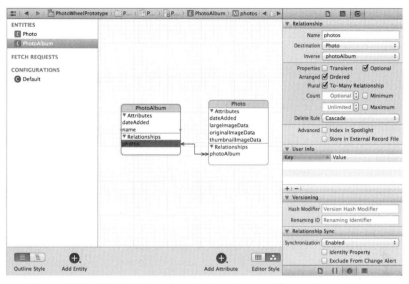

Figure 13.7   Model editor showing the `photoAlbum` relationship on
the `Photo` entity

files, it looks at the existing entities and the class names configured for each one. If any entity has a class other than `NSManagedObject`, it offers to create a custom subclass for that entity.

Before you do that, let's continue the discussion from earlier about thinking ahead when designing a data model. Suppose in version 1.1 of PhotoWheel you want to add new attributes to one or both of the entities. Maybe you would add location information so that you could show photos on a map. Recall also from the earlier discussion the idea that you might want to add custom methods to your model classes to implement model-specific behavior.

These two requirements conflict if you have Xcode generate your subclasses. When Xcode generates managed object classes, it overwrites the existing file and replaces it with one matching the current state of the entities in the data model. If you have added custom methods, those will be wiped away. On the other hand, creating and managing your subclasses by hand is tedious and error-prone. You would need to update the subclass code anytime you update the entity, making the same change in two different places.

How can you resolve this? With a little bit of trickery, you use generated subclasses without overwriting your custom code. It works by creating two classes for each entity, one that will be generated by Xcode and the other that will be a subclass of the first. Then Xcode can generate your model classes, and you can add methods without conflict. You'll do this by temporarily renaming the entity subclasses.

1. In the model editor, change the name of the PhotoAlbum entity's class to _PhotoAlbum.

2. In the model editor, change the name of the Photo entity's class to _Photo.

3. Click one of the entities, and then **Shift-Click** on the other so that both entities are selected.

4. On Xcode's **File** menu, select **New File**.

5. In the new file window, select Core Data from the list on the left, and NSManagedObject subclass from the options on the right (Figure 13.8) and click **Next**.

6. Save the new files. This will produce four new files, both header and implementation files for each of the _Photo and _PhotoAlbum classes. These define two subclasses of NSManagedObject.

7. On Xcode's **File** menu, select **New File**. Create an Objective-C class. When Xcode asks you what Photo's superclass should be, type in "_Photo" (Figure 13.9). Name the class Photo. This creates a subclass of _Photo called Photo.

8. Repeat the previous step, creating a class named PhotoAlbum whose superclass is _PhotoAlbum.

9. Go back to the model editor and change the Photo entity's class name back to Photo and the PhotoAlbum entity's class name back to PhotoAlbum.

What did you just do? You used Xcode to automatically create two classes, _Photo and _PhotoAlbum, that match the entities you created earlier. You also created two

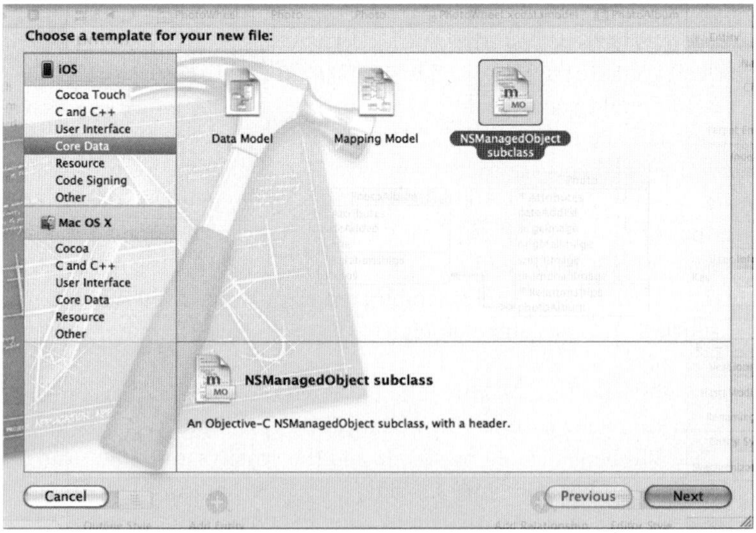

Figure 13.8   Creating custom NSManagedObject subclasses in Xcode

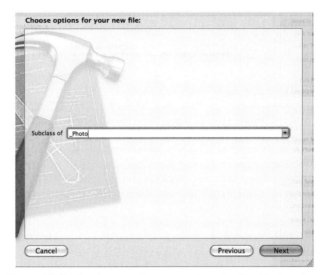

Figure 13.9   Setting a custom superclass for the Photo class

subclasses, Photo and PhotoAlbum. Xcode generated the superclasses, and your custom code will go in the subclasses. This keeps your code separate from code generated by Xcode. Keep in mind that you'll have to repeat the temporary renaming process if you change the entities later.

Why not just leave the class names with the underscored names? The class names saved in the model are the classes Core Data will return when creating managed objects. If the PhotoAlbum entity's class were named _PhotoAlbum, Core Data would create instances of _PhotoAlbum that would not contain any custom behaviors added in the PhotoAlbum subclass. With the name changed back, Core Data provides PhotoAlbum instances that contain the custom code.

Take a look at the generated code. Xcode creates properties for each of the entity's attributes and relationships. For to-many relationships, it also creates custom accessor methods for adding and removing Photos. Listing 13.19 shows the generated code for _PhotoAlbum.h. The photos property contains all of the album's photos and can be accessed to look up the album contents. For adding and removing individual photos you would use the accessor methods addPhotosObject and removePhotosObject.

Listing 13.19 **Automatically Generated Code in** _PhotoAlbum.h

```
#import <Foundation/Foundation.h>
#import <CoreData/CoreData.h>

@class _Photo;

@interface _PhotoAlbum : NSManagedObject
```

```
@property (nonatomic, retain) NSString * name;
@property (nonatomic, retain) NSDate * dateAdded;
@property (nonatomic, retain) NSOrderedSet *photos;
@end

@interface _PhotoAlbum (CoreDataGeneratedAccessors)

- (void)insertObject:(_Photo *)value inPhotosAtIndex:(NSUInteger)idx;
- (void)removeObjectFromPhotosAtIndex:(NSUInteger)idx;
- (void)insertPhotos:(NSArray *)value atIndexes:(NSIndexSet *)indexes;
- (void)removePhotosAtIndexes:(NSIndexSet *)indexes;
- (void)replaceObjectInPhotosAtIndex:(NSUInteger)idx withObject:(_Photo *)value;
- (void)replacePhotosAtIndexes:(NSIndexSet *)indexes withPhotos:(NSArray *)values;
- (void)addPhotosObject:(_Photo *)value;
- (void)removePhotosObject:(_Photo *)value;
- (void)addPhotos:(NSOrderedSet *)values;
- (void)removePhotos:(NSOrderedSet *)values;
@end
```

If you look at the implementation file _PhotoAlbum.m_ (Listing 13.20), you'll see that there is not much there. All of the properties are listed as `@dynamic` declarations, and that's it. Declaring properties as `@dynamic` implies that the necessary method declarations will be created at run time, or that dynamic method resolution will be used to handle calls to the method. `NSManagedObject` takes care of that. These are a couple of the interesting features of Objective-C, that new methods can be created while an app is running, and that calls to nonexistent methods can be handled dynamically.

Listing 13.20   **Automatically Generated Code in** _PhotoAlbum.m_

```
#import "_PhotoAlbum.h"
#import "_Photo.h"


@implementation _PhotoAlbum
@dynamic name;
@dynamic dateAdded;
@dynamic photos;

@end
```

Alternative Subclass Generation: mogenerator

The multistep process for keeping generated code separate from custom code (described in the previous section) is effective but can be error-prone. If you regenerate the class files without first changing the class names, you could accidentally wipe out custom code. Good version control software is a must when doing this, so that code can be recovered if necessary.

There's an open source tool written by Jonathan "Wolf" Rentzsch called mogenerator that can simplify this process. It serves as an alternative means for generating `NSManagedObject` subclasses. It follows the same general approach as a two-level class system in which one contains generated class files based on entities and the other subclasses the first. mogenerator includes an Xcode plug-in called Xmo'd and works automatically. It's easy to use, but if there's a team of people working on an app, everyone must install it. Both mogenerator and Xmo'd are available from Rentzsch at **rentzsch.github.com/mogenerator/**. As of this writing Xmo'd has not yet been updated to work with Xcode 4, but development continues and updates are planned. mogenerator does work with Xcode 4, and it's the more important part of the system.

Adding Custom Code to Model Objects

Now that we have a place to safely add custom code, what code do we need? You may have noticed earlier that all of the image-related attributes on the `Photo` entity used the binary data type. In Cocoa Touch this corresponds to an instance of `NSData`. In order to draw images on the screen we'll need `UIImage` instances. Adding custom code to translate between the `NSData` in the data store and the `UIImages` needed for the user interface is an obvious choice.

Start with code to handle a new picture from the camera. You'll have a `UIImage`, and you need to create several images of differing sizes and save all of them. Add a method declaration in *Photo.h*:

```
- (void)saveImage:(UIImage *)newImage;
```

The method definition goes in *Photo.m* and is shown in Listing 13.21. The listing also includes two methods that resize images, since we'll use multiple image sizes. We won't discuss these in detail here. If you would like to investigate them in more detail, consult Xcode's built-in documentation for the methods and functions they use.

The –saveImage: method starts off by converting the `UIImage` to an `NSData` object using JPEG compression and saving that as the original image data. Next, the method converts the image to other sizes, using the image-scaling methods discussed earlier. In each case, the code scales the incoming `UIImage` to a smaller size, converts it to `NSData`, and calls one of the generated accessor methods.

Listing 13.21   **Saving a New Photo in Multiple Sizes in an** `NSManagedObject`
Subclass

```
- (UIImage *)image:(UIImage *)image scaleAspectToMaxSize:(CGFloat)newSize {
  CGSize size = [image size];
  CGFloat ratio;
  if (size.width > size.height) {
    ratio = newSize / size.width;
```

```
    } else {
       ratio = newSize / size.height;
    }

    CGRect rect = CGRectMake(0.0, 0.0, ratio * size.width, ratio * size.height);
    UIGraphicsBeginImageContext(rect.size);
    [image drawInRect:rect];
    UIImage *scaledImage = UIGraphicsGetImageFromCurrentImageContext();
    return scaledImage;
}

- (UIImage *)image:(UIImage *)image scaleAndCropToMaxSize:(CGSize)newSize {
    CGFloat largestSize =
        (newSize.width > newSize.height) ? newSize.width : newSize.height;
    CGSize imageSize = [image size];

    // Scale the image while maintaining the aspect and making sure
    // the scaled image is not smaller than the given new size. In
    // other words, we calculate the aspect ratio using the largest
    // dimension from the new size and the smallest dimension from the
    // actual size.
    CGFloat ratio;
    if (imageSize.width > imageSize.height) {
       ratio = largestSize / imageSize.height;
    } else {
       ratio = largestSize / imageSize.width;
    }

    CGRect rect =
        CGRectMake(0.0, 0.0, ratio * imageSize.width, ratio * imageSize.height);
    UIGraphicsBeginImageContext(rect.size);
    [image drawInRect:rect];
    UIImage *scaledImage = UIGraphicsGetImageFromCurrentImageContext();

    // Crop the image to the requested new size, maintaining
    // the innermost parts of the image.
    CGFloat offsetX = 0;
    CGFloat offsetY = 0;
    imageSize = [scaledImage size];
    if (imageSize.width < imageSize.height) {
       offsetY = (imageSize.height / 2) - (imageSize.width / 2);
    } else {
       offsetX = (imageSize.width / 2) - (imageSize.height / 2);
    }

    CGRect cropRect = CGRectMake(offsetX, offsetY,
                                 imageSize.width - (offsetX * 2),
                                 imageSize.height - (offsetY * 2));
```

```
    CGImageRef croppedImageRef =
        CGImageCreateWithImageInRect([scaledImage CGImage], cropRect);
    UIImage *newImage = [UIImage imageWithCGImage:croppedImageRef];
    CGImageRelease(croppedImageRef);

    return newImage;
}
- (void)saveImage:(UIImage *)newImage;
{
    NSData *originalImageData = UIImageJPEGRepresentation(newImage, 0.8);
    [self setOriginalImageData:originalImageData];
    // Save thumbnail
    CGSize thumbnailSize = CGSizeMake(75.0, 75.0);
    UIImage *thumbnailImage = [self image:newImage
                    scaleAndCropToMaxSize:thumbnailSize]];
    NSData *thumbnailImageData = UIImageJPEGRepresentation(thumbnailImage, 0.8);
    [self setThumbnailImageData:thumbnailImageData];

    // Save large (screen-size) image
    CGRect screenBounds = [[UIScreen mainScreen] bounds];
    // Calculate size for retina displays
    CGFloat scale = [[UIScreen mainScreen] scale];
    CGFloat maxScreenSize = MAX(screenBounds.size.width,
        screenBounds.size.height) * scale;

    CGSize imageSize = [newImage size];
    CGFloat maxImageSize = MAX(imageSize.width, imageSize.height) * scale;

    CGFloat maxSize = MIN(maxScreenSize, maxImageSize);
    UIImage *largeImage = [self image:newImage scaleAspectToMaxSize:maxSize];
    NSData *largeImageData = UIImageJPEGRepresentation(largeImage, 0.8);
    [self setLargeImageData:largeImageData];
}
```

Going in the other direction, it would be convenient to be able to ask a Photo for a UIImage even though the image is saved in the data store as binary data. Add the following convenience method declarations to *Photo.h*:

```
- (UIImage *)originalImage;
- (UIImage *)largeImage;
- (UIImage *)thumbnailImage;
```

The method definitions in *Photo.m* are straightforward and are shown in Listing 13.22.

Listing 13.22   **Convenience Methods to Get `UIImage` Objects from Binary Data in the Data Store**

```
- (UIImage *)originalImage;
{
    return [UIImage imageWithData:[self originalImageData]];
}


- (UIImage *)largeImage;
{
    return [UIImage imageWithData:[self largeImageData]];
}


- (UIImage *)thumbnailImage;
{
    return [UIImage imageWithData:[self thumbnailImageData]];
}
```

The `PhotoAlbum` class has a few custom methods of its own. First, you'll override `NSManagedObject`'s `awakeFromInsert` method (Listing 13.23). This method gets called when a managed object is first inserted into a managed object context and is guaranteed to be called only once on any object. You'll use this method to set the photo album's add date.

Listing 13.23   **Setting the Add Date on Insertion into the Managed Object Context**

```
- (void)awakeFromInsert
{
    [super awakeFromInsert];
    [self setDateAdded:[NSDate date]];
}
```

Next, you'll add a convenience method for creating a new photo album (Listing 13.24). This method takes two arguments: the desired album name and the managed object context into which the new album should be inserted. The second argument is used because this is a class method rather than an instance method. Instances of `PhotoAlbum` have a reference to their managed object context, which can be looked up using the `managedObjectContext` property. The `PhotoAlbum` class does not have this property since it could be used in more than one context, so the managed object context needs to be passed in by the caller of this method.

Listing 13.24   **Adding a New Photo Album to a Managed Object Context**

```
+ (PhotoAlbum *)newPhotoAlbumWithName:(NSString *)albumName
        inContext:(NSManagedObjectContext *)context
{
```

```
PhotoAlbum *newAlbum = [NSEntityDescription
    insertNewObjectForEntityForName:@"PhotoAlbum"
    inManagedObjectContext:context];
[newAlbum setName:albumName];

NSMutableOrderedSet *photos = [newAlbum mutableOrderedSetValueForKey:@"photos"];
for (int index=0; index<10; index++) {
    Photo *placeholderPhoto = [NSEntityDescription
        insertNewObjectForEntityForName:@"Photo"
        inManagedObjectContext:context];
    [photos addObject:placeholderPhoto];
}
return newAlbum;
}
```

The code starts off by creating a new `PhotoAlbum` and setting its name. The add
date will be set automatically in `awakeFromInsert`. Next, the code fills out the
album with placeholder objects. As with the property list implementation, this is done
so that photos can be added to the album at any index instead of only at the end of the
current photo list. The new `Photo` instances won't have any of their properties set and
will use minimal memory.

Since this code makes use of the `Photo` class, make sure to import the header file
for that class at the top of the file:

```
#import "Photo.h"
```

`PhotoAlbum` also has a custom method to look up all albums in a managed object
context (Listing 13.25). This will be used when `MasterViewController` first loads,
so that it can display the full album list.

Listing 13.25 Looking Up All Photo Albums in a Managed Object Context

```
+ (NSMutableArray *)allPhotoAlbumsInContext:(NSManagedObjectContext *)context
{
    NSFetchRequest *fetchRequest = [[NSFetchRequest alloc]
        initWithEntityName:@"PhotoAlbum"];

    NSArray *sortDescriptors = [NSArray arrayWithObject:
        [NSSortDescriptor sortDescriptorWithKey:@"name"
            ascending:YES]];
    [fetchRequest setSortDescriptors:sortDescriptors];

    NSError *error = nil;
    NSArray *photoAlbums = [context executeFetchRequest:fetchRequest
        error:&error];

    if (photoAlbums != nil) {
        return [photoAlbums mutableCopy];
```

```
    } else {
        return [NSMutableArray array];
    }
}
```

The first thing this code does is create a fetch request for the entity named Photo-
Album. The entity name used here is just an NSString, but an entity with that name
must be present in the managed object context when the fetch request executes. The
sort descriptor requests that the results of the request be ordered by name. Sorting is
handled internally by Core Data; all that's necessary is to provide the key or keys by
which you want to sort.

The method then executes the fetch. If any albums are found, the code creates
a mutable copy of the array and returns it. This method returns a mutable array so
that the caller can add new albums. If the managed object context doesn't contain
any albums yet, the result will be nil, and in that case the method returns an empty
mutable array.

Make sure to add declarations in *PhotoAlbum.h* that correspond to the methods just
defined.

Reading and Saving Photo Albums with Core Data

Working with photo albums is a little simpler here than it was with property lists,
because a lot of the management work is handled by Core Data. Initially you need to
add nearly the same code to the top of *MasterViewController.m* (Listing 13.26). In addition, make sure to change the type of the MasterViewController's data property
from NSMutableOrderedSet to NSMutableArray, just as you did in the property
list section of this chapter.

Listing 13.26   **Import Statement and Class Extension for** MasterViewController

```
#import "PhotoAlbum.h"

@interface MasterViewController ()
@property (readwrite, assign) NSUInteger currentAlbumIndex;
@end
```

The first line imports the header for the PhotoAlbum class, which you need so that
MasterViewController can work with albums. The rest declares the property cur-
rentAlbumIndex, which will be used to keep track of the album being displayed in
the detail view, so that MasterViewController can show the user which one is currently selected.

Setting up the list of albums can be done in viewDidLoad. Listing 13.27 shows an
updated version of *MasterViewController.m*'s –viewDidLoad that handles this.

Listing 13.27   **Setting Up the List of Photo Albums**

```objc
- (void)viewDidLoad
{
   [super viewDidLoad];
   // Do any additional setup after loading the view, typically from a nib.

   self.title = NSLocalizedString(@"Photo Albums", @"Photo albums title");

   [self setData:
      [PhotoAlbum allPhotoAlbumsInContext:[self managedObjectContext]]];

   if ([[self data] count] == 0) {
      PhotoAlbum *newAlbum = [PhotoAlbum
                                 newPhotoAlbumWithName:@"First album"
                              inContext:[self managedObjectContext]];
      [self setData:[NSMutableArray arrayWithObject:newAlbum]];
      [[self managedObjectContext] save:nil];
   }

   [self.tableView selectRowAtIndexPath:[NSIndexPath indexPathForRow:0
                                                           inSection:0]
                               animated:NO
                         scrollPosition:UITableViewScrollPositionMiddle];

   UIBarButtonItem *addButton = [[UIBarButtonItem alloc]
            initWithBarButtonSystemItem:UIBarButtonSystemItemAdd
                                 target:self
                                 action:@selector(add:)];
   [[self navigationItem] setRightBarButtonItem:addButton];
   [[self navigationItem] setLeftBarButtonItem:[self editButtonItem]];

   [[self detailViewController] setPhotoAlbum:[[self data] objectAtIndex:0]];
}
```

The first highlighted line loads all existing photo albums into `MasterViewController`'s `data` array, using the convenience method defined earlier. The following code handles the first-run scenario when no albums exist yet. If there are no albums, the code creates an initial album and saves it in the `data` array. Then it tells the managed object context to save changes so that this new album will be recorded in the data store.

It's also good to show the user which album is currently selected, so change the cell configuration section of `tableView:cellForRowAtIndexPath:` to match the code in Listing 13.28.

Listing 13.28   **Configuring Table Cells to Show Photo Album Information**

```
// Configure the cell.
PhotoAlbum *album = [[self data] objectAtIndex:[indexPath row]];
[[cell textLabel] setText:[album name]];

if ([indexPath row] == [self currentAlbumIndex]) {
    [cell setAccessoryType:UITableViewCellAccessoryCheckmark];
} else {
    [cell setAccessoryType:UITableViewCellAccessoryNone];
}
```

This code looks up a photo album corresponding to the current table index path and sets the cell's text to that album's name. Next, it shows a check mark if the album is the currently selected album.

You also need to change the code that handles editing photo album names to handle Core Data entities properly. First, change the code in *MasterViewController.m* that loads the NameEditorViewController to look like Listing 13.29.

Listing 13.29   **Loading the Name Editor for a Core Data Photo Album Entity**

```
- (void)tableView:(UITableView *)tableView
accessoryButtonTappedForRowWithIndexPath:(NSIndexPath *)indexPath
{
    NameEditorViewController *newController =
    [[NameEditorViewController alloc] initWithDefaultNib];
    [newController setDelegate:self];
    [newController setEditing:YES];
    [newController setIndexPath:indexPath];
    NSString *name = [[[self data] objectAtIndex:[indexPath row]]
        valueForKey:@"name"];
    [newController setDefaultNameText:name];
    [newController setModalPresentationStyle:UIModalPresentationFormSheet];
    [self presentModalViewController:newController animated:YES];
}
```

The only change in Listing 13.29 is that the code now looks up the name property of the selected photo album, which is defined on the PhotoAlbum entity.

You also need to update the callback from NameEditorViewController to handle new album names and new albums. Make the method look like Listing 13.30.

Listing 13.30   **Handling Photo Album Name Editor Callbacks with Core Data**

```
- (void)nameEditorViewControllerDidFinish:(NameEditorViewController *)controller
{
    NSString *newName = [[controller nameTextField] text];
    if (newName && [newName length] > 0) {
```

```
    if ([controller isEditing]) {
      PhotoAlbum *album = [[self data]
          objectAtIndex:[[controller indexPath] row]];
      [album setName:newName];
    } else {
      PhotoAlbum *newAlbum = [PhotoAlbum
          newPhotoAlbumWithName:newName
          inContext:[self managedObjectContext]];
      [[self data] addObject:newAlbum];
    }
    [[self managedObjectContext] save:nil];
    [[self tableView] reloadData];
  }
}
```

If the controller was editing an album name, this code finds the PhotoAlbum being edited and updates its name. If the controller was not editing an album name, the code creates a new PhotoAlbum with the requested name and adds it to the data array.

In either case the code tells the managedObjectContext to save the change that was just made.

Adding New Photos to an Album with Core Data

Now let's see how to get pictures into photo albums when using Core Data. As with the property list approach, the first thing we need to do is give DetailView-Controller a reference to the currently selected photo album. Add a new property to *DetailViewController.h* to hold this reference, only this time make it an instance of PhotoAlbum:

```
@property (strong, nonatomic) PhotoAlbum *photoAlbum;
```

In the property list code photoAlbum was an NSMutableDictionary, which is one of the core Cocoa Touch classes. Here it is a custom class that is part of the Photo-WheelPrototype project, so you also need to add a declaration for the class for the code to compile. Add this declaration at the top of *DetailViewController.h*, above the @interface line:

```
@class PhotoAlbum;
```

Add a @synthesize statement for this property in *DetailViewController.m*. Also, be sure to import *PhotoAlbum.h* so that the compiler will know where the class is defined:

```
#import "PhotoAlbum.h"
```

Now you need to tell DetailViewController what album is selected. You'll do this back in MasterViewController where the album selection is managed. First, add a line to MasterViewController's viewDidLoad, telling the detail view controller to use the first album in the list. Make this the last line in the method, so that it happens after the data property has been initialized.

```
[[self detailViewController] setPhotoAlbum:[[self data] objectAtIndex:0]];
```

Next, fill in MasterViewController's implementation of -tableView: didSelectRowAtIndexPath: so that both the detail and master views will update appropriately when the user taps on a photo album (Listing 13.31).

Listing 13.31   **Changing the Selected Album Using Core Data**

```
- (void)tableView:(UITableView *)tableView
   didSelectRowAtIndexPath:(NSIndexPath *)indexPath
{
   NSIndexPath *oldCurrentAlbumIndexPath = [NSIndexPath
       indexPathForRow:[self currentAlbumIndex]
       inSection:0];
   [self setCurrentAlbumIndex:[indexPath row]];
   [tableView reloadRowsAtIndexPaths:
          [NSArray arrayWithObjects:indexPath, oldCurrentAlbumIndexPath, nil]
       withRowAnimation:UITableViewRowAnimationNone];

   PhotoAlbum *selectedAlbum = [[self data] objectAtIndex:[indexPath row]];
   [[self detailViewController] setPhotoAlbum:selectedAlbum];
}
```

The first part of this code handles updating the current album index and updating the table view to show the new selection. It saves the old selected index in an NSIndexPath and then updates the selection. Then it tells the table view to reload data at both the previous and new selection values. This will lead to calls to -tableView:cellForRowAtIndexPath: for both of those index paths, and that will remove the check mark at the old selected row and add one at the new selection.

The rest of the method looks up the PhotoAlbum in the data array and tells detailViewController that the selection has changed.

Getting new photos from the camera or photo library again happens in *DetailViewController.m* in the UIImagePickerController delegate callback, though things work differently with Core Data from the way they did with property lists (Listing 13.32).

Listing 13.32   **Adding New Photos to a Photo Album Using Core Data**

```
- (void)imagePickerController:(UIImagePickerController *)picker
   didFinishPickingMediaWithInfo:(NSDictionary *)info
{
   // If the popover controller is available,
   // assume the photo is selected from the library
   // and not from the camera.
   BOOL takenWithCamera = ([self popoverController] == nil);
```

```
   // Dismiss the popover controller if available,
   // otherwise dismiss the camera view.
   if ([self masterPopoverController]) {
      [[self masterPopoverController] dismissPopoverAnimated:YES];
      [self setMasterPopoverController:nil];
   } else {
      [self dismissModalViewControllerAnimated:YES];
   }


   UIImage *image = [info objectForKey:UIImagePickerControllerOriginalImage];
   [[self selectedPhotoWheelViewCell] setImage:image];

   Photo *targetPhoto = [[[self photoAlbum] photos]
      objectAtIndex:[self selectedWheelViewCellIndex]];
   [targetPhoto saveImage:image];
   [targetPhoto setDateAdded:[NSDate date]];

   NSError *error = nil;
   [[[self photoAlbum] managedObjectContext] save:&error];

if (takenWithCamera) {
    UIImageWriteToSavedPhotosAlbum(image, nil, nil, nil);
   }
}
```

This code looks up the "target" photo in the album using the index of the selected cell view. The new image is saved using Photo's -saveImage: method, which was discussed earlier. This creates multiple photo sizes as JPEG data and saves that data in the target photo. The code then sets the photo's add date to the current date and time.

The code then asks the managed object context to save the new changes. Unlike with the property list version, no notification is posted here, because changes can be saved directly instead of via MasterViewController.

As with the property list version, you need to add a property in DetailView-Controller called selectedWheelViewCellIndex. It is an integer that saves the index of the thumbnail view the user tapped on. Add the declaration to *DetailViewController.h*, and add a corresponding @synthesize statement in *DetailViewController.m*:

```
@property (assign, nonatomic) NSUInteger selectedWheelViewCellIndex;
```

The code in Listing 13.32 uses the Photo class, so be sure to import the header for that class at the top of *DetailViewController.m*:

```
#import "Photo.h"
```

Displaying Photos in an Album with Core Data

When the user selects a new album, `DetailViewController` needs to update its view to show photos from that album. Since `MasterViewController` is already setting `DetailViewController`'s photoAlbum property when that happens, the best place to handle this is again in a custom setter method for that property (Listing 13.33).

Listing 13.33   **Updating the Wheel View When a New Photo Album Is Selected**

```
- (void)setPhotoAlbum:(PhotoAlbum *)photoAlbum
{
    _photoAlbum = photoAlbum;

    UIImage *defaultPhoto = [UIImage imageNamed:@"defaultPhoto.png"];
    for (NSUInteger index=0; index<10; index++) {
        PhotoWheelViewCell *cell = [[self data] objectAtIndex:index];
        Photo *photo = [[[self photoAlbum] photos] objectAtIndex:index];
        UIImage *thumbnail = [photo thumbnailImage];
        if (thumbnail != nil) {
            [cell setImage:thumbnail];
        } else {
            [cell setImage:defaultPhoto];
        }
    }
}
```

The first line in this method handles the actual setting of the new value of the photo album property. The rest of the code runs through the album, updating the wheel view as it goes. At each pass through the loop the code finds both the cell view and the photo corresponding to the loop counter. If the photo has a thumbnail, the code displays that thumbnail in the cell. Otherwise it displays a default image, indicating that no photo exists at that index.

With these changes the app is again ready for use as a prototype, now using Core Data to store photos and albums instead of property lists.

In this version, the app uses Core Data to automatically sort photo albums based on album properties. We have not added undo management, but if you wanted to do so, Core Data would work directly with `NSUndoManager` to simplify the process.

Using SQLite Directly

Core Data is extremely useful as an app's model layer, but it's not ideal in all cases. In some situations your needs might more closely match those of a database rather than an object store. For example, if you routinely need to update a flag on a large collection of records, it is difficult to do so efficiently in Core Data. In those cases you might prefer to work with SQLite directly. In most cases Core Data will be easier, but in cases where it is not a good match, you can create and use your own SQLite files.

SQLite offers a powerful API but it can be intimidating at first. It is written in C, so you'll have to do some work to convert between database records and your own model objects. You can simplify this somewhat by using an Objective-C wrapper for SQLite. Two open source projects, FMDB and PLDatabase,[1] can greatly simplify using SQLite in Objective-C code but otherwise don't come between your code and the database. You'll still have to put some effort into converting between your model objects and database records, but if the advantage of more direct database access is important enough, it may be worth doing so.

Summary

This chapter presented different approaches to implementing the model layer of an iPad app, and two alternatives were implemented. Core Data is frequently though not always the better choice. At this point the PhotoWheelPrototype project can get new photos, display them, and manage the albums that contain them. Next, you'll move on to implementing the rest of the user interface and other useful app features.

Exercises

1. Update the method `-tableView:commitEditingStyle:forRowAtIndex-Path:` found in *MasterViewController.m* to delete the photo album from the Core Data store. Hint: You can use the `-deleteObject:` method found on the `NSManagedObjectContext` object.

---

1. FMDB can be found at **github.com/ccgus/fmdb**, and PLDatabase can be found at **code .google.com/p/pldatabase/**.

14

Storyboarding in Xcode

Up to this point, you have been working on building the prototype app for PhotoWheel. Certain design concepts were proven and development techniques explored, and you learned more about building apps for the iPad. Now it's time to use what you learned by starting to build the "real" PhotoWheel app. To start things off, let's talk about a new way of designing the user interface using a feature called a storyboard.

What Is a Storyboard?

In the previous chapters, you learned how to create the user interface using IB and NIB files. Mac and iOS developers have been creating user interfaces for years using this approach. But the approach could be better. Imagine, for example, how helpful it would be to see the entire user interface of your application on one screen, or to view related screens at once.

And how cool would it be if you didn't have to write the code to transition from one screen to another? Imagine creating a user interface that displays a button, and when that button is tapped it transitions the screen to a new view. Now imagine doing this without writing any code. This is exactly what Apple has done with the new storyboard feature in Xcode 4.2.

Apple engineers have improved the way iOS developers can create user interfaces. They have made it possible for developers to see the entire makeup of an app's user interface, and they have eliminated the need for the trivial code used to transition from one screen to another. This is all done within a storyboard; but what is a storyboard?

Storyboarding, which was introduced with Xcode 4.2 and iOS 5, streamlines the process of creating user interfaces and defines the transitions between view controllers. Under the hood, a storyboard still uses NIB files, but instead of having multiple NIBs within your project, you now have a single storyboard file that contains all the information that would otherwise be found in multiple NIBs. And with a storyboard, you're still using Interface Builder to design the UI because, after all, it's all based on NIBs.

This means that everything you already know about using IB applies to a storyboard. The same inspectors are available. The same Object library is available. You still have view controllers, and you still define outlets and actions. You connect objects to outlets and actions the same way you always have (**Control–click** and drag, Assistant editor, etc.). With a storyboard, you create your user interface exactly the same way you did with individual NIBs; the only difference is that you now can *see* all of the screens at one time.

> **Note**
>
> You are not limited to a single storyboard within a project. A project can contain as many storyboards as needed. Larger projects, for example, may have multiple storyboards, each representing a collection of related screens or specific areas of the application. Think of a storyboard as a collection of related NIBs (or screens) stored in a single file.

Using a Storyboard

You use a storyboard in much the same way you use a NIB. The only difference is that instead of multiple NIB files in your project, you have a single storyboard containing a collection of NIBs. You can, however, intermix storyboards and NIBs within your project. Using a storyboard does not lock you into a single approach for UI design.

When creating a new project, most of the project templates give you the option to use a storyboard or not. The generated template code will differ based on this option. Say, for example, you create a new project called MyAwesomeApp. This will generate the *plist* file *MyAwesomeApp-Info.plist*. This *plist* file contains settings about the app used by the operating system and the runtime environment. The file includes settings such as the name of the app, which is displayed on the iPad's Home screen. The app name is determined by a setting named Bundle Display Name (or `CFBundleDisplayName`, if you look at the raw key).

> **Note**
>
> When viewing the *Info.plist* for a project, you have the option to view the key name in plain English (as in Bundle Display Name) or as the raw key name (`CFBundleDisplay-Name`). To switch between the two view options, **Control-click** (or right-click) the *plist* editor and select **Show Raw Keys/Values** from the popup menu (see Figure 14.1).

A project that uses a NIB file as the starting UI for the app (i.e., a project created from a template with the Use Storyboard option turned off) will have the raw key `NSMainNibFile` setting in its *Info.plist*. The key's value is the NIB file name that is used when the app is launched. A project using a storyboard as the starting UI will have the `UIMainStoryboardFile` setting defined in the *Info.plist* with the storyboard file name as the key's value.

Another notable difference between an app that launches with a NIB and one that launches with a storyboard is the main window. All iOS applications have a main

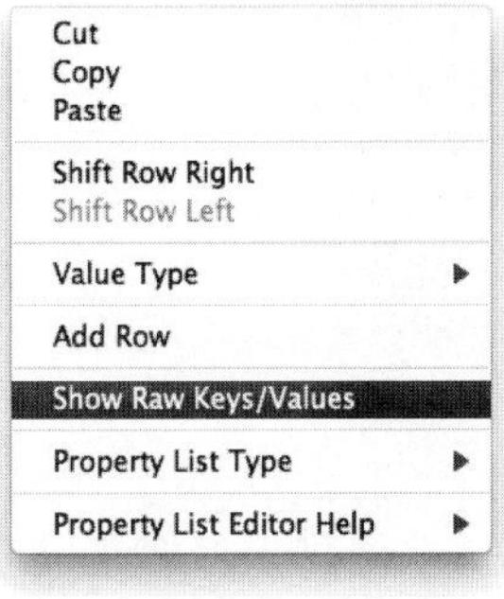

Figure 14.1   Use the popup menu to show and hide raw key values.

window. The main window contains the root view controller that manages the initial screen of the app. The generated project template for a NIB-based project will include a NIB and outlet for the main window. This is not the case with a storyboard project. When the app launches with a storyboard, the main window is not defined in the project. Instead, it is automatically created when the storyboard loads.

> **Note**
>
> To better understand the difference, create two new single view application projects. In one, turn on the Use Storyboard option and turn off the option in the other. Take a look at the generated project files. The storyboard-based project doesn't have any NIB files, only a single *MainStoryboard.storyboard* file. The code in the app delegate is also differ-ent. In the `application:didFinishLaunchingWithOptions:` method for the NIB-based project, you see that the `rootViewController` is set for the window. This code is not present in storyboard-based projects as it is done behind the scenes.

Scenes

Storyboarding introduces two new concepts to UI design: a scene and a segue.

A scene is a view controller representing a particular aspect of the screen. For iPhone applications, a scene typically represents the full screen of the device. The same can be true for iPad apps. However, a scene for the iPad may also represent only a por-tion of the screen where a collection of scenes is used to form the entire screen at run time. In other words, multiple scenes are displayed simultaneously to form the whole screen. (You learn how to break up the screen into multiple scenes in Chapter 15, "Doing More with View Controllers.")

Each scene is managed by a view controller, and every storyboard file has one and only one view controller flagged as the initial view controller (Figure 14.2). The ini-tial view controller is the first scene displayed by the storyboard when it is loaded.

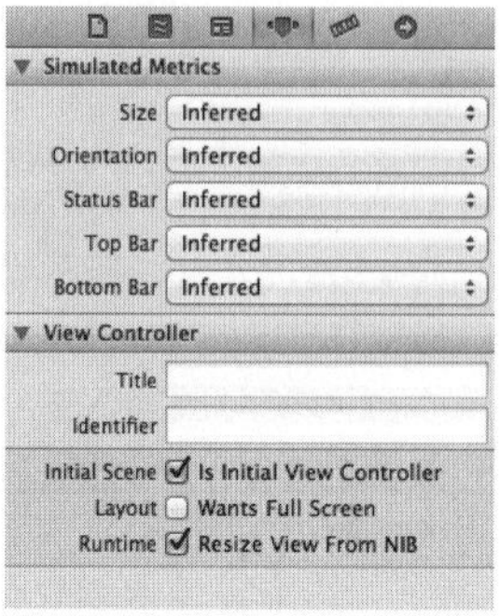

Figure 14.2   Is Initial View Controller flag available in the Attributes inspector

Segues

The other new concept introduced with storyboards is that of a segue. A segue represents the transition between two scenes (see Figure 14.3). It provides the magic needed to produce an animated transition from one scene to another without writing code.

A segue performs a transition from one scene to another when some event or action occurs within the first scene. For example, when a button is tapped in one scene, a

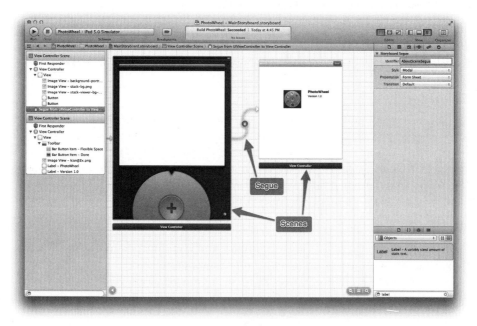

Figure 14.3   Sample storyboard with two scenes and one segue

segue performs the necessary work to display the next scene. The transition is often animated, with the new scene sliding up from the bottom or sliding in from right to left, similar to what you might see in a Keynote presentation. Other animated transitions are available as well, and you can even create your own custom animation sequence for a segue (which you will do later in this chapter).

What makes a segue cool—at least from the developer's perspective—is that the relationship between the two scenes and the transition are defined visually using Interface Builder. In other words, you don't have to write the code for it.

Granted, we as developers know that at some point code is needed, and this is true with segues. While a segue manages the transition between two scenes, it doesn't have the smarts to pass data between the scenes. And often a new scene must be told by the previous scene what content to display. Thankfully there is an event, `prepareForSegue:sender:`, that you override should you need to pass data between scenes. (You'll learn more about this method and using segues in the next chapter.)

Storyboarding PhotoWheel

So now you know: A storyboard is a visual design canvas for creating user interfaces consisting of scenes (view controllers) and segues (transitions between scenes). But to really understand a storyboard, you have to give it a go. Fortunately for you, you're at a place in the book where it's time to create the real PhotoWheel application, so using a storyboard for the UI design seems appropriate. While we're at it, now is also a good time to introduce another new feature in Xcode 4.2 called workspace.

Workspace

An Xcode workspace is a container for one or more related projects. It provides the following benefits:

- The Project navigator provides quick access to related projects.
- Xcode automatically detects dependencies between projects and builds them in the correct sequence.
- Project files are visible to other projects, so there is no need to copy shared libraries into project folders.
- The scope of Xcode's content-aware features, such as code completion, extends across all projects within the workspace.

A workspace can also contain related projects that don't necessarily share code and are not dependent on one another. You can, for example, create a workspace containing the PhotoWheel prototype and the new PhotoWheel project. The two projects are related but not dependent on each other. With the workspace, you will be able to switch quickly between the projects, make changes to either project, and build and run the projects, all from a single workspace window.

To create a new workspace, select **File > New > New Workspace** (or **Control-⌘-N**). Name the workspace "PhotoWheel" and save it to the same directory containing the PhotoWheelPrototype Xcode project. You should now have an empty workspace window.

Select **File > Add Files to "PhotoWheel"** (or **Option-⌘-A**). Select the Photo-WheelPrototype Xcode project file and click the **Add** button (see Figure 14.4). You now have one project contained in the PhotoWheel workspace.

Now add a new project to the workspace. To do this, select **File > New > New Project** (or **Shift-⌘-N**). Alternatively, you can **Control-click** the Project navigator and select **New Project** from the popup menu. Select the Empty Application template under **iOS > Application**. Click the **Next** button to continue.

For the project options, enter "PhotoWheel" as the Product Name, select iPad for the Device Family, and select the Use Core Data option. Also, select the Use Automatic Reference Counting option. Click the **Next** button. Save the project to the same directory containing the prototype project and the PhotoWheel workspace. Make sure the PhotoWheel workspace is selected as the group, as seen in Figure 14.5.

Click the **Create** button to create the new project. This will also add the project to the workspace. You should now have a PhotoWheel workspace containing two projects, PhotoWheel and PhotoWheelPrototype, as seen in Figure 14.6.

Did you notice that there was no option for a storyboard? The Empty Application template creates a bare-bones project. At the moment, the project does not support a main storyboard or NIB. This is something you do manually with a few simple steps, and while we're at it, let's do a couple of other things to the project so that you can concentrate on development.

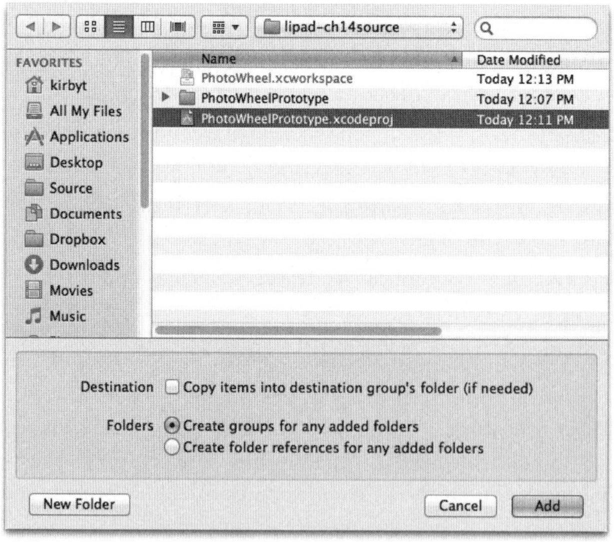

Figure 14.4   Add the PhotoWheelPrototype project to the workspace.

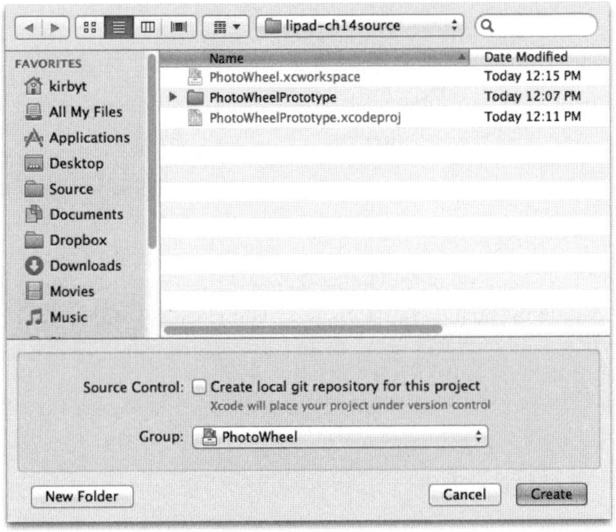

Figure 14.5   Create a new project in the PhotoWheel workspace. Make
sure you select the PhotoWheel workspace as the group.

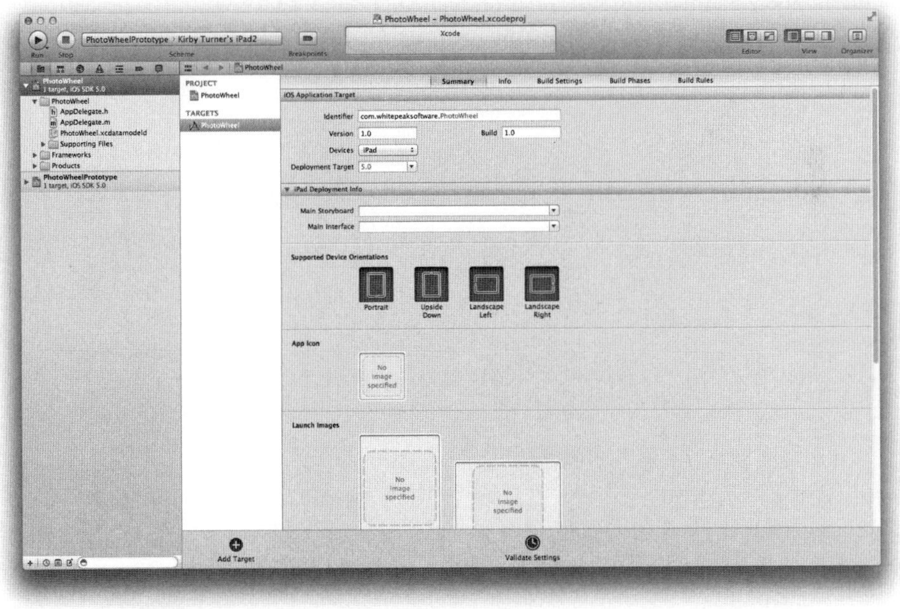

Figure 14.6   The PhotoWheel workspace contains two projects,
PhotoWheel and PhotoWheelPrototype.

Why Are We Using the Empty Application Template?

Xcode's application templates are a great way to quickly get started on a new project. The same is true for file templates such as the `UIViewController` subclass. The template generates the necessary code so that you can quickly get started, but you'll often find yourself deleting generated project files, renaming files, and deleting template code you won't ever use. And it's not uncommon for templates to change with each release of Xcode, which means you must relearn what the template will and won't do for you.

Sometimes it's just easier to work with empty templates. This means that you do all the work, but over time you'll find that it saves time since you do not have to clean up the files and code generated by the template. This is why many developers choose to use empty templates instead.

Add the Main Storyboard

You need to set up the project to use a storyboard, which means that the first thing you must do is add the main storyboard to the project. Select the PhotoWheel project or any of its files in the Project navigator. Type **⌘-N** to create a new file. Select Storyboard as the file type (found under **iOS > User Interface**, as shown in Figure 14.7). Click the **Next** button. Select iPad as the device family, and click **Next** again. Name the storyboard "MainStoryboard," then click the **Create** button. The new storyboard file is added to the PhotoWheel project.

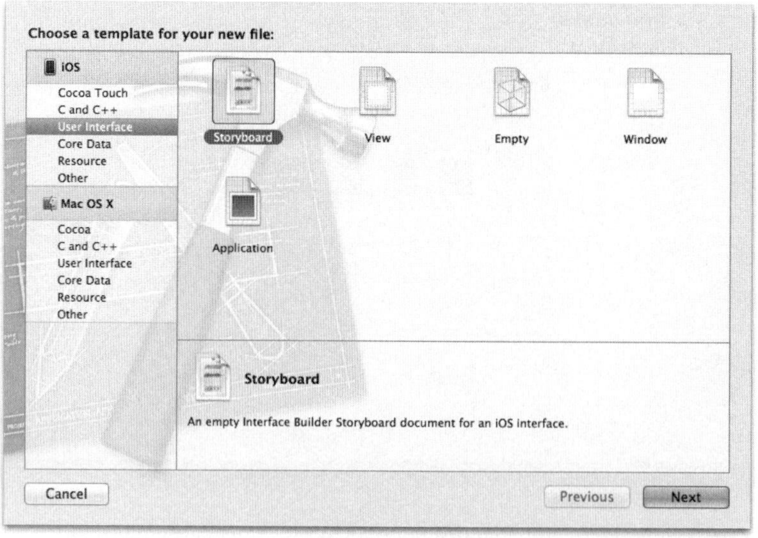

Figure 14.7   Add a new storyboard to the project. Storyboard is found under **iOS > User Interface**.

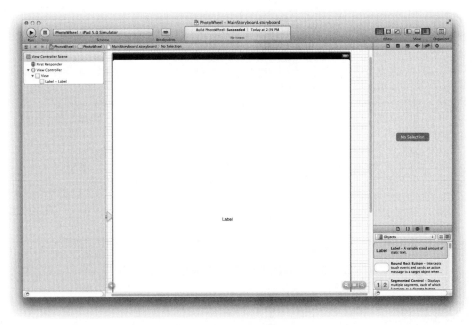

Figure 14.8   Screen shot of the PhotoWheel workspace with the main
storyboard open in the IB editor

Before the storyboard can be used, it needs an initial view controller representing
the initial scene. Select MainStoryboard in the Project navigator to open it. Open the
Object library found in the Utilities area (**Control-Option-⌘-3**). Drop a view controller object onto the storyboard's designer canvas. Next, drop a label onto the view
managed by the view controller. This will give you something visual when you test
that the storyboard is loading properly. Your storyboard should look similar to the one
in Figure 14.8.

One thing you quickly realize when working with iPad scenes is that they tend to
take up a lot of screen real estate. A helpful tip is to hide parts of the workspace that
you are not using while working on a storyboard. For instance, hide the Navigator
area (**⌘-0**) and the Utilities area (**Option-⌘-0**). You can also double-click the design
canvas to zoom in and out. This is helpful when you want to view multiple scenes at
once. You can also use the hover buttons at the bottom left and right corners of the
designer to show and hide the IB dock and to zoom in and out. Just be aware that
when you zoom out on a storyboard, edits cannot be performed. You must zoom in
on a scene to make edits, add and remove objects, and so on.

Set `UIMainStoryboardFile`

Next, you need to tell the project to use the storyboard. In the Project navigator, select the file *PhotoWheel-Info.plist*. It can be found under the Supporting Files group. **Control-click** (or right-click) the Editor area to display the popup menu. Select **Add Row** from the menu, as shown in Figure 14.9. If you are viewing the keys in plain English, type "Main Storyboard file base name" as the key for the new row. (The editor should find the key for you if you simply type "Main story.") If you are viewing the raw keys, the key name is `UIMainStoryboardFile`.

Next, enter "MainStoryboard" for the value. This is the name of the storyboard file you just created. However, do not include the file extension; it will be added for you at run time. The setting is shown in Figure 14.10. Be sure to save (⌘-S) your changes to the file.

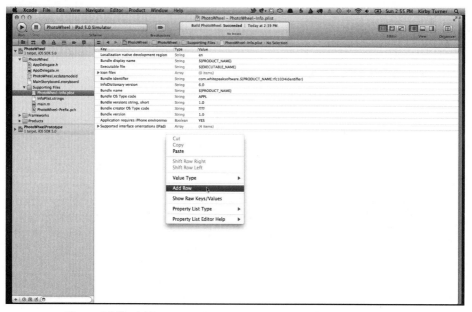

Figure 14.9   Add a row to the *plist* by **Control-clicking** the editor and selecting **Add Row** from the popup menu.

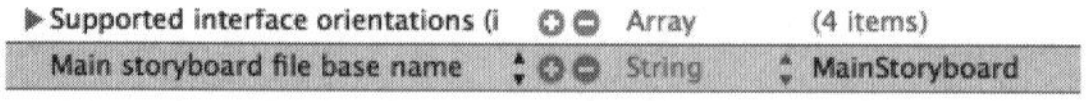

Figure 14.10   Set the "Main Storyboard file base name" to "MainStoryboard."

Update *AppDelegate*

The final step of the process is to change the `application:didFinishLaunching-WithOptions:` method in *AppDelegate.m* to *not* create the main window. This may seem odd given that all iOS applications must have a main window, but the window is created automatically when the main storyboard is loaded. If the code in the app delegate were to remain, the main storyboard would not be attached to the correct window.

Open the file *AppDelegate.m* found in the Project navigator. Delete the first few lines of code in the `application:didFinishLaunchingWithOptions:` method so that it matches the code in Listing 14.1.

Listing 14.1   **Changes to** *AppDelegate.m*

```
- (BOOL)application:(UIApplication *)application
didFinishLaunchingWithOptions:(NSDictionary *)launchOptions
{
    [self.window makeKeyAndVisible];
    return YES;
}
```

Save your changes and run the app. Make sure you have set the active scheme to PhotoWheel and the run destination to iPad 5.0 Simulator, as shown in Figure 14.11. You'll see PhotoWheel running in the simulator with its one scene containing the label. This tells you that the project has been properly set up to use the main storyboard.

> **Note**
>
> This work is done automatically when you select a project template that has the Use Storyboard option turned on. But since the option is not available with the Empty Application template, you are left with doing the setup yourself.

Add Images

One more thing must happen before you start work on the PhotoWheel app. A number of images are used in the app, everything from the app icon to background images for views. Instead of adding the images piecemeal as you read the rest of the book,

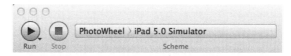

Figure 14.11   Select PhotoWheel as the active scheme, and select iPad
5.0 Simulator as the run destination.

let's add those images now. This will save you steps later, and it will save trees (as in printed pages) because we won't have to tell you to add an image here and there.

> ### Download the Images
>
> The images used to create PhotoWheel can be downloaded from the book's Web site, located at **learnipadprogramming.com/files/2011/08/lipad-pw-images.zip**. Download the *.zip* file containing the images, and unzip the archive on your system.

Now that you have downloaded the images used in PhotoWheel (you just did that, right?), it's time to add them to the PhotoWheel project. With the PhotoWheel project selected, select **File > Add Files to "PhotoWheel"** (**Option-⌘-A**). Navigate to and select the *lipad-pw-images* folder that was created when you unpacked the *.zip* file. Be sure to select the Destination option "Copy items into destination group's folder (if needed)" as shown in Figure 14.12; this copies the images into the PhotoWheel project directory. Click the **Add** button to add the images to the project.

The images needed to complete PhotoWheel are now part of the project, and they will be available when you need them. There's no need to worry about adding images to the project in later parts of the book.

Figure 14.12   Add images to the PhotoWheel project.

App Icon

With the images in place, there's no better time than the present to add the app icon to the project. When looking at the images, you may notice that there are multiple icon files (*Icon*.png*). Each of these represents the app icon; they are just at different resolutions. iPhone app icons are 57 × 57 pixels in size. iPad app icons are 72 × 72. And other sizes are used for things such as Spotlight's search icon, the Settings icon, and on iOS devices with a retina display (which, at the time of this writing, is just the iPhone 4). The different sizes enable the app icon designer to add and remove detail as needed to make the best-looking icon for the particular size.

iOS knows which icon to use for display. If, for example, the app icon is displayed in the Settings app, iOS looks for a 29 × 29-pixel icon. If that image isn't found, iOS will use the main app icon (72 × 72 for iPad and 57 × 57 for iPhone) and scale it down to the appropriate size. If you have the app icon stored at different sizes, you can tell iOS about them by adding icon references in the project's *Info.plist*.

To accomplish this with the PhotoWheel app, open *PhotoWheel-Info.plist* and add the entries shown in Figure 14.13 to the *plist*. This tells iOS about the different-size app icons for PhotoWheel.

Initial View Controller

As previously mentioned, each storyboard will have an initial view controller. This is the first scene displayed when the storyboard is loaded. MainStoryboard has only one scene at the moment, so it is the initial view controller. If, however, there are multiple scenes in the storyboard, you can change the initial view controller by selecting the view controller and selecting the Initial Scene setting in the Attributes inspector, as shown in Figure 14.14. But MainStoryboard has only one scene for the moment, so you do not need to worry about changing this setting. Instead, let's focus on setting up the storyboard.

Open MainStoryboard and select the one and only scene. Delete the label object added earlier, as it is no longer needed. You now have a clean slate to work with.

Drop an image view (`UIImageView`) onto the view managed by the scene's view controller. Set the image view to fill the entire view. A quick way to accomplish this is to open the Size inspector (**Option-⌘-5**) and set the X, Y, Width, and Height values, as shown in Figure 14.15.

Executable file		String	${EXECUTABLE_NAME}
Icon files	⇕ ⊕ ⊖	Array	⇕ (4 items)
Item 0		String	Icon.png
Item 1		String	Icon72x72.png
Item 2		String	IconSmall-50x50.png
Item 3		String	IconSmall.png
Bundle identifier		String	com.whitepeaksoftware.${PRODUCT_NAME}

Figure 14.13   Add the list of icon file names to the *PhotoWheel-Info.plist*.

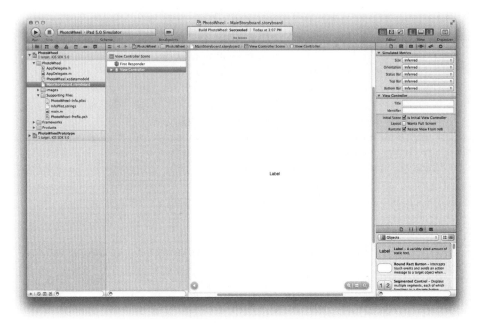

Figure 14.14   A storyboard with one scene flagged as the initial
view controller

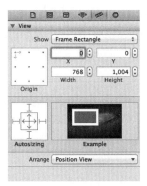

Figure 14.15   Size inspector values for the image view

Next, open the Attributes inspector (**Option-⌘-4**) and set the Image name to
background-portrait-grooved.png. You can open the drop-down list to see the list of available images. These are the images added to the project earlier.

Now add two more image views. The settings you want to use are listed in Table
14.1.

Table 14.1 `UIImageView` **Settings**

Image Name	X	Y	Width	Height
stack-viewer-bg-portrait.png	26	18	716	717
stack-bg.png	109	680	551	550

Next, add a button to the view. The button is listed in the Object library as Round Rect Button, or you can filter on "Button" or "`UIButton`." In the Attributes inspector, set the Type to Custom and set the Image to *stack-add.png*; this image is used when the button is in a normal state. To add the image representing the button in a down state, change the State Config from Default to Highlighted. Now set the Image to *stack-add-down.png*. The button, which is displayed as an image, now has visible normal and down states.

Switch to the Size inspector and set the following for the button: X to 295, Y to 846, and Height and Width each to 178. You should now see a round **+** button at the bottom of the scene.

One more visual addition to the scene is needed. Drop another Round Rect Button (`UIButton`) onto the view. Change its Type to Info Light. Set X to 722 and Y to 959; you cannot change its Width and Height because those are controlled by the system.

The main scene is now complete. Run the app and take a look at your work. The scene should look like Figure 14.16.

Figure 14.16   The PhotoWheel app running with the main scene displayed in the simulator

> **Note**
>
> If the arrow pointing to the wheel is not visible, you may need to reorder the images. You can accomplish this by selecting the image view for *stack-viewer-bg-portrait.png* and then selecting **Editor > Arrange > Send to Front** from the menu bar.

Another Scene

Another scene is needed, one that is displayed when the info button (the *i* button at the lower right of the UI) is tapped. Create the new scene in MainStoryboard by dropping in a new view controller from the Object library. You may want to zoom out so that you can see the two views side by side, as shown in Figure 14.17.

This new scene displays the About screen for the app when the user taps the info button found on the main scene. The first thing to add is a toolbar that is displayed across the top of the scene. Find the toolbar in the Object library, drop it onto the view of the new scene, and place it at the top of the view.

By default, a toolbar anchors itself to the bottom of the view. This is determined by the autosizing settings found in the Size inspector. Autosizing plays an important role when the device is rotated. It allows objects on the screen to automatically size and position themselves when the device rotates. This is covered in more detail in Chapter 18, "Supporting Device Rotation." For now, just know that you need to anchor the toolbar to the top of the view.

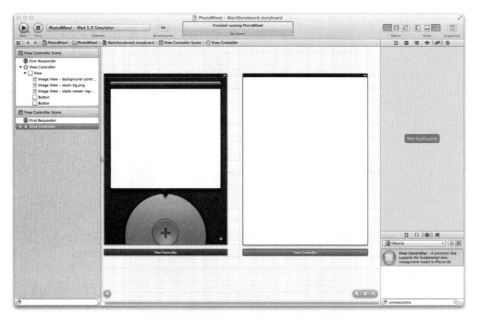

Figure 14.17   Storyboard with two scenes, zoomed out to see both at the same time

To accomplish this, open the Size inspector. Click on the dashed red constraint bar at the top of the Autosizing settings area. This anchors the object to the top of its current position. In other words, if the top position changes when the user rotates his iPad, the object adjusts its position to whatever is the top of the display. Next, click on the solid red I beam at the bottom, turning it into a dotted I beam. This prevents the toolbar from anchoring to the bottom. The Size inspector should look like Figure 14.18.

The toolbar comes with a default button labeled **Item**. Let's move the item to the right side of the toolbar. Filter the Object library with the word "Flexible." This shows the flexible space bar button item in the object list. Drop this object just to the left of the **Item** button in the toolbar. This moves the **Item** button to the far right.

Note

There is also a fixed space bar button item that you can use if you ever want to separate toolbar items by a specific set of pixels.

The **Item** button is now positioned correctly, but we need to change it to read "Done." One way to do this is by changing the title of the button, but a better way is to change the button's identifier. Select the **Item** button, and then open the Attributes inspector. Open the Identifier drop-down list to see the list of available system buttons. This list covers the most common buttons used in iOS apps, including the **Done** button. Change the Identifier from Custom to Done. This changes the display style of the button and sets its label to "Done."

Why Is This Better?

Setting a button's identifier in the Attributes inspector is better because your app will use system-provided buttons whenever possible. One benefit here is that the buttons have already been localized and internationalized by Apple. Also, using system-provided buttons helps ensure consistency between apps, reducing the learning curve for the user.

Let's display the information about the app on the About scene. This scene will include the app icon in an image view along with the name of the app and its version number. To

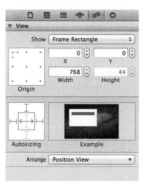

Figure 14.18   The Size inspector values for the toolbar

accomplish this, drop an image view onto the view. Set the image name to *Icon@2x.png*. From the Size inspector, set X to 160, Y to 190, and the Width and Height to 114.

Now add a label (`UILabel`) to the view, and set its Text to "PhotoWheel." In the Attributes inspector, set the Font to System Bold 24.0. (You can click the T icon in the Font field to display the popover with font settings, as shown in Figure 14.19.) Last, resize the label's width so that the text, "PhotoWheel," is not truncated. You can eyeball the position of the label or set the size manually (X to 317, Y to 190, Width to 193, and Height to 21).

Place another label below the PhotoWheel label. Set its Text to "Version 1.0" and its Font to System 18. Use the alignment guides (covered in Chapter 3, "Getting Started with Interface Builder") to position and size the label based on the PhotoWheel label, or set the size manually (X to 317, Y to 219, Width to 193, and Height to 21). The scene should look similar to the one in Figure 14.20.

Creating a Segue

The storyboard now has two scenes, but there is no segue (also known as a transition) between the two. What we want is to have the About scene display when the user taps the info button on the main scene. This can be accomplished without writing a single line of code.

Adjust the designer display so that you can see both scenes. You do not need to zoom completely out, but you do need to see portions of both scenes at the same time. Next, **Control-click** on the info button (*i*) in the main scene and drag it anywhere on the About scene. This displays the Storyboard Segues HUD, showing the `performSegueWithIdentifier:sender:` method. Select this method to create a segue between the info button and the About scene. A line with an arrow at the end is drawn between the two scenes. This arrow represents the segue and shows the relationship between the two scenes.

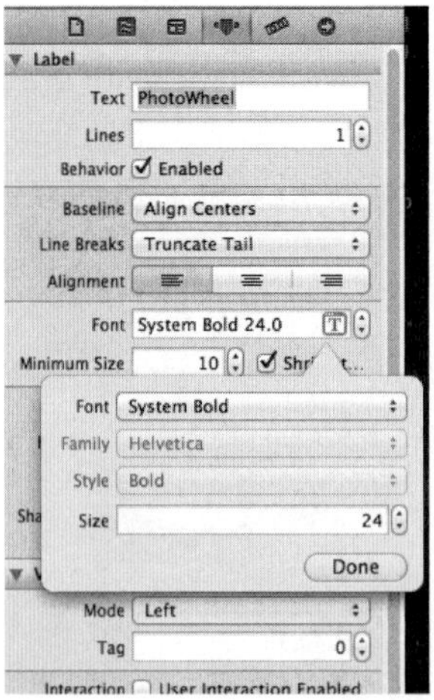

Figure 14.19   Font settings popover

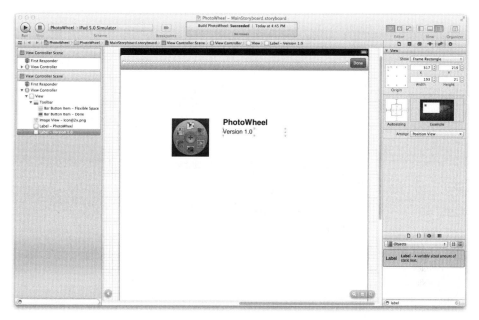

Figure 14.20   The About scene as it looks in the storyboard

> **Note**
>
> If your segue is not working when you run the app, it's possible that the segue was not created from the info button. The easiest way to fix this is to delete the segue and create it again, making sure you **Control-click** and drag from the info button to the About scene.

You can fine-tune the transition managed by the segue by clicking the segue arrow and then opening the Attributes inspector. Set the Identifier to AboutSceneSegue. The Identifier can be used to perform segues programmatically. Next, set the style, presentation, and transition for the segue.

We want the segue Style to be Modal; this displays the About scene on top of the main scene. Set the Presentation to Form Sheet. This resizes the About scene to the smaller form size. Finally, leave the Transition set to Default (although you should play with other transition styles so that you can see how they differ). The storyboard should now look like it does in Figure 14.21.

Run the app and take a look at your handiwork. The app displays the main scene when launched, and the About scene is displayed when the info button is tapped, as shown in Figure 14.22. All of this was accomplished without writing a single line of code. Of course, you'll quickly see that code is needed to dismiss the About scene when the **Done** button is tapped. You'll learn how to add code behind a scene in the next chapter, so for now you must quit the app to dismiss the About scene.

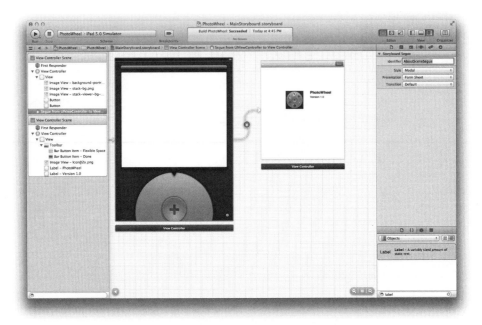

Figure 14.21   The storyboard with two scenes and a segue

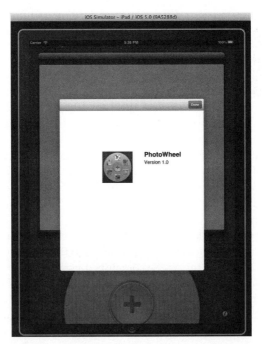

Figure 14.22   The completed app when run in the simulator

Summary

This chapter introduced you to a new way of creating user interfaces called story-boarding. A storyboard is built on top of Interface Builder, so everything you already know about building a UI in IB still applies. You also learned how to set up an empty application project to support storyboarding, and you were introduced to workspaces, a way to quickly access related projects from the same workspace window.

Exercises

1. Open *PhotoWheel-Info.plist*. Switch between the plain English and raw key values views.

2. Create a single view application project. Select the Use Storyboard option. Now create a second project, but this time do not select the Use Storyboard option. Compare the two projects.

3. Create a workspace and add the two projects created in the previous exercise to the workspace.

4. Open MainStoryboard and change the style, presentation, and transitions for the AboutSceneSegue.

Doing More with View Controllers

In Chapter 14, "Storyboarding in Xcode," you learned how to use a storyboard to build the initial user interface for PhotoWheel. You created the main storyboard, added two scenes to it, and used a segue to display the About scene from the main scene. All of this was accomplished without writing a single line of code; but we developers know an app cannot really be useful unless there is code.

This chapter will show you how to do more with your scenes by writing custom view controller classes, with each view controller managing a storyboard scene. You will also learn how to create and use custom segues to give your app that special somethin'-somethin'.

Implementing a View Controller

You learned early on in the book that when using a NIB for a screen, a view controller class is implemented to coordinate the interactions between the view and model classes. You do the same with a storyboard. Each scene in the storyboard has its own view controller. In fact, to create a scene in a storyboard, you drop a view controller object from the Object library onto the IB design canvas. This means that each scene, at a minimum, has a view controller, which is of type UIViewController. But to do more, you will need to create your own UIViewController subclass.

Let's take a look at the About scene created in the last chapter. A segue connects the About scene to the main scene by way of the info button found in the lower right corner of the main scene. When the user taps the button, the About scene is displayed. To close the About scene, the user taps the **Done** button, but it doesn't work. That's because you have not told the **Done** button what to do when the button is tapped.

How do you tell the **Done** button to dismiss the About scene? You might be thinking, "Use another segue," but unfortunately that will not work here. A segue guides the user forward through the app's UI, not backward. There is no segue for dismissing a modal view controller. Instead, a bit of code is needed.

A custom view controller is needed for the About scene. This view controller will have an action for the **Done** button. The implementation of this action dismisses the About scene when **Done** is tapped.

To make this happen, create a new view controller class. Select the PhotoWheel project in the workspace. Type ⌘-N to create a new file. Select the Objective-C class template and click the **Next** button. Name the class `AboutViewController` and make it a subclass of `UIViewController` (see Figure 15.1). Click the **Next** button, and save the class file in the project directory by clicking the **Create** button. The `AboutViewController` has been added to the PhotoWheel project.

Note

You can use the `UIViewController` subclass template instead of the Objective-C class template if you like. This will generate additional code for you, which is not needed at this time.

An action is needed for the **Done** button, so open the file *AboutViewController.h* and add the declaration for the action method `done:`. The source code is shown in Listing 15.1.

Listing 15.1   *AboutViewController.h* **with the New Action Method** `done:`

```
#import <UIKit/UIKit.h>

@interface AboutViewController : UIViewController

- (IBAction)done:(id)sender;

@end
```

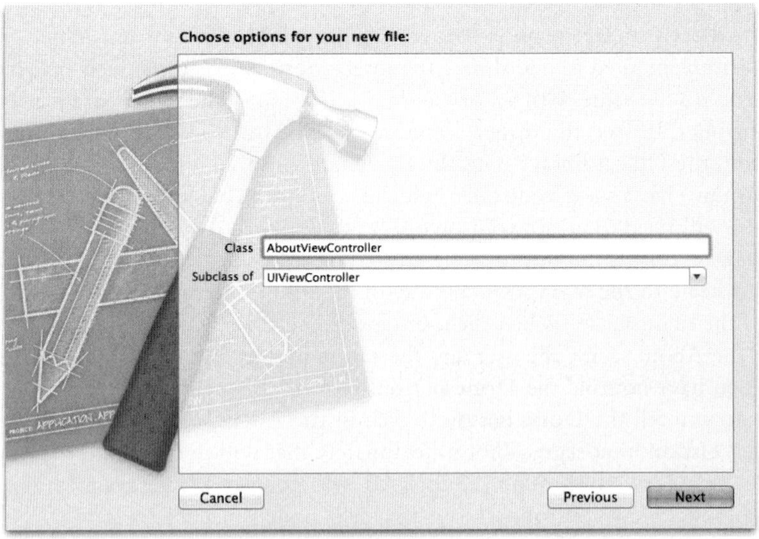

Figure 15.1   Create a new class named `AboutViewController`, which is a subclass of `UIViewController`.

Next, you need to implement `done:`. Open *AboutViewController.m* (**Control-⌘-Up** or **Control-⌘-Down** to switch between the counterpart files) and add the `done:` implementation, shown in Listing 15.2.

Listing 15.2   *AboutViewController.m* **with the** `done:` **Implementation**

```
#import "AboutViewController.h"

@implementation AboutViewController

- (IBAction)done:(id)sender
{
    [self dismissModalViewControllerAnimated:YES];
}

@end
```

The implementation is straightforward. It calls the `-dismissModalViewControllerAnimated:` method on itself. This closes the About scene and returns the user to the main scene.

With the view controller now in place, it's time to update the About scene so that it knows about and uses the `AboutViewController` class. Open the *MainStoryboard.storyboard* file. Select the view controller for the About scene. If the document outline is visible (**Editor > Show Document Outline**), you can click the View Controller object in the IB dock. Otherwise click the View Controller object in the object bar below the scene (see Figure 15.2).

Open the Identity inspector (**Option-⌘-3**). The Class defaults to `UIViewController`. Change this to `AboutViewController`. Now the scene is aware of the `AboutViewController` you created. Now connect the **Done** button to the `done:` action declared in `AboutViewController`. One way to accomplish this is to **Control-click** and drag from the **Done** button to the `AboutViewController` object displayed in either the IB dock or in the object bar. Note that because the **Done** button is inside the toolbar, you must click the **Done** button twice to select it. Or you can expand the document structure and select the **Done** button, as shown in Figure 15.3.

> **Note**
>
> Yet another way of declaring the `done:` action and making the connection is to use the Assistant editor. Refer to Chapter 3, "Getting Started with Interface Builder," for instructions on using the Assistant editor.

That's it. The **Done** button is now connected to the `done:` action method, and the `done:` action method dismisses the modal view, which is the About scene. Save your changes and run the app. Tap the info button to display the About scene. Tap the **Done** button on the About scene to close it and return to the main scene.

Everything should work smoothly now.

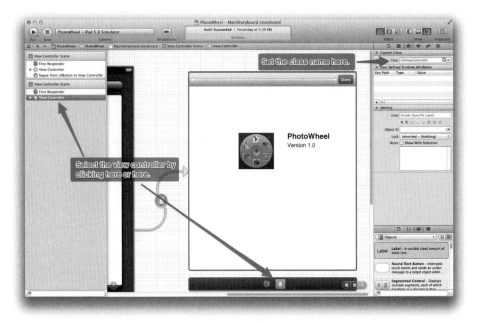

Figure 15.2   The About View Controller Scene in the main storyboard

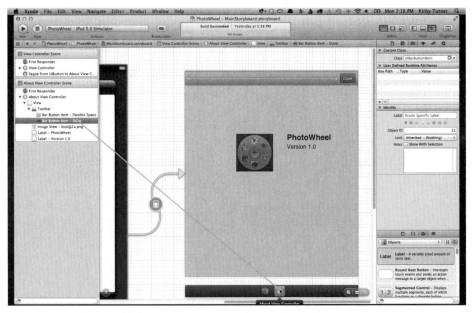

Figure 15.3   Connect the **Done** button to the `done:` action.

Segue

As you may recall, a segue manages the transition between two scenes. A segue is defined visually within the storyboard, and you use the Attributes inspector to fine-tune it. You fine-tune the segue by combining its style, presentation, and transition. For instance, the `AboutSceneSegue` created in Chapter 14, "Storyboarding in Xcode," uses the style Modal, presentation Form Sheet, and transition Default. When the segue is used to display the About scene, the scene animates up from the bottom (transition). It fills only the center portion of the screen; it does not take over the full screen (presentation). And it's a modal view (style), meaning it sits on top of the underlying view, and user interaction with the underlying view is disabled.

> **Note**
>
> Not all segue types have the same three properties: style, presentation, and transition. A push segue, for example, has style and destination, and a popover segue has style, direction, anchor, and pass-through.

The combination of properties defines the segue and its behavior. The combination you use depends on the design of the scene and app. For example, if the app was using a navigation controller, a push segue would be used to push a new scene (view controller) onto the navigation stack. Or a popover segue can be used to display a view within a popover. There's even a replace-style segue that replaces one scene with another.

But what if you cannot find the ideal segue for your app's needs? For this you can create a custom segue.

Creating a Custom Segue

A custom segue is a segue that you implement to suit the needs of your app. Creating a custom segue gives you complete control over the segue's behavior. Say you want to have an explosion-style animation that starts from the center of the screen when transitioning from one scene to another. (Not that you would, but let's use that as an example.) The iOS SDK doesn't provide a segue for this type of effect, so you will need to create one.

To create a custom segue, you create a new class that subclasses `UIStoryboard-Segue`. In the class implementation, override the `-(void)perform` method to perform the custom transition. The segue provides access to both the source and destination view controllers, so you can change the transition based on these two controllers.

Let's take a closer look at a custom segue by creating one.

Setting the Scene

PhotoWheel needs a way to display a photo browser when a photo is tapped, and the photo browser needs a way to return to the main scene with a tap of a finger. But unlike the About scene, the photo browser should not be modal; it should fill the entire screen.

iOS provides a controller class named `UINavigationController` which manages a stack of view controllers. The top view controller in the stack is the visible controller. A new controller is added to the stack with a push (the `-pushViewController: animated:` method). This makes the new controller the top controller, which in turn makes it the visible controller. To return to a previous controller in the stack, a pop is performed. The navigation controller enables an app to pop the top controller (`-popViewControllerAnimated:`) or pop to a specific controller within the stack (`-popToViewController:animated:`), including the root view controller (`-popToRootViewControllerAnimated:`), which is at the bottom of the stack.

The navigation controller is *perfect* for PhotoWheel! The main view controller is the root controller on the navigation stack since it's the first controller displayed. When the user taps a photo, the photo browser view controller is pushed onto the navigation stack. This displays the photo browser.

To get back to the main scene, the user needs to tap a **Back** button, which is provided by the navigation controller. The navigation controller displays a navigation bar at the top of the screen. A **Back** button is displayed on the left that enables the user to navigate back to the previous view controller in the stack.

Before you implement the custom segue, let's add the photo browser scene to the storyboard. And let's use the standard push segue to transition between the main scene and the photo browser scene.

Open the *MainStoryboard.storyboard* file and drop a Round Rect Button somewhere onto the main scene. The button is temporarily used to test the transition from the main scene to the photo browser scene. Next, create a new scene by dropping a view controller object onto the design canvas. **Control-click** the button on the main scene and drag to the new scene to create a new segue between the two scenes. Click the segue and open the Attributes inspector. Set the Style to Push and the Destination to Current.

If you run the app, you might be surprised to learn that the new scene does not appear when the button in the main scene is tapped. This is because the new scene is pushed onto the navigation stack, but the storyboard does not have a scene with a navigation controller. You can quickly remedy this by selecting the main scene in the storyboard and choosing **Editor > Embed In > Navigation Controller** from the menu bar. This creates a new scene for the navigation controller, and it sets the scene as the initial view controller.

Run the app to see the navigation controller in action. When you tap the button in the main scene (at the center on the left of Figure 15.4), the photo browser scene is pushed onto the stack (at the right in Figure 15.4). You can return to the main scene by tapping the **Back** button displayed in the navigation bar at the top of the screen. Figure 15.4 shows the two scenes side by side.

Navigation and the transition between the two scenes are working, but some things are not quite right. The navigation bar at the top of the main scene looks out of place. Not only that, it causes the rest of the screen to shift downward. You can fix this by hiding the navigation bar, but if you hide it, it won't be visible in the second scene.

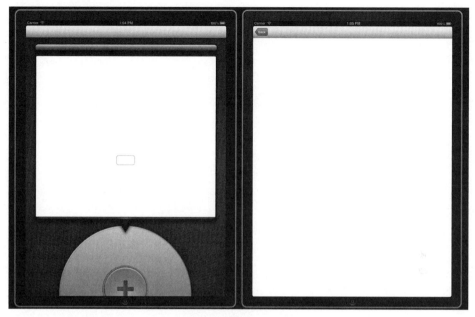

Figure 15.4   Side-by-side view of the main and photo browser scenes

And if it is not visible, the user will have no way of returning to the main scene from the photo browser scene.

The other issue is the transition from the main scene to the photo browser scene. While the default transition of sliding the next view from right to left is fine for many apps, it won't look so great once PhotoWheel displays the pictures. The effect we want is to have the transition explode from the touch point, so that when you touch a PhotoWheel, the images fan out in a view. This is the perfect job for a custom segue.

First things first: Let's fix the navigation bar display, then move on to the custom segue.

The navigation bar should have a black style. This makes it blend in better with the PhotoWheel look and feel. To change the style, you need to open the Document Outline, select the Navigation Controller Scene, and click on the disclosure icon for the Navigation Controller object. Click on the navigation bar object to select it, then open the Attributes inspector (**Option-⌘-4**). In the Inspector, set the Style from Default to Black Translucent.

Next, you want to hide the navigation bar so that it does not appear on the main screen. To hide the navigation bar, open the *MainStoryboard.storyboard* file and select the Navigation Controller Scene. Open the Attributes inspector (**Option-⌘-4**) and deselect the Shows Navigation Bar attribute (shown in Figure 15.5). You can see that the navigation bar is hidden in the storyboard scenes when you deselect this option.

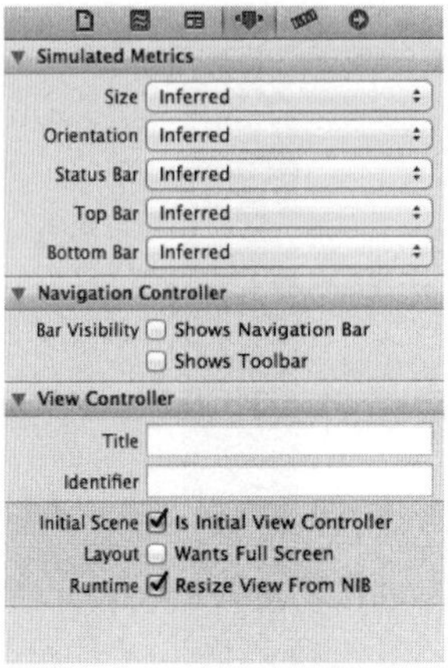

Figure 15.5   Deselect the Show Navigation Bar option to hide the
navigation bar.

Now that the navigation bar is hidden, the user will not have a way to return to the
main scene from the photo browser scene. There are two possible ways to solve this:

- Show the navigation bar in -viewWillAppear: for the photo browser view
  controller.
- Include the showing of the navigation bar in the custom segue.

In PhotoWheel, we have chosen the second option because that enables you to control
the animation sequence for presenting the navigation bar. Let's implement that custom
segue.

Implementing a Custom Segue

A custom segue is needed to override the default visual transition provided by the
push segue. To use a custom segue, you change the segue attributes using the Attributes inspector. Open the main storyboard if it isn't already open. Select the segue
that is performed when the button is tapped, and open the Attributes inspector
(**Option-⌘-4**). Change the Style from Push to Custom, and set the segue Class to
CustomPushSegue. Now when the button is tapped, the custom push segue is used
and handles the transition from the main scene to the photo browser scene.

But where is the class CustomPushSegue? Answer: You need to create it.

Start by creating a new Objective-C class. Type **⌘-N** and select Objective-C class
from the list of file templates. Name the class CustomPushSegue and set it as a subclass of UIStoryboardSegue. Finally, save the new class to the PhotoWheel project.

A UIStoryboardSegue subclass must override the -perform method. This is
where the animation for the transition takes place. The -perform implementation for
CustomPushSegue is given in Listing 15.3. Open *CustomPushSegue.m* and make the
changes to your code.

Listing 15.3 *CustomPushSegue.m*

```objc
#import "CustomPushSegue.h"
#import "UIView+PWCategory.h"                                    // 1

@implementation CustomPushSegue

- (void)perform
{
   UIView *sourceView = [[self sourceViewController] view];     // 2
   UIView *destinationView = [[self destinationViewController] view];   // 3

   UIImageView *sourceImageView;
   sourceImageView = [[UIImageView alloc]
                      initWithImage:[sourceView pw_imageSnapshot]];     // 4

   UIImageView *destinationImageView;
   destinationImageView = [[UIImageView alloc]
                           initWithImage:[destinationView pw_imageSnapshot]];
   CGRect originalFrame = [destinationImageView frame];
   [destinationImageView setFrame:CGRectMake(originalFrame.size.width/2,
                                             originalFrame.size.height/2,
                                             0,
                                             0)];
   [destinationImageView setAlpha:0.3];                         // 5


   UINavigationController *navController;
   navController = [[self sourceViewController] navigationController];   // 6
   [navController pushViewController:[self destinationViewController]
                           animated:NO];                        // 7

   UINavigationBar *navBar = [navController navigationBar];     // 8
   [navController setNavigationBarHidden:NO];
   [navBar setFrame:CGRectOffset(navBar.frame,
                                 0,
                                 -navBar.frame.size.height)];   // 9

   [destinationView addSubview:sourceImageView];                // 10
   [destinationView addSubview:destinationImageView];           // 11

   void (^animations)(void) = ^ {                               // 12
      [destinationImageView setFrame:originalFrame];            // 13
      [destinationImageView setAlpha:1.0];                      // 14

      [navBar setFrame:CGRectOffset(navBar.frame,
                                    0,
                                    navBar.frame.size.height)]; // 15
   };
```

```
    void (^completion)(BOOL) = ^(BOOL finished) {          // 16
        if (finished) {
            [sourceImageView removeFromSuperview];
            [destinationImageView removeFromSuperview];
        }
    };

    [UIView animateWithDuration:0.6
                     animations:animations
                     completion:completion];               // 17
}

@end
```

Let's walk through the code and see what is happening:

1. On the second line, you see #import "UIView+PWCategory.h". This is a category on UIView that you will implement momentarily. (It will have a method named pw_imageSnapshot.) This method takes a screen shot of the view and returns the screen shot as a UIImage. Screen shot images of the source and destination views are used to simplify the animation sequence for this segue.

2–3. At the top of -perform, two local variables are set, one for the source view and another for the destination view. The local variables make referencing the views easier later in the code.

4. This is followed by setting local variables for image views that contain the source and destination screen shot images. These image views, not the actual images, are what will be animated.

5. Next, the original frame for the destination image view is saved to a local variable. The destination image view frame is then set with a Width and Height of 0 and is placed in the center of the screen. The alpha for the destination image view is set to 0.3. This gives the view a transparent look. Setting the alpha to 0.0 will hide the view and setting it to 1.0 will make it fully visible. As part of the animation sequence, this view will go from a transparent look (alpha 0.3) to fully visible (alpha 1.0).

Note

The ultimate goal will be to perform the segue animation sequence from the photo that has been touched, but no photos are displayed in PhotoWheel yet. Therefore, the animation sequence starts from the center of the screen. The code for the segue will evolve over time as you build the app, and eventually the animation sequence will start from the appropriate location.

6–7. The next line of code saves a reference to the navigation controller to a local variable. Then the navigation controller is used to push the destination view controller onto the navigation controller stack. Note that the animated flag is set to NO. This means that the default animation used during a push is turned off. The default animation sequence is not needed since the segue is performing the animation sequence.

8. Following the push of the destination view controller, a reference to the navigation bar is saved. The navigation bar is then unhidden. Remember, we need the navigation bar to be displayed on the destination view controller, aka the photo browser scene. Without it, the user will have no way to return to the main scene.

9. Simply showing the navigation bar during the animation sequence is okay, but having it slide down from the top would look even better. After the navigation bar is unhidden, it is moved off the top of the screen. CGRectOffset() is used to adjust the frame for the navigation bar. It returns a rectangle that is offset from the source rectangle. In this case, the offset is the negative of the navigation bar's height, which moves it off the top of the screen by the same number of pixels as the height.

Note

CGRectOffset is but one of many helper functions found in CGGeometry, which makes working with and manipulating CGRect, CGSize, and CGPoint variables easier. For a complete list of functions, take a look at the *CGGeometry Reference* document (**developer.apple.com/library/ios/#documentation/GraphicsImaging/Reference/ CGGeometry/Reference/reference.html**).

10–11. Next, the source image view (containing the screen shot of the source view) and the destination image view (containing the screen shot of the destination view) are added to the view hierarchy of the destination view controller. Why do this?

The destination view controller has been pushed onto the navigation stack. That makes the destination view controller the topmost controller, which means its view is the visible view. Adding the screen shot images from the source and destination views to the destination view controller's view hierarchy makes these image views the visible elements on the screen. And since the destination image view starts out as an alpha of 0.3, the source image view shows through the transparency of the destination image view.

12. The destination view controller having been set up, it's now time to define the animation sequence. An animation block is defined for the animation sequence, which performs three primary steps.

13. It resizes the destination image view to its original size. The resize is animated, so the visual effect is that the view grows in size.

14. The destination image view goes from a transparent visual state to a fully visible state by setting the alpha to 1.0. This too is animated, so the transition from transparent to fully visible is gradual through the animation sequence. The source image view is hidden once the destination image view is fully visible.

15. The navigation bar slides down from the top of the screen. Here `CGRect-Offset` is used again, this time to move the navigation bar to the top of the screen. Because the move is animated, the user sees a slide-down effect.

16. That's it for the animation sequence. Following it is the block completion declaration. The completion block is called once the animation sequence is complete. The completion block removes the source and destination image views from the destination view controller's view hierarchy. These static images of the screens are no longer needed, which is why they are removed. Since it is the destination image view that is the visible element on the screen, and since it is an exact screen shot of the destination view, removing the image views is not noticeable to the user.

17. The final line of code in -`perform` executes the animation sequence. The duration for the sequence is set to 0.6 seconds, and the animation and completion blocks are passed in.

Slow Motion

To see the animation sequence in slow motion, change the duration to some number of seconds longer than 0.6 seconds, such as 20 or 30 seconds.

Before You Compile

Before you compile and run the app, you still need to add the `UIView+PWCategory` to the PhotoWheel project. Type ⌘-N to create a new file. This time select the Objective-C category template instead of the class template. Name the category "PWCategory" and set "Category on" to `UIView`, as seen in Figure 15.6. Then add the category to the project.

Open *UIView+PWCategory.h* and add the code in Listing 15.4.

Listing 15.4   *UIView+PWCategory.h*

```
#import <UIKit/UIKit.h>

@interface UIView (PWCategory)

- (UIImage *)pw_imageSnapshot;

@end
```

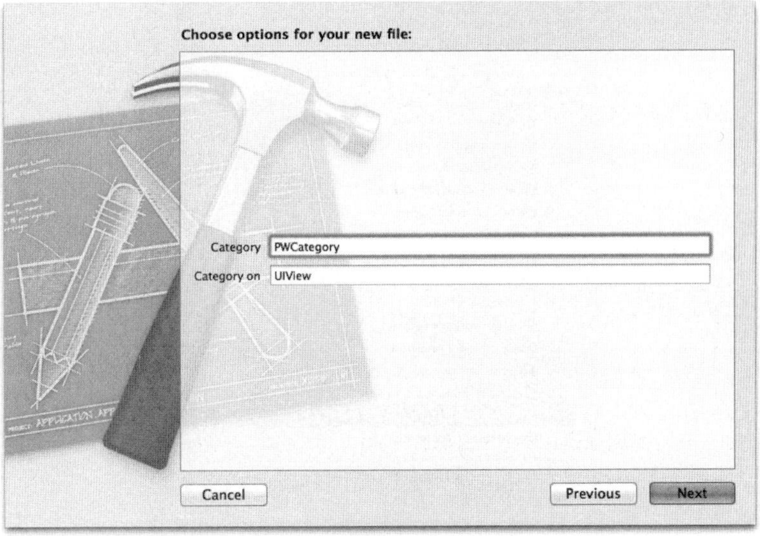

Figure 15.6   Select the Objective-C category template.

Now open *UIView+PWCategory.m* and add the code in Listing 15.5.

Listing 15.5   *UIView+PWCategory.m*

```
#import "UIView+PWCategory.h"
#import <QuartzCore/QuartzCore.h>

@implementation UIView (PWCategory)

- (UIImage *)pw_imageSnapshot
{
    UIGraphicsBeginImageContext([self bounds].size);
    [[self layer] renderInContext:UIGraphicsGetCurrentContext()];
    UIImage *image = UIGraphicsGetImageFromCurrentImageContext();
    UIGraphicsEndImageContext();

    return image;
}

@end
```

> **Note**
>
> A category extends a class. Because you are not the owner of the class, it is always a good idea to prefix category method names. This reduces the chances of a conflict should the class owner, which in this case is Apple, decides to add a method name `imageSnapshot`.

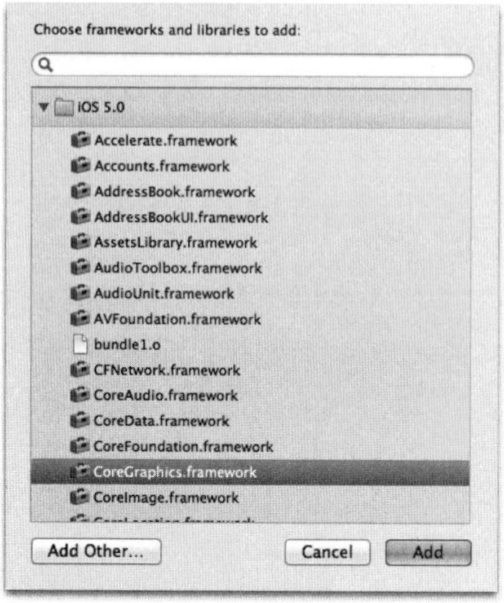

Figure 15.7   Add the Core Graphics framework to the
PhotoWheel project.

One more change is needed before you can compile the application. The function
CGRectOffset is defined in the Core Graphics framework. You must add this frame-
work to the PhotoWheel project, as shown in Figure 15.7. (Refer to Chapter 13, "Data
Persistence," if you need a refresher on how to add a framework to an Xcode project.)

You should now be able to compile and run the app. When you do, tap the button
that invokes CustomPushSegue and watch your handiwork in action.

Customizing the Pop Transitions

A segue is a great way to visually represent a transition between two scenes. However,
in the case of a navigation-based app (an app, such as PhotoWheel, that uses a navigation controller), a segue defines the transition for pushing only. There is no way to
define a segue for *popping* a view controller from the navigation controller stack.

If you can't use a segue for the pop transition, what other options are there? You
could roll your own navigation controller model, but that would be time-consuming.
After all, who really wants to reinvent that wheel? (No pun intended.) The easier
approach is to subclass UINavigationController.

Subclassing the navigation controller is an easy way to override the default behavior
provided by the class. But keep in mind that UINavigationController does a lot
for you, and it can be easy to mess something up by subclassing it. In fact, the documentation for UINavigationController says, "This class is not intended for subclassing." This statement doesn't mean you *can't* subclass it, but it is a warning to *deter*
you from doing it.

That said, there is no other way, other than subclassing, to override the default transition from a pop on the navigation controller. To have a pop transition that is consistent with the push segue, you must subclass `UINavigationController`. There is no getting around it.

To subclass `UINavigationController`, create a new class (⌘-N) using the Objective-C class template. Name the class `CustomNavigationController` and make it a subclass of `UINavigationController`.

To change the pop transition, you override the `-popViewControllerAnimated:` method. The new implementation is shown in Listing 15.6. Open *CustomNavigation-Controller.m* and add the code from the listing to your class implementation.

Listing 15.6   *CustomNavigationController.m*

```
#import "CustomNavigationController.h"
#import "UIView+PWCategory.h"

@implementation CustomNavigationController

- (UIViewController *)popViewControllerAnimated:(BOOL)animated
{
    UIViewController *sourceViewController = [self topViewController];

    // Animates image snapshot of the view
    UIView *sourceView = [sourceViewController view];
    UIImage *sourceViewImage = [sourceView pw_imageSnapshot];
    UIImageView *sourceImageView = [[UIImageView alloc]
                                    initWithImage:sourceViewImage];

    NSArray *viewControllers = [self viewControllers];
    NSInteger count = [viewControllers count];
    NSInteger index = count - 2;

    UIViewController *destinationViewController;
    destinationViewController = [viewControllers objectAtIndex:index];
    UIView *destinationView = [destinationViewController view];
    UIImage *destinationViewImage = [destinationView pw_imageSnapshot];
    UIImageView *destinationImageView = [[UIImageView alloc]
                                         initWithImage:destinationViewImage];

    [super popViewControllerAnimated:NO];

    [destinationView addSubview:destinationImageView];
    [destinationView addSubview:sourceImageView];

    CGRect frame = [destinationView frame];
    CGPoint shrinkToPoint = CGPointMake(frame.size.width / 2,
                                        frame.size.height / 2);
```

```
void (^animations)(void) = ^ {
    [sourceImageView setFrame:CGRectMake(shrinkToPoint.x,
                                         shrinkToPoint.y,
                                         0,
                                         0)];
    [sourceImageView setAlpha:0.0];

    // Animate the nav bar too
    UINavigationBar *navBar = [self navigationBar];
    [navBar setFrame:CGRectOffset(navBar.frame, 0, -navBar.frame.size.height)];
};

void (^completion)(BOOL) = ^(BOOL finished) {
    [self setNavigationBarHidden:YES];
    // Reset the nav bar position
    UINavigationBar *navBar = [self navigationBar];
    [navBar setFrame:CGRectOffset(navBar.frame, 0, navBar.frame.size.height)];

    [sourceImageView removeFromSuperview];
    [destinationImageView removeFromSuperview];
};

[UIView transitionWithView:destinationView
                  duration:0.3
                   options:UIViewAnimationOptionTransitionNone
                animations:animations
                completion:completion];

    return sourceViewController;
}

@end
```

The code in Listing 15.6 is similar to the code for CustomPushSegue, so a thorough walk-through is not necessary. The primary difference is that the code for –popViewControllerAnimated: reverses the animation sequence found in CustomPushSegue. Also, –popViewControllerAnimated: returns a reference to the view controller that is popped from the navigation stack. The rest of the code should look familiar to you.

To use the new CustomNavigationController class, we need to change the class name for the navigation controller created in the initial view controller defined in the storyboard. Open the file *MainStoryboard.storyboard*. Select the navigation controller in the Navigation Controller Scene, then open the Identity inspector. Change the class from UINavigationController to CustomNavigationController, as shown in Figure 15.8.

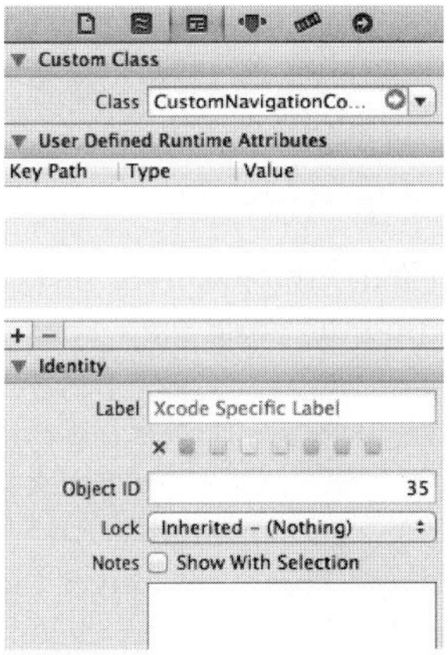

Figure 15.8   Set the class name for the navigation view controller.

Run the app again and check out the new pop transition. That looks much better.

Container View Controller

A container view controller is a view controller containing one or multiple child view controllers. It is used as a way to present content from a combination of different view controllers. `UINavigationController`, `UITabBarController`, and `UISplitViewController` are examples of container view controllers. A container view controller is the parent to the controllers it contains, forwarding messages and events to its children.

Using a custom container view controller in your iPad app is really useful as it enables you to break down the entire screen into smaller parts, each of which is managed by its own view controller. In this way, each view controller becomes more focused in its role within the application. The code for each view controller becomes smaller and easier to maintain, and the view controllers can become reusable components within the application.

Note

Using a container view controller to separate pieces of the UI into smaller parts managed independently is not a new concept. The pattern has been around for some time now, especially in the Web world where it is known as a composite view.

To make your own container view controller, you create a new class that subclasses `UIViewController`. Within your view controller class, you make use of the containment view methods provided by `UIViewController`. These methods are

- `-addChildViewController:`
- `-removeFromParentViewController`

- -transitionFromViewController:toViewController:duration:options: animations:completion:
- -willMoveToParentViewController:
- -didMoveToParentViewController:

UIViewController also includes the property childViewControllers, which is a read-only NSArray containing the child view controllers for the container view controller.

A key feature of the container view controller is message forwarding. Prior to iOS 5's enhancements to UIViewController for container view controllers, it was up to the developer to roll her own containment model. And building in reliable message forwarding was difficult to achieve. This is no longer the case. Important messages and events are forwarded to each child view controller, including rotation messages and view events such as -viewWillAppear:, -viewDidAppear:, -viewWillDisappear:, and -viewDidDisappear:.

Message forwarding can be turned off by overriding the method -automatically-ForwardAppearanceAndRotationMethodsToChildViewControllers in the container view controller. Return NO and messages will not be forwarded to the child view controllers.

> **Warning**
>
> If you do turn off forwarding, it is up to you to forward the appropriate messages to the child view controllers.

Using a container view controller is as simple as calling -addChildView-Controller:, adding an instance of another view controller. When the view controller is added as a child, it receives the message -willMoveToParentView-Controller:, which includes the parent view controller as a parameter. You override this method in the child view controller to perform any necessary logic prior to the view controller becoming a child of the parent controller. It is then up to your code to perform any transitions needed for the presentation of the child view controller.

Once the transition is complete, your code must call -didMoveToParentView-Controller: on the child view controller. This method is *not* called automatically because the parent view controller does not know about the transition, if any, for the child view controller. You can override this method in your child view controller to perform any necessary logic after the view controller has become a child of the parent controller.

Removing a child view controller from the parent follows a reverse workflow. When you call -removeFromParentViewController within a child view controller, you must first call -willMoveToParentViewController:, and when you do, -removeFromParentViewController automatically calls -didMoveToParent-ViewController:.

Create a Container View Controller

Let's take advantage of containment views in PhotoWheel. The main screen has two distinct areas: the photo album viewer at the top and the photo album wheel at the bottom. Managing both of these areas within the same view controller will result in a very lengthy view controller class that will be hard to maintain. To get around this problem, let's make the main view controller a container view controller and separate the other two areas into child view controllers of the main controller.

Start by creating a new `UIViewController` subclass named `MainViewController`. By now, the steps to create a new class should be familiar to you, but as a quick reminder, enter ⌘-N and select the Objective-C class template. Name the class `Main-ViewController` and make it a subclass of `UIViewController`. Then save it to the PhotoWheel project directory.

While you're at it, you might as well create the view controller classes for the photo album viewer and the photo album's wheel. Let's call the photo album view controller, which is the area at the top of the screen, `PhotoAlbumViewController`. And let's call the photo albums wheel, displayed at the bottom of the screen, `PhotoAlbumsViewController`. Follow the same steps as you did when creating `MainViewController`.

Add the Child Scenes

`PhotoAlbumViewController` and `PhotoAlbumsViewController` are the view controller classes for two new scenes, which means that the scenes must be added to the main storyboard. There is no way within the storyboard to indicate that a scene is a child to another scene, so while the storyboard contains all the scenes for the Photo-Wheel app, you still need to write some code to add the new scenes as child view controllers to `MainViewController`. But first things first:

1. Open the *MainStoryboard.storyboard* file and drag two view controllers onto the design canvas to create the new scenes.

2. Select one view controller and change its class name from `UIViewController` to `PhotoAlbumViewController` (**Option-⌘-3** to open the Identity inspector).

3. Next—and this is very important—you need to set the identifier for this scene. Open the Attributes inspector (**Option-⌘-4**) and set the Identifier attribute to PhotoAlbumScene.

   Why is setting the identifier important? The identifier will be used to programmatically load the scene from the storyboard. As you will soon see, this is how the scene is added to the main view controller as a child view controller.

4. Next, select the other view controller. Set its class name to `PhotoAlbumsView-Controller` and its identifier to PhotoAlbumsScene.

5. Finally, select the view controller that represents the main screen. Set its class name to `MainViewController` and its identifier to MainScreen.

An example of the storyboard with the new scenes is shown in Figure 15.9.

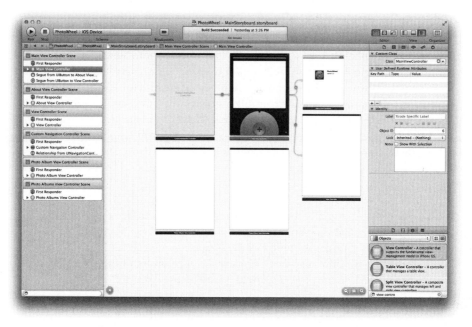

Figure 15.9 New scenes added to the main storyboard

Size Doesn't Matter

It's important to note that as of right now, IB does not allow you to resize a scene manually. This means that although the child scenes will use only a subset of the entire screen real estate, within IB the child scene is represented as a full-screen view. Don't worry; adjustments will be made in code to get around this sizing limitation.

While you have the main storyboard open, go ahead and add the visual elements to each new scene. In the `PhotoAlbumsViewController` scene, add the `UIImageView` for the disc and add the **+** button. You'll follow the same steps as you did in Chapter 14, "Storyboarding in Xcode." The only difference is that you want to place the disc and the **+** button at the top of the scene instead of at the bottom. The actual placement for this view will be determined at run time in code as the child view controller is added to the parent view controller.

Do the same for the `PhotoAlbumViewController` scene. Add the `UIImageView` for the photo album viewer and add the button used to test the segue to the photo browser scene.

Hint

You can copy and paste the objects from the main scene into the child scene as a time-saver. When you paste the objects into the child scene, be sure that they are positioned in the top left corner of the scene.

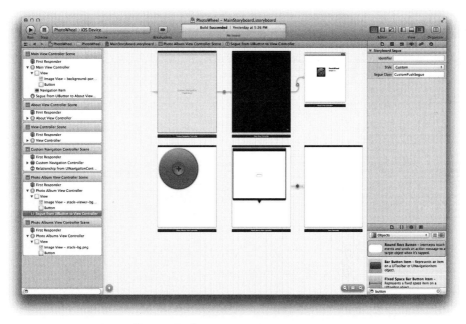

Figure 15.10   The completed storyboard

Once you are finished, remove the objects represented in the child scenes from the Main View Controller Scene. Note that when you remove the button attached to the segue to the photo browser scene, the segue is also removed. This is a good thing because the button has moved. It is now in the `PhotoAlbumViewController` scene. This also means that you need to create a new segue from the button in the Photo Album View Controller Scene to the photo browser scene, which you should do now. Be sure to set up the segue as a custom segue using the class `CustomPushSegue`.

Once you are finished, the storyboard should look like the screen shot in Figure 15.10.

Add Child View Controllers

A bit of code is needed to add the new scenes as child view controllers to the main view controller. It would be nice if this could be performed within the storyboard, and maybe one day that feature will exist. But for now, writing a bit of code is needed.

To add the new scenes as children of the main scene, you must get the instance of each child view controller from the storyboard. The instance is then added to the array of child controllers on the main view controller. Once the child view controller is added, a call is made to `-didMoveToParentViewController:` on the child view controller. Finally, the child view controller overrides `-didMoveToParentViewController:` so that it can set its position within the view hierarchy. That's it. So let's make it happen in PhotoWheel.

The -viewDidLoad of MainViewController is a good place to add the child view controllers, so open *MainViewController.m* and add the code given in Listing 15.7.

Listing 15.7   **Adding Child View Controllers to** MainViewController

```
#import "MainViewController.h"                                      // 1
#import "PhotoAlbumViewController.h"
#import "PhotoAlbumsViewController.h"

@implementation MainViewController

- (void)viewDidLoad                                                 // 2
{
[super viewDidLoad];

    UIStoryboard *storyboard = [self storyboard];                   // 3


    PhotoAlbumsViewController *photoAlbumsScene;                     // 4
    photoAlbumsScene =
        [storyboard instantiateViewControllerWithIdentifier:@"PhotoAlbumsScene"];
    [self addChildViewController:photoAlbumsScene];                 // 5
    [photoAlbumsScene didMoveToParentViewController:self];          // 6

    PhotoAlbumViewController *photoAlbumScene;                       // 7
    photoAlbumScene = [storyboard
                    instantiateViewControllerWithIdentifier:@"PhotoAlbumScene"];
    [self addChildViewController:photoAlbumScene];                  // 8
    [photoAlbumScene didMoveToParentViewController:self];           // 9
}

@end
```

Let's take a look at the code in Listing 15.7:

1. It starts off by importing the header files (*MainViewController.h*, *PhotoAlbumViewController.h*, and *PhotoAlbumsViewController.h*), followed by the @implementation statement for MainViewController and the @end statement at the end of the listing for the implementation.

2. The piece we're most interested in is the override for -viewDidLoad. This method is called when the content view for the view controller is loaded. Once the view is loaded, all of its objects—including outlets, if any—are available to the code in the view controller class.

3. The content view for this view controller is loaded from the main storyboard. The view controller has a property named storyboard, which is a reference to the storyboard used to load the content view. You use this reference to access

resources in the storyboard, including other view controllers and segues. To make the code more readable, the local variable `storyboard` is set to the view controller's `storyboard` property value.

4. The next thing that happens is that an instance of the `PhotoAlbumsView-Controller` is created from the storyboard. Note that the view controller instance is created using the identifier set earlier in this chapter. If the identifier is not found in the storyboard, an invalid argument exception is thrown when the app is run.

5. The instance of the `PhotoAlbumsViewController` is stored in a local variable. The local variable is used to add the view controller as a child view controller to `MainViewController`. `[self addChildViewController:photoAlbum-Scene]` is the line of code that adds the photo albums view controller as a child.

6. After the controller is added, you can perform a transition to present the child view controller. The transition can be animated or not. That's up to you. In the particular case of PhotoWheel, a transition is not performed. Instead, we'll let the child view controller size and position itself within the parent view during the `-didMoveToParentViewController:` call, which is called immediately after the view controller is added as a child.

There is no reason why sizing and positioning of the child view controller can't be handled as part of the transition in the main view controller. Depending on the requirements of the app, that might make perfect sense. A combination of `-willMoveToParentViewController:`, `-didMoveToParentView-Controller:`, and transitioning within the parent view controller can even be used. For instance, the `-willMoveToParentViewController:` could be implemented in the child view controller to set the size of its content view. An animation sequence could be implemented in the parent view controller that fades in and positions the child view controller. And the `-didMoveTo-ParentViewController:` could be implemented in the child view controller to retrieve data from a Web service. It's up to you to decide the best approach and design for your app.

> **Note**
>
> `-willMoveToParentViewController:` is called automatically on a view controller when it is added as a child. However, `-didMoveToParentViewController:` is not automatically called. It's up to you to make that call in your code.

7–9. The same steps are performed again, but this time for the photo album scene. An instance of `PhotoAlbumViewController` is returned from the storyboard. The instance is added as a child view controller. And the `-didMoveToParentView-Controller:` method is called on the photo album view controller.

At this point, the view controllers for the photo albums and photo album scenes are children of the main view controller. However, if you were to run the app, these scenes would not be visible. Each scene needs to be sized and positioned before being added to the view hierarchy managed by the main view controller.

To accomplish this, open *PhotoAlbumsViewController.m* and add the code in Listing 15.8. This code has the implementation for -didMoveToParentViewController:. In this implementation, the content view for the view controller is added to the parent's view hierarchy. Next, the size and position of the child content view are set. This will make the child scene visible when the app is run.

Listing 15.8   Setting the Size and Position in *PhotoAlbumsViewController.m*

```
#import "PhotoAlbumsViewController.h"

@implementation PhotoAlbumsViewController

- (void)didMoveToParentViewController:(UIViewController *)parent
{
    // Position the view within the new parent
    [[parent view] addSubview:[self view]];
    CGRect newFrame = CGRectMake(109, 680, 551, 550);
    [[self view] setFrame:newFrame];

    [[self view] setBackgroundColor:[UIColor clearColor]];
}

@end
```

The last statement in the -didMoveToParentViewController: implementation sets the background color for the view to clear. This makes the background transparent.

This setting can be made in code (as shown in Listing 15.8) or in the storyboard using IB. To set it in IB, select the view, open the Attributes inspector, and change the Background attribute to Clear Color. However, the clear color is not visible in IB, so this is a case where explicitly setting the background color in code makes it clear (pun intended) what background color is used.

Similar code is added to *PhotoAlbumViewController.m*. Open this file and add the code in Listing 15.9.

Listing 15.9   Setting the Size and Position in *PhotoAlbumViewController.m*

```
#import "PhotoAlbumViewController.h"

@implementation PhotoAlbumViewController

- (void)didMoveToParentViewController:(UIViewController *)parent
{
    // Position the view within the new parent
    [[parent view] addSubview:[self view]];
```

```
    CGRect newFrame = CGRectMake(26, 18, 716, 717);
    [[self view] setFrame:newFrame];

    [[self view] setBackgroundColor:[UIColor clearColor]];
}

@end
```

At this point, you have a main view controller that contains two child view controllers. When you run the app, the main screen looks like it did before, so you may be wondering why the main scene was separated into two child scenes. The benefits of this will become apparent in Chapter 16, "Building the Main Screen." It is in Chapter 16 that you will implement the view controllers for each scene. When the scenes are separated into individual view controllers, the code is easier to write and maintain.

Another thing you will notice when you run the app is that the custom segue is not animating correctly. The custom segue assumes that the source view controller represents the entire screen. This is no longer the case. The source view controller is PhotoAlbumViewController, and it is only a subset of the entire screen. Therefore, a fix to the custom segue is needed.

Fix the Custom Push Segue

The local variable sourceView is pointing to the content view of the PhotoAlbumViewController. To correct the animation sequence, you need to change the sourceView to reference the content view from the MainViewController, which it so happens is the parent view controller.

This one-line fix is shown in Listing 15.10. Open *CustomPushSegue.m* and apply the fix.

Listing 15.10   **Fix Applied to the Custom Push Segue**

```
#import "CustomPushSegue.h"
#import "UIView+PWCategory.h"

@implementation CustomPushSegue

- (void)perform
{
    // Replace:
    // UIView *sourceView = [[self sourceViewController] view];
    // with:
    UIView *sourceView = [[[self sourceViewController] parentViewController] view];

    // Other code left out for brevity

@end
```

Run the app and check your handiwork.

Summary

In this chapter, you learned how to implement view controllers for scenes defined in the main storyboard. Storyboarding is a powerful feature, and it helps reduce source code. But it does not completely eliminate the need for source code, as you now know.

You also learned how to use view controller containment to separate a screen into multiple scenes that are pieced together by code forming the full screen. With containment, you end up with view controllers that are focused on a particular purpose. This makes the code easier to maintain, and it makes it possible to reuse the view controller, if needed, in other parts of the application.

Exercises

1. Slow down the animation sequence in `CustomPushSegue` and observe how the animation sequence works.

2. Change the background color for the photo browser scene to black or some other color to see the `CustomPushSegue` animation sequence better. Set the background color using the Attributes inspector, and then set it to a different color in code.

3. Update the About view controller scene to programmatically display the version number. Hint: You want to add an outlet to the `AboutViewController` that is connected to the version label defined in the scene. Then in the `-viewDidLoad` event for the view controller, retrieve the version number from the application bundle and set the label. The code to retrieve the version number is `[[[NSBundle mainBundle] infoDictionary] objectForKey:@"CFBundleVersion"]`.

16

Building the Main Screen

Welcome to the longest chapter in the book. This chapter is long because it walks you through building the core piece of PhotoWheel. It is not broken into multiple chapters because this core piece focuses on one area: the main screen of the application. This chapter also provides the foundation needed for the remaining chapters. As a reward for completing it, you'll have a functioning photo app that you can show off to others. If you thought you could work through this chapter over your morning coffee, you might find that it's time for lunch by the time you have completed it.

To better understand why this chapter is so long—and why it isn't broken into multiple chapters—here is a list of the things you will learn and accomplish:

- ***Reusing the prototype code***

  A good amount of code presented in this chapter originated in the prototype app. However, tweaks to the code are needed in places.

- ***Setup of the PhotoWheel Core Data model***

  Like the reusable code, the Core Data model is copied from the prototype. However, tweaks are needed to support PhotoWheel.

- ***Making changes to the WheelView class***

  The original implementation of this class suited the needs of the prototype app, but PhotoWheel is no prototype app. The WheelView class will be beefed up to be more powerful and flexible.

- ***Completing the photo album scene***

  This is the child scene displayed at the top of the screen. You will complete the UI design and implementation for this scene. In other words, you will finally be able to view photos stored within a photo album.

- ***Building a functional photo album manager***

  This includes adding and removing photo albums, and adding photos to albums.

- ***Building a custom grid view***

  You will build a custom grid view, which is modeled after UITableView, to display a collection of photos in a series of rows and columns.

The extra time spent on this chapter is worthwhile. By the end, you will have a function-ing photo app that you can show off to family and friends. Not only that; you will have built the foundation needed for the remainder of the book. After completing this chapter, you can focus on adding cool new features to PhotoWheel, such as importing photos from Flickr, syncing with iCloud, and displaying a slideshow of your photos using AirPlay.

Now top off your coffee mug, get settled in your favorite comfy chair, and prepare to build the main screen of PhotoWheel.

Reusing Prototype Code

Starting with Chapter 8, "Creating a Master-Detail App," you implemented various concepts that ultimately will roll into the PhotoWheel app. While the prototype app itself is a throwaway, that doesn't mean that all of the code has to be tossed. On the contrary, there are some real gems in the prototype app that can and will be used in PhotoWheel.

To reuse the code, you must copy the files from the PhotoWheelPrototype proj-ect into the PhotoWheel project. One way to copy the files is to drag and drop the file references from the PhotoWheelPrototype project into the PhotoWheel project within the PhotoWheel workspace. However, this copies only file references, not the actual files. While this might be fine when you want to share files between projects, that's not what you need to do here, because additional changes need to be made to files common to the two projects. You don't want a change needed for PhotoWheel to break your PhotoWheelPrototype app (and vice versa), so the best solution is to copy the files, not just the file references. Unfortunately, this cannot be done in Xcode, so you will need to use Finder instead.

Copy Files

Open Finder and navigate to the PhotoWheelPrototype project directory. A quick way to do this is to **Control-click** (or right-click) any file in the PhotoWheelPrototype project, then select **Show in Finder** from the popup menu. Next, select the following files in Finder and drop them into the PhotoWheel project in Xcode (see Figure 16.1):

- *_Photo.h* and *.m*
- *_PhotoAlbum.h* and *.m*
- *Photo.h* and *.m*
- *PhotoAlbum.h* and *.m*
- *PhotoWheelViewCell.h* and *.m*
- *SpinGestureRecognizer.h* and *.m*
- *WheelView.h* and *.m*

Xcode prompts you for options when copying files into a new project, shown in Fig-ure 16.2. Make sure you check "Copy items into destination group's folder (if needed)."

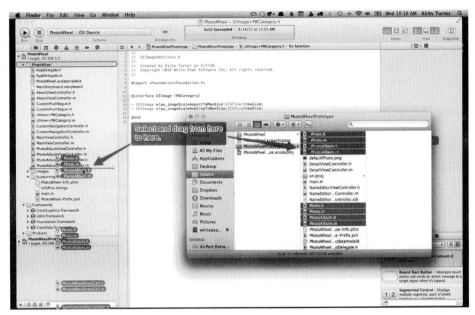

Figure 16.1   Dropping files into the PhotoWheel Xcode project

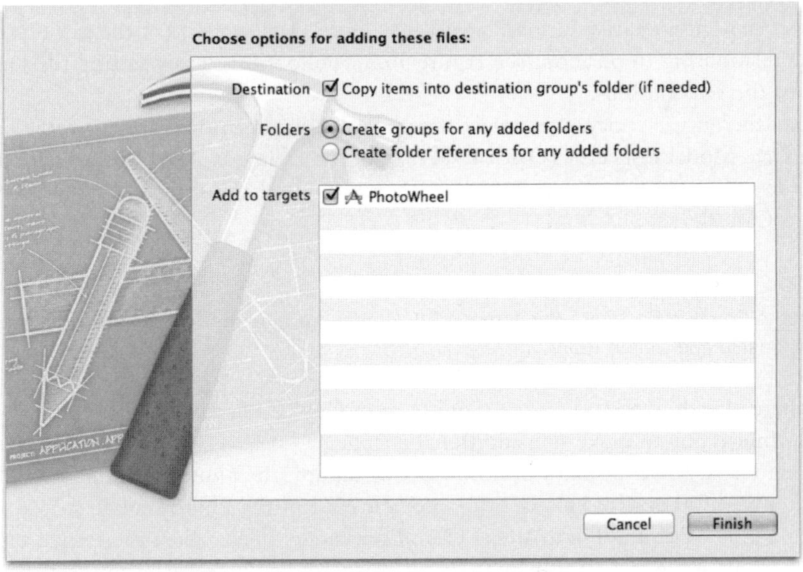

Choose options for adding these files:

Destination ☑ Copy items into destination group's folder (if needed)

Folders ⦿ Create groups for any added folders
○ Create folder references for any added folders

Add to targets ☑ ⚔ PhotoWheel

Cancel   Finish

Figure 16.2   Copy file options. Be sure to select the "Copy items into destination group's folder (if needed)" option.

With this option selected, the files from the PhotoWheelPrototype project directory are copied into the PhotoWheel project directory. If you do not select the option, the files will remain in the PhotoWheelPrototype project directory and file references will be added to the PhotoWheel project. Future changes to the files will be reflected in both projects, which is not what is wanted here.

Core Data Model

One file you do not want to copy is the Core Data model file (*PhotoWheelPrototype .xcdatamodeld*). This is an inappropriate file name for the PhotoWheel project, and renaming a Core Data model is not the easiest task to accomplish. Besides, the Photo-Wheel project already has a data model file name, *PhotoWheel.xcdatamodeld*.

While the original Core Data model file isn't needed, you *do* want to use the same data model in PhotoWheel as was used in the prototype app. One option is to re-create the entries in the PhotoWheel data model, but an easier way is to copy and paste the entries from the prototype data model into the PhotoWheel data model.

Open the *PhotoWheelPrototype.xcdatamodeld* data model in the PhotoWheelPrototype project. Select the entities Photo and PhotoAlbum and copy them to the clipboard (⌘-C). Next, open the *PhotoWheel.xcdatamodeld* file in the PhotoWheel project and paste (⌘-V) the entities.

The Core Data model for PhotoWheel now includes the entities needed by the app. However, the copy-paste trick doesn't copy all the settings. Inverse relationships and Delete Rules must be set up again.

Select the Photo entity in the PhotoWheel Core Data model. Set the photoAlbum inverse relationship to photos (see Figure 16.3). Follow this up by setting the Delete Rule for the relationships.

Select the Photo entity, then select the photoAlbum relationship within the entity. In the Data Model inspector (**Option-⌘-3**), set the Delete Rule to Nullify. Next, select the PhotoAlbum entity, then select the photos relationship, and set its Delete Rule to Cascade.

> **Note**
>
> Refer to Chapter 13, "Data Persistence," if you need a refresher on setting the inverse relationship and Delete Rule.

You are already working on the Core Data model for PhotoWheel, so now is as good a time as any to make one additional change.

When PhotoWheel displays a photo from an album, the photo thumbnail will be sized at 100 × 100 pixels. This size does not yet exist in the Photo model, so you will need to add it. With the PhotoWheel Core Data model open, select the Photo entity. Add a new attribute to Photo named smallImageData and set its Type to Binary Data. Save the Core Data model file.

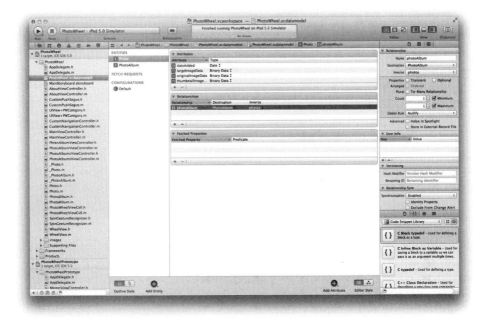

Figure 16.3   Set the inverse relationship.

At this point, you can regenerate the _Photo model class, but since it is only one field, it's faster to make the class change by hand. Open _Photo.h and add a new declared property named smallImageData. Next, open _Photo.m and add the @dynamic statement for smallImageData. The updated _Photo.h and .m files are shown in Listing 16.1.

Listing 16.1   **Updated** _Photo **Class**

```
///////
// _Photo.h
///////
#import <Foundation/Foundation.h>
#import <CoreData/CoreData.h>

@class _PhotoAlbum;

@interface _Photo : NSManagedObject {
@private
}
@property (nonatomic, retain) NSDate * dateAdded;
@property (nonatomic, retain) NSData * originalImageData;
@property (nonatomic, retain) NSData * thumbnailImageData;
```

```
@property (nonatomic, retain) NSData * largeImageData;
@property (nonatomic, retain) NSData * smallImageData;
@property (nonatomic, retain) _PhotoAlbum *photoAlbum;

@end



///////
//   _Photo.m
///////
#import "_Photo.h"
#import "_PhotoAlbum.h"


@implementation _Photo
@dynamic dateAdded;
@dynamic originalImageData;
@dynamic thumbnailImageData;
@dynamic largeImageData;
@dynamic smallImageData;
@dynamic photoAlbum;

@end
```

Now open the *Photo.h* model class and add a method named -smallImage that returns a pointer to a UIImage. Then open *Photo.m*, add the implementation for -smallImage, and update the -saveImage: method to save the small image as a 100 × 100-pixel image. The updated source code is given in Listing 16.2.

Listing 16.2 **Updated** Photo **Class**

```
///////
//   Photo.h
///////
#import "_Photo.h"

@interface Photo : _Photo

- (void)saveImage:(UIImage *)newImage;

- (UIImage *)originalImage;
- (UIImage *)largeImage;
- (UIImage *)thumbnailImage;
- (UIImage *)smallImage;

@end
```

```
///////
//  Photo.m
///////
#import "Photo.h"

@implementation Photo

- (UIImage *)image:(UIImage *)image scaleAspectToMaxSize:(CGFloat)newSize
{
   CGSize size = [image size];
   CGFloat ratio;
   if (size.width > size.height) {
      ratio = newSize / size.width;
   } else {
      ratio = newSize / size.height;
   }

   CGRect rect = CGRectMake(0.0, 0.0, ratio * size.width, ratio * size.height);
   UIGraphicsBeginImageContext(rect.size);
   [image drawInRect:rect];
   UIImage *scaledImage = UIGraphicsGetImageFromCurrentImageContext();
   return scaledImage;
}

- (UIImage *)image:(UIImage *)image scaleAndCropToMaxSize:(CGSize)newSize
{
   CGFloat largestSize =
      (newSize.width > newSize.height) ? newSize.width : newSize.height;
   CGSize imageSize = [image size];

   // Scale the image while maintaining the aspect and making sure
   // the scaled image is not smaller than the given new size. In
   // other words, we calculate the aspect ratio using the largest
   // dimension from the new size and the smaller dimension from the
   // actual size.
   CGFloat ratio;
   if (imageSize.width > imageSize.height) {
      ratio = largestSize / imageSize.height;
   } else {
      ratio = largestSize / imageSize.width;
   }

   CGRect rect =
      CGRectMake(0.0, 0.0, ratio * imageSize.width, ratio * imageSize.height);
   UIGraphicsBeginImageContext(rect.size);
   [image drawInRect:rect];
   UIImage *scaledImage = UIGraphicsGetImageFromCurrentImageContext();
```

```
      // Crop the image to the requested new size, maintaining
      // the innermost parts of the image.
      CGFloat offsetX = 0;
      CGFloat offsetY = 0;
      imageSize = [scaledImage size];
      if (imageSize.width < imageSize.height) {
         offsetY = (imageSize.height / 2) - (imageSize.width / 2);
      } else {
         offsetX = (imageSize.width / 2) - (imageSize.height / 2);
      }

      CGRect cropRect = CGRectMake(offsetX, offsetY,
                                   imageSize.width - (offsetX * 2),
                                   imageSize.height - (offsetY * 2));

      CGImageRef croppedImageRef
         = CGImageCreateWithImageInRect([scaledImage CGImage], cropRect);
      UIImage *newImage = [UIImage imageWithCGImage:croppedImageRef];
      CGImageRelease(croppedImageRef);

      return newImage;
   }

   - (void)saveImage:(UIImage *)newImage;
   {
      NSData *originalImageData = UIImageJPEGRepresentation(newImage, 0.8);
      [self setOriginalImageData:originalImageData];
      // Save thumbnail
      CGSize thumbnailSize = CGSizeMake(75.0, 75.0);
      UIImage *thumbnailImage = [self image:newImage
                       scaleAndCropToMaxSize:thumbnailSize];
      NSData *thumbnailImageData = UIImageJPEGRepresentation(thumbnailImage, 0.8);
      [self setThumbnailImageData:thumbnailImageData];

      // Save small image
      CGSize smallSize = CGSizeMake(100.0, 100.0);
      UIImage *smallImage = [self image:newImage scaleAndCropToMaxSize:smallSize];
      NSData *smallImageData = UIImageJPEGRepresentation(smallImage, 0.8);
      [self setSmallImageData:smallImageData];

      // Save large (screen-size) image
      CGRect screenBounds = [[UIScreen mainScreen] bounds];
      // Calculate size for retina displays
      CGFloat scale = [[UIScreen mainScreen] scale];
      CGFloat maxScreenSize = MAX(screenBounds.size.width,
                                  screenBounds.size.height) * scale;
```

```
    CGSize imageSize = [newImage size];
    CGFloat maxImageSize = MAX(imageSize.width, imageSize.height) * scale;

    CGFloat maxSize = MIN(maxScreenSize, maxImageSize);
    UIImage *largeImage = [self image:newImage scaleAspectToMaxSize:maxSize];
    NSData *largeImageData = UIImageJPEGRepresentation(largeImage, 0.8);
    [self setLargeImageData:largeImageData];
}

- (UIImage *)originalImage;
{
    return [UIImage imageWithData:[self originalImageData]];
}

- (UIImage *)largeImage;
{
    return [UIImage imageWithData:[self largeImageData]];
}

- (UIImage *)thumbnailImage;
{
    return [UIImage imageWithData:[self thumbnailImageData]];
}

- (UIImage *)smallImage
{
    return [UIImage imageWithData:[self smallImageData]];
}

@end
```

The Core Data model is now ready for use. Next up: updating the WheelView class to make it more useful.

Changes to WheelView

PhotoWheel is different from the prototype app in that the spinning wheel of photos contains thumbnails of each photo album, whereas in the prototype app the spinning wheel displayed photos from within the selected photo album.

To support the needs of PhotoWheel, a few changes are needed to the WheelView class. The current implementation limits the number of cells displayed in the wheel. Sure, an app can tell WheelView to display 200 photos, but it would be unusable. The cells would be crammed together, making it impossible to find and view the desired photo album's thumbnail.

PhotoWheel will not limit the number of photo albums. The user can create as many photo albums as he desires. So the WheelView class must be updated to support a finite number of visible cells (photo album thumbnails). While this change is easy to implement, it leads to a bigger issue. If the wheel view has been configured with seven visible cells and the data source has more than seven cells, how are all the cells displayed? A wrapping feature is needed.

The wrapping feature displays the first cell when the end has been reached. But more important, it continuously displays cells in sequential order within the bounds of the visible cells. As the user spins the wheel, the last of the visible cells is replaced with the next cell to display. And because only the top two-thirds of the wheel is displayed in PhotoWheel, the user never sees this replacement. Instead, the user sees a continuous flow of photo album thumbnails moving in a circular fashion.

The WheelView class also needs another change related to the display of an unknown number of cells. In the prototype app, the DetailViewController class managed a cache of WheelViewCell instances. The cache loads all the needed cells into memory during the -viewDidLoad event. While this is fine for the prototype app, this will not fly for PhotoWheel. The user may have 200 photo albums. Loading 200 wheel view cells is wasteful, especially considering that only seven will be displayed at any given time.

The WheelView class needs updating to manage the cell cache. This will help conserve valuable system resources and simplify the code in the view controller class. But managing the cache is only one part of the update needed. The WheelView class must support dequeuing of unused cells to improve performance, and it must notify a delegate when a cell has been selected. In other words, it needs to behave like the UITableView class.

Make the changes to WheelView by opening the file *WheelView.h* and applying the changes shown in Listing 16.3.

> **Note**
>
> The complete source code for the WheelView class is shown in Listings 16.3 and 16.4. This makes it easier to follow the code while reading instead of looking at just the changes.

Listing 16.3   **Updated** *WheelView.h*

```
#import <UIKit/UIKit.h>

@protocol WheelViewDataSource;
@protocol WheelViewDelegate;
@class WheelViewCell;

typedef enum {
   WheelViewStyleWheel,
   WheelViewStyleCarousel,
} WheelViewStyle;
```

```
@interface WheelView : UIView

@property (nonatomic, strong) IBOutlet id<WheelViewDataSource> dataSource;
@property (nonatomic, strong) IBOutlet id<WheelViewDelegate> delegate;
@property (nonatomic, assign) WheelViewStyle style;
@property (nonatomic, assign) NSInteger selectedIndex;              // 1

- (id)dequeueReusableCell;                                          // 2
- (void)reloadData;                                                 // 3
- (WheelViewCell *)cellAtIndex:(NSInteger)index;                    // 4

@end


@protocol WheelViewDataSource <NSObject>
@required
- (NSInteger)wheelViewNumberOfCells:(WheelView *)wheelView;
- (WheelViewCell *)wheelView:(WheelView *)wheelView cellAtIndex:(NSInteger)index;
@optional
- (void)wheelView:(WheelView *)wheelView
   didSelectCellAtIndex:(NSInteger)index;                           // 5
@end

@protocol WheelViewDelegate <NSObject>                              // 6
@optional
- (NSInteger)wheelViewNumberOfVisibleCells:(WheelView *)wheelView;
@end


@interface WheelViewCell : UIView
@end
```

Now let's run through the code:

1–4. The updated class interface isn't much different from the original. A new
   selectedIndex property has been added along with three methods.
   -dequeueReusableCell returns a reusable WheelViewCell to the caller. The
   method -reloadData reinitializes and loads data into the wheel view. And
   -cellAtIndex: returns the WheelViewCell instance for the specific index.

5. The WheelViewDataSource protocol has been updated with the new optional
   message -wheelView:didSelectCellAtIndex:. This message is received by
   the data source when the user selects a cell in the wheel view.

6. Finally, a new protocol has been added, WheelViewDelegate. It has one
   optional method, -wheelViewNumberOfVisibleCells:. If this method is
   not implemented in the delegate, WheelView will display all cells. This default

behavior is overridden by implementing the new method in the delegate, returning the number of cells to display. This is used in conjunction with the wrapping
feature mentioned earlier.

Changes to the `WheelView` class interface are minor compared to those in the
implementation. While the original logic for the display of each cell and style setting
is still in place, a number of other changes have been made. The complete source code
listing is shown in Listing 16.4. Update your code to match it.

Listing 16.4   **Updated** *WheelView.m*

```
#import "WheelView.h"
#import <QuartzCore/QuartzCore.h>
#import "SpinGestureRecognizer.h"

#pragma mark - WheelViewCell

@interface WheelViewCell ()                                     // 1
@property (nonatomic, assign) NSInteger indexInWheelView;       // 2
@end

@implementation WheelViewCell                                   // 3
@synthesize indexInWheelView = indexInWheelView_;
@end



#pragma mark - WheelView

@interface WheelView ()
@property (nonatomic, assign) CGFloat currentAngle;
@property (nonatomic, strong) NSMutableSet *reusableCells;      // 4

// The visible cell indexes are stored in a mutable dictionary
// instead of a mutable array because the number of visible cells
// can change. Using an array requires additional logic to maintain
// the dimensions of the array. This is avoided by using the
// dictionary where the key represents the element index number.
@property (nonatomic, strong) NSMutableDictionary *visibleCellIndexes;   // 5
@end

@implementation WheelView

@synthesize dataSource = _dataSource;
@synthesize delegate = _delegate;
@synthesize style = _style;
@synthesize currentAngle = _currentAngle;
@synthesize selectedIndex = _selectedIndex;                     // 6
```

```objc
@synthesize reusableCells = _reusableCells;
@synthesize visibleCellIndexes = _visibleCellIndexes;

- (void)commonInit                                                      // 7
{
   [self setSelectedIndex:-1];
   [self setCurrentAngle:0.0];

   [self setVisibleCellIndexes:[[NSMutableDictionary alloc] init]];

   SpinGestureRecognizer *spin = [[SpinGestureRecognizer alloc]
                                initWithTarget:self action:@selector(spin:)];
   [self addGestureRecognizer:spin];

   self.reusableCells = [[NSMutableSet alloc] init];
}

- (id)init                                                              // 8
{
   self = [super init];
   if (self) {
      [self commonInit];
   }
   return self;
}

- (id)initWithCoder:(NSCoder *)aDecoder
{
   self = [super initWithCoder:aDecoder];
   if (self) {
      [self commonInit];
   }
   return self;
}

- (id)initWithFrame:(CGRect)frame
{
   self = [super initWithFrame:frame];
   if (self) {
      [self commonInit];
   }
   return self;
}

- (NSInteger)numberOfCells                                              // 9
{
   NSInteger cellCount = 0;
```

```objc
   id<WheelViewDataSource> dataSource = [self dataSource];
   if ([dataSource respondsToSelector:@selector(wheelViewNumberOfCells:)]) {
      cellCount = [dataSource wheelViewNumberOfCells:self];
   }
   return cellCount;
}


- (NSInteger)numberOfVisibleCells                                  // 10
{
   NSInteger cellCount = [self numberOfCells];
   NSInteger numberOfVisibleCells = cellCount;
   id<WheelViewDelegate> delegate = [self delegate];
   if (delegate &&
       [delegate respondsToSelector:@selector(wheelViewNumberOfVisibleCells:)])
   {
      numberOfVisibleCells = [delegate wheelViewNumberOfVisibleCells:self];
   }
   return numberOfVisibleCells;
}


- (BOOL)isSelectedItemForAngle:(CGFloat)angle                      // 11
{
   // The selected item is one whose angle is
   // at or near 0 degrees.
   //
   // To calculate the selected item based on the
   // angle, we must convert the angle to the
   // relative angle between 0 and 360 degrees.

   CGFloat relativeAngle = fabsf(fmodf(angle, 360.0));

   // Pad the selection point so it does not
   // have to be exact.
   CGFloat padding = 20.0;   // Allow 20 degrees on either side.

   BOOL isSelectedItem =
      relativeAngle >= (360.0 - padding) || relativeAngle <= padding;
   return isSelectedItem;
}

- (BOOL)isIndexVisible:(NSInteger)index                            // 12
{
   NSNumber *cellIndex = [NSNumber numberWithInteger:index];
   __block BOOL visible = NO;
   void (^enumerateBlock) (id, id, BOOL *) = ^(id key, id obj, BOOL *stop) {
      if ([obj isEqual:cellIndex]) {
         visible = YES;
```

```
                *stop = YES;
            }
        };
        [[self visibleCellIndexes] enumerateKeysAndObjectsUsingBlock:enumerateBlock];
        return visible;
}


- (void)queueNonVisibleCells                                        // 13
{
    NSArray *subviews = [self subviews];
    for (id view in subviews) {
        if ([view isKindOfClass:[WheelViewCell class]]) {
            NSInteger index = [(WheelViewCell *)view indexInWheelView];
            BOOL visible = [self isIndexVisible:index];
            if (!visible) {
                [[self reusableCells] addObject:view];
                [view removeFromSuperview];
            }
        }
    }
}


- (NSInteger)cellIndexForIndex:(NSInteger)index                     // 14
{
    NSInteger numberOfCells = [self numberOfCells];
    NSInteger numberOfVisibleCells = [self numberOfVisibleCells];
    NSInteger offset = MAX([self selectedIndex], 0);

    NSInteger cellIndex;
    if (index < (numberOfVisibleCells/2)) {
        cellIndex = index + offset;
        if (cellIndex > numberOfCells - 1) cellIndex = cellIndex - numberOfCells;
    } else {
        cellIndex = offset - (numberOfVisibleCells - index);
        if (cellIndex < 0) cellIndex = numberOfCells + cellIndex;
    }

    return cellIndex;
}


- (NSSet*)cellIndexesToDisplay                                      // 15
{
    NSInteger numberOfVisibleCells = [self numberOfVisibleCells];
    NSMutableSet *cellIndexes =
        [[NSMutableSet alloc] initWithCapacity:numberOfVisibleCells];
    for (NSInteger index = 0; index < numberOfVisibleCells; index++)
    {
```

```
        NSInteger cellIndex = [self cellIndexForIndex:index];
        [cellIndexes addObject:[NSNumber numberWithInteger:cellIndex]];
    }
    return cellIndexes;
}


- (void)setAngle:(CGFloat)angle                                        // 16
{
    [self queueNonVisibleCells];                                       // 17
    NSSet *cellIndexesToDisplay = [self cellIndexesToDisplay];         // 18

    // The following code is inspired by the carousel example at
    // http://stackoverflow.com/questions/5243614/3d-carousel-effect-on-the-ipad

    CGPoint center = CGPointMake(CGRectGetMidX([self bounds]),
                                 CGRectGetMidY([self bounds]));
    CGFloat radiusX = MIN([self bounds].size.width,
                          [self bounds].size.height) * 0.35;
    CGFloat radiusY = radiusX;
    if ([self style] == WheelViewStyleCarousel) {
        radiusY = radiusX * 0.30;
    }

    NSInteger numberOfVisibleCells = [self numberOfVisibleCells];
    float angleToAdd = 360.0f / numberOfVisibleCells;

    // If there are more cells than the number of visible cells,
    // we wrap the cells. Wrapping allows all cells to display
    // within a finite number of visible cells. Cells are displayed in
    // sequential order. When the end is reached, the display wraps
    // to the beginning.
    //
    // Because there is a finite number of visible cells, one cell
    // is replaced with a wrapping cell as the user scrolls through
    // (spins) the wheel. At any given time there is one and only one
    // cell that requires replacing. The cell to replace is determined
    // by comparing the contents of visibleCellIndexes to
    // cellIndexesToDisplay.
    // visibleCellIndexes can contain one index not found in
    // cellIndexesToDisplay.
    // This is the index that is replaced. It is replaced with the one
    // index in cellIndexesToDisplay not found in visibleCellIndexes.

    BOOL wrap = [self numberOfCells] > numberOfVisibleCells;           // 19

    // Lay out visible cells.
    for (NSInteger index = 0; index < numberOfVisibleCells; index++)
```

```
{
    NSNumber *cellIndexNumber;
    if (wrap) {
        cellIndexNumber = [[self visibleCellIndexes]
                          objectForKey:[NSNumber numberWithInteger:index]];
        if (cellIndexNumber == nil) {
            // First time through, visibleCellIndexes is empty, hence the nil
            // cellIndexNumber. Initialize it with the appropriate cell
            // index.
            cellIndexNumber =
                [NSNumber numberWithInteger:[self cellIndexForIndex:index]];
        }
    } else {
        // Cell indexes are sequential when wrapping is turned off.
        cellIndexNumber = [NSNumber numberWithInteger:index];
    }


    if (wrap && ![cellIndexesToDisplay containsObject:cellIndexNumber]) {
        // Replace the wrapping cell index.
        __block NSNumber *replacementNumber = nil;
        NSArray *array = [[self visibleCellIndexes] allValues];
        void (^enumerateBlock) (id, BOOL *) = ^(id obj, BOOL *stop) {
            if (![array containsObject:obj]) {
                replacementNumber = obj;
                *stop = YES;
            }
        };
        [cellIndexesToDisplay enumerateObjectsUsingBlock:enumerateBlock];

        cellIndexNumber = replacementNumber;
    }

    NSInteger cellIndex = [cellIndexNumber integerValue];
    WheelViewCell *cell = [self cellAtIndex:cellIndex];

    if (cell == nil) {
        cellIndex = -1;    // No cell, no cell index.
    }

    // If index is not within the visible indexes, the
    // cell is missing from the view and it must be added.
    BOOL visible = [self isIndexVisible:cellIndex];
    if (!visible) {
        [[self visibleCellIndexes] setObject:cellIndexNumber
                                 forKey:[NSNumber numberWithInteger:index]];
```

```
    [cell setIndexInWheelView:cellIndex];
    [self addSubview:cell];
}


// Set the selected index if it has changed.
if (cellIndex != [self selectedIndex] &&
    [self isSelectedItemForAngle:angle])                        // 20
{
    [self setSelectedIndex:cellIndex];
    if ([[self dataSource]
        respondsToSelector:@selector(wheelView:didSelectCellAtIndex:)])
    {
        [[self dataSource] wheelView:self didSelectCellAtIndex:cellIndex];
    }
}


float angleInRadians = (angle + 180.0) * M_PI / 180.0f;         // 21


// Get a position based on the angle
float xPosition = center.x + (radiusX * sinf(angleInRadians))
                - (CGRectGetWidth([cell frame]) / 2);
float yPosition = center.y + (radiusY * cosf(angleInRadians))
                - (CGRectGetHeight([cell frame]) / 2);


float scale = 0.75f + 0.25f * (cosf(angleInRadians) + 1.0);


// Apply location and scale
if ([self style] == WheelViewStyleCarousel) {
    [cell setTransform:CGAffineTransformScale(
            CGAffineTransformMakeTranslation(xPosition, yPosition),
            scale, scale)];
    // Tweak alpha using the same system as applied for scale, this time
    // with 0.3 the minimum and a semicircle range of 0.5
    [cell setAlpha:(0.3f + 0.5f * (cosf(angleInRadians) + 1.0))];

} else {
    [cell setTransform:CGAffineTransformMakeTranslation(xPosition,
                                                        yPosition)];
    [cell setAlpha:1.0];
}


[[cell layer] setZPosition:scale];


// Work out what the next angle is going to be
angle += angleToAdd;
    }
}
```

```
- (void)layoutSubviews                                              // 22
{
  [self setAngle:[self currentAngle]];
}


- (void)setStyle:(WheelViewStyle)newStyle                           // 23
{
  if (_style != newStyle) {
    _style = newStyle;

    [UIView beginAnimations:@"WheelViewStyleChange" context:nil];
    [self setAngle:[self currentAngle]];
    [UIView commitAnimations];
  }
}


- (void)spin:(SpinGestureRecognizer *)recognizer                   // 24
{
  CGFloat angleInRadians = -[recognizer rotation];
  CGFloat degrees = 180.0 * angleInRadians / M_PI;   // Radians to degrees
  [self setCurrentAngle:[self currentAngle] + degrees];
  [self setAngle:[self currentAngle]];
}


- (id)dequeueReusableCell                                          // 25
{
  id view = [[self reusableCells] anyObject];
  if (view != nil) {
    [[self reusableCells] removeObject:view];
  }
  return view;
}


- (void)queueReusableCells                                        // 26
{
  for (UIView *view in [self subviews]) {
    if ([view isKindOfClass:[WheelViewCell class]]) {
      [[self reusableCells] addObject:view];
      [view removeFromSuperview];
    }
  }

  [[self visibleCellIndexes] removeAllObjects];
  [self setSelectedIndex:-1];
}
```

```
- (void)reloadData                                                // 27
{
    [self queueReusableCells];
    [self layoutSubviews];
}

- (WheelViewCell *)cellAtIndex:(NSInteger)index                   // 28
{
    if (index < 0 || index > [self numberOfCells] - 1) {
        return nil;
    }

    WheelViewCell *cell = nil;
    BOOL visible = [self isIndexVisible:index];
    if (visible) {
        for (id view in [self subviews]) {
            if ([view isKindOfClass:[WheelViewCell class]]) {
                if ([view indexInWheelView] == index) {
                    cell = view;
                    break;
                }
            }
        }
    }

    if (cell == nil) {
        cell = [[self dataSource] wheelView:self cellAtIndex:index];
    }

    return cell;
}

@end
```

Let's walk though the code together, highlighting the changes:

1–3. The implementation for WheelViewCell has been moved to the top of the source code file. Also, a new private declared property named indexInWheel-View has been added. This private property is used by WheelView to track the index for the cell, which may be different from the display index. Remember, the new WheelView can have fewer visible cells than the total number of cells.

Note
The WheelViewCell class extension and implementation were moved to the top to make the compiler aware of the class within the WheelView implementation. If the code remained at the bottom, the WheelView class would not compile.

4–5. Two new declared properties have been added to the `WheelView` class extension: `reusableCells` and `visibleCellIndexes`. `reusableCells` is a mutable set used to manage the cache of reusable `WheelViewCell` instances. `visibleCellIndexes` is a mutable dictionary of indexes representing the visible cells.

5. You might be wondering why `visibleCellIndexes` is declared as `NSMutableDictionary` instead of `NSMutableArray`. Admittedly, it does seem strange, but there's a good reason for this approach.

The number of visible cells can change. If an array were used, a change in the number of visible cells would require a change to the array's dimension. Also, the indexes for cells to display are not necessarily calculated in sequential order. They are displayed sequentially, but that doesn't mean each cell to display is determined sequentially. Therefore, if an array were used, additional code would be needed to ensure that elements were added to the array to fill holes that might exist as each cell is processed.

The dictionary eliminates the need for additional array management code, and since a dictionary's contents are not order dependent, `WheelView` doesn't need to worry about checking the bounds of an array and filling holes in it. Instead, the class stores the index value as an `NSNumber`, which is used as the key to the dictionary. Note that this index is an index within the range of visible cell indexes. In other words, it is a value between 0 and the number of visible cells.

The object stored in the dictionary for the visible cell index key is the actual cell index. It too is stored as an `NSNumber` since `NSDictionary` can store only object references. The actual cell index value is some number between 0 and the total number of cells.

6–8. Continuing with the changes... The new declared properties are synthesized. The method `-commonInit` is updated to initialize the selected index, `visibleCellIndexes`, and `reusableCells` properties. The remaining `init*` methods remain the same as before.

9–10. The init methods are followed by two helper methods, `-numberOfCells` and `-numberOfVisibleCells`. Each returns a value retrieved from the data source. These values are used throughout the `WheelView` class. The helper methods were created to eliminate the duplication of code in `WheelView`.

11. The method `-isSelectedItemForAngle:` is responsible for determining if a wheel view cell is "selected" based on the specified angle. A cell is considered selected when it is displayed at the top of the wheel, at degree `0.0` plus or minus `20.0` degrees.

12. Another helper method named `-isIndexVisible:` has been added. This method enumerates the `visibleCellIndexes` to see if it contains the specific cell index. A block is used to perform the enumeration. If a number is found in the `visibleCellIndexes` that matches the cell index number, the cell is visible and `YES` is returned to the caller; otherwise `NO` is returned.

13. The next method is -queueNonVisibleCells. The method removes any nonvisible wheel view cells from the view and places them into the local cache reusableCells.

14–15. The next two methods are -cellIndexForIndex: and -cellIndexesTo-Display. The first, -cellIndexForIndex:, converts a visible cell index (a number between 0 and the number of visible cells) to a cell index (a number between 0 and the total number of cells). This method is used by -cell-IndexesToDisplay, which returns an NSSet of cell indexes to display. As you will see in a moment, this set is compared to visibleCellIndexes to find the cell that is replaced during wrapping.

16–21. The method -setAngle: has been updated to queue nonvisible cells, retrieve the set of cell indexes to display, support cell wrapping, and set the selected index. The code to transform a cell to a particular position as the wheel spins remains the same as before.

22–24. The methods -layoutSubviews, -setStyle:, and -spin: remain unchanged from the earlier implementation. The remaining methods, however, are new to this implementation.

25. -dequeueReusableCell returns a reusable cell from the cache. It grabs any object from the cache. It doesn't matter which object is grabbed since all are available for reuse. The object is then removed from the cache and returned to the caller. If there are no available objects in the cache, nil is returned to the caller, and the caller is expected to create a new instance of the cell.

26. The method -queueReusableCells is called when data is reloaded in the wheel view. This method takes all the visible cells currently in the view and moves them to the reusable cell cache.

27. -reloadData queues any reusable cells and calls -layoutSubviews, which in turn starts the process of displaying cells within the view.

28. Finally, there's -cellAtIndex:. This method returns a reference to the cell at the specified index. It is used internally by the WheelView class and can be used externally by others such as a view controller.

Now that the new WheelView class is in place, it's time to put it to good use displaying photo albums.

Displaying Photo Albums

The next thing you want to tackle is the display of photo albums. In PhotoWheel, photo albums are displayed as thumbnails in the disc at the bottom of the screen. This is different from the prototype app where the albums were displayed in a table view. Luckily, the WheelView class has been implemented as a generic view class, which means that you can use it to display the photo album thumbnails.

Open the main storyboard and select the Photo Albums View Controller Scene. This is the scene with the image of the disc. Drag a `UIView` into this scene. Set its position and size—X to 31, Y to 33, Width to 488, and Height to 484—and anchor the view to the top left corner using the autosizing settings.

The new view should appear on top of the disc image view but under the round + button. To accomplish this, you need to rearrange the views in the view hierarchy. Open the Document Outline (**Editor > Show Document Outline**) and expand the view hierarchy for the scene. Drag and drop the views to rearrange the view order within the hierarchy. The order should match the order shown in Figure 16.4.

After the view hierarchy has been set, the new view will partially hide the disc image view, so set the Background color to Clear (found in the Attributes inspector) for the new view.

The new view is of type `UIView`. You need to change this to the `WheelView` class. Open the Identity inspector and change the class from `UIView` to `WheelView`. Now that the view is of type `WheelView`, its `dataSource` and delegate outlets can be set. Connect the `WheelView` `dataSource` to the Photo Albums View Controller Scene. Remember, you can accomplish this by **Control-clicking** (right-clicking) the view and dragging the `dataSource` connector to the view controller, or you can **Control-click** and hold, then drag from the view to the view controller to make the connection. Both approaches work.

Do the same for the `WheelView` delegate, connecting it to the `PhotoAlbumsView-Controller`.

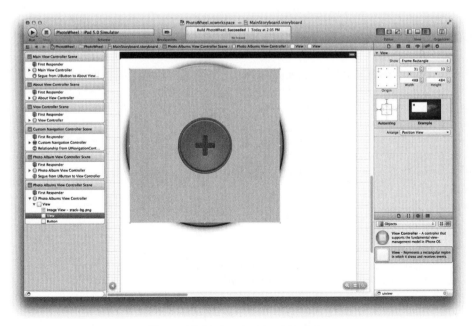

Figure 16.4   Set the view hierarchy.

Implementing the Photo Albums View Controller

With the wheel view in place, it's time to implement the `PhotoAlbumsView-Controller`. This controller is the data source and delegate for the `WheelView` instance, which means it must implement code conforming to the `WheelViewDataSource` and `WheelViewDelegate` protocols.

Start with the interface file, *PhotoAlbumsViewController.h*. Let the compiler know that the class conforms to these two protocols. Also add `NSFetchedResultsControllerDelegate` to the list of protocols, as a fetched results controller will be used to retrieve the photo albums. Next, add an outlet for the `WheelView` object. This will be used in the implementation of the view controller. Finally, add a new property for the managed object context, and an action for the **+** button that adds a new photo album. The source code is shown in Listing 16.5.

Listing 16.5   **Updated** *PhotoAlbumsViewController.h*

```
#import <UIKit/UIKit.h>
#import "WheelView.h"

@interface PhotoAlbumsViewController : UIViewController
<NSFetchedResultsControllerDelegate, WheelViewDataSource, WheelViewDelegate>

@property (nonatomic, strong) NSManagedObjectContext *managedObjectContext;
@property (nonatomic, strong) IBOutlet WheelView *wheelView;

- (IBAction)addPhotoAlbum:(id)sender;

@end
```

While you are making changes, be sure you return to the Photo Albums View Controller Scene in the main storyboard and connect the `WheelView` object to the `wheelView` outlet and the **+** button to the `addPhotoAlbum:` action. Otherwise the app will not display and add photo albums properly.

And make sure to connect the `addPhotoAlbum:` action to the Touch Up Inside event of the button. This is done for you when you **Control-click** and drag to make the connection. You must manually select the event if you use the popup HUD to make the connection.

> **Note**
>
> You may be wondering how and when the `managedObjectContext` property is set. It will be set in the `MainViewController` at the time the `PhotoAlbumsViewController` instance is created from the storyboard. You'll implement this code once the implementation for `PhotoAlbumsViewController` is complete.

With the interface complete, it's time to shift your attention to the implementation. Open *PhotoAlbumsViewController.m* and update it with the code in Listing 16.6.

Listing 16.6   **Updated** *PhotoAlbumsViewController.m*

```objc
#import "PhotoAlbumsViewController.h"
#import "PhotoWheelViewCell.h"                               // 1
#import "PhotoAlbum.h"
#import "Photo.h"

@interface PhotoAlbumsViewController ()                       // 2
@property (nonatomic, strong)
   NSFetchedResultsController *fetchedResultsController;      // 3
@end

@implementation PhotoAlbumsViewController

@synthesize managedObjectContext = _managedObjectContext;
@synthesize wheelView = _wheelView;                          // 4
@synthesize fetchedResultsController = _fetchedResultsController;

- (void)didMoveToParentViewController:(UIViewController *)parent    // 5
{
   // Position the view within the new parent.
   [[parent view] addSubview:[self view]];
   CGRect newFrame = CGRectMake(109, 680, 551, 550);
   [[self view] setFrame:newFrame];

   [[self view] setBackgroundColor:[UIColor clearColor]];
}

- (void)viewDidUnload                                        // 6
{
   [self setWheelView:nil];
   [super viewDidUnload];
}

#pragma mark - Actions

- (IBAction)addPhotoAlbum:(id)sender                         // 7
{

}

#pragma mark - NSFetchedResultsController and NSFetchedResultsControllerDelegate

- (NSFetchedResultsController *)fetchedResultsController     // 8
{
   if (_fetchedResultsController) {                          // 9
      return _fetchedResultsController;
   }
```

```
    NSString *cacheName = NSStringFromClass([self class]);              // 10
    NSFetchRequest *fetchRequest =
       [NSFetchRequest fetchRequestWithEntityName:@"PhotoAlbum"];       // 11

    NSSortDescriptor *sortDescriptor =
       [NSSortDescriptor sortDescriptorWithKey:@"dateAdded"
                                      ascending:YES];                    // 12
    [fetchRequest setSortDescriptors:[NSArray arrayWithObject:sortDescriptor]];

    NSFetchedResultsController *newFetchedResultsController =
       [[NSFetchedResultsController alloc]
         initWithFetchRequest:fetchRequest
         managedObjectContext:[self managedObjectContext]
           sectionNameKeyPath:nil
                    cacheName:cacheName];                               // 13
    [newFetchedResultsController setDelegate:self];                     // 14

    NSError *error = nil;
    if (![newFetchedResultsController performFetch:&error])             // 15
    {
       /*
        Replace this implementation with code to handle the error appropriately.

        abort() causes the application to generate a crash log and terminate.
        You should not use this function in a shipping application, although it
        may be useful during development. If it is not possible to recover from
        the error, display an alert panel that instructs the user to quit the
        application by pressing the Home button.
        */
       NSLog(@"Unresolved error %@, %@", error, [error userInfo]);
       abort();
    }

    [self setFetchedResultsController:newFetchedResultsController];     // 16
    return _fetchedResultsController;                                   // 17
 }

- (void)controller:(NSFetchedResultsController *)controller
   didChangeObject:(id)anObject
       atIndexPath:(NSIndexPath *)indexPath
     forChangeType:(NSFetchedResultsChangeType)type
      newIndexPath:(NSIndexPath *)newIndexPath                          // 18
{
    [[self wheelView] reloadData];
}
```

```
#pragma mark - WheelViewDataSource and WheelViewDelegate methods       // 19


- (NSInteger)wheelViewNumberOfVisibleCells:(WheelView *)wheelView       // 20
{
    return 7;
}


- (NSInteger)wheelViewNumberOfCells:(WheelView *)wheelView              // 21
{
    NSArray *sections = [[self fetchedResultsController] sections];
    NSInteger count = [[sections objectAtIndex:0] numberOfObjects];
    return count;
}


- (WheelViewCell *)wheelView:(WheelView *)wheelView
                cellAtIndex:(NSInteger)index                            // 22
{
    PhotoWheelViewCell *cell = [wheelView dequeueReusableCell];         // 23
    if (!cell) {
        cell = [[PhotoWheelViewCell alloc]
                initWithFrame:CGRectMake(0, 0, 75, 75)];               // 24
    }

    NSIndexPath *indexPath = [NSIndexPath indexPathForRow:index inSection:0];
    PhotoAlbum *photoAlbum = [[self fetchedResultsController]
                              objectAtIndexPath:indexPath];            // 25
    Photo *photo = [[photoAlbum photos] lastObject];                   // 26
    UIImage *image = [photo thumbnailImage];
    if (image == nil) {
        image = [UIImage imageNamed:@"defaultPhoto.png"];              // 27
    }
    [cell setImage:image];                                             // 28


    return cell;                                                       // 29
}

- (void)wheelView:(WheelView *)wheelView
didSelectCellAtIndex:(NSInteger)index                                  // 30
{

}

@end
```

Now let's walk through the code to see what is happening:

1–3. The first things you notice are the additional `#import` statements. These are followed by the class extension for `PhotoAlbumsViewController`. The class extension adds a private declared property named `fetchedResultsController`. The fetched results controller is used to populate the wheel view with photo albums.

4–5. The first things in the `@implement` section are the `@synthesize` statements for the new declared properties. These are followed by the method `-didMoveToParentViewController:`, which is unchanged from the original implementation of `PhotoAlbumsViewController`.

6. The `-viewDidUnload` method is added. It sets the outlet `wheelView` to `nil` when the view unloads. You should always explicitly set outlets to `nil` in the `-viewDidUnload` method. This conserves memory resources when the view is no longer loaded. If you do not set the outlet to `nil`, it will remain in memory until the view controller is released. This is because the outlet is a declared property with a strong reference.

7. The next method in Listing 16.6 is `-addPhotoAlbum:`. This action is connected to the **+** button in the Photo Albums View Controller Scene. The implementation is empty for the moment. You'll add the code that adds a new photo album momentarily.

8. The action is followed by the custom fetched results controller getter method `-fetchedResultsController`. `NSFetchedResultsController` manages the results of a Core Data fetched request. It is optimized for the mobile platform and designed to be used with `UITableView`. However, since `WheelView` is modeled after `UITableView`, the fetched results controller can be used with it as well.

9. The first thing the getter method does is check to see if the ivar for the fetched results controller has already been set. If it has, the reference to the ivar is returned. If the ivar has not been set (its value is `nil`), the getter method initializes it.

10. `NSFetchedResultsController` can optionally use a cache. The cache reduces the overhead of figuring out section and index information managed by the controller. The cache name used in this getter method is the view controller class name. The class name is returned by the C function `NSStringFromClass()`.

11. A new fetch request object is created next using the class method `+ fetchRequestWithEntityName:`. This method provides a convenient way to create an `NSFetchRequest` object that is configured for a particular entity without having to use an `NSEntityDescription` object. Here the fetch request is configured for the `PhotoAlbum` entity. Note that this name must match the entity name defined in the PhotoWheel Core Data model.

12. A sort descriptor is created and added to the fetch request. The sort descriptor tells Core Data how to sort fetched results. In this particular case, the fetched results are sorted by the `dateAdded` field in ascending order.

13–14. The fetch request is then added to the fetched results controller, and the view controller is made the delegate of the fetched results controller. This means that `PhotoAlbumsViewController` will receive messages from the fetched results controller as needed (such as when new data is added to the fetched results controller).

15–17. Finally, the fetched results controller is told to perform the fetch. This retrieves the data from Core Data so that it can be used within the view controller. Also, the declared property `fetchedResultsController` is set to the new fetched results controller. This in turn sets the ivar `_fetched-ResultsController`, which is returned at the end of the method.

18. Following the fetched results controller getter method is the `-controller:didChangeObject:atIndexPath:forChangeType:newIndexPath:` method. This is an `NSFetchedResultsControllerDelegate` method called by the fetched results controller whenever data changes in the fetched results. The implementation is simple. It reloads the data in `wheelView`. As a result, the display is automatically updated to show the changes the moment they happen. For example, when the user taps the + button, the new photo album displays immediately. No additional coding is needed, just the call to `-reloadData`.

> **Note**
>
> Had you used a `UITableView` instead of `WheelView`, you could do a number of things other than `-reloadData` to show the data change. `UITableView` has methods to insert and remove individual rows, and to update particular rows. These enhanced behaviors are not implemented in the `WheelView` class, however, so `reloadData` will have to do.

19. The last code changes to the `PhotoAlbumsViewController` class are the `WheelViewDataSource` and `WheelViewDelegate` protocol methods. These methods are called by `WheelView` to display cells within the view, and to report back to the view controller which cell has been selected by the user.

20. The first of these methods is `-wheelViewNumberOfVisibleCells:`. It returns the value 7. This means that no more than seven photo album thumbnails are displayed at once in the wheel view. More than seven cells can exist, but at the most, only seven cells will be displayed.

21. The next method is `-wheelViewNumberOfCells:`. This method returns the total number of cells, or in the case of PhotoWheel, the total number of photo albums. The count is retrieved from the fetched results controller. The sections array contains the data for each section. Remember, the fetched results controller is designed for `UITableView`, which can have one or more sections.

There is always only one section when using the WheelView, so the section at index zero contains the list of photo albums.

22–29.   The method -wheelView:cellAtIndex: is responsible for constructing WheelViewCell, setting its properties, and returning it to the caller, which happens to be the wheelView. This method first retrieves a reusable cell, if any are available. If no reusable cells are available, a new cell is created. Next, the photo album model object is retrieved from the fetched results by way of the fetched results controller. The last photo of the photo album is used as the thumbnail of the photo album. If there is no photo or thumbnail for the photo, the *defaultPhoto.png* image is used as the thumbnail. The image is added to the cell for display, and the cell is returned to the caller.

30.   And finally, there is the -wheelView:didSelectCellAtIndex: method. This method is called when the user selects a new photo album in the wheel view. A photo album is selected when the arrow from the photos popover image points to a cell (see Figure 16.5). For now, leave the implementation of this method empty.

Setting the Managed Object Context

Before the app will run, one other change is needed. The PhotoAlbumsView-Controller needs a reference to the managed object context set up by the app delegate. This view controller is decoupled from the app delegate, so it expects that its managedObjectContext property will be set by the user of the object.

Figure 16.5   The top photo album cell is the selected cell.

> **Note**
>
> When possible, it's always a good thing to decouple view controllers, and classes in general, from one another. This will make the design of your application more flexible. One way to decouple a view controller from other dependencies is to pass references into the controller, as is done with the managed object context.

The appropriate place to set the `managedObjectContext` property of Photo-AlbumsViewController is at the time the controller instance is created. This happens in `MainViewController` in the `-viewDidLoad` event. Open *MainViewController.m* and update the code to set the `managedObjectContext` property for the `Photo-AlbumsViewController` instance, as shown in Listing 16.7.

Listing 16.7   Updated *MainViewController.m*

```
#import "MainViewController.h"
#import "PhotoAlbumViewController.h"
#import "PhotoAlbumsViewController.h"
#import "AppDelegate.h"

@implementation MainViewController

- (void)viewDidLoad
{
    [super viewDidLoad];

    AppDelegate *appDelegate =
        (AppDelegate *)[[UIApplication sharedApplication] delegate];      // 1
    NSManagedObjectContext *managedObjectContext =
        [appDelegate managedObjectContext];                               // 2

    UIStoryboard *storyboard = [self storyboard];

    PhotoAlbumsViewController *photoAlbumsScene =
        [storyboard instantiateViewControllerWithIdentifier:@"PhotoAlbumsScene"];
    [photoAlbumsScene setManagedObjectContext:managedObjectContext];      // 3
    [self addChildViewController:photoAlbumsScene];
    [photoAlbumsScene didMoveToParentViewController:self];

    PhotoAlbumViewController *photoAlbumScene =
        [storyboard instantiateViewControllerWithIdentifier:@"PhotoAlbumScene"];
    [self addChildViewController:photoAlbumScene];
    [photoAlbumScene didMoveToParentViewController:self];
}

@end
```

Now let's walk through the code in Listing 16.7:

1. In order for the managed object context property to be set, it must first be retrieved from the app delegate. The `AppDelegate` class contains the code that initializes the managed object context. To retrieve the app delegate, you use the `UIApplication` class. It has a class method named `+sharedApplication`, which returns a reference to the current application object. You call the delegate property on the current application object to get the reference to the App-Delegate instance.

2. Once you have a reference to the `AppDelegate`, a reference to the managed object context provided by the `AppDelegate` is stored in the local variable `managedObjectContext`.

3. The local reference to the managed object context is then used to set the `managedObjectContext` property of the `photoAlbumsScene`.

> **Note**
>
> Decoupling the app delegate from the main view controller is often the preferred approach. However, the two are coupled in Listing 16.7 to show you how to retrieve a reference to the app delegate should you ever need it.

At this point, PhotoWheel will compile and run. However, you will not see any photo albums. That is because there are no photo albums in the Core Data persistent store. You need to implement the action for adding a photo album first before you can see photo albums in the wheel view.

> **Note**
>
> The Core Data model has changed in the chapter. Therefore, the first time the app is run and it references the managed object context, an exception is thrown, indicating that the data model has changed. To fix this, delete previous versions of PhotoWheel from the simulator and iPad before running the app. You need to do this only once as the data model will not change again.

Adding Photo Albums

Before the user can see a photo album in the wheel view, he needs to add one to the data store. But before that can happen, you must implement the `-addPhotoAlbum:` action method in *PhotoAlbumsViewController.m*. Open *PhotoAlbumsViewController.m* and scroll to the `-addPhotoAlbum:` method. Add the implementation shown in Listing 16.8.

Listing 16.8 Updated `-addPhotoAlbum:` **Implementation in** *PhotoAlbumsViewController.m*

```
- (IBAction)addPhotoAlbum:(id)sender
{
    NSManagedObjectContext *context = [self managedObjectContext];        // 1
```

```
PhotoAlbum *photoAlbum = [NSEntityDescription
                        insertNewObjectForEntityForName:@"PhotoAlbum"
                        inManagedObjectContext:context];          // 2
[photoAlbum setDateAdded:[NSDate date]];                          // 3

// Save the context.
NSError *error = nil;
if (![context save:&error])                                       // 4
{
    /*
     Replace this implementation with code to handle the error appropriately.

     abort() causes the application to generate a crash log and terminate.
     You should not use this function in a shipping application, although
     it may be useful during development. If it is not possible to recover
     from the error, display an alert panel that instructs the user to quit
     the application by pressing the Home button.
     */
    NSLog(@"Unresolved error %@, %@", error, [error userInfo]);
    abort();
}
}
```

Now when the user taps the **+** button at the bottom of the PhotoWheel screen, a new photo album is added. The code to accomplish this is straightforward:

1. A local variable stores a reference to the managed object context.

2. A new entity description is inserted for the entity name PhotoAlbum.

3. The dateAdded property for the entity is set to the current date.

4. The context is saved.

Because a fetched results controller is used to manage the data, PhotoAlbums-
ViewController automatically receives a message from the fetched results controller telling it to update the wheel view display.

Run the app and test that photo albums can be added. Check your work if you cannot add new photo albums. Remember, if nothing is happening, check the outlet and action connections defined in the Photo Albums View Controller Scene. Nothing will happen if the connections are missing.

Managing Photo Albums

You have updated PhotoWheel to add and display photo albums, but more work is needed. The user should be able to select a photo album to view its photos. The user may also want to give the photo album a name. And the user will certainly want to remove any photo albums accidentally created.

This is as good a time as any to implement these features, starting with the selection of a photo album.

Selecting the Photo Album

Most of the work of selecting a photo album has already been done. The `Wheel-View` class knows how to detect the selected cell, and it knows when the selected cell changes. It also sends a message to its delegate when the selected cell changes. All that is needed to implement the features is to implement the `WheelViewDelegate` method `-wheelView:didSelectCellAtIndex:` found in *PhotoAlbumsViewController.m*.

What should this implementation do? It should notify the `PhotoAlbumView-Controller`—that's the other child view controller displayed at the top of the screen—that a different photo album has been selected. The `PhotoAlbumView-Controller` is responsible for displaying the details of the photo album; this includes displaying the title and the photos contained within the album. It is also responsible for deleting a photo album, adding photos to the album, and setting the album title. But first things first.

The `PhotoAlbumsViewController` needs to know about the `PhotoAlbum-ViewController`. Without a reference to the photo album view controller, the photo albums view controller will not be able to tell it when a photo album has been selected.

The best place to inform `PhotoAlbumsViewController` about the existence of `PhotoAlbumViewController` is in the `MainViewController` at the time the view controllers are created. Open *MainViewController.m* and add the last line of code at the bottom of `-viewDidLoad` in Listing 16.9.

This line of code simply sets a declared property on `PhotoAlbumsViewController` to `photoAlbumScene`, which is an instance of `PhotoAlbumViewController`. The full implementation of `-viewDidLoad` is shown in Listing 16.9.

Listing 16.9 *MainViewController's* `-viewDidLoad` **Implementation**

```
- (void)viewDidLoad
{
    [super viewDidLoad];

    AppDelegate *appDelegate =
        (AppDelegate *)[[UIApplication sharedApplication] delegate];
    NSManagedObjectContext *managedObjectContext =
        [appDelegate managedObjectContext];

    UIStoryboard *storyboard = [self storyboard];

    PhotoAlbumsViewController *photoAlbumsScene =
        [storyboard instantiateViewControllerWithIdentifier:@"PhotoAlbumsScene"];
    [photoAlbumsScene setManagedObjectContext:managedObjectContext];
```

```
[self addChildViewController:photoAlbumsScene];
[photoAlbumsScene didMoveToParentViewController:self];

PhotoAlbumViewController *photoAlbumScene =
    [storyboard instantiateViewControllerWithIdentifier:@"PhotoAlbumScene"];
[self addChildViewController:photoAlbumScene];
[photoAlbumScene didMoveToParentViewController:self];

[photoAlbumsScene setPhotoAlbumViewController:photoAlbumScene];
}
```

Next, you must add the declared property photoAlbumViewController to the
PhotoAlbumsViewController class. Open *PhotoAlbumsViewController.h* and add the
declared property photoAlbumViewController with the type PhotoAlbumView-
Controller. Because this view controller does not yet know about the PhotoAlbum-
ViewController class, you'll need to add a forward @class declaration for it at the
top. Take a look at Listing 16.10 for the changes.

Listing 16.10   **Updated** *PhotoAlbumsViewController.h*

```
#import <UIKit/UIKit.h>
#import "WheelView.h"

@class PhotoAlbumViewController;

@interface PhotoAlbumsViewController : UIViewController
<NSFetchedResultsControllerDelegate, WheelViewDataSource, WheelViewDelegate>

@property (nonatomic, strong) NSManagedObjectContext *managedObjectContext;
@property (nonatomic, strong) IBOutlet WheelView *wheelView;
@property (nonatomic, strong) PhotoAlbumViewController *photoAlbumViewController;

- (IBAction)addPhotoAlbum:(id)sender;

@end
```

In *PhotoAlbumsViewController.m*, you must add the #import statement for
PhotoAlbumViewController.h. You must also add the @synthesize statement for the
new declared property. Last, you need to add the implementation for the -wheelView
:didSelectCellAtIndex: method. The changes are shown in Listing 16.11.

Listing 16.11   **Updated** *PhotoAlbumsViewController.m*

```
#import "PhotoAlbumsViewController.h"
#import "PhotoWheelViewCell.h"
#import "PhotoAlbum.h"
```

```objc
#import "Photo.h"
#import "PhotoAlbumViewController.h"

// Other code left out for brevity's sake.

@implementation PhotoAlbumsViewController

// Other code left out for brevity's sake.

@synthesize photoAlbumViewController = _photoAlbumViewController;

// Other code left out for brevity's sake.

- (void)wheelView:(WheelView *)wheelView didSelectCellAtIndex:(NSInteger)index
{
    // Retrieve the photo album from the fetched results.
    NSIndexPath *indexPath = [NSIndexPath indexPathForRow:index
                                                inSection:0];          // 1
    PhotoAlbum *photoAlbum = nil;
    // index = -1 means no selected cell and nothing to retrieve
    // from the fetched results.
    if (index >= 0) {
        photoAlbum = [[self fetchedResultsController]
                    objectAtIndexPath:indexPath];
    }

    // Pass the current managed object context and object id for the
    // photo album to the photo album view controller.
    PhotoAlbumViewController *photoAlbumViewController =
        [self photoAlbumViewController];
    [photoAlbumViewController
        setManagedObjectContext:[self managedObjectContext]];          // 2
    [photoAlbumViewController setObjectID:[photoAlbum objectID]];       // 3
    [photoAlbumViewController reload];                                  // 4
}

@end
```

Now let's run through the code in Listing 16.11:

1. The implementation for -wheelView:didSelectCellAtIndex: starts by retrieving the photo album model object from the fetched results. This is accomplished by calling objectAtIndexPath: on the fetched results controller. Remember, section 0 is used because the WheelView class always has only one section.

2–3. After the photo album model object is retrieved, the current managed object context and object ID for the photo album are passed to the PhotoAlbumView-Controller instance. This is but one of many different implementations that could have been used to share model data between two view controllers. For instance, instead of passing the managed object context and object ID, the photo album model object could be passed. After all, the model object knows its object ID, and the managed object context can be retrieved from the model object.

Why use the approach of passing the managed object context and object ID? This approach is used to illustrate a point. The managed object context can be a separate context. Granted, in this case it's the same as the one retrieved from the `AppDelegate` instance, but it can be different.

The other point illustrated here is that each model object has a unique identifier named `objectID`. The object ID can be used to retrieve an object from a different managed object context (from the same persistent store). An example of where this is common is with background threads.

`NSManagedObjectContext` is not thread safe. You should never use a managed object context created in a different thread. You should only use a context created in the current thread. Instead of passing the context between threads, you pass the persistent store coordinator, then create a new context instance using the store coordinator in the secondary thread. And you can pass the `objectID` to the secondary thread should it need to operate on a particular object.

> **Note**
>
> Read *Core Data: Apple's API for Persisting Data on Mac OS X*, by Marcus Zarra (Pragmatic Bookshelf, 2009), for more on using Core Data in multithreaded applications.

4. Back to `PhotoAlbumsViewController`. Once the managed object context and object ID have been passed to the `PhotoAlbumViewController` instance, the `-reload` method is called on the same controller instance. `-reload` presents the photo album data for the object ID retrieved from the managed object context.

This, of course, means that you need to add these properties (`managedObject-Context` and `objectID`) to the `PhotoAlbumViewController` class along with the `-reload` method. Open *PhotoAlbumViewController.h* and update it with the code shown in Listing 16.12.

Listing 16.12   Updated *PhotoAlbumViewController.h*

```
#import <UIKit/UIKit.h>

@interface PhotoAlbumViewController : UIViewController

@property (nonatomic, strong) NSManagedObjectContext *managedObjectContext;
@property (nonatomic, strong) NSManagedObjectID *objectID;

- (void)reload;

@end
```

When you are finished with the interface, open *PhotoAlbumViewController.m* and add the implementation as shown in Listing 16.13. The -reload method is empty for the moment. You'll work on the implementation of this method as the view controller is enhanced.

Listing 16.13   **Updated** *PhotoAlbumViewController.m*

```
#import "PhotoAlbumViewController.h"

@implementation PhotoAlbumViewController

@synthesize managedObjectContext = _managedObjectContext;
@synthesize objectID = _objectID;

- (void)didMoveToParentViewController:(UIViewController *)parent
{
    // Position the view within the new parent.
    [[parent view] addSubview:[self view]];
    CGRect newFrame = CGRectMake(26, 18, 716, 717);
    [[self view] setFrame:newFrame];

    [[self view] setBackgroundColor:[UIColor clearColor]];
}

- (void)reload
{

}

@end
```

At this point, the user can add a photo album and select an album by spinning the wheel.

Naming the Photo Album

A nice feature to give the user is the ability to name a photo album. The name can be displayed in the toolbar at the top of the photo album view. This area can also be used to edit the album name. Simply tap the name and it becomes editable.

But the toolbar does not yet exist. You must add it. You also need to add a text field to the toolbar for the photo album name. And you need to add two bar button items to the toolbar. One bar button item is displayed on the left side of the toolbar and the other on the right. The left button is an action button that will display a menu of action items. The right button is the add button that's used to add a photo to the album.

Implement these requirements in your app.

Open *MainStoryboard.storyboard*. Select the Photo Album View Controller in the Photo Album View Controller Scene. Delete the Round Rect Button that was used to test the custom push segue. It's no longer needed.

Next, drop a `UIToolbar` onto the scene. Position it at the top of the popover image view in the area that looks like a toolbar area (set the position and size: X to 9, Y to 6, Width to 698, and Height to 44). Anchor the toolbar to the top by changing the autoresizing properties, and turn off autosizing for the width. Set the Style for the toolbar to Black Opaque, and set its Background color to Clear.

Now add two buttons (`UIBarButtonItem`) and a text field (`UITextField`) to the toolbar. Use the flexible spacing object to position the buttons and text field. There should be buttons on the left and right of the text field. The text field should be in the middle of the toolbar. Set the text field Width to 533. Set the Placeholder property to "Tap to edit." Set the Alignment to Center and the Border Style to nothing. Finally, set the Text Color to White and the Background to Clear.

Change the Identifier for the left button to Action, and change the Identifier for the right-side button to Add. The finished scene should look like the screen shot in Figure 16.6.

Now open *PhotoAlbumViewController.h* and add the following outlets and actions. You can do this by hand, or use the Assistant editor. Be sure to connect the outlets and actions. The code changes are shown in Listing 16.14.

- Outlet named `toolbar` of type `UIToolbar`

- Outlet named `textField` of type `UITextField`

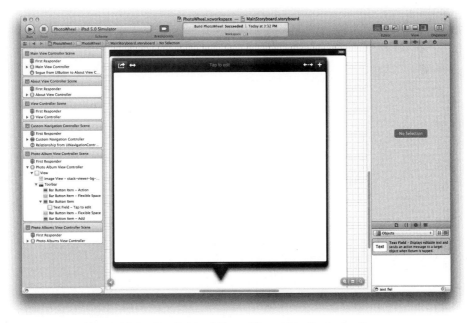

Figure 16.6   The finished Photo Album View Controller Scene

- Outlet named `addButton` of type `UIBarButtonItem`
- Action named `showActionMenu`
- Action named `addPhoto`

Listing 16.14   Updated `PhotoAlbumViewController` **Class**

```
///////
//  PhotoAlbumViewController.h
///////
#import <UIKit/UIKit.h>

@interface PhotoAlbumViewController : UIViewController

@property (nonatomic, strong) NSManagedObjectContext *managedObjectContext;
@property (nonatomic, strong) NSManagedObjectID *objectID;
@property (nonatomic, strong) IBOutlet UIToolbar *toolbar;
@property (nonatomic, strong) IBOutlet UITextField *textField;
@property (nonatomic, strong) IBOutlet UIBarButtonItem *addButton;

- (void)reload;
- (IBAction)showActionMenu:(id)sender;
- (IBAction)addPhoto:(id)sender;

@end

///////
//  PhotoAlbumViewController.m
///////
#import "PhotoAlbumViewController.h"

@implementation PhotoAlbumViewController

@synthesize managedObjectContext = _managedObjectContext;
@synthesize objectID = _objectID;
@synthesize toolbar = _toolbar;
@synthesize textField = _textField;
@synthesize addButton = _addButton;

- (void)didMoveToParentViewController:(UIViewController *)parent
{
    // Position the view within the new parent.
    [[parent view] addSubview:[self view]];
    CGRect newFrame = CGRectMake(26, 18, 716, 717);
    [[self view] setFrame:newFrame];

    [[self view] setBackgroundColor:[UIColor clearColor]];
}
```

```
- (void)viewDidUnload
{
   [self setToolbar:nil];
   [self setTextField:nil];
   [self setAddButton:nil];
   [super viewDidUnload];
}

- (void)reload
{

}

#pragma mark - Actions

- (IBAction)showActionMenu:(id)sender
{

}

- (IBAction)addPhoto:(id)sender
{

}

@end
```

One last connection is needed in the Photo Album View Controller Scene. **Control-click** and drag the text field to the Photo Album View Controller object, and make the view controller the delegate of the text field.

With the scene in place, turn your attention to the implementation of Photo-AlbumViewController. A number of things must happen to prepare the class to manage a photo album. First, the -reload method must be implemented. It should retrieve the photo album and present the photo album data to the user. If there is no photo album, the toolbar should be hidden. This prevents the user from manipulating a nil photo album.

PhotoAlbumViewController must also respond to UITextFieldDelegate methods. These responses control the user experience editing the photo album name, and they tell the controller when to save the updated album name. The updated version of *PhotoAlbumViewController.m* is given in Listing 16.15. Apply these changes to your code.

Listing 16.15   **Updated** *PhotoAlbumViewController.m*

```
#import "PhotoAlbumViewController.h"
#import "PhotoAlbum.h"                                          // 1
```

```
@interface PhotoAlbumViewController ()                          // 2
@property (nonatomic, strong) PhotoAlbum *photoAlbum;           // 3
@end

@implementation PhotoAlbumViewController

@synthesize managedObjectContext = _managedObjectContext;
@synthesize objectID = _objectID;
@synthesize toolbar = _toolbar;
@synthesize textField = _textField;
@synthesize addButton = _addButton;
@synthesize photoAlbum = _photoAlbum;

- (void)didMoveToParentViewController:(UIViewController *)parent
{
    // Position the view within the new parent.
    [[parent view] addSubview:[self view]];
    CGRect newFrame = CGRectMake(26, 18, 716, 717);
    [[self view] setFrame:newFrame];

    [[self view] setBackgroundColor:[UIColor clearColor]];
}

- (void)viewDidLoad                                             // 4
{
    [super viewDidLoad];
    [self reload];
}

- (void)viewDidUnload                                           // 5
{
    [self setToolbar:nil];
    [self setTextField:nil];
    [self setAddButton:nil];
    [super viewDidUnload];
}

#pragma mark - Photo album management

- (void)reload                                                 // 6
{
    if ([self managedObjectContext] && [self objectID]) {      // 7
        self.photoAlbum = (PhotoAlbum *)[self.managedObjectContext
                                  objectWithID:[self objectID]]; // 8
        [[self toolbar] setHidden:NO];                         // 9
        [[self textField] setText:[self.photoAlbum name]];     // 10
    } else {
        [self setPhotoAlbum:nil];
```

```
      [[self toolbar] setHidden:YES];
      [[self textField] setText:@""];
   }
}

- (void)saveChanges                                           // 11
{
   // Save the context.
   NSManagedObjectContext *context = [self managedObjectContext];
   NSError *error = nil;
   if (![context save:&error])
   {
      /*
       Replace this implementation with code to handle the error appropriately.

       abort() causes the application to generate a crash log and terminate.
       You should not use this function in a shipping application, although
       it may be useful during development. If it is not possible to recover
       from the error, display an alert panel that instructs the user to quit
       the application by pressing the Home button.
       */
      NSLog(@"Unresolved error %@, %@", error, [error userInfo]);
      abort();
   }
}

#pragma mark - UITextFieldDelegate methods                    // 12

- (BOOL)textFieldShouldBeginEditing:(UITextField *)textField  // 13
{
   [textField setBorderStyle:UITextBorderStyleRoundedRect];
   [textField setTextColor:[UIColor blackColor]];
   [textField setBackgroundColor:[UIColor whiteColor]];
   return YES;
}

- (void)textFieldDidEndEditing:(UITextField *)textField       // 14
{
   [textField setBackgroundColor:[UIColor clearColor]];
   [textField setTextColor:[UIColor whiteColor]];
   [textField setBorderStyle:UITextBorderStyleNone];

   [[self photoAlbum] setName:[textField text]];
   [self saveChanges];
}

- (BOOL)textFieldShouldReturn:(UITextField *)textField        // 15
{
```

```
    [textField resignFirstResponder];
    return NO;
}

#pragma mark - Actions

- (IBAction)showActionMenu:(id)sender
{

}

- (IBAction)addPhoto:(id)sender
{

}

@end
```

Let's run through the code in Listing 16.15:

1–3. *PhotoAlbum.h* is imported. A class extension is defined, and the declared property named `photoAlbum` is added. The declared property is synthesized in the `@implementation` section.

4–5. The method `-viewDidLoad` is added. It calls the `-reload` method to initialize the presentation at startup. `-viewDidUnload` is also added, and it releases outlets when the view unloads.

6–10. The implementation for `-reload` has changed. It checks to see if the controller has a managed object context and object ID. If so, it retrieves the photo album and displays the name in the toolbar. If the managed object context or object ID is missing, the toolbar is hidden. This prevents the user from manipulating a `nil` photo album.

11. The method `-saveChanges` is a helper method. Saving the context is needed throughout the controller, so having a common save changes method is helpful.

12–13. The save helper method is followed by the `UITextFieldDelegate` methods. This is the meat of what you are trying to accomplish at the moment. The first delegate method, `-textFieldShouldBeginEditing:`, is called just before editing in the text field begins. Here the code changes the text field border style, text color, and background to give the appearance of being in an edit mode.

14. The edit mode appearance is reset in the `-textFieldDidEndEditing:` method. This method is called after editing in the text field has ended. In addition to the visual appearance of the text field being reset, the edited text is saved as the photo album's name.

15. The last of the UITextFieldDelegate methods used in this controller is
    -textFieldShouldReturn:. This method is called when the user taps the
    Return button in the virtual keyboard. The implementation of this method
    dismisses the keyboard. The method -resignFirstResponder on the text
    field is called to dismiss the keyboard.

Congratulations! The app now supports editing the photo album name. Build and
run the app, and test the new feature.

Fixing the Toolbar Display

When you ran the app, you may have noticed that the toolbar looks a little odd. The
background for the toolbar has been set to clear, but it's not clear. Instead, the toolbar
sits on top of the image and hides the rounded corners of the background image. To
fix this, a little hackery is needed.

You are going to create a custom toolbar that controls the drawing of the toolbar's
background. Or rather, it prevents the drawing of the background.

Add a new Objective-C class to the PhotoWheel project. Name the class
ClearToolbar, and make it a subclass of UIToolbar. Then open *ClearToolbar.m* and
override -drawRect: with a blank implementation. The complete code is given in
Listing 16.16.

Listing 16.16 ClearToolbar **Class**

```
///////
// ClearToolbar.h
///////
#import <UIKit/UIKit.h>

@interface ClearToolbar : UIToolbar

@end


///////
// ClearToolbar.m
///////
#import "ClearToolbar.h"

@implementation ClearToolbar

- (void)drawRect:(CGRect)rect
{
    // Intentionally left blank.
}

@end
```

Figure 16.7   The cleaned-up version of the toolbar

Now tell the Photo Album View Controller Scene to use `ClearToolbar` instead of `UIToolbar`. You accomplish this by opening *MainStoryboard.storyboard*, selecting the toolbar in the Photo Album View Controller Scene, and changing the class name from `UIToolbar` to `ClearToolbar` in the Identity inspector.

Save your changes, then build and run the app again. The toolbar should look much better, as shown in Figure 16.7.

Removing the Photo Album

If the user can add a photo album, surely he will want to remove one. PhotoWheel needs a way for the user to delete a photo album. The action button on the left side of the toolbar is a good place to display a menu of actions, including Delete Photo Album. When the user taps this action item, the app should prompt for confirmation; otherwise the user may end up deleting his favorite set of photos accidentally.

To make all of this happen, open *PhotoAlbumViewController.m* and scroll to the `-showActionMenu:` action method. Create a `UIActionSheet` and add a button with the title "Delete Photo Album." Then show the action sheet from the action button. You must also set the view controller as the delegate for the action sheet. This means that you also need to open *PhotoAlbumViewController.h* and add `UIActionSheet-Delegate` to the list of conforming protocols.

Finally, display the `UIAlertView` to confirm the delete with the user. This is the user's last chance to back out of the action before the photo album is gone forever.

The code changes to accomplish all of this are shown in Listing 16.17.

Listing 16.17   Updated `PhotoAlbumViewController` **with Photo Album Deletion**
Support

```
///////
// PhotoAlbumViewController.h
///////
#import <UIKit/UIKit.h>

@interface PhotoAlbumViewController : UIViewController <UIActionSheetDelegate>

// Other code left out for brevity's sake.

@end

///////
// PhotoAlbumViewController.m
///////
#import "PhotoAlbumViewController.h"
#import "PhotoAlbum.h"

// Other code left out for brevity's sake.

@implementation PhotoAlbumViewController

// Other code left out for brevity's sake.

#pragma mark - Actions

- (IBAction)showActionMenu:(id)sender
{
    UIActionSheet *actionSheet = [[UIActionSheet alloc] init];
    [actionSheet setDelegate:self];
    [actionSheet addButtonWithTitle:@"Delete Photo Album"];
    [actionSheet showFromBarButtonItem:sender animated:YES];
}

- (IBAction)addPhoto:(id)sender
{

}

#pragma mark - Confirm and delete photo album

- (void)confirmDeletePhotoAlbum
{
    NSString *message;
```

```objc
    NSString *name = [[self photoAlbum] name];
    if ([name length] > 0) {
        message = [NSString stringWithFormat:
                    @"Delete the photo album \"%@\". This action cannot be undone.",
                    name];
    } else {
        message = @"Delete this photo album? This action cannot be undone.";
    }
    UIAlertView *alertView = [[UIAlertView alloc]
                                initWithTitle:@"Delete Photo Album"
                                message:message
                                delegate:self
                                cancelButtonTitle:@"Cancel"
                                otherButtonTitles:@"OK", nil];
    [alertView show];
}

#pragma mark - UIAlertViewDelegate methods

- (void)alertView:(UIAlertView *)alertView
clickedButtonAtIndex:(NSInteger)buttonIndex
{
    if (buttonIndex == 1) {
        [self.managedObjectContext deleteObject:[self photoAlbum]];
        [self setPhotoAlbum:nil];
        [self setObjectID:nil];
        [self saveChanges];
        [self reload];
    }
}

#pragma mark - UIActionSheetDelegate methods

- (void)actionSheet:(UIActionSheet *)actionSheet
clickedButtonAtIndex:(NSInteger)buttonIndex
{
    // Do nothing if the user taps outside the action
    // sheet (thus closing the popover containing the
    // action sheet).
    if (buttonIndex < 0) {
        return;
    }

    [self confirmDeletePhotoAlbum];
}

@end
```

That's it. Photo albums can now be deleted.

A Better Photo Album Thumbnail

The photo album thumbnails look okay, but there's room for improvement. For instance, the thumbnail icons don't exactly convey a collection of photos to the user. And the photo album name is not even displayed. It's time to change this.

Open *PhotoWheelViewCell.h* and replace the interface code with the code in Listing 16.18.

Listing 16.18   **Updated** *PhotoWheelViewCell.h*

```
#import "WheelView.h"

@interface PhotoWheelViewCell : WheelViewCell

@property (nonatomic, strong) IBOutlet UIImageView *imageView;
@property (nonatomic, strong) IBOutlet UILabel *label;

+ (PhotoWheelViewCell *)photoWheelViewCell;

@end
```

By now, the code change shouldn't look too foreign to you. Two outlets are added as declared properties. The image view is used to display the thumbnail, and the label is used to display the photo album name.

What might look a little different to you is the class method +photoWheelView-Cell. The + at the start indicates that this is a class method, not an instance method. The method is used to return a photo wheel view cell.

> **Note**
>
> Methods like +photoWheelViewCell are sometimes called convenience methods. They are called convenience methods because they are provided as a matter of convenience. In this particular case, the method makes it more convenient to create a new PhotoWheelViewCell instance.

Now open *PhotoWheelViewCell.m* and update the implementation with the code given in Listing 16.19. This new code replaces all of the old code.

Listing 16.19   **Updated** *PhotoWheelViewController.m*

```
#import "PhotoWheelViewCell.h"

@implementation PhotoWheelViewCell

@synthesize imageView = _imageView;
@synthesize label = _label;
```

```
+ (PhotoWheelViewCell *)photoWheelViewCell
{
   NSString *nibName = NSStringFromClass([self class]);
   UINib *nib = [UINib nibWithNibName:nibName bundle:nil];
   NSArray *nibObjects = [nib instantiateWithOwner:nil options:nil];
   // Verify that the top-level object is in fact of the correct type.
   NSAssert2([nibObjects count] > 0 &&
             [[nibObjects objectAtIndex:0] isKindOfClass:[self class]],
             @"Nib '%@' does not contain top-level view of type %@.",
             nibName, nibName);
   return [nibObjects objectAtIndex:0];
}

@end
```

The implementation starts by synthesizing the declared properties. That's nothing new. But what is new is the implementation for +photoWheelViewCell.

The previous implementation of PhotoWheelViewCell used a CALayer to draw an image onto the view. The new PhotoWheelViewCell uses a NIB to define the view layout. The code in +photoWheelViewCell returns an instance of the cell created in the NIB *PhotoWheelViewCell.xib*, which you have not created yet.

The first line of code retrieves the name of the class. The class name will be the name of the NIB. The next line of code sets a local variable to the NIB instance. The class method nibWithNibName:bundle: found on UINib is used to retrieve the NIB instance. The NIB is then instantiated, and an array of objects found in the NIB is returned. A quick verification check is performed to ensure that the array has at least one object and the top-level object is of the expected class type, which is Photo-WheelViewCell. The top-level object is then returned to the caller.

Once you complete the code changes, create a new NIB file and add it to the PhotoWheel project. Creating a NIB file is similar to creating other project files. Type **⌘-N** to create a new file. Select **iOS > User Interface**, then select the Empty file template, as shown in Figure 16.8. Click the **Next** button, then select iPhone as the Device Family. Click the **Next** button, and save the NIB file as *PhotoWheelViewCell*.

Why Select iPhone as the Device Family?

The photo wheel view cell is a small view. By selecting iPhone as the device family, IB creates a smaller view than it would have if iPad had been selected.

Open the NIB file *PhotoWheelViewCell.xib*. Drag a view onto the design canvas. Change the class name for the view to PhotoWheelViewCell. Set the Background color to Clear, and give the view a Width of 97 and a Height of 117.

Drop a UIImageView into the view. Set the image name to *defaultPhoto.png* and set the frame position and size: X to 12, Y to 10, Width to 75, and Height to 75. **Control-click** and drag the image view to the photo wheel view cell view object, and

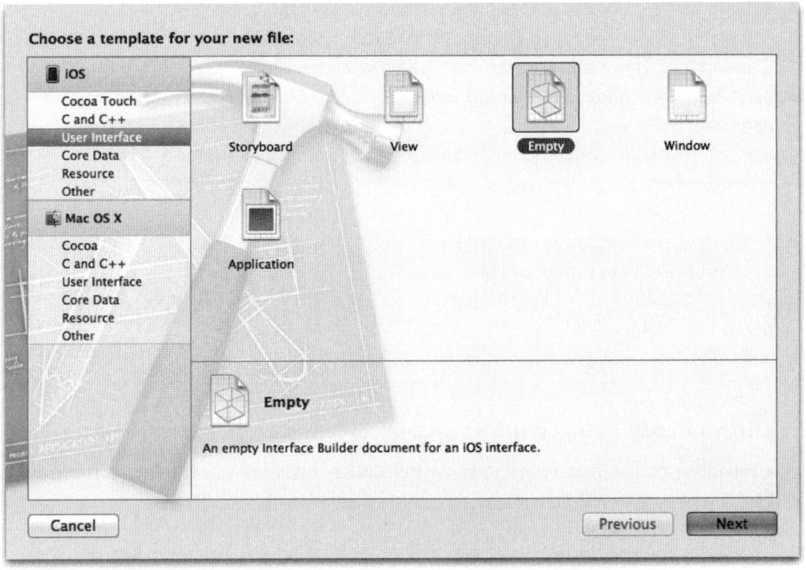

Figure 16.8   Create a new NIB using the Empty file template

connect it to the `imageView` outlet. This is the image view that displays the photo album thumbnail image.

Drag another `UIImageView` onto the view. Set the image name to *stack-overlay.png*, and set the frame position and size: X to 0, Y to 0, Width to 97, and Height to 97.

Finally, drag a `UILabel` onto the view. In the Attributes inspector, set Line Breaks to Truncate Middle and Alignment to Center. Set the Text Color to Default (or Black) and the Font size to 14. In the Size inspector, set the frame: X to 0, Y to 90, Width to 97, and Height to 21. Now **Control-click** and drag the label to the photo wheel view cell, connecting it to the label outlet.

The final results should look like Figure 16.9.

To use the new and improved `PhotoWheelViewCell`, open *PhotoAlbumsView-Controller.m* and scroll to the method `-wheelView:cellAtIndex:`. Replace the implementation with the code in Listing 16.20.

Listing 16.20   **Updated** `-wheelView:cellAtIndex:` **Method**

```
- (WheelViewCell *)wheelView:(WheelView *)wheelView cellAtIndex:(NSInteger)index
{
PhotoWheelViewCell *cell = [wheelView dequeueReusableCell];
    if (!cell) {
        cell = [PhotoWheelViewCell photoWheelViewCell];                // 1
    }

    NSIndexPath *indexPath = [NSIndexPath indexPathForRow:index inSection:0];
```

```
PhotoAlbum *photoAlbum = [[self fetchedResultsController]
                          objectAtIndexPath:indexPath];
Photo *photo = [[photoAlbum photos] lastObject];
UIImage *image = [photo thumbnailImage];
if (image == nil) {
   image = [UIImage imageNamed:@"defaultPhoto.png"];
}

[[cell imageView] setImage:image];                          // 2
[[cell label] setText:[photoAlbum name]];                   // 3

return cell;
}
```

Three lines of code changed in the update, so let's take a look at those:

1. If a reusable cell is not returned, a new cell is created using the convenience method +photoWheelViewCell on PhotoWheelViewCell.

2. The second change replaces [cell setImage:image] with [[cell imageView] setImage:image]. The previous implementation of the photo wheel view cell handled drawing the image on the layer, but the new implementation uses an image view instead.

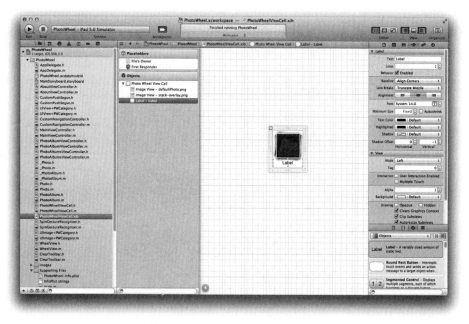

Figure 16.9   UI for the PhotoWheelViewCell NIB

Figure 16.10   PhotoWheel with the new thumbnail display style

3. The third and final change is the addition of the line [[cell label] setText:[photoAlbum name]]. This change displays the photo album name in the wheel.

Run the app to see how the new thumbnail looks—a definite improvement, as you can see in Figure 16.10.

Adding Photos

You have accomplished a lot in this chapter so far, but there is a bit more that must be done. The last major component missing from PhotoWheel is the display of photos. But before the app can display photos, the user must have a way to add them.

You already added the + button (aka add button) to the toolbar, and in the prototype app you wrote code to pick an image from the Photos app library or the camera. It's time to pull those pieces together and give the user a way to add photos to the photo album.

Start by opening *PhotoAlbumViewController.h* and adding UIImagePicker-ControllerDelegate and UINavigationControllerDelegate to the list of conforming protocols. Yes, it seems strange to include UINavigationControllerDelegate in the list of protocols, but it's required to be a delegate of `UIImagePickerController`. It's not a big deal, though. All of the methods of `UINavigationControllerDelegate` are optional, so there are no `UINavigationControllerDelegate` methods to implement.

The updated *PhotoAlbumViewController.h* is shown in Listing 16.21.

Listing 16.21   Updated *PhotoAlbumViewController.h*

```
#import <UIKit/UIKit.h>

@interface PhotoAlbumViewController : UIViewController <UIActionSheetDelegate,
UIImagePickerControllerDelegate, UINavigationControllerDelegate>

@property (nonatomic, strong) NSManagedObjectContext *managedObjectContext;
@property (nonatomic, strong) NSManagedObjectID *objectID;
@property (nonatomic, strong) IBOutlet UIToolbar *toolbar;
@property (nonatomic, strong) IBOutlet UITextField *textField;
@property (nonatomic, strong) IBOutlet UIBarButtonItem *addButton;

- (void)reload;
- (IBAction)showActionMenu:(id)sender;
- (IBAction)addPhoto:(id)sender;

@end
```

Now turn your attention to the implementation file *PhotoAlbumViewController.m*. You have already written the code that makes it possible for a user to add a photo to the photo album. The code is in the prototype app, but for the sake of completeness, the updated *PhotoAlbumViewController.m* is shown in Listing 16.22. You need to apply the same changes to your code.

Listing 16.22   Updated *PhotoAlbumViewController.m*

```
#import "PhotoAlbumViewController.h"
#import "PhotoAlbum.h"
#import "Photo.h"                                                      // 1

@interface PhotoAlbumViewController ()

// Other code left out for brevity's sake.

@property (nonatomic, strong) UIImagePickerController *imagePickerController; // 2
@property (nonatomic, strong) UIPopoverController *imagePickerPopoverController; // 3

- (void)presentPhotoPickerMenu;                                       // 4
@end
```

```
@implementation PhotoAlbumViewController

// Other code left out for brevity's sake.

@synthesize imagePickerController = _imagePickerController;            // 5
@synthesize imagePickerPopoverController = _imagePickerPopoverController;

// Other code left out for brevity's sake.

- (UIImagePickerController *)imagePickerController                     // 6
{
   if (_imagePickerController) {
      return _imagePickerController;
   }

   self.imagePickerController = [[UIImagePickerController alloc] init];
   [self.imagePickerController setDelegate:self];

   return _imagePickerController;
}

// Other code left out for brevity's sake.

- (IBAction)addPhoto:(id)sender                                       // 7
{
   if ([self imagePickerPopoverController]) {
      [[self imagePickerPopoverController] dismissPopoverAnimated:YES];
   }

   [self presentPhotoPickerMenu];
}

// Other code left out for brevity's sake.

#pragma mark - UIActionSheetDelegate methods

- (void)actionSheet:(UIActionSheet *)actionSheet clickedButtonAtIndex:(NSInteger)
buttonIndex                                                           // 8
{
   // Do nothing if the user taps outside the action
   // sheet (thus closing the popover containing the
   // action sheet).
   if (buttonIndex < 0) {
      return;
   }

   NSMutableArray *names = [[NSMutableArray alloc] init];             // 9
```

```
   if ([actionSheet tag] == 0) {
      [names addObject:@"confirmDeletePhotoAlbum"];

   } else {
      BOOL hasCamera = [UIImagePickerController
         isSourceTypeAvailable:UIImagePickerControllerSourceTypeCamera];
      if (hasCamera) [names addObject:@"presentCamera"];
      [names addObject:@"presentPhotoLibrary"];
   }

   SEL selector = NSSelectorFromString([names objectAtIndex:buttonIndex]);
   [self performSelector:selector];
}

#pragma mark - Image picker helper methods

- (void)presentCamera
{
   // Display the camera.
   UIImagePickerController *imagePicker = [self imagePickerController];
   [imagePicker setSourceType:UIImagePickerControllerSourceTypeCamera];
   [self presentModalViewController:imagePicker animated:YES];
}

- (void)presentPhotoLibrary
{
   // Display assets from the photo library only.
   UIImagePickerController *imagePicker = [self imagePickerController];
   [imagePicker setSourceType:UIImagePickerControllerSourceTypePhotoLibrary];

   UIPopoverController *newPopoverController =
      [[UIPopoverController alloc] initWithContentViewController:imagePicker];
   [newPopoverController presentPopoverFromBarButtonItem:[self addButton]
                              permittedArrowDirections:UIPopoverArrowDirectionAny
                                               animated:YES];
   [self setImagePickerPopoverController:newPopoverController];
}

- (void)presentPhotoPickerMenu
{
   UIActionSheet *actionSheet = [[UIActionSheet alloc] init];
   [actionSheet setDelegate:self];
   BOOL hasCamera = [UIImagePickerController
               isSourceTypeAvailable:UIImagePickerControllerSourceTypeCamera];
   if (hasCamera) {
      [actionSheet addButtonWithTitle:@"Take Photo"];
   }
```

```
    [actionSheet addButtonWithTitle:@"Choose from Library"];
    [actionSheet setTag:1];
    [actionSheet showFromBarButtonItem:[self addButton] animated:YES];
}


#pragma mark - UIImagePickerControllerDelegate methods

- (void)imagePickerController:(UIImagePickerController *)picker
didFinishPickingMediaWithInfo:(NSDictionary *)info
{
    // If the popover controller is available,
    // assume the photo is selected from the library
    // and not from the camera.
    BOOL takenWithCamera = ([self imagePickerPopoverController] == nil);

    if (takenWithCamera) {
        [self dismissModalViewControllerAnimated:YES];
    } else {
        [[self imagePickerPopoverController] dismissPopoverAnimated:YES];
        [self setImagePickerPopoverController:nil];
    }

    // Retrieve and display the image.
    UIImage *image = [info objectForKey:UIImagePickerControllerOriginalImage];

    NSManagedObjectContext *context = [self managedObjectContext];
    Photo *newPhoto =
        [NSEntityDescription insertNewObjectForEntityForName:@"Photo"
                                      inManagedObjectContext:context];
    [newPhoto setDateAdded:[NSDate date]];
    [newPhoto saveImage:image];
    [newPhoto setPhotoAlbum:[self photoAlbum]];

    [self saveChanges];
}

@end
```

Now for the walk-through, highlighting the changes:

1–5. *Photo.h* is added to the list of imports. Two declared properties have been added to the class extension. The first is a reference to the image picker and the second is a reference to the popover controller used to present the image picker. The method declaration -presentPhotoPickerMenu has also been added to the class extension to make its location in the @implementation section unimportant. And speaking of the implementation section, the new declared properties are synthesized in the @implementation section.

6. A custom getter method has been created for `imagePickerController`. It lazy loads the `UIImagePickerController` instance used by the view controller.

7. The getter is followed by `-addPhoto:`. Previously its implementation was empty, but now it starts the process for picking an image. It also dismisses the popover controller if it is open.

8. The method `-actionSheet:clickedButtonAtIndex:`, which is a callback for the `UIActionSheetDelegate` protocol, has been modified to support more than one action sheet. The action button displays one action sheet, and the add button displays the other. Both use the `PhotoAlbumViewController` instance as their delegates, so the same callback method is called regardless of the sending action sheet. The tag property on the action sheet is used to distinguish between the two action sheets. A tag value of 0 indicates that the action sheet is used by the action button. A tag value of 1 indicates that the action sheet is used by the add button.

9. To make the code in `-actionSheet:clickedButtonAtIndex:` more maintainable, a mutable array is used to list the selector names for each menu item within the action sheet. The `buttonIndex` is then used to retrieve the selector name from the array, and `-performSelector:` is called to invoke the selector. This dynamic approach to calling selectors is a powerful feature of Objective-C not found in many other compiled programming languages.

> **Note**
>
> The PhotoWheel project uses ARC to transfer responsibility for memory management of objects to the compiler. Because the selector is unknown in the `-performSelector:` call, a "possible memory leak" warning message is reported by the compiler. This warning is legitimate given that ARC does not know the selector. The selector is determined at run time. But the code in question does not cause a leak. There is, unfortunately, no way to turn off this warning, so for now the warning message must be a part of the compiler output.

The remaining code in Listing 16.22 is similar to the code you wrote for the prototype app for picking an image. Refer to Chapter 12, "Adding Photos," if you need a refresher on what the code is doing.

Displaying Photos

The final piece missing from PhotoWheel is the display of photos. A nice way to present the photos is to lay them out in a grid, but iOS doesn't provide a grid view. This means it's up to you to write the code for a grid view. Writing a grid view from scratch should not be too difficult since some of the core concepts have already been implemented in the `WheelView` class.

Like the `WheelView` class, the grid view will be modeled after `UITableView`. It will rely on a data source protocol to communicate to a controller, and it will manage an internal cache of reusable cells.

To create the grid view, start by creating a new Objective-C class. Name the class `GridView`, make it a subclass of `UIScrollView`, and add the new class to the Photo-Wheel project.

`UIScrollView`, the superclass for your `GridView` class, displays content in a view that is larger than the visible display area. The user scrolls through the content using swiping gestures. A PhotoWheel user may have many photos stored within a single photo album, many more photos than the app can display at one time. Therefore, basing the `GridView` class on the scroll view gives you lots of display behavior for free.

After creating the `GridView` class, open the file *GridView.h* and add the code shown in Listing 16.23.

Listing 16.23   *GridView.h*

```
#import <UIKit/UIKit.h>

@class GridViewCell;                                          // 1
@protocol GridViewDataSource;                                 // 2


@interface GridView : UIScrollView <UIScrollViewDelegate>     // 3

@property (nonatomic, strong) IBOutlet id<GridViewDataSource> dataSource;// 4
@property (nonatomic, assign) BOOL allowsMultipleSelection;   // 5


- (id)dequeueReusableCell;                                    // 6
- (void)reloadData;                                           // 7
- (GridViewCell *)cellAtIndex:(NSInteger)index;               // 8
- (NSInteger)indexForSelectedCell;                            // 9
- (NSArray *)indexesForSelectedCells;                         // 10

@end


@protocol GridViewDataSource <NSObject>
@required
- (NSInteger)gridViewNumberOfCells:(GridView *)gridView;
- (GridViewCell *)gridView:(GridView *)gridView cellAtIndex:(NSInteger)index;
- (CGSize)gridViewCellSize:(GridView *)gridView;

@optional
- (NSInteger)gridViewCellsPerRow:(GridView *)gridView;
- (void)gridView:(GridView *)gridView didSelectCellAtIndex:(NSInteger)index;
```

```
- (void)gridView:(GridView *)gridView didDeselectCellAtIndex:(NSInteger)index;
@end


@interface GridViewCell : UIView
@property (nonatomic, assign, getter = isSelected) BOOL selected;        // 11
@end
```

1. The interface for the GridView class should look familiar. It uses a pattern similar to the one you used to implement the WheelView class. A GridView-Cell is declared as a forward declaration. Its interface is declared at the bottom of the source code listing. This class provides a known base class that is used by the GridView class.

2. It is followed by the declaration for the GridViewDataSource protocol. Its interface is also defined toward the bottom of the source code listing. This protocol is used to enable communication between the grid view and a view controller. The protocol has the methods you would expect after working with UITableView and WheelView. There is a method to retrieve the number of cells, a method to get the cell size, a method to get the number of cells to display per row, and of course a method to get the cell that is displayed in the grid.

3. The interface for GridView is straightforward. It subclasses UIScrollView, and it conforms to the UIScrollViewDelegate protocol. As you will see shortly, the GridView is its own delegate for managing scroll events.

4–5. The GridView class has two properties: dataSource and allowsMultiple-Selection. dataSource is a reference to an object (typically a view controller) that conforms to the GridViewDataSource protocol. allowsMultiple-Selection is a flag indicating whether the GridView should manage multiple selections or not. When this flag is set to YES, one or more cells can be selected at the same time. When the flag is set to NO, only one cell is marked as selected.

> **Note**
>
> The GridView class presented here implements the multi-select feature. However, you will not use this feature until Chapter 21, "Web Services."

6–8. The GridView class has a set of methods that should be familiar to you. The methods -dequeueReusableCell, -reloadData, and -cellAtIndex: are also found in the WheelView class.

9–10. Two additional methods are provided in the GridView class for reporting the selected cell or cells: -indexForSelectedCell and -indexesFor-SelectedCells. The first returns the index to the selected cell, and the second returns an array of selected cells. The second method is meaningful only when the `allowsMultipleSelection` flag is set to YES.

11. The declared property `selected` is a Boolean (BOOL) indicating whether the cell is selected or not.

Now for the implementation. Open *GridView.m* and update it with the code found in Listing 16.24.

Listing 16.24   *GridView.m*

```
#import "GridView.h"

#pragma mark - GridViewCell

@interface GridViewCell ()                                      // 1
@property (nonatomic, assign) NSInteger indexInGrid;
@end

@implementation GridViewCell                                    // 2
@synthesize selected = selected_;
@synthesize indexInGrid = indexInGrid_;
@end



#pragma mark - GridView

@interface GridView ()                                          // 3
@property (nonatomic, strong) NSMutableSet *reusableViews;
@property (nonatomic, assign) NSInteger firstVisibleIndex;
@property (nonatomic, assign) NSInteger lastVisibleIndex;
@property (nonatomic, assign) NSInteger previousItemsPerRow;
@property (nonatomic, strong) NSMutableSet *selectedCellIndexes;
@end

@implementation GridView                                        // 4

@synthesize dataSource = _dataSource;
@synthesize reusableViews = _reusableViews;
@synthesize firstVisibleIndex = _firstVisibleIndex;
@synthesize lastVisibleIndex = _lastVisibleIndex;
@synthesize previousItemsPerRow = _previousItemsPerRow;
@synthesize selectedCellIndexes = _selectedCellIndexes;
@synthesize allowsMultipleSelection = _allowsMultipleSelection;

- (void)commonInit                                              // 5
{
    // We keep a collection of reusable views. This
    // improves scrolling performance by not requiring
```

```objc
    // creation of the view each and every time.
    self.reusableViews = [[NSMutableSet alloc] init];

    // We have no views visible at first so we
    // set index values high and low to trigger
    // the display during layoutSubviews.
    [self setFirstVisibleIndex:NSIntegerMax];
    [self setLastVisibleIndex:NSIntegerMin];
    [self setPreviousItemsPerRow:NSIntegerMin];

    [self setDelaysContentTouches:YES];                    // 6
    [self setClipsToBounds:YES];                           // 7
    [self setAlwaysBounceVertical:YES];                    // 8

    [self setAllowsMultipleSelection:NO];                  // 9
    self.selectedCellIndexes = [[NSMutableSet alloc] init];  // 10

    UITapGestureRecognizer *tap = [[UITapGestureRecognizer alloc]
            initWithTarget:self action:@selector(didTap:)];  // 11
    [self addGestureRecognizer:tap];
}

- (id)init                                                 // 12
{
    self = [super init];
    if (self) {
        [self commonInit];
    }
    return self;
}

- (id)initWithCoder:(NSCoder *)aDecoder
{
    self = [super initWithCoder:aDecoder];
    if (self) {
        [self commonInit];
    }
    return self;
}

- (id)initWithFrame:(CGRect)frame
{
    self = [super initWithFrame:frame];
    if (self) {
        [self commonInit];
    }
    return self;
}
```

```objc
- (id)dequeueReusableCell                                    // 13
{
    id view = [[self reusableViews] anyObject];
    if (view != nil) {
        [[self reusableViews] removeObject:view];
    }
    return view;
}


- (void)queueReusableCells                                   // 14
{
    for (UIView *view in [self subviews]) {
        if ([view isKindOfClass:[GridViewCell class]]) {
            [[self reusableViews] addObject:view];
            [view removeFromSuperview];
        }
    }

    [self setFirstVisibleIndex:NSIntegerMax];
    [self setLastVisibleIndex:NSIntegerMin];
    [[self selectedCellIndexes] removeAllObjects];
}


- (void)reloadData                                           // 15
{
    [self queueReusableCells];
    [self setNeedsLayout];
}


- (GridViewCell *)cellAtIndex:(NSInteger)index               // 16
{
    GridViewCell *cell = nil;
    if (index >= [self firstVisibleIndex] && index <= [self lastVisibleIndex]) {
        for (id view in [self subviews]) {
            if ([view isKindOfClass:[GridViewCell class]]) {
                if ([view indexInGrid] == index) {
                    cell = view;
                    break;
                }
            }
        }
    }

    if (cell == nil) {
        cell = [[self dataSource] gridView:self cellAtIndex:index];
    }
```

```
    return cell;
}

- (void)layoutSubviews                                          // 17
{
    [super layoutSubviews];

    CGRect visibleBounds = [self bounds];                       // 18
    NSInteger visibleWidth = visibleBounds.size.width;
    NSInteger visibleHeight = visibleBounds.size.height;

    CGSize viewSize = [[self dataSource] gridViewCellSize:self];  // 19

    // Do some math to determine which rows and columns
    // are visible.
    NSInteger itemsPerRow = NSIntegerMin;                       // 20
    if ([[self dataSource] respondsToSelector:@selector(gridViewCellsPerRow:)]) {
        itemsPerRow = [[self dataSource] gridViewCellsPerRow:self];
    }
    if (itemsPerRow == NSIntegerMin) {
        // Calculate the number of items per row.
        itemsPerRow = floor(visibleWidth / viewSize.width);
    }
    if (itemsPerRow != [self previousItemsPerRow]) {
        // Force reload of grid views. Unfortunately this means
        // visible views will reload, which can hurt performance
        // when the view isn't cached. Need to find a better
        // approach someday.
        [self queueReusableCells];
    }
    [self setPreviousItemsPerRow:itemsPerRow];

    // Ensure a minimum amount of space between views.
    NSInteger minimumSpace = 5;
    if (visibleWidth - itemsPerRow * viewSize.width < minimumSpace) {
        itemsPerRow--;
    }

    if (itemsPerRow < 1) itemsPerRow = 1;  // Ensure at least one view per row.

    NSInteger spaceWidth =
        round((visibleWidth - viewSize.width * itemsPerRow) / (itemsPerRow + 1));
    NSInteger spaceHeight = spaceWidth;

    // Calculate the content size for the scroll view.
    NSInteger viewCount = [[self dataSource] gridViewNumberOfCells:self];
    NSInteger rowCount = ceil(viewCount / (float)itemsPerRow);
```

```
NSInteger rowHeight = viewSize.height + spaceHeight;
CGSize contentSize = CGSizeMake(visibleWidth,
                                (rowHeight * rowCount + spaceHeight));
[self setContentSize:contentSize];                              // 21

NSInteger numberOfVisibleRows = visibleHeight / rowHeight;
NSInteger topRow = MAX(0, floorf(visibleBounds.origin.y / rowHeight));
NSInteger bottomRow = topRow + numberOfVisibleRows;

CGRect extendedVisibleBounds =
    CGRectMake(visibleBounds.origin.x,
               MAX(0, visibleBounds.origin.y),
               visibleBounds.size.width,
               visibleBounds.size.height + rowHeight);

// Recycle all views that are no longer visible.
for (UIView *view in [self subviews]) {                         // 22
    if ([view isKindOfClass:[GridViewCell class]]) {
        CGRect viewFrame = [view frame];

        // If the view doesn't intersect, it's not visible, so recycle it.
        if (!CGRectIntersectsRect(viewFrame, extendedVisibleBounds)) {
            [[self reusableViews] addObject:view];
            [view removeFromSuperview];
        }
    }
}


////////////
// Whew! We're now ready to lay out the subviews.                // 23

NSInteger startAtIndex = MAX(0, topRow * itemsPerRow);
NSInteger stopAtIndex = MIN(viewCount,
                            (bottomRow * itemsPerRow) + itemsPerRow);

// Set the initial origin.
NSInteger x = spaceWidth;
NSInteger y = spaceHeight + (topRow * rowHeight);

// Iterate through the needed views, adding any views that are missing.
for (NSInteger index = startAtIndex; index < stopAtIndex; index++) {

    // Set the frame so the view is placed in the correct position.
    GridViewCell *view = [self cellAtIndex:index];
    CGRect newFrame = CGRectMake(x, y, viewSize.width, viewSize.height);
    [view setFrame:newFrame];
```

```
         // If the index is between the first and last, the
         // view is not missing.
         BOOL isViewMissing =
            !(index >= [self firstVisibleIndex] && index < [self lastVisibleIndex]);
         if (isViewMissing) {
            BOOL selected = [[self selectedCellIndexes]
                             containsObject:[NSNumber numberWithInteger:index]];
            [view setSelected:selected];
            [view setIndexInGrid:index];
            [self addSubview:view];
         }

         // Adjust the position.
         if ((index+1) % itemsPerRow == 0) {
            // Start new row.
            x = spaceWidth;
            y += viewSize.height + spaceHeight;
         } else {
            x += viewSize.width + spaceWidth;
         }
      }

   // Finally, remember which view indexes are visible.
   [self setFirstVisibleIndex:startAtIndex];
   [self setLastVisibleIndex:stopAtIndex];
}

- (void)didTap:(UITapGestureRecognizer *)recognizer                  // 24
{
   // Need to figure out if the user tapped a cell or not.
   // If a cell was tapped, let the data source know
   // which cell was tapped.

   CGPoint touchPoint = [recognizer locationInView:self];

   for (id view in [self subviews]) {
      if ([view isKindOfClass:[GridViewCell class]]) {
         if (CGRectContainsPoint([view frame], touchPoint)) {          // 25

            NSInteger previousIndex = -1;                              // 26
            NSInteger selectedIndex = -1;

            NSMutableSet *selectedCellIndexes = [self selectedCellIndexes];
            if ([self allowsMultipleSelection] == NO) {
               // Out with the old.
               if ([selectedCellIndexes count] > 0) {
                  previousIndex = [[selectedCellIndexes anyObject] integerValue];
```

```
                [[self cellAtIndex:previousIndex] setSelected:NO];
                [selectedCellIndexes removeAllObjects];
            }

            // And in with the new.
            selectedIndex = [view indexInGrid];
            [view setSelected:YES];
            [selectedCellIndexes
                addObject:[NSNumber numberWithInteger:selectedIndex]];

        } else {
            NSInteger indexInGrid = [view indexInGrid];
            NSNumber *numberIndexInGrid =
                [NSNumber numberWithInteger:indexInGrid];
            if ([selectedCellIndexes containsObject:numberIndexInGrid]) {
                previousIndex = indexInGrid;
                [view setSelected:NO];
                [selectedCellIndexes removeObject:numberIndexInGrid];
            } else {
                selectedIndex = indexInGrid;
                [view setSelected:YES];
                [selectedCellIndexes addObject:numberIndexInGrid];
            }
        }

        id <GridViewDataSource> dataSource = [self dataSource];      // 27
        if (previousIndex >= 0) {
            if ([dataSource
                    respondsToSelector:@selector(gridView:didDeselectCellAtIndex:)])
            {
                [dataSource gridView:self didDeselectCellAtIndex:previousIndex];
            }
        }
        if (selectedIndex >= 0) {
            if ([dataSource
                    respondsToSelector:@selector(gridView:didSelectCellAtIndex:)])
            {
                [dataSource gridView:self didSelectCellAtIndex:selectedIndex];
            }
        }

        break;
    }
  }
 }
}
```

```
- (NSInteger)indexForSelectedCell                                    // 28
{
  NSInteger selectedIndex = -1;
  NSMutableSet *selectedCellIndexes = [self selectedCellIndexes];
  if ([selectedCellIndexes count] > 0) {
    selectedIndex = [[selectedCellIndexes anyObject] integerValue];
  }
  return selectedIndex;
}


- (NSArray *)indexesForSelectedCells                                 // 29
{
  NSArray *selectedIndexes = nil;
  NSMutableSet *selectedCellIndexes = [self selectedCellIndexes];
  if ([selectedCellIndexes count] > 0) {
    NSSortDescriptor *sortDescriptor = [NSSortDescriptor
                                  sortDescriptorWithKey:@"self"
                                  ascending:YES];
    selectedIndexes = [selectedCellIndexes
      sortedArrayUsingDescriptors:[NSArray arrayWithObject:sortDescriptor]];
  }
  return selectedIndexes;
}


@end
```

Much of the code in Listing 16.24 is conceptually familiar, so instead of a thorough code walk-through, only key parts are highlighted.

1–2. At the top of *GridView.m* is a class extension and the implementation for GridViewCell. It has a private property indexInGrid that is used by the GridView class to maintain the cell index within the grid.

3. Following GridViewCell is a class extension for GridView. The class extension has a set of properties used to manage the cache of reusable cells, the display of cells, and the set of selected cell indexes.

4–5. The implementation for GridView starts, as you might expect, with the synthesizing of the declared properties. This is followed by -commonInit. This method is called by the other init* methods, and it is responsible for initializing the GridView instance. It allocates the reusableViews set. It then sets property values used to control the display layout.

The properties delaysContentTouches, clipsToBounds, and always-BounceVertical are set to YES. These properties are inherited from UIScrollView. This is why you do not see their declarations in the GridView class.

6. The property `delaysContentTouches` tells the scroll view to delay the handling of touch-down gestures. The handling is delayed until the scroll view can determine if scrolling is the intent of the gesture. The delay is needed to give the tap gesture (also instantiated in -`commonInit`) a chance to handle the gesture.

7–8. The property `clipsToBounds` confines the subviews (aka cells) to the bounds of the scroll view. This ensures that the cells are not displayed outside the visible area of the grid view. And `alwaysBounceVertical` always bounces the scroll area when the content has reached an end.

9–10. -`commonInit` also sets the `allowMultipleSelection` flag to `NO`, which is the default behavior for the `GridView` class. It then instantiates the mutable set used to maintain the collection of selected cell indexes.

11. A tap gesture is created and added to the grid view. The tap gesture is used to determine when a cell in the grid view has been tapped.

12. Additional `init*` methods are provided, enabling a `GridView` object to be created by different approaches common to Cocoa. For instance, -`initWith-Coder:` is called when the `GridView` is defined in a NIB or storyboard, and it is loaded at run time.

13–16. The methods following the inits (i.e., -`dequeueReusableCell`, -`queueReusableCells`, -`reloadData`, and -`cellAtIndex:`) are essentially the same as ones (with the same names) found in the `WheelView` class, and the code is self-explanatory. The method following those, -`layoutSubviews`, is not.

17–19. The method -`layoutSubviews` is the workhorse of the `GridView` class. This method is responsible for displaying the cells in a grid layout. The method starts by setting local variables to the bounds and size of the grid view. It then requests the size of the cell from the data source, which the data source is required to provide. These sizes, along with other variables, are used to calculate the rows and columns as well as the overall layout for the grid.

20. Next, the number of items per row is calculated. The calculation evenly distributes the cells within the row. The data source has the option to override this calculation and instead specify a specific number of items per row.

21–22. Once the calculations have been performed, the content size for the scroll view is set. The content size can be larger than the view port displaying the grid. After this, the bounds of the grid are calculated. These are used to determine whether a cell is visible or not. Cells that are not visible are queued for reuse.

23. It is at this point that -`layoutSubviews` can finally lay out the subviews. The subviews are the individual cells that make up the grid. A loop is created that iterates through the cells to be displayed. If a cell is missing from the

display, it is added. The cells are then positioned within the grid to form the grid layout of rows and columns.

24–25. The -layoutSubviews method is followed by the -didTap: method. This method handles the tap events from the tap gestures created in -commonInit. The method iterates through the collection of subviews looking for the cell, if any, displayed at the user's touch point. CGRectContainsPoint() is used to determine if the cell has been tapped or not.

26–27. If it is determined that a cell has been tapped, logic is applied to determine if the cell is being selected or deselected. If multiple selection support is turned off, a tapped cell is instantly made the selected cell. If, however, multiple selection is turned on, a tap on a nonselected cell will select it, and a tap on a selected cell will deselect it. Once the code determines if a cell has been selected or deselected, a callback to the data source is made informing it about the selection change.

28. The last two methods in the GridView implementation return selected index information. The method -indexForSelectedCell returns the selected index. If there are no cells marked as selected, -1 is returned. If allow-MultipleSelection is set to YES, the index of any one selected cell is returned. The same logic is used to return the selected cell index when allowMultipleSelection is turned off. This works because the selected-CellIndexes set contains one and only one cell index when allow-MultipleSelection is turned off.

29. And finally there is the -indexesForSelectedCells method. This method returns the list of indexes for selected cells. If no cells are selected, nil is returned.

And that, my friends, is a high-level overview of the GridView class and its implementation.

Using the GridView **Class**

You use the GridView class the same way you used the WheelView class. You place a view in a NIB or storyboard scene, change its class name in the Identity inspector, and connect a view controller as its data source. In fact, let's do that now.

Open *MainStoryboard.storyboard*. Select the Photo Album View Controller Scene and drag a new UIView onto the scene's content view. Change the name of the class from UIView to GridView, and set the frame position and size: X to 9, Y to 51, Width to 698, and Height to 597. Make the photo album view controller the data source for the grid view by **Control-clicking** and dragging the grid view to the view controller.

You must also connect the grid view as an outlet to the view controller. Open *PhotoAlbumViewController.h*, import *GridView.h*, and add a new outlet named gridView of type GridView. Be sure to update the -viewDidUnload method in the view controller's implementation with [self setGridView:nil]. Alternatively, you can use the Assistant editor to create and connect the new outlet.

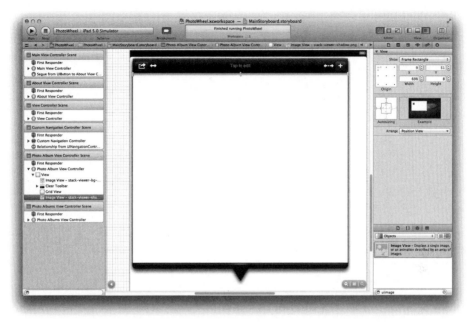

Figure 16.11   Completed scene with grid view and drop shadow

Also, `PhotoAlbumViewController` will be the data source for the `GridView`, and it will use an `NSFetchedResultsController`. Therefore, you need to add `GridViewDataSource` and `NSFetchedResultsControllerDelegate` to the list of protocols implemented by the `PhotoAlbumViewController` class.

There's one last visual change to make. To soften the look as a user scrolls the grid up, place a drop shadow under the toolbar. The easiest way to accomplish this is to drag a `UIImageView` into the scene. Set the image name to *stack-viewer-shadow.png*, and set its frame position and size: X to 9, Y to 51, Width to 698, and Height to 8. Last, turn off autosizing for the image view.

The completed scene should look like the one in Figure 16.11.

The updated code for the `PhotoAlbumViewController` class is shown in Listing 16.25. Review the listing to make sure you made the same changes to your code.

Listing 16.25   Updated `PhotoAlbumViewController` **Class**

```
///////
// PhotoAlbumViewController.h
///////
#import <UIKit/UIKit.h>
#import "GridView.h"

@interface PhotoAlbumViewController : UIViewController
<UIActionSheetDelegate, UIImagePickerControllerDelegate,
```

```objc
UINavigationControllerDelegate, NSFetchedResultsControllerDelegate,
GridViewDataSource>

// Other code left out for brevity's sake.

@property (nonatomic, strong) IBOutlet GridView *gridView;

// Other code left out for brevity's sake.

@end


///////
//  PhotoAlbumViewController.m
///////
#import "PhotoAlbumViewController.h"
#import "PhotoAlbum.h"
#import "Photo.h"
#import "ImageGridViewCell.h"

@interface PhotoAlbumViewController ()

// Other code left out for brevity's sake.

@property (nonatomic, strong) NSFetchedResultsController
*fetchedResultsController;

// Other code left out for brevity's sake.

@end

@implementation PhotoAlbumViewController

// Other code left out for brevity's sake.

@synthesize gridView = _gridView;
@synthesize fetchedResultsController = _fetchedResultsController;

// Other code left out for brevity's sake.

- (void)reload
{
    if ([self managedObjectContext] && [self objectID]) {
        self.photoAlbum = (PhotoAlbum *)[self.managedObjectContext
                                    objectWithID:[self objectID]];
        [[self toolbar] setHidden:NO];
        [[self textField] setText:[self.photoAlbum name]];
```

```
   } else {
      [self setPhotoAlbum:nil];
      [[self toolbar] setHidden:YES];
      [[self textField] setText:@""];
   }

   [self setFetchedResultsController:nil];
   [[self gridView] reloadData];
}

// Other code left out for brevity's sake.

#pragma mark - NSFetchedResultsController and NSFetchedResultsControllerDelegate

- (NSFetchedResultsController *)fetchedResultsController
{
   if (_fetchedResultsController) {
      return _fetchedResultsController;
   }

   NSManagedObjectContext *context = [self managedObjectContext];
   if (!context) {
      return nil;
   }

   NSString *cacheName = [NSString stringWithFormat:@"%@-%@",
                          [self.photoAlbum name], [self.photoAlbum dateAdded]];
   NSFetchRequest *fetchRequest = [[NSFetchRequest alloc] init];
   NSEntityDescription *entityDescription =
      [NSEntityDescription entityForName:@"Photo"
                 inManagedObjectContext:context];
   [fetchRequest setEntity:entityDescription];

   NSSortDescriptor *sortDescriptor =
      [NSSortDescriptor sortDescriptorWithKey:@"dateAdded" ascending:YES];
   [fetchRequest setSortDescriptors:[NSArray arrayWithObject:sortDescriptor]];

   [fetchRequest setPredicate:[NSPredicate predicateWithFormat:@"photoAlbum = %@",
                               [self photoAlbum]]];

   NSFetchedResultsController *newFetchedResultsController =
      [[NSFetchedResultsController alloc] initWithFetchRequest:fetchRequest
                                       managedObjectContext:context
                                          sectionNameKeyPath:nil
                                                  cacheName:cacheName];
   [newFetchedResultsController setDelegate:self];
   [self setFetchedResultsController:newFetchedResultsController];
```

```
        NSError *error = nil;
        if (![[self fetchedResultsController] performFetch:&error])
        {
            /*
              Replace this implementation with code to handle the error appropriately.

              abort() causes the application to generate a crash log and terminate.
              You should not use this function in a shipping application, although
              it may be useful during development. If it is not possible to recover
              from the error, display an alert panel that instructs the user to quit
              the application by pressing the Home button.
            */
            NSLog(@"Unresolved error %@, %@", error, [error userInfo]);
            abort();
        }

    return _fetchedResultsController;
}

- (void)controllerDidChangeContent:(NSFetchedResultsController *)controller
{
    [[self gridView] reloadData];
}

#pragma mark - GridViewDataSource methods

- (NSInteger)gridViewNumberOfCells:(GridView *)gridView
{
    NSInteger count = [[[[self fetchedResultsController] sections]
                        objectAtIndex:0] numberOfObjects];
    return count;
}

- (GridViewCell *)gridView:(GridView *)gridView cellAtIndex:(NSInteger)index
{
    ImageGridViewCell *cell = [gridView dequeueReusableCell];
    if (cell == nil) {
        cell = [ImageGridViewCell imageGridViewCellWithSize:CGSizeMake(100, 100)];
    }

    NSIndexPath *indexPath = [NSIndexPath indexPathForRow:index inSection:0];
    Photo *photo = [[self fetchedResultsController] objectAtIndexPath:indexPath];
    [[cell imageView] setImage:[photo smallImage]];

    return cell;
}
```

```
- (CGSize)gridViewCellSize:(GridView *)gridView
{
    return CGSizeMake(100, 100);
}

- (void)gridView:(GridView *)gridView didSelectCellAtIndex:(NSInteger)index
{

}

@end
```

The code in Listing 16.25 follows the same pattern you have already learned using `WheelView`, so a code walk-through is not necessary. The time is better spent creating another new Objective-C class.

The cell type returned in the `-gridView:cellAtIndex:` method is `Image-GridViewCell`. This class does not yet exist, which is why the app will not compile (assuming you did try to compile it). `ImageGridViewCell` is similar to the `PhotoWheelViewCell` created in the prototype app. The difference here is that `ImageGridViewCell` supports a selected state. A selected cell will display a visual indicator. A nonselected cell will not.

Note

The visual indicator for selected cells is not used in this chapter, but it's important to get the code in place now. It will be used in Chapter 21, "Web Services."

By now, you can probably guess what is coming, but just in case...

Building the Image Grid View Cell

Create a new Objective-C class. Name it `ImageGridViewCell`, and make it a subclass of `GridViewCell`. Add it to the PhotoWheel project, and then copy the code from Listing 16.26.

Listing 16.26   `ImageGridViewCell` **Class**

```
///////
// ImageGridViewCell.h
///////
#import "GridView.h"

@interface ImageGridViewCell : GridViewCell

@property (nonatomic, strong, readonly) UIImageView *imageView;        // 1
@property (nonatomic, strong, readonly) UIImageView *selectedIndicator; // 2
```

```
+ (ImageGridViewCell *)imageGridViewCellWithSize:(CGSize)size;          // 3
- (id)initWithSize:(CGSize)size;

@end



/////////
//  ImageGridViewCell.m
/////////
#import "ImageGridViewCell.h"

@interface ImageGridViewCell ()                                          // 4
@property (nonatomic, strong, readwrite) UIImageView *imageView;
@property (nonatomic, strong, readwrite) UIImageView *selectedIndicator;
@end

@implementation ImageGridViewCell

@synthesize imageView = _imageView;                                      // 5
@synthesize selectedIndicator = _selectedIndicator;

- (void)commonInitWithSize:(CGSize)size                                  // 6
{
    CGRect frame = CGRectMake(0, 0, size.width, size.height);
    [self setBackgroundColor:[UIColor clearColor]];

    self.imageView = [[UIImageView alloc] initWithFrame:frame];
    [self addSubview:[self imageView]];

    NSInteger baseSize = 29;
    self.selectedIndicator =
        [[UIImageView alloc] initWithFrame:CGRectMake(size.width - baseSize - 4,
                                                      size.height - baseSize - 4,
                                                      baseSize,
                                                      baseSize)];
    [[self selectedIndicator] setHidden:YES];

    [self addSubview:[self selectedIndicator]];
}

- (id)init                                                               // 7
{
    CGSize size = CGSizeMake(100, 100);
    self = [self initWithSize:size];
    if (self) {

    }
```

```
    return self;
}

- (id)initWithSize:(CGSize)size                                    // 8
{
    CGRect frame = CGRectMake(0, 0, size.width, size.height);
    self = [super initWithFrame:frame];
    if (self) {
        [self commonInitWithSize:size];
    }
    return self;
}

- (void)setSelected:(BOOL)selected                                 // 9
{
    [super setSelected:selected];
    [[self selectedIndicator] setHidden:!selected];
}

+ (ImageGridViewCell *)imageGridViewCellWithSize:(CGSize)size       // 10
{
    ImageGridViewCell *newCell = [[ImageGridViewCell alloc] initWithSize:size];
    return newCell;
}

@end
```

Now let's review the code:

1–2. The class interface for `ImageGridViewCell` has three properties: `imageView`, `selectedIndicator`, and `selected`. The `imageView` contains the photo that is displayed in the cell. The `selectedIndicator` property is a 29 × 29-pixel image view displayed in the lower right corner of the image view when the cell is selected.

3. A convenience method named `+imageGridViewCellWithSize:` is provided to create a new cell of a specified size. Of course, you are not required to use the convenience method. You can call `-initWithSize:` directly, which is also included in the class interface.

4. The implementation for `ImageGridViewCell` starts with a class extension. The class extension defines the properties `imageView` and `selectedIndicator`. In the public interface, these properties are read-only, but in the redeclaration these properties are made read-writable. This allows the internals of the class to change the property values while preventing users of the class from doing the same.

   What this means for `ImageGridViewCell` is that users of the class cannot replace the image view or selector indicator view. However, users of the class can change values within these two properties. In other words, the user can set the image for both `imageView` and `selectorIndicator`. The only thing the class user can't do is replace the reference to the image views created by the `ImageGridViewCell` class itself.

5–6. Continuing with the implementation of `ImageGridViewCell`, you see that the declared properties are synthesized. The `-commitInit` method is provided to initialize the class upon creation. It allocates the image views used within the class and adds each to the container view.

7–8. The methods `-init` and `-initWithSize:` provide different ways to create an instance of the class.

9. The `-setSelected:` method overrides the setter method for the `selected` property defined in the `GridViewCell` class. It updates the setter method to show and hide the `selectedIndicator` image view based on the `selected` value.

10. Finally, the convenience method `+imageGridViewCellWithSize:` is provided for creating new instances of the `ImageGridViewCell`.

With this class in place, you can now compile PhotoWheel and run it to see all the changes in action. The finished app will look something like Figure 16.12.

Figure 16.12   The finished app

> **Note**
>
> You maybe wondering why `ImageGridViewCell` does not use a NIB yet `Photo-WheelViewCell` does. The choice not to use a NIB for `ImageGridViewCell` was based on where my mind was at the time the code was written. Certainly a NIB can be used for `ImageGridViewCell`, but at the moment the code was written it was crystal-clear to me how to create the cell in code. Had it been a different day and had my mind been in a different place, I might have used a NIB for the class.

Summary

Congratulations! You made it through the book's longest chapter. Go on, pat yourself on the back; you deserve it. You have accomplished quite a bit in this chapter.

You took advantage of existing code from the prototype to help speed up development. You made the `WheelView` class more robust, and you implemented a new `GridView` class, both of which you can now use in other apps. And you have, for the first time, a functional photo app that is worth showing off.

Award yourself for a job well done by taking a break. When you're feeling refreshed and ready, we'll tackle adding new features to PhotoWheel in Chapter 17, "Creating a Photo Browser."

Exercises

1. Modify the add photo logic in `PhotoAlbumViewController` to save new photos to the camera roll. (Refer to Chapter 12, "Adding Photos," for pointers on how to do this.)

2. Enable multiple selection support on the grid view managed by the `Photo-AlbumViewController` view controller class. You will need to set the image for the cell's `selectedIndicator` image view if you want to see a visual indicator displayed on each selected cell. Use *addphoto.png* as the selector indicator image.

Creating a Photo Browser

In this chapter, you will add a full-screen photo browser to PhotoWheel. You will also learn more ways to use the UIScrollView class.

The UIScrollView class provides a way to present a view that is larger than the visible area on the screen. Swiping touch gestures are used to scroll the content area horizontally and vertically, and the pinch gesture is used to zoom in and out. As you build the photo browser, you will learn how to use the scroll view to scroll content and zoom in and out of the view. It's time to get started.

Using the Scroll View

You use the scroll view for two different purposes as you build the photo browser. First, you use the class to build a full-screen photo browser. This browser enables users to flick through an album of photos by swiping left and right with a finger. Later, you use the UIScrollView class to enable the user to zoom in and out on a photo.

To begin, you need a view controller for the photo browser. Create a new Objective-C class named PhotoBrowserViewController, which is a subclass of UIViewController. The class will respond to scroll events, so add UIScrollViewDelegate to the list of protocols supported by the class. The class will also need an outlet for the scroll view itself, so add an outlet named scrollView and make it a pointer to the UIScrollView type.

The photo browser will be launched from the main screen when a photo is tapped. The photo browser will display the tapped photo, and the user can scroll left and right through the other photos. To support this feature, the view controller must be told the index to the starting photo. So add a declared property of type NSInteger with the name startAtIndex.

The photo browser must also know what photos to display. One approach is to pass in the photo album model object to the view controller. Another approach, which you have already used, is to pass in the managed object context and object ID for the model object. But let's go with a third approach that is a bit more flexible and makes the photo browser view controller reusable for other projects.

The class `PhotoBrowserViewController` will have a delegate property. The delegate object must conform to the protocol `PhotoBrowserViewController-Delegate`, which you must create. The delegate will provide methods to retrieve the number of photos within the album and retrieve the photo image for a specified index. This approach enables the photo browser view controller to work in any project, not just PhotoWheel, as long as a delegate object conforming to `PhotoBrowserView-ControllerDelegate` is provided.

The interface code for these requirements is shown in Listing 17.1.

Listing 17.1   *PhotoBrowserViewController.h*

```
#import <UIKit/UIKit.h>

@protocol PhotoBrowserViewControllerDelegate;

@interface PhotoBrowserViewController : UIViewController <UIScrollViewDelegate>

@property (nonatomic, strong) IBOutlet UIScrollView *scrollView;
@property (nonatomic, strong) id<PhotoBrowserViewControllerDelegate> delegate;
@property (nonatomic, assign) NSInteger startAtIndex;

@end

@protocol PhotoBrowserViewControllerDelegate <NSObject>
@required
- (NSInteger)photoBrowserViewControllerNumberOfPhotos:
(PhotoBrowserViewController *)photoBrowser;
- (UIImage *)photoBrowserViewController:(PhotoBrowserViewController *)photoBrowser
                      imageAtIndex:(NSInteger)index;

@end
```

With the easy part out of the way, it's time to add the implementation, shown in Listing 17.2. You must copy this code into your controller class. An explanation of the code is provided after the listing.

Listing 17.2   *PhotoBrowserViewController.m*

```
#import "PhotoBrowserViewController.h"

@interface PhotoBrowserViewController ()
@property (nonatomic, assign) NSInteger currentIndex;            // 1
@property (nonatomic, strong) NSMutableArray *photoViewCache;    // 2

- (void)initPhotoViewCache;                                      // 3
- (void)setScrollViewContentSize;
- (void)scrollToIndex:(NSInteger)index;
```

```objc
- (void)setTitleWithCurrentIndex;
- (CGRect)frameForPagingScrollView;
- (CGRect)frameForPageAtIndex:(NSUInteger)index;
@end

@implementation PhotoBrowserViewController

@synthesize scrollView = _scrollView;                                // 4
@synthesize delegate = _delegate;
@synthesize startAtIndex = _startAtIndex;
@synthesize currentIndex = _currentIndex;
@synthesize photoViewCache = _photoViewCache;

- (void)viewDidLoad                                                  // 5
{
    [super viewDidLoad];

    // Make sure to set wantsFullScreenLayout or the photo
    // will not display behind the status bar.
    [self setWantsFullScreenLayout:YES];                            // 6

    // Set the view's frame size. This ensures that the scroll view
    // autoresizes correctly and avoids surprises when retrieving
    // the scroll view's bounds later.
    CGRect frame = [[UIScreen mainScreen] bounds];                  // 7
    [[self view] setFrame:frame];

    UIScrollView *scrollView = [self scrollView];                  // 8
    // Set the initial size.
    [scrollView setFrame:[self frameForPagingScrollView]];
    [scrollView setDelegate:self];
    [scrollView setBackgroundColor:[UIColor blackColor]];
    [scrollView setAutoresizingMask:UIViewAutoresizingFlexibleWidth |
      UIViewAutoresizingFlexibleHeight];
    [scrollView setAutoresizesSubviews:YES];
    [scrollView setPagingEnabled:YES];
    [scrollView setShowsVerticalScrollIndicator:NO];
    [scrollView setShowsHorizontalScrollIndicator:NO];

    [self initPhotoViewCache];                                      // 9
}

- (void)viewDidUnload                                                // 10
{
    [self setScrollView:nil];
    [super viewDidUnload];
}
```

```
- (void)viewWillAppear:(BOOL)animated                            // 11
{
    [super viewWillAppear:animated];
    [self setScrollViewContentSize];
    [self setCurrentIndex:[self startAtIndex]];
    [self scrollToIndex:[self startAtIndex]];
    [self setTitleWithCurrentIndex];
}


#pragma mark - Delegate callback helpers

- (NSInteger)numberOfPhotos                                      // 12
{
    NSInteger numberOfPhotos = 0;
    id<PhotoBrowserViewControllerDelegate> delegate = [self delegate];
    if (delegate && [delegate respondsToSelector:
                    @selector(photoBrowserViewControllerNumberOfPhotos:)])
    {
        numberOfPhotos = [delegate photoBrowserViewControllerNumberOfPhotos:self];
    }
    return numberOfPhotos;
}


- (UIImage*)imageAtIndex:(NSInteger)index                        // 13
{
    UIImage *image = nil;
    id<PhotoBrowserViewControllerDelegate> delegate = [self delegate];
    if (delegate && [delegate respondsToSelector:
                    @selector(photoBrowserViewController:imageAtIndex:)])
    {
        image = [delegate photoBrowserViewController:self imageAtIndex:index];
    }
    return image;
}


#pragma mark - Helper methods

- (void)initPhotoViewCache                                       // 14
{
    // Set up the photo's view cache. We keep only three views in
    // memory. NSNull is used as a placeholder for the other
    // elements in the view cache array.

    NSInteger numberOfPhotos = [self numberOfPhotos];;
    [self setPhotoViewCache:
     [[NSMutableArray alloc] initWithCapacity:numberOfPhotos]];
    for (int i=0; i < numberOfPhotos; i++) {
        [self.photoViewCache addObject:[NSNull null]];
```

```
    }
}

- (void)setScrollViewContentSize                                    // 15
{
    NSInteger pageCount = [self numberOfPhotos];
    if (pageCount == 0) {
        pageCount = 1;
    }

    CGRect bounds = [[self scrollView] bounds];
    CGSize size = CGSizeMake(bounds.size.width * pageCount,
                             // Divide in half to prevent horizontal
                             // scrolling.
                             bounds.size.height / 2);
    [[self scrollView] setContentSize:size];
}

- (void)scrollToIndex:(NSInteger)index                             // 16
{
    CGRect bounds = [[self scrollView] bounds];
    bounds.origin.x = bounds.size.width * index;
    bounds.origin.y = 0;
    [[self scrollView] scrollRectToVisible:bounds animated:NO];
}

- (void)setTitleWithCurrentIndex                                   // 17
{
    NSInteger index = [self currentIndex] + 1;
    if (index < 1) {
        // Prevents the title from showing 0 of n when the user
        // attempts to scroll the first page to the right.
        index = 1;
    }
    NSInteger count = [self numberOfPhotos];
    NSString *title = title = [NSString stringWithFormat:@"%1$i of %2$i",
                                 index, count, nil];
    [self setTitle:title];
}

#pragma mark - Frame calculations
#define PADDING  20

- (CGRect)frameForPagingScrollView                                // 18
{
    CGRect frame = [[UIScreen mainScreen] bounds];
    frame.origin.x -= PADDING;
    frame.size.width += (2 * PADDING);
```

```
        return frame;
    }

    - (CGRect)frameForPageAtIndex:(NSUInteger)index                         // 19
    {
        CGRect bounds = [[self scrollView] bounds];
        CGRect pageFrame = bounds;
        pageFrame.size.width -= (2 * PADDING);
        pageFrame.origin.x = (bounds.size.width * index) + PADDING;
        return pageFrame;
    }

    #pragma mark - Page management

    - (void)loadPage:(NSInteger)index                                       // 20
    {
        if (index < 0 || index >= [self numberOfPhotos]) {
            return;
        }

        id currentView = [[self photoViewCache] objectAtIndex:index];
        if ([currentView isKindOfClass:[UIImageView class]] == NO) {
            // Load the photo view.
            CGRect frame = [self frameForPageAtIndex:index];
            UIImageView *newView = [[UIImageView alloc] initWithFrame:frame];
            [newView setContentMode:UIViewContentModeScaleAspectFit];
            [newView setBackgroundColor:[UIColor clearColor]];
            [newView setImage:[self imageAtIndex:index]];

            [[self scrollView] addSubview:newView];
            [[self photoViewCache] replaceObjectAtIndex:index withObject:newView];
        }
    }

    - (void)unloadPage:(NSInteger)index                                     // 21
    {
        if (index < 0 || index >= [self numberOfPhotos]) {
            return;
        }

        id currentView = [[self photoViewCache] objectAtIndex:index];
        if ([currentView isKindOfClass:[UIImageView class]]) {
            [currentView removeFromSuperview];
            [[self photoViewCache] replaceObjectAtIndex:index withObject:[NSNull null]];
        }
    }
```

```
- (void)setCurrentIndex:(NSInteger)newIndex                          // 22
{
    _currentIndex = newIndex;

    [self loadPage:_currentIndex];
    [self loadPage:_currentIndex + 1];
    [self loadPage:_currentIndex - 1];
    [self unloadPage:_currentIndex + 2];
    [self unloadPage:_currentIndex - 2];

    [self setTitleWithCurrentIndex];
}

#pragma mark - UIScrollViewDelegate

- (void)scrollViewDidScroll:(UIScrollView *)scrollView               // 23
{
    if ([scrollView isScrollEnabled]) {
        CGFloat pageWidth = scrollView.bounds.size.width;
        float fractionalPage = scrollView.contentOffset.x / pageWidth;
        NSInteger page = floor(fractionalPage);
        if (page != [self currentIndex]) {
            [self setCurrentIndex:page];
        }
    }
}

@end
```

Let's take a closer look at the implementation:

1. A class extension for PhotoBrowserViewController is added. It has two declared properties: currentIndex and photoViewCache. The first property, currentIndex, is the index value for the photo currently displayed.

2. The second property is photoViewCache. This property is a mutable array of photo views. Each photo view is an instance of UIImageView. A photo album can contain a large number of photos. Therefore, loading each photo into memory increases the chance of out-of-memory crashes for PhotoWheel. To conserve memory and help avoid memory-related crashes, the photo browser will store up to three photo views in memory at any given time. The photoViewCache property contains the reference to the array containing the three photo views.

3. Following the declared properties is a set of forwardly declared methods. These declarations are included in the class extension so their placement within the implementation is not important.

4. The implementation section begins with the @synthesize statements for each declared property.

5. The -viewDidLoad method is added so that additional setup for the view can be performed.

6. The photo browser will display photos full-screen. This means that the photo will display behind the status bar. To make this happen, you must set the wantsFullScreenLayout flag to YES. This gives the photo browser a full 768 × 1024 set of pixels to work with.

7. The view controller's top view is sized and positioned to use the entire screen, including the pixels behind the status bar. Explicitly setting the frame for the view helps ensure that autoresizing views like the scroll view will be sized correctly. This becomes much more important in Chapter 18, "Supporting Device Rotation," when you modify PhotoWheel to support all device orientations.

8. Properties for an outlet can be set in a storyboard or NIB, but they can also be set in code. Sometimes setting outlet properties in code is preferred since it makes clear what property values have been changed. It is not always easy to see this when looking at the inspectors for an outlet object in a storyboard or NIB.

   This is why property values for the scroll view are set in the -viewDidLoad method. It makes it clear what values have changed to accommodate the needs of the photo browser.

9. This is followed by the initialization of the photo view cache. The details of what happens in the method are discussed momentarily.

10. The next method is -viewDidUnload, which sets the scroll view outlet to nil.

11. The method -viewWillAppear is added to set the scroll view content size and current index. It also scrolls the view to the starting index, which is the index of the photo thumbnail tapped on the main screen. The title, which is displayed at the center of the navigation bar, is updated to display the current index.

12–13. A couple of wrapper methods are provided calling the PhotoBrowserView-Controller delegate to retrieve the number of photos and the image at a particular index.

14. The method -initPhotoViewCache, which was just mentioned, creates the instance of the mutable array and initializes it with NSNull objects. NSNull is a singleton class that represents null objects. It is used in places where nil is not allowed, such as in the contents for NSArray, NSDictionary, and NSSet.

15. The method -setScrollViewContentSize determines the content size (i.e., the scrollable area) based on the number of photos. Each photo represents a page, hence the local variable name pageCount.

16. The method -scrollToIndex: does as its name implies. It scrolls the scroll view to a specific index, where the index is the index value for a photo.

17. The method -setTitleWithCurrentIndex updates the display for the title in the navigation bar.

18. The next method is -frameForPagingScrollView. This method is called in -viewDidLoad, and it sets the frame (position and size) for the scroll view. This is not the content size but the actual size of the viewable area of the scroll view. However, there is a little sleight of hand going on here. The viewable area of the scroll view (that is, the frame) is actually 40 pixels wider than the iPad's screen. There are exactly 20 pixels to the left and right of the scroll view.

Why do this? We want to have a bit of space between the photos when scrolling, 20 pixels of space to be precise. The 20 pixels are specified in the macro PADDING. By setting the scroll view's frame to be 40 pixels (2 * PADDING) wider, and taking into account the padding when calculating the frame for each photo, we can produce a visual effect whereby the scroll view and photo appear full-screen but in fact are wider than the physical screen. The effect is achieved by allowing the visible area of the scroll view to be clipped by the physical dimensions of the iPad's screen (Figure 17.1), thus making the 20-pixel spacing visible only when scrolling.

Figure 17.1   Illustration of the scroll view frame

19. The method -frameForPageAtIndex: calculates the frame (position and size within the content area of the scroll view) for the page (aka the photo) at a specified index. The calculation takes into account the padding used to space out the photos when scrolling.

20. The method -loadPage: loads the page (aka the photo) into memory and adds it to the scroll view. It starts by verifying that the index is within the range of available photo indexes. It then retrieves a reference to the view from the photoViewCache. If the reference points to an instance of UIImageView, nothing happens. The image view already contains the photo to display. However, if the reference is an NSNull object and not UIImageView, a new image view is created, configured to display the photo at the specified index, and added to the scroll view. The photoViewCache is also updated, replacing the NSNull object with the UIImageView object.

21. The method -unloadPage: does the opposite of -loadPage:. It removes UIImageView from memory and from the scroll view, and it updates the photoViewCache, replacing the image view with an NSNull object.

22. The method -setCurrentIndex: is the final piece of the sleight-of-hand magic trick. It is here, in this custom getter method for currentIndex, that pages are loaded and unloaded. The current, previous, and next pages are always loaded. And the previous set of pages is unloaded, leaving only three photos loaded into memory at any given time.

23. The implementation for PhotoBrowserViewController wraps up with the implementation of the UIScrollViewDelegate callback method -scroll-ViewDidScroll:. This method determines the index for the current photo and sets the currentIndex property accordingly. This fires the custom setCurrentIndex getter method, which in turns loads and unloads the appropriate pages.

Setting Up the Photo Browser UI

Now that the PhotoBrowserViewController class is completed, it's time to update the user interface for the photo browser. Open the *MainStoryboard.storyboard* file and select the View Controller Scene that you used earlier to test the custom segue. Highlight the view controller, open the Identity inspector, and change the class from UIViewController to PhotoBrowserViewController.

Next, add a scroll view to the scene. Size it to fill the entire container view, and then connect it to the scrollView outlet defined in the PhotoBrowserView-Controller class.

Finally, add a segue between the Photo Album View Controller Scene and the Photo Browser View Controller Scene. One way to do this is to **Control-click** and drag the PhotoAlbumViewController to the PhotoBrowserViewController in the Document Outline area. After creating the segue, open the Attributes inspector for

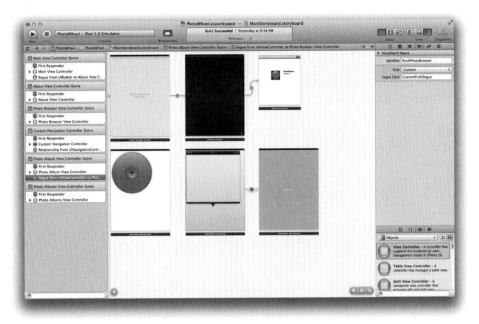

Figure 17.2   Updated storyboard with new segue

the segue and set the Identifier to PushPhotoBrowser, set the Style to Custom, and set the Segue Class to `CustomPushSegue`.

Take a look at Figure 17.2 for an example of what the updated storyboard looks like.

Launching the Photo Browser

To launch the photo browser, the user taps a photo thumbnail displayed on the main screen. To make this possible for the user, your code must perform the segue programmatically. Open the *PhotoAlbumViewController.m* file and scroll to the `-gridView:didSelectCellAtIndex:` method. The empty stub for this method was created in Chapter 16, "Building the Main Screen." Replace the stub with the new implementation shown in Listing 17.3.

Listing 17.3   **Performing the Segue Programmatically**

```
- (void)gridView:(GridView *)gridView didSelectCellAtIndex:(NSInteger)index
{
    [self performSegueWithIdentifier:@"PushPhotoBrowser" sender:self];
}
```

This one line of code tells the storyboard to perform the segue. The identifier string literal must match the identifier set in the Attributes inspector for the segue.

While this line of code starts the segue, it does not prepare the photo browser with the needed information to display the photos. The photo browser view controller expects a delegate object and a startAtIndex value.

To set this information, you override the -prepareForSegue:sender: method in the PhotoAlbumViewController class. This method provides a reference to the segue, which, as you may remember from building the CustomPushSegue class, has references to the source and destination view controllers. *This is your one opportunity to provide additional information to the source and destination view controllers prior to the execution of the segue.*

In the particular case of the PhotoAlbumViewController class, the segue needs to update the destination controller with a delegate and startAtIndex. The code listing to accomplish this is shown in Listing 17.4. This code should be added to the bottom of *PhotoAlbumViewController.m*.

Listing 17.4   **Preparing the Destination Controller**

```
#pragma mark - Segue

- (void)prepareForSegue:(UIStoryboardSegue *)segue sender:(id)sender
{
    PhotoBrowserViewController *destinationViewController =
        [segue destinationViewController];
    [destinationViewController setDelegate:self];
    NSInteger index = [[self gridView] indexForSelectedCell];
    [destinationViewController setStartAtIndex:index];
}
```

The code stores a local variable reference to the destination view controller, which is casted to PhotoBrowserViewController. The delegate property is set to self, but it can also be set to [segue sourceViewController] since self and the source view controller are the same. Finally, startAtIndex is set on the photo browser to the selected cell index. This tells the photo browser which photo to display first.

Because self is the delegate to the photo browser, and self is an instance of PhotoAlbumViewController, the PhotoAlbumViewController class must be updated to conform to the PhotoBrowserViewControllerDelegate protocol. The updated source code is shown in Listing 17.5. Apply these changes to your code.

Listing 17.5   **Updated** PhotoAlbumViewController **Class**

```
///////
//  PhotoAlbumViewController.h
///////
#import <UIKit/UIKit.h>
#import "GridView.h"
#import "PhotoBrowserViewController.h"                              // 1
```

```
@interface PhotoAlbumViewController : UIViewController
<UIActionSheetDelegate, UIImagePickerControllerDelegate,
UINavigationControllerDelegate, NSFetchedResultsControllerDelegate,
GridViewDataSource, PhotoBrowserViewControllerDelegate>            // 2

// Other code left out for brevity's sake.

@end



////////
//  PhotoAlbumViewController.m
////////
@implementation PhotoAlbumViewController

// Other code left out for brevity's sake.

#pragma mark - PhotoBrowserViewControllerDelegate methods

- (NSInteger)photoBrowserViewControllerNumberOfPhotos:
(PhotoBrowserViewController *)photoBrowser                         // 3
{
    NSInteger count = [[[[self fetchedResultsController] sections]
                    objectAtIndex:0] numberOfObjects];
    return count;
}

- (UIImage *)photoBrowserViewController:(PhotoBrowserViewController *)photoBrowser
                    imageAtIndex:(NSInteger)index                  // 4
{
    NSIndexPath *indexPath = [NSIndexPath indexPathForRow:index inSection:0];
    Photo *photo = [[self fetchedResultsController] objectAtIndexPath:indexPath];
    return [photo largeImage];
}

@end
```

Walking through the code, you see the following:

1. The *PhotoBrowserViewController.h* header file is imported in the interface file.

2. The PhotoBrowserViewControllerDelegate is added to the list of conforming protocols.

3. The delegate method -photoBrowserViewControllerNumberOfPhotos: is implemented. It returns the number of photos based on the data in the fetched results controller.

4. The delegate method -photoBrowserViewController:imageAtIndex: returns the image from the photo retrieved from the fetched results controller.

You now have a basic full-screen photo browser included in the app. Build and run the app to see the photo browser in action.

Improving the Push and Pop

The push and pop of the photo browser are nice, but there is room for improvement. For a better user experience, the push should start when the photo thumbnail is tapped, and the pop should return to the same location. To accomplish this, the push location must be stored somewhere so that it can be used by both the CustomPush-Segue and CustomNavigationController classes. Each of these classes knows about the PhotoAlbumViewController. It is the sourceViewController in the custom segue, and it is the destination view controller in the custom navigation controller. So the PhotoAlbumViewController is a good place to store the tap-from location.

As it so happens, the location is already stored for you. It is the frame of the grid view cell displaying the photo thumbnail. You just need to expose the cell frame via the PhotoAlbumViewController's public interface. While you are at it, expose another method that returns the UIImage of the selected photo. The custom segue will use it to make the animation smoother during the view transition.

Open *PhotoAlbumViewController.h* and add two methods. The first is -selected-Image, which returns a pointer to UIImage. The second is -selectedCellFrame, which returns the CGRect for the cell frame. Next, open *PhotoAlbumViewController.m* and add the implementation for the new methods. The code changes are shown in Listing 17.6.

Listing 17.6   **Updated** PhotoAlbumViewController **Class**

```
///////
//  PhotoAlbumViewController.h
///////

// Other code left out for brevity's sake.

@interface PhotoAlbumViewController : UIViewController
<UIActionSheetDelegate, UIImagePickerControllerDelegate,
UINavigationControllerDelegate, NSFetchedResultsControllerDelegate,
GridViewDataSource, PhotoBrowserViewControllerDelegate>


// Other code left out for brevity's sake.

- (UIImage *)selectedImage;
- (CGRect)selectedCellFrame;

@end
```

```
///////
//   PhotoAlbumViewController.m
///////

// Other code left out for brevity's sake.

- (NSInteger)indexForSelectedGridCell
{
   GridView *gridView = [self gridView];
   NSInteger selectedIndex = [gridView indexForSelectedCell];
   NSInteger count = [[[[self fetchedResultsController] sections]
                      objectAtIndex:0] numberOfObjects];
   if (selectedIndex < 0 && count > 0) {
      selectedIndex = 0;
   }
   return selectedIndex;
}




- (UIImage *)selectedImage
{
   UIImage *selectedImage = nil;
   NSInteger selectedIndex = [self indexForSelectedGridCell];
   if (selectedIndex >= 0) {
      NSIndexPath *indexPath = [NSIndexPath indexPathForRow:selectedIndex
                                                  inSection:0];
      Photo *photo = [[self fetchedResultsController]
                      objectAtIndexPath:indexPath];
      selectedImage = [photo largeImage];
   }
   return selectedImage;
}


- (CGRect)selectedCellFrame
{
   CGRect rect;
   GridView *gridView = [self gridView];
   NSInteger selectedIndex = [self indexForSelectedGridCell];
   if (selectedIndex >= 0) {
      GridViewCell *cell = [gridView cellAtIndex:selectedIndex];
      UIView *parentView = [[self parentViewController] view];
      rect = [parentView convertRect:[cell frame] fromView:gridView];
   } else {
      CGRect gridFrame = [gridView frame];
      rect = CGRectMake(CGRectGetMidX(gridFrame),
                        CGRectGetMidY(gridFrame), 0, 0);
   }
```

```
        return rect;
}

@end
```

The code change starts with the helper method -indexForSelectedGridCell. This method retrieves the index of the selected grid cell. If there is no selected cell in the grid and the grid has at least one cell, the index to the first cell is returned; otherwise -1 is returned. This is necessary because the selected cell may have been deleted. How can this be when the user has no way to delete a photo? It's true that at this moment the user has no way to delete a photo, but that will change by the end of this chapter.

The next two methods are similar. Both call the helper method -indexForSelectedGridCell to get the cell index. But then the two methods start to differ.

The first method, -selectedImage, retrieves the photo model object from the fetched results controller, then returns the large image from the photo. The second method, -selectedCellFrame, retrieves the grid view cell of the tapped photo. It then converts the cell frame from the grid view coordinate system to the MainViewController's view coordinate system. The conversion makes it possible for the custom segue to use the correct screen location when placing the images used to animate the view transition.

Next, the custom push segue must be updated to use the new methods on the photo album view controller. The new implementation is similar to the previous one, except instead of using a snapshot of the destination view controller's view, the selected image returned from the photo album view controller is used. This will make the animation sequence smoother for the view transition.

Open *CustomPushSegue.m* and replace the implementation with the one provided in Listing 17.7.

Listing 17.7 Updated CustomPushSegue Implementation

```
#import "CustomPushSegue.h"
#import "UIView+PWCategory.h"
#import "PhotoAlbumViewController.h"                              // 1

@implementation CustomPushSegue

- (void)perform
{
    id sourceViewController = [self sourceViewController];        // 2

    UIView *sourceView = [[sourceViewController parentViewController] view];
    UIImageView *sourceImageView = [[UIImageView alloc]
                          initWithImage:[sourceView pw_imageSnapshot]];
```

```
BOOL isLandscape = UIInterfaceOrientationIsLandscape(
    [sourceViewController interfaceOrientation]);                  // 3

CGRect statusBarFrame = [[UIApplication sharedApplication]
                        statusBarFrame];                           // 4
CGFloat statusBarHeight;
if (isLandscape) {                                                 // 5
    statusBarHeight = statusBarFrame.size.width;
} else {
    statusBarHeight = statusBarFrame.size.height;
}
CGRect newFrame = CGRectOffset([sourceImageView frame], 0, statusBarHeight);
[sourceImageView setFrame:newFrame];                               // 6


CGRect destinationFrame = [[UIScreen mainScreen] bounds];
if (isLandscape) {                                                 // 7
    destinationFrame.size = CGSizeMake(destinationFrame.size.height,
                                       destinationFrame.size.width);
}

UIImage *destinationImage = [sourceViewController selectedImage];
UIImageView *destinationImageView = [[UIImageView alloc]
                                initWithImage:destinationImage];
[destinationImageView setContentMode:UIViewContentModeScaleAspectFit];
[destinationImageView setBackgroundColor:[UIColor blackColor]];
[destinationImageView setFrame:[sourceViewController selectedCellFrame]];
[destinationImageView setAlpha:0.3];

UINavigationController *navController =
    [sourceViewController navigationController];
[navController pushViewController:[self destinationViewController]
                        animated:NO];

UINavigationBar *navBar = [navController navigationBar];
[navController setNavigationBarHidden:NO];
[navBar setFrame:CGRectOffset(navBar.frame, 0, -navBar.frame.size.height)];

UIView *destinationView = [[self destinationViewController] view];
[destinationView addSubview:sourceImageView];
[destinationView addSubview:destinationImageView];

void (^animations)(void) = ^ {
    [destinationImageView setFrame:destinationFrame];
    [destinationImageView setAlpha:1.0];

    [navBar setFrame:CGRectOffset(navBar.frame, 0, navBar.frame.size.height)];
};
```

```
void (^completion)(BOOL) = ^(BOOL finished) {
    if (finished) {
        [sourceImageView removeFromSuperview];
        [destinationImageView removeFromSuperview];
    }
};

[UIView animateWithDuration:0.6 animations:animations completion:completion];
}

@end
```

Let's walk through the key changes to the custom push segue:

1. The *PhotoAlbumViewController.h* header file is imported.

2. A local variable is used to store a reference to the `sourceViewController`. This makes later code more readable.

3–5. The photo browser uses the entire screen. This means that the frame used to display the `sourceImageView` must be offset by the height of the status bar. If the offset does not happen, the image will jump during the animation sequence.

   You retrieve the status bar frame from the application, which is retrieved from `UIApplication`. Although device orientation and rotation have not been covered yet, the code here takes orientation into consideration. The current orientation mode is checked. If the device orientation is landscape, the status bar height is actually the width value from the frame. Otherwise it is the height value from the frame. Why? The frame size does not change when the device is rotated. Therefore, you must make the necessary adjustment based on the current orientation.

6. The `sourceImageView` frame is set to include the offset from the status bar height.

7. The last change to point out is the adjustment made to the destination frame. It too must be adjusted to support the landscape orientation. (Chapter 18, "Supporting Device Rotation," provides full coverage of rotation and orientation support.)

A similar change is needed for the `CustomNavigationController` class. Open *CustomNavigationController.m* and update it so that it uses the `-selectedCellFrame` method on the destination view controller. The needed code changes are shown in Listing 17.8.

Listing 17.8 Updated `CustomNavigationController` Class

```
#import "CustomNavigationController.h"
#import "UIView+PWCategory.h"
#import "PhotoAlbumViewController.h"                              // 1
```

```
@implementation CustomNavigationController

- (UIViewController *)popViewControllerAnimated:(BOOL)animated
{
    UIViewController *sourceViewController = [self topViewController];

    // Animates image snapshot of the view.
    UIView *sourceView = [sourceViewController view];
    UIImage *sourceViewImage = [sourceView pw_imageSnapshot];
    UIImageView *sourceImageView = [[UIImageView alloc]
                                    initWithImage:sourceViewImage];

    // Offset the sourceImageView frame by the height of the status bar.
    // This prevents the image from dropping down after the view controller
    // is popped from the stack.
    BOOL isLandscape = UIInterfaceOrientationIsLandscape(
        [sourceViewController interfaceOrientation]);                    // 2
    CGRect statusBarFrame = [[UIApplication sharedApplication] statusBarFrame];
    CGFloat statusBarHeight;
    if (isLandscape) {
        statusBarHeight = statusBarFrame.size.width;
    } else {
        statusBarHeight = statusBarFrame.size.height;
    }
    CGRect newFrame = CGRectOffset([sourceImageView frame], 0, -statusBarHeight);
    [sourceImageView setFrame:newFrame];


    NSArray *viewControllers = [self viewControllers];
    NSInteger count = [viewControllers count];
    NSInteger index = count - 2;

    UIViewController *destinationViewController =[viewControllers
                                                  objectAtIndex:index];
    UIView *destinationView = [destinationViewController view];
    UIImage *destinationViewImage = [destinationView pw_imageSnapshot];
    UIImageView *destinationImageView = [[UIImageView alloc]
                                         initWithImage:destinationViewImage];

    [super popViewControllerAnimated:NO];

    [destinationView addSubview:destinationImageView];
    [destinationView addSubview:sourceImageView];

    // We need the selectedCellFrame from the PhotoAlbumViewController. This
    // controller is a child of the destination controller.
    CGRect selectedCellFrame = CGRectZero;                              // 3
    for (id childViewController in [destinationViewController childViewControllers])
```

```objc
{
    if ([childViewController isKindOfClass:[PhotoAlbumViewController class]]) {
        selectedCellFrame = [childViewController selectedCellFrame];
        break;
    }
}
CGPoint shrinkToPoint = CGPointMake(CGRectGetMidX(selectedCellFrame),
                                    CGRectGetMidY(selectedCellFrame));

void (^animations)(void) = ^ {
    [sourceImageView setFrame:CGRectMake(shrinkToPoint.x, shrinkToPoint.y,
                                         0, 0)];
    [sourceImageView setAlpha:0.0];

    // Animate the nav bar too.
    UINavigationBar *navBar = [self navigationBar];
    [navBar setFrame:CGRectOffset(navBar.frame, 0, -navBar.frame.size.height)];
};

void (^completion)(BOOL) = ^(BOOL finished) {
    [self setNavigationBarHidden:YES];
    // Reset the nav bar's position.
    UINavigationBar *navBar = [self navigationBar];
    [navBar setFrame:CGRectOffset(navBar.frame, 0, navBar.frame.size.height)];

    [sourceImageView removeFromSuperview];
    [destinationImageView removeFromSuperview];
};

[UIView transitionWithView:destinationView
                  duration:0.3
                   options:UIViewAnimationOptionTransitionNone
                animations:animations
                completion:completion];

    return sourceViewController;
}

@end
```

The changes include the following:

1. Import the *PhotoAlbumViewController.h* header file.

2. The `sourceImageView` frame is offset by the height of the status bar. This prevents the image from jumping during the animation.

3. The final change calculates the `shrinkToPoint`. It is calculated based on the `selectedCellFrame` provided by the `PhotoAlbumViewController`.

However, this view controller is not the source controller. Its parent is the source view controller. So you must loop through the child view controllers, looking for the `PhotoAlbumViewController`. Once it is found, the `selectedCell-Frame` can be set and used to calculate the `shrinkToPoint`.

Build and run the app to test the changes. Tap a photo thumbnail to animate the push from the tapped photo cell. And when the user closes the photo browser (by tapping the **Back** button), the animation ends at the same tapped photo cell. This bit of extra polish really enhances the user experience.

Adding Chrome Effects

If you have played with the iPad's Photos app, you have noticed that it is a full-screen photo browser that autohides the chrome. In the case of PhotoWheel's photo browser, the chrome is the combination of the status and navigation bars at the top of the screen. You'll need to add this autohide feature to the PhotoWheel photo browser, too, so that the UI looks smooth and elegant without the user even noticing.

An `NSTimer` is used to determine when it's time to hide the chrome. The `NSTimer` class creates a timer that waits for a certain interval to elapse, then fires, sending a message (action) to an object (target).

The code changes made to *PhotoBrowserViewController.m* to manage the display of the chrome are shown in Listing 17.9. Apply these changes to your code. And, of course, an explanation of the changes is provided after the listing.

Listing 17.9   **Autohiding the Chrome**

```
#import "PhotoBrowserViewController.h"

@interface PhotoBrowserViewController ()

// Other code left out for brevity's sake.

@property (nonatomic, assign, getter = isChromeHidden) BOOL chromeHidden; // 1
@property (nonatomic, strong) NSTimer *chromeHideTimer;                   // 2
@property (nonatomic, assign) CGFloat statusBarHeight;                    // 3

// Other code left out for brevity's sake.

- (void)toggleChrome:(BOOL)hide;                                         // 4
- (void)hideChrome;                                                      // 5
- (void)startChromeDisplayTimer;                                         // 7
- (void)cancelChromeDisplayTimer;                                        // 8

@end
```

```
@implementation PhotoBrowserViewController

// Other code left out for brevity's sake.

@synthesize chromeHidden = _chromeHidden;                              // 9
@synthesize chromeHideTimer = _chromeHideTimer;                        // 10
@synthesize statusBarHeight = _statusBarHeight;                        // 11


// Other code left out for brevity's sake.

- (void)viewDidLoad
{
   // Other code left out for brevity's sake.

   // Must store the status bar size while it is still visible.
   CGRect statusBarFrame = [[UIApplication sharedApplication]
                       statusBarFrame];                                // 12
   if (UIInterfaceOrientationIsLandscape([self interfaceOrientation])) {
      [self setStatusBarHeight:statusBarFrame.size.width];
   } else {
      [self setStatusBarHeight:statusBarFrame.size.height];
   }
}

// Other code left out for brevity's sake.

- (void)viewWillAppear:(BOOL)animated
{
   // Other code left out for brevity's sake.

   [self startChromeDisplayTimer];                                     // 13
}

- (void)viewWillDisappear:(BOOL)animated                              // 14
{
   [self cancelChromeDisplayTimer];
   [super viewWillDisappear:animated];
}

// Other code left out for brevity's sake.

#pragma mark - Page management

- (void)loadPage:(NSInteger)index
{
```

```objc
  if (index < 0 || index >= [self numberOfPhotos]) {
    return;
  }

  id currentView = [[self photoViewCache] objectAtIndex:index];
  if ([currentView isKindOfClass:[UIImageView class]] == NO) {
    // Load the photo view.
    CGRect frame = [self frameForPageAtIndex:index];
    UIImageView *newView = [[UIImageView alloc] initWithFrame:frame];
    [newView setContentMode:UIViewContentModeScaleAspectFit];
    [newView setBackgroundColor:[UIColor clearColor]];
    [newView setImage:[self imageAtIndex:index]];

    UITapGestureRecognizer *tap = [[UITapGestureRecognizer alloc]
                                    initWithTarget:self
                                    action:@selector(imageTapped:)];   // 15
    [newView addGestureRecognizer:tap];                                // 16
    [newView setUserInteractionEnabled:YES];                           // 17

    [[self scrollView] addSubview:newView];
    [[self photoViewCache] replaceObjectAtIndex:index withObject:newView];
  }
}


// Other code left out for brevity's sake.

#pragma mark - UIScrollViewDelegate

// Other code left out for brevity's sake.

- (void)scrollViewWillBeginDragging:(UIScrollView *)scrollView       // 18
{
   [self hideChrome];
}

#pragma mark - Chrome helpers

- (void)toggleChromeDisplay                                          // 19
{
   [self toggleChrome:![self isChromeHidden]];
}

- (void)toggleChrome:(BOOL)hide                                      // 20
{
   [self setChromeHidden:hide];
   if (hide) {
     [UIView beginAnimations:nil context:nil];
```

```
      [UIView setAnimationDuration:0.4];
   }

   CGFloat alpha = hide ? 0.0 : 1.0;

   UINavigationBar *navbar = [[self navigationController] navigationBar];
   [navbar setAlpha:alpha];

   [[UIApplication sharedApplication] setStatusBarHidden:hide];

   if (hide) {
      [UIView commitAnimations];
   }

   if ( ! [self isChromeHidden] ) {
      [self startChromeDisplayTimer];
   }
}

- (void)hideChrome                                             // 21
{
   NSTimer *timer = [self chromeHideTimer];
   if (timer && [timer isValid]) {
      [timer invalidate];
      [self setChromeHideTimer:nil];
   }
   [self toggleChrome:YES];
}

- (void)startChromeDisplayTimer                                // 22
{
   [self cancelChromeDisplayTimer];
   NSTimer *timer = [NSTimer scheduledTimerWithTimeInterval:5.0
                                            target:self
                                          selector:@selector(hideChrome)
                                          userInfo:nil
                                           repeats:NO];
   [self setChromeHideTimer:timer];
}

- (void)cancelChromeDisplayTimer                               // 23
{
   if ([self chromeHideTimer]) {
      [[self chromeHideTimer] invalidate];
      [self setChromeHideTimer:nil];
   }
}
```

```
#pragma mark - Gesture handlers

- (void)imageTapped:(UITapGestureRecognizer *)recognizer              // 24
{
    [self toggleChromeDisplay];
}


@end
```

Walking through the changes, you'll note the following:

1–2. The class extension for `PhotoBrowserViewController` has been updated with two new declared properties: `chromeHidden` and `chromeHideTimer`. The `chromeHidden` property is a Boolean flag indicating the current status for the chrome, hidden or visible. The `chromeHideTimer` property is a reference to the current `NSTimer` used to autohide the chrome.

3. A third property, `statusBarHeight`, has been added to the class extension. The status bar height is stored during the `-viewDidLoad` method while the status bar is still visible. Once it is hidden, the status bar frame will no longer be available, which is why the height is saved to this property.

4–8. Also added to the class extension is a set of chrome-related helper methods, which will be discussed momentarily.

9–11. In the implementation section of the class, the newly declared properties are synthesized.

12. The status bar height is saved for use later. A check for the interface orientation is made. If the orientation is landscape, the width value in the status bar frame is the actual height; otherwise the status bar frame height is the height.

13. An override for the method `-viewWillAppear:` is updated with a call to `-startChromeDisplayTimer`. This, of course, starts the timer used to autohide the chrome.

14. Another override method, this time on `-viewWillDisappear:`, is added. Here the `-cancelChromeDisplayTimer` is called to cancel the timer prior to the view disappearing.

15–16. The user should be able to show and hide the chrome with a tap of the finger. So a tap gesture recognizer is added to the `UIImageView` that displays the photo. The recognizer calls the `-imageTapped:` method defined at the end of the listing.

17. Even though the tap gesture recognizer has been added to the image view, the tap won't work until the `userInteractionEnabled` flag on the image view is set to `YES`. This flag is `NO` by default, which means the view does not receive any touch events.

18. Another `UIScrollViewDelegate` callback method is added, `-scrollView-WillBeginDragging:`. Here the chrome is told to hide when the user begins to scroll through the photos.

19. The first of the chrome-related helper methods is `-toggleChromeDisplay`. This method does as its name implies; it toggles the chrome display. If the chrome is hidden, calling this method will show it. If the chrome is visible, calling this method will hide it.

20. The method `-toggleChrome:` will toggle the chrome based on the hide flag. Pass in `YES` and the chrome is hidden. Pass in `NO` and the chrome is made visible. This is also where the animation for showing and hiding the chrome is performed.

21. The method `-hideChrome` forces the chrome to hide. It also invalidates the timer, which means it will stop firing. The chrome is hidden so the timer is no longer needed. The timer calls this method when it fires.

22. The `-startChromeDisplayTimer` method creates a timer that runs for 5 seconds (5.0). The timer calls `-hideChrome` when it fires.

23. The last chrome-related helper method is `-cancelChromeDisplayTimer`. This invalidates the timer, causing it to stop firing.

24. The last change to the `PhotoBrowserViewController` class is the addition of the `-imageTapped:` method. This is called when the user taps the photo.

After you have added the changes to your code, build and run the app. Display the photo browser, and see how the chrome display works. When the chrome is displayed, it autohides after 5 seconds. Tap the photo to toggle between showing and hiding the chrome. Scrolling while the chrome is visible will also hide it. Check your work if you do not see these behaviors.

Zooming

Your photo browser is coming along nicely, and it is already pretty useful. But let's not stop here. Let's add another feature that users will expect. Let's make it possible for users to zoom in and out on the photo by double tapping and pinching.

To accomplish this, you will use another `UIScrollView`. You can implement your own zoom using tap and pinch gestures, but why do that when the `UIScrollView` provides most of the functionality for you?

Currently, the `UIImageView` class is used to display the photo within the browser. You will replace this with a new custom class derived from `UIScrollView`. But before you can replace the `UIImageView` used in the `PhotoBrowserViewController` class, you need to create the new scroll view subclass.

Create a new Objective-C class. Name the class `PhotoBrowserPhotoView`, and make it a subclass of `UIScrollView`. Next, add the source code for the interface and implementation files as shown in Listing 17.10.

Listing 17.10   PhotoBrowserPhotoView **Class**

```
///////
//  PhotoBrowserPhotoView.h
///////
#import <UIKit/UIKit.h>

@class PhotoBrowserViewController;                             // 1

@interface PhotoBrowserPhotoView : UIScrollView <UIScrollViewDelegate>  // 2


@property (nonatomic, assign) NSInteger index;                // 3
@property (nonatomic, weak) PhotoBrowserViewController
*photoBrowserViewController;                                   // 4

- (void)setImage:(UIImage *)newImage;                         // 5
- (void)turnOffZoom;                                          // 6


@end


///////
//  PhotoBrowserPhotoView.m
///////
#import "PhotoBrowserPhotoView.h"
#import "PhotoBrowserViewController.h"                         // 7

@interface PhotoBrowserPhotoView ()                           // 8
@property (nonatomic, strong) UIImageView *imageView;         // 9

- (void)loadSubviewsWithFrame:(CGRect)frame;                  // 10
- (BOOL)isZoomed;                                             // 11
@end

@implementation PhotoBrowserPhotoView

@synthesize photoBrowserViewController = _photoBrowserViewController;  // 12
@synthesize imageView = _imageView;

@synthesize index = _index;
```

```objc
- (id)initWithFrame:(CGRect)frame                                            // 13
{
    self = [super initWithFrame:frame];
    if (self) {
        [self setDelegate:self];
        [self setMaximumZoomScale:5.0];
        [self setShowsHorizontalScrollIndicator:NO];
        [self setShowsVerticalScrollIndicator:NO];
        [self loadSubviewsWithFrame:frame];
        [self setBackgroundColor:[UIColor clearColor]];
        [self setAutoresizingMask:UIViewAutoresizingFlexibleWidth|
         UIViewAutoresizingFlexibleHeight];

        UITapGestureRecognizer *doubleTap = [[UITapGestureRecognizer alloc]
                                             initWithTarget:self
                                             action:@selector(doubleTapped:)];
        [doubleTap setNumberOfTapsRequired:2];
        [self addGestureRecognizer:doubleTap];

        UITapGestureRecognizer *tap = [[UITapGestureRecognizer alloc]
                                       initWithTarget:self
                                       action:@selector(tapped:)];
        [tap requireGestureRecognizerToFail:doubleTap];
        [self addGestureRecognizer:tap];
    }
    return self;
}


- (void)loadSubviewsWithFrame:(CGRect)frame                                  // 14
{
    frame.origin = CGPointMake(0, 0);
    UIImageView *newImageView = [[UIImageView alloc] initWithFrame:frame];
    [newImageView setAutoresizingMask:UIViewAutoresizingFlexibleWidth|
     UIViewAutoresizingFlexibleHeight];
    [newImageView setContentMode:UIViewContentModeScaleAspectFit];
    [self addSubview:newImageView];

    [self setImageView:newImageView];
}


- (void)setImage:(UIImage *)newImage                                         // 15
{
    [[self imageView] setImage:newImage];
}


- (BOOL)isZoomed                                                            // 16
{
```

```
      return !([self zoomScale] == [self minimumZoomScale]);
}

- (CGRect)zoomRectForScale:(float)scale withCenter:(CGPoint)center       // 17
{
    // The following is derived from the ScrollViewSuite sample project
    // provided by Apple:
    // http://bit.ly/pYoPat

    CGRect zoomRect;

    // The zoom rect is in the content view's coordinates.
    // At a zoom scale of 1.0, it would be the size of the
    // imageScrollView's bounds.
    // As the zoom scale decreases, so more content is visible,
    // the size of the rect grows.
    zoomRect.size.height = [self frame].size.height / scale;
    zoomRect.size.width = [self frame].size.width  / scale;

    // Choose an origin so as to get the right center.
    zoomRect.origin.x = center.x - (zoomRect.size.width  / 2.0);
    zoomRect.origin.y = center.y - (zoomRect.size.height / 2.0);

    return zoomRect;
}

- (void)zoomToLocation:(CGPoint)location                                 // 18
{
    float newScale;
    CGRect zoomRect;
    if ([self isZoomed]) {
        zoomRect = [self bounds];
    } else {
        newScale = [self maximumZoomScale];
        zoomRect = [self zoomRectForScale:newScale withCenter:location];
    }

    [self zoomToRect:zoomRect animated:YES];
}

- (void)turnOffZoom                                                      // 19
{
    if ([self isZoomed]) {
        [self zoomToLocation:CGPointZero];
    }
}
```

```
#pragma mark - Touch gestures

- (void)doubleTapped:(UITapGestureRecognizer *)recognizer                // 20
{
    [self zoomToLocation:[recognizer locationInView:self]];
}

- (void)tapped:(UITapGestureRecognizer *)recognizer                      // 21
{
    [[self photoBrowserViewController] toggleChromeDisplay];
}

#pragma mark - UIScrollViewDelegate methods

- (UIView *)viewForZoomingInScrollView:(UIScrollView *)scrollView        // 22
{
    return [self imageView];
}


@end
```

Let's walk through the code and see what is happening, starting with the header file *PhotoBrowserPhotoView.h*:

1. The forward declaration for the class PhotoBrowserViewController is made.

2. The PhotoBrowserPhotoView class is the delegate to itself, the scroll view. Therefore, UIScrollViewDelegate is added to the list of protocols.

3. The class also has a property named index. This is the index to the photo displayed in the scroll view.

4. The property photoBrowserViewController is added. This weak reference to the photo browser enables the photo view to talk back to the browser.

5. The method -setImage: is called by the photo browser. It passes an image reference for the photo that is displayed.

6. The method -turnOffZoom is provided so that the photo browser can turn off zooming when the user begins to scroll through the collection of photos.

The interface in Listing 17.10 is followed by the implementation. The changes to the implementation include the following:

7. The *PhotoBrowserViewController.h* header file is imported.

8. A class extension for PhotoBrowserPhotoView is declared.

9. An image view is added. This is the image view responsible for displaying the photo.

10. The method -loadSubviewsWithFrame: is called during object initialization. It loads the image view used to display the photo.

11. The method -isZoomed indicates whether the view is currently zoomed in or not.

12. The @implementation section starts by synthesizing the declared properties.

13. This is followed by -initWithFrame:. This override method initializes the view, setting properties on the scroll view, and adds tap and double-tap gestures.

14. The method -loadSubviewsWithFrame: is responsible for creating the image view used to display the photo.

15. The method -setImage: sets the image for the image view. The photo browser calls this method.

16. The method -isZoomed returns YES when the user has zoomed in on the photo; otherwise it returns NO.

17. The method -zoomRectForScale:withCenter: is responsible for calculating the zoom rect based on a center point.

18. The method -zoomToLocation: does as the name implies. It zooms to a location within the photo.

19. The method -turnOffZoom is provided so that the photo browser can request that the zoom be turned off during scrolling.

20–21. Two touch gestures are assigned to the view: a double tap and a tap. The double tap will zoom to the tapped location within the photo. The tap toggles the chrome display. The tap gesture is managed in the PhotoBrowserPhotoView class instead of the photo browser because it relies on the double-tap gesture failing first.

22. The last method of the class is -viewForZoomingInScrollView:. This is a UIScrollViewDelegate method, and it returns a reference to the view that is used for zooming within the scroll view. For this particular case, that view is the image view.

With the new class in place, it's time to replace UIImageView used in the photo browser with PhotoBrowserPhotoView. In addition to replacing the image view with the new photo view, the -toggleChromeDisplay method must be made public so that it can be used in the PhotoBrowserPhotoView class.

Open the PhotoBrowserViewController class and apply the changes in Listing 17.11.

Listing 17.11 Changes to the PhotoBrowserViewController Class

```
///////
// PhotoBrowserViewController.h
///////
```

```objc
@interface PhotoBrowserViewController : UIViewController <UIScrollViewDelegate>

// Other code left out for brevity's sake.

- (void)toggleChromeDisplay;                                            // 1

@end

///////
//  PhotoBrowserViewController.m
///////
#import "PhotoBrowserViewController.h"
#import "PhotoBrowserPhotoView.h"                                       // 2

// Other code left out for brevity's sake.

@implementation PhotoBrowserViewController

// Other code left out for brevity's sake.

#pragma mark - Page management

- (void)loadPage:(NSInteger)index
{
    if (index < 0 || index >= [self numberOfPhotos]) {
        return;
    }

    id currentView = [[self photoViewCache] objectAtIndex:index];
    if ([currentView isKindOfClass:[PhotoBrowserPhotoView class]] == NO) { // 3
        // Load the photo view.
        CGRect frame = [self frameForPageAtIndex:index];
        PhotoBrowserPhotoView *newView = [[PhotoBrowserPhotoView alloc]
                                          initWithFrame:frame];         // 4
        [newView setBackgroundColor:[UIColor clearColor]];             // 5
        [newView setImage:[self imageAtIndex:index]];                  // 6
        [newView setPhotoBrowserViewController:self];                  // 7
        [newView setIndex:index];                                      // 8

        [[self scrollView] addSubview:newView];
        [[self photoViewCache] replaceObjectAtIndex:index withObject:newView];
    } else {
        [currentView turnOffZoom];
    }
}

- (void)unloadPage:(NSInteger)index
{
```

```
    if (index < 0 || index >= [self numberOfPhotos]) {
        return;
    }

    id currentView = [[self photoViewCache] objectAtIndex:index];
    if ([currentView isKindOfClass:[PhotoBrowserPhotoView class]]) {        // 9
        [currentView removeFromSuperview];
        [[self photoViewCache] replaceObjectAtIndex:index withObject:[NSNull null]];
    }
}

// Other code left out for brevity's sake.

@end
```

Here is a quick rundown of the changes to the `PhotoBrowserViewController` class:

1. The `-toggleChromeDisplay` method declaration has been added to the public interface.

2. The *PhotoBrowserPhotoView.h* header file is imported in the *PhotoBrowserViewController.m* implementation file.

3. The check for the `UIImageView` class in the `-loadPage:` method has been changed to check for the `PhotoBrowserPhotoView` class.

4–8. The `UIImageView` code has been replaced with `PhotoBrowserPhotoView` code. The background color is set to clear. The image is set to the current photo. And the photo browser reference is set to enable callbacks to the view controller.

9. The `UIImageView` class check found in the `-unloadPage:` has been replaced with a check for the `PhotoBrowserPhotoView` class.

And with that, your photo browser now supports zooming on a photo. As always, build and run the app to test the changes. Check your work if zooming isn't working properly.

Note
Hold down the **Option** key and use your mouse to simulate a pinch gesture when using the iPad Simulator.

Deleting a Photo

Before moving on, you need to add one more feature to the photo browser. In addition to adding the new delete feature, you will be laying the foundation for future enhancements to the photo browser. The feature to add at this time is a "Delete Photo" action. This action asks the user to confirm the deletion of the photo. The delete action is made available to the user as a button on the navigation bar displayed at the top of the screen.

More actions will be added in later chapters, so an action button will be displayed in the navigation bar. This involves a little trickery since the navigation bar does not support more than two buttons, one on the left and one on the right. In PhotoWheel, however, three buttons are needed: one on the left for the **Back** button, and two on the right, one for delete and the other for the action menu. But to make it more fun, let's not stop with two buttons on the right. Let's make it three, one each for delete, action, and Slideshow.

> **Note**
>
> This chapter walks you through the steps to delete a photo. Chapter 19, "Printing with AirPrint," and Chapter 20, "Sending Email," show how to implement additional actions. Chapter 23, "Producing a Slideshow with AirPlay," shows you how to implement the slide-show feature.

First, the additional buttons must be added to the navigation bar. Open the file *PhotoBrowserViewController.m* and add the new method -addButtonsToNavigation-Bar. Next, update the -viewDidLoad method to call the -addButtonsToNaviga-tionBar method. The complete set of code changes is shown in Listing 17.12, with a full explanation of the changes to follow.

Listing 17.12   **Updates to** *PhotoBrowserViewController.m*

```
///////
//  PhotoBrowserViewController.h
///////

@interface PhotoBrowserViewController : UIViewController <UIScrollViewDelegate,
UIActionSheetDelegate>                                                  // 1

// Other code left out for brevity's sake.

@end

@protocol PhotoBrowserViewControllerDelegate <NSObject>
@required

// Other code left out for brevity's sake.

@optional
- (void)photoBrowserViewController:(PhotoBrowserViewController *)photoBrowser
             deleteImageAtIndex:(NSInteger)index;                      // 2

@end
```

```
///////
//   PhotoBrowserViewController.m
///////
#import "PhotoBrowserViewController.h"
#import "PhotoBrowserPhotoView.h"
#import "ClearToolbar.h"                                          // 3

#define ACTIONSHEET_TAG_DELETE 1                                  // 4
#define ACTIONSHEET_TAG_ACTIONS 2                                 // 5

@interface PhotoBrowserViewController ()

// Other code left out for brevity's sake.

@property (nonatomic, strong) UIBarButtonItem *actionButton;     // 6

- (void)addButtonsToNavigationBar;                               // 7

// Other code left out for brevity's sake.

@end

@implementation PhotoBrowserViewController

// Other code left out for brevity's sake.

@synthesize actionButton = _actionButton;                        // 8

- (void)viewDidLoad
{
    [super viewDidLoad];

    // Make sure to set wantsFullScreenLayout or the photo
    // will not display behind the status bar.
    [self setWantsFullScreenLayout:YES];

    // Set the view's frame size. This ensures that the scroll view
    // autoresizes correctly and avoids surprises when retrieving
    // the scroll view's bounds later.
    CGRect frame = [[UIScreen mainScreen] bounds];
    [[self view] setFrame:frame];

    UIScrollView *scrollView = [self scrollView];
    // Set the initial size.
    [scrollView setFrame:[self frameForPagingScrollView]];
    [scrollView setDelegate:self];
```

```
   [scrollView setBackgroundColor:[UIColor blackColor]];
   [scrollView setAutoresizingMask:UIViewAutoresizingFlexibleWidth |
    UIViewAutoresizingFlexibleHeight];
   [scrollView setAutoresizesSubviews:YES];
   [scrollView setPagingEnabled:YES];
   [scrollView setShowsVerticalScrollIndicator:NO];
   [scrollView setShowsHorizontalScrollIndicator:NO];

   [self addButtonsToNavigationBar];                              // 9
   [self initPhotoViewCache];


   // Must store the status bar size while it is still visible.
   CGRect statusBarFrame = [[UIApplication sharedApplication]
                            statusBarFrame];
   if (UIInterfaceOrientationIsLandscape([self interfaceOrientation])) {
      [self setStatusBarHeight:statusBarFrame.size.width];
   } else {
      [self setStatusBarHeight:statusBarFrame.size.height];
   }
}

// Other code left out for brevity's sake.

#pragma mark - Helper methods

- (void)addButtonsToNavigationBar                                 // 10
{
   // Add buttons to the navigation bar. The nav bar allows
   // one button on the left and one on the right. Optionally,
   // a custom view can be used instead of a button. To get
   // multiple buttons we must create a short toolbar containing
   // the buttons we want.

   UIBarButtonItem *trashButton = [[UIBarButtonItem alloc]
                     initWithBarButtonSystemItem:UIBarButtonSystemItemTrash
                     target:self
                     action:@selector(deletePhoto:)];
   [trashButton setStyle:UIBarButtonItemStyleBordered];

   UIBarButtonItem *actionButton = [[UIBarButtonItem alloc]
                      initWithBarButtonSystemItem:UIBarButtonSystemItemAction
                      target:self
                      action:@selector(showActionMenu:)];
   [actionButton setStyle:UIBarButtonItemStyleBordered];
   [self setActionButton:actionButton];
```

```
    UIBarButtonItem *slideshowButton = [[UIBarButtonItem alloc]
                                    initWithTitle:@"Slideshow"
                                    style:UIBarButtonItemStyleBordered
                                    target:self
                                    action:@selector(slideshow:)];

    UIBarButtonItem *flexibleSpace = [[UIBarButtonItem alloc]
                  initWithBarButtonSystemItem:UIBarButtonSystemItemFlexibleSpace
                  target:nil
                  action:nil];


    NSMutableArray *toolbarItems = [[NSMutableArray alloc] initWithCapacity:3];
    [toolbarItems addObject:flexibleSpace];
    [toolbarItems addObject:slideshowButton];
    [toolbarItems addObject:actionButton];
    [toolbarItems addObject:trashButton];

    UIToolbar *toolbar = [[ClearToolbar alloc]
                        initWithFrame:CGRectMake(0, 0, 200, 44)];
    [toolbar setBackgroundColor:[UIColor clearColor]];
    [toolbar setBarStyle:UIBarStyleBlack];
    [toolbar setTranslucent:YES];

    [toolbar setItems:toolbarItems];

    UIBarButtonItem *customBarButtonItem = [[UIBarButtonItem alloc]
                                    initWithCustomView:toolbar];
    [[self navigationItem] setRightBarButtonItem:customBarButtonItem
                                    animated:YES];
}

// Other code left out for brevity's sake.

#pragma mark - Actions

- (void)deletePhotoConfirmed                                    // 11
{
    id<PhotoBrowserViewControllerDelegate> delegate = [self delegate];
    if (delegate && [delegate respondsToSelector:
                    @selector(photoBrowserViewController:deleteImageAtIndex:)])
    {
        NSInteger count = [self numberOfPhotos];
        NSInteger indexToDelete = [self currentIndex];
        [self unloadPage:indexToDelete];
        [delegate photoBrowserViewController:self deleteImageAtIndex:indexToDelete];
```

```
        if (count == 1) {
            // The one and only photo was deleted. Pop back to
            // the previous view controller.
            [[self navigationController] popViewControllerAnimated:YES];
        } else {
            NSInteger nextIndex = indexToDelete;
            if (indexToDelete == count) {
                nextIndex -= 1;
            }
            [self setCurrentIndex:nextIndex];
            [self setScrollViewContentSize];
        }
    }
}


- (void)deletePhoto:(id)sender                                          // 12
{
    [self cancelChromeDisplayTimer];
    UIActionSheet *actionSheet = [[UIActionSheet alloc] initWithTitle:nil
                                                        delegate:self
                                                   cancelButtonTitle:nil
                                              destructiveButtonTitle:@"Delete
Photo"
                                                     otherButtonTitles:nil, nil];
    [actionSheet setTag:ACTIONSHEET_TAG_DELETE];
    [actionSheet showFromBarButtonItem:sender animated:YES];
}


- (void)showActionMenu:(id)sender                                       // 13
{
    NSLog(@"%s", __PRETTY_FUNCTION__);
}


- (void)slideshow:(id)sender                                            // 14
{
    NSLog(@"%s", __PRETTY_FUNCTION__);
}


#pragma mark - UIActionSheetDelegate methods

- (void)actionSheet:(UIActionSheet *)actionSheet
clickedButtonAtIndex:(NSInteger)buttonIndex                             // 15
{
    [self startChromeDisplayTimer];

    // Do nothing if the user taps outside the action
    // sheet (thus closing the popover containing the
```

```
    // action sheet).
    if (buttonIndex < 0) {
        return;
    }

    if ([actionSheet tag] == ACTIONSHEET_TAG_DELETE) {
        [self deletePhotoConfirmed];
    }
}
```

@end

Let's walk through the code changes together:

1. Two action sheets are used in the photo browser. To respond to the action sheets, the photo browser must implement methods from the UIAction-SheetDelegate protocol. The protocol is added to the list of conforming protocols so that the compiler can do the appropriate checks to ensure conformity with the protocols.

2. The PhotoBrowserViewControllerDelegate protocol defined in the *PhotoBrowserViewController.h* file has been modified to include a new optional method, -photoBrowserViewController:deleteImageAtIndex:. Remember, the photo browser knows only how to display photos. It doesn't actually know anything about the origins of the photos, so it is up to the photo browser delegate to perform the actual deletion of a photo.

3. The *ClearToolbar.h* header file is imported. To get more than one button on the right side of the navigation bar, a toolbar is needed. But the embedded toolbar should be invisible to the user, which is why the ClearToolbar class is used.

4–5. Two #defines are created, representing each action sheet. Each action sheet will have a tag value matching one of these C macros.

6. A new declared property is added to the PhotoBrowserViewController class extension. The property, actionButton, is a reference to the action button displayed in the toolbar embedded in the navigation bar.

7. Also added to the class extension is the method -addButtonsToNavigation-Bar. This method is called at the time the view is loaded. It is responsible for embedding the toolbar of buttons into the right bar button item of the navigation bar.

8. The new declared property actionButton is synthesized.

9. The -viewDidLoad method is updated to include a call to the -addButtons-ToNavigationBar method.

10. The method -addButtonsToNavigationBar is responsible for creating a clear toolbar, adding buttons to the toolbar, and then adding the toolbar as

the right bar button item of the navigation bar. While a navigation bar cannot contain more than one button on the right, it can contain a custom view. This feature of the navigation bar is used to create a toolbar of additional buttons that is added to the right bar button item.

11. The method -deletePhotoConfirmed is called after the user has confirmed the delete request. This method checks that the delegate responds to the -photoBrowserViewController:deleteImageAtIndex: method. If it does, it instructs the delegate to delete the current photo. If the photo deleted is the last one in the photo album, the photo browser is popped from the navigation stack and the user returns to the main screen. Otherwise, adjustments are made to the browser's scroll view to accommodate the new number of photos.

12. The method -deletePhoto: is called when the user taps the delete button in the navigation bar. It creates and displays an action sheet. The action sheet has one item, Delete Photo. The user must tap this item to confirm the delete request. This method also stops the chrome display timer. The chrome must remain visible while the action sheet is displayed.

13–14. Stub methods for the action menu and slideshow have been added. The implementation for these methods will be completed in later chapters.

15. The UIActionSheetDelegate method -actionSheet:clickedButtonAtIndex: is next in the class implementation. This method starts the chrome display timer. The action sheet is no longer visible; therefore, the chrome should autohide in 5 seconds. Next, it checks that a button was tapped, and if so, it calls the -deletePhotoConfirmed method. The -actionSheet:clickedButtonAtIndex: method will have additional enhancements in later chapters, which is why the action sheet tag value is checked within the method's implementation.

At this point, you should build and run the app to test the changes. Don't worry about deleting a photo. Nothing is deleted right now. Before a photo can be deleted, the photo browser delegate object must be modified to implement the optional -photoBrowserViewController:deleteImageAtIndex: method.

Test your changes. Ensure that each button is calling the appropriate action method, and verify that the delete confirmation action sheet is displayed when the user taps the delete button.

After you verify the changes, update the PhotoAlbumViewController class. An instance of this class is the delegate for the photo browser, and it must be modified to include the delete image at index callback.

Open the file *PhotoAlbumViewController.m*. Add the implementation shown in Listing 17.13.

Listing 17.13   **Updated** *PhotoAlbumViewController.m*

```
- (void)photoBrowserViewController:(PhotoBrowserViewController *)photoBrowser
deleteImageAtIndex:(NSInteger)index
{
   NSIndexPath *indexPath = [NSIndexPath indexPathForRow:index inSection:0];
   Photo *photo = [[self fetchedResultsController] objectAtIndexPath:indexPath];
   NSManagedObjectContext *context = [self managedObjectContext];
   [context deleteObject:photo];
   [self saveChanges];
}
```

This method retrieves the photo model object from the fetched results controller, then deletes the object from the managed object context. Finally, the change is saved.

Congratulations! Your PhotoWheel app now has a full-screen photo browser complete with zooming and delete functionality as seen in Figure 17.3.

Figure 17.3   Screen shot of the PhotoWheel photo browser

Summary

In this chapter, you learned two more ways to leverage `UIScrollView`. You learned how to use it to display scrollable content as pages in a memory-efficient manner, and you learned how the scroll view can be used to zoom in on content. You also provided a few additional enhancements to the app, such as launching the photo browser from the tapped photo thumbnail and deleting a photo. But don't stop working on Photo-Wheel just yet. There are more features just itching to be written by you as you continue reading this book.

But first, there's an important issue to resolve. When the user rotates the iPad, the PhotoWheel UI does not rotate to match the device orientation. This is not good and must be fixed, which is exactly what you will do in the next chapter.

Exercise

1. Modify the pop animation for the photo browser so that the animation ends on the cell for the photo currently displayed in the browser.

18

Supporting Device Rotation

It is important that iPad apps support all device orientations. But what does this actually mean? It means that your application should rotate the user interface to match the orientation of the device. Most iPhone applications can get away with not rotating because of the small form factor of the phone and the way users hold it. But the same is not true for the iPad.

An iPhone user tends to hold the device in a portrait orientation with the Home button at the bottom. An iPad user, on the other hand, will hold the iPad in different orientations based on how she picks it up. If your app does not rotate based on the current orientation, the user is forced to rotate her iPad, which is not an ideal user experience.

This chapter shows you how to support device rotation within your app. Along the way, you will update PhotoWheel so that it can be used regardless of how the user is holding the iPad—with the Home button on the bottom, top, left, or right.

How to Support Rotation

Supporting rotation, or rather, enabling rotation for your app, is simple. To rotate a screen, your view controller subclass overrides the `-shouldAutorotateToInterfaceOrientation:` method and returns `YES` for the supported orientations. This may be all you need to do if you correctly use autoresizing properties for the views that make up the UI. The PhotoWheel prototype app you wrote earlier in the book (in Chapters 8 through 13) supports rotation, and it required nothing more than returning `YES` on the `-shouldAutorotateToInterfaceOrientation:` method.

There are, however, times when additional work is needed. You may wish to disable a feature during rotation, or you may want to perform custom animation during the rotations. Or the user interface is simply too complex to rely solely on the autoresizing properties to support rotation. Whatever the situation might be, there are additional methods that you can override to handle the unique needs of your app.

Say you wish to disable a feature during a rotation. Override the method `-willRotateToInterfaceOrientation:duration:` and turn off the feature. Override the method `-didRotateFromInterfaceOrientation:` to turn the feature back on.

If you want to perform custom animations during a rotation, your view controller subclass overrides the `-willAnimateRotationToInterfaceOrientation: duration:` method. This method is called within the animation block used to rotate the view. You override this method when you need to set additional view properties that can animate. Say, for example, you need to move a button from one location to another during rotation. Set the frame for the button during this method call, and it will animate to its final destination.

> **Note**
>
> Prior to iOS 3, a two-step process was used to animate changes during a rotation. For the two-step approach, your view controller subclass would override the methods `-will-AnimateFirstHalfOfRotationToInterfaceOrientation:duration:` and `-willAnimateSecondHalfOfRotationFromInterfaceOrientation: duration:`. This approach is no longer recommended. You should use the one-step process, as it tends to be faster.

Supported Orientations

There are six *device* orientations:

- Portrait
- Portrait upside down
- Landscape left
- Landscape right
- Face up
- Face down

Upside down, left, and right indicate the position of the Home button on the iPad. Portrait upside down, for example, is when the device is held in portrait mode and the Home button is at the top. Landscape left is when the device is held in landscape mode and the Home button is on the right, and landscape right has the Home button on the left.

Did you catch the comment about landscape left and right? The device orientation is landscape left when the Home button is on the right, and the device orientation is landscape right when the button is on the left. The device orientation is based on how the device is rotated. Hold your iPad in your hands with the Home button at the bottom. Now rotate it to the left (turning the device counterclockwise). Where is the Home button? It's on the right, and the device orientation is landscape left.

Adding to the confusion are the four *interface* orientations: portrait, portrait upside down, landscape left, and landscape right. The Home button positions for the interface orientations portrait and portrait upside down are the same as the device orientations portrait and portrait upside down. But the Home button position for the two interface orientation landscape modes is the opposite of the landscape device orientations. The interface orientation landscape left means the Home button is on the left of the device, and landscape right means the Home button is on the right. This is the opposite of the landscape modes for device orientation.

Under most circumstances, an iPad app needs to concern itself only with the interface orientation, not the device orientation. And most iPad apps do not care if the device is face up or face down. Because of this, the typical iPad app relies on the view controller rotation mechanism described in the last section to support rotation.

You may be wondering how this rotation mechanism is used when your app is launched and the device is in landscape mode. By default, applications are launched in portrait mode. This is why you tend to initially design your UI in portrait. After the -application:didFinishLaunchingWithOptions: method (found on the app delegate) returns, the app's root view controller receives the -shouldAutorotate-ToInterfaceOrientation: method call. If YES is returned, the view controller receives the other rotation method calls, which in turn cause the user interface to rotate. The UI is fully rotated by the time the user sees it.

Using Autoresizing

By far the easiest way to support rotation within your app is to rely on autoresizing. If the views in your app are correctly configured with autoresizing, all that is needed to support rotation is to respond YES in the -shouldAutorotateToInterface-Orientation: method. This sounds simple, but getting autoresizing configured properly can be a challenge involving some trial and error.

You can set the autoresizing property for a view using the Size inspector in IB, shown in Figure 18.1, or you can set it in code. For example, the following code snippet assigns a flexible width and height to an image view. This means that the width and height expand and shrink as the container view resizes.

```
[imageView setAutoresizingMask:UIViewAutoresizingFlexibleWidth|
UIViewAutoresizingFlexibleHeight]
```

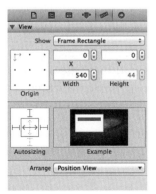

Figure 18.1 The Size inspector with the Autosizing settings

Use any combination of the following to define how a view is autoresized:

- `UIViewAutoresizingNone`
- `UIViewAutoresizingFlexibleLeftMargin`
- `UIViewAutoresizingFlexibleWidth`
- `UIViewAutoresizingFlexibleRightMargin`
- `UIViewAutoresizingFlexibleTopMargin`
- `UIViewAutoresizingFlexibleHeight`
- `UIViewAutoresizingFlexibleBottomMargin`

If you do not wish to have a view resize its subviews, you can turn off resizing by setting the property `autoresizesSubviews` to `NO`. The default value for this property is `YES`.

Customized Rotation

Relying solely on autoresizing for rotation support may not be an option for your app. In addition to resizing a screen element, maybe an element needs to change positions, such as moving from the top of the screen to the far right side. This is something autoresizing will not do for you. When autoresizing alone doesn't properly rotate your app's user interface, it's time to customize the rotation.

> **Note**
>
> You should rely on autoresizing as much as possible. Even if your app requires customizing the rotation sequence, try using autoresizing on subviews to help reduce the amount of code you have to write. You'll likely find that you use a combination of autoresizing and customized rotation to produce the best user experience. In fact, PhotoWheel does this. It uses a combination to provide a nice animated rotation sequence.

The UI for PhotoWheel uses background images for visual effects. The UI has a top-down look to it where the contents of a photo album are displayed at the top and the list of photo albums is displayed at the bottom. There are other visual effects such as the arrow pointing to the selected photo album.

If PhotoWheel were to rely solely on autoresizing to support a landscape UI, the UI would look odd. The photo album wheel, for example, would be stretched and distorted. Therefore, you will need to customize the rotation in addition to using autoresizing to properly display PhotoWheel in landscape mode.

To start, open the file *MainViewController.m* and add the method `-shouldAutorotate-ToInterfaceOrientation:`. Have the method return `YES` to support all interface orientations. The method will look like this:

```
- (BOOL)shouldAutorotateToInterfaceOrientation:
(UIInterfaceOrientation)toInterfaceOrientation
```

```
{
    return YES;
}
```

Run the app and rotate the device. If you are using the simulator, you can type **⌘-Left** and **⌘-Right** to rotate. As expected, the UI looks a mess, as you can see in Figure 18.2. Autoresizing is used on the background image displayed in the

Figure 18.2   At the top is PhotoWheel with a messy landscape UI.
The bottom screen shot is what it should look like when the UI is
properly rotated.

MainViewController view. The views for the child view controllers do not use autoresizing, so their position and size remain the same. However, the photo album wheel is barely visible, and the UI simply looks bad.

A number of changes are required to clean up the UI for landscape mode. Additional outlets must be defined for existing screen elements. Then code must be added to the view controller classes to manipulate the screen elements that require new sizes, new positions, and, in the case of image views, new images.

Let's start with the view for the MainViewController. It has a background image and an *i* info button. The background must change to the landscape version of the artwork. The info button must also move to a new location on the screen, aligning itself with the placeholder area found in the landscape version of the artwork. This means that the MainViewController class must have outlets for the background image view and the info button. Open *MainViewController.h* and add the new outlets. Remember to connect the outlets to the objects defined in the storyboard scene for the main view controller, and remember to synthesize the declared properties in the class implementation file. The updated header file is shown in Listing 18.1.

Listing 18.1   **Updated** *MainViewController.h*

```
#import <UIKit/UIKit.h>

@interface MainViewController : UIViewController

@property (nonatomic, strong) IBOutlet UIImageView *backgroundImageView;
@property (nonatomic, strong) IBOutlet UIButton *infoButton;

@end
```

Now open the file *MainViewController.m* and override the method -willAnimate-RotationToInterfaceOrientation:duration:. The implementation for this method checks the interface orientation. If the iPad is held landscape (with the Home button on either the left or the right side), a landscape layout is used for the UI; otherwise a portrait layout is used. The code is shown in Listing 18.2. Make the same code changes to your MainViewController class.

Listing 18.2   **Updated** *MainViewController.m*

```
#import "MainViewController.h"
#import "PhotoAlbumViewController.h"
#import "PhotoAlbumsViewController.h"
#import "AppDelegate.h"

@implementation MainViewController

@synthesize backgroundImageView = _backgroundImageView;          // 1
@synthesize infoButton = _infoButton;                            // 2
```

```objc
- (void)viewDidLoad                                              // 3

{
    [super viewDidLoad];

    AppDelegate *appDelegate =
        (AppDelegate *)[[UIApplication sharedApplication] delegate];
    NSManagedObjectContext *managedObjectContext =
        [appDelegate managedObjectContext];

    UIStoryboard *storyboard = [self storyboard];

    PhotoAlbumsViewController *photoAlbumsScene =
        [storyboard instantiateViewControllerWithIdentifier:@"PhotoAlbumsScene"];
    [photoAlbumsScene setManagedObjectContext:managedObjectContext];
    [self addChildViewController:photoAlbumsScene];
    [photoAlbumsScene didMoveToParentViewController:self];

    PhotoAlbumViewController *photoAlbumScene =
        [storyboard instantiateViewControllerWithIdentifier:@"PhotoAlbumScene"];
    [self addChildViewController:photoAlbumScene];
    [photoAlbumScene didMoveToParentViewController:self];

    [photoAlbumsScene setPhotoAlbumViewController:photoAlbumScene];
}

- (void)viewDidUnload                                            // 4
{
    [self setBackgroundImageView:nil];
    [self setInfoButton:nil];
    [super viewDidUnload];
}

#pragma mark - Rotation support

- (BOOL)shouldAutorotateToInterfaceOrientation:
(UIInterfaceOrientation)toInterfaceOrientation                   // 5
{
    return YES;
}

- (void)layoutForLandscape                                       // 6
{
    UIImage *backgroundImage = [UIImage
                        imageNamed:@"background-landscape-right-grooved.png"];
    [[self backgroundImageView] setImage:backgroundImage];
```

```
    CGRect frame = [[self infoButton] frame];
    frame.origin = CGPointMake(981, 712);
    [[self infoButton] setFrame:frame];
}


- (void)layoutForPortrait                                            // 7
{
    UIImage *backgroundImage = [UIImage
                             imageNamed:@"background-portrait-grooved.png"];
    [[self backgroundImageView] setImage:backgroundImage];

    CGRect frame = [[self infoButton] frame];
    frame.origin = CGPointMake(723, 960);
    [[self infoButton] setFrame:frame];
}


- (void)willAnimateRotationToInterfaceOrientation:
(UIInterfaceOrientation)toInterfaceOrientation
duration:(NSTimeInterval)duration                                    // 8
{
    if (UIInterfaceOrientationIsLandscape(toInterfaceOrientation)) {
        [self layoutForLandscape];
    } else {
        [self layoutForPortrait];
    }
}


@end
```

Let's review the changes:

1–2. The declared properties for the outlets are @synthesized.

3. The method -viewDidLoad remains unchanged.

4. The method -viewDidUnload is added. It sets the outlets to nil.

5. The method -shouldAutorotateToInterfaceOrientation: is implemented. It always returns YES since all interface orientations are supported.

6. The helper method -layoutForLandscape is used to lay out the screen elements for landscape mode. First, the background image is replaced with *back-
ground-landscape-right-grooved.png*. The landscape view for PhotoWheel positions
the wheel on the right of the screen, and this background image reflects this
change. The info button must also be repositioned. The frame for the button is
retrieved, and the origin is changed to reflect the new location. Finally, the button's frame is updated with the adjusted frame values.

7. The helper method -layoutForPortrait does the same thing as the previous method except it is used to lay out the screen elements for portrait mode.

8. The -willAnimateRotationToInterfaceOrientation:duration: method is overridden. It checks the interface orientation mode, then calls the appropriate layout helper method.

Checking the Interface Orientation

When checking the interface orientation, you can use the macros UIInterface-OrientationIsLandscape and UIInterfaceOrientationIsPortrait. UIInterfaceOrientationIsLandscape checks that the interface orientation is landscape left or right, and UIInterfaceOrientationIsPortrait checks that the orientation is portrait or portrait upside down. You can use the UIInterface-Orientation enumeration if you need to perform a more specific check, for example, if (toInterfaceOrientation == UIInterfaceOrientation-PortraitUpsideDown).

The UIInterfaceOrientation options are

- UIInterfaceOrientationPortrait
- UIInterfaceOrientationPortraitUpsideDown
- UIInterfaceOrientationLandscapeLeft
- UIInterfaceOrientationLandscapeRight

Build and run the app to test your changes. Rotate the device. If the background image or the info button remains unchanged, it's likely you forgot to connect the objects to the outlets in the storyboard scene.

Rotating the Photo Albums Scene

Next up is adding rotation support to the photo albums scene. This scene is displayed at the bottom of the screen when the iPad is in portrait mode. It consists of the photo album wheel and round + button; its view controller class is PhotoAlbumsViewController.

Because PhotoAlbumViewController is a child view controller to MainView-Controller, it automatically receives the rotation-related messages. This means that the PhotoAlbumsViewController class does not need to override the -should-AutorotateToInterfaceOrientation: method. Instead, it only needs to override the -willAnimateRotationToInterfaceOrientation:duration: method. And because the contents of the PhotoAlbumsViewController view do not change size or position within the view, the only thing that needs to happen is to move the controller's view based on the landscape or portrait interface orientation.

Simply put, in code, you just need to add the following method to the *PhotoAlbums-ViewController.m* file:

```
- (void)willAnimateRotationToInterfaceOrientation:
(UIInterfaceOrientation)toInterfaceOrientation duration:(NSTimeInterval)duration
{
    CGRect newFrame;
    if (UIInterfaceOrientationIsLandscape(toInterfaceOrientation)) {
        newFrame = CGRectMake(700, 100, 551, 550);
    } else {
        newFrame = CGRectMake(109, 680, 551, 550);
    }
    [[self view] setFrame:newFrame];
}
```

All this does is to move the view to a new position based on the interface's orientation.

> **Note**
>
> By default, appearance and rotation messages are forwarded to child view controllers for view controllers that implement containment logic. This behavior can be turned off by overriding the method - (BOOL)automaticallyForwardAppearanceAnd-RotationMethodsToChildViewControllers and returning NO in the parent view controller.

Rotating the Photo Album Scene

Rotating the photo album scene is a bit more involved. A new background image will be displayed for landscape mode. This new image has new dimensions that make using autoresizing of subviews impossible. This means that each subview in the PhotoAlbumViewController view must be explicitly resized and positioned in code. This also means that outlets must be defined for each screen element.

Outlets for the toolbar and grid view have already been declared. This leaves you with the task of adding an outlet for the background and shadow images. The objects in the toolbar do not need to be declared as outlets. Autoresizing will take care of resizing and positioning the objects in the toolbar.

Open *PhotoAlbumViewController.h* and add an outlet for the background image. Add another outlet for the shadow image, which is displayed below the toolbar. The code for the declared properties is

```
@property (nonatomic, strong) IBOutlet UIImageView *backgroundImageView;
@property (nonatomic, strong) IBOutlet UIImageView *shadowImageView;
```

Remember to open *PhotoAlbumViewController.m* and @synthesize the new declared properties. While you're at it, be sure to connect the outlets to the appropriate UIImageView objects created in the Photo Album View Controller Scene in the main storyboard.

Next, open *PhotoAlbumViewController.m* and add the rotation-related methods, shown in Listing 18.3.

Listing 18.3   **Rotation-Related Methods for** `PhotoAlbumViewController`

```
- (void)layoutForLandscape
[[self view] setFrame:CGRectMake(18, 20, 738, 719)];
   [[self backgroundImageView] setImage:[UIImage
                          imageNamed:@"stack-viewer-bg-landscape-right.png"]];
   [[self backgroundImageView] setFrame:[[self view] bounds]];
   [[self shadowImageView] setFrame:CGRectMake(9, 51, 678, 8)];
   [[self gridView] setFrame:CGRectMake(20, 52, 654, 632)];
   [[self toolbar] setFrame:CGRectMake(9, 6, 678, 44)];
}

- (void)layoutForPortrait
{
   [[self view] setFrame:CGRectMake(26, 18, 716, 717)];
   [[self backgroundImageView] setImage:[UIImage
                              imageNamed:@"stack-viewer-bg-portrait.png"]];
   [[self backgroundImageView] setFrame:[[self view] bounds]];
   [[self shadowImageView] setFrame:CGRectMake(9, 51, 698, 8)];
   [[self gridView] setFrame:CGRectMake(20, 51, 678, 597)];
   [[self toolbar] setFrame:CGRectMake(9, 6, 698, 44)];
}

- (void)willAnimateRotationToInterfaceOrientation:
(UIInterfaceOrientation)toInterfaceOrientation duration:(NSTimeInterval)duration
{
   if (UIInterfaceOrientationIsLandscape(toInterfaceOrientation)) {
      [self layoutForLandscape];
   } else {
      [self layoutForPortrait];
   }
}
```

The code here is pretty straightforward. There are helper methods for portrait and landscape layouts. Each layout method positions and sizes the view and subviews based on the current interface's orientation.

At this point, PhotoWheel's main screen fully supports rotation.

Or does it?

Tweaking the `WheelView` Class

Visually the main screen rotates, but the wheel view for the photo album still has an issue. The wheel view does not make appropriate adjustments for landscape. In portrait mode, the selected photo album is displayed at the top of the wheel (0.0 degrees). In landscape mode, the selected photo album should be displayed at the left of the wheel (–90.0 or 270.0 degrees). A tweak is needed to the `WheelView` class to offset the wheel by a certain number of degrees.

Open the *WheelView.h* file. Add a new declared property named `angleOffset` of type `CGFloat`. The property declaration should look like this:

```
@property (nonatomic, assign) CGFloat angleOffset;
```

Next, open the file *WheelView.m* and synthesize the `angleOffset` property. At the bottom of the implementation section, add the following custom setter method:

```
- (void)setAngleOffset:(CGFloat)angleOffset
{
    if (_angleOffset != -angleOffset) {
        _angleOffset = -angleOffset;
        [self layoutSubviews];
    }
}
```

This method adjusts the given angle offset. This adjustment is needed because, internally, 0.0 degrees of the wheel view is actually at the bottom of the view, not the top. However, we tend to think of a circle's 0-degree point as the top of the circle. The setter method also calls `-layoutSubviews`. This forces the wheel view to redraw the contents each time the angle offset is set.

Finally, scroll to the middle of the method `-(void)setAngle:(CGFloat)angle` and replace the line of code that reads

```
float angleInRadians = (angle + 180.0) * M_PI / 180.0f;
```

with the following line of code:

```
float angleInRadians = ((angle + [self angleOffset]) + 180.0) * M_PI / 180.0f;
```

The `WheelView` class now supports an angle offset that can be used to control the "virtual top" of the wheel. You want to set this property in the `-willAnimate-RotationToInterfaceOrientation:duration:` method in the `PhotoAlbums-ViewController` class. The angle offset should be set to 0.0 for portrait mode and 270.0 (or -90.00) for landscape mode. Make the change to your code; Listing 18.4 shows an example of the modified code.

Listing 18.4   **Update to the** *PhotoAlbumsViewController.m* **File**

```
- (void)willAnimateRotationToInterfaceOrientation:
(UIInterfaceOrientation)toInterfaceOrientation duration:(NSTimeInterval)duration
{
    CGRect newFrame;
    CGFloat angleOffset;
    if (UIInterfaceOrientationIsLandscape(toInterfaceOrientation)) {
        newFrame = CGRectMake(700, 100, 551, 550);
        angleOffset = 270.0;
    } else {
        newFrame = CGRectMake(109, 680, 551, 550);
        angleOffset = 0.0;
    }
```

```
    [[self view] setFrame:newFrame];
    [[self wheelView] setAngleOffset:angleOffset];
}
```

Rotating the About View

The main screen is not the only screen that needs to support rotation. The About screen is another. Open the implementation file for the `AboutViewController` class and add the override method `-shouldAutorotateToInterfaceOrientation:` so that the method always returns `YES`.

Rotating the Photo Browser

The photo browser needs the same change. Open the implementation file for the `PhotoBrowserViewController` class and add the `-shouldAutorotateTo-InterfaceOrientation:` method so that it always returns `YES`.

Unfortunately, though, the photo browser requires a little more work to properly support rotation. The navigation bar and the scroll view are properly autoresized, but the contents of the scroll view do not resize properly. We'll get to those next.

Fixing the Trouble Spots

Adding rotation support is never easy unless the app relies solely on autoresizing. PhotoWheel has issues with rotation that are not uncommon in other apps. First of all, the contents of the photo browser scroll view do not resize properly during a rotation. Another issue is seen when you launch the photo browser from portrait mode, rotate the device to landscape mode, then tap the **Back** button to return to the main screen. In this scenario, the main screen never rotates.

You need to fix these trouble spots, starting with the photo browser content area.

Fixing the Photo Browser

The photo browser is not your standard iOS screen. It displays a scroll view, which contains one or more scroll views. Each sub–scroll view displays a photo that the user may or may not have zoomed in on. In addition to this, the photo browser shows and hides chrome. The combination of these points makes the photo browser a bit more challenging to rotate.

The best way to describe what needs to happen is to show you the updated source code, then walk you through it. You will need to update your source code with the same set of changes. Start with the `PhotoBrowserPhotoView` class. It needs a number of new methods to reposition the photo after the content size for the scroll view changes, which happens when the device is rotated.

Open the header file for the `PhotoBrowserPhotoView` class and add the new method declarations shown in Listing 18.5.

Listing 18.5   **New Method Declarations for the** PhotoBrowserPhotoView **Class**

```
@interface PhotoBrowserPhotoView : UIScrollView <UIScrollViewDelegate>

// Other code left out for brevity's sake.

- (CGPoint)pointToCenterAfterRotation;
- (CGFloat)scaleToRestoreAfterRotation;
- (void)setMaxMinZoomScalesForCurrentBounds;
- (void)restoreCenterPoint:(CGPoint)oldCenter scale:(CGFloat)oldScale;

@end
```

Now open the implementation file for the PhotoBrowserPhotoView class and add the implementation for the new methods; the code is shown in Listing 18.6.

Listing 18.6   **New Method Implementations for** PhotoBrowserPhotoView

```
#pragma mark - Rotation methods

/**
 ** Methods called during rotation to preserve the zoomScale and the visible
 ** portion of the image.
 **
 ** The following code comes from the Apple sample project PhotoScroller
 ** available at
 ** http://bit.ly/qSUDOH
 **
 **/

- (void)setMaxMinZoomScalesForCurrentBounds
{
    CGSize boundsSize = self.bounds.size;
    CGSize imageSize = [[self imageView] bounds].size;

    // Calculate min/max zoom scale:
    // the scale needed to perfectly fit the image width-wise
    CGFloat xScale = boundsSize.width / imageSize.width;
    // the scale needed to perfectly fit the image height-wise
    CGFloat yScale = boundsSize.height / imageSize.height;
    // use minimum of these to allow the image to become fully visible
    CGFloat minScale = MIN(xScale, yScale);

    // On high-resolution screens we have double the pixel density,
    // so we will be seeing every pixel if we limit the maximum
    // zoom scale to 0.5.
    CGFloat maxScale = 1.0 / [[UIScreen mainScreen] scale];
```

```objc
    // Don't let minScale exceed maxScale. (If the image is smaller
    // than the screen, we don't want to force it to be zoomed.)
    if (minScale > maxScale) {
        minScale = maxScale;
    }

    self.maximumZoomScale = maxScale;
    self.minimumZoomScale = minScale;
}

// Returns the center point, in image coordinate space, to try
// to restore after rotation.
- (CGPoint)pointToCenterAfterRotation
{
    CGPoint boundsCenter = CGPointMake(CGRectGetMidX(self.bounds),
                                       CGRectGetMidY(self.bounds));
    return [self convertPoint:boundsCenter toView:[self imageView]];
}

// Returns the zoom scale to attempt to restore after rotation.
- (CGFloat)scaleToRestoreAfterRotation
{
    CGFloat contentScale = self.zoomScale;

    // If we're at the minimum zoom scale, preserve that by returning 0,
    // which will be converted to the minimum allowable scale when the
    // scale is restored.
    if (contentScale <= self.minimumZoomScale + FLT_EPSILON)
        contentScale = 0;

    return contentScale;
}

- (CGPoint)maximumContentOffset
{
    CGSize contentSize = self.contentSize;
    CGSize boundsSize = self.bounds.size;
    return CGPointMake(contentSize.width - boundsSize.width,
                       contentSize.height - boundsSize.height);
}

- (CGPoint)minimumContentOffset
{
    return CGPointZero;
}
```

```
// Adjusts content offset and scale to try to preserve the old
// zoom scale and center.
- (void)restoreCenterPoint:(CGPoint)oldCenter scale:(CGFloat)oldScale
{
    // Step 1: Restore zoom scale, first making sure it is within
    // the allowable range.
    self.zoomScale = MIN(self.maximumZoomScale, MAX(self.minimumZoomScale,
                                                        oldScale));


    // Step 2: Restore center point, first making sure it is within
    // the allowable range.

    // Step 2a: Convert the desired center point back to our own
    // coordinate space.
    CGPoint boundsCenter = [self convertPoint:oldCenter fromView:[self imageView]];
    // Step 2b: Calculate the content offset that would yield that center
    // point.
    CGPoint offset = CGPointMake(boundsCenter.x - self.bounds.size.width / 2.0,
                                boundsCenter.y - self.bounds.size.height / 2.0);
    // Step 2c: Restore the offset, adjusted to be within the allowable
    // range.
    CGPoint maxOffset = [self maximumContentOffset];
    CGPoint minOffset = [self minimumContentOffset];
    offset.x = MAX(minOffset.x, MIN(maxOffset.x, offset.x));
    offset.y = MAX(minOffset.y, MIN(maxOffset.y, offset.y));
    self.contentOffset = offset;
}
```

This code comes from the PhotoScroller sample app made available by Apple. It does the job of repositioning the image while at the same time preserving the zoom scale for the image. The code is well documented with comments, so there's no need to walk through the method. Instead, it's time to put the changes to work.

Open the file *PhotoBrowserViewController.m* and add the changes shown in Listing 18.7.

Listing 18.7   Adding Rotation Support to the `PhotoBrowserViewController` **Class**

```
#import "PhotoBrowserViewController.h"
#import "PhotoBrowserPhotoView.h"
#import "ClearToolbar.h"


// Other code left out for brevity's sake.


@interface PhotoBrowserViewController ()


// Other code left out for brevity's sake.
```

```
@property (nonatomic, assign) NSInteger firstVisiblePageIndexBeforeRotation; // 1
@property (nonatomic, assign) NSInteger percentScrolledIntoFirstVisiblePage; // 2

// Other code left out for brevity's sake.

@end

@implementation PhotoBrowserViewController

// Other code left out for brevity's sake.

@synthesize firstVisiblePageIndexBeforeRotation =
_firstVisiblePageIndexBeforeRotation;                                        // 3
@synthesize percentScrolledIntoFirstVisiblePage =
_percentScrolledIntoFirstVisiblePage;                                       // 4


// Other code left out for brevity's sake.

#pragma mark - Rotation support
/**
 **
 ** Portions of the rotation code come from the Apple sample project
 ** PhotoScroller available at
 ** http://bit.ly/qSUD0H
 **
 **/

- (BOOL)shouldAutorotateToInterfaceOrientation:
(UIInterfaceOrientation)toInterfaceOrientation
{
   return YES;
}

- (void)willRotateToInterfaceOrientation:
(UIInterfaceOrientation)toInterfaceOrientation
duration:(NSTimeInterval)duration                                           // 5
{
   [[self scrollView] setScrollEnabled:NO];

   // Here, our pagingScrollView bounds have not yet been updated for the
   // new interface orientation. So this is a good place to calculate the
   // content offset that we will need in the new orientation.
   CGFloat offset = [self scrollView].contentOffset.x;
   CGFloat pageWidth = [self scrollView].bounds.size.width;
```

```
    if (offset >= 0) {
        [self setFirstVisiblePageIndexBeforeRotation:floorf(offset / pageWidth)];
        [self setPercentScrolledIntoFirstVisiblePage:
        (offset - ([self firstVisiblePageIndexBeforeRotation] * pageWidth))
         / pageWidth];
    } else {
        [self setFirstVisiblePageIndexBeforeRotation:0];
        [self setPercentScrolledIntoFirstVisiblePage:offset / pageWidth];
    }
}


- (void)layoutScrollViewSubviews                                        // 6
{
    [self setScrollViewContentSize];

    NSArray *subviews = [[self scrollView] subviews];

    for (PhotoBrowserPhotoView *view in subviews) {
        CGPoint restorePoint = [view pointToCenterAfterRotation];
        CGFloat restoreScale = [view scaleToRestoreAfterRotation];
        [view setFrame:[self frameForPageAtIndex:[view index]]];
        [view setMaxMinZoomScalesForCurrentBounds];
        [view restoreCenterPoint:restorePoint scale:restoreScale];
    }

    // Adjust contentOffset to preserve page location based on
    // values collected prior to location.
    CGRect bounds = [[self scrollView] bounds];
    CGFloat pageWidth = bounds.size.width;
    CGFloat newOffset = ([self firstVisiblePageIndexBeforeRotation] * pageWidth)
        + ([self percentScrolledIntoFirstVisiblePage] * pageWidth);
    [[self scrollView] setContentOffset:CGPointMake(newOffset, 0)];
}


- (void)willAnimateRotationToInterfaceOrientation:
(UIInterfaceOrientation)toInterfaceOrientation
duration:(NSTimeInterval)duration                                       // 7
{
    [self layoutScrollViewSubviews];

    // If the chrome is hidden, the navigation
    // bar must be repositioned under the status
    // bar.
    if ([self isChromeHidden]) {
        UINavigationBar *navbar = [[self navigationController] navigationBar];
        CGRect frame = [navbar frame];
        frame.origin.y = [self statusBarHeight];
```

```
        [navbar setFrame:frame];
    }
}

- (void)didRotateFromInterfaceOrientation:
(UIInterfaceOrientation)fromInterfaceOrientation
{
    [[self scrollView] setScrollEnabled:YES];
    [self startChromeDisplayTimer];
}

@end
```

Let's take a closer look at the changes:

1–2. Two properties are added to the PhotoBrowserViewController class extension. These properties store values needed during the rotation and repositioning
of the photo scroll views.

3–4. The new properties are synthesized.

5. The -willRotateToInterfaceOrientation:duration: method calculates the first visible page index and the percentage scrolled. The calculations
are based on the position in the scroll view's content area and the width of the
scroll view prior to resizing. This method also turns off scrolling. This prevents
the scroll view from changing pages during recalculations that occur during the
rotation. The check for whether scrolling is enabled or not is performed in the
-scrollViewDidScroll: callback method that you implemented earlier.

6. The method -layoutScrollViewSubviews is called during the rotation. It
repositions each photo within the scroll view while retaining the current zoom
scale. It then calculates and sets the new content offset for the scroll view.

7. The method -willAnimateRotationToInterfaceOrientation:duration:
calls -layoutScrollViewSubviews to reposition the photos within the scroll
view. It also repositions the navigation bar when the chrome is hidden. If the
navigation bar were not repositioned, autoresizing would have moved it off the
screen, making it unavailable to the user when the chrome is shown again.

8. The method -didRotateFromInterfaceOrientation: is called at the end
of the rotation sequence. It reenables scrolling for the user and starts the chrome
display timer.

And with that, the photo browser now supports all six possible interface orientations. Build the app, run it, and test the latest set of changes. Feel free to take your
iPad for a "spin." ☺

Fixing the Main Screen

Another rotation-related problem exists with the main screen. To see the problem, hold your iPad in portrait mode. Launch PhotoWheel and then tap on a photo to launch the photo browser. Now rotate the iPad to landscape mode. Tap the **Back** button to close the photo browser. The main screen did not rotate, as you can see in Figure 18.3.

The problem is caused by a design flaw with `UINavigationController` and the way it forwards rotation events. `UINavigationController` forwards rotation events only to the top view controller, so when using a `UINavigationController`, only the visible view controller receives the rotation events. This means that other view controllers on the stack do not receive the event notifications, and for those view controllers with views that rely on receiving the rotation events, the UI never rotates to the new interface orientation.

> **Note**
>
> If your view relies solely on autoresizing, this is not an issue for you.

Luckily, the fix is rather simple. The main screen receives appearance events including `-viewWillAppear:` when the top view controller is popped from the stack. You can use this opportunity to force the UI to rotate. The code to accomplish this is given in Listing 18.8. Just open the file *MainViewController.m* and add the code for the `-viewWillAppear:` method.

Figure 18.3   The main screen using the portrait layout in landscape mode

Listing 18.8 **Update to the** *MainViewController.m* **File**

```objc
@interface MainViewController ()
@property (nonatomic, assign) BOOL skipRotation;
@end

@implementation MainViewController

// Other code left out for brevity's sake.

@synthesize skipRotation = _skipRotation;

- (void)viewDidLoad
{
   // Other code left out for brevity's sake.

   [self setSkipRotation:YES];
}

- (void)viewWillAppear:(BOOL)animated
{
   [super viewWillAppear:animated];

   if ([self skipRotation] == NO) {
      UIInterfaceOrientation interfaceOrientation = [self interfaceOrientation];
      NSTimeInterval interval = 0.35;

      void (^animation)() = ^ {
         [self willAnimateRotationToInterfaceOrientation:interfaceOrientation
                                        duration:interval];
         for (UIViewController *childController in [self childViewControllers]) {
            [childController
            willAnimateRotationToInterfaceOrientation:interfaceOrientation
            duration:interval];
         }
      };

      [UIView animateWithDuration:interval animations:animation];
   }
   [self setSkipRotation:NO];
}

// Other code left out for brevity's sake.

@end
```

Let's spend a moment reviewing the code.

A class extension is added. The extension defines a new Boolean property named `skipRotation`. The property is used to bypass the forced rotation the first time `-viewWillAppear:` is called. Why do this? Tests of PhotoWheel showed that launching the app while the device is in landscape mode caused a slightly delayed animation sequence the first time the main screen was displayed. So this property was added to skip the rotation the first time.

> **Note**
>
> Set `skipRotation` to `NO` in the `-viewDidLoad` method to see the problem firsthand.

The other piece of code added to the `MainViewController` class is the `-viewWillAppear:` method. This method is called just prior to the view appearing on the screen. This means that the method is called when the photo browser is popped from the navigation stack.

This method creates an animation sequence that calls the rotation methods for the main view controller and each of its child view controllers. The reason this is done as an animation sequence is to make the visual transition from one orientation mode to another appear smooth.

It is important to point out that that while a view controller that uses containment will automatically forward rotation and appearance events to its child controllers, this autoforwarding does not happen when you explicitly call one of the rotation methods. Therefore, it is up to you to forward the calls to each child view controller.

Once you finish making the code changes, build and run the app. The main screen now rotates when the interface orientation changes while the photo browser is displayed.

Launch Images

One last topic related to orientation is the use of launch images. A launch image is an image that is displayed the moment the user taps the app icon on the Home screen. iOS is responsible for displaying the launch image and hiding it when your app is ready to run. Using a launch image gives the user the perception that the app has launched quickly even though it may still be loading.

> **Note**
>
> You may be tempted to use the launch image as a splash screen for your app. *Don't!* Users don't want to see your splash screen. They want to use your app. Need some convincing? Listen to Mike Lee's talk on *Making Apps That Don't Suck* (**www.infoq.com/ presentations/Making-Apps-That-Dont-Suck**).

A launch image is not a splash screen. It is an image representing the initial launch state of your app. It typically looks like the first screen of your app with no content.

An easy way to make a screen shot of your app is to use Organizer. With your device connected to your computer, open Organizer and select Devices, then select Screenshots under the section for your device. With your app running, click the **New Screenshot** button in Organizer. This takes a screen shot of your app's current screen, as shown in Figure 18.4. You can also click **Save as Launch Image** to add the image to your project.

When you create the launch image for your iPad app, you actually need to create two images, one image each for portrait and landscape modes. iOS will use the appropriate image based on the device orientation when the app is launched. The recommended size for the portrait launch image is 768 × 1004 pixels, and the recommended size for the landscape image is 1024 × 748 pixels. This leaves 20 pixels at the top to display the status bar.

Once you have the launch images, you need to tell your app about them. Add the launch images to your Xcode project, then open the *info.plist* file for the project. Add a new row with the key Launch Image (or Launch Image (iPad)) and set the value to the file name of the portrait version of your launch image, as shown in Figure 18.5.

You can skip the *info.plist* step by naming the portrait image *Default.png* and the landscape image *Default-Landscape.png*. The iPad will look for these images when the launch image is not defined in the *info.plist*. If, however, you wish to use a different name for the launch images, you must update the project's *info.plist* file.

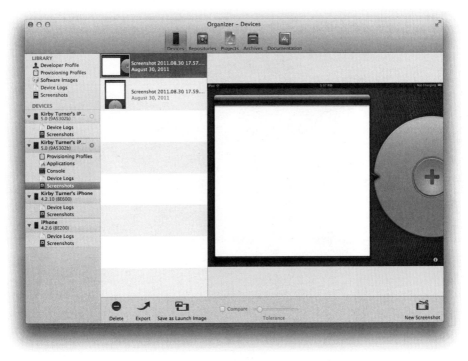

Figure 18.4   Screenshots available in Organizer

Key	Type	Value
Localization native development region	String	en
Bundle display name	String	${PRODUCT_NAME}
Executable file	String	${EXECUTABLE_NAME}
▶ Icon files	Array	(4 items)
Bundle identifier	String	com.whitepeaksoftware.${PRODUCT_NAME:rfc1034identifier}
InfoDictionary version	String	6.0
Bundle name	String	${PRODUCT_NAME}
Bundle OS Type code	String	APPL
Bundle versions string, short	String	1.0
Bundle creator OS Type code	String	????
Bundle version	String	1.0
Application requires iPhone environmer	Boolean	YES
▶ Supported interface orientations (iPad)	Array	(4 items)
Main storyboard file base name	String	MainStoryboard
Launch image (iPad)	String	Default.png

Figure 18.5   Specify the launch image in the project's *info.plist*.

The launch images for PhotoWheel are included in the set of images you added to the project back in Chapter 14, "Storyboarding in Xcode." The images are named *PW-Default.png* and *PWDefault-Landscape.png*. Find these files under the Images group in the Project navigator. Click each file name and rename it by removing the *PW* at the beginning of each name (Figure 18.6). PhotoWheel will now use these images as the launch images.

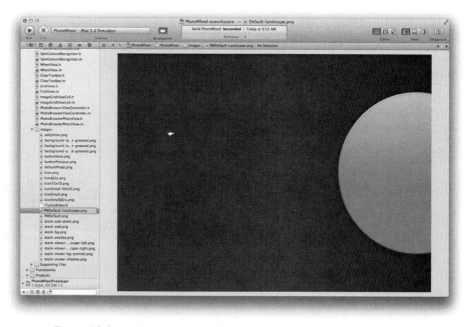

Figure 18.6   Use the Project navigator to rename the launch image files.

Summary

So there you have it, rotation and orientation in a nutshell. Armed with the knowledge from this chapter, you have no excuse for not supporting each interface orientation in your iPad apps. When adding rotation to your apps, remember to use autoresizing as much as possible. It will save you time and code. But do not just lock your app into portrait mode if autoresizing won't work for you. Take the time needed to support portrait and landscape in your UI. Your reward for the extra time and effort will be the satisfied users of your app.

Exercises

1. Change the landscape UI layout such that the photo album wheel is displayed on the left side instead of the right. Use the images *background-landscape-left-grooved.png* and *stack-viewer-bg-landscape-left.png* for the left-handed landscape layout.
2. Take screen shots of PhotoWheel and other apps using Organizer.

19

Printing with AirPrint

AirPrint is a feature added to iOS in version 4.2 that makes it possible to print wireless from the iPad. This is a welcome feature for many iPad users who prefer having a hard copy of content such as receipts from online purchases, documents, and images.

In this chapter, you will learn about the printing subsystem provided by iOS and how to incorporate printing into your own apps.

How Printing Works

Printing is a feature you build into your app. It is not something that is automatically provided to users of each and every app on the device. Your app must provide a way for the user to request that content be printed. This is usually a tap on a button displayed in a navigation bar or toolbar. When a user wants to print from your app, he taps the button (or whatever mechanism is provided by your app), which presents the printer options. The user then selects the desired printer and number of copies to print (Figure 19.1). And with a tap on the **Print** button, the content is sent to the printer.

> **Note**
>
> On the iPad, the Printer Options view is displayed in a popover, which you present from the button or view tapped by the user. The Printer Options view slides up from the bottom to fill the entire screen when presented on an iPhone or iPod touch.

Figure 19.1   The Printer Options view displayed in a popover on the iPad

Each print request issued by the user creates a print job. A print job is the combination of the content to print and the information needed to print, such as the printer name, name of the print job, and number of copies to print.

A print job is sent to the printing subsystem where the data is saved to storage (i.e., the data is spooled). The print job is then placed in the print queue where it waits for its turn to be printed. The print queue operates on a first-in first-out basis, and multiple applications on the same device can submit multiple print jobs to the printing subsystem. This means that a user can print from your app and while waiting for the print job to complete, print again from another app.

Print Center

The user can check the status of a print job that is printing or waiting to print by double tapping the Home button and selecting the Print Center app in the multitasking UI (Figure 19.2). Print Center is a background system application that is available only when a print job is processing. The Print Center makes it possible for the user to view detailed information about each print job and cancel jobs that are printing or waiting.

Requirements for Printing

Printing is available on any iOS device that supports multitasking and is running iOS version 4.2 or greater. If the device does not meet these minimum requirements, printing won't be available. In your app, it is up to you to check whether the device supports printing or not. If printing isn't supported, your app should not give the user an option to print (i.e., you need to hide the **Print** button). You will learn how to do this in a moment.

Figure 19.2   Print Center showing the details of a print job

Printing API

The programmatic interface for printing is provided by UIKit. The UIKit Printing API provides classes and a protocol giving you complete control of printing content from your application. Printing is managed through the shared instance of `UIPrintInteractionController`. The controller contains information about the print job (`UIPrintInfo`) and the paper (`UIPrintPaper`). It also contains the content to be printed. The content can be a single image or PDF document, an array of images or PDF documents, a print formatter (`UIPrintFormatter`), or a page renderer (`UIPrintPageRenderer`). The controller can also have a delegate object that conforms to the `UIPrintInteractionControllerDelegate` protocol.

The content types that are easiest to print are images and PDF documents. The content is an object reference to a `UIImage`, `NSData`, `NSURL`, or `ALAsset`. An `NSURL` object referring to the location of an image or PDF document must use the `file:` or `asset-library:` scheme or any scheme capable of returning an `NSData` object. To print an image or PDF document, set the `printingItem` property on the shared `UIPrintInteractionController` instance. To print a collection of images or PDF documents, store the object references in an `NSArray` and set the `printingItems` property.

To print slightly complex content that does not require headers and footers and can span multiple pages, you use one of the `UIPrintFormatter` concrete subclasses. These subclasses include `UISimpleTextPrintFormatter`, `UIMarkupTextPrintFormatter`, and `UIViewPrintFormatter`. Create an instance of the appropriate formatter object, then set the `printFormatter` property on the shared `UIPrintInteractionController` instance.

For complex content that can include headers and footers, use a custom class derived from `UIPrintPageRenderer`. A print renderer object draws pages of content to be printed, with or without using formatter objects. This is definitely the hardest way to print content, but it also gives you the maximum level of control over the printed output.

Adding Printing to PhotoWheel

PhotoWheel displays photos, and printing images is something that is easy with the `UIPrintInteractionController` class. So let's give the PhotoWheel user the option to print a photo from the photo browser.

The navigation bar in the photo browser already has an action button. This is the perfect place to display an action menu with a print option. (You'll add a send email option in the next chapter, which is why an action sheet is used here.) Here is how it should work from the point of view of the user.

The user taps the action button to display the action menu. Then the user taps the **Print** menu item. The Printer Options view is displayed. The user selects the printer, then taps the **Print** button. The current photo is sent to the printer, and the printer produces a copy of the photo.

The code to make this happen is simple. The -showActionMenu: method in the PhotoBrowserViewController class is changed to display the action sheet. The action sheet delegate callback -actionSheet:clickedButtonAtIndex: checks which menu item is tapped. If it is the **Print** action menu item, -printCurrent-Photo is called. This new method prepares the shared UIPrintInteraction-Controller instance, then displays it so that the user can print the photo.

That's all it takes to print a photo.

The code to accomplish the steps just described is shown in Listing 19.1. Apply the same code changes to your version of the *PhotoBrowserViewController.m* file.

Listing 19.1   **Add Print Support to the** PhotoBrowserViewController **Class**

```
- (void)showActionMenu:(id)sender                                    // 1
{
    [self cancelChromeDisplayTimer];
    UIActionSheet *actionSheet = [[UIActionSheet alloc] init];
    [actionSheet setDelegate:self];
    [actionSheet setTag:ACTIONSHEET_TAG_ACTIONS];
    if ([UIPrintInteractionController isPrintingAvailable]) {
        [actionSheet addButtonWithTitle:@"Print"];
    }

    [actionSheet showFromBarButtonItem:sender animated:YES];
}

#pragma mark - Printing

- (void)printCurrentPhoto
{
    [self cancelChromeDisplayTimer];                                 // 2
    UIImage *currentPhoto = [self imageAtIndex:[self currentIndex]]; // 3

    UIPrintInteractionController *controller =
        [UIPrintInteractionController sharedPrintController];        // 4
    if(!controller){
        NSLog(@"Couldn't get shared UIPrintInteractionController!");
        return;
    }

    UIPrintInteractionCompletionHandler completionHandler =
        ^(UIPrintInteractionController *printController, BOOL completed,
          NSError *error)
    {
        [self startChromeDisplayTimer];
```

```
        if(completed && error)
           NSLog(@"FAILED! due to error in domain %@ with error code %u",
                   error.domain, error.code);
    };                                                              // 5


    UIPrintInfo *printInfo = [UIPrintInfo printInfo];              // 6
    [printInfo setOutputType:UIPrintInfoOutputPhoto];             // 7
    [printInfo setJobName:[NSString stringWithFormat:@"photo-%i",
                           [self currentIndex]]];                  // 8


    [controller setPrintInfo:printInfo];                          // 9
    [controller setPrintingItem:currentPhoto];                    // 10


    [controller presentFromBarButtonItem:[self actionButton]
                               animated:YES
                      completionHandler:completionHandler];        // 11
}



#pragma mark - UIActionSheetDelegate methods

- (void)actionSheet:(UIActionSheet *)actionSheet
clickedButtonAtIndex:(NSInteger)buttonIndex
{
   [self startChromeDisplayTimer];

   // Do nothing if the user taps outside the action
   // sheet (thus closing the popover containing the
   // action sheet).
   if (buttonIndex < 0) {
      return;
   }

   if ([actionSheet tag] == ACTIONSHEET_TAG_DELETE) {
      [self deletePhotoConfirmed];
   } else if ([actionSheet tag] == ACTIONSHEET_TAG_ACTIONS) {      // 12
      [self printCurrentPhoto];
   }
}
```

Let's take a closer look at the code in Listing 19.1:

1. The NSLog() statement originally in -showActionMenu: is replaced with
   code that creates and shows an action sheet. A check is performed to make sure
   the device supports printing. If the device does not, the **Print** menu item is not
   added to the action sheet.

The chrome display timer is also turned off. The chrome should remain visible while the action sheet is displayed.

2. The method -printCurrentPhoto is the workhorse of the print feature for the photo browser. It starts by canceling the chrome display timer. The chrome should remain visible while the Printer Options view is displayed.

3. A reference to the current photo is retrieved; this is the content to be printed.

4. A reference to the shared UIPrintInteractionController is retrieved. This is followed by a check to ensure that a valid reference is returned. If it is not, an error message is logged to the console.

5. A completion block is created. This block is called when the print request completes. Within the block, the chrome display timer is started again, and if an error occurred, it is logged to the console.

6–8. A new instance of UIPrintInfo is created. The output type is set to UIPrint-InfoOutputPhoto, which produces the best-quality output for images, and the print job is named. Naming the print job is optional, but you should give the job a name that the user will recognize should the user need to cancel something he has queued up to print.

9. The printInfo object is assigned to the printInfo property found on the shared UIPrintInteractionController object.

10. The printingItem property for the shared UIPrintInteractionController is set to the photo reference, which is a pointer to UIImage. This tells the controller what content to print.

11. Finally, the Printer Option view is presented to the user.

The code change is ready to test, but how do you test printing? One option that saves paper and doesn't require a physical printer is to use the Printer Simulator.

The Printer Simulator

Included with Xcode is the Printer Simulator (Figure 19.3). The Printer Simulator registers different simulated printer types that can be used from your app to test printing, as shown in Figure 19.4.

The Printer Simulator is launched from the iOS Simulator by selecting the **File > Open Printer Simulator** menu item. The simulated printers are available to your app running in the iOS Simulator and on your iPad (as long as your iPad and the Printer Simulator are on the same network). The simulated printers remain available as long as the Printer Simulator is running. When you quit the simulator, the simulated printers are unregistered and no longer available to your app.

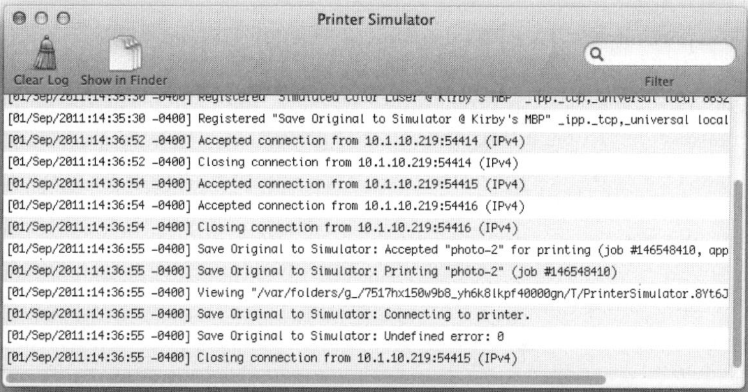

Figure 19.3   The Print Simulator running on a development
Mac computer

Figure 19.4   A list of simulated printers made available courtesy of the
Printer Simulator

Summary

This chapter gave you a basic understanding of how printing works in iOS. You
also got to see printing in action by adding a print feature to PhotoWheel. This
only scratches the surface of printing in iOS. To learn more, read the Printing section of the *Drawing and Printing Guide for iOS* (**developer.apple.com/library/
ios/#documentation/2DDrawing/Conceptual/DrawingPrintingiOS/
Introduction/Introduction.html**).

Exercises

1. Add a print option to the main screen that allows the user to print all photos.
2. Enable multi-selection on the photos grid view, and change the print option on the main screen to print only the selected photos.

20

Sending Email

Email is a common feature found in many iPad apps. There are two main reasons for this:

1. *Users want to share your app's content with their friends.*
2. *Email is easy to implement in iOS apps.*

PhotoWheel is no different. Users will want to share their favorite photos with others. And since adding email support is so simple, it would be a disservice to PhotoWheel users if we didn't include the feature. That is the focus of this chapter: to show you how to send email from your iPad app.

How It Works

iOS includes the Message UI Framework, which provides specialized view controllers for composing email and SMS messages. Once the user finishes composing an email, her message is sent to the appropriate subsystem where it is then sent out for delivery to the recipients.

Note

SMS messages are text-based only. Because PhotoWheel is a photo app, there isn't a strong use case for it to support SMS, so it is not covered in this book. Conceptually, however, sending an SMS message is no different from sending an email message. So learning how to send an email message points you in the right direction for sending SMS messages.

Warning

The subsystem for sending an email message is the Mail app within each iOS device. To send email from your app, the user must configure the device with a default email account. If the device is not set up with email, your app won't be able to send mail messages, and therefore your app should not give the user the option to send mail.

To send an email from your app (on a properly configured device), the app first displays the mail composition view (Figure 20.1). The `MFMailComposeView-Controller` class found in the Message UI Framework provides this view. The app can provide initial information for the email message such as a subject, recipients, message body, and attachments. The user can add to, change, and even delete the app-provided information in the mail composition view.

To send the message, the user simply taps the **Send** button and off it goes. This sends the email message to the Mail app, where it is placed into the Outbox. The Mail app is then responsible for sending the email message when there is an available network connection.

If the user decides not to send the email while in the message composition view, she needs to tap the **Cancel** button. The **Cancel** button gives her two choices: to delete the draft or to save it as a draft message where it can later be edited and sent (or deleted). Deleting the draft means that the mail message is gone forever. A deleted message is never sent to the Mail app. A saved draft, on the other hand, is sent to the Mail app. The user can decide later to edit and send the email from within the Mail app.

The Message UI Framework is designed in such a way that it leverages iOS's Mail app to handle the complexities of composing, queuing, and sending messages. From a developer's perspective, the Message UI Framework enables you to focus on what is

Figure 20.1   Screen shot of the mail composition view

important—building your app—without getting bogged down with having to write an entire messaging interface for your app. The best part is that all of this simplicity is transparent to the user. The Message UI Framework allows users to compose and send messages from your app, regardless of whether they are connected to a network. When a user isn't connected to a network (for example, when her iPad is in Airplane mode), messages are stored in Mail's Outbox until the user connects to a 3G or Wi-Fi network. The next time the user connects to a network and launches Mail, any messages in the queue from your app and others will be sent.

The `MFMailComposeViewController` Class

The `MFMailComposeViewController` class provides a standard email composition view that is displayed within your app. Since this view is provided by the system, the user sees the same view regardless of which app she is using. This consistency across third-party apps makes it easier for users to send email because the email experience remains the same.

To send an email from your app, your app creates an instance of the `MFMailComposeViewController` class. Initial message information, such as the list of recipients, subject, and message body, are set using this class. The view controller is then presented to the user as a modal view controller. The user edits the message (if any) and sends it on its way. Your app must provide a delegate object that conforms to the `MFMailComposeViewControllerDelegate` protocol. The delegate object is responsible for dismissing the view presented by the `MFMailComposeViewController` at the appropriate time.

Let's take a look at some code to better understand how sending email from your app works.

The `SendEmailController` Class

As part of learning how to send email, you will update PhotoWheel to allow users to email their photos. Users can send email from two different places within PhotoWheel:

- From the photo browser, the user will be able to send an email containing the current photo.
- From the photo album child view (displayed within the main screen), the user will be able to send an email containing all photos in a photo album.

To implement this, you add the code that uses the `MFMailComposeViewController` class to both the `PhotoBrowserViewController` and the `PhotoAlbumViewController`. The code needed in the two view controllers is the same, so rather than implement this twice, a better design is to consolidate redundant code by creating a new controller class to handle message sending.

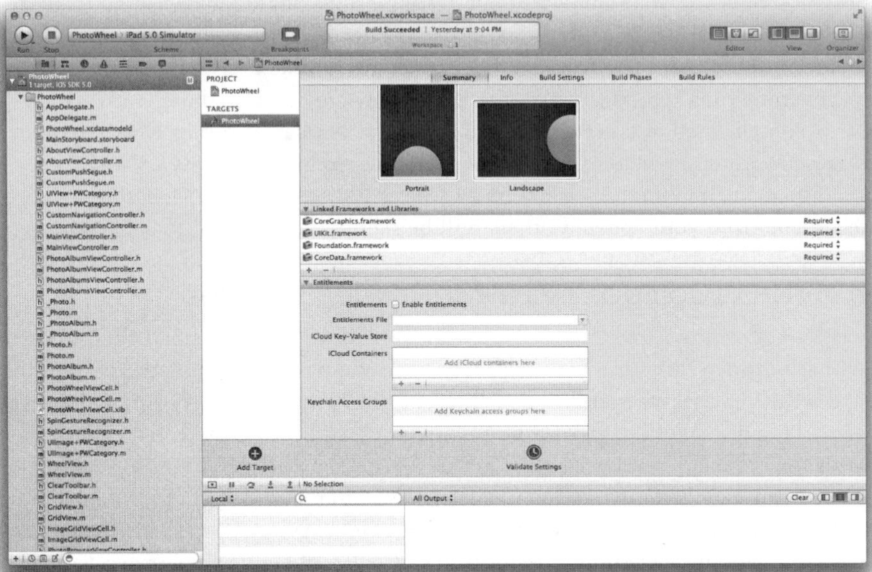

Figure 20.2   The project summary editor

But before you can create a new controller class, you need to add the Message UI Framework to the project. In the Project navigator, click the PhotoWheel project. In the Editor area, select the PhotoWheel target, then select the Summary tab. Scroll down to view the list of Linked Frameworks and Libraries (shown in Figure 20.2). Click the **+** button under the Linked Frameworks and Libraries section, and add *MessageUI.framework* to the project.

Now you are ready to create the new controller class for sending emails.

Introducing the `SendEmailController` Class

The new controller, `SendEmailController`, has a simple interface with two properties (`viewController` and `photos`), as shown in Listing 20.1. The `viewController` property is a reference to the view controller using the `SendEmailController` class. This view controller must conform to the `SendEmailControllerDelegate` protocol. The `photos` property is a reference to the set of photos to send.

> **Note**
>
> This new controller class is not a view controller, but it is still called a controller class because it controls the setup, display, and dismissal of the `MFMailComposeViewController` class.

The `SendEmailController` class also has two instance methods: `-initWith-`
`ViewController:` and `-sendEmail`. The first method is used to initialize the class
instance. The second method displays the mail composition view managed by the
`MFMailComposeViewController` class instance.

The class method `+canSendMail` wraps the `[MFMailComposeViewController`
`canSendMail]` call. It is provided so that the photo browser and photo album view
controller classes do not have to include the Message UI Framework header files.

The class interface is followed by the `SendEmailControllerDelegate` protocol
definition. The protocol has one required method that the delegate view controller
must implement, `-sendEmailControllerDidFinish:`. This method is called to
inform the view controller that the send email request was completed.

Now that you know what the interface to the class looks like, it's time to create it.
Start by adding a new Objective-C class to the project. Name the class `SendEmail-`
`Controller` and make it a subclass of `NSObject`. After the class files are added to the
project, update the *SendEmailController.h* file with the code in the Listing 20.1. Be sure
to include the header files from the Message UI Framework.

Listing 20.1   *SendEmailController.h*

```
#import <Foundation/Foundation.h>
#import <MessageUI/MessageUI.h>
#import <MessageUI/MFMailComposeViewController.h>


@protocol SendEmailControllerDelegate;


@interface SendEmailController : NSObject <MFMailComposeViewControllerDelegate>

@property (nonatomic, strong) UIViewController<SendEmailControllerDelegate>
*viewController;
@property (nonatomic, strong) NSSet *photos;


- (id)initWithViewController:(UIViewController<SendEmailControllerDelegate> *)
viewController;
- (void)sendEmail;

+ (BOOL)canSendMail;

@end


@protocol SendEmailControllerDelegate <NSObject>
@required
- (void)sendEmailControllerDidFinish:(SendEmailController *)controller;
@end
```

Next, open the file *SendEmailController.m* and add the implementation code shown in Listing 20.2.

Listing 20.2   *SendEmailController.m*

```objc
#import "SendEmailController.h"
#import "Photo.h"

@implementation SendEmailController

@synthesize viewController = _viewController;
@synthesize photos = _photos;

- (id)initWithViewController:(UIViewController<SendEmailControllerDelegate> *)
viewController
{
   self = [super init];
   if (self) {
      [self setViewController:viewController];
   }
   return self;
}

- (void)sendEmail
{
   MFMailComposeViewController *mailer = [[MFMailComposeViewController alloc]
                                          init];
   [mailer setMailComposeDelegate:self];
   [mailer setSubject:@"Pictures from PhotoWheel"];

   __block NSInteger index = 0;
   [[self photos] enumerateObjectsUsingBlock:^(id photo, BOOL *stop) {
      index++;
      UIImage *image;
      if ([photo isKindOfClass:[UIImage class]]) {
         image = photo;
      } else if ([photo isKindOfClass:[Photo class]]) {
         image = [photo originalImage];
      }

      if (image) {
         NSData *imageData = UIImageJPEGRepresentation(image, 1.0);
         NSString *fileName = [NSString stringWithFormat:@"photo-%1", index];
         [mailer addAttachmentData:imageData
                          mimeType:@"image/jpeg"
                          fileName:fileName];
      }
   }];
```

```
      [[self viewController] presentModalViewController:mailer animated:YES];
}


- (void)mailComposeController:(MFMailComposeViewController*)controller
          didFinishWithResult:(MFMailComposeResult)result
                        error:(NSError*)error
{
   UIViewController<SendEmailControllerDelegate> *viewController =
      [self viewController];
   [viewController dismissModalViewControllerAnimated:YES];
   if (viewController && [viewController respondsToSelector:
                            @selector(sendEmailControllerDidFinish:)])
   {
      [viewController sendEmailControllerDidFinish:self];
   }
}

+ (BOOL)canSendMail
{
   return [MFMailComposeViewController canSendMail];
}

@end
```

The implementation file starts by importing *Photo.h*. The Photo class is used to retrieve the photo, as you will see momentarily. Also toward the top of the listing are the synthesize statements for the declared properties defined in the class interface. These are followed by the -initWithViewController: method. This method is provided as a matter of convenience. All it does is set the viewController property to the view controller reference passed in on the method call.

The -sendEmail method is the juicy goodness that uses the Message UI Framework. The method begins by creating a local instance of the MFMailComposeView-Controller class. The SendEmailController class instance is set as the delegate to the view controller, and the subject is set to a string literal.

Next, the method enumerates the set of photos using a block. To make this class more flexible, the photo set can contain either UIImage or Photo object references. A check is performed on the object class type, and a local variable for the image is set based on the outcome of the class check. The image is then added as an attachment to the email message.

Once the enumeration block completes, the mail compose view controller is presented to the user. It is presented from the view controller provided at the time the SendEmailController class is initialized.

> **Why Support** `UIImage` **and** `Photo` **Objects?**
>
> The photo browser does not know about `Photo` objects. It only knows about `UIImage` objects. So when it wants to send an email, it needs to pass a `UIImage` object in the photo set.
>
> The `PhotoAlbumViewController` can do the same. It can build the photo set using `UIImage` object references instead of `Photo` model objects, but this would require the allocation of a `UIImage` object for each photo. This could cause a memory problem, so references to the managed model object are passed instead. The assumption here, be it a good one or bad, is that `MFMailComposeViewController` will manage the memory for attaching a potentially large number of images to an email message.

The next method in the listing is `-mailComposeController:didFinishWith-Result:error:`. This is a delegate method of the `MFMailComposeViewController-Delegate` protocol. The implementation dismisses the mail composition view, then informs the `SendEmailControllerDelegate` view controller that the send email request has finished.

The last method of the `SendEmailController` class is the class method `+canSendMail`. It is a wrapper for the class method of the same name on the `MFMailComposeViewController` class. This method returns `YES` if the device has been properly configured to send email; otherwise `NO` is returned.

Using `SendEmailController`

It's time now to update the `PhotoBrowserViewController` and `PhotoAlbum-ViewController` classes to use the new `SendEmailController` class. Start with the `PhotoBrowserViewController` class. The class interface must be modified to tell the compiler that it adopts the `SendEmailControllerDelegate` protocol. The class implementation must be modified to display an Email action item on the action button action sheet, and the action sheet callback must be modified to present the mail message composition view to the user by way of the `SendEmailController`.

The code changes are shown in Listing 20.3. Be sure to make these same changes to your copy of the `PhotoBrowserViewController` class.

Listing 20.3   Updated `PhotoBrowserViewController` **Class**

```
///////
// PhotoBrowserViewController.h
///////
#import <UIKit/UIKit.h>
#import "SendEmailController.h"                                      // 1

// Other code left out for brevity's sake.

@interface PhotoBrowserViewController : UIViewController <UIScrollViewDelegate,
UIActionSheetDelegate, SendEmailControllerDelegate>                  // 2
```

```
// Other code left out for brevity's sake.

@end


///////
//  PhotoBrowserViewController.m
///////

@interface PhotoBrowserViewController ()

// Other code left out for brevity's sake.

@property (nonatomic, strong) SendEmailController *sendEmailController;     // 3

// Other code left out for brevity's sake.

- (void)emailCurrentPhoto;                                                 // 4

@end

@implementation PhotoBrowserViewController

// Other code left out for brevity's sake.

@synthesize sendEmailController = _sendEmailController;                     // 5

// Other code left out for brevity's sake.

- (void)showActionMenu:(id)sender
{
   [self cancelChromeDisplayTimer];
   UIActionSheet *actionSheet = [[UIActionSheet alloc] init];
   [actionSheet setDelegate:self];
   [actionSheet setTag:ACTIONSHEET_TAG_ACTIONS];

   if ([SendEmailController canSendMail]) {                                 // 6
      [actionSheet addButtonWithTitle:@"Email"];
   }

   if ([UIPrintInteractionController isPrintingAvailable]) {
      [actionSheet addButtonWithTitle:@"Print"];
   }

   [actionSheet showFromBarButtonItem:sender animated:YES];
}
```

```objc
// Other code left out for brevity's sake.

#pragma mark - UIActionSheetDelegate methods

- (void)actionSheet:(UIActionSheet *)actionSheet
clickedButtonAtIndex:(NSInteger)buttonIndex
{
   [self startChromeDisplayTimer];

   // Do nothing if the user taps outside the action
   // sheet (thus closing the popover containing the
   // action sheet).
   if (buttonIndex < 0) {
      return;
   }

   if ([actionSheet tag] == ACTIONSHEET_TAG_DELETE) {
      [self deletePhotoConfirmed];

   } else if ([actionSheet tag] == ACTIONSHEET_TAG_ACTIONS) {
      // Button index 0 can be Email or Print. It depends on whether or
      // not the device supports that feature.
      if (buttonIndex == 0) {                                              // 7
         if ([SendEmailController canSendMail]) {
            [self emailCurrentPhoto];
         } else if ([UIPrintInteractionController isPrintingAvailable]) {
            [self printCurrentPhoto];
         }
      } else {
         // If there is a button index 1, it
         // will also be Print.
         [self printCurrentPhoto];
      }
   }
}

// Other code left out for brevity's sake.

#pragma mark - Email and SendEmailControllerDelegate methods

- (void)emailCurrentPhoto                                                  // 8
{
   UIImage *currentPhoto = [self imageAtIndex:[self currentIndex]];
   NSSet *photos = [NSSet setWithObject:currentPhoto];

   SendEmailController *controller = [[SendEmailController alloc]
                                      initWithViewController:self];
```

```
    [controller setPhotos:photos];
    [controller sendEmail];

    [self setSendEmailController:controller];
}

- (void)sendEmailControllerDidFinish:(SendEmailController *)controller    // 9
{
    if ([controller isEqual:[self sendEmailController]]) {
        [self setSendEmailController:nil];
    }
}

@end
```

Reviewing the code, you will notice the following:

1–2. The *SendEmailController.h* header file is imported, and the SendEmail-ControllerDelegate protocol is listed as one of the protocols supported by the PhotoBrowserViewController class.

3. In the implementation file, the sendEmailController declared property is added to the class extension. A reference to the SendEmailController class instance is kept while it is being used.

4. A new method, -emailCurrentPhoto, is added to the class extension. This method is called when the user taps the Email action item.

5. The sendEmailController property is synthesized.

6. The action sheet displaying the list of action items is updated to include Email if the device is able to send email messages.

7. The action sheet callback is updated to check for the Email action item. The item is at button index 0 if the device supports sending email; otherwise it is not available. The method -emailCurrentPhoto is called when it is determined that the user has indeed tapped the Email action item.

8. The method -emailCurrentPhoto grabs a reference to the current photo and adds it to an NSSet object. Then it creates a new instance of the class Send-EmailController, passes the photo set, and tells the controller to send email. This in turn presents the mail composition view to the user. Last, -email-CurrentPhoto sets the private declared property sendEmailController to the instance just created.

9. The method -sendEmailControllerDidFinish: is called by the Send-EmailController instance, informing the photo browser that the send email request has finished. At this point, the property reference to the SendEmail-Controller instance is set to nil, releasing it from memory.

A similar set of changes is made to the `PhotoAlbumViewController` class. The only difference is that instead of sending a `UIImage` object reference in the photo set, the photo set contains the collection of `Photo` model object references from the photo album. The code changes for the `PhotoAlbumViewController` class are shown in Listing 20.4. Be sure to make the same changes to your project.

Listing 20.4   **Updated** `PhotoAlbumViewController` **Class**

```
///////
//  PhotoAlbumViewController.h
///////
#import <UIKit/UIKit.h>
#import "GridView.h"
#import "PhotoBrowserViewController.h"
#import "SendEmailController.h"

@interface PhotoAlbumViewController : UIViewController
<UIActionSheetDelegate, UIImagePickerControllerDelegate,
UINavigationControllerDelegate, NSFetchedResultsControllerDelegate,
GridViewDataSource, PhotoBrowserViewControllerDelegate,
SendEmailControllerDelegate>

// Other code left out for brevity's sake.

@end



///////
//  PhotoAlbumViewController.h
///////

// Other code left out for brevity's sake.

@interface PhotoAlbumViewController ()

// Other code left out for brevity's sake.

@property (nonatomic, strong) SendEmailController *sendEmailController;

// Other code left out for brevity's sake.

- (void)emailPhotos;

@end

@implementation PhotoAlbumViewController
```

```objc
// Other code left out for brevity's sake.

@synthesize sendEmailController = _sendEmailController;

// Other code left out for brevity's sake.

- (IBAction)showActionMenu:(id)sender
{
   UIActionSheet *actionSheet = [[UIActionSheet alloc] init];
   [actionSheet setDelegate:self];

   if ([SendEmailController canSendMail]) {
      [actionSheet addButtonWithTitle:@"Email Photo Album"];
   }

   [actionSheet addButtonWithTitle:@"Delete Photo Album"];
   [actionSheet showFromBarButtonItem:sender animated:YES];
}

// Other code left out for brevity's sake.

- (void)actionSheet:(UIActionSheet *)actionSheet
clickedButtonAtIndex:(NSInteger)buttonIndex
{
   // Do nothing if the user taps outside the action
   // sheet (thus closing the popover containing the
   // action sheet).
   if (buttonIndex < 0) {
      return;
   }

   NSMutableArray *names = [[NSMutableArray alloc] init];

   if ([actionSheet tag] == 0) {
      if ([SendEmailController canSendMail]) [names addObject:@"emailPhotos"];
      [names addObject:@"confirmDeletePhotoAlbum"];

   } else {
      BOOL hasCamera = [UIImagePickerController
               isSourceTypeAvailable:UIImagePickerControllerSourceTypeCamera];
      if (hasCamera) [names addObject:@"presentCamera"];
      [names addObject:@"presentPhotoLibrary"];
   }

   SEL selector = NSSelectorFromString([names objectAtIndex:buttonIndex]);
   [self performSelector:selector];
}
```

```
// Other code left out for brevity's sake.

#pragma mark - Email and SendEmailControllerDelegate methods

- (void)emailPhotos
{
    NSManagedObjectContext *context = [self managedObjectContext];
    PhotoAlbum *album = (PhotoAlbum *)[context objectWithID:[self objectID]];
    NSSet *photos = [[album photos] set];

    SendEmailController *controller = [[SendEmailController alloc]
                                        initWithViewController:self];
    [controller setPhotos:photos];
    [controller sendEmail];

    [self setSendEmailController:controller];
}

- (void)sendEmailControllerDidFinish:(SendEmailController *)controller
{
    if ([controller isEqual:[self sendEmailController]]) {
        [self setSendEmailController:nil];
    }
}

@end
```

Congratulations! Your version of PhotoWheel now supports email. This will *surely* delight the users.

Summary

As you just learned, it is not that difficult to configure your iPad apps to handle email. The Message UI Framework and iOS's Mail app handle most of the work for you. Your app only needs to prepare the mail message and display the mail composition view provided by the MFMailComposeViewController class.

Exercises

1. Modify the code to send the large image instead of the original image.
2. Enable multi-selection on the photos grid view, and change the send email feature on the main screen to send only the selected photos.

Web Services

Many of today's apps have some level of integration with Web servers and services hosted on the Internet. There are many reasons why an iPad app may need to talk with a Web server. For instance, the app may need to download an image or a movie file, or maybe it needs to upload a file to a server. Other examples include calling a Web service to perform calculations, to update leaderboards, or to request data that gets displayed in your app. Whatever the reason may be, chances are good that one day you will need to incorporate Web services into your app.

This chapter gives you a basic introduction to using Web services. The focus is on the most common type of Web services in use today: RESTful Web services. This chapter does not attempt to cover every aspect of communicating with a Web server, but it does provide a jump start to using Web services within your app.

In this introduction to Web services, you will learn how to communicate with a Web server using the Cocoa classes, and you will learn how to parse JSON data. You will also learn how to use blocks to simplify your code for asynchronous processing and concurrent programming.

Let's get started.

The Basics

The term *Web service* means different things to different people. Say "Web service" to a C# programmer and SOAP-based services will likely come to mind. Say "Web service" to a Ruby programmer and REST-based services will likely be the first thing to come to mind. To some, a Web site is a Web service, and to others, a Web service is an API.

Why does this happen? Why does *Web service* mean different things to different people?

Technology people tend to think differently when hearing the term *Web service* because they tend to think in terms of the technology they are most familiar with. The technologies we are most comfortable with tend to influence our technical decisions and our way of thinking. A C# programmer, for example, writing a client-server solution where .NET is used on both ends will mostly likely use SOAP-based Web services because this is the preferred approach of .NET. To this programmer, a Web service is a SOAP-based service. But ask that same programmer to build a version of the same client app on the Mac desktop and iOS device. His eyes will be opened to a new approach to Web services as SOAP-based services are not the preferred approach in the Cocoa world.

So, what is a Web service?

From a generic point of view, a Web service is a method for communicating between two systems over a network, typically using HTTP. The rest of the techno-mumbo-jumbo surrounding Web services consists of approaches, protocols, and techniques built on top of this generic definition. This is not to belittle the mumbo-jumbo. On the contrary, it plays a very important role in deciding how communication between the two systems is achieved.

This being said, it is important to clarify the focus of this chapter with regard to Web services. This chapter teaches you how to use REST-compliant Web services, often called RESTful Web services. REST, or representational state transfer, is the style of architecture used by the Web and HTTP. Roy Fielding introduced the term *REST* in his doctoral dissertation released in 2000. A RESTful Web service has four basic design principles:

- It uses HTTP methods explicitly (GET, POST, PUT, and DELETE).
- It is stateless.
- It uses directory-structure-like URLs.
- It transfers data in XML or JSON (JavaScript Object Notation).

These design principles are not always strictly followed. For instance, a RESTful Web service is not limited to transferring data using XML or JSON. Data coming back from the server can be plain text, CSV-formatted, or another format other than XML and JSON.

The adoption of RESTful Web services was slow, but REST has become a popular choice for the majority of Web services hosted on the Internet today. This is because of its ease of use. Whereas other Web service methods such as SOAP require a toolkit or framework (typically provided by the programming environment's vendor), RESTful Web services can be used without any toolkit. That is not to say there are no RESTful frameworks. In fact, there are many for many different programming languages. But the power of REST comes from the fact that a framework is not needed. Any programming environment that can make an HTTP call can make use of RESTful Web services. Even a Web browser can be used to call a RESTful Web service.

RESTful Web Services Using Cocoa

Cocoa does not provide a RESTful framework, but it does provide the classes that make it possible to call and consume RESTful Web services from your iOS app. These classes are

- NSURL
- NSURLRequest

- `NSURLConnection`
- `NSXMLParser`
- `NSJSONSerialization`

`NSURL` is the object containing the URL to the Web service you want to call. The `NSURLRequest` object is used to build the HTTP request, and an `NSURL-Connection` object is used to submit the request over the network. When using the `NSURLConnection` object, you assign it a delegate object that conforms to the `NSURLConnectionDelegate` protocol. This protocol provides optional methods for interacting with the connection object as its state changes (e.g., authentication challenges and blocks of incoming data are received).

Once all the data has been received, you use either the `NSXMLParser` or `NSJSONSerialization` class to parse the contents of the data. `NSXMLParser` is an event-driven XML parser that works in a similar fashion to a SAX parser. It notifies a delegate about the items (e.g., elements, attributes, etc.) found as it processes the XML document.

The `NSJSONSerialization` class converts JSON data to Foundation objects (such as `NSDictionary`, `NSArray`, `NSString`, and `NSNumber`) and Foundation classes into JSON data. This class was introduced into the iOS SDK with the release of iOS 5. Prior to iOS 5, developers relied on open source libraries such as JSON Framework (**github.com/stig/json-framework/**) and TouchJSON (**github.com/TouchCode/TouchJSON**).

Armed with these five classes, you should be able to interact with any RESTful Web service available today, including Flickr.

Flickr

Flickr is a Web site for publishing and sharing photos. Flickr also provides a RESTful-Web-service-based API that developers like you can use in apps like PhotoWheel. In fact, that is what you will do now. You will update PhotoWheel so that users can search Flickr for photos and add photos to a PhotoWheel photo album.

Before the code presented in this chapter will work, you must set up a Flickr account and request a Flickr API Key, which Flickr uses to identify your app. The key is free for noncommercial use with the following conditions (published at **www.flickr.com/services/apps/create/apply**):

- Your app doesn't make money.
- Your app makes money, but you're a family-run, small, or independent business.
- You're developing a product that is not currently commercial but might be in the future.
- You're building a personal Web site or blog where you are using only your own images.

Note

A commercial key is available to organizations working the major brands or looking to make a profit from products and services related to Flickr beyond that of a family-run, small, or independent business.

To request a Flickr API Key, you must first sign up with Flickr. Go to **www.flickr.com**, click Sign Up, and follow the instructions for creating a new account. Once you have a Flickr account, sign in to your account and go to **www.flickr.com/services/apps/create/apply**. Click the button for **Apply for Non-Commercial Key** and tell Flickr about your app (Figure 21.1). You will receive the key within minutes of submitting your application information. You can find the key by opening the **You** drop-down menu and selecting **Your Apps** (Figure 21.2). The key is used by your app to make calls to the Flickr Web services.

Figure 21.1   Screen shot of the Flickr "Tell us about your app" Web page

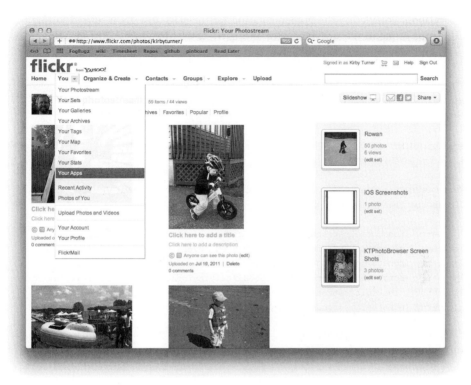

Figure 21.2   Find your API keys under the **You > Your Apps** menu item.

Adding Flickr to PhotoWheel

Once you have your Flickr API Key, you can update PhotoWheel to display and save photos from Flickr. To accomplish this, you need to make a number of changes to PhotoWheel, including the following:

- Add a new scene and view controller for the Flickr photo display.
- Add a search feature to the Flickr scene.
- Add a class wrapper for the Flickr API calls used by PhotoWheel.
- Parse the Flickr JSON response data.
- Download photos from Flickr asynchronously.

Start with adding the new view controller. Create a new Objective-C class named `FlickrViewController` and make it a subclass of `UIViewController`. Add the outlets and actions shown in Listing 21.1. Be sure to add `GridViewDataSource` and `UISearchBarDelegate` as protocols to the `FlickrViewController` class. Do not worry about completing the implementation for the class. Just get it started so that the UI can be set up in the storyboard (or alternatively use the Assistant editor while piecing together the UI). The stubbed view controller code is shown in Listing 21.1.

Listing 21.1   **Stubbed** FlickrViewController **Class**

```
///////
//  FlickrViewController.h
///////
#import <UIKit/UIKit.h>
#import "GridView.h"

@interface FlickrViewController : UIViewController <GridViewDataSource,
UISearchBarDelegate>

@property (nonatomic, strong) IBOutlet GridView *gridView;
@property (nonatomic, strong) IBOutlet UIView *overlayView;
@property (nonatomic, strong) IBOutlet UISearchBar *searchBar;
@property (nonatomic, strong) IBOutlet UIActivityIndicatorView *activityIndicator;
@property (nonatomic, strong) NSManagedObjectContext *managedObjectContext;
@property (nonatomic, strong) NSManagedObjectID *objectID;

- (IBAction)save:(id)sender;
- (IBAction)cancel:(id)sender;

@end


///////
//  FlickrViewController.m
///////
#import "FlickrViewController.h"

@implementation FlickrViewController

@synthesize gridView = _gridView;
@synthesize overlayView = _overlayView;
@synthesize searchBar = _searchBar;
@synthesize activityIndicator = _activityIndicator;
@synthesize managedObjectContext = _managedObjectContext;
@synthesize objectID = _objectID;

- (BOOL)shouldAutorotateToInterfaceOrientation:
(UIInterfaceOrientation)toInterfaceOrientation
{
    return YES;
}
```

```
#pragma mark - Actions

- (IBAction)save:(id)sender
{

}

- (IBAction)cancel:(id)sender
{

}

@end
```

A new class is added to the view controller that you have not used before: the `UISearchBar` class. This class provides a text field that can be used for text-based searches. It is used in the Flickr scene to capture search terms from the user.

The declared property `overlayView` may have you scratching your head, too. This is a dark, transparent view that is displayed on top of the grid view to prevent the user from interacting with the grid view during searches.

Another new class included in the `FlickrViewController` class interface is `UIActivityIndicatorView`. This displays a spinning wheel to indicate to the user that something is happening in the app and to please wait.

Updating the Flickr View Controller Scene

With the Flickr view controller class started, it's time to update the storyboard to include the new Flickr scene. Open the file *MainStoryboard.storyboard*. Drag a new view controller object into the storyboard to create a new scene. Select the view controller in the Document Outline, open the Identity inspector, and change the class name to `FlickrViewController`.

Add a toolbar to the top of the Flickr scene. Be sure to anchor the toolbar to the top using the Size inspector. Next, add a **Cancel** button on the left side of the toolbar and a **Save** button on the right side. Use the Attributes inspector for each button to set the Identifiers to Cancel and Save respectively. Use a flexible spacing bar button item to set the spacing for the two buttons.

Connect the **Save** button to the -save: action defined in the `FlickrView-Controller` class. Connect the **Cancel** button to the -cancel: action.

Add a search bar under the toolbar, then connect it to the `searchBar` outlet defined in the `FlickrViewController` class. Also set `FlickrViewController` as the delegate to the search bar object. If the delegate is not set, the search bar will not function properly.

Add a `UIView` object to the Flickr scene. This view should fill the remaining space of the container view. You can change the background color to green to make the view easier to see while you resize it. Just be sure to change it back to Default when you are finished. Also, set the autosizing property so that the view always fills the available space. This means turning on each autosizing constraint so that all are displayed as red. Finally, rename the class from `UIView` to `GridView`. This is used to display the photos retrieved from Flickr.

Add another `UIView` object that sits on top of the grid view. Make sure the new view also has its autosizing property set to always fill the area, and set its background color to black.

Now connect the grid view to the `gridView` outlet, and connect the `UIView` sitting on top of the grid view to the `overlayView` outlet. Also, set the `dataSource` for the `gridView` to the `FlickrViewController` object. If you don't do this, the search results won't appear.

Next, drag an activity indicator object to the Flickr scene and position it in the center of the screen. In the Attributes inspector for the activity indicator, turn on the Hides When Stopped option. And in the Size inspector, turn off all the autosizing constraints. When you have finished, connect the activity indicator to the `activity-Indicator` outlet defined in the `FlickrViewController` class.

Last, create a new segue between the photo album scene and the Flickr scene. The segue should be a modal segue. Set its Identifier to PushFlickrScene and the Presentation to Form Sheet. Leave the Transition as Default.

The updated storyboard should look like the one in Figure 21.3.

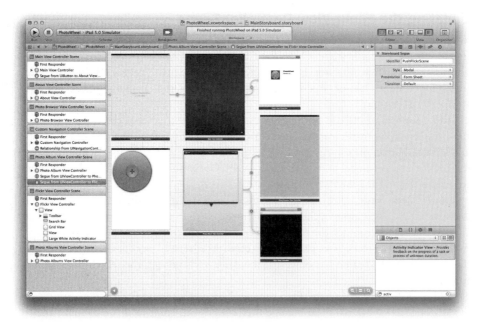

Figure 21.3 Updated storyboard

> **Note**
>
> Make sure the view hierarchy has the grid view, the overlay view, and the activity indicator at the levels shown in Figure 21.3. If a different view hierarchy is used, the scene may not display properly.

Displaying the Flickr Scene

To make sure the Flickr scene displays properly, add a new action item to the add button displayed in the photo album scene. In case you do not remember, this button calls the -addPhoto: action method, which in turn calls the -presentPhotoPickerMenu method.

Open the file *PhotoAlbumViewController.m* and apply the changes shown in Listing 21.2.

Listing 21.2   *PhotoAlbumViewController.m* **Changes**

```
#import "PhotoAlbumViewController.h"
#import "PhotoAlbum.h"
#import "Photo.h"
#import "ImageGridViewCell.h"
#import "FlickrViewController.h"                                    // 1

// Other code left out for brevity's sake.

@implementation PhotoAlbumViewController

// Other code left out for brevity's sake.

- (void)actionSheet:(UIActionSheet *)actionSheet
clickedButtonAtIndex:(NSInteger)buttonIndex
{
    // Do nothing if the user taps outside the action
    // sheet (thus closing the popover containing the
    // action sheet).
    if (buttonIndex < 0) {
        return;
    }

    NSMutableArray *names = [[NSMutableArray alloc] init];

    if ([actionSheet tag] == 0) {
        if ([SendEmailController canSendMail]) [names addObject:@"emailPhotos"];
        [names addObject:@"confirmDeletePhotoAlbum"];

    } else {
        BOOL hasCamera = [UIImagePickerController
                isSourceTypeAvailable:UIImagePickerControllerSourceTypeCamera];
```

```
            if (hasCamera) [names addObject:@"presentCamera"];
            [names addObject:@"presentPhotoLibrary"];
            [names addObject:@"presentFlickr"];                        // 2
        }

        SEL selector = NSSelectorFromString([names objectAtIndex:buttonIndex]);
        [self performSelector:selector];
    }

    // Other code left out for brevity's sake.

    - (void)presentFlickr                                               // 3
    {
        [self performSegueWithIdentifier:@"PushFlickrScene" sender:self];
    }

    - (void)presentPhotoPickerMenu
    {
        UIActionSheet *actionSheet = [[UIActionSheet alloc] init];
        [actionSheet setDelegate:self];
        BOOL hasCamera = [UIImagePickerController
                    isSourceTypeAvailable:UIImagePickerControllerSourceTypeCamera];
        if (hasCamera) {
            [actionSheet addButtonWithTitle:@"Take Photo"];
        }
        [actionSheet addButtonWithTitle:@"Choose from Library"];
        [actionSheet addButtonWithTitle:@"Choose from Flickr"];        // 4
        [actionSheet setTag:1];
        [actionSheet showFromBarButtonItem:[self addButton] animated:YES];
    }

    // Other code left out for brevity's sake.

    - (void)prepareForSegue:(UIStoryboardSegue *)segue sender:(id)sender   // 5
    {
        if ([[segue destinationViewController]
            isKindOfClass:[PhotoBrowserViewController class]])
        {
            PhotoBrowserViewController *destinationViewController =
                [segue destinationViewController];
            [destinationViewController setDelegate:self];
            NSInteger index = [[self gridView] indexForSelectedCell];
            [destinationViewController setStartAtIndex:index];
        } else if ([[segue destinationViewController]
                    isKindOfClass:[FlickrViewController class]])
        {
            [[segue destinationViewController]
                setManagedObjectContext:[self managedObjectContext]];
```

```
        [[segue destinationViewController] setObjectID:[self objectID]];
    }
}

// Other code left out for brevity's sake.

@end
```

Let's take a look at the changes:

1. The *FlickrViewController.h* header is imported.
2. The `presentFlickr` selector name is added to the array of selectors available for the add action sheet.
3. The `-presentFlickr` method is added. It is responsible for performing the segue PushFlickrScene.
4. The "Choose from Flickr" action item is added to the action sheet.
5. The biggest change is to the `-prepareForSegue:sender:` method. More than one segue can be performed; therefore, a check is required to make sure that the appropriate prep work is performed. The original code is enclosed in a check of the `destinationViewController`'s class type. If it is a `PhotoBrowser-ViewController` class, the original code is executed; otherwise a check for the `FlickrViewController` class is made.

   If the destination view controller is the `FlickrViewController` class, the managed object context and object ID values are passed. The `objectID`, in case you have forgotten, is the object ID for the selected photo album.

You can build and run the app if you like, but note that the Flickr scene will not dismiss when you tap the **Cancel** or **Save** buttons. This is because the `FlickrView-Controller` class has not been properly implemented yet. But before this class can be implemented, a couple of other new classes must be created and implemented.

Wrapping the Flickr API

Before the `FlickrViewController` can display photos from Flickr, the app must know how to communicate with Flickr. PhotoWheel will use the Flickr RESTful Web service API to communicate with Flickr. Because the Web service is RESTful, PhotoWheel relies on using standard Cocoa classes for communicating with the Flickr Web server.

> ### Note
>
> The Flickr API class presented here is a basic wrapper for some Flickr API calls. If you need to add full Flickr support to your app, consider using a Flickr API framework such as ObjectiveFlickr (**github.com/lukhnos/objectiveflickr**).

PhotoWheel uses only one Flickr API: the search API. For illustration purposes, however, the simple Flickr API wrapper class you are about to create supports four API calls. The extra calls are implemented to show you how you would update the class should you need to support additional API calls.

> **Note**
>
> The Flickr API documentation is available at **www.flickr.com/services**/api/. Please read the documentation if you want a better understanding of how each API works.

The Flickr API wrapper will be an Objective-C class, so add a new Objective-C class to the PhotoWheel project. Name the class `SimpleFlickrAPI` and make it a subclass of `NSObject`. The class will wrap four API calls, as shown in Listing 21.3.

Listing 21.3   *SimpleFlickrAPI.h*

```
#import <Foundation/Foundation.h>

@interface SimpleFlickrAPI : NSObject

// Returns a set of photos matching the search string.
- (NSArray *)photosWithSearchString:(NSString *)string;

// Returns the Flickr NSID for the given user name.
- (NSString *)userIdForUsername:(NSString *)username;

// Returns a Flickr photo set for the user. userId is the Flickr NSID
// of the user.
- (NSArray *)photoSetListWithUserId:(NSString *)userId;

// Returns the photos for a Flickr photo set.
- (NSArray *)photosWithPhotoSetId:(NSString *)photoSetId;

@end
```

Naturally, the implementation for the `SimpleFlickrAPI` class is more involved. The implementation code is provided in Listing 21.4. Add the code to your version of *SimpleFlickrAPI.m*, then return here for a walk-through of the code.

Listing 21.4   *SimpleFlickrAPI.m*

```
#import "SimpleFlickrAPI.h"
#import <Foundation/NSJSONSerialization.h>                              // 1

// Changes this value to your own application key. More info
// at http://www.flickr.com/services/api/misc.api_keys.html.
#define flickrAPIKey @"YOUR_FLICKR_APP_KEY"                            // 2

#define flickrBaseURL @"http://api.flickr.com/services/rest/?format=json&" // 3
```

```objc
#define flickrParamMethod @"method"                                        // 4
#define flickrParamAppKey @"api_key"
#define flickrParamUsername @"username"
#define flickrParamUserid @"user_id"
#define flickrParamPhotoSetId @"photoset_id"
#define flickrParamExtras @"extras"
#define flickrParamText @"text"


#define flickrMethodFindByUsername @"flickr.people.findByUsername"          // 5
#define flickrMethodGetPhotoSetList @"flickr.photosets.getList"
#define flickrMethodGetPhotosWithPhotoSetId @"flickr.photosets.getPhotos"
#define flickrMethodSearchPhotos @"flickr.photos.search"



@interface SimpleFlickrAPI ()                                              // 6
- (id)flickrJSONSWithParameters:(NSDictionary *)parameters;
@end

@implementation SimpleFlickrAPI

- (NSArray *)photosWithSearchString:(NSString *)string                     // 7
{
    NSDictionary *parameters = [NSDictionary dictionaryWithObjectsAndKeys:
                                flickrMethodSearchPhotos, flickrParamMethod,
                                flickrAPIKey, flickrParamAppKey,
                                string, flickrParamText,
                                @"url_t, url_s, url_m, url_sq", flickrParamExtras,
                                nil];                                       // 8
    NSDictionary *json = [self flickrJSONSWithParameters:parameters];      // 9
    NSDictionary *photoset = [json objectForKey:@"photos"];                // 10
    NSArray *photos = [photoset objectForKey:@"photo"];                    // 11
    return photos;                                                         // 12
}


- (NSString *)userIdForUsername:(NSString *)username                       // 13
{
    NSDictionary *parameters = [NSDictionary dictionaryWithObjectsAndKeys:
                                flickrMethodFindByUsername, flickrParamMethod,
                                flickrAPIKey, flickrParamAppKey,
                                username, flickrParamUsername,
                                nil];
    NSDictionary *json = [self flickrJSONSWithParameters:parameters];
    NSDictionary *userDict = [json objectForKey:@"user"];
    NSString *nsid = [userDict objectForKey:@"nsid"];

    return nsid;
}
```

```objc
- (NSArray *)photoSetListWithUserId:(NSString *)userId              // 14
{
    NSDictionary *parameters = [NSDictionary dictionaryWithObjectsAndKeys:
                                flickrMethodGetPhotoSetList, flickrParamMethod,
                                flickrAPIKey, flickrParamAppKey,
                                userId, flickrParamUserid,
                                nil];
    NSDictionary *json = [self flickrJSONSWithParameters:parameters];
    NSDictionary *photosets = [json objectForKey:@"photosets"];
    NSArray *photoSet = [photosets objectForKey:@"photoset"];
    return photoSet;
}


- (NSArray *)photosWithPhotoSetId:(NSString *)photoSetId            // 15
{
    NSDictionary *parameters = [NSDictionary dictionaryWithObjectsAndKeys:
                              flickrMethodGetPhotosWithPhotoSetId, flickrParamMethod,
                              flickrAPIKey, flickrParamAppKey,
                              photoSetId, flickrParamPhotoSetId,
                              @"url_t, url_s, url_m, url_sq", flickrParamExtras,
                              nil];
    NSDictionary *json = [self flickrJSONSWithParameters:parameters];
    NSDictionary *photoset = [json objectForKey:@"photoset"];
    NSArray *photos = [photoset objectForKey:@"photo"];
    return photos;
}


#pragma mark - Helper methods

- (NSData *)fetchResponseWithURL:(NSURL *)URL                      // 16
{
    NSURLRequest *request = [NSURLRequest requestWithURL:URL];      // 17
    NSURLResponse *response = nil;                                  // 18
    NSError *error = nil;                                           // 19
    NSData *data = [NSURLConnection sendSynchronousRequest:request
                                         returningResponse:&response
                                                     error:&error];  // 20
    if (data == nil) {                                             // 21
        NSLog(@"%s: Error: %@", __PRETTY_FUNCTION__, [error localizedDescription]);
    }
    return data;                                                   // 22
}

- (NSURL *)buildFlickrURLWithParameters:(NSDictionary *)parameters  // 23
{
    NSMutableString *URLString = [[NSMutableString alloc]
                                    initWithString:flickrBaseURL];
```

```objc
   for (id key in parameters) {
      NSString *value = [parameters objectForKey:key];
      [URLString appendFormat:@"%@=%@&", key,
        [value stringByAddingPercentEscapesUsingEncoding:NSUTF8StringEncoding]];
   }
   NSURL *URL = [NSURL URLWithString:URLString];
   return URL;
}

- (NSString *)stringWithData:(NSData *)data                          // 24
{
   NSString *result = [[NSString alloc] initWithBytes:[data bytes]
                                         length:[data length]
                                       encoding:NSUTF8StringEncoding];
   return result;
}

- (NSString *)stringByRemovingFlickrJavaScript:(NSData *)data        // 25
{
   // Flickr returns a JavaScript function containing the JSON data.
   // We need to strip out the JavaScript part before we can parse
   // the JSON data. Ex: jsonFlickrApi(JSON-DATA-HERE).

   NSMutableString *string = [[self stringWithData:data] mutableCopy];
   NSRange range = NSMakeRange(0, [@"jsonFlickrApi(" length]);
   [string deleteCharactersInRange:range];
   range = NSMakeRange([string length] - 1, 1);
   [string deleteCharactersInRange:range];

   return string;
}

- (id)flickrJSONSWithParameters:(NSDictionary *)parameters          // 26
{
   NSURL *URL = [self buildFlickrURLWithParameters:parameters];
   NSData *data = [self fetchResponseWithURL:URL];
   NSString *string = [self stringByRemovingFlickrJavaScript:data];
   NSData *jsonData = [string dataUsingEncoding:NSUTF8StringEncoding];

   NSLog(@"%s: json: %@", __PRETTY_FUNCTION__, string);

   NSError *error = nil;
   id json = [NSJSONSerialization JSONObjectWithData:jsonData
                                     options:NSJSONReadingAllowFragments
                                       error:&error];
   if (json == nil) {
      NSLog(@"%s: Error: %@", __PRETTY_FUNCTION__, [error localizedDescription]);
   }
```

```
    return json;
}

@end
```

Let's walk through the code so that you understand what is happening:

1. The NSJSONSerialization header file is imported. The Flickr API supports both XML and JSON. JSON is used by the SimpleFlickrAPI class because it is easier to parse and use than XML.

2. This #define is where your Flickr API Key is stored. This must match the key provided by Flickr.

3. Each RESTful API uses the same base URL. The base URL is stored as a macro, making it easy to change should Flickr ever change the URL. Also note the query string parameter format. It is set to json, which tells the Flickr API to return data formatted with JSON. You can change the parameter value to xml if you want XML returned by Flickr.

4. The Flickr API uses different parameter names. Instead of the Flickr API parameter names being hard-coded throughout, they are defined here as macros. The Flickr API parameters are defined as query string parameters on the HTTP GET request.

5. The Flickr API includes a parameter named *method*. This parameter defines which API method is called. The API methods supported by this simple wrapper are defined here as macros.

6. A class extension for SimpleFlickrAPI is defined. It declares the instance method -flickrJSONWithParameters:. This method takes a dictionary of parameters, calls Flickr, and returns the parsed JSON data.

7. The first Flickr API wrapped by the class is flickr.photos.search. It is wrapped in the method -photosWithSearchString:. This method takes a search string, asks Flickr to find any matching photos, and then returns an array of photos to the caller.

8. The first thing this method does is create a dictionary of Flickr parameters. This key-value pairing is used to construct the query string that is used when calling the Flickr Web server. The API method and key are the first two parameters in the dictionary. The search string provided by the caller follows this. The Flickr parameter extras provides a way for calling apps to request additional data to be included in the response data. The value url_t tells the Flickr API to include the thumbnail of the photo. url_s is a small version of the photo, _m is the medium-size version, and _sq returns a square (75 × 75-pixel) version of the photo.

   One thing that should be noted here is that the API does not actually return the photo image file. Instead, the response data includes the URL to the photo image. By telling the API to include the `url_t`, `url_s`, `url_m`, and `url_sq` photos in the `extras` parameter, you are telling the Flickr API to return the URLs to these photos.

9. The parameters are passed to the method `-flickrJSONWithParameters:`. As you will see in a moment, the method is responsible for making the call to the Flickr Web server. It also gathers the response data from the Web server and parses it into Foundation objects (i.e., `NSDictionary`, `NSArray`, `NSString`, etc.) using the `NSJSONSerialization` object.

10–11. The JSON data from Flickr for this API is converted into an `NSDictionary` object by the `NSJSONSerialization` class. The dictionary contains a key named `photos`, which represents the Flickr photo set for the search results. The `photoset` is another dictionary containing the key photo, and `photo` is an `NSArray` of photos. Each photo in the array is a dictionary containing data about the photo, including the URLs requested in the `extras` parameter.

12. The `photos` array is returned to the caller.

13–15. Examples of calling other Flickr API methods are provided. These methods are not used by PhotoWheel but are provided here as examples of how to make other API calls. You can see from these examples that a specific design pattern is followed: A dictionary of parameters is created. The parameters are passed off to the method that communicates with Flickr. The response data is returned and parsed, and the requested data is returned to the caller.

16. The method `-fetchResponseWithURL:` is responsible for making the actual Web service call to the Flickr Web server. The URL passed in is the Flickr API URL with parameters.

17. This method first creates an `NSURLRequest` object for the given URL.

18. A `nil` `NSURLResponse` object is also created. The response object is used to retrieve additional information, such as headers, from the HTTP response.

19. A `nil` pointer to an `NSError` is created. This pointer is set to a valid object reference if an error occurs during the request.

20. The `NSURLConnection` is used to call the Flickr Web server synchronously for the given request. The `response` and `error` pointers are set to valid object references if any are created during the request process. The synchronous call returns the data as an `NSData` object. This is a stream of the response data coming from the Flickr Web server, which is formatted as JSON.

21. If `nil` is returned for the response data, an error occurred during the request. The error is logged to the console. A more robust Flickr framework would return the error to the caller so that the caller can log it or report the error to the user.

22. Finally, the data is returned.

23. The method -buildFlickrURLWithParameters: takes the dictionary of parameters and creates the URL to the API call. This is done by appending each key-value pair in the dictionary as a query string parameter to the base Flickr API URL.

24. The method -stringWithData: converts the contents of an NSData object to a string. As you will see momentarily, the response data from Flickr requires a bit of tweaking before NSJSONSerialization can parse it.

25. The method -stringByRemovingFlickrJavaScript: returns a cleaned-up version of the Flickr API response data. The Flickr API wraps the response data in a JavaScript function, but the SimpleFlickrAPI wants only the JSON data. So the response data is converted from an NSData object to an NSString object. The JavaScript function is then stripped from the string, resulting in the string containing only the JSON-formatted data.

26. The method -flickrJSONWithParameters: is the method called by the wrapper methods defined at the top of the class. This method pulls all the pieces together to make the API call. It uses the parameters to create the API URL. It uses the URL to fetch the response data from Flickr. It removes the JavaScript function provided by Flickr. It then uses the NSJSONSerialization class to convert the JSON data into Foundation objects, which are returned to the caller. The method also logs the JSON data to the console so that you can see what the data looks like coming from Flickr.

That's it for making the Flickr API Web service call. As you can see, the majority of the code in the class centers on preparing the request and parsing the response. The actual Web service call takes only a few lines of code, as seen in the method -fetchResponseWithURL:. No additional toolkit or framework (beyond what is provided by the iOS SDK) is needed to make the API call. There is no converting the data into a SOAP message or any of that mess. Instead, a standard HTTP GET request with query string parameters is made and the response data is returned. Easy-peasy.

Downloading Photos Asynchronously

The Flickr API wrapper class SimpleFlickrAPI makes a synchronous call to the Flickr Web server. However, more times than not, you will need to make asynchronous calls to a Web server. PhotoWheel can get away with making a synchronous call to the Flickr API because the app waits for the Flickr call to return a list of photos. But there are times when you don't want your users waiting. One such time is when PhotoWheel is displaying the photos from Flickr.

Once the search completes and the list of photos is returned, the Flickr scene must display the photos in the grid view. It is here that the photos should be downloaded asynchronously, for two primary reasons:

- You want the app to remain responsive to the user. It should not appear frozen. The user should be allowed to do things such as tap the **Cancel** button to close the Flickr scene without having to wait until all the photos have downloaded.

- The search results can include more than one photo, and often there will be many more. Downloading and displaying 100 photos synchronously would take a long time, which in turn annoys the user. However, the user will perceive downloading the same number of photos asynchronously as fast because, well, it *is* faster.

One way to download the photos asynchronously is to create a separate thread for each download request, which downloads an image synchronously within the secondary thread. While this approach works, it is not necessary.

NSURLConnection uses the CFNetwork framework, which is extremely efficient at handling hundreds, if not thousands, of download requests without blocking the main thread of the app. This is due, in part, to the combination of the run loop and threads created as needed by the CFNetwork framework.

What Is the Runtime Loop?

When an iOS application is launched, a main thread is created for the app. The main thread is the primary thread running the app. The app is able to respond to events that are detected by the default run loop created on the main thread. The run loop is always running, performing various tasks from updating the UI to checking for hardware input to processing NSTimer object events. One of the tasks performed by the run loop is to check for incoming network data requested by NSURLConnection objects.

To learn more about this, read **developer.apple.com/library/ios/#DOCUMENTATION/ General/Conceptual/Devpedia-CocoaApp/MainEventLoop.html in the Apple documentation.**

The efficiencies of the CFNetwork framework combined with the run loop on the main thread make it possible to have simultaneous downloads without your explicitly creating and managing threads in your app.

Note

For more information on simultaneous downloads without creating your own threads, read the blog post *Downloading Images for a Table without Threads* by Jeff LaMarche (**iphonedevelopment.blogspot.com/2010/05/downloading-images-for-table-without.html**). This blog post is also the inspiration for the ImageDownloader class you create in this chapter.

Theory aside, how do you download multiple images (or any data, for that matter) from a Web server simultaneously without creating your own thread? For starters, you use NSURLConnection, but instead of making the call synchronously as you did in the SimpleFlickrAPI class, you make the call asynchronously. The asynchronous call still runs on the main thread, but it does not block the app thanks to the run loop and the secret sauce in CFNetwork.

As the NSURLConnection object receives data from the network, it calls its delegate object. The delegate object implements the optional methods from the NSURL-ConnectionDelegate protocol.

How would this work in the Flickr scene, which displays the downloaded photos in the grid view? One approach is to define an array of NSURLConnection objects in the FlickrViewController. The array contains the same number of NSURL-Connection objects as there are photos in the search results. The problem, however, is that the code becomes very messy, very fast.

Each NSURLConnection object calls the same set of delegate methods, and each delegate method needs to know that the downloaded data belongs to a particular photo. Not only that, but each downloaded photo must be displayed in the appropriate grid view cell, which only further complicates the code.

A much cleaner approach is to create a new class that is responsible for downloading an image. Instead of the FlickrViewController class managing an array of NSURLConnection objects, it can manage an array of this new image downloader object. One problem still exists, however: *The image download is asynchronous.* The new image download class needs to notify the FlickrViewController that the image has downloaded and is ready for display. The view controller must then display the image in the correct grid view cell. The image downloader class could use a delegate object, but it would introduce the same unnecessary mess in the view controller as was introduced by the NSURLConnection delegate.

It would be great if the view controller could tell the image downloader class to execute a particular snippet of code upon completion of the download. With blocks, you can do *exactly* that. You can define a block of code that is executed by the image downloader object after the download has completed.

Let's take a look at the code in Listing 21.5.

Listing 21.5   ImageDownloaderClass

```
///////
//  ImageDownloader.h
///////
#import <Foundation/Foundation.h>

typedef void(^ImageDownloaderCompletionBlock)(UIImage *image, NSError *); // 1

@interface ImageDownloader : NSObject

@property (nonatomic, strong, readonly) UIImage *image;                    // 2

- (void)downloadImageAtURL:(NSURL *)URL
            completion:(ImageDownloaderCompletionBlock)completion;        // 3

@end
```

```
///////
//  ImageDownloader.m
///////
#import "ImageDownloader.h"

@interface ImageDownloader ()
@property (nonatomic, strong, readwrite) UIImage *image;              // 4
@property (nonatomic, strong) NSMutableData *receivedData;            // 5
@property (nonatomic, strong) ImageDownloaderCompletionBlock completion;  // 6
@end

@implementation ImageDownloader

@synthesize image = _image;
@synthesize completion = _completion;
@synthesize receivedData = _receivedData;

- (void)downloadImageAtURL:(NSURL *)URL
              completion:(void(^)(UIImage *image, NSError*))completion // 7
{
   if (URL) {
      [self setCompletion:completion];
      [self setReceivedData:[[NSMutableData alloc] init]];
      NSURLRequest *request = [NSURLRequest requestWithURL:URL];
      NSURLConnection *connection = [[NSURLConnection alloc]
                                 initWithRequest:request
                                 delegate:self
                                 startImmediately:NO];
      [connection scheduleInRunLoop:[NSRunLoop currentRunLoop]
                        forMode:NSRunLoopCommonModes];        // 8
      [connection start];                                     // 9
   }
}

#pragma mark - NSURLConnection delegate methods              // 10

- (void)connection:(NSURLConnection *)connection
didReceiveResponse:(NSURLResponse *)response                 // 11
{
   [[self receivedData] setLength:0];
}

- (void)connection:(NSURLConnection *)connection
    didReceiveData:(NSData *)data                            // 12
{
   [[self receivedData] appendData:data];
}
```

```
- (void)connectionDidFinishLoading:(NSURLConnection *)connection          // 13
{
    [self setImage:[UIImage imageWithData:[self receivedData]]];
    [self setReceivedData:nil];

    ImageDownloaderCompletionBlock completion = [self completion];
    completion([self image], nil);
}

- (void)connection:(NSURLConnection *)connection
  didFailWithError:(NSError *)error                                       // 14
{
    [self setReceivedData:nil];

    ImageDownloaderCompletionBlock completion = [self completion];
    completion(nil, error);
}

@end
```

You need to add the ImageDownloader class to your PhotoWheel project. Create a new Objective-C class. Name the class ImageDownloader, make it a subclass of NSObject, and then copy in the code from Listing 21.5. Here is an explanation of the code you are copying:

1. The ImageDownloader class stores a completion block that is called once the image has been downloaded. To make the code more readable, the Image-DownloaderCompletionBlock typedef is defined. This avoids having to redeclare the block definition everywhere it is used.

2. The declared property image is a read-only property that returns the reference to the UIImage object containing the downloaded image. Its value is nil if the image has not been downloaded.

3. The ImageDownloader class has one public method, -downloadImageAtURL :completion:. It takes two parameters: the URL to the image and the completion block.

4. A class extension is defined for use internally. The first declared property of the class extension is image. image is redeclared as a writable property to allow updates internal to the class.

5. The declared property receivedData contains the data downloaded by the NSURLConnection object. The data can be received over the network in blocks (or batches). This is why receivedData is mutable. It allows the class to append data to the property as data is received from the network.

6. The declared property completion stores a reference to the code block provided by the caller. This block is called once the download has completed.

7. The first method found in the implementation is -downloadImageAtURL:
completion:. This is the public method that is called by the FlickrView-
Controller. It checks that a URL is provided, and if so, it stores the reference
to the completion block. It also starts the download request.

The download request is similar to what you saw when implementing the
SimpleFlickrAPI class. The difference here is that the NSURLConnection
object is set up for asynchronous instead of synchronous use. The receiveData
property is allocated with a new NSMutableData object. The NSURLRequest
object is created with the given URL. And the NSURLConnection object is
created and initialized with the request object and the ImageDownloader class
instance as the delegate. The startImmediately flag is set to NO to give the
class time to do more setup before starting the download.

8. Because you told the NSURLConnection object not to start immediately, the
run loop for the object can be changed. The default run loop for an NSURL-
Connection object is the run loop for the current thread. The call
[NSRunLoop currentRunLoop] returns the same run loop, the one for the
current thread. So the run loop for this NSURLConnection object does not
actually change. What does change, however, is the mode.

There are two modes for a run loop: NSDefaultRunLoopMode and NSRun-
LoopCommonModes. NSDefaultRunLoopMode is the most commonly used run
loop mode. It is intended to deal with objects other than NSURLConnection.
NSRunLoopCommonMode, on the other hand, is used to register objects with
all run loop modes in a common mode set. In essence, an object added to the
common run loop mode is monitored by all run loops in the common mode
set. Therefore, you should always use NSRunLoopCommonModes when using
NSURLConnection asynchronously. Without it, the responsiveness of NSURL-
Connection will not be as good and your Web service calls will seem slower to
respond.

9. Once the run loop mode for the connection object has been set, the connection
object starts the request process to download the image.

10. The remaining methods in the ImageDownloader class are callback methods
from the NSURLConnect object.

11. The method -connection:didReceiveResponse: is called when the Web
server responds to the request. The method might be called multiple times, as
is the case when the original request results in one or more redirects. When the
method is called, the receivedData property is reset with a length of zero,
clearing any previously stored data. This ensures that only the data received from
the final request is captured.

12. The method -connection:didReceiveData: is called as data is received from
the network. The method can be called multiple times during a single request.
The data is appended to the data already stored in the receivedData property.

13. The method -connectionDidFinishLoading: is called after the request has completed and all data has been received. This method converts the data stored in receivedData to a UIImage object. It then calls the completion block, passing a reference to the UIImage object.

14. The last method of the class, -connection:didFailWithError:, is called if an error is detected at any time during the download process. When this method is called, the error message is forwarded to the completion block.

And that, my friend, is how you make an asynchronous call to a Web server. You create an NSURLRequest object for an NSURL. You create an NSURLConnection object and initialize it with a request and delegate object. You set the run loop mode to common modes, then start the request process. Finally, you implement methods from the NSURLConnectionDelegate protocol that responds to events from the NSURLConnection object.

Although the ImageDownloader class is designed to download an image, the same pattern can be used to download other types of data.

Image Caching

One concept not presented here is caching downloaded images. In the real world, you don't want to keep downloading the same image over and over. Instead, you want to store the downloaded image (or whatever the asset might be) to the file system. As you will see momentarily, the FlickrViewController class uses a poor man's approach to caching the image. If the ImageDownloader object already has an image, that image is used instead of downloading it again.

If image caching is important to your app, you should roll your own cache manager or use an open source framework such as SDWebImage (**github.com/rs/SDWebImage**), which provides image caching for you.

Implementing FlickrViewController

With the SimpleFlickrAPI and ImageDownloader classes complete, you can once again turn your attention to the FlickrViewController class and complete its implementation.

The FlickrViewController class is responsible for performing a number of tasks. It searches Flickr for photos matching the search criteria provided by the user. It displays the matching photos in the grid view. It allows the user to select and deselect photos. And finally, it saves selected photos to the current photo album.

The code to accomplish all of this is shown in Listing 21.6. Open the file *FlickrViewController.m* in your PhotoWheel project and add the code from this listing.

As you add the code, you may notice that a good amount of it looks familiar. The GridViewDataSource methods, for example, follow the same pattern you have seen over and over in earlier chapters. The only real difference is how the grid view cell *retrieves* the image.

Listing 21.6 **Updated** *FlickrViewController.m* **File**

```objc
#import "FlickrViewController.h"                                        // 1
#import "ImageGridViewCell.h"
#import "SimpleFlickrAPI.h"
#import "ImageDownloader.h"
#import "Photo.h"
#import "PhotoAlbum.h"

@interface FlickrViewController ()
@property (nonatomic, strong) NSArray *flickrPhotos;                    // 2
@property (nonatomic, strong) NSMutableArray *downloaders;              // 3
@property (nonatomic, assign) NSInteger showOverlayCount;              // 4
@end

@implementation FlickrViewController

@synthesize gridView = _gridView;
@synthesize overlayView = _overlayView;
@synthesize searchBar = _searchBar;
@synthesize activityIndicator = _activityIndicator;
@synthesize managedObjectContext = _managedObjectContext;
@synthesize objectID = _objectID;
@synthesize flickrPhotos = _flickrPhotos;
@synthesize downloaders = _downloaders;
@synthesize showOverlayCount = _showOverlayCount;

- (void)viewDidLoad
{
    [super viewDidLoad];
    self.flickrPhotos = [NSArray array];
    [[self overlayView] setAlpha:0.0];                                 // 5

    UITapGestureRecognizer *tap = [[UITapGestureRecognizer alloc]
                                   initWithTarget:self
                                   action:@selector(overlayViewTapped:)];   // 6
    [[self overlayView] addGestureRecognizer:tap];

    [[self gridView] setAlwaysBounceVertical:YES];
    [[self gridView] setAllowsMultipleSelection:YES];                  // 7
}

- (void)viewDidUnload
{
    [self setGridView:nil];
    [self setOverlayView:nil];
    [self setSearchBar:nil];
```

```objc
    [self setActivityIndicator:nil];
    [super viewDidUnload];
}

- (BOOL)shouldAutorotateToInterfaceOrientation:
(UIInterfaceOrientation)toInterfaceOrientation
{
    return YES;
}

- (BOOL)disablesAutomaticKeyboardDismissal                          // 8
{
    return NO;
}

#pragma mark - Save photos

- (void)saveContextAndExit
{
    NSManagedObjectContext *context = [self managedObjectContext];
    NSError *error = nil;
    if (![context save:&error])
    {
        /*
         Replace this implementation with code to handle the error appropriately.

         abort() causes the application to generate a crash log and terminate.
         You should not use this function in a shipping application, although
         it may be useful during development. If it is not possible to recover
         from the error, display an alert panel that instructs the user to quit
         the application by pressing the Home button.
         */
        NSLog(@"Unresolved error %@, %@", error, [error userInfo]);
        abort();
    }

    [self dismissModalViewControllerAnimated:YES];
}

- (void)saveSelectedPhotos
{
    NSManagedObjectContext *context = [self managedObjectContext];
    id photoAlbum = [context objectWithID:[self objectID]];

    NSArray *indexes = [[self gridView] indexesForSelectedCells];
    __block NSInteger count = [indexes count];                      // 9
```

```
   if (count == 0) {                                              // 10
      [self dismissModalViewControllerAnimated:YES];
      return;
   }

   ImageDownloaderCompletionBlock completion =
      ^(UIImage *image, NSError *error) {                         // 11
      NSLog(@"block: count: %i", count);
      if (image) {
         Photo *newPhoto = [NSEntityDescription
                            insertNewObjectForEntityForName:@"Photo"
                            inManagedObjectContext:context];
         [newPhoto setDateAdded:[NSDate date]];
         [newPhoto saveImage:image];
         [newPhoto setPhotoAlbum:photoAlbum];
      } else {
         NSLog(@"%s: Error: %@", __PRETTY_FUNCTION__,
               [error localizedDescription]);
      }

      count--;                                                    // 12
      if (count == 0) {
         [self saveContextAndExit];
      }
   };

   for (NSNumber *indexNumber in indexes) {                       // 13
      NSInteger index = [indexNumber integerValue];
      NSDictionary *flickrPhoto = [[self flickrPhotos] objectAtIndex:index];
      NSURL *URL = [NSURL URLWithString:[flickrPhoto objectForKey:@"url_m"]];
      NSLog(@"URL: %@", URL);
      ImageDownloader *downloader = [[ImageDownloader alloc] init];
      [downloader downloadImageAtURL:URL completion:completion];

      [[self downloaders] addObject:downloader];
   }
}

#pragma mark - Actions

- (IBAction)save:(id)sender                                       // 14
{
   [[self overlayView] setUserInteractionEnabled:NO];

   void (^animations)(void) = ^ {
      [[self overlayView] setAlpha:0.4];
      [[self activityIndicator] startAnimating];
   };
```

```
    [UIView animateWithDuration:0.2 animations:animations];

    [self saveSelectedPhotos];
}


- (IBAction)cancel:(id)sender
{
    [self dismissModalViewControllerAnimated:YES];
}



#pragma mark - Overlay methods

- (void)showOverlay:(BOOL)showOverlay                                  // 15
{
    BOOL isVisible = ([[self overlayView] alpha] > 0.0);
    if (isVisible != showOverlay) {
        CGFloat alpha = showOverlay ? 0.4 : 0.0;
        void (^animations)(void) = ^ {
            [[self overlayView] setAlpha:alpha];
            [[self searchBar] setShowsCancelButton:showOverlay animated:YES];
        };

        void (^completion)(BOOL) = ^(BOOL finished) {
            if (finished) {
                // Do other cleanup if needed.
            }
        };

        [UIView animateWithDuration:0.2 animations:animations
                         completion:completion];
    }
}

- (void)showOverlay                                                    // 16
{
    self.showOverlayCount += 1;
    BOOL showOverlay = (self.showOverlayCount > 0);
    [self showOverlay:showOverlay];
}

- (void)hideOverlay                                                    // 17
{
    self.showOverlayCount -= 1;
    BOOL showOverlay = (self.showOverlayCount > 0);
    [self showOverlay:showOverlay];
```

```objc
    if (self.showOverlayCount < 0) {
       self.showOverlayCount = 0;
    }
}

- (void)overlayViewTapped:(UITapGestureRecognizer *)recognizer          // 18
{
    [self hideOverlay];
    [[self searchBar] resignFirstResponder];
}

#pragma mark - Flickr

- (void)fetchFlickrPhotoWithSearchString:(NSString *)searchString
{
    [[self activityIndicator] startAnimating];                          // 19
    [self showOverlay];
    [[self overlayView] setUserInteractionEnabled:NO];

    SimpleFlickrAPI *flickr = [[SimpleFlickrAPI alloc] init];
    NSArray *photos = [flickr photosWithSearchString:searchString];     // 20

    NSMutableArray *downloaders = [[NSMutableArray alloc]
                                 initWithCapacity:[photos count]];
    for (NSInteger index = 0; index < [photos count]; index++) {
       ImageDownloader *downloader = [[ImageDownloader alloc] init];     // 21
       [downloaders addObject:downloader];
    }

    [self setDownloaders:downloaders];                                  // 22
    [self setFlickrPhotos:photos];                                      // 23

    [[self gridView] reloadData];                                       // 24
    [self hideOverlay];
    [[self overlayView] setUserInteractionEnabled:YES];
    [[self searchBar] resignFirstResponder];
    [[self activityIndicator] stopAnimating];
}

#pragma mark - UISearchBarDelegate methods                              // 25

- (BOOL)searchBarShouldBeginEditing:(UISearchBar *)searchBar
{
    [self showOverlay];
    return YES;
}
```

```objc
- (void)searchBarTextDidEndEditing:(UISearchBar *)searchBar
{
  [searchBar resignFirstResponder];
  [self hideOverlay];
}


- (void)searchBarSearchButtonClicked:(UISearchBar *)searchBar        // 26
{
  [self fetchFlickrPhotoWithSearchString:[searchBar text]];
}


- (void)searchBarCancelButtonClicked:(UISearchBar *)searchBar
{
  [searchBar resignFirstResponder];
  [self hideOverlay];
}


#pragma mark - GridViewDataSource methods                            // 27

- (NSInteger)gridViewNumberOfCells:(GridView *)gridView
{
  NSInteger count = [[self flickrPhotos] count];
  return count;
}

- (GridViewCell *)gridView:(GridView *)gridView cellAtIndex:(NSInteger)index
{
  ImageGridViewCell *cell = [gridView dequeueReusableCell];
  if (cell == nil) {
    cell = [ImageGridViewCell imageGridViewCellWithSize:CGSizeMake(75, 75)];
    [[cell selectedIndicator] setImage:
     [UIImage imageNamed:@"addphoto.png"]];                          // 28
  }


  ImageDownloaderCompletionBlock completion =
    ^(UIImage *image, NSError *error) {                              // 29
    if (image) {
       [[cell imageView] setImage:image];
    } else {
       NSLog(@"%s: Error: %@", __PRETTY_FUNCTION__, [error
localizedDescription]);
    }
  };


  ImageDownloader *downloader = [[self downloaders] objectAtIndex:index];
  UIImage *image = [downloader image];                               // 30
```

```
    if (image) {
        [[cell imageView] setImage:image];
    } else {
        NSDictionary *flickrPhoto = [[self flickrPhotos] objectAtIndex:index];
        NSURL *URL = [NSURL URLWithString:[flickrPhoto objectForKey:@"url_sq"]];
        [downloader downloadImageAtURL:URL completion:completion];
    }

    return cell;
}

- (CGSize)gridViewCellSize:(GridView *)gridView
{
    return CGSizeMake(75, 75);
}

- (void)gridView:(GridView *)gridView didSelectCellAtIndex:(NSInteger)index
{
    id cell = [gridView cellAtIndex:index];
    [cell setSelected:YES];
}

- (void)gridView:(GridView *)gridView didDeselectCellAtIndex:(NSInteger)index
{
    id cell = [gridView cellAtIndex:index];
    [cell setSelected:NO];
}

@end
```

Even though a lot of the code looks familiar, let's still walk through it, just to make sure you understand everything that's going on:

1. The various header files for classes used by the view controller are imported. These include the two new classes you created, `SimpleFlickrAPI` and `ImageDownloader`.

2. The property `flickrPhotos` stores a local copy of the photo data returned from Flickr.

3. The property `downloaders` stores an `ImageDownloader` object for each photo in the `flickrPhotos` array. This is a quick-and-dirty attempt at caching the downloaded images. Each image is downloaded once for each photo for the life of the view controller. The images are cached to memory, which could lead to out-of-memory errors. But the Flickr API is returning a maximum of only 100 photos per request, so the potential for memory errors is low for this particular app.

4. The property showOverlayCount stores a stack count of the show and hide requests for the overlay. This is used to ensure that the overlay is not prematurely hidden.

5. The alpha for the overlay view is set to 0.0, which makes the view invisible.

6. A tap gesture is added to the overlay view; this is for usability's sake only. When the view controller is in search mode, the user can tap the overlay view to exit the mode.

7. The grid is configured for multiple selections. Multi-select is used to save more than one photo at a time to the photo album.

8. The method -disablesAutomaticKeyboardDismissal is an override method for NSViewController. This method is used to determine if the input view (i.e., the virtual keyboard) is automatically dismissed when changing controls. By default, the method returns NO except when the presentation style is UIModalPresentationFormSheet, where the default return value is YES.

   The problem with the default behavior in the FlickrViewController class is that the keyboard does not dismiss when [[self searchBar] resignFirstResponder] is called. This happens because the presentation style for the view controller is UIModalPresentationFormSheet. This is not the desired behavior for this view controller, so the method is overridden to return NO.

9. The number of selected cells is stored in the local variable count. The __block directive is used to make the variable mutable within the completion block defined a few lines down.

10. If the number of selected cells is zero, the view controller is dismissed and program control exits the method. Nothing else needs to be done.

11. The completion block for the ImageDownloader object is defined. If the block receives an image, a new Photo model object is created and its properties are set.

12. The local variable count is decremented by one. Since the variable was declared with the __block directive, it is mutable within the block. When the count reaches zero, all images have been downloaded and added to the photo album. Now the managed object context is saved and the view controller is dismissed.

13. Outside of the block is a for loop that downloads the medium-size image for each photo found in the Flickr search results. The downloaders are added to the downloaders array to ensure that they stay alive until the view controller is dismissed.

14. The method -save: is called when the user taps the **Save** button. Its primary role is to call the -saveSelectedPhotos method (described in code lines

9–13). It also turns off user interaction on the overlay view. This prevents the user from tapping the view, which normally will hide the overlay. It displays the overlay view to prevent the user from interacting with the grid view, and it displays the activity indicator informing the user that work is in progress.

15. The method -showOverlay: is called to show and hide the overlay when the search bar is in use. Pass in YES to show the overlay view, and NO to hide it.

16–17. The methods -showOverlay and -hideOverlay manage the display of the overlay view. Each call to -showOverlay increments the showOverlay-Count property, and each call to -hideOverlay decrements the count. When the count is greater than zero, the overlay view is visible; otherwise it is hidden.

18. When the overlay view is tapped, the gesture recognizer calls the -overlay-ViewTapped: method. This method hides the overlay view and the keyboard if displayed.

19–24. The method -fetchFlickrPhotoWithSearchString: is called to search Flickr. It displays the activity indicator telling the user that something is happening. It creates an instance of the SimpleFlickrAPI, then performs the search. When the search completes, the property downloaders is populated with instances of the ImageDownloader objects. The download process has not started, though. The photos returned from the Flickr API call are stored in the flickrPhotos property. Last, the grid view data is reloaded with the photos returned from Flickr.

25. Callback methods for the UISearchBarDelegate are implemented. These methods control the user experience when using the search bar.

26. The callback method -searchBarSearchButtonClicked: is called when it is time to perform the search. It calls the -fetchFlickrPhotoWithSearch-String: method.

27. The callback methods for GridViewDataSource are implemented. Each method uses the property flickrPhotos as the data.

28. The grid view is set up to support multi-selection. When a cell is allocated, the selected indicator image is set to the image *addphoto.png*.

29. Each cell displays an image of the photo from Flickr. However, the image must be downloaded first. The completion block for the ImageDownloader object is defined. The completion block sets the cell's image to the image passed in to the block.

30. If, however, the image was previously downloaded, the cell's image is set right away. There is no reason to download it again.

Those are the highlights from Listing 21.6. Build and run the app to test your changes.

```
All Output ÷                                                                    Clear
GNU gdb 6.3.50-20050815 (Apple version gdb-1708) (Mon Aug  8 20:32:45 UTC 2011)
Copyright 2004 Free Software Foundation, Inc.
GDB is free software, covered by the GNU General Public License, and you are
welcome to change it and/or distribute copies of it under certain conditions.
Type "show copying" to see the conditions.
There is absolutely no warranty for GDB.  Type "show warranty" for details.
This GDB was configured as "x86_64-apple-darwin".sharedlibrary apply-load-rules all
Attaching to process 11066.
2011-09-05 17:31:11.625 PhotoWheel[11066:15203] -[SimpleFlickrAPI flickrJSONSWithParameters:]: json:
{"stat":"fail", "code":100, "message":"Invalid API Key (Key has invalid format)"}
```

Figure 21.4 Invalid API key error message displayed in the debug console window

> **Note**
>
> If the Flickr search is not working, check to ensure that the outlet and delegate connections for the search bar have been made. Also verify the outlet and data source connections for the grid view. Finally, check your Flickr API Key. If it is missing or invalid, the search will fail with an "Invalid API Key (Key has invalid format)" message from Flickr. You can see this message in the debug console window shown in Figure 21.4.

One More Thing

When you ran PhotoWheel to test the Flickr changes, did you notice how the app freezes while searching Flickr? Even the activity indicator does not appear.

The problem is the synchronous call to Flickr made by the `SimpleFlickrAPI` object. Unlike the asynchronous call to the Flickr Web server in the `ImageDownloader` class, the synchronous call in `SimpleFlickrAPI` is blocking the main thread from performing additional steps in the run loop. This is why, for example, the activity indicator never displays. A quick solution to the problem is to use the `SimpleFlickrAPI` object on a background thread, but there's a better way.

Grand Central Dispatch (GCD) is a C-level API for concurrent programming. GCD offers three benefits over traditional multithreaded programming: It is easy to use, it is efficient, and performance is better. The GCD API makes heavy use of blocks. These make it easier to define a unit of work in code as compared to creating a thread. They also make your code more readable since the unit of work is coded in one place. When using threads, the unit of work is usually spread across multiple functions or even in a separate class file.

GCD uses dispatch queues to process units of work. Three types of dispatch queues are found in GCD: the main queue, global queues, and custom queues. The main queue executes on the main thread, and it is the same as performing a task on the main thread such as updating the UI. Global queues are concurrent queues shared throughout the lifetime of the app. Custom queues are queues you create.

To prevent blocking on the main thread during the Flickr fetch process, you can dispatch the fetch process to a global asynchronous queue. Once the process completes, you dispatch another unit of work to the main queue to update the UI. The code to accomplish this is shown in Listing 21.7.

Listing 21.7   **Updated Save Process to Use GCD**

```
- (void)fetchFlickrPhotoWithSearchString:(NSString *)searchString
{
   [[self activityIndicator] startAnimating];
   [self showOverlay];
   [[self overlayView] setUserInteractionEnabled:NO];

   dispatch_async(dispatch_get_global_queue(DISPATCH_QUEUE_PRIORITY_DEFAULT, 0),
^{
      SimpleFlickrAPI *flickr = [[SimpleFlickrAPI alloc] init];
      NSArray *photos = [flickr photosWithSearchString:searchString];

      NSMutableArray *downloaders = [[NSMutableArray alloc]
                                initWithCapacity:[photos count]];
      for (NSInteger index = 0; index < [photos count]; index++) {
         ImageDownloader *downloader = [[ImageDownloader alloc] init];
         [downloaders addObject:downloader];
      }

      [self setDownloaders:downloaders];
      [self setFlickrPhotos:photos];

      dispatch_async(dispatch_get_main_queue(), ^{
         [[self gridView] reloadData];
         [self hideOverlay];
         [[self overlayView] setUserInteractionEnabled:YES];
         [[self searchBar] resignFirstResponder];
         [[self activityIndicator] stopAnimating];
      });
   });
}
```

This code is almost identical to the original code. The exceptions are the two dispatch calls. The first dispatch call, `dispatch_async`, queues the unit of work in a global asynchronous queue. The global queue is retrieved by the function `dispatch_get_global_queue`.

Inside the block defining the first unit of work is another `dispatch_async` call. This time the main queue is used. This means that the unit of work defined in the second block is performed on the main thread, which is required since the unit of work is updating the user interface.

Apply this change to your version of the `FlickrViewController` class. Then build and run the app to see the difference made by using GCD.

What's Missing

Because this chapter is a basic overview, a number of topics were left out. Authentication and security are two topics that come to mind. Another is reachability.

Reachability is a term often used by iOS programmers to refer to a network's accessibility. The word *reachability* comes from the name of a class found in a networking sample provided by Apple (**developer.apple.com/library/ios/#samplecode/Reachability/Introduction/Intro.html**). The `Reachability` class is used to determine the current state of the network and to monitor changes in the network state. Apple recommends that any app using the network check the status of the network and gracefully handle situations where the network is not available.

Keep an eye on the *Learning iPad Programming* blog (**learnipadprogramming.com/blog/**) and the PhotoWheel source code repository (**github.com/kirbyt/PhotoWheel**) to see how other Web-service-related improvements are made to the app over time.

Summary

This chapter provided a basic overview of making RESTful Web service calls using the classes provided by Cocoa. It was just an introduction to using Web services and by no means a complete guide to using Web services in iOS apps. Full coverage of Web services would fill an entire book, but the topics covered in this chapter should point you in the right direction for building more robust support for Web services within your apps.

Exercises

1. It is possible for the Flickr search to return no photos. Included in the JSON data is the photo count. Update the app to check the photo count, and if the count is zero, display a "No photos found" message to the user.

2. Set your iPad to Airplane mode and run PhotoWheel. Try searching Flickr and see what happens. What changes can be made to improve the user experience?

22

Syncing with iCloud

At this point PhotoWheel is pretty useful. Users can work with their photos in a variety of ways. But the app is limited to a single device. It is increasingly common for people to have more than one iOS device and often a Mac as well. Wouldn't it be great if PhotoWheel could sync its data across multiple devices so that users could have their app data available on any of their devices? In this chapter we'll expand PhotoWheel to use Apple's iCloud service to sync photos and albums to different devices via the Internet. The technique we'll cover makes Core Data into a cloud-enabled data storage system.

Syncing Made Simple

In earlier releases of iOS, syncing data from one device to another was difficult. There were no standard, drop-in frameworks that would easily manage syncing data across multiple devices. App developers came up with various schemes, mostly for single apps. The bottom line was: *Syncing is hard*. It often seems simple enough at first, but in practice it is very tricky to get it right. Resolving conflicts without losing user data is a challenge that has defeated many developers.

Syncing also requires some means of transmitting an app's data from one device to another. This has been implemented by means such as building a Web server into an app so that data could be requested from other devices or by running an online service of some kind to handle syncing. Some apps used online services such as Dropbox to make data available across different devices. While quite useful, these services didn't really provide sync mechanisms.

Beginning with iOS 5.0, Apple introduced an online service called iCloud. With iCloud, users get access to a variety of cloud-based services such as automatic device backup and syncing of music, contacts, and other data across devices. The feature we're most interested in for PhotoWheel is built-in support for third-party apps that want to sync their own app data across iOS devices. With iCloud, Apple has (mostly) solved the syncing problem for you, providing both API support for your apps as well as the online server support necessary to make syncing happen.

Apple provides a free iCloud account to any user with an iOS 5 device, so your users can easily access this service at no extra charge.

iCloud Concepts

The key concept when working with iCloud is ubiquitous content. Data is said to be ubiquitous if the iCloud service monitors it and ensures that it is kept in sync among multiple devices that use the same iCloud account. This is in contrast to local content, which exists only in the app and is not synced via iCloud. Up to now, PhotoWheel has used only local content, but in this chapter we'll make it ubiquitous.

The general flow for creating ubiquitous content is to first create the content locally and then tell the operating system that it should be transferred to ubiquitous storage. The data will then be moved to a new location on the device. Uploading to the cloud is asynchronous and may not happen instantly, even if the device has a good network connection. When your app modifies the content locally, the iCloud daemon periodically updates the cloud-based copy of the data. If the user has installed the same app on other devices that use the same iCloud account, the updates are then available on those devices.

On the receiving end, the iCloud daemon will download updates to the app's data and then notify the app that new changes are available. Apps using iCloud are then responsible for reading the new data and updating views as needed.

File Coordinators and Presenters

Ubiquitous content can be read and written both by the app that created the content and by the iCloud daemon. In order to coordinate access to the data, iOS 5 introduces the concept of a file coordinator and a file presenter.

A file coordinator is just an instance of NSFileCoordinator. It acts as a read/write lock for file access. Multiple read requests can proceed simultaneously, but writing to a file requires an exclusive lock. When using a file coordinator, an app requests either read or write access to the data before accessing it, and the framework uses a read/write lock to keep the data intact.

A file presenter is any object that implements the NSFilePresenter protocol. If data is changed in a write action managed by an NSFileCoordinator, the file presenter for that data is notified of the change. It can then make whatever updates are necessary to present the new data to the user. You might implement this protocol on your model objects, your view controllers, or both, depending on how your app needs to respond to changes to its data.

The file presenter protocol also declares methods that notify your app of any sync conflicts. Although iCloud resolves most conflicts internally, it is not always possible to handle conflicts automatically. When this happens, your app will be notified of a new version of the data via the file presenter. The app must then resolve the conflicts, asking the user for help if it can't handle the conflict silently.

Combining these two, then, if an app using iCloud needs to update its data, it requests a write lock from an NSFileCoordinator and makes its changes. Another copy of the app, on a different device, receives a notification of this change via objects that implement NSFilePresenter.

UIDocument **and** UIManagedDocument

You don't necessarily need to use file coordinators and presenters in your own code, though. As a convenience, iOS 5 also introduces the UIDocument class for managing document-based data. Document-based data is any data that can be considered as individual, independent documents rather than as a single data store for an entire application. Word processors and spreadsheets are examples of apps that have document-based data. Calendars and to-do list applications usually are not document-based.

UIDocument implements the NSFilePresenter protocol and uses file coordinators to handle data access. To use UIDocument, you create a custom subclass that can manage your app's document data. UIDocument will create and use file coordinators as needed. Your subclass will need to implement the file coordinator methods, though, since UIDocument's implementations of these methods mostly do nothing.

If you have document-based data and you're using Core Data, you can use UIManagedDocument, which is a subclass of UIDocument. It creates and manages its own Core Data stack. By default it searches the app bundle for managed object models. It creates a persistent store coordinator and managed object context based on the file URL you provide when instantiating UIManagedDocument. This process can be customized if necessary.

It is worth noting that neither UIDocument nor UIManagedDocument is actually tied to iCloud. Each can be used for purely local document-based data that is never synced.

Ubiquitous Persistent Stores

If you're using Core Data but your data doesn't fit the document paradigm, you also can simplify the process of working with iCloud. Rather than create file coordinators and presenters, it is possible to simply configure the persistent store coordinator to make its data store ubiquitous. Setting up the Core Data stack is more or less the same as when you're not using Core Data. The major change is adding code to handle incoming changes from iCloud. The iCloud daemon will update the data store automatically, and the app will need to respond to these changes. Using this method is convenient for apps that already have Core Data stores, since existing data stores can be easily moved to iCloud storage.

When a ubiquitous persistent store is used, incoming changes are reconciled with local data on a record-by-record basis, preserving changes to individual attributes of entities. Core Data already incorporates conflict management, since handling Core Data conflicts is necessary when working with multiple threads. Conflicts are handled either automatically based on a merge policy you choose or by custom code you write to resolve conflicts.

This is the approach Apple recommends for "shoebox" apps—apps that contain a collection of related data but where the data doesn't fit the document paradigm or where the app simply does not expose documents to the user. PhotoWheel matches this description, so this is the approach taken in making PhotoWheel work with iCloud.

Device Provisioning, Revisited

Chapter 6, "Provisioning Your iPad," discussed setting up an App ID and a provisioning profile for use when developing apps. Before you can start working with iCloud, you need to make some changes to the App ID configuration and update your provisioning profile. Apps cannot access iCloud services unless the App ID has been configured for iCloud and the provisioning profile has been generated with this configuration. There are several steps you need to follow to enable an app to use iCloud, described in the following sections.

Configuring the App ID

Up to now, everything you have done with PhotoWheel could have been done using a wildcard App ID, that is, one with an *, which can be used with multiple applications. That is certainly convenient, but it won't work with iCloud. If you're using a wildcard App ID, you need to replace it with an explicit App ID. The differences and the process for creating an App ID are discussed in Chapter 6, "Provisioning Your iPad."

Once you have an explicit App ID, you need to configure it for use with iCloud. Start by logging in to the iOS Developer Center and going to the Provisioning Portal. In the portal, click App IDs in the navigation section on the left (Figure 22.1). In App

You'll see a list of your App IDs. Find the PhotoWheel App ID. The Provisioning Portal shows various capabilities available with this App ID (Figure 22.2). In App

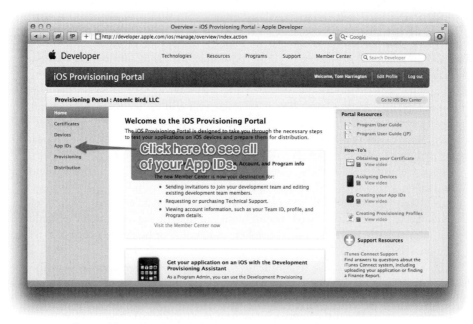

Figure 22.1   Finding the App IDs section of the provisioning profile

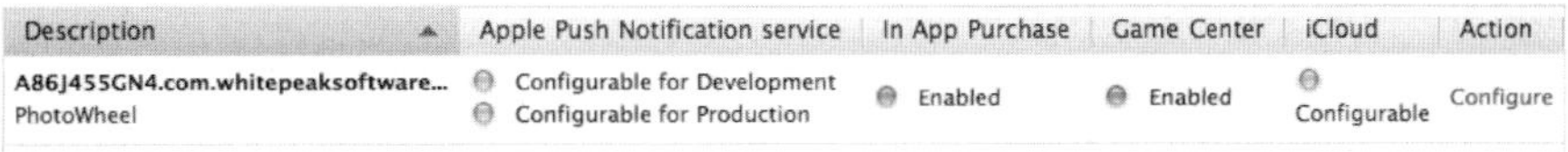

Description	Apple Push Notification service	In App Purchase	Game Center	iCloud	Action
A86J455GN4.com.whitepeaksoftware... PhotoWheel	⊖ Configurable for Development ⊖ Configurable for Production	⊜ Enabled	⊜ Enabled	⊖ Configurable	Configure

Figure 22.2   Current configuration of the PhotoWheel App ID

Purchase and Game Center are enabled by default with explicit App IDs. Push Notifications and iCloud are disabled but configurable. Click the **Configure** link in the rightmost column of the table to start configuring iCloud.

Once you do this, you'll see options to configure the App ID for use with Apple Push Notifications and for iCloud. Click the "Enable for iCloud" check box (Figure 22.3), and then click **Done**.

Figure 22.3   Configuration options for the PhotoWheel App ID

Provisioning for iCloud

Next, you need to regenerate your provisioning profile so that it includes the correct entitlements for the app to use iCloud. The Provisioning Portal doesn't have an option to simply regenerate an existing provisioning profile. To force it to regenerate the profile, you'll need to edit the profile and make a simple, even meaningless, change— adding or removing a device, for example. You can even remove a device and then add it back. Changing the name is a good idea since doing so makes it easy to distinguish the previous profile from the regenerated one.

Find the provisioning profile in the portal and click the **Edit** link, and then click **Modify** in the popup window (Figure 22.4).

Make your change to the provisioning profile and click **Submit**. Download the revised profile. To replace the previous copy, find it in Xcode's Organizer window (see Chapter 6, "Provisioning Your iPad," if you're not sure how). Select the old version and click the − button to delete it, then install the new version.

Figure 22.4   Modifying a provisioning profile

If you didn't previously generate a provisioning profile, you need to create one now, but it is not necessary to regenerate it to enable iCloud. Once you have enabled iCloud for the App ID as described earlier, all new provisioning profiles will include iCloud.

> **Note**
>
> The iPad Simulator does not support working with iCloud. When testing iCloud code, you must use a real iOS device (iPad, iPhone, or iPod touch).

Configuring iCloud Entitlements

Finally, the app needs a custom entitlements file. Entitlements files are XML property list files used by iOS that contain metadata about an application. To use iCloud, you need one that contains information about how the app will use iCloud. Specifically, the entitlements file will list container identifiers, which are used to determine where iCloud data is stored.

First, though, you need to get your development team's ID, since the container ID must contain the team ID. You can find this in the Member Center section of Apple's developer Web site. When you're logged in to the iOS Dev Center or the Provisioning Portal, there is a link at the top labeled **Member Center**. Click this link (Figure 22.5).

Figure 22.5   Getting to the Member Center

In the Member Center, click on **Your Account**, and then find Organization Profile. This page has a variety of information about your developer account. You need the value shown for Company/Organization ID, which is a 10-character code (Figure 22.6).

Now switch over to Xcode to add the entitlements file. Select the PhotoWheel project in the navigator, and then the PhotoWheel app target in the editor. If you scroll down to the bottom of the editor pane, you'll see a section named Entitlements (Figure 22.7).

Check the Enable Entitlements box. When you do, Xcode creates a new file in the project, called *PhotoWheel.entitlements*.

One of the entitlements sections is labeled iCloud Containers. Click the **+** button at the bottom of this section to add a container entry. This adds a blank line for the container identifier for the app.

The container identifier uses the team ID that you looked up earlier, plus a unique string that the app will use to manage iCloud content. Choose a custom container identifier of the form `<Team ID>.<Custom string>`. The custom string can be any string that makes sense to you, but it is convenient to make it the same as the app's Bundle ID. If your team ID is `A1B2C3D4E5` and the Bundle ID is `com.example.PhotoWheel`, a good choice for the container identifier would be `A1B2C3D4E5.com.example.PhotoWheel`.

Enter your container identifier on the blank line. The entitlements section should now resemble Figure 22.8.

Figure 22.6   Finding your team ID

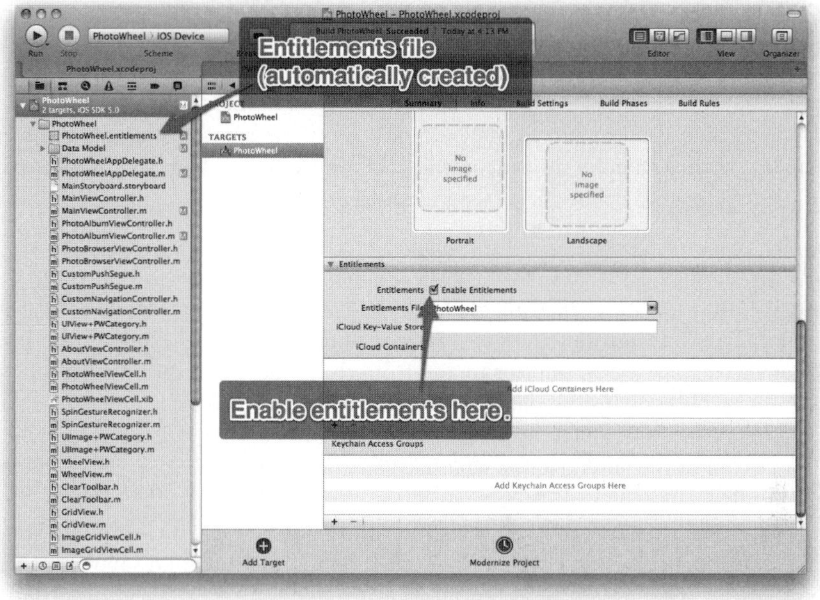

Figure 22.7   Enabling custom entitlements

Figure 22.8   iCloud entitlements for PhotoWheel

iCloud Considerations for PhotoWheel

Now that PhotoWheel is ready to use iCloud, you could start adding code to sync the app's data between devices. The existing Core Data model will work as is, with no changes. You'll need to add a couple of extra configuration options when the app starts up and code to handle new incoming changes from the cloud. Before doing that, though, let's give a little thought to whether that is really the best approach.

Don't Sync More Than You Need to Sync

Although iCloud accounts are available for free to any iOS 5 user, the data storage is not unlimited. A free account is capped at 5GB of data, and this includes space taken up by device backups. Also, transfer to and from the cloud is not instant. An iOS device might still be on a slow mobile phone network, but you still want syncing to happen as fast as possible. As a result, it's a good idea to consider whether you really want to sync all of the app's data or whether you could sync some of it and generate the rest locally.

You may recall that PhotoWheel saves four different versions of each photo: the original photo as well as three scaled versions. If you just add iCloud support to the current model, everything will be synced. But it is not really necessary to sync all of them—the scaled versions can be created from the original photo. The app could sync just the original photo and generate the scaled versions whenever it receives a new original from iCloud. The original is of course the largest of the images, but syncing the original is necessary to replicate the same data on all devices.

Using Transient Core Data Attributes

We'll still be using Core Data to manage the data model, but now we don't want Core Data to save the scaled images in the data store. Core Data has a "transient" attribute type that is designed for this purpose. Transient attributes are managed by Core Data while the app is running but are not actually saved to the data store. They are intended for data that can be generated at run time, such as data that can be derived from other attributes.

In Xcode, select the Core Data model file from the navigation pane. Click on the Photo entity's largeImageData attribute. In the Inspector, enable the Transient check box for this property (Figure 22.9).

Repeat this process for the smallImageData and thumbnailImageData attributes and save the data model. You don't need to regenerate the model class for the Photo entity, because the generated code is the same for transient and permanent attributes.

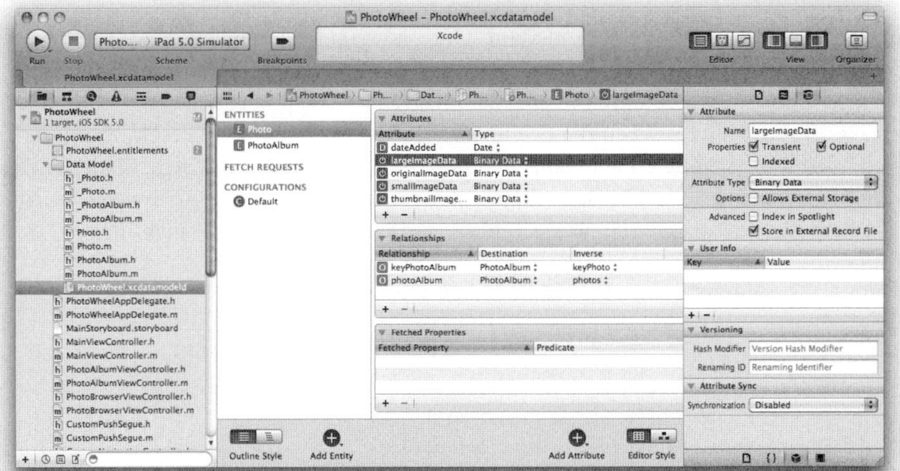

Figure 22.9   Making the `largeImageData` attribute transient

Changing Core Data Models

When creating a Core Data stack, it is crucial that the entities defined in the data model exactly match instances stored in any existing data stores. Any model change, no matter how minor, will prevent Core Data from initializing the stack without some help. This help takes the form of data model migration, which can be simple or complex depending on how much the model has changed.

If the app has not been released yet, it is common to bypass this by simply removing the app from the iPad and starting with a fresh copy. The first time the new build of the app runs, there is no data store and therefore no compatibility issues. That's what you'll do here, so after you change the model, make sure to remove the app from your iPad before attempting to compile and run it again. If you don't, the app will raise an exception as soon as it tries to load the data store.

Of course, if the app had already been released, this wouldn't be an acceptable solution. You would need to handle model migration so that your users' data would be preserved when they upgraded to the latest version of your app.

Updating PhotoWheel for iCloud

Now that the scaled image attributes are transient, you need to make some code changes to deal with keeping these images in external files. The original image is unchanged, but the other images need new code.

First you'll need to change the –saveImage: method in *Photo.m* to move the image-scaling code to a separate method. Until now the scaled images have been created only when the original image is first saved. With iCloud, new images delivered from the cloud will have only the original image, so the app needs to create the scaled images for those photos when the original image already exists. As a result, the app needs to run the scaling code independently of saving the original image. Code for this is shown in Listing 22.1. The only change this makes is breaking up –saveImage: into two methods: one to save the original image and one to create the scaled images.

Listing 22.1   Moving Image-Scaling Code into a Separate Method

```
- (void)saveImage:(UIImage *)newImage;
{
    NSData *originalImageData = UIImageJPEGRepresentation(newImage, 0.8);
    [self setOriginalImageData:originalImageData];
    [self createScaledImagesForImage:newImage];
}

- (void)createScaledImagesForImage:(UIImage *)originalImage
{
    // Save thumbnail
    CGSize thumbnailSize = CGSizeMake(75.0, 75.0);
    UIImage *thumbnailImage = [originalImage
        pw_imageScaleAndCropToMaxSize:thumbnailSize];
    NSData *thumbnailImageData = UIImageJPEGRepresentation(thumbnailImage, 0.8);
    [self setThumbnailImageData:thumbnailImageData];

    // Save large (screen-size) image
    CGRect screenBounds = [[UIScreen mainScreen] bounds];
    // Calculate size for retina displays.
    CGFloat scale = [[UIScreen mainScreen] scale];
    CGFloat maxScreenSize = MAX(screenBounds.size.width,
        screenBounds.size.height) * scale;

    CGSize imageSize = [originalImage size];
    CGFloat maxImageSize = MAX(imageSize.width, imageSize.height) * scale;

    CGFloat maxSize = MIN(maxScreenSize, maxImageSize);
    UIImage *largeImage = [originalImage pw_imageScaleAspectToMaxSize:maxSize];
    NSData *largeImageData = UIImageJPEGRepresentation(largeImage, 0.8);
    [self setLargeImageData:largeImageData];

    // Save small image
    CGSize smallSize = CGSizeMake(100.0, 100.0);
    UIImage *smallImage = [originalImage pw_imageScaleAndCropToMaxSize:smallSize];
    NSData *smallImageData = UIImageJPEGRepresentation(smallImage, 0.8);
    [self setSmallImageData:smallImageData];
}
```

Next, the app needs a method that returns the file path to use for one of the scaled image attributes. This method is used by both getter and setter methods to read and write the file. This is shown in Listing 22.2. Add this method to *Photo.m*.

Listing 22.2 Generating a Unique Path for an Attribute of a Managed Object

```
- (NSURL *)fileURLForAttributeNamed:(NSString *)attributeName
{
    if ([[self objectID] isTemporaryID]) {
        NSError *error = nil;
        [[self managedObjectContext]
            obtainPermanentIDsForObjects:[NSArray arrayWithObject:self]
            error:&error];
    }
    NSUInteger filenameID = [[[[self objectID] URIRepresentation]
        absoluteURL] hash];
    NSString *filename = [NSString stringWithFormat:@"%@-%ld",
        attributeName, filenameID];
    NSURL *documentsDirectory = [[[NSFileManager defaultManager]
            URLsForDirectory:NSDocumentDirectory
            inDomains:NSUserDomainMask]
        lastObject];
    return [documentsDirectory URLByAppendingPathComponent:filename];
}
```

This method generates a file name unique to the current photo by looking up the photo's `objectID`. The `objectID` is a unique identifier that is part of every managed object. The first part of the method checks to see if the `objectID` is temporary. When a managed object is first created, it has a temporary `objectID`. That ID is replaced with a permanent value when you save changes to the managed object context. If you need a permanent `objectID` before saving, you can ask the managed object context to make the conversion early. You need a permanent ID so that the generated file name won't change when you save changes.

The managed object ID is opaque but can be converted to a URI. The code does this and then asks `NSString` to calculate a hash value for the absolute URI string. This results in an integer unique to the current photo. The method uses this file ID to create a file name by combining it with the attribute name. For example, if the attribute name is `thumbnailImageData`, and the file name ID is `1234567890`, the file name would be `thumbnailImageData-1234567890`.

The file name is then added to the app's document directory path to produce a full path to a file that can be used for data owned by a specific `Photo` instance and that contains a specific attribute's image data.

Next, you need to add custom accessor methods for the `largeImage`, `small-Image`, and `thumbnailImage` attributes, which handle getting the data to and from files. The first step here is to create the setters. You'll need one setter per scaled image attribute; these are called `-setLargeImageData:`, `-setSmallImageData:`, and

-setThumbnailImageData:. These methods are identical except for the attribute name, so most of the code can be put in a common method used by all three setters. That makes four new methods, shown in Listing 22.3. Add these methods to *Photo.m*.

Listing 22.3 **Custom Attribute Setters for Scaled Image Attributes**

```
- (void)setImageData:(NSData *)imageData forAttributeNamed:(NSString *)
attributeName
{
    // Do the set
    [self willChangeValueForKey:attributeName];
    [self setPrimitiveValue:imageData forKey:attributeName];
    [self didChangeValueForKey:attributeName];

    // Now write to a file, since the attribute is transient.
    [imageData writeToURL:
        [self fileURLForAttributeNamed:attributeName] atomically:YES];
}

- (void)setLargeImageData:(NSData *)largeImageData
{
    [self setImageData:largeImageData forAttributeNamed:@"largeImageData"];
}

- (void)setSmallImageData:(NSData *)smallImageData
{
    [self setImageData:smallImageData forAttributeNamed:@"smallImageData"];
}

- (void)setThumbnailImageData:(NSData *)thumbnailImageData
{
    [self setImageData:thumbnailImageData forAttributeNamed:@"thumbnailImageD
ata"];
}
```

The incoming data is saved on the managed object using the -setPrimitiveValue: forKey: method of NSManagedObject. This method is used when overriding setters on managed objects. It sets the value on the managed object directly without implicitly calling any other setter method. The calls to -willChangeValueForKey: and -didChangeValueForKey: are a necessary detail of writing a custom Core Data setter method, and they ensure that features such as undo management work. Normally they would be handled by the dynamically generated setter method.

Along with custom setter methods, we need custom getters as well. As with the setters, the actual work of getting the data is identical for all three keys; the only difference is the attribute name. The code will therefore follow the same pattern of putting the common code in a single method called by all three of the attribute-specific getters. This code is shown in Listing 22.4.

Listing 22.4   Custom Getter Methods for Nonsynced Image Data

```objc
- (NSData *)imageDataForAttributeNamed:(NSString *)attributeName
{
    // Get the existing data for the attribute, if possible.
    [self willAccessValueForKey:attributeName];
    NSData *imageData = [self primitiveValueForKey:attributeName];
    [self didAccessValueForKey:attributeName];

    // If we don't already have image data, get it.
    if (imageData == nil) {
        NSURL *fileURL = [self fileURLForAttributeNamed:attributeName];
        if ([[NSFileManager defaultManager] fileExistsAtPath:[fileURL path]]) {
            // Read image data from the appropriate file, if it exists.
            imageData = [NSData dataWithContentsOfURL:fileURL];
            [self willChangeValueForKey:attributeName];
            [self setPrimitiveValue:imageData forKey:attributeName];
            [self didChangeValueForKey:attributeName];
        } else {
            // If the file doesn't exist, create it.
            [self createScaledImagesForImage:[self originalImage]];
            [self willAccessValueForKey:attributeName];
            imageData = [self primitiveValueForKey:attributeName];
            [self didAccessValueForKey:attributeName];
        }
    }

    return imageData;
}

- (NSData *)largeImageData
{
    return [self imageDataForAttributeNamed:@"largeImageData"];
}

- (NSData *)smallImageData
{
    return [self imageDataForAttributeNamed:@"smallImageData"];
}

- (NSData *)thumbnailImageData
{
    return [self imageDataForAttributeNamed:@"thumbnailImageData"];
}
```

The -imageDataForAttributeNamed: method handles a variety of cases to get the image data. First, it just checks to see if the image data has already been loaded, and if so, it returns it. If the image data has not already been loaded, the method looks for a file containing image data, using the -fileURLForAttributeNamed: method discussed earlier. If that file exists, the method loads image data from it. If the file doesn't exist, this implies that the external files have not been created yet, which would be the case if the photo had just been received from iCloud. In that case the method calls the –createScaledImagesForImage: method discussed earlier. Recall that it creates the scaled images and the files and also calls the setter methods for the scaled image attributes.

This method also includes extra code necessary when using a custom getter method on a managed object. In this case it uses –primitiveValueForKey:, the getter complement to –setPrimitiveValue:forKey:. It also uses –willAccessValue-ForKey: and –didAccessValueForKey: to notify the superclass that the method is accessing the attribute value directly. Again, this would normally be called by the dynamically generated getter.

Syncing Photos with iCloud

PhotoWheel now has the changes it needs to minimize the amount of data it syncs via iCloud. Now you can make the changes needed to actually sync the data. You'll make two types of changes: one to make the app's persistent store coordinator work with ubiquitous data and one to make the app respond to incoming changes from the cloud.

Making the Persistent Store Coordinator Ubiquitous

The only requirement to make a persistent store coordinator work with iCloud is that you must provide a value for the NSPersistentStoreUbiquitousContentNameKey option at creation time. This option just indicates the name that should be used for the data in iCloud. You may optionally also set a value for NSPersistentStore-UbiquitousContentURLKey, which allows control over where the ubiquitous data is stored. If you don't provide a value for this key, one will be generated.

To enable cloud storage on the persistent store coordinator, replace the existing –persistentStoreCoordinator method with the version from Listing 22.5.

Listing 22.5 Configuring the Persistent Store Coordinator to Work with iCloud

```
- (NSPersistentStoreCoordinator *)persistentStoreCoordinator
{
   if (__persistentStoreCoordinator != nil)
   {
      return __persistentStoreCoordinator;
   }

    __persistentStoreCoordinator = [[NSPersistentStoreCoordinator alloc]
         initWithManagedObjectModel: [self managedObjectModel]];

   NSURL *storeURL = [[self applicationDocumentsDirectory]
      URLByAppendingPathComponent:@"PhotoWheel.sqlite"];
```

```objc
dispatch_async(dispatch_get_global_queue(DISPATCH_QUEUE_PRIORITY_DEFAULT, 0), ^{

   // Build a URL to use as NSPersistentStoreUbiquitousContentURLKey
   NSURL *cloudURL = [[NSFileManager defaultManager]
      URLForUbiquityContainerIdentifier:nil];

   NSDictionary *options = nil;

   if (cloudURL != nil) {
      NSString* coreDataCloudContent = [[cloudURL path]
         stringByAppendingPathComponent:@"photowheel"];
      cloudURL = [NSURL fileURLWithPath:coreDataCloudContent];

      options = [NSDictionary dictionaryWithObjectsAndKeys:
         @"com.mycompany.photowheel",
         NSPersistentStoreUbiquitousContentNameKey,
         cloudURL,
         NSPersistentStoreUbiquitousContentURLKey,
         nil];
   }

   NSError *error = nil;
   [__persistentStoreCoordinator lock];
   if (![__persistentStoreCoordinator
      addPersistentStoreWithType:NSSQLiteStoreType
      configuration:nil
      URL:storeURL
      options:options
      error:&error])
   {
      NSLog(@"Unresolved error %@, %@", error, [error userInfo]);
      abort();
   }
   [__persistentStoreCoordinator unlock];

   dispatch_async(dispatch_get_main_queue(), ^{
      NSLog(@"asynchronously added persistent store!");
      [[NSNotificationCenter defaultCenter]
         postNotificationName:kRefetchAllDataNotification
         object:self
         userInfo:nil];
   });
});

   return __persistentStoreCoordinator;
}
```

This version of `-persistentStoreCoordinator` starts off the same way the old version did, but then it uses `dispatch_async` to finish setting up the coordinator on a background thread. Everything in the block passed to `dispatch_async` will happen asynchronously on a different thread. It does this to avoid blocking the main thread, which controls the user interface. If this is the first time the app runs on a device and there is a lot of preexisting iCloud data, it might take a long time to get all the data. Putting it on a background thread lets the user interface stay responsive while the background thread waits. This means that any fetch requests the app runs to manage the UI will return no results at first, since the persistent store coordinator doesn't have a data store yet.

The first thing that happens in the background is building `cloudURL`, the URL where iCloud data will go. The code starts off by passing the iCloud container ID to `NSFileManager`'s `URLForUbiquityContainerIdentifier` method. This asks iOS for the appropriate iCloud location to store iCloud data for your container ID. If you pass `nil` for the container ID, the method uses the first container ID found in the app's entitlements. You can't choose the URL's location—although you can create files and directories below this URL. The code does just that by appending *photowheel* to the URL and then setting `cloudURL` to the combined path.

Note that this is not the same location as the actual data store file. That location is in `storeURL` and is still in the app's documents directory. With `cloudURL`, you're configuring how the persistent store coordinator works with iCloud, but the actual data store is in the same place it has always been. This is very convenient because it means that you can add iCloud support to an app that already uses Core Data but still use the same data store. That would simplify the upgrade process for anyone using an older non-iCloud version of the app.

The method then creates a dictionary to contain the various options that the persistent store coordinator will use. It sets `cloudURL` as the value of `NSPersistentStoreUbiquitousContentURLKey` and `com.mycompany.photowheel` as the value of `NSPersistentStoreUbiquitousContentNameKey`. It is not necessary to use the app's Bundle ID for this key but it's convenient. Really, it can be anything that makes sense to you and to other developers on your team. There are other options you could use when configuring a persistent store coordinator, which you can read about in the class documentation.

If `URLForUbiquityContainerIdentifier` returns `nil`, the app leaves `options` set to `nil`. This would happen if the user has not configured an iCloud account. It would also happen if the user did configure an account but did not enable Documents & Data, which would mean that apps were not permitted to store data in the iCloud account. In this case the app continues just as it would without iCloud, using local-only data. If the user later adds an iCloud account or enables Documents & Data, the app's data would automatically start syncing to iCloud the next time the user runs the app.

Now that the options are configured, the method creates the persistent store coordinator. Since this code is running in a background thread, it locks and unlocks the coordinator before making the change. Persistent store coordinators are not thread safe, but they have their own locking mechanism in case you need to access one from a different thread.

Once that is done, the code posts a notification to tell the rest of the app that the data store is now available. View controllers can listen for this notification and update their views. Up until this point, the persistent store coordinator didn't have a data store, so fetches would return no data. Now that the data store is available, view controllers need to refetch data in order to get data from the store. The method does this in another dispatch_async call, which calls back from the background to the main thread. It does this because the user interface should be updated only on the main thread.

The notification name is kRefetchAllDataNotification, which isn't defined yet. This notification will be posted by the app delegate and received in view controllers, so the notification name needs to be defined somewhere available to all of those classes. A convenient place to do this is in *PhotoWheel-Prefix.pch*, which is automatically included in all source files in the project. Add this one line to *PhotoWheel-Prefix.pch*:

```
#define kRefetchAllDataNotification @"RefetchAllDatabaseData"
```

Now you can use this notification name anywhere it is needed. It is a common convention to name constant variables or defined constants with names that start with k, but it is not required.

Of course, that notification won't do any good unless the view controllers are actually listening for it. Both PhotoAlbumsViewController and PhotoAlbumViewController manage views using data from the data store, so both of them need to receive this notification and update their view. Add the code from Listing 22.6 to *PhotoAlbumsViewController.m*, in the viewDidLoad method.

Listing 22.6 Updating PhotoAlbumsViewController When the Persistent Store Coordinator Has Loaded the Data Model

```
[[NSNotificationCenter defaultCenter]
   addObserverForName:kRefetchAllDataNotification
              object:[[UIApplication sharedApplication] delegate]
               queue:[NSOperationQueue mainQueue]
          usingBlock:^(NSNotification *__strong note) {

       [self setFetchedResultsController:nil];
       [[self wheelView] reloadData];
   }];
```

When the notification is posted, this code gets rid of the existing fetched results controller and then tells wheelView to reload its data. The fetched results controller is re-created on demand in the -fetchedResultsController method, which is called when wheelView starts asking for data. This time the fetch returns data found in the data store.

There are a couple of related changes you need to make to avoid having
NSNotificationCenter try to call the block when the view has been unloaded or
when the view controller doesn't exist. In those cases the view controller should unregis-
ter for the notification. Add a –viewDidUnload method to *PhotoAlbumsViewController.m*
with the code from Listing 22.7. This handles the case where the view has been removed
because of low-memory situations.

Listing 22.7   Unregistering for Notifications in `PhotoAlbumsViewController`

```
- (void)viewDidUnload
{
    [super viewDidUnload];
    [[NSNotificationCenter defaultCenter]
        removeObserver:self
        name:kRefetchAllDataNotification
        object:nil];
}
```

Also, add a dealloc method that does the same thing. This is called whenever the
view controller is de-allocated. The dealloc method is shown in Listing 22.8.

Listing 22.8   dealloc Method for `PhotoAlbumsViewController`

```
- (void)dealloc
{
    [[NSNotificationCenter defaultCenter]
        removeObserver:self
        name:kRefetchAllDataNotification
        object:nil];
}
```

You need to make the same changes in `PhotoAlbumViewController`. The
changes there are nearly identical to the ones just given, except that

- Instead of calling [[self wheelView] reloadData] when the notification is
  posted, the block should call [self reload] to reload the photo grid view.
- Add the –removeObserver call to the –viewDidUnload and –dealloc
  methods.

Receiving Changes from iCloud

Great! Now the app can send data to iCloud. That's half the battle. Now you need to
make it notice incoming changes from the cloud for changes made on other devices.

When new changes are available, the iCloud daemon will download them in the
background. These changes are saved to the data store automatically. Once this is complete, the persistent store coordinator will post a notification with the ungainly name of

`NSPersistentStoreDidImportUbiquitousContentChangesNotification`. At that point the data store is up-to-date with the latest iCloud changes, but these don't automatically show up in your app. Any managed objects that have been loaded are still valid, and their values don't change. The app needs to tell any managed object contexts that it is using to get the incoming changes, and the app can then update its objects and views to reflect the new data.

To listen for this notification, change the `–managedObjectContext` method in *PhotoWheelAppDelegate.m* to look like Listing 22.9.

Listing 22.9 Updated Code to Create the Managed Object Context

```
- (NSManagedObjectContext *)managedObjectContext
{
    if (__managedObjectContext != nil)
    {
        return __managedObjectContext;
    }

    NSPersistentStoreCoordinator *coordinator = [self persistentStoreCoordinator];
    if (coordinator != nil)
    {
        __managedObjectContext = [[NSManagedObjectContext alloc]
            initWithConcurrencyType:NSMainQueueConcurrencyType];
        [__managedObjectContext performBlockAndWait:^(void) {
            [__managedObjectContext setPersistentStoreCoordinator:coordinator];

            [__managedObjectContext
                setMergePolicy:NSMergeByPropertyObjectTrumpMergePolicy];

            [[NSNotificationCenter defaultCenter]
                addObserver:self
                selector:@selector(mergeChangesFrom_iCloud:)
                name:
                    NSPersistentStoreDidImportUbiquitousContentChangesNotification
                object:coordinator];
        }];
    }
    return __managedObjectContext;
}
```

This makes a couple of changes from the previous version. First, it changes the initialization of the context to use `NSMainQueueConcurrencyType`. This means that any code executed by the managed object context will be performed on the main thread. However, to make that happen, it is necessary to enclose any code that uses the context in a block, and to execute that block using either `–performBlock:` or `–performBlockAndWait:`. So, after creating the context, that is what the code does.

Previously the code didn't indicate what concurrency type to use, which means that the managed object context used the default concurrency type of NSConfinement-ConcurrencyType. That doesn't add any threading help; it just means that you assume responsibility for making sure that the context is used on only one thread.

The next change is that this version of the method explicitly sets the context's merge policy. Merge policies are used when you need to tell a managed object context about changes to the data store that were made somewhere else, for example, by a different managed object context—or on a different device, in which case the changes would arrive from iCloud. The merge policy determines how conflicts will be resolved. By default, conflicts cause an exception. The NSMergeByProperty-ObjectTrumpMergePolicy option means that if there are changes in memory that conflict with objects loaded by the context, the in-memory changes should take priority. NSManagedObjectContext defines several other automatic merge policies that you can choose from depending on your app's requirements.

Once the context exists, the code adds self as an observer for incoming iCloud changes and arranges for notifications to call a method named –mergeChangesFrom_iCloud:. That method is shown in Listing 22.10.

Listing 22.10   **Callback for** NSPersistentStoreDidImportUbiquitous-
                 ContentChangesNotification

```
- (void)mergeChangesFrom_iCloud:(NSNotification *)notification {
    NSDictionary* userInfo = [notification userInfo];
    NSManagedObjectContext* moc = [self managedObjectContext];

    [moc performBlock:^{
        [self mergeiCloudChanges:userInfo forContext:moc];
    }];
}
```

The code in –mergeChangesFrom_iCloud: doesn't handle the incoming changes itself. It is just a "trampoline" method that uses –performBlock: to pass data from the incoming notification over to the main thread. Notifications are received on the thread that posted the notification, and there is no guarantee that this notification was posted on the main thread. This method gets the change information from the notification's userInfo property and passes that on to the main thread to be merged.

Next, you need to handle actually merging in the changes. The nice thing about this is that managed object contexts already know how to merge in data changes that were made in other places. This is often necessary even without iCloud, in cases where an app needs more than one managed object context. For example, an app might use a background thread to import a lot of data that should not be available to the main thread until all the changes have been saved. In that case it could use a secondary managed object context for the import and then merge those changes to the main thread when it finished. There is a built-in merging system designed to make one managed object context notice changes made in a different context, but it works just as well no matter where the changes actually come from. That makes it ideal for use with iCloud.

The catch is that the changes provided by `NSPersistentStoreDidImport-UbiquitousContentChangesNotification` are not in the format required by managed object context change merging. So, you need to add some code to run through the incoming changes and repackage them in a different format. This code goes in the `-mergeiCloudChanges:forContext:` method, shown in Listing 22.11.

Listing 22.11   **Merging Incoming Changes from iCloud**

```
- (void)mergeiCloudChanges:(NSDictionary*)noteInfo
  forContext:(NSManagedObjectContext*)moc
{
    @autoreleasepool {
        NSMutableDictionary *localUserInfo = [NSMutableDictionary dictionary];

        NSString* materializeKeys[] = { NSDeletedObjectsKey, NSInsertedObjectsKey
};
        int c = (sizeof(materializeKeys) / sizeof(NSString*));
        for (int i = 0; i < c; i++) {
            NSSet* set = [noteInfo objectForKey:materializeKeys[i]];
            if ([set count] > 0) {
                NSMutableSet* objectSet = [NSMutableSet set];
                for (NSManagedObjectID* moid in set) {
                    [objectSet addObject:[moc objectWithID:moid]];
                }
                [localUserInfo setObject:objectSet forKey:materializeKeys[i]];
            }
        }

        NSString* noMaterializeKeys[] = { NSUpdatedObjectsKey,
            NSRefreshedObjectsKey, NSInvalidatedObjectsKey };
        c = (sizeof(noMaterializeKeys) / sizeof(NSString*));
        for (int i = 0; i < 2; i++) {
            NSSet* set = [noteInfo objectForKey:noMaterializeKeys[i]];
            if ([set count] > 0) {
                NSMutableSet* objectSet = [NSMutableSet set];
                for (NSManagedObjectID* moid in set) {
                    NSManagedObject* realObj = [moc objectRegisteredForID:moid];
                    if (realObj) {
                        [objectSet addObject:realObj];
                    }
                }
                [localUserInfo setObject:objectSet forKey:noMaterializeKeys[i]];
            }
        }
```

```
        NSNotification *fakeSave = [NSNotification
            notificationWithName:NSManagedObjectContextDidSaveNotification
            object:self
            userInfo:localUserInfo];
        [moc mergeChangesFromContextDidSaveNotification:fakeSave];

        [moc processPendingChanges];
    }
}
```

The two loops in this method run through the incoming changes and repackage them in a form that NSManagedObjectContext can handle automatically. The first loop handles instances that have been added or deleted by the change, which are always merged in to the managed object context. The second loop handles changes to existing objects. These are merged in to the managed object context only if they have already been loaded from the data store. If they have not, there is no need to merge the change, because the new values will be read from the data store if and when the entity is loaded.

The key part of the method is at the end, with the fakeSave notification. When a managed object context saves changes, it posts a notification named NSManaged-ObjectContextDidSaveNotification. If the app has any other managed object contexts, it can listen for this notification and then tell the other contexts to merge in the changes contained in the notification. NSManagedObjectContext has a method called mergeChangesFromContextDidSaveNotification that handles this. Here, the method builds up an NSDictionary called localUserInfo that has the same format as the information contained in NSManagedObjectContextDidSave-Notification. It passes this to the managed context *as if the changes had come from another managed object context,* even though they came from iCloud. The managed object context merges the data automatically.

Merging happens automatically according to the merge policy set earlier on the managed object context. If one of the automatic merge policies is appropriate for your app, the code in Listing 22.11 will handle updating the managed object context. If none of those policies seems right for your app, you can replace the code with custom merge code that has whatever logic you need.

How do you make the view controllers update their views to show the new changes? Believe it or not, we have already covered that. In PhotoWheel, the view controllers interact with Core Data using NSFetchedResultController. One of the great things about that class is that it notices changes in the managed object context automatically and notifies its delegate. Since both MainViewController and Photo-AlbumViewController act as delegates to their NSFetchedResultController, they are already configured to automatically receive any changes sent from iCloud.

Summary

Syncing is hard, not just from a technical standpoint but for logistical reasons as well. Many developers have made the mistake of thinking that it would be simple, only to end up with code that never quite works right or with code that is still unfinished even after long development periods. With iCloud most of the heavy lifting is done for you, at no extra charge. PhotoWheel now syncs its photos via iCloud, so it can be used on multiple devices with the same data. It is details like this that really make an app appealing.

In the next chapter we'll cover displaying photos over a wireless connection to external displays using Apple's AirPlay technology, so that PhotoWheel can present a slideshow of its photos.

Exercises

1. Merging changes from iCloud makes use of the managed object context's merge policy. Investigate the merge options defined by the NSMergePolicy class and choose one to use in PhotoWheel. Most likely you'd want to use NSMergeBy-PropertyObjectTrumpMergePolicyType, which gives priority to unsaved local changes, but you might prefer one of the other options. You set a merge policy using the -setMergePolicy: method on the managed object context.

2. iCloud also has a key-value store that can be used to sync simple data about app state across devices, in the NSUbiquitousKeyValueStore class. Investigate the key-value store and use it to save the current photo to iCloud. You'll need to add a new iCloud entitlement to the app.

Producing a Slideshow
with AirPlay

Browsing through photos on the iPad's built-in screen works pretty well, but wouldn't it be nice to put on a slideshow with fancy transitions? Even better: to be able to show this slideshow on a larger external display, such as that big HDTV in your living room? Maybe even using an Apple TV to run the show over a wireless link?

In this chapter, you'll learn how to add a slideshow to PhotoWheel and make it work with external displays, whether connected via a video adapter or via wireless connections to AirPlay destinations.

External Display Options

All iPads support external displays. With the original iPad, video output worked with apps that were specifically coded to detect and use external displays. Displays had to use wired connections via a video adapter plugged into the iPad's 30-pin dock connector. Several adapters exist, for digital video out, VGA displays, and other formats.

With the iPad 2, however, the system was *greatly* enhanced. The iPad 2 can automatically mirror the internal display to a wired external display, so everything that happens on the built-in screen also happens on the external display. Also, the iPad 2 added support for AirPlay destinations such as the Apple TV, making it possible to use wireless video connections to external displays.

In all cases, using an external display changes a requirement that is otherwise absolute: the screen size. External displays will have different sizes and aspect ratios from the built-in display. Apps using external displays need to avoid making assumptions about screen size.

App Requirements for External Displays

In the simplest case, then, if your app is running on an iPad 2, you don't actually need to do anything at all to use an external display. Whatever your app does on its main screen will automatically appear on an external display so long as the user has enabled device mirroring.

However, we can do a whole lot better than that. The most obvious reason is that many people still use the original iPad. Even though it is no longer a current model, it is never a good idea to set system requirements higher than necessary. If an app doesn't do anything that specifically requires iPad 2 hardware, there is no good reason to exclude the earlier model. PhotoWheel would seem to require a camera and therefore need the iPad 2, but it works just fine with photos from your photo library. If a person uses iCloud's Photo Stream, chances are good she'll have new photos appearing on her original iPad all the time, even without a built-in camera. PhotoWheel doesn't actually need an iPad 2, so it shouldn't be (and isn't) coded to require a camera.

Also, simply mirroring the internal display often isn't the best user experience. If the external display doesn't have a touch-sensitive screen—and it almost certainly does not—it doesn't make sense to display user interface controls there. What is necessary and useful on the internal display becomes distracting clutter for someone sitting across the room watching a display that wouldn't handle touch events even if she were close enough to reach it. A better app would make more appropriate use of an external display by leaving out useless content.

For apps that update their user interface based on device orientation, device rotation must also be considered when using an external display. The external display won't rotate when the iPad does, so you should consider whether the external display's content should adjust to match the device orientation. In some cases it will, but in many cases it won't.

External Display API

Fortunately, the API to make an app work with a wired external display is almost exactly the same as the API for wireless AirPlay displays. The only difference is adding a UI control for the user to select an AirPlay device. Once the iPad connects to the device, though, it becomes available to apps in exactly the same way as a wired display connection.

The starting point for working with external displays is the UIScreen class. It provides a class method +screens that returns an array containing UIScreen instances for all currently available screens (Listing 23.1).

Listing 23.1   **Getting a List of All Currently Connected Screens**

```
NSArray *screens = [UIScreen screens];
if ([screens count] > 1) {
    NSLog(@"External display is connected");
}
```

The internal screen is guaranteed to be the first entry in the screens array. If the array contains more than one item, an external display is connected and available for use. It isn't currently possible to have more than one external display; only one AirPlay device can be selected at a given time. Furthermore, if you connect a wired external display, the AirPlay connection is automatically terminated.

UIScreen provides methods and properties that provide details about the screen. The bounds property tells you the screen resolution. Some displays support more than one resolution. The availableModes property is an array of screen modes, each of which contains a supported screen resolution. By default the UIScreen instance for an external display has its mode set to the one in the preferredMode property. That is usually the display's native resolution. Apps can change the mode and therefore the resolution if necessary, but only to modes defined in availableModes.

UIScreen posts notifications to let your app know when displays are connected or removed, the appropriately named UIScreenDidConnectNotification and UIScreenDidDisconnectNotification. Both of these pass the newly connected or disconnected screen as the notification's object. It is important to listen for these notifications because displays can come and go at any time.

The typical flow when using an external display is therefore:

1. When the app is ready to use an external display, it calls [UIScreen screens] to find out if one is currently connected. If so, it can start using it.

2. If the app receives UIScreenDidDisconnectNotification, it stops trying to use the external display.

3. If the app receives UIScreenDidConnectNotification, it gets the new screen and starts using it.

To put content on an external screen, an app creates a new instance of UIWindow. Normally you have just one UIWindow, but an external display needs its own instance. iPads don't support spanning a single window across multiple displays, so the existing window isn't enough. Once you have created the new UIWindow, you move it to the external display by setting its screen property to the right UIScreen instance.

Adding a Slideshow to PhotoWheel

Based on the discussion in the previous section, PhotoWheel's slideshow will make use of two view controllers:

- SlideShowViewController

  This class is used for external displays. It handles displaying photos and transitions between them but doesn't provide any user interface controls, and it won't respond to device rotation.

- MainSlideShowViewController

  This class is used for the main screen. The main screen shows the same slideshow as the external display, so MainSlideShowViewController will be a subclass of SlideShowViewController. That way it inherits the code to display slides.

This subclass adds code to detect and manage external displays and to create instances of `SlideShowViewController` as needed. It also adds user interface controls to allow the user to control the slideshow and runs the timer to automatically advance to the next photo. It responds to device rotation (as you would normally expect an iPad app to respond) by rotating the display and controls.

`MainSlideShowViewController` is in charge of the slideshow. Instances of `SlideShowViewController` will update their display only when instructed to do so by `MainSlideShowViewController`.

Let's start by creating these two classes. Don't forget to make `MainSlideShow-ViewController` a subclass of `SlideShowViewController`!

Updating the Storyboard

The existing `PhotoBrowserViewController` already has a **Slideshow** button that was added in Chapter 17, "Creating a Photo Browser." We'll build on that to load the slideshow. Edit *MainStoryboard.storyboard* and add a new view controller, with a push segue from `PhotoBrowserViewController` (Figure 23.1).

Make the new view controller an instance of `MainSlideShowViewController`, and name the segue `SlideshowSegue`. Set the background color of the new view to black.

We'll implement the rest of the slideshow in code.

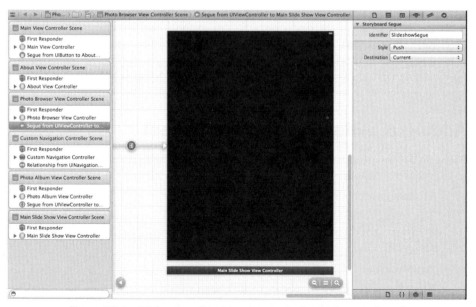

Figure 23.1 Adding the slideshow view controller to the storyboard

Adding the Slideshow Display

The first code we'll add is implementing `SlideShowViewController`. This class handles displaying photos and transitions between them, and it is the superclass of `MainSlideShowViewController`.

To display photos, the class needs some way to look up photos in the album. Fortunately, we already have this, in the form of the `PhotoBrowserViewController-Delegate` protocol. This protocol was designed for use in the photo browser, but it works just as well for the slideshow. `SlideShowViewController` will have a delegate that implements this protocol and will use it in exactly the same way as the photo browser. We'll discuss how the delegate gets set a little later on.

Make *SlideShowViewController.h* look like Listing 23.2.

Listing 23.2   **Interface for** `SlideShowViewController`

```
#import <UIKit/UIKit.h>

@protocol PhotoBrowserViewControllerDelegate;

@interface SlideShowViewController : UIViewController

@property (nonatomic, strong) id<PhotoBrowserViewControllerDelegate> delegate;
@property (nonatomic, assign) NSInteger currentIndex;
@property (nonatomic, assign) NSInteger startIndex;
@property (nonatomic, strong) UIView *currentPhotoView;

@end
```

The `@protocol` line declares the `PhotoBrowserViewControllerDelegate` protocol. There is no implementation in this file, but that's okay because it exists elsewhere in the project. As long as we tell the compiler it exists, we can declare that the delegate implements it. The next two instance variables deal with the starting and current indexes in the photo album in the same way as the photo browser. As in the photo browser, `startIndex` is the initial photo index when the slideshow loads, and `currentIndex` is the index of the currently displayed photo.

The last instance variable is a `UIView`, which displays the current photo. In most cases we would declare `currentPhotoView` in the implementation file instead of in the header. In this case, though, the subclass needs to know about it. Putting it in the header file allows code in `MainSlideShowViewController` to access the view. If it were in the implementation file, it would be private, even from subclasses.

The slideshow display is handled in the custom setter method for `currentIndex`. Each time the photo index changes, this method updates the display to show the newly current photo. This method is shown in Listing 23.3.

Listing 23.3   **Custom Setter Method for** `currentIndex` **in**
`SlideShowViewController`

```
- (void)setCurrentIndex:(NSInteger)rawNewCurrentIndex
{
   if ((rawNewCurrentIndex == [self currentIndex]) &&
      ([[[self view] subviews] count] != 0))
   {
      return;
   }
   // If the new index is outside the existing range, wrap
   // around to the other end.
   NSInteger photoCount = [[self delegate]
      photoBrowserViewControllerNumberOfPhotos:nil];
   NSInteger newCurrentIndex = rawNewCurrentIndex;
   if (newCurrentIndex >= photoCount) {
      newCurrentIndex = 0;
   }
   if (newCurrentIndex < 0) {
      newCurrentIndex = photoCount - 1;
   }

   // Create a new image view for the current photo
   UIImage *newImage = [[self delegate]
      photoBrowserViewController:nil
      imageAtIndex:newCurrentIndex];
   UIImageView *newPhotoView = [[UIImageView alloc] initWithImage:newImage];
   [newPhotoView setContentMode:UIViewContentModeScaleAspectFit];
   [newPhotoView setFrame:[[self view] bounds]];
   [newPhotoView setAutoresizingMask:
      (UIViewAutoresizingFlexibleWidth|UIViewAutoresizingFlexibleHeight)];

   if ([self currentPhotoView] == nil) {
      // If there's no photo view yet, just add it
      [[self view] addSubview:newPhotoView];
   } else {
      // If there is a photo view, do a nice animation
      NSInteger transitionOptions;
      // Use the original value of the new index to decide if
      // we're moving forward or backward through the photos.
      // Curl up for moving forward, down for moving backward.
      if (rawNewCurrentIndex > [self currentIndex]) {
         transitionOptions = UIViewAnimationOptionTransitionCurlUp;
      } else {
         transitionOptions = UIViewAnimationOptionTransitionCurlDown;
      }
```

```
    // Replace the current photo view with the new one on screen
    [UIView transitionFromView:[self currentPhotoView]
                        toView:newPhotoView
                      duration:1.0
                       options:transitionOptions
                    completion:^(BOOL finished) {

                    }];
    }
    [self setCurrentPhotoView:newPhotoView];

    // Finally, do the actual set
    currentIndex_ = newCurrentIndex;
}
```

First the setter checks the incoming value to see if it is the same as the current value. If so, it's best to skip the rest of the method with its work of looking up a photo and creating a view for it. But it continues if [self view] doesn't have any subviews yet, because that indicates that no photo is currently displayed. This will happen the first time the setter is called, if the slideshow starts with the photo at index 0.

Next, the setter checks the new value for currentIndex to make sure it is valid. The index can't be less than zero, and the upper limit depends on the number of photos in the album. Next, it asks the delegate for a UIImage containing the current photo and creates a UIImageView to display it. The content mode tells the image view to scale the photo to fit the display subject to the constraint that the aspect ratio (shape) cannot change. The autoresizing mask tells the image view that its size and shape should change when its parent view's size and shape change, so that it always fills the parent view.

If currentPhotoView is nil, it implies that no photo is being displayed. This would be the case when the slideshow first loads. In that case the code just adds new-PhotoView to the view hierarchy. Otherwise, the code arranges to replace current-PhotoView with newPhotoView using a fancy visual transition. If the new index is greater than the old one or if the index has wrapped around to zero, the transition is a page curl upward. If the new index is less than the old one or if the index has wrapped around to the upper end of the range, the transition is a page curl downward. The code chooses the transition by comparing the original incoming new index value to the current index.

The code replaces the old photo view with the new one using a UIView class method that replaces one view with another in the view hierarchy. One line of code removes currentPhotoView from the view hierarchy and inserts newPhotoView in its place. The options argument specifies how the change should occur. The last argument takes a block that executes on completion, but we don't need to do anything when that happens so we leave it empty. The code then updates the values of currentPhotoView and currentIndex.

That takes care of most of `SlideShowViewController`, but there are a couple of minor details to cover. One is that we need to set the initial value of `current-Index` based on the provided value of `startIndex`. This works the same as in `PhotoBrowserViewController`. The other is that we want to ignore device rotation in this class, so that the external display won't rotate when the device does. Add the two methods in Listing 23.4 to `SlideShowViewController` to implement these behaviors.

Listing 23.4   Setting the Slideshow's Initial Photo Index, and Disabling Autorotation on External Displays

```
- (void)viewWillAppear:(BOOL)animated
{
    [super viewWillAppear:animated];
    [self setCurrentIndex:[self startIndex]];
}

- (BOOL)shouldAutorotateToInterfaceOrientation:
        (UIInterfaceOrientation)interfaceOrientation
{
    return NO;
}
```

Managing External Displays

Now that the app can display slideshow photos, let's add the internal screen component that will handle detecting and managing external displays.

`MainSlideShowViewController` subclasses `SlideShowViewController` but does not add any new public instance variables. It does add several private instance variables in a class extension. Add the declarations in Listing 23.5 to *MainSlideShow-ViewController.m*, and then add corresponding @synthesize statements.

Listing 23.5   Private Instance Variables in `MainSlideShowViewController`

```
@interface MainSlideShowViewController ()
@property (nonatomic, strong) NSTimer *slideAdvanceTimer;
@property (nonatomic, assign, getter = isChromeHidden) BOOL chromeHidden;
@property (nonatomic, strong) NSTimer *chromeHideTimer;
@property (nonatomic, strong) SlideShowViewController \
    *externalDisplaySlideshowController;
@property (nonatomic, strong) UIWindow *externalScreenWindow;
@end
```

The new instance variables serve the following purposes:

- **slideAdvanceTimer:** This periodically calls a method that automatically advances to the next photo while the slideshow is running.

- **chromeHidden, chromeHideTimer:** These are used to make the user interface controls show and hide automatically. They work just like the ones in `Photo-BrowserViewController`, so we won't spend any time on them here.

- **externalDisplaySlideshowController:** When an external display is connected, this will point to the `SlideShowViewController` displaying photos on that display.

- **externalScreenWindow:** When an external display is connected, this will point to the `UIWindow` instance managing content on that display.

To detect and configure external displays we'll add two methods to `MainSlide-ShowViewController`. The code in Listing 23.6 looks for any external displays and returns the result. If no external displays are found, it returns `nil`. `MainSlide-ShowViewController` calls this method from `−viewDidLoad:` to see if an external display is already available.

Listing 23.6   Detecting External Displays

```
- (UIScreen *)getExternalScreen
{
   NSArray *screens = [UIScreen screens];
   UIScreen *externalScreen = nil;
   if ([screens count] > 1) {
      // The internal screen is guaranteed to be at index 0.
      externalScreen = [screens lastObject];
   }
   return externalScreen;
}
```

When an external display is connected, `MainSlideShowViewController` will call the `−configureExternalScreen:` method in Listing 23.7 to create the display's window and view controller.

Listing 23.7   Configuring an External Display

```
- (void)configureExternalScreen:(UIScreen *)externalScreen
{
   // Clear any existing external screen items
   [self setExternalDisplaySlideshowController:nil];
   [self setExternalScreenWindow:nil];

   // Create a new window and move it to the external screen
   [self setExternalScreenWindow:[[UIWindow alloc]
      initWithFrame:[externalScreen applicationFrame]]];
   [[self externalScreenWindow] setScreen:externalScreen];
```

```
    // Create a SlideShowViewController to handle slides on the
    // external screen
    SlideShowViewController *externalSlideController =
        [[SlideShowViewController alloc] init];
    [self setExternalDisplaySlideshowController:externalSlideController];
    [externalSlideController setDelegate:[self delegate]];
    [externalSlideController setStartIndex:[self currentIndex]];

    // Add the external slideshow view to the external window and
    // resize it to fit
    [[self externalScreenWindow] addSubview:[externalSlideController view]];
    [[externalSlideController view] setFrame:[[self externalScreenWindow] frame]];

    // Set the external screen view's background color to match the
    // one configured in the storyboard
    [[externalSlideController view]
        setBackgroundColor:[[self view] backgroundColor]];

    // Show the window
    [[self externalScreenWindow] makeKeyAndVisible];
}
```

This method begins by checking to see if a window and view controller already exist for an external screen. Since the app will be detecting display connect and disconnect events, these objects should already be nil. With AirPlay, though, it's sometimes possible to receive multiple connection events with no intervening disconnect event, so it's best to make sure that the app starts "clean" here.

This method then creates a UIWindow for the external display. The window's frame is the same as the applicationFrame property of the screen, which is the area available for use by the app. This window is then moved to the new screen. You can move a window to a new screen at any time, but if the window already has content, it can be an expensive operation. It's best to move the window first and add content to it later.

Next we create a SlideShowViewController to display slides on the external display. Since this is a new instance, we also need to set the delegate and the startIndex of the new view controller to match self's values. They need to be the same as the ones in MainSlideShowViewController so that the internal and external displays will show the same photos.

Once the view controller exists, we add its view to the UIWindow we just created and resize the view to match the window's size. Since external displays come in a variety of sizes, we don't know the size in advance, so we need to set it here. Then we set the view's background color to match [self view]'s background color, which is the one configured in the storyboard. Finally, call –makeKeyAndVisible to make the new window visible on the external display. This is when the slideshow actually appears there.

We'll make use of these methods in –viewDidLoad. We need to check whether an external display is already connected and register for notifications of screens being connected and disconnected. Use the code in Listing 23.8 for MainSlideShowView-Controller's –viewDidLoad.

Listing 23.8 **Setting Up External Screen Management in**
              MainSlideShowViewController

```objc
- (void)viewDidLoad
{
    [super viewDidLoad];

    [self updateNavBarButtonsForPlayingState:YES];

    // Check for an extra screen existing right now
    UIScreen *externalScreen = [self getExternalScreen];
    if (externalScreen != nil) {
        [self configureExternalScreen:externalScreen];
    }

    NSNotificationCenter *notificationCenter = [NSNotificationCenter
defaultCenter];
    // Add observers for screen connect/disconnect
    [notificationCenter addObserverForName:UIScreenDidConnectNotification
                                    object:nil
                                     queue:[NSOperationQueue mainQueue]
                                usingBlock:^(NSNotification *note)
    {
        UIScreen *newExternalScreen = [note object];
        [self configureExternalScreen:newExternalScreen];
    }];

    [notificationCenter addObserverForName:UIScreenDidDisconnectNotification
                                    object:nil
                                     queue:[NSOperationQueue mainQueue]
                                usingBlock:^(NSNotification *note)
    {
        [self setExternalDisplaySlideshowController:nil];
        [self setExternalScreenWindow:nil];
    }];
}
```

The first part of this code calls the –getExternalScreen method from previously to look for external displays. If one is found, it calls –configureExternalScreen to set up the display's contents.

Following this, the code registers for UIScreenDidConnectNotification and
UIScreenDidDisconnectNotification to track screen events. If a new display is
connected, the code calls -configureExternalScreen to add content to it. If one
is disconnected, the code disposes of the externalDisplaySlideshowController
and externalScreenWindow instance variables, since they aren't needed anymore.

Advancing to the Next Photo

The app is now displaying slideshow-related view controllers on one or more displays.
To actually have a slideshow we need to add a timer to automatically advance to the
next slide at regular intervals. We also need to arrange for the main screen slideshow
controller to tell the external display when to change photos. We'll do this in Main-
SlideShowViewController, since it is always present during slideshows.

Create another custom setter method for currentIndex so that setting the current index on the main screen slideshow controller also updates the external display, if
there is one. This setter is given in Listing 23.9.

Listing 23.9   Custom Setter for currentIndex **in**
          MainSlideShowViewController

```
- (void)setCurrentIndex:(NSInteger)currentIndex
{
    [super setCurrentIndex:currentIndex];
    [[self externalDisplaySlideshowController] setCurrentIndex:currentIndex];

    [[self currentPhotoView] setUserInteractionEnabled:YES];
    UITapGestureRecognizer *photoTapRecognizer =
        [[UITapGestureRecognizer alloc]
            initWithTarget:self
            action:@selector(photoTapped:)];
    [[self currentPhotoView] addGestureRecognizer:photoTapRecognizer];
}
```

First, of course, the setter calls super's implementation, which we discussed earlier.
Then it calls -setCurrentIndex on the external display's view controller to update
the photo displayed there. If there isn't an external display, [self externalDisplay-
SlideShowController] will be nil. As you probably recall, sending a message to nil
in Objective-C is valid and is equivalent to doing nothing, so we don't need to check for
nil first.

The code does a little more setup for currentPhotoView, adding a tap gesture
recognizer which calls the -photoTapped: method. As with PhotoBrowserView-
Controller, this is part of the chrome-hiding system. Buttons will automatically hide
after a few seconds but will reappear when the user taps on the screen.

Advancing to the next photo is managed by an NSTimer, which periodically updates currentIndex. Create the timer in –viewWillAppear: using the code in Listing 23.10.

Listing 23.10   Creating a Timer to Automatically Move to the Next Photo

```
NSTimer *timer = [NSTimer scheduledTimerWithTimeInterval:5.0
                                    target:self
                                    selector:@selector(advanceSlide:)
                                    userInfo:nil
                                    repeats:YES];
[self setSlideAdvanceTimer:timer];
```

This creates an NSTimer that calls the –advanceSlide: method on self every 5 seconds. The –advanceSlide: method is shown in Listing 23.11.

Listing 23.11   Advancing to the Next Photo

```
- (void)advanceSlide:(NSTimer *)timer
{
    [self setCurrentIndex:[self currentIndex] + 1];
}
```

This method just increments currentIndex by one. Doing so calls both self and super's custom setter methods, which in turn update the photo display on both internal and external displays. This method doesn't bother checking whether the new value is valid, because that is handled in the setter.

It's also important to make sure that MainSlideShowViewController cleans up after itself when it leaves the screen. It needs to remove the slideshow and chrome timers as well as objects that manage the external display. This should happen in –viewWillDisappear, which will be called anytime the user ends a slideshow. Make MainSlideShowViewController's –viewWillDisappear method look like Listing 23.12.

Listing 23.12   Cleaning Up MainSlideShowViewController Data When a Slide Show Ends

```
- (void)viewWillDisappear:(BOOL)animated
{
    [self cancelChromeDisplayTimer];
    [[self slideAdvanceTimer] invalidate];
    [self setSlideAdvanceTimer:nil];
    [self setExternalDisplaySlideshowController:nil];
    [self setExternalScreenWindow:nil];
}
```

Adding Slideshow User Interface Controls

The main screen slideshow display will include some basic user interface controls. Users will be able to pause or resume slideshows and to manually advance to the next or previous photo in the album. We'll do this with buttons on the navigation bar, again using an approach similar to `PhotoBrowserViewController`.

The `-updateNavBarButtonsForPlayingState` method in Listing 23.13 creates these buttons. It takes one argument, a `BOOL` that indicates whether the navigation bar should include a play button or a pause button.

Listing 23.13   **Adding Slideshow Controls**

```
- (void)updateNavBarButtonsForPlayingState:(BOOL)playing
{
    UIBarButtonItem *rewindButton = [[UIBarButtonItem alloc]
                initWithBarButtonSystemItem:UIBarButtonSystemItemRewind
                target:self
                action:@selector(backOnePhoto:)];
    [rewindButton setStyle:UIBarButtonItemStyleBordered];
    UIBarButtonItem *playPauseButton;
    if (playing) {
        playPauseButton = [[UIBarButtonItem alloc]
                initWithBarButtonSystemItem:UIBarButtonSystemItemPause
                target:self
                action:@selector(pause:)];
    } else {
        playPauseButton = [[UIBarButtonItem alloc]
                initWithBarButtonSystemItem:UIBarButtonSystemItemPlay
                target:self
                action:@selector(resume:)];
    }
    [playPauseButton setStyle:UIBarButtonItemStyleBordered];
    UIBarButtonItem *forwardButton = [[UIBarButtonItem alloc]
                initWithBarButtonSystemItem:UIBarButtonSystemItemFastForward
                target:self
                action:@selector(forwardOnePhoto:)];
    [forwardButton setStyle:UIBarButtonItemStyleBordered];

    NSArray *toolbarItems = [NSArray arrayWithObjects:
        rewindButton, playPauseButton, forwardButton, nil];

    UIToolbar *toolbar = [[ClearToolbar alloc]
        initWithFrame:CGRectMake(0, 0, 200, 44)];
    [toolbar setBackgroundColor:[UIColor clearColor]];
    [toolbar setBarStyle:UIBarStyleBlack];
    [toolbar setTranslucent:YES];
    [toolbar setItems:toolbarItems];
```

```
UIBarButtonItem *customBarButtonItem =
  [[UIBarButtonItem alloc] initWithCustomView:toolbar];
[[self navigationItem]
  setRightBarButtonItem:customBarButtonItem
  animated:YES];
}
```

The general idea in this method is the same as in PhotoBrowserView-Controller's –addButtonsToNavigationBar method. The code creates several UIBarButtonItem instances, adds them to a UIToolbar, and then places that toolbar in the navigation item. The biggest change is that the collection of buttons depends on the playing argument. If playing is YES, the toolbar includes a pause button. If playing is NO, the toolbar includes a play button.

The actions triggered by these buttons are shown in Listing 23.14.

Listing 23.14   **Actions for Slideshow Controls**

```
- (void)pause:(id)sender
{
  [[self slideAdvanceTimer] setFireDate:[NSDate distantFuture]];
  [self updateNavBarButtonsForPlayingState:NO];
}

- (void)resume:(id)sender
{
  [[self slideAdvanceTimer] setFireDate:[NSDate date]];
  [self updateNavBarButtonsForPlayingState:YES];
}

- (void)backOnePhoto:(id)sender
{
  [self pause:nil];
  [self setCurrentIndex:[self currentIndex] - 1];
}

- (void)forwardOnePhoto:(id)sender
{
  [self pause:nil];
  [self setCurrentIndex:[self currentIndex] + 1];
}
```

In the –pause: method we want to stop the automatic photo advance timer. There is more than one way we could do this. In this case we do it by manually changing the timer's fire time. Normally it repeats at regular intervals, but it is possible to give it a specific date for its next fire time. It then sits idle until that time occurs. Here, we set the time to [NSDate distantFuture]. The exact meaning of distantFuture is not documented except to say that it is centuries into the future. For our purposes we can regard this as meaning "never," which effectively pauses the timer. This method also updates the toolbar buttons so that the pause button will be replaced by a play button.

When -resume: is called, we undo the effects of -pause:. To resume automatic slide advancement we again update the timer's fire date, this time telling it to fire immediately. It will then continue at its scheduled interval. We again update the toolbar buttons, this time putting the pause button back.

The -backOnePhoto: and -forwardOnePhoto: methods move to the previous and next photos respectively by changing currentIndex. Again, we don't bother checking whether the new values for currentIndex are valid here since the setter method will take care of that. In both cases we also pause the auto-advance timer, since tapping either of these buttons implies that the user wants to take control of the photo display.

Updating the Photo Browser

Great, we now have a slideshow! Except ... we don't have any code to load it yet. We need to do something about that.

PhotoBrowserViewController already has a placeholder method called -slideshow: which is connected to the **Slideshow** button. And we now have a segue named SlideshowSegue that loads the slideshow. The obvious thing to do, then, is connect these two by implementing -slideshow:, as shown in Listing 23.15.

Listing 23.15   **Loading the Slideshow from** PhotoBrowserViewController

```
- (void)slideshow:(id)sender
{
    [self performSegueWithIdentifier:@"SlideshowSegue" sender:self];
}
```

We also need to tell the new slideshow what photo it should start at and provide it with a delegate so that it can load photos. We'll do this by implementing -prepareForSegue: in PhotoBrowserViewController, as shown in Listing 23.16.

Listing 23.16   **Configuring the Slideshow in** PhotoBrowserViewController

```
- (void)prepareForSegue:(UIStoryboardSegue *)segue sender:(id)sender
{
    if ([[segue destinationViewController] isKindOfClass:
        [MainSlideShowViewController class]]) {
        [self setSlideShowController:
            (MainSlideShowViewController *)[segue destinationViewController]];
        [[self slideShowController] setDelegate:[self delegate]];
        [[self slideShowController] setStartIndex:[self currentIndex]];
    }
}
```

This method is straightforward; all it does is provide the new `MainSlideShow-VideoController` with a delegate and a starting point. Note that this code assumes the existence of an instance variable to hold that controller, which we'll provide by adding a declaration to the class continuation:

```
@property (nonatomic, strong) MainSlideShowViewController *slideShowController;
```

Why do we need to keep a reference to the slideshow controller anyway? There's one more thing we really should do, for consistency of user experience. The slideshow will start with whatever photo is being displayed in the photo browser. When the slideshow finishes, the photo browser should show the last photo displayed. Going back to the initial photo would be slightly jarring since it would unexpectedly change photos when the slideshow finishes. We'll do this by changing –viewWillAppear:, replacing the lines that set `currentIndex` and scrolling to that index with the lines shown in Listing 23.17.

Listing 23.17 Updated Code to Set `currentIndex` in PhotoBrowserViewController's –viewDidAppear:

```
if ([self slideShowController] != nil) {
    [self setCurrentIndex:[[self slideShowController] currentIndex]];
    [self scrollToIndex:[[self slideShowController] currentIndex]];
    [self setSlideShowController:nil];
} else {
    [self setCurrentIndex:[self startAtIndex]];
    [self scrollToIndex:[self startAtIndex]];
}
```

In this updated code, if the view is appearing for the first time, it proceeds as before. It sets `currentIndex` to the value of `startIndex` and updates the scroll view. But if the view is loading because a slideshow has just finished, it instead updates `currentIndex` to the slideshow's index value. This way, the photo browser shows whatever photo was just shown in the slideshow.

A Note on Testing and Debugging

When you work with code that can use external displays, you may run into a conundrum when attempting to test the code. You install and test apps on a device using Xcode via a USB cable connected to the iPad's dock connector. But if you're using a wired display, you need to use that dock connector for the video adapter! You can't connect the device to both the Mac and the display at the same time, and as a result you can't run the debugger or even see the device console while the app is running.

One approach is to insert a lot of `NSLog()` statements, run the app, and then reconnect the device to the Mac. You can then inspect the device console in Xcode and see what messages were printed. It's awkward, but it does give insight into what is happening on the device.

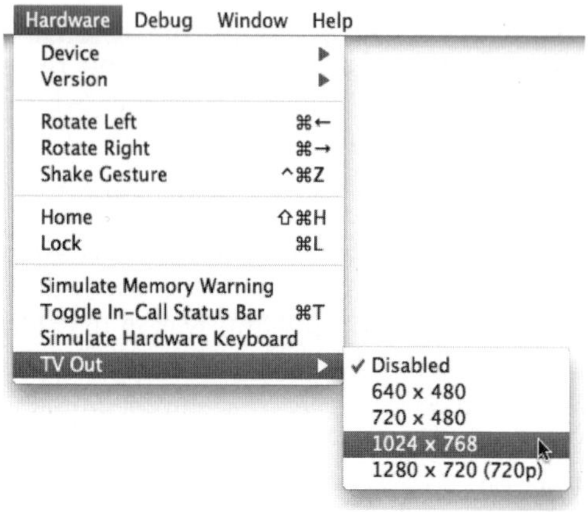

Figure 23.2   External display options in the iOS Simulator

Perhaps surprisingly, the simulator proves quite useful in this scenario. The simulator's **Hardware** menu has an entry labeled **TV Out**, which lists several screen resolutions (Figure 23.2).

If you select one of the **TV Out** options, the iOS Simulator opens a new window matching the size you've selected. This window acts as an external display connected to the simulator. It's not a perfect solution. There is no automatic mirroring, making the simulator more like the original iPad than the iPad 2. Also, you can't simulate connecting and disconnecting displays while the app is running, because changing the **TV Out** option causes the app to quit. Still, it's extremely convenient if you're debugging code that uses an external display.

Of course, if you're working with an AirPlay device, this is not an issue. Just leave the device connected to the Mac and work with the app normally.

Adding AirPlay Support

The external display code we have added works the same with AirPlay destinations as with wired external displays. The only extra detail we need for AirPlay support is some way for the user to select an AirPlay destination to use as the external display.

The `MediaPlayer` framework has a class called `MPVolumeView` that includes the option to select AirPlay destinations. The class is capable of showing a volume slider and a route button that can be used to select AirPlay devices. Both of these are optional, so in this case we'll use the route button but turn off the volume slider.

First you'll need to add the `MediaPlayer` framework to the app. Do this in the build phases settings for the app, just like in Chapter 13 when you added the Core Data framework. Then, import *MediaPlayer.h* into *MainSlideShowViewController.m* so that you can use `MPVolumeView`:

```
#import <MediaPlayer/MediaPlayer.h>
```

We'll add MPVolumeView to the toolbar at the top of the screen, next to the play/pause, back, and forward buttons. Therefore, we'll make some additions to the –updateNavBarButtonsForPlayingState: method we discussed earlier. The new version is shown in Listing 23.18.

Listing 23.18   New Code to Add an AirPlay Destination Selector

```
- (void)updateNavBarButtonsForPlayingState:(BOOL)playing
{
   UIBarButtonItem *rewindButton = [[UIBarButtonItem alloc]
      initWithBarButtonSystemItem:UIBarButtonSystemItemRewind
      target:self
      action:@selector(backOnePhoto:)];
   [rewindButton setStyle:UIBarButtonItemStyleBordered];
   UIBarButtonItem *playPauseButton;
   if (playing) {
      playPauseButton = [[UIBarButtonItem alloc]
         initWithBarButtonSystemItem:UIBarButtonSystemItemPause
         target:self
         action:@selector(pause:)];
   } else {
      playPauseButton = [[UIBarButtonItem alloc]
         initWithBarButtonSystemItem:UIBarButtonSystemItemPlay
         target:self
         action:@selector(resume:)];
   }
   [playPauseButton setStyle:UIBarButtonItemStyleBordered];
   UIBarButtonItem *forwardButton = [[UIBarButtonItem alloc]
      initWithBarButtonSystemItem:UIBarButtonSystemItemFastForward
      target:self
      action:@selector(forwardOnePhoto:)];
   [forwardButton setStyle:UIBarButtonItemStyleBordered];

   // Add the AirPlay selector
   MPVolumeView *airPlaySelectorView = [[MPVolumeView alloc] init];
   [airPlaySelectorView setShowsVolumeSlider:NO];
   [airPlaySelectorView setShowsRouteButton:YES];
   CGSize airPlaySelectorSize = [airPlaySelectorView
      sizeThatFits:CGSizeMake(44.0, 44.0)];
   [airPlaySelectorView setFrame:
      CGRectMake(0, 0, airPlaySelectorSize.width,
         airPlaySelectorSize.height)];
   UIBarButtonItem *airPlayButton = [[UIBarButtonItem alloc]
      initWithCustomView:airPlaySelectorView];

   NSArray *toolbarItems = [NSArray arrayWithObjects:
      airPlayButton, rewindButton, playPauseButton, forwardButton, nil];
```

```
UIToolbar *toolbar = [[ClearToolbar alloc]
    initWithFrame:CGRectMake(0, 0, 200, 44)];
[toolbar setBackgroundColor:[UIColor clearColor]];
[toolbar setBarStyle:UIBarStyleBlack];
[toolbar setTranslucent:YES];
[toolbar setItems:toolbarItems];

UIBarButtonItem *customBarButtonItem = [[UIBarButtonItem alloc]
    initWithCustomView:toolbar];
[[self navigationItem]
    setRightBarButtonItem:customBarButtonItem
    animated:YES];
}
```

The new code adds a new button on the toolbar, which contains an `MPVolumeView`. Since the code turns off the volume slider and enables the route button, the resulting `MPVolumeView` is a small button-size view. Its exact size is not documented, but we can ask it how big it needs to be using the `-sizeThatFits:` method. When the user taps this button, she'll be presented with a popup menu listing available AirPlay destinations.

One nice feature about `MPVolumeView`'s route button is that it automatically hides itself if no AirPlay destinations are available. That way users don't get a useless button in the app in those situations. If you don't have an Apple TV, you won't see the button even after adding the code in Listing 23.18.

Using AirPlay

Running the slideshow via AirPlay requires turning on device mirroring for the iPad. As the term suggests, when device mirroring is active, the iPad's internal screen is mirrored to the AirPlay destination just as with a wired external display. It may seem strange that device mirroring is required when the slideshow is designed specifically to not use mirroring, but that's how Apple has implemented the API.

To enable device mirroring via AirPlay, double-tap the iPad's Home button to show the application switcher, and drag to show the audio controls. If an AirPlay device is available, these will include an AirPlay menu (Figure 23.3).

You'll need to select the AirPlay device from the popup menu and enable mirroring. If device mirroring is not turned on, `[UIScreen screens]` returns only a single `UIScreen` instance representing the internal screen. What's more, `UIScreenDidConnectNotification` is never posted. If you enable device mirroring while a slideshow is running, `UIScreenDidConnectNotification` will be posted.

Figure 23.3   Enabling device mirroring over AirPlay

Summary

Showing a slideshow on an external display is a great way to share photos with a group of people. (Just don't overdo it on the vacation photos.) In this chapter, we covered how to run a slideshow and how to make use of both wired and wireless external displays. The code for making use of external displays would work with any kind of content and uses the same Cocoa Touch APIs you're already familiar with. You can also take AirPlay further and send audio or video over the wireless link. Many apps can benefit from intelligent use of external displays, and now PhotoWheel is among them.

Next we'll explore the new-to-iOS Core Image framework. We'll add fun and entertaining image transformations and see how to make PhotoWheel locate and zoom in on faces in a picture.

Exercises

1. The slideshow transition in –setCurrentIndex: uses a page-curl effect when changing slides. Experiment with other transition effects, like the flip-style transitions offered by UIViewAnimationOptionTransitionFlipFromRight and UIViewAnimationOptionTransitionFlipFromLeft.

2. This chapter's code didn't set the animation timing to use when changing slides, so it used the default setting of UIViewAnimationOptionCurveEaseInOut. Look up some other view animation options in the documentation for UIView and try different timing options. Try some others, such as UIViewAnimation-OptionCurveEaseIn or UIViewAnimationOptionCurveLinear.

24

Visual Effects with Core Image

Sometimes photos don't come out as well as you hoped. The image is too dark, or too light, or the people have red eyes. Most photo management software includes basic editing features to help you deal with these problems, as well as visual effects that can be applied to change photos in fun and interesting ways. Wouldn't it be nice if PhotoWheel could do that too? Well, it will by the end of this chapter: Enter Core Image.

In this chapter we'll use Core Image to add these features and more. We'll explore creating filters to create visual effects and to automatically enhance photos. We'll also see how Core Image can locate faces in a picture.

Core Image Concepts

Core Image has been around for OS X, and it has been introduced in iOS 5 to provide visual effects for use with both photos and video. It includes a variety of color alterations and enhancements, image compositing effects for combining multiple images, automatic photo enhancement including red-eye repair, and face detection. It works nondestructively on images, and effects can be chained together for more complex transformations.

We'll focus mainly on CIFilter, the Core Image Filter class. A CIFilter typically takes one or two images and one or more configuration parameters as inputs and produces a single output image. iOS includes numerous built-in filters that perform different image operations. CIFilters work on instances of CIImage, which is the class Core Image uses to store images. Figure 24.1 shows a simple example.

CIFilters can be chained together by simply connecting the output image of one filter to the input image of another. By doing this you can combine multiple effects to get more complex results. Figure 24.2 shows an example of using multiple filters on the same original image.

An important concept when using Core Image is that a CIImage instance does not actually contain an image. It contains an image *recipe*, that is, instructions for how to create a particular image. Setting up filters defines the steps from input image to

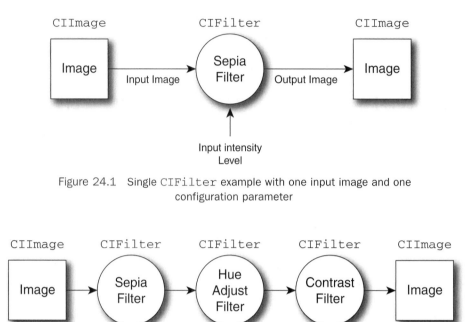

Figure 24.1   Single `CIFilter` example with one input image and one
configuration parameter

Figure 24.2   Chaining multiple `CIFilter`s for more complex effects

output but does not actually render the filtered output image. Getting the output
image from a `CIFilter` doesn't apply the filter; rather it creates a recipe for a filtered
image.

Rendering filtered images is the responsibility of a `CIContext`. `CIContext`s do the
work of carrying out the `CIImage`'s recipe and producing the final image. Once the
final image is rendered, you can get a `UIImage` to display on the screen or save to a
file or to the user's photo library.

CPU or GPU?

`CIContext`s can process images on either the CPU or the GPU, giving a choice
between software and hardware image rendering. It's tempting to think that the GPU
would always be the better choice, since it's dedicated to graphics processing and
leaves the CPU free for other work.

That's not always the case, though. Both CPU and GPU `CIContext`s have limits on
the size of their input and output images, and the GPU limit is much smaller than the
CPU limit. Also, Core Animation uses the GPU, so if your app is doing animations, the
GPU may already be busy with other work. Finally, CPU rendering uses higher-precision
math and can produce more accurate results.

Introducing `CIFilter`

iOS 5 includes numerous built-in filters. You could read about them in the documentation, but you can also ask the runtime environment what is available. You can get a list of all filter names directly from `CIFilter`:

```
NSArray *filterNames = [CIFilter filterNamesInCategory:kCICategoryBuiltIn];
```

As the method name implies, there are various filter categories. Some filters belong to more than one category. This line of code asks for all built-in filters. For Photo-Wheel we might look up filters in the `kCICategoryStillImage` category instead, which contains all filters that work on still images.

Filter names are strings. Some examples include `CIHueAdjust`, `CICrop`, and `CIColorInvert`. `CIFilter` can also provide detailed information about how to use each filter via its `attributes` method. The attributes describe each of the filter's inputs, including acceptable values. For example, the code in Listing 24.1 looks up information on the `CISepiaTone` filter.

Listing 24.1 **Looking Up Attributes of the** `CISepiaTone` **Filter**

```
CIFilter *sepiaFilter = [CIFilter filterWithName:@"CISepiaTone"];
NSLog(@"CISepiaTone attributes: %@", [sepiaFilter attributes]);
```

The result of running this code is shown in Listing 24.2.

Listing 24.2 **Attributes of** `CISepiaTone` **Filter**

```
2011-07-29 17:02:31.833 CIDemo[13727:207] CISepiaTone attributes: {
    CIAttributeFilterCategories =     (
        CICategoryColorEffect,
        CICategoryVideo,
        CICategoryInterlaced,
        CICategoryNonSquarePixels,
        CICategoryStillImage,
        CICategoryBuiltIn
    );
    CIAttributeFilterDisplayName = "Sepia Tone";
    CIAttributeFilterName = CISepiaTone;
    inputImage =     {
        CIAttributeClass = CIImage;
        CIAttributeType = CIAttributeTypeImage;
    };
    inputIntensity =     {
        CIAttributeClass = NSNumber;
        CIAttributeDefault = 1;
        CIAttributeIdentity = 0;
        CIAttributeMax = 1;
```

```
            CIAttributeMin = 0;
            CIAttributeSliderMax = 1;
            CIAttributeSliderMin = 0;
            CIAttributeType = CIAttributeTypeScalar;
        };
}
```

From this we see that CISepiaTone has two inputs. The first is an image to filter and the second is the intensity of the sepia tone effect. The attributes dictionary includes the expected class for each argument and a Core Image type field. For the intensity input it also includes a variety of details about acceptable values, including minimum, maximum, default, and suggestions for what values to use on a slider-style UI control. The attributes even include a suggested display name suitable for presenting to users. By inspecting filter attributes it is possible to generate user interface controls for filters dynamically, without hard-coding any of the information about the filter.

Filter Types

Built-in filters are grouped into over a dozen different categories, but in general they fall into three distinct groups:

- **Filters that alter single images.** These filters take one input image and zero or more configuration parameters. They include filters that change an image's colors or that apply an affine transform to an image.

- **Filters that combine images.** These filters take two input images and combine them using one of a variety of image compositing or blending techniques.

- **Filters that generate images.** These filters have no input image but take one or more configuration parameters. They create new images that contain gradients, checkerboards, or other designs whose appearance is determined by the input values.

In this chapter we'll expand PhotoWheel to include some fun image effects that users can apply to pictures in their library.

Using CIFilter

Basic CIFilter usage is quite simple, though it does involve new classes and concepts. CIFilters work on and produce instances of CIImage. Final images are rendered not by the filter or the image, but by a CIContext. Listing 24.3 shows a simple example of using the CISepiaTone filter to apply a sepia tint to an image. This example also shows how you can convert between UIImage and CIImage, which is useful when you're working with UIKit.

Listing 24.3   **Using the** CISepiaTone **Filter with a** UIImage

```
- (UIImage *)sepiaImageFromImage:(UIImage *)myImage
{
    CIImage *myCIImage = [CIImage imageWithCGImage:[myImage CGImage]];

    CIFilter *sepiaFilter = [CIFilter filterWithName:@"CISepiaTone"];
    [sepiaFilter setValue:myCIImage forKey:kCIInputImageKey];
    [sepiaFilter setValue:[NSNumber numberWithFloat:0.9]
        forKey:@"inputIntensity"];

    CIImage *sepiaImage = [sepiaFilter outputImage];

    CIContext *context = [CIContext contextWithOptions:[NSDictionary
        dictionaryWithObject:[NSNumber numberWithBool:NO]
        forKey:kCIContextUseSoftwareRenderer]];
    CGImageRef sepiaCGImage = [context createCGImage:sepiaImage
        fromRect:[sepiaImage extent]];
    UIImage *sepiaUIImage = [UIImage imageWithCGImage:sepiaCGImage];
    CFRelease(sepiaCGImage);

    return sepiaUIImage;
}
```

The first thing this method does is convert the incoming UIImage to a CIImage so that CIFilter can work with it. This is done using the CGImage format defined by Core Graphics. Both UIImage and CIImage work with CGImages, so here it takes the role of the transfer point from one class to another.

Next, the code creates the CIFilter, looking it up by name. As seen earlier, CISepiaTone takes two parameters: an input image and an intensity level. The code sets both of these via key-value coding.

The code assigns the result of the filter to sepiaImage, which is another CIImage. Recall from earlier that this doesn't actually contain an image; it instead contains a recipe for creating an image. At this point the code has defined the path from the original image to the result via the filter but has not actually applied the filter and rendered the output image.

Rendering the result is the CIContext's job. The method creates a CIContext, setting the kCIContextUseSoftwareRenderer option to NO. This means that the CIContext will use the GPU to render the image instead of the CPU. Creating a CIContext on the fly like this is okay if you'll need it only occasionally, but if you expect to be doing a lot of Core Image work, it's best to make the context an instance variable and reuse it whenever you need it. The final image is rendered as a CGImage in the call to -createCGImage:fromRect:. The first argument is the CIImage just created, and the second is that image's extent, or size and location.

The rendered image is converted back to a `UIImage` and returned. Since ARC manages only Objective-C objects, it is necessary to explicitly release the interim `CGImageRef sepiaCGImage`.

Image Analysis

Filters are useful and often fun, but Core Image goes further, into features that require analyzing the source image instead of merely processing its pixels. One is the auto-enhance feature you have probably noticed in iOS 5's camera app, which includes red-eye elimination. The other is face detection, which locates any faces found in an image as well as specific facial features like the person's eyes and mouth.

Automatic Enhancement

Image enhancement uses a series of `CIFilters`. Rather than create the filters your-self, though, you ask `CIImage` to create them for you. A `CIImage` instance analyzes its image to determine what enhancements might be needed and returns an array of `CIFilters`. You then chain these filters together to produce the enhanced image. List-ing 24.4 shows an example of applying auto-enhance filters to a `UIImage`.

Listing 24.4   **Auto-enhancing a** `UIImage`

```
- (UIImage *)autoEnhancedVersionOfImage:(UIImage *)myImage
{
    CIImage *myCIImage = [CIImage imageWithCGImage:[myImage CGImage]];

    NSArray *autoAdjustmentFilters = [myCIImage autoAdjustmentFilters];
    CIImage *enhancedCIImage = myCIImage;
    for (CIFilter *filter in autoAdjustmentFilters) {
        [filter setValue:enhancedCIImage forKey:kCIInputImageKey];
        enhancedCIImage = [filter outputImage];
    }

    CGImageRef enhancedCGImage = [[self ciContext]
        createCGImage:enhancedCIImage
        fromRect:[enhancedCIImage extent]];
    UIImage *enhancedImage = [UIImage imageWithCGImage:enhancedCGImage];
    CFRelease(enhancedCGImage);

    return enhancedImage;
}
```

As with the previous example, the code in Listing 24.4 starts by converting the incoming `UIImage` to a `CIImage`.

Next, it asks the `CIImage` to analyze the image and determine what, if any, fil-ters are needed to enhance it. This step is processor intensive, especially with larger images, so you should consider doing it on a background thread. The result is several CIFilters collected in an array. In this case the code asks for all possible auto-adjust filters, which may include red-eye correction. If you don't think you'll need that, you can speed up the analysis by turning that enhancement off. In that case you would use -autoAdjustmentFiltersWithOptions: and set the kCIImageAutoAdjustRed-Eye option to NO.

To get the enhanced image you need to apply each of these filters to the original image. The easiest way to do that is to chain them end to end. Then you can process the entire filter chain at once when you render the final image. The code does this using the CIImage enhancedCIImage, which is initially set to the original image. That becomes the input to the first filter. At each stage in the for loop the code sets the current filter's input to the current value of enhancedImage. Then it updates enhancedImage to point to the current filter's outputImage. When the loop completes, enhancedImage points to the output of the final enhancement filter.

In this case the CIImage has a more complex image recipe than in the earlier CISepiaTone example, but it's still just a recipe and not the final rendered image. The rest of the method renders the result and converts it to UIImage. The only rendering difference in this method is that the code uses an instance variable called ciContext that contains a CIContext instance owned by the class.

Face Detection

Detecting faces also requires analyzing the image, but in this case no CIFilters are involved. Instead, you use the CIDetector class. CIDetector is designed to analyze images and find specific types of features. As of iOS 5, there is only one detector, which locates faces.

CIDetector analyzes an image to locate features and returns an array of CIFeature instances corresponding to those features. When detecting faces, the array contains instances of CIFaceFeature, which is a subclass of CIFeature. Each CIFaceFeature contains the overall bounds of the detected face. It may also contain eye and mouth locations, when they can be determined. Listing 24.5 shows a code snippet that finds faces in a CIImage.

Listing 24.5   Detecting Faces in an Image

```
NSDictionary *detectorOptions = [NSDictionary
    dictionaryWithObject:CIDetectorAccuracyLow
    forKey:CIDetectorAccuracy];
CIDetector *faceDetector = [CIDetector detectorOfType:CIDetectorTypeFace
    context:nil
    options:detectorOptions];

NSArray *faces = [faceDetector featuresInImage:[self filteredCIImage]
    options:nil];
```

```
if ([faces count] > 0) {
    for (CIFaceFeature *face in faces) {
        NSLog(@"Found face at %@", NSStringFromCGRect([face bounds]));
    }
}
```

The code starts by creating a `dictionary`, which holds options for the face detector. Currently the only option is the accuracy, which can be high or low. Higher accuracy takes longer to calculate. The code then creates a `CIDetector` of type `CIDetectorTypeFace` using these options.

Face detection happens during the call to `-featuresInImage:options:`. Analyzing the image to find faces may be processor intensive, so you may want to dispatch the process to a background thread. This method returns an array of `CIFaceFeatures` representing faces in the image. If no faces were found, the array will be empty.

When this call completes, the code runs through any faces that were found and prints their bounds.

Adding Core Image Effects to PhotoWheel

Now it's time to add these features to PhotoWheel. We'll be adding the following options to the photo browser:

- A collection of `CIFilter` effects that modify the image in various ways

  The filters will be configured with random attribute values, producing a range of effects. The app will show small preview images demonstrating the effect the filter would have.

- Automatic image enhancement
- Automatically zooming an image to focus on faces

The effects will be cumulative, so that the user can apply multiple effects sequentially.

> **Note**
>
> In addition to the code changes presented in this chapter, you must add `CoreImage.framework` to the PhotoWheel project.

New Delegate Methods

Since the app will show a small preview of each of the `CIFilter` effects, `PhotoBrowserViewController` needs to be able to look up the small image for the current photo. Also, since we are adding the ability to edit an image and save the changes, the `PhotoBrowserViewController` needs to be able to replace an existing image with a new one. For each of these we'll need to add a new method to the `PhotoBrowserViewControllerDelegate` protocol. First change the protocol declaration in *PhotoBrowserViewController.m* to look like Listing 24.6.

Listing 24.6   **New Delegate Methods to Support Image Editing**

```
@protocol PhotoBrowserViewControllerDelegate <NSObject>
@required
- (NSInteger)photoBrowserViewControllerNumberOfPhotos:
      (PhotoBrowserViewController *)photoBrowser;
- (UIImage *)photoBrowserViewController:
      (PhotoBrowserViewController *)photoBrowser
   imageAtIndex:(NSInteger)index;
- (UIImage *)photoBrowserViewController:
      (PhotoBrowserViewController *)photoBrowser
   smallImageAtIndex:(NSInteger)index;
- (void)photoBrowserViewController:
      (PhotoBrowserViewController *)photoBrowser
   deleteImageAtIndex:(NSInteger)index;
- (void)photoBrowserViewController:
      (PhotoBrowserViewController *)photoBrowser
   updateToNewImage:(UIImage *)image atIndex:(NSInteger)index;
@end
```

The implementations of these methods go in *PhotoAlbumViewController.m*, since that class is acting as the delegate. They are shown in Listing 24.7.

Listing 24.7   **New Delegate Method Implementations**

```
- (UIImage *)photoBrowserViewController:
      (PhotoBrowserViewController *)photoBrowser
   smallImageAtIndex:(NSInteger)index
{
    NSIndexPath *indexPath = [NSIndexPath indexPathForRow:index inSection:0];
    Photo *photo = [[self fetchedResultsController] objectAtIndexPath:indexPath];
    UIImage *image = [photo smallImage];
    return image;
}

- (void)photoBrowserViewController:(PhotoBrowserViewController *)photoBrowser
      updateToNewImage:(UIImage *)image
      atIndex:(NSInteger)index;
{
    NSIndexPath *indexPath = [NSIndexPath indexPathForRow:index inSection:0];
    Photo *photo = [[self fetchedResultsController] objectAtIndexPath:indexPath];
    [photo saveImage:image];
    [[self gridView] reloadData];
}
```

The first method looks up the Photo's small image. It is nearly identical to the existing delegate method that looks up the large image.

The second method is used when the user wants to save changes to an image. It looks up the Photo at the requested index and calls its –saveImage: method. Recall that this method will create a new scaled version of the image. The method then tells its grid view to reload data, so that it will show the new version of the thumbnail.

Instance Variables for Filter Management

The photo browser needs a few new instance variables to manage the filtering process. Add the property declarations in Listing 24.8 to the PhotoBrowserViewController class extension at the top of *PhotoBrowserViewController.m*.

Listing 24.8   **New Instance Variable Declarations for**
                PhotoBrowserViewController

```
@property (readwrite, strong) CIContext *ciContext;
@property (nonatomic, strong) NSMutableArray *imageFilters;
@property (nonatomic, strong) NSMutableArray *filteredThumbnailPreviewImages;
@property (nonatomic, strong) UIImage *filteredThumbnailImage;
@property (nonatomic, strong) UIImage *filteredLargeImage;
```

These variables serve the following purposes:

- ciContext is a persistent CIContext that is used every time a new image is rendered.

- imageFilters contains a collection of CIFilters. The same filter instances are used to create small preview images and full-size filtered images, so they are created once for the previews and saved in imageFilters so that they can be reused for the full-size image.

- filteredThumbnailPreviewImages contains the filter preview images, which are displayed in the UI.

- filteredThumbnailImage is the same as the raw, unfiltered thumbnail image at first. As the user applies filters to the image, filteredThumbnailImage is updated to contain the results of the most recent filter. Each time the user applies a filter, filteredThumbnailImage updates with a new value selected from filteredThumbnailPreviewImages.

- Initially, filteredLargeImage is the same as the raw, unfiltered full-size image. As the user applies filters to the image, filteredLargeImage updates to contain the results of the most recent filter.

Be sure to add @synthesize statements for all of the new properties.

User Interface Additions

Now we need to add the various UI elements the app needs to provide for the user to control the effects. The effects UI goes in PhotoBrowserViewController, since that is where the user views individual images.

The updated UI will have several additional buttons corresponding to instance methods as well as new instance variables that will be used to control the UI's appearance. Start by updating *PhotoBrowserViewController.h* to look like Listing 24.9.

Listing 24.9   **New IBOutlets and IBActions in** *PhotoBrowserViewController.h*

```
@interface PhotoBrowserViewController : UIViewController <UIScrollViewDelegate>

@property (nonatomic, strong) id<PhotoBrowserViewControllerDelegate> delegate;
@property (nonatomic, assign) NSInteger startAtIndex;
@property (nonatomic, assign, getter = pushedFromFrame) CGRect pushFromFrame;

- (void)toggleChromeDisplay;

@property (strong, nonatomic) IBOutlet UIView *filterViewContainer;
@property (strong, nonatomic) IBOutletCollection(UIButton) NSArray *filterButtons;

// Actions that modify the image
- (IBAction)enhanceImage:(id)sender;
- (IBAction)zoomToFaces:(id)sender;
- (IBAction)applyFilter:(id)sender;

// Actions that save or restore the image
- (IBAction)revertToOriginal:(id)sender;
- (IBAction)saveImage:(id)sender;
- (IBAction)cancel:(id)sender;

@end
```

The `filterViewContainer` property will refer to an overall container view for the Core Image effects view. The `filterButtons` array is something new, an `IBOutletCollection` instead of an `IBOutlet`. An `IBOutletCollection` is similar to an `IBOutlet` except that it can refer to multiple user interface elements and can be connected to all of them in the storyboard. In this case the `filterButtons` collection will point to several `UIButtons` in the UI that correspond to different `CIFilter` effects.

The first three `IBActions` will be used to apply Core Image effects to the image. The rest of the new `IBActions` will provide the necessary options to revert changes, save changes, or simply cancel image editing.

Also be sure to add `@synthesize` directives in *PhotoBrowserViewController.m* for the new `IBOutlets`.

Now we'll add the actual UI elements corresponding to the new `IBOutlets` and `IBActions`. In *MainStoryboard.storyboard*, locate the photo browser view controller. The new UI elements will go at the bottom of the main view and will look like those in Figure 24.3.

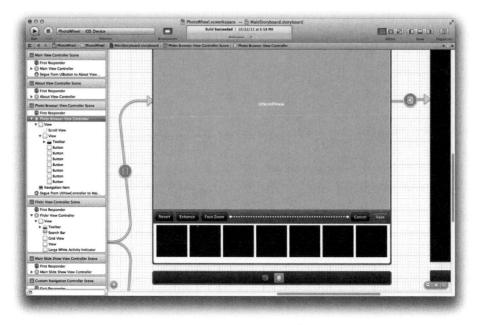

Figure 24.3　New UI elements for Core Image effects

The new elements include a UIToolbar and several UIButtons, contained in an overall container view for filter-related UI.

The toolbar contains five UIBarButtonItems and a flexible space. Add those to the toolbar. To make the **Save** button stand out in blue, make sure its Style is set to Done in the Attributes inspector. Connect these five buttons to the corresponding IBAction methods declared in *PhotoBrowserViewController.h*.

The buttons at the bottom should be 100 × 100 pixels, which is the same as Photo-Wheel's small image size. Set the button Type for the buttons to Custom in the Attributes inspector so that they won't automatically be drawn with a rounded border. Set the background color to something other than white so that they stand out against the background. The buttons will display the images contained in filteredThumbnail-PreviewImages. Since the buttons are the same size as the preview images, the button color won't be visible, but it is helpful to change the color so that you can see them when editing the user interface.

Go through the buttons and set the tag for each one to values from 0 to 6, starting at 0 on the left and working up to 6 on the right. You may need to scroll the Attributes inspector downward to find the Tag option (Figure 24.4). We'll use the tag values later to determine which button was pressed.

Connect the new filterViewContainer IBOutlet to the container view just as you would connect any other IBOutlet. Connecting the filterButtons collection works almost the same way, except that since it is a collection, you can now make multiple connections from the same outlet (Figure 24.5).

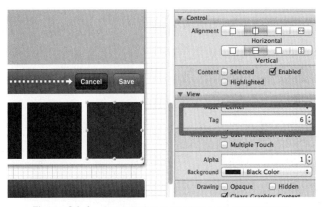

Figure 24.4   Setting the tag value on a `UIButton`

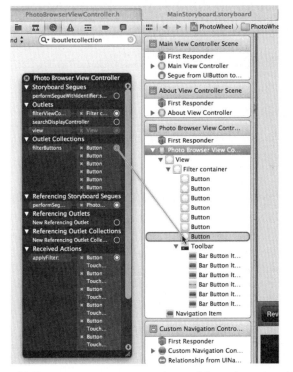

Figure 24.5   Connecting an `IBOutletCollection` to multiple
UI elements

Next, we need to add code to control when the new filter container view is visible. It shouldn't be visible all the time, only when the user wants to use the filters. At other times it should disappear. The first change, then, is to make the view hidden when the photo browser first appears. Do this by adding a line of code in –viewWillAppear that sets the container's alpha to zero:

```
[[self filterViewContainer] setAlpha:0.0];
```

To make the filter container show and hide, add the methods in Listing 24.10 to *PhotoBrowserViewController.m.*

Listing 24.10   **Showing and Hiding the Filter Overlay View**

```
- (void)showFilters:(id)sender
{
   if ([self imageFilters] == nil) {
      [self setImageFilters:
         [NSMutableArray arrayWithCapacity:[[self filterButtons] count]]];

      [self setCiContext:[CIContext contextWithOptions:nil]];

      [self setFilteredThumbnailPreviewImages:[NSMutableArray array]];
   }

   [self setFilteredThumbnailImage:[[self delegate]
      photoBrowserViewController:self
      smallImageAtIndex:[self currentIndex]]];
   UIImage *largeImage = [[self delegate]
      photoBrowserViewController:self
      imageAtIndex:[self currentIndex]];
   [self setFilteredLargeImage:largeImage];

   [self randomizeFilters];

   [[self view] bringSubviewToFront:[self filterViewContainer]];
   [UIView animateWithDuration:0.3 animations:^(void) {
      [[self filterViewContainer] setAlpha:1.0];
   }];
}

- (void)hideFilters
{
   // Hide filter container
   [UIView animateWithDuration:0.3 animations:^(void) {
      [[self filterViewContainer] setAlpha:0.0];
   }];
}
```

The showFilters method handles more than just displaying the filter container. If this is the first time the user has asked to use filters, the method initializes some of the instance variables added earlier, creating empty arrays and the CIContext that will render images. It also sets the initial values of filteredThumbnailImage and filteredLargeImage to images retrieved from the delegate. It creates a collection of CIFilters using the new randomizeFilters method and then displays the filter container view. The code fades the filter container gradually into view by animating its alpha value.

The hideFilters method just makes the filter container invisible by animating its alpha value back to zero.

Now that we have code to show the filter container, we need some way for the user to trigger that code. We'll add a button to the navigation bar to call the -showFilters: method. We already have a method called -addButtonsToNavigationBar that sets up buttons there, and we'll add one more button. Listing 24.11 shows the updated version of this method, with new code highlighted.

Listing 24.11   Updated Toolbar Buttons, Including a Button to Show the Filter Container

```objc
- (void)addButtonsToNavigationBar
{
   UIBarButtonItem *trashButton = [[UIBarButtonItem alloc]
      initWithBarButtonSystemItem:UIBarButtonSystemItemTrash
      target:self
      action:@selector(deletePhoto:)];
   [trashButton setStyle:UIBarButtonItemStyleBordered];

   UIBarButtonItem *actionButton = [[UIBarButtonItem alloc]
      initWithBarButtonSystemItem:UIBarButtonSystemItemAction
      target:self action:@selector(showActionMenu:)];
   [actionButton setStyle:UIBarButtonItemStyleBordered];
   [self setActionButton:actionButton];

   UIBarButtonItem *slideshowButton = [[UIBarButtonItem alloc]
      initWithTitle:@"Slideshow"
      style:UIBarButtonItemStyleBordered
      target:self
      action:@selector(slideshow:)];

   UIBarButtonItem *flexibleSpace = [[UIBarButtonItem alloc]
      initWithBarButtonSystemItem:UIBarButtonSystemItemFlexibleSpace
      target:nil
      action:nil];

   UIBarButtonItem *filterButton = [[UIBarButtonItem alloc]
      initWithTitle:@"Edit"
      style:UIBarButtonItemStyleBordered
```

```
    target:self
    action:@selector(showFilters:)];

NSMutableArray *toolbarItems = [[NSMutableArray alloc]
    initWithCapacity:4];
[toolbarItems addObject:flexibleSpace];
[toolbarItems addObject:filterButton];
[toolbarItems addObject:slideshowButton];
[toolbarItems addObject:actionButton];
[toolbarItems addObject:trashButton];

UIToolbar *toolbar = [[ClearToolbar alloc]
    initWithFrame:CGRectMake(0, 0, 250, 44)];
[toolbar setBackgroundColor:[UIColor clearColor]];
[toolbar setBarStyle:UIBarStyleBlack];
[toolbar setTranslucent:YES];

[toolbar setItems:toolbarItems];

UIBarButtonItem *customBarButtonItem = [[UIBarButtonItem alloc]
    initWithCustomView:toolbar];
[[self navigationItem] setRightBarButtonItem:customBarButtonItem animated:YES];
}
```

This code is mostly the same as before except for the extra button and the wider size when creating the `UIToolbar`.

One other UI management detail that we need to handle is sorting the buttons in the `filterButtons` array. Using `IBOutletCollection` is convenient for grouping the buttons into an array. But unfortunately the order of the array is not guaranteed. In order to make sure the array is sorted so that it corresponds to the tag values, we'll override the setter method for `filterButtons` and sort the array by button tag. This method is given in Listing 24.12.

Listing 24.12 Sorting the `filterButtons` Array by Button Tag Values

```
- (void)setFilterButtons:(NSArray *)filterButtonsFromIB
{
    -filterButtons = [filterButtonsFromIB sortedArrayUsingComparator:
      ^NSComparisonResult(UIButton *button1, UIButton *button2) {
        return [button1 tag] > [button2 tag];
      }];
}
```

This method takes the incoming array `filterButtonsFromIB`, which contains the buttons in some unknown order, and sorts it using an `NSComparator` block. The block looks at the tag values for a pair of buttons and returns the result of comparing them. `NSArray` calls the block repeatedly with different pairs of buttons and produces a new sorted array. The result is an array where the contents are sorted by tag value. The code assigns this result to `filterButtons`.

Creating the `CIFilter` Effects

PhotoWheel will use several different filters for different visual effects. To provide some variety in these effects, we'll use random values for numeric and color filter parameters. First, we need to get random numbers. Add the `RAND_IN_RANGE` macro to the top of *PhotoBrowserViewController.m*:

```
#define RAND_IN_RANGE(low,high) (low + (high - low) * \
    (arc4random_uniform(RAND_MAX) / (double)RAND_MAX))
```

This macro produces a random number in the range from `low` to `high`, which can be either integer or floating-point values. With `arc4random_uniform`, it isn't necessary to seed the random number generation process, so we won't add code for that.

We'll use this macro to create random colors for use in filters. Core Image uses its own `CIColor` class to represent colors. `CIColor` can be instantiated with RGB or RGBA values, so we'll use two methods that use random values for the color parameters. These are shown in Listing 24.13. Add them to *PhotoBrowserViewController.m*.

Listing 24.13 Creating Random `CIColor`s

```
- (CIColor *)randomCIColor
{
   CIColor *randomColor = [CIColor colorWithRed:RAND_IN_RANGE(0.0, 1.0)
                                          green:RAND_IN_RANGE(0.0, 1.0)
                                           blue:RAND_IN_RANGE(0.0, 1.0)];
   return randomColor;
}


- (CIColor *)randomCIColorAlpha
{
   CIColor *randomColor = [CIColor colorWithRed:RAND_IN_RANGE(0.0, 1.0)
                                          green:RAND_IN_RANGE(0.0, 1.0)
                                           blue:RAND_IN_RANGE(0.0, 1.0)
                                          alpha:RAND_IN_RANGE(0.0, 1.0)];
   return randomColor;
}
```

The `randomCIColor` method creates a `CIColor` with random red, green, and blue values. In `randomCIColorAlpha` this is expanded slightly to include a value for alpha, which allows for partially transparent colors.

Now we'll create the actual `CIFilters`. The user interface has seven buttons for different filters. But filters have different effects depending on how they are configured, so there are only five methods for creating different filters. These are shown in Listing 24.14.

Listing 24.14   Creating Randomly Configured `CIFilters`

```objc
- (CIFilter *)hueAdjustFilter
{
    CIFilter *hueAdjust = [CIFilter filterWithName:@"CIHueAdjust"];
    CGFloat inputAngle = RAND_IN_RANGE(-M_PI, M_PI);
    [hueAdjust setValue:[NSNumber numberWithFloat: inputAngle]
        forKey:@"inputAngle"];
    return hueAdjust;
}


- (CIFilter *)colorTintFilter
{
    CIColor *tintColor = [self randomCIColor];
    CIFilter *tintFilter = [CIFilter filterWithName:@"CIColorMonochrome"];
    [tintFilter setValue:tintColor forKey:@"inputColor"];
    return tintFilter;
}


- (CIFilter *)falseColorFilter
{
    CIColor *color0 = [self randomCIColor];
    CIColor *color1 = [CIColor colorWithRed:(1.0 - [color0 red])
                                      green:(1.0 - [color0 green])
                                       blue:(1.0 - [color0 blue])];
    CIFilter *falseColor = [CIFilter filterWithName:@"CIFalseColor"];
    [falseColor setValue:color0 forKey:@"inputColor0"];
    [falseColor setValue:color1 forKey:@"inputColor1"];
    return falseColor;
}


- (CIFilter *)invertColorFilter
{
    CIFilter *invertFilter = [CIFilter filterWithName:@"CIColorInvert"];
    return invertFilter;
}


- (CIFilter *)filterWithAffineTransform:(CGAffineTransform)transform
{
    CIFilter *transformFilter = [CIFilter filterWithName:@"CIAffineTransform"];
    [transformFilter setDefaults];
    [transformFilter setValue:[NSValue valueWithCGAffineTransform:transform]
        forKey:@"inputTransform"];
    return transformFilter;
}
```

The methods in Listing 24.14 create the following types of filters:

- **CIHueAdjust:** Rotates the color cube used in the image by an angle measured in radians. The effect is that all the colors in the image shift their hue by a fixed amount.

- **CIColorMonochrome:** Tints the image using a single color, giving the effect of seeing the image though a color filter.

- **CIFalseColor:** Alters image colors over a range defined by two colors based on brightness. Brighter colors shift toward one of the color parameters and darker colors toward the other parameter.

- **CIColorInvert:** Inverts image colors. Note that this filter is not actually random since there are no numeric parameters.

- **CIAffineTransform:** Applies an affine transform to the image, which can change its shape or size via matrix math. Affine transforms can rotate images or flip or skew them depending on the affine transform. This method will be used repeatedly with different transform types.

We now have everything we need to create the filters and set up the thumbnail preview images in the user interface. This happens in the randomizeFilters method mentioned earlier, which was called from showFilters. This method is shown in Listing 24.15.

> **Note**
>
> All of these filters are independent of their input image. That means that they can be used repeatedly, on different images, exactly as they are. As a result, we can use them to create preview thumbnail images and then reuse them later on the large image.

Listing 24.15 **Creating New Randomized Filters**

```
- (void)randomizeFilters
{
    [[self imageFilters] removeAllObjects];
    [[self filteredThumbnailPreviewImages] removeAllObjects];

    // Hue adjust filter
    CIFilter *hueAdjustFilter = [self hueAdjustFilter];
    [[self imageFilters] addObject:hueAdjustFilter];

    // Color tint filter
    CIFilter *tintFilter = [self colorTintFilter];
    [[self imageFilters] addObject:tintFilter];

    // False color filter
    CIFilter *falseColorFilter = [self falseColorFilter];
    [[self imageFilters] addObject:falseColorFilter];
```

```objectivec
    // Invert color filter
    CIFilter *invertFilter = [self invertColorFilter];
    [[self imageFilters] addObject:invertFilter];

    // Rotate 180 degrees filter
    CIFilter *rotateFilter = [self filterWithAffineTransform:
      CGAffineTransformMakeRotation(M_PI)];
    [[self imageFilters] addObject:rotateFilter];

    // Mirror image filter
    CIFilter *mirrorFilter = [self filterWithAffineTransform:
      CGAffineTransformMakeScale(-1, 1)];
    [[self imageFilters] addObject:mirrorFilter];

    // Skew filter
    CIFilter *skewFilter = [self filterWithAffineTransform:
      CGAffineTransformMake(1, tan(M_PI/12), tan(M_PI/16), 1, 0, 0)];
    [[self imageFilters] addObject:skewFilter];

    CIImage *thumbnailCIImage = [CIImage imageWithCGImage:
      [[self filteredThumbnailImage] CGImage]];

    dispatch_apply([[self imageFilters] count],
      dispatch_get_global_queue(DISPATCH_QUEUE_PRIORITY_DEFAULT, 0),
      ^(size_t i) {

      CIFilter *filter = [[self imageFilters] objectAtIndex:i];
      [filter setValue:thumbnailCIImage forKey:kCIInputImageKey];
      CIImage *filterResult = [filter outputImage];

      CGImageRef filteredCGImage = [[self ciContext]
         createCGImage:filterResult
         fromRect:[filterResult extent]];
      UIImage *filteredImage = [UIImage imageWithCGImage:filteredCGImage];
      CFRelease(filteredCGImage);

      [[self filteredThumbnailPreviewImages] addObject:filteredImage];

      dispatch_async(dispatch_get_main_queue(), ^(void) {
         UIButton *filterButton = [[self filterButtons] objectAtIndex:i];
         [filterButton setImage:filteredImage forState:UIControlStateNormal];
      });
    });
}
```

A lot happens in this method, but it is not as complex as it might seem at first. The first thing the method does is clear out any previously existing filters and filter preview images by clearing the arrays that hold them. The method then runs through the `CIFilter` methods described earlier, creating several filters and collecting them in the `imageFilters` array. Notice that this method calls `-filterWithAffine-Transform:` three times with different transforms, to get different effects. A full discussion of `CGAffineTransform` is beyond the scope of this book, but Core Graphics provides convenience functions for common transforms like rotating or scaling images. For the mirror image filter we use a scale filter that scales the X-axis by −1 and leaves the Y-axis unchanged. This effectively flips the image without changing its size.

The method then converts the current image in `filteredThumbnailImage` to a `CIImage` so that it can be used with `CIFilters`.

To create the preview images the method makes use of `dispatch_apply`. This is a GCD function that works sort of like a `for` loop, in that it calls its block of code multiple times. Unlike a `for` loop, though, `dispatch_apply` can use multiple processor cores to run more than one pass through the block at the same time. That can be a big advantage on multicore systems, provided the block code is thread safe. The first argument to `dispatch_apply` tells it how many times to run the block. The block takes one argument, an integer that tells it which pass-through the block is running. This argument takes the place of a `for` loop's index value.

The first thing the block does is look up a `CIFilter` in the `imageFilters` array, set its input image to the current thumbnail, and get its output image. It then renders that image as a `CGImageRef` and converts the rendered image to a `UIImage`. This `UIImage` goes into the `filteredThumbnailPreviewImages` array.

Updating the user interface needs to be done on the main thread, so the block uses `dispatch_apply` to call back to the main thread and update the current `filter-Button` with the new preview image.

Applying the Filters

Now that we're creating filters and preview images, we're ready to apply filters to the original large image. Recall from earlier that all seven of the new filter buttons at the bottom of the photo browser are connected to the `applyFilter` method. The implementation of this method is shown in Listing 24.16.

Listing 24.16 **Applying Filters from the Seven Filter Preview Buttons**

```
- (void)applySpecifiedFilter:(CIFilter *)filter
{
    CIImage *filteredLargeImage = [filter outputImage];
    CGImageRef filteredLargeCGImage = [[self ciContext]
        createCGImage:filteredLargeImage
        fromRect:[filteredLargeImage extent]];
    UIImage *filteredImage = [UIImage imageWithCGImage:filteredLargeCGImage];
    [[[self photoViewCache] objectAtIndex:[self currentIndex]]
        setImage:filteredImage];
```

```
    [self setFilteredLargeImage:filteredImage];
    CFRelease(filteredLargeCGImage);
}

- (IBAction)applyFilter:(id)sender {
    CIFilter *filter = [[self imageFilters] objectAtIndex:[sender tag]];
    [self applySpecifiedFilter:filter];
    [self setFilteredThumbnailImage:
      [[self filteredThumbnailPreviewImages] objectAtIndex:[sender tag]]];
    [self randomizeFilters];
}
```

The `applyFilter` method looks up the selected filter based on the tag value of the button tapped by the user. Recall that the tag values on the preview buttons range from 0 to 6. These values correspond to the index values used to look up entries in `imageFilters`.

The `applySpecifiedFilter` method does the work of applying the selected filter to the large image, following the pattern described earlier. The resulting image is displayed in the user interface and saved in `filteredLargeImage`. Saving the filtered image in an instance variable makes the filter effects cumulative, since this saved image always contains the result of the most recently applied filter.

Back in `applyFilter`, the code sets the current value of `filteredThumbnail-Image` to one of the previously rendered images in `filteredThumbnailPreview-Images`. Again, this is so that the filter effects will be cumulative. Finally, the code calls `randomizeFilters` to create new filter options and update the preview thumbnails.

Implementing Auto-Enhance

Using the auto-enhance capability is comparatively simple and not that different from the sample auto-enhance code presented earlier. The implementation of `enhance-Image` is shown in Listing 24.17.

Listing 24.17   PhotoWheel's Image Auto-enhance Method

```
- (IBAction)enhanceImage:(id)sender {
    CIImage *largeCIImage = [CIImage imageWithCGImage:
      [[self filteredLargeImage] CGImage]];
    NSArray *autoAdjustmentFilters = [largeCIImage autoAdjustmentFilters];
    CIImage *enhancedImage = largeCIImage;
    for (CIFilter *filter in autoAdjustmentFilters) {
        [filter setValue:enhancedImage forKey:kCIInputImageKey];
        enhancedImage = [filter outputImage];
    }
    [self applySpecifiedFilter:[autoAdjustmentFilters lastObject]];
}
```

As discussed earlier in the section on auto-enhancement, this method asks the large CIImage for a full set of enhancement filters, chains those filters together, and gets the final resulting CIImage. It passes the final filter in the chain to applySpecified-Filter, which handles updating the UI and saving the new image so that further filters can be applied.

Implementing Face Zoom

Earlier we discussed how to locate faces in a photo, but in PhotoWheel we'll take that a little further. Once we find faces, we'll automatically zoom the photo in on the faces, based on the face locations found during image analysis. Listing 24.18 shows the method that implements this.

Listing 24.18 **Finding Faces and Zooming In on Them**

```
- (IBAction)zoomToFaces:(id)sender {
  NSDictionary *detectorOptions = [NSDictionary
      dictionaryWithObject:CIDetectorAccuracyLow
      forKey:CIDetectorAccuracy];
  CIDetector *faceDetector = [CIDetector
      detectorOfType:CIDetectorTypeFace
      context:nil
      options:detectorOptions];

  CIImage *largeCIImage = [CIImage imageWithCGImage:
      [[self filteredLargeImage] CGImage]];
  NSArray *faces = [faceDetector featuresInImage:largeCIImage options:nil];

  if ([faces count] > 0) {
    CGRect faceZoomRect = CGRectNull;

    for (CIFaceFeature *face in faces) {
      if (CGRectEqualToRect(faceZoomRect, CGRectNull)) {
        faceZoomRect = [face bounds];
      } else {
        faceZoomRect = CGRectUnion(faceZoomRect, [face bounds]);
      }
    }

    faceZoomRect = CGRectIntersection([largeCIImage extent],
      CGRectInset(faceZoomRect, -50.0, -50.0)) ;

    CIFilter *cropFilter = [CIFilter filterWithName:@"CICrop"];
    [cropFilter setValue:largeCIImage forKey:kCIInputImageKey];
    [cropFilter setValue:[CIVector
      vectorWithCGRect:faceZoomRect] forKey:@"inputRectangle"];
```

```
      [self applySpecifiedFilter:cropFilter];
    } else {
      UIAlertView *noFacesAlert = [[UIAlertView alloc]
        initWithTitle:@"No Faces"
        message:@"Sorry, I couldn't find any faces in this picture."
        delegate:nil
        cancelButtonTitle:@"OK"
        otherButtonTitles:nil];
      [noFacesAlert show];
    }
}
```

Detecting faces in −zoomToFaces: is the same as we discussed earlier. What is new here is what we do with the face information.

We can get the bounds of each face in the image. In order to zoom in on the faces, we need to calculate a rectangle that encompasses all of them. The code uses the faceZoomRect variable for this. Initially the code sets it to CGRectNull, which is a constant defining a rectangle with no valid location or size. For each face, the code checks to see if faceZoomRect has changed. If not, it saves the current face location in faceZoomRect. If faceZoomRect has changed, the code calculates the union of the faceZoomRect and the new face location. In this way faceZoomRect grows to encompass all faces in the photo.

Next the code adjusts faceZoomRect a little. It uses CGRectInset to expand faceZoomRect by 50 pixels on all sides, to widen the zoom slightly. This isn't strictly needed, but the unmodified faceZoomRect can lead to a zoom that feels somewhat cramped. If there are faces close to the edge of the picture, adjusting the zoom might result in a rectangle whose bounds go beyond the edge of the picture. The code uses CGRectIntersection to ensure that the final value of faceZoomRect doesn't go beyond the large image's extent.

Now that we have a rectangle containing the faces, we need to crop the image. The code does this using the CICrop filter, using faceZoomRect as the crop area.

> **Note**
>
> Core Image once again has its own type to represent the filter parameters. In this case Core Image needs a CIVector to represent the crop area, so the code makes the conversion and applies the filter.

If no faces were found, the faces array will be empty. The code then skips the zooming code and just displays a message to the user. A different approach you might want to try is to detect faces in advance and, if none are found, either disable or hide the **Face Zoom** button.

Other Necessary Methods

We need a few utility methods to make the filter view fully useful. Users need to be able to save filtered images or discard them, or revert the filtered image to the original and start over. These methods are shown in Listing 24.19.

Listing 24.19   **Filter Utility Methods**

```
- (IBAction)revertToOriginal:(id)sender {
    [self setFilteredThumbnailImage:[[self delegate]
       photoBrowserViewController:self
       smallImageAtIndex:[self currentIndex]]];
    [self randomizeFilters];
    UIImage *originalImage = [[self delegate]
       photoBrowserViewController:self
       imageAtIndex:[self currentIndex]];
    [[[self photoViewCache] objectAtIndex:[self currentIndex]]
       setImage:originalImage];
    [self setFilteredLargeImage:originalImage];
}

- (IBAction)saveImage:(id)sender {
    // Save the filtered large image
    if ([self filteredLargeImage] != nil) {
        [[self delegate] photoBrowserViewController:self
           updateToNewImage:[self filteredLargeImage]
           atIndex:[self currentIndex]];
    }

    [self hideFilters];
}

- (IBAction)cancel:(id)sender {
    // Restore original large image
    UIImage *originalImage = [[self delegate]
       photoBrowserViewController:self
       imageAtIndex:[self currentIndex]];
    [[[self photoViewCache] objectAtIndex:[self currentIndex]]
       setImage:originalImage];

    [self hideFilters];
}
```

The -revertToOriginal: method reloads the original images from the delegate, displays them, and generates new filters using randomizeFilters. It leaves the filter buttons visible so that the user can continue exploring the filter effects.

The -saveImage: method replaces the current original image with the filtered large image, saving changes via the delegate. It hides the filter view, since this completes filtering for this photo.

The -cancel: method restores the original image but, unlike -revertTo-Original:, it doesn't restore the thumbnail or generate new filters. Instead, it simply hides the filter container.

Summary

Core Image frequently inspires more than a little trepidation at first. Basic Core Image filtering is surprisingly easy, though, and it can improve images or be used for fun and interesting visual effects. As often happens with iOS development, the really hard work is already complete and built into the frameworks. In this chapter, we leveraged the framework to enhance PhotoWheel with features that might appear complex but are surprisingly straightforward.

Up until now, we have mostly assumed that the app is working as expected. Of course, often that's not the case. Despite your best efforts, it is extremely rare to get your code right on the first try. In the next chapter we'll explore tools available to find and fix bugs in your code. We'll also see how to monitor and analyze an app's performance to make sure it runs efficiently and stays responsive.

Exercises

1. Add a new effect using the CIExposureAdjust filter. To create the filter, add a new method called -exposureAdjustFilter, similar to the other filter creation methods described in this chapter. CIExposureAdjust takes two arguments. One is the same input image argument described for other filters in this chapter. The other is called inputEV, which adjusts exposure and takes values in a range from -10 to 10. To show this filter on the screen you can either replace one of the existing filters or add another thumbnail view to the user interface. If you choose to add a new thumbnail, you will need to make the existing thumbnails smaller so that there's room for a new one. Don't forget to set the tag on the new thumbnail button!

2. Try a more complex multistage effect. One good example is to use the CICheckerboardGenerator filter to create a semitransparent image that you then overlay on the original image. As with the previous exercise, you'll need to either replace one of the existing effects or make room for a new one, and you should add a new method that generates a randomly configured version of the effect. To add this effect, you'll need three filters chained together:

   a. A CICheckerboardGenerator filter to create the checkerboard. This filter has two color arguments, inputColor0 and inputColor1. Use the

-randomCIColorAlpha method described in this chapter for these arguments. It also has an inputWidth argument that should be somewhere from 50 to 100 pixels, and an inputSharpness argument that should be a random number from 0 to 1.

b. A CICrop filter to make the generated checkerboard image the same size as the original image. The generated checkerboard goes on forever, and this step converts it to be the size of the original image. The input image should be the output from the CICheckerboardGenerator in the previous step, and the inputRectangle argument should be the original image's size (recall that this is called the extent for CIImage).

c. A CISourceOverCompositing filter to combine the original image and the checkerboard into a new image. Make the input image the cropped checkerboard from the previous filter, and make the inputBackground-Image argument the original image.

Part III
The Finishing Touches

25

Debugging

As you develop an app, you'll find at times that the app isn't behaving quite as you expected. Maybe the screen layout seems off, or maybe the app is just crashing. Xcode provides a number of useful tools for finding and fixing bugs. In this chapter we'll discuss these tools as well as the more general question of narrowing down and finding the source of problems.

Understand the Problem

The first thing you need to do when confronted with a bug is to get the most detailed, accurate picture of the problem that you can. Getting a clear picture of the bug from the outside is a crucial first step in understanding what is wrong on the inside. Diving right into the code is rarely the best approach.

What Went Wrong?

The first step is making sure you understand exactly what happened that was unexpected and what steps the user had taken when this happened. If you're testing the app yourself, you may have a pretty good idea already. If someone else was testing the app, try to get as much detail as possible. Without a good description of what seemed to be wrong with the app, it can be almost impossible to track the cause. A bug description needs to be very specific. Longtime developers have all seen at one time or another a bug report that reads something like "I was using the app and it crashed." Unfortunately, that statement is entirely useless when it comes to fixing the problem. Unless the app is crashing constantly, you don't have anything to go on to find the problem. And if the app *is* crashing constantly, you're probably painfully aware of that fact already.

Reproducing Bugs

Once you have that clear picture, it's time to reproduce the problem. Occasionally there will be situations where you're familiar with the code to the point that the bug description makes it obvious where the code is going wrong. More commonly, though, the cause of the problem is not immediately obvious. In those cases, sit down with the app and *make the bug happen*. Explore different ways of using the app to see if there are other circumstances that could cause the problem. Maybe taking a slightly different set of steps prevents the bug from appearing or makes it worse. Try to find the minimal test case that gets directly to the bug as quickly as possible with as little extra work as possible.

If you find that you can't reproduce the bug, you have a problem. It is extremely difficult to fix a problem that you can't see. If nothing else, you may not be able to tell if you have fixed the problem even if you change the code. Subtle or intermittent problems may require considerable detective work to uncover where things go awry. You might need to make your test data resemble the user's test data. In extreme cases you might need to get the user's data onto your own device. Bugs can also depend on timing or in unusual cases even the time of day.

Debugging Concepts

Xcode includes a built-in debugger. New developers often underestimate or misunderstand the use of debuggers and avoid them, but they don't know what they are missing. In this section we'll cover some of the tools and techniques debuggers offer. If you have used debuggers on other platforms, you can skip ahead to the following section, which discusses how Xcode's debugger works.

Without a doubt, *the debugger is the second-most important tool in your arsenal as a developer.* The only tool that is more important is the compiler itself. If you're not using the debugger to investigate your code, you're missing out on an incredibly useful tool. If you haven't used one before, debuggers can seem daunting at first. But whatever time you take to learn to use a good debugger will be repaid many times over in the time saved finding and fixing bugs.

What Is a "Debugger" Anyway?

A debugger is a specialized tool that can run another application and control and monitor that application's progress. It's like opening the hood on a car engine to inspect and make adjustments while the motor is running. You'll use a debugger to investigate what is actually happening in your code while that code is running. You can understand a lot by reading and thinking about the code, but you'll almost always learn a lot more when you can see every step of the code as it really happens.

Breakpoints

Probably the most common use of a debugger is to set breakpoints in code. A breakpoint is just a line in the code where you want to see what is happening. You'll set breakpoints on lines you suspect of buggy behavior. Once you have added a breakpoint for a line, you run the code in the debugger and interact with the app normally.

When the code reaches the line with the breakpoint, it stops. It's as though time has suddenly stopped for the app, but not for you. At this point you can use the debugger to inspect the state of the program and see if it is operating the way it should. You can see the values of variables and change them, and even call functions while paused at the breakpoint.

When you're finished, you can tell the debugger to continue running the program, and it picks up where it left off. You can also have the debugger run through the code one line at a time, breaking after each one. Doing this can give you a very clear picture of what is happening in the code.

Another kind of breakpoint affects specific conditions instead of specific lines of code. The effect is the same as a breakpoint, but the program stops because of an event or situation rather than because it reaches the right line. A good example is an exception breakpoint. Certain kinds of bugs in code cause exceptions to be thrown, and if the exceptions aren't handled, the app will crash. An exception breakpoint is one that stops the app whenever an exception is thrown, regardless of where it happened. You can also create what's called a watchpoint to track changes to a variable. With a watchpoint, the debugger will break any time the value of a variable changes. If you're not sure when or why a value changed, watching the variable will help uncover the problem.

Debugging in Xcode

Now let's investigate how you can use these techniques in Xcode.

Setting and Managing Breakpoints

Xcode's options for setting breakpoints are shown in Figure 25.1.

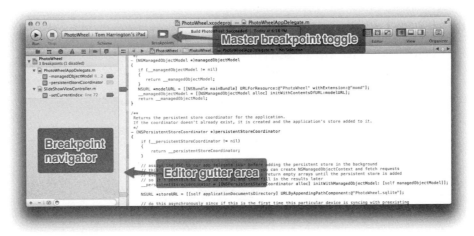

Figure 25.1   Setting breakpoints in Xcode

The quickest way to set a breakpoint on a line is in the editor's gutter, which is the vertical band on the left side of the source code pane. To set a breakpoint on a line, click in the gutter next to the line. A blue pointer appears next to the line. You can disable and reenable a breakpoint by clicking this blue indicator. Figure 25.1 shows two breakpoints in *PhotoWheelAppDelegate.m*. The first, in -managedObjectModel, is enabled. The second, in -persistentStoreCoordinator, is disabled.

To remove a breakpoint in the editor gutter, drag the blue pointer out of the gutter.

On the left side of the window is the Breakpoint navigator. This lists all breakpoints, including those that are disabled. Breakpoints are organized by source file. Clicking on one of them opens the corresponding source file at the line where the breakpoint is set. You can also disable and reenable breakpoints here, by clicking on the blue pointer icon. To delete a breakpoint in the Breakpoint navigator, either drag it out of the navigator or select it and press the **Delete** key.

At the top of the window is the master breakpoint toggle button (**⌘-Y**). This button controls whether the app will run with breakpoints or without them. Clicking this button affects the overall run environment when the app is running. It does not affect whether individual breakpoints are enabled; instead it determines whether any breakpoints will be used while the app is running. You can change this state while the app is running.

Customizing Breakpoints

If you right-click on a breakpoint in the Breakpoint navigator and select Edit Breakpoint from the popup menu, a popover appears that you can use to customize the breakpoint's behavior (Figure 25.2).

This popover offers the following options:

- Specify a condition that must be true for the breakpoint to stop the app. If you want to stop the app only when a variable has a specific value, you can enter a test for this condition here.

- Tell Xcode that it should ignore the breakpoint some number of times before stopping. This can be useful for breakpoints in loops, if you want to stop in the loop but only after, say, 50 passes through. Without this you would have to hit the breakpoint 50 times and continue after each one.

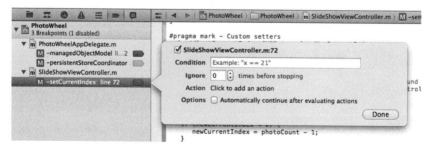

Figure 25.2   Editing a breakpoint

- Configure a variety of automatic actions to take when the breakpoint is hit (more on this later).
- Tell Xcode that it should automatically continue after executing any custom actions the breakpoint has.

Why would you want to have Xcode automatically continue when it hits a breakpoint? It turns out that breakpoints can do a number of useful things even if the app keeps running. You configure these in the Action section of the popover.

One good use for breakpoint actions is to replace the NSLog statements that are so common when code is in development. Often you want to know that a method has been called or find out the value of a variable at a particular line, but you don't necessarily want to stop the app to find this out. It's enough just to get the information. Or you might be investigating a bug that depends on getting just the right timing, and stopping the app ends up preventing the bug from happening. Developers commonly add an NSLog that prints out the information of interest, which is simple and effective. But it's also messy and can get confusing. NSLog statements have a way of sticking around long after their usefulness has expired, leading to extremely verbose output that can make it hard to find the one line you're interested in. They also really need to be cleaned out before the app is released so as not to fill up the system console on people's iPads.

One of the breakpoint actions is the Log Message action, which just prints a message to the device console. It's more or less the same as using NSLog except that it doesn't clutter up the source code. This action can also speak the text aloud using speech synthesis instead of printing the message, so you can listen for it instead of watching the console. Figure 25.3 shows an example of this. In this case the breakpoint is in the –managedObjectModel method. When the code reaches the line with the breakpoint, it says, "Starting managedObjectModel" and then continues without stopping the app.

A similar option is to have Xcode play a sound when the code hits the breakpoint (Figure 25.4). This can be used similarly to having Xcode speak a message. It is useful for monitoring code when you expect to hit a breakpoint frequently. As you use

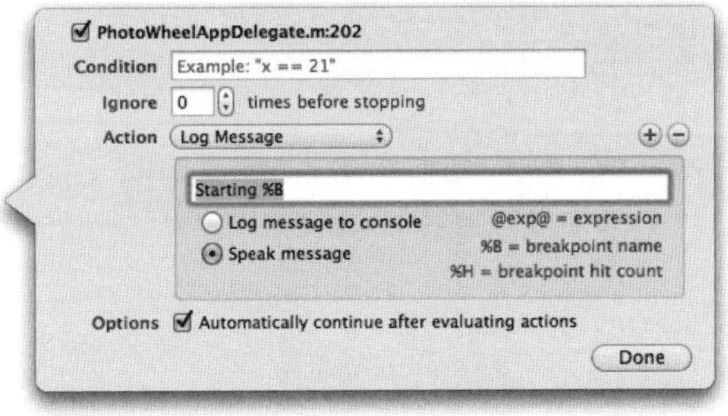

Figure 25.3   Adding a Log Message action to a breakpoint

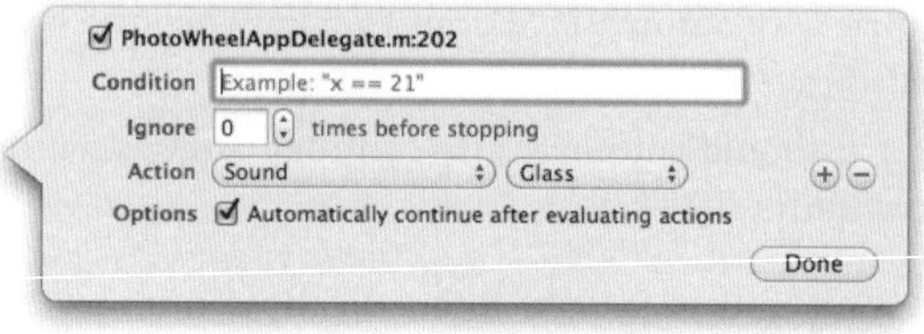

Figure 25.4   Configuring a breakpoint to play a sound and continue

the app, the sounds will often form a rhythm, and if the rhythm breaks, it's a clue that something isn't happening the way it should.

You can add multiple actions to a breakpoint by clicking the **+** button on the right side of the popover.

Hitting a Breakpoint

When the app hits a breakpoint and stops, Xcode will look like Figure 25.5.

There are a number of things of interest in this window:

- **Current line.** The current line in the app is highlighted in the editor, so that you always know where you are in the app. The highlighted line has not been executed yet—the highlighting indicates the next line that would run if the app were to continue.

- **Debug navigator.** This shows the current state of all threads in the app. In Figure 25.5 we see that the app is stopped at a breakpoint in [PhotoWheel-AppDelegate managedObjectModel], which is in thread 1. The information displayed under the thread 1 heading is a call stack, showing the method that

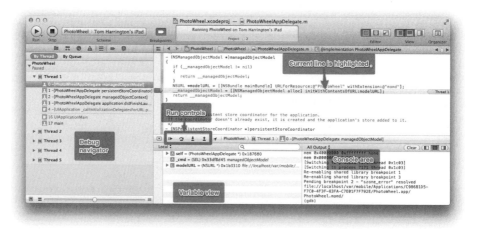

Figure 25.5   Xcode window when stopped at a breakpoint

called –managedObjectModel, and the one that called *that* method, and so on. Methods that are part of iOS frameworks rather than the app are grayed out.

You can explore the call stack by clicking on different methods. When you do, the code editor will update to show the current line in that method. In this case we could immediately jump to the line that called –managedObjectModel, for example.

The slider at the bottom of the Debug navigator controls how much detail is included in the call stack. Xcode normally tries to limit the information to methods that are likely to be of interest (i.e., those that are part of your app). You can adjust the level of detail to show more or less information.

- **Run controls.** These four buttons allow you to control what happens next in the program's flow. The first button tells Xcode to continue running the app normally from the current line. The app continues until it reaches another breakpoint, if there are others. Next to this is the "step over" button, which steps forward one line and *does not* step into functions or methods that might be called. After that, the "step into" button also steps forward one line but will step into any functions or methods that are called, if the source code is available (it won't step into system framework methods since you don't have the source for them). Finally, the "step out" button tells Xcode that the app should continue running but only until the current function or method ends.

- **Variable view.** This pane normally displays the value of any local variables. In Figure 25.5 you see that modelURL is included here, since it is local to the current method. There's a popup menu at the top of the variable view that selects different modes such as displaying global variables as well as locals.

- **Console.** The console displays messages from the debugger about the app's state, as well as the output from any NSLog or other printing statements. The console also has a command-line interface to the debugger which can be used to control the debug session and to inspect and change variable values. We'll talk about some debugger commands a little later. In Figure 25.5 the breakpoint was configured to print the value of modelURL when the app hit the breakpoint, so you can see the full value in the console.

Checking on Variables

Often the variable view is all you need to check on variables. In Figure 25.5, you can see the URL stored in modelURL—some of it, anyway—and you could get more by dragging the split between the variable view and the console area to the right. You could also hover the mouse pointer over modelURL in the code editor and look at a popup window that has a little more space (Figure 25.6).

The variable view doesn't always have enough information, though. In Figure 25.7, for example, the variable view tells us that options is a dictionary and that it has two key-value pairs. That's nice, and sometimes that's all you need to know.

Figure 25.6   Displaying a variable's value by hovering the mouse pointer over it

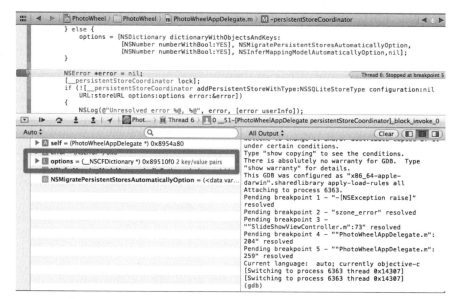

Figure 25.7   Variable view information about an NSDictionary

But you might want to know what data is actually saved in those key-value pairs. Hovering the mouse pointer over options doesn't help in this case either (Figure 25.8).

Fortunately there are a couple of other options. One way is to select the variable in the variable view and right-click. The contextual popup menu includes an option to print a description of the variable (Figure 25.9). It also includes some other useful things, like the ability to set a watchpoint on the selected variable.

If you select this menu item, the description is printed in the console area (Figure 25.10).

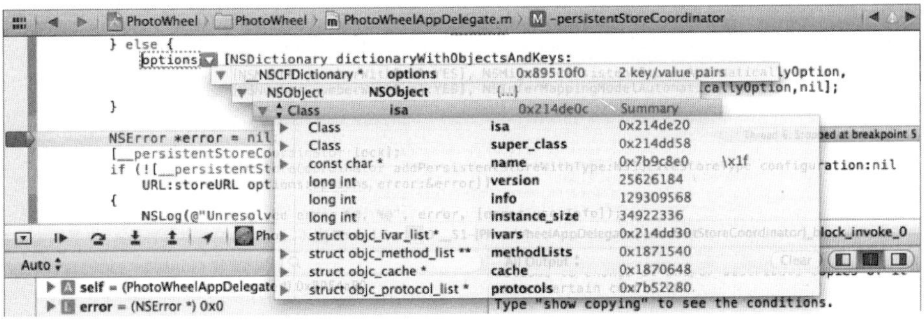

Figure 25.8   Hovering the mouse pointer over an `NSDictionary`

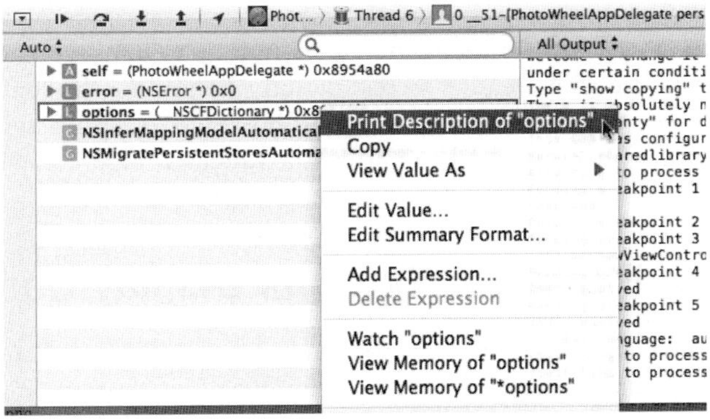

Figure 25.9   The variable view contextual menu

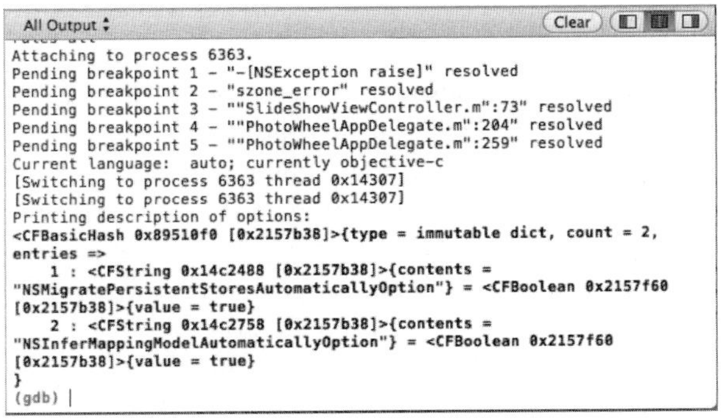

Figure 25.10   Console output after selecting the Print Description
menu item

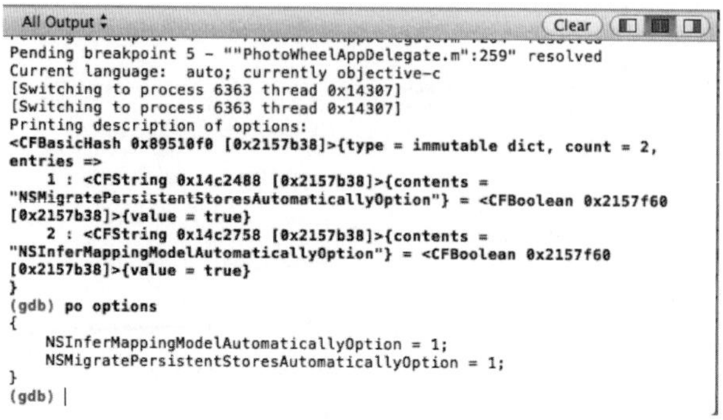

Figure 25.11 Using the `po` command in the debug console

That might be more information than you really want to know about `options`, but the keys and values are all present. A second option is to just use the console command line directly. The `po` command in the console is shorthand for "print object." It calls the object's `-description` method and prints the result. As Figure 25.11 shows, it is sometimes easier to understand than the contextual menu's version.

Debugging Example: External Display Code

While writing Chapter 23's sample code for using external displays, there was a puzzling bug at one point. Although the app was running a slideshow on an external display, the images were off-center. They were too low and off to the left, leaving a large black L-shaped space along the top and right side of the display.

Experimenting with different ways to reproduce the bug didn't turn up a lot of information. The problem occurred anytime a slideshow started, and always in the same way. Well, almost always.

The bug first showed up when using a 720p television as an external display via AirPlay. This meant that the external display resolution was 1280 × 720. At that size, the L-shaped black area was approximately half the width of the screen and half the height. It might have been exactly half but it was hard to be sure it wasn't off by a few pixels. That might suggest a math error, or that the code might somehow be accidentally using the center point of the window someplace where it should have been using the origin. But on iOS the origin is at the top left corner—using the center instead of the origin would move the photo down and to the right, not down and to the left as was happening.

Further investigation showed that the bug varied depending on the size of the screen. By running the app in the iOS Simulator, I could simulate several different external display sizes. With a simulated 1024 × 768 display, the L-shaped area was thinner, occupying maybe one-quarter of the display width and one-third of the height. With a 720 × 480 or 640 × 480 simulated display, the photos disappeared completely, although the page-curl animation still occurred.

It seemed possible that the code in SlideShowViewController that displays the photos might be at fault. The code looked okay, but plainly something was not right. Maybe the photo view was off-center for some reason. I set a breakpoint in -setCurrentIndex:, just after setting the photo view's frame. When the app reached the breakpoint, I checked the frame in the debug console (Figure 25.12).

Look at the debug command in Figure 25.12. The p command is shorthand for "print." Here I'm printing the value of newPhotoView's frame. When using p, you usually need to typecast the result so that the debugger knows how to format its output. A UIView's frame is a CGRect, so that's what I used here. Another detail to notice is that the command is calling a method on newPhotoView to get the frame. I'm making Objective-C method calls right from the console, which interprets and executes them and then prints the result.

In Figure 25.12 the frame's size is 768 × 1004. That indicates that the view is on the internal display, since the simulated external display was 1024 × 768. So I hit the continue button and the code hit the breakpoint again. This time the frame matched the external display size, so I knew it was the right view (Figure 25.13).

The frame's size is okay, but the origin is way off. The photo's origin should be at (0, 0), the same as the display origin. In the code editor you'll see that the previous line of code set newPhotoView's frame to be the same as [self view]'s frame. That meant that [self view]'s frame must also have a bad origin value, and checking on it confirmed that this was the case.

Now I needed to check where the view's origin was set. This happens over in MainSlideShowViewController, in the -configureExternalScreen: method.

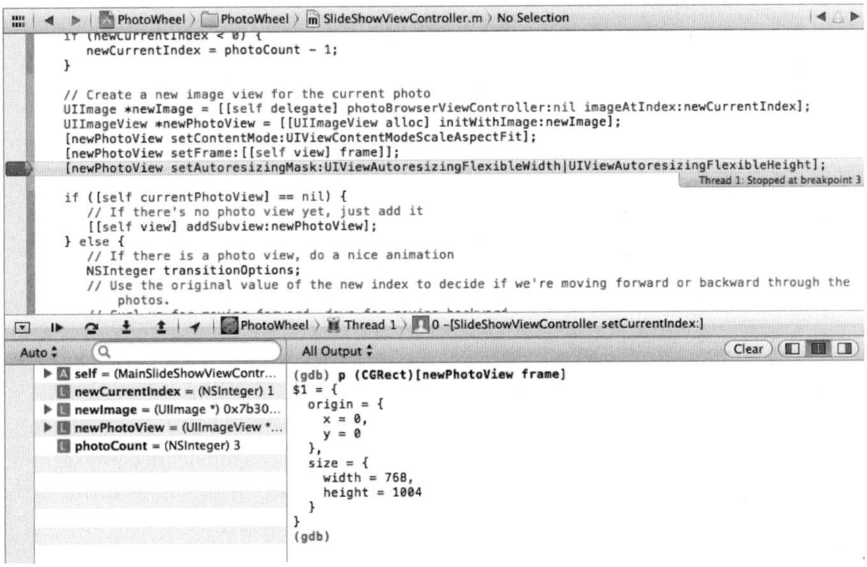

Figure 25.12   Checking a view's frame in the debug console, first pass

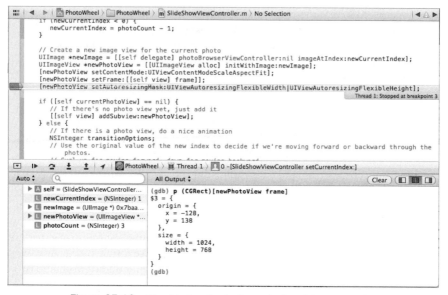

Figure 25.13   Checking a view's frame in the debug console,
second pass

That method creates a new UIWindow and a new view controller and adjusts the
view controller's view to fit the screen. I wasn't sure which step might be wrong, so I
decided to set a breakpoint at the beginning of the method and step through it line by
line, checking on each part of the process.

As I stepped through the method, I found that the window was the right size. The
CGRect I was using to set the external display's view also looked correct. I found this
in the console, as shown in Figure 25.14.

The view controller's view was off-center, though, in the same way as the photo
view. What could have caused that? Looking through the code, I decided that this line
was suspect:

```
[[externalSlideController view] setBounds:externalViewFrame];
```

The problem with that line is that it mixes up a view's bounds with its frame.
These are closely related but they are not the same. A view's frame uses its parent
view's coordinate system, while its bounds uses its own coordinate system. The frame's
origin gives the view's location in its parent view, and the bounds origin is usually
(though not always) at (0, 0). Mixing up bounds and frame is a bad idea and can lead
to weirdly misplaced views. Sound familiar? Sometimes this happens because although
the bounds origin is usually (0, 0), the frame origin usually is not. When this is the
case, setting the bounds origin to the frame origin usually won't do what you want.
Here, though, we already know that the frame origin in externalViewFrame is

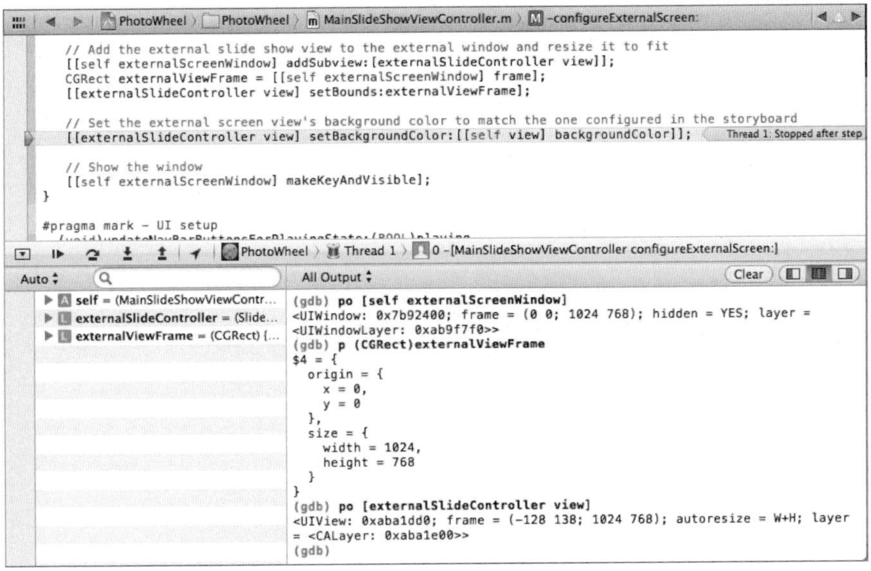

Figure 25.14   Investigating the external display bug

at (0, 0), so that shouldn't be a problem. The other factor is that changing a view's bounds will change its size relative to its *center point*, not relative to its origin. That seemed more likely to be the cause of this bug.

Based on this, I suspected that I would fix the bug if I changed the suspect line to read

```
[[externalSlideController view] setFrame:externalViewFrame];
```

I could use the debugger to verify this hypothesis, without restarting the app and without editing code until I was sure of what I needed (Figure 25.15).

The first command in the console executes the new line of code, as if it were in the app. The `call` command is used to call functions and methods in code. As with p, you need to tell the debugger what the return type of the function or method is. Here there is no return value, so I used `void`.

On the second line I checked the view to make sure the frame was what it should be. It was! I pressed the continue button and the slideshow started. This time the external display images were in the right place, so I changed the code.

Before declaring the problem to be fixed, I went through the tests I had done earlier. In the simulator, I tried the app on multiple external display sizes. Then I tried it using an iPad and a real external display. It still looked good, so I decided the bug was now fixed.

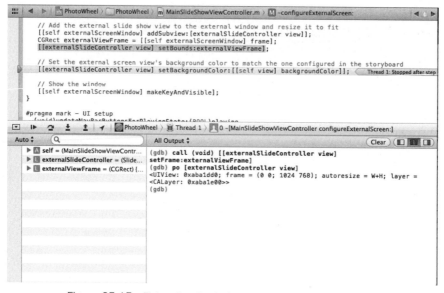

Figure 25.15   Fixing the view's frame in the debugger console

When You Really Need NSLog

Despite all the power the debugger offers, sometimes you just really need to use NSLog. Even the most experienced developers do, at least some of the time. The problems mentioned earlier still exist, though. NSLog statements have a way of outliving their usefulness and cluttering up code. They also fill up the device console with needless messages if you leave them in place when you release the app.

The second problem, at least, is easy to address. Using a compiler macro and a definition, you can arrange for NSLog statements to appear automatically only in debug builds. Here the basic macro is called DLog, for "debug log," and is shown in Listing 25.1. You can call it whatever you like.

Listing 25.1   **Defining a Macro for Debug-Only** NSLog

```
#ifdef DEBUG
#define DLog(...) NSLog(__VA_ARGS__)
#else
#define DLog(...)
#endif
```

Figure 25.16   Compiler flags in Xcode

This creates a macro called `DLog`. A compiler macro tells the compiler that some defined text should be replaced by some other text. The replacement happens before the code is compiled, as part of the preprocessing stage.

In this case, if `DEBUG` is defined in the app, any use of `DLog` will be replaced by a call to `NSLog`. It is not simply equivalent to calling `NSLog`; it literally is a call to `NSLog` once preprocessing is complete. Any arguments to `DLog` will become `NSLog` arguments. If `DEBUG` is not defined, any call to `NSLog` is replaced by an empty string—so when the code compiles, the `NSLog` is already gone. There are numerous variations on this macro online that modify or add to the `NSLog` arguments. In this case what you get is exactly what you would get if you used `NSLog`, but only when `DEBUG` is defined.

If you put this code in your project's precompiled header file (the *.pch* file), it will be available throughout the app without requiring any extra `#import` statements.

To use `DLog` you need to arrange for `DEBUG` to be defined for debug builds but not for any other builds. You do this in the app's Build Settings, by adding a new compiler flag that will be used only in debug builds. The easiest way to find the flags section is to type `cflags` in the Build Settings search field (Figure 25.16).

Xcode automatically creates both debug and release configurations. If you double-click next to Debug in the Other C Flags section, a popover view appears where you can add custom flags (Figure 25.17).

The compiler option to create a `#define` is –D, and we want to define `DEBUG`, so adding –DDEBUG as shown in Figure 25.17 will make the `DLog` macro work. With this bit of setup, turning `NSLog` on for debug builds only is completely automatic.

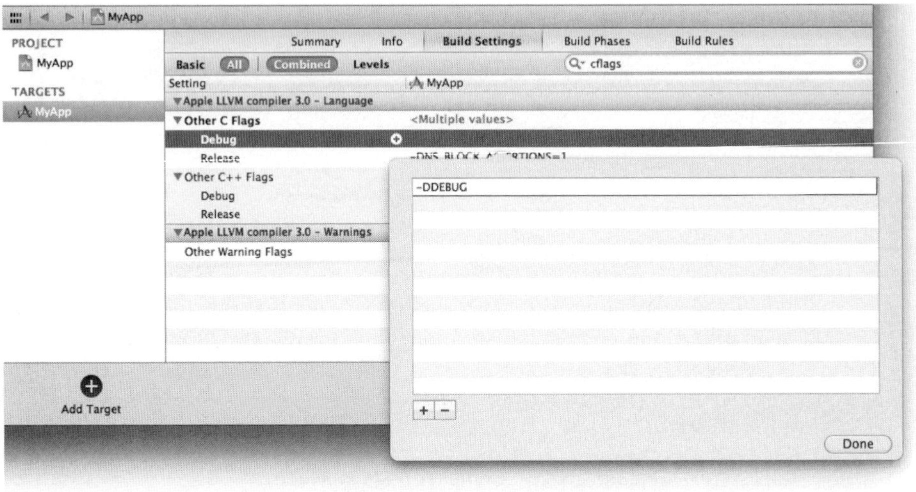

Figure 25.17   Defining DEBUG for debug builds

Profiling Code with Instruments

Some code bugs don't show up as incorrect data or screen layouts. Maybe the app is using more memory than you think it should. Maybe it is just too slow in places. The debugger won't help much with this kind of issue.

Xcode includes a separate tool called Instruments, designed for cases just like this. Instruments is a graphical profiling tool that helps you understand what is really happening when an app runs. A profiler, like the debugger, is a tool that can run another application and monitor its activities. It is unlike the debugger in that it doesn't work with breakpoints or do anything that would stop the app. Instead, it sits back and lets you interact with the app while it collects data, such as how much memory is in use or how much time the app spends in each method. Instruments provides graphs and detailed statistics about the app's behavior, which can give deep insights into where performance issues occur and how to fix them.

It is common to think that you can prevent performance issues by writing better code. Some code seems obviously inefficient and in need of speed improvements. This is often a mistake and can lead to what is known as premature optimization. The code that looks as if it should be slow is often not a bottleneck, but it's easy to spend a lot of time optimizing it based on incorrect assumptions. There are a variety of reasons for this. Modern compilers are capable of quite a bit of optimization, so inefficiencies in source code may not remain once the app is compiled. Other times, the code that actually takes more time is not obviously any less efficient than other code. As a result of this, profiling code should be an integral part of any attempts at optimization. It's better to see what is actually slow instead of spending lots of time analyzing your code only to find out that your guess was wrong.

Even before profiling, though, consider whether you actually have a problem. It is almost always possible to find a way to make code run a little faster, but it doesn't always make sense to do so. If the app has no appreciable performance problems, it is often not worth the time to try to make it even more efficient. You want to have a great app, of course, but you also want to release it someday, and optimization can be a never-ending challenge. Better code is, well, better, but it's important to keep things in perspective.

Instruments works with both simulator and device builds. You should work with a device whenever possible. Performance on simulator builds is very different from that of device builds. Even relative performance, such as finding that one method takes longer than another without considering absolute time, can be different. Memory issues will usually be more similar, but they probably won't be identical.

To start Instruments, select **Product > Profile** in Xcode (or press **⌘-I**). Xcode builds the app, if needed, and launches Instruments. Instruments starts by showing a scrollable window with various profiling options, as shown in Figure 25.18.

Instruments offers numerous profiling tools. The Allocations and Leaks tools monitor memory usage over time. The Time Profiler tool monitors the time spent in each

Figure 25.18   Startup options for Instruments

function or method in the app, to help find performance bottlenecks. Other tools monitor overall system usage, network activity, and graphics performance. You can use more than one tool during the same run if you need data in multiple areas. The startup window lets you select only one, but once Instruments is running, others can be added.

Once you select a tool, Instruments starts the app and shows its main window (Figure 25.19). The current tools are shown on the left, next to graphs showing activity over time. The bottom part of the window is the data display, which shows statistics related to the currently selected tool and options for configuring and filtering those numbers.

It's also possible to attach Instruments to an app that is already running. This is handy because often you want to monitor only a specific action in an app. Collecting data from the time the app starts until you reach the area of interest can fill up Instruments with data that is not relevant to the problem you're investigating. To do this, you first start the app, then click the Target popup menu. In the **Attach to Process** section of the menu, locate your app. Instruments starts recording data for the app. Figure 25.20 shows how you might do this for a simulator build.

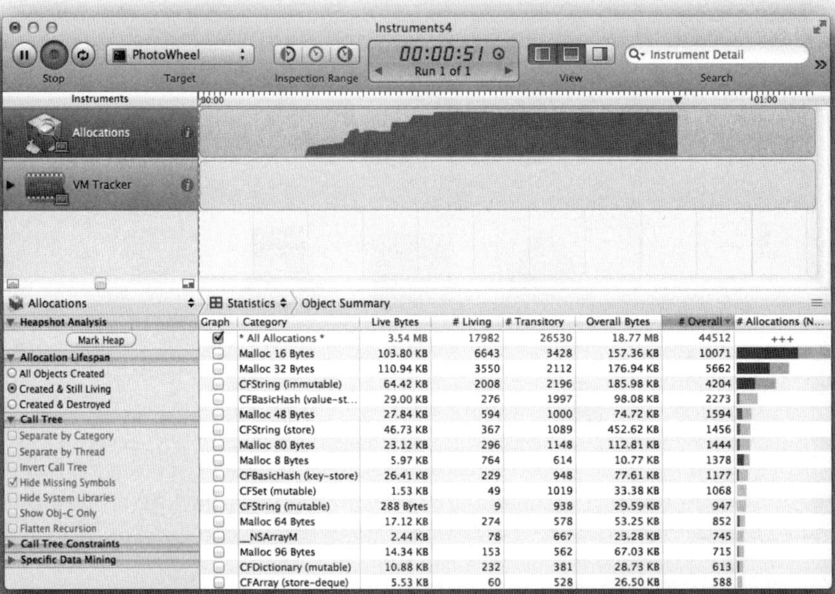

Figure 25.19   Main Instruments window, with the Allocations tool

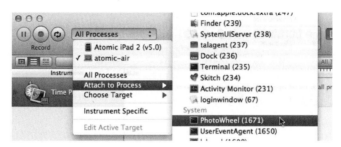

Figure 25.20   Attaching Instruments to a running process

Profiling Example: Slideshow UI Control Updates

One area that looks ripe for performance improvement is in the code that handles the play/pause buttons in the slideshow. As you may recall, when the user presses "play" or "pause" in the slideshow, the app rebuilds the entire set of buttons. The buttons aren't cached or reused; they're thrown out and replaced. Even the forward and back buttons get replaced, and they never change. It doesn't seem as if the app is running slowly here, but at the same time the code is clearly doing more work than it needs to do. What changes might make it better?

The code of interest executes whenever the user presses "play" or "pause." To make Instruments collect data that focuses on this task, let's use Instruments as follows:

1. Start up the app and navigate to the slideshow.

2. Start Instruments using the Time Profiler tool and attach it to the running process.

3. Press "play" and "pause" over and over for a while.

4. Click on the **Stop** button in Instruments to make it stop recording data.

The effect is that while Instruments is running, the app is spending most of its time in the code under investigation. After doing this, Instruments looks like Figure 25.21.

The graph next to the Time Profiler tool shows CPU activity over time. Below the graph is a list of call trees found while Instruments was recording data. The list shows the deepest method call and can be expanded to show more detail. In this case you can see that the call to -updateNavBarButtonsForPlayingState: consumed the most CPU at 159ms. Instruments also shows that this method was called from two other methods, -pause: and -play:, and that the 159ms was close to evenly distributed between calls from those methods. Several other call trees are listed, but they didn't use anywhere near as much time.

The box on the lower left has several check boxes that control how call tree information is displayed. Two that are often useful when finding slow points in your code are

- **Hide System Libraries**. This option limits the display so that it includes only methods and functions in your code. When this is unchecked, the call tree area

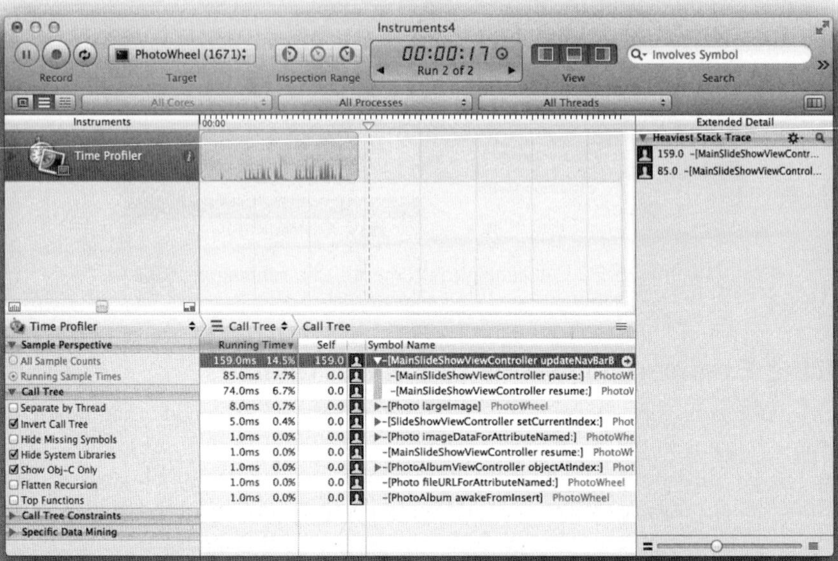

Figure 25.21   Instruments showing time profile results for PhotoWheel's slideshow

includes entries that relate to code used by iOS and frameworks but that your code did not directly call. This can be interesting to see, but it can also mean you have a lot of detail that is not directly relevant to the problem you're trying to solve.

- **Show Obj-C Only**. When this option is checked, the call tree display filters out detail that is not directly related to Objective-C method calls. Again, this can be useful information, but it often includes unnecessary detail.

The section on the right shows the stack trace with the greatest impact on the selected call tree. In Figure 25.21 this would show the call from –pause: to –updateNavBarButtonsForPlayingState:. The call from –play: is also important, but it took slightly less CPU time overall, so it is not the "heaviest" stack trace.

None of this is really surprising yet. The steps taken pretty much guaranteed that –updateNavBarButtonsForPlayingState: would take the most time, since that is the method that updates the slideshow control buttons. The goal was to find out what parts of that method are consuming most of the time when that method executes.

To get this information, double-click on that method in the Heaviest Stack Trace display. Instruments then replaces the call tree area with the source code for the method. Every line that took a significant portion of the method's run time is

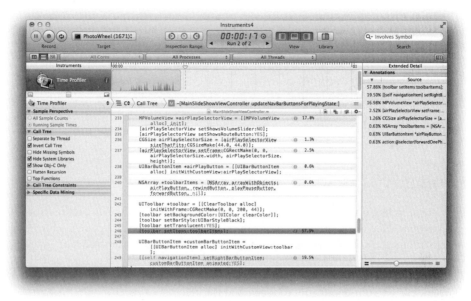

Figure 25.22   Source code display in Instruments

highlighted. A number by these lines shows the percentage of time taken by that line. Figure 25.22 shows the results for this method.

The code shown covers creating the AirPlay button, adjusting it to fit, and then updating the toolbar with a new set of buttons. One surprising finding is that the code to re-create the back, play, pause, and forward buttons takes so little time that none of the lines were highlighted. They are not shown here, but that's because Instruments reported nothing of interest for them. Re-creating them is redundant but takes hardly any time compared to other parts of the method.

The most expensive line is the one updating the toolbar items, at 57.9 percent of the total in this method. That is probably unavoidable unless we redesign the buttons completely. This time wouldn't be reduced by caching copies of buttons or other tricks—as long as we're updating the toolbar's buttons, we need this line. If this method were presenting a significant slowdown, the time taken by this line would be a good argument for reconsidering how the buttons are managed.

One area that *could* be optimized is creating the AirPlay button. Creating the button is 17 percent of the total method time. Add in other lines that resize the button and create a UIBarButtonItem for it and the total comes to 21.4 percent. But this button never changes. We could create it once and then reuse the existing copy. Of all the toolbar button items, this is the only one for which changing the code would improve the overall speed of the method.

A possible extra optimization is the last line shown, where the code updates the navigation item with the new buttons. As it stands, the code creates a new

`UIBarButtonItem` each time it runs, with a custom view containing the toolbar. Then it sets this item as the right bar button item on the navigation item. But the `customView` property of `UIBarButtonItem` is writable. It might be faster to keep a reference to `customBarButtonItem` around and just update its `customView` in this method. The benefit here is not as obvious as with the AirPlay button, because we would be replacing relatively slow code with different code. That new code might be just as slow or even slower. It's not obvious how much time it takes to update `customView`. If we made this change, we would need to do some more profiling to check whether it improved things.

Summary

Bugs are an unfortunate fact of any software developer's life. The real question is how effective a developer is at finding and fixing those problems. With Xcode's debugger and Instruments, you are well equipped to deal with unexpected problems in code. Logic errors, incorrect data and settings, and a variety of performance issues can be diagnosed by examining and manipulating code while it is running. When you see a problem, put on your debugging tool belt and fix it!

Effective debugging is crucial not just for a good user experience; it is also a fundamental part of launching an app. An app crashing during Apple's review testing is grounds for immediate rejection. Except in extreme cases, poor performance usually doesn't stop an app from being approved. But it is one of the easiest ways to rack up one-star reviews in the App Store, and that in turn is one of the easiest ways to make an app flop. Take it seriously and deal with performance problems in advance. Fixing bugs and improving performance can be a challenge, but it's far, far better to deal with problems privately instead of publicly.

Speaking of the App Store, the next chapter discusses how to get your app ready for submission to Apple so that you can sell it through the App Store.

Distributing Your App

Finally, PhotoWheel is complete! Or at least it's ready for a good round of beta testing. So far you have learned how to build and install PhotoWheel on your own iPad, but eventually you'll want to make it available to other people. During development you'll want to have other people test the app, both while you're working on finishing it and as a final test stage before releasing it to the world. When your app is ready, you'll want to upload it to the App Store for approval.

This chapter covers how you can prepare and distribute your app for testing and approval.

Distribution Methods

Until now you have deployed apps from Xcode to your own devices. Preparing your app to run on other people's devices requires some extra steps. You can distribute apps using one of two methods:

- **Ad Hoc distribution:** You use this method to distribute your app to testers. Ad Hoc distribution does not go through the App Store. Instead, you build the app and provide copies to testers by whatever means you find convenient. Ad Hoc builds can only go to devices listed in your iOS Provisioning Portal account, which limits the number of testers. Testers install the app on their devices using iTunes. People who install Ad Hoc builds of apps don't need to belong to the iOS Developer Program; anyone with a device that supports the app can be a tester.

- **App Store distribution:** You use this method when the app is ready to be released to the App Store. An App Store build of the app can't be installed directly on any devices. Instead, you upload the build to Apple. Apple reviews the app and, if accepted, it becomes available through the App Store.

This chapter covers both methods.

The first thing you need to do, for either distribution method, is set up a new signing certificate for distribution builds. The steps to do this are nearly the same as those discussed in Chapter 6, "Provisioning Your iPad," for development certificates. There are two differences. One is that in the Certificates section of the Provisioning Portal, you click the **Distribution** tab instead of **Development**. The process of creating and downloading a certificate is the same. The second difference is that distribution certificates can be created only by the Team Agent, who is normally the person who created the iPhone Developer Program account. If you're working independently, this is you, but if you're part of a team, it might be someone else.

Building for Ad Hoc Distribution

Now let's tackle the process for Ad Hoc distribution. You'll need to set up provisioning and prepare an Ad Hoc build of the app before you can send it out for testing.

Provisioning for Ad Hoc Distribution

Provisioning for Ad Hoc builds is very similar to provisioning for development. There are only a couple of minor differences. To create an Ad Hoc provisioning profile, use the Provisioning section of the Provisioning Portal site, and the **Distribution** tab within that section (Figure 26.1).

When you click **New Profile**, the screen that appears is similar to the one used for development profiles, but not quite. Next to Distribution Method, select the Ad Hoc option (Figure 26.2). From this point forward, the provisioning process is the same as for development builds. Name the profile and select an App ID and whichever devices should be included, and then create the profile as in Chapter 6, "Provisioning Your iPad." If you're planning to send the build to other people for testing, you'll need to have their device IDs in your account and include them in the profile.

Prepare the (Ad Hoc) Build!

To build an app for Ad Hoc distribution, you need to use the new Ad Hoc provisioning profile. You could just switch between Development and Ad Hoc distribution profiles in Xcode, but that's going to get awkward pretty fast. You can't just use one

Figure 26.1   Distribution Provisioning profile section of the Provisioning Portal

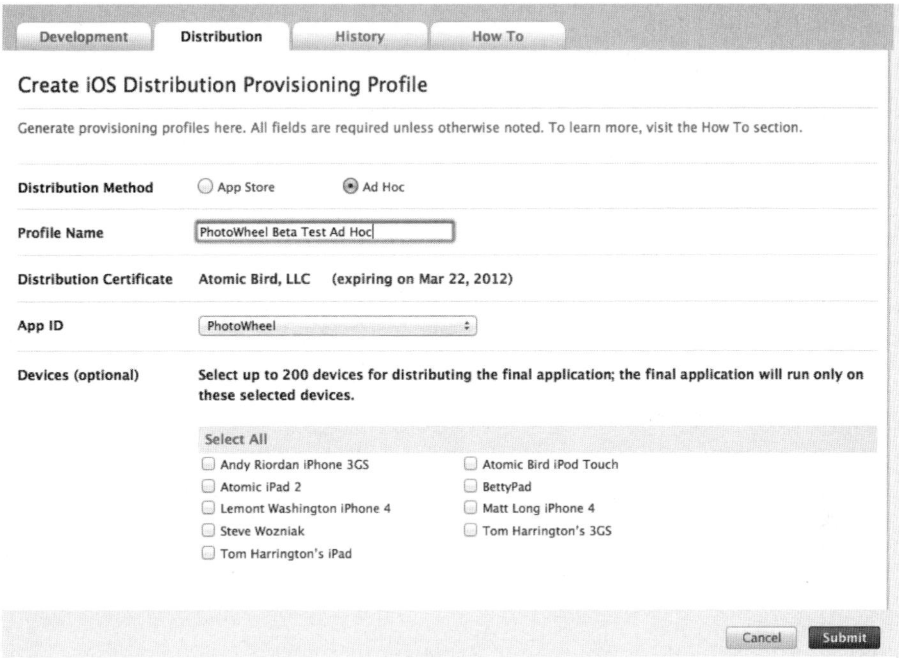

Figure 26.2   Creating an Ad Hoc distribution profile

profile either. While it is possible to build and run with an Ad Hoc profile, you can't debug an app built this way. Conversely, it's not possible to distribute an app built with a development profile. You need to have both profiles available for different build requirements. Fortunately, Xcode provides a way to use both in the project and have the right one selected automatically when you build the app.

When building for Ad Hoc distribution, what you'll actually build is an archive file. The archive contains the compiled app and the provisioning profile and can be used by testers to install the app on their iOS device. Archive settings are found in the default scheme for the project (Figure 26.3). You can display the scheme editor by selecting **Product > Edit Scheme** (⌘-<) in Xcode's menu bar.

By default the archive section of the scheme uses the Release build configuration. Since you'll build an archive for Ad Hoc distribution, the Release configuration will determine what provisioning profile is used. If you take a look at the Test section of the scheme editor, you'll see that it uses the Debug build configuration instead. Xcode automatically creates these configurations when you create a new project.

Code signing settings for the Debug and Release configurations are found in the Build Settings for the app. To use the Ad Hoc provisioning profile for archive builds, you need to tell Xcode to use that profile for the Release configuration.

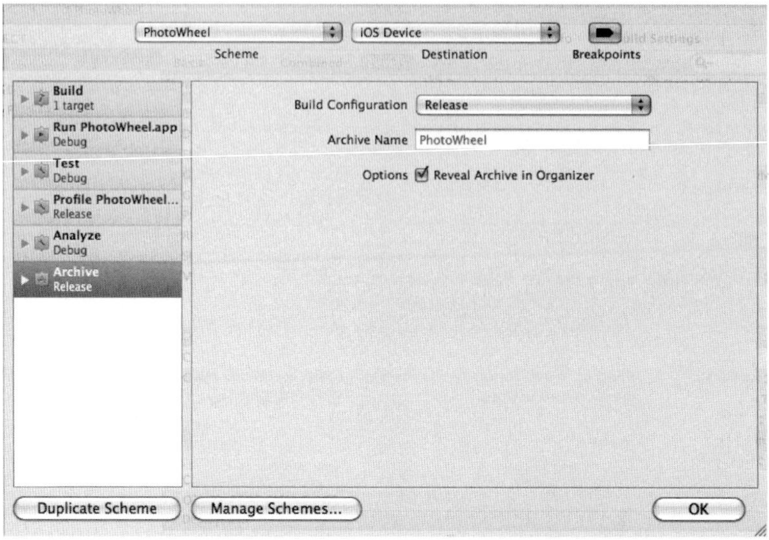

Figure 26.3   Archive settings in the default build scheme

Figure 26.4 shows the configurations for PhotoWheel. These settings are part of the project settings for the PhotoWheel project.

To build the Ad Hoc archive, select **Product > Archive** in Xcode. Xcode builds the app, creates the archive file, and opens the Organizer window to show the archive (Figure 26.5). The window also lists both current and previous archives.

The archive is what you will send to testers. You do this by saving the archive as a file. Click the **Share...** button, shown in Figure 26.5. Select "iOS App Store Package (.ipa)" for the contents, and then select your Ad Hoc provisioning profile from the Identity popup menu (Figure 26.6).

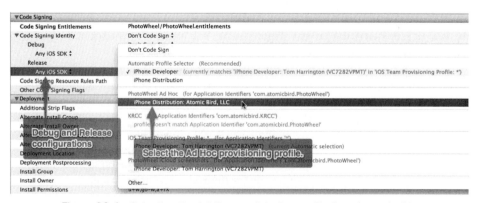

Figure 26.4   Selecting the Ad Hoc provisioning profile for release builds

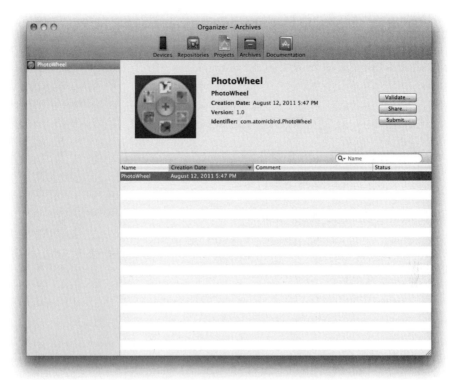

Figure 26.5   Xcode's Organizer window showing an archived build

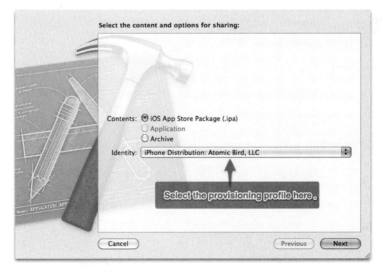

Figure 26.6   Exporting an app archive from Xcode

When you click **Next**, Xcode prompts you to save the file somewhere. Xcode auto-matically adds the *.ipa* extension to the file name.

When you're ready to send a build to testers, all you need to do is send them this file. They can install it on their devices by dragging it into iTunes and then syncing their device.

Building for App Store Distribution

The build process for the App Store is very similar to the Ad Hoc build process. You'll need to complete a slightly different provisioning process. You'll also need to update the project settings for the new build type.

Provisioning for the App Store

Getting an app ready for the App Store requires yet another provisioning profile. Start off as for the Ad Hoc profile. This time, select App Store as the distribution method (Figure 26.7).

This time the devices are grayed out. App Store profiles aren't tied to specific devices, so there is no need to select them. Create and download the profile, and drag it into Xcode.

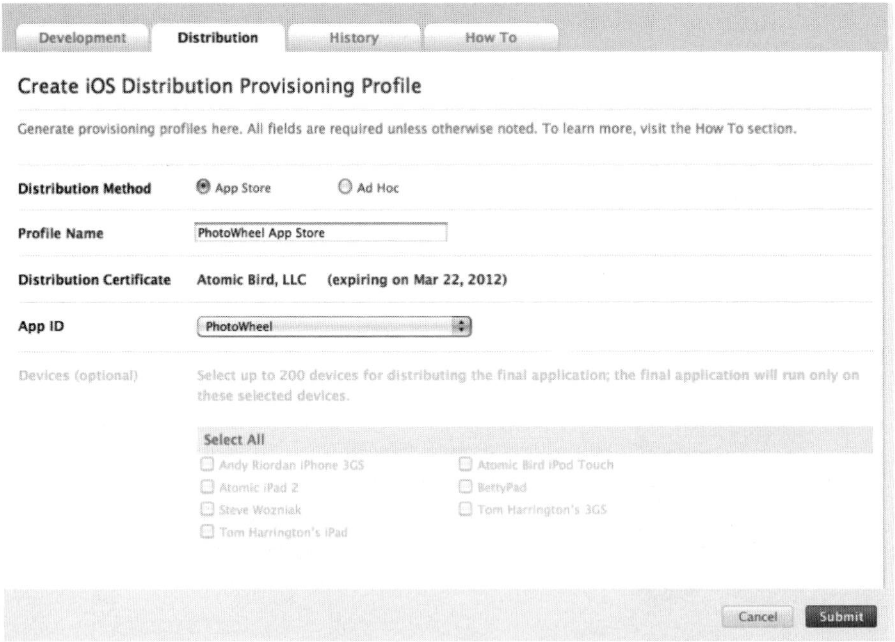

Figure 26.7   Creating an App Store distribution profile

Prepare the (App Store) Build!

Building for the App Store, as with Ad Hoc builds, involves creating an archive. But we have already used the archive setting in the current build scheme for Ad Hoc builds. Again, you could switch back and forth between provisioning profiles, choosing either the Ad Hoc or the App Store profile as needed. A much better solution would be to create a new build scheme and make its archive setting use the new App Store profile. Switching between schemes is much more convenient than changing provisioning profiles within a scheme.

In Xcode's menu, select **Product > Manage Schemes**. The scheme manager window appears, showing the original build scheme you have been using (Figure 26.8).

Select the existing profile, and then click on the gear menu at the bottom of the window and select Duplicate. The scheme editor appears. Name the scheme something obvious, like PhotoWheel App Store, and then click **OK** to save the new scheme. Once you have done this, you'll be able to choose which scheme to use from the popup menu at the top of Xcode's main window (Figure 26.9). Choose the original PhotoWheel scheme for development and Ad Hoc builds, and choose the new Photo-Wheel App Store scheme for App Store builds. Now whenever you build the app, the settings for the currently selected build scheme apply automatically.

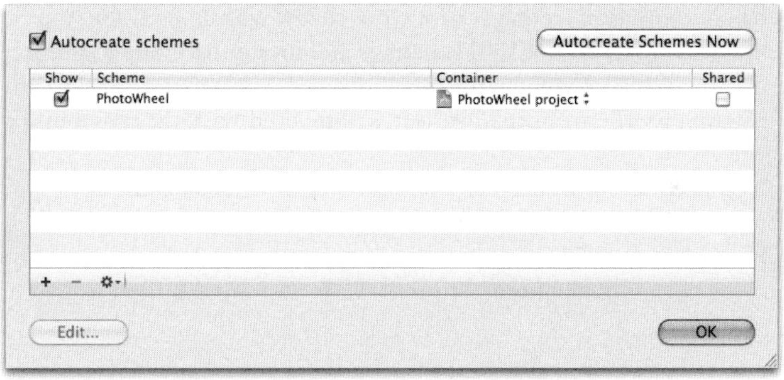

Figure 26.8   Managing build schemes

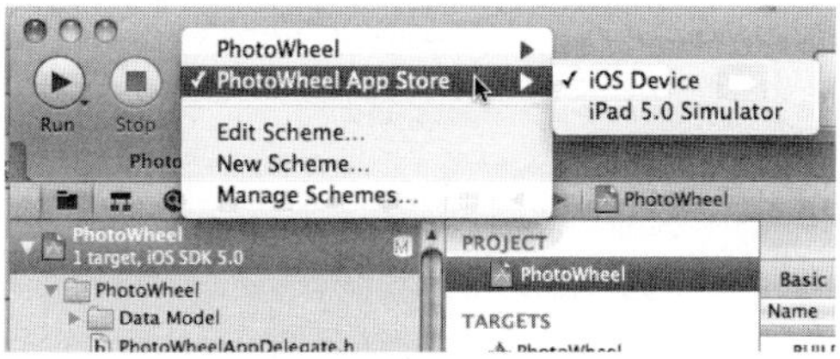

Figure 26.9   Selecting a build scheme

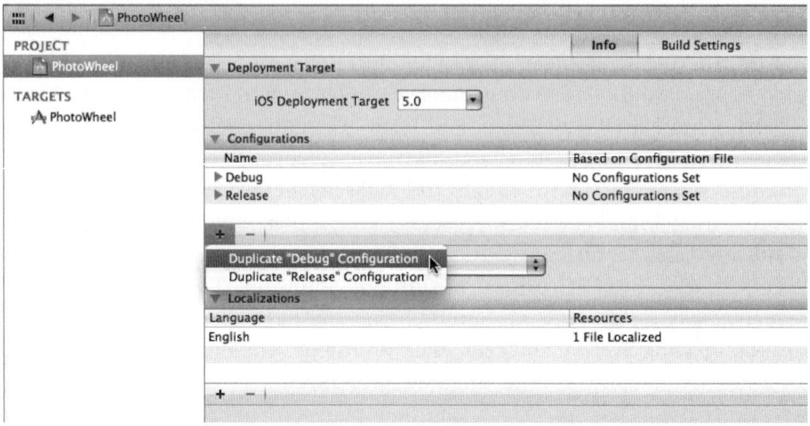

Figure 26.10   Adding a new build configuration

To go with the new build scheme, you'll also need a new build configuration. In the project settings, select the **Info** tab. In the Configurations section, click the **+** button at the bottom of the list, and then select Duplicate "Release" Configuration from the popup (Figure 26.10).

Name the configuration so that it is obvious that it will be used for App Store builds. Next, switch over to the Build Settings and locate the Code Signing settings. You'll see that there is a new entry for the new build configuration. Select the App Store provisioning profile from the list so it will be used with the new build configuration (Figure 26.11).

Finally, you need to configure the App Store build scheme to use the App Store build configuration for archive builds. This works the same as with the Ad Hoc changes, discussed earlier. This time make sure you're editing the new App Store build scheme, and set the archive options to use the new App Store build configuration.

Figure 26.11   Changing Code Signing settings for the App Store
build configuration

Next Steps

Submitting apps to the App Store takes a lot more than just building the app. Launching software always does. For iPad apps, you need to prepare all of the other information that will appear in the App Store listing. If the app isn't free, you need to set up banking information with Apple so that you can get paid. You also need to be ready to provide support for your app's users. And all of that is just to get the app into the App Store; you also need to consider how to market the app and find your audience. The next sections will cover the various requirements before you can submit your app to Apple.

The App Store Process

If you have never submitted an app to the App Store, the process can seem opaque and confusing at first. There are several steps that need to be done in the right order to complete the process. These steps are as follows:

1. Build the app for the App Store, as described earlier. You can do this at any time during the app development process. It's worth setting up your project for this early to avoid last-minute confusion. You might want to deal with this at the same time as you begin sending out Ad Hoc builds to testers. You'll be working with certificates and provisioning profiles at that point already, and the App Store requirements are similar.

2. Gather or create various metadata and images related to the app. You'll need to provide everything that will be visible in the store as well as other information used by the store to categorize the app and help people search for apps. These requirements are described in the following sections. It's a good idea to get this started in parallel with app development if possible to avoid rushing the process at the last second.

3. Log in to iTunes Connect and create a listing for the application. You'll need all of the information from the previous step here. This creates an entry in Apple's app database with information about the app but doesn't begin the approval process yet.

4. If your app is not free, go to the Contracts, Tax, and Banking section of iTunes Connect. You'll need to approve the iOS Paid Applications contract, which is a legal agreement between Apple and you or your company. It basically allows Apple to sell your app in the App Store, but you should review the contract before agreeing to it. You'll also need to enter banking information so that Apple can send payments for app sales.

5. Back in Xcode, build an app archive and use the built-in app submission tool. Xcode will validate the app and upload it to iTunes Connect. *This is when the app review process begins.* (This process is described in more detail later in this section.)

6. Wait. Apple will review your app to decide whether to allow it into the App Store. Apple doesn't guarantee that the review will be done in any specific time

frame. Typically, it takes about a week. In some cases it can be much quicker or, unfortunately, much longer. Apple sends automatic emails as your app moves through the approval process, notifying you of events such as when the review process has started and when it has finished.

If Apple approves your app, the final status is Ready for Sale. Congratulations! Your app is public!

What If Apple Rejects the App?

Apple has the final say over whether an app is permitted into the App Store. The vast majority of apps are accepted, but not all. If your app is rejected, Apple will notify you and describe the reasons for the rejection. Apple provides a detailed list of restrictions in the iOS Developer Program Agreement. You should review these restrictions carefully. Be aware, though, that this is not a complete list. Apple can reject an app for any reason it feels is appropriate, and the company has been known to reject apps for previously unknown reasons.

The most common reasons for rejection are purely technical. Usually this means that the app crashed while being reviewed. Crashing is grounds for automatic rejection. Another common technical issue is nonfunctional user interface items—buttons that are visible and appear enabled but that don't work, for example. With technical issues you generally have a clear picture of what is wrong. Fix the issues and resubmit the app.

If you have used undocumented APIs in your app, it's more than just a technical issue. Apple provides detailed documentation of frameworks and other APIs available to applications. iOS has many more methods that are not documented, which are intended for internal use by Apple. It's possible to write software that uses these APIs, but doing so is specifically against App Store rules. If you have used undocumented APIs, you need to rewrite code so that you don't use them anymore. How difficult this is depends on what specifically the API does and how hard it is to write replacement code.

Apps can also be rejected because of content included with the app. For example, Apple specifically forbids pornographic material. Again, the rejection notice will be clear about the reasons, and you can take steps to address those issues.

If your app has been rejected for what you believe to be invalid reasons, you can appeal the rejection. Ultimately, though, Apple is not obligated to accept your app. As noted earlier, most apps are accepted, and it's unlikely yours will be rejected unless you have done something egregious.

App Information for the App Store

When you submit your app to Apple, you'll need to provide a variety of information related to the app. This section summarizes the information needed. Except where noted, all of these are required.

❑ **App name.** You probably already know this. If you haven't yet decided among multiple possibilities, it's time to do so. Make sure you are not infringing any copyrights or trademarks in the name, as this is grounds to reject the app. The app name can't be one that someone else is already using.

❑ **SKU number.** This is any unique code you want to use to identify your app. It is your own product ID for the app, and it will appear in sales reports. You can use any text that makes sense to you, but think ahead to when you might have multiple apps. You might choose to number apps sequentially, or use a date string or any other string that will help you keep track of your apps. SKU numbers are not displayed in the App Store.

❑ **Bundle ID.** You will need to know the Bundle ID of the app. This corresponds to the App ID in the Provisioning Portal for your account.

❑ **Availability date.** You can indicate the date when your app should appear in the store. This is the earliest possible date when this can happen, but the actual date could be later. If Apple has not approved your app by this date, the app won't automatically go into the App Store. Instead, it will appear as soon as it has been approved.

❑ **Price.** If your app isn't free, this is where you set the price. You don't get to specify the actual price; instead, you decide which price tier should be used. Each tier corresponds to a specific price in a variety of world currencies. For example, tier 2 corresponds to $1.99 in the United States, Canada, and Australia; €1.59 in most of Europe; £1.49 in the UK, and so on.

❑ **Availability by country.** Apple operates the App Store in most countries in the world. Not all apps are available in all countries. You decide in which countries your app should be available. Most apps are available in all stores. If your app contains content that you have licensed for use, you may need to restrict availability based on that license.

❑ **Version number.** The version number for your app is up to you, but it's best to follow typical versioning schemes to avoid confusing users. This information will be displayed in the App Store.

❑ **App description.** This is where you tell potential customers about your app. The text you provide will appear in the App Store and will be one of the factors people use to decide whether to buy your app. You have up to 4,000 characters. Proofread the text carefully, since spelling or grammar errors will make the app seem amateurish.

❑ **Primary and secondary category.** The category determines where the app will appear in the App Store. Every app must have a primary category and may also have a secondary category. To get an idea of what apps go in what categories, visit the App Store in iTunes and tap the Categories tab. If you're not sure what category to use, browse the categories and see which ones seem most appropriate. For PhotoWheel the primary category would be "Photography" and the secondary might be "Lifestyle."

❑ **Keywords.** Decide on one or more keywords that describe the app. Keywords are used when people search for apps in the store, so choose yours carefully. Keep in mind that Apple forbids using the names of other apps in the keyword list, so don't list competing apps in the hope of getting more notice in search results. The keyword list is limited to 100 characters.

❑ **Copyright.** This describes the ownership of the app and will appear in the App Store. Don't include the copyright symbol (©), which is added automatically.

❑ **Contact email address.** Apple will use this address to get in touch with you about the app if necessary. This address will not be displayed in the store.

❑ **Support URL.** Supply the URL that users can visit for support issues related to your app. This will be a clickable link in the App Store.

❑ **App URL.** This is the app's home page, with information about the app. This will be a clickable link in the App Store and is optional.

❑ **Review notes.** Use this area for any information Apple's app review team might need when evaluating your app. If your app requires login information of some kind, include information on a testing account here. This information is optional.

❑ **Rating.** You'll need to rate your app in a variety of categories so that Apple can determine an age rating for it. Age ratings go from 4+, which is available to anyone, to 17+ for apps that contain more mature content. The categories include things like violent or sexual content. In each area you can rate your app as having the content never, infrequently, or frequently.

❑ **EULA (End User License Agreement).** You can provide your own license agreement for your app, if Apple's standard EULA doesn't meet your needs. If you do, the agreement will be visible in the App Store. This is optional.

App Store Assets

In addition to metadata about the app, you'll need to have several images ready when you submit the app. These are listed here:

- **Large app icon.** You already have an icon that is used by the app, but you need a much larger version for the App Store. The App Store will use this icon for fancy screen layouts if your app is chosen as one of the featured apps. The large icon must be 512 × 512 pixels and can be saved as JPEG, TIFF, or PNG. *This is required.*

- **Screen shots.** When users browse the App Store, they'll want to see what your app looks like. Since the App Store doesn't allow users to try apps before buying them, this is one of the main factors people will use when deciding whether to buy your app. Your screen shots should highlight your app's features. Ideally they should cover all of the most interesting ones. Try to make the screen shots resemble how users might actually use the app. For PhotoWheel that would mean naming albums with names people might actually use on photo albums instead of fake names you might have used in testing. The app will seem more appealing with album names such as "Vacation in Hawaii" or "First Day of School," rather than with names like "Test Album 1," "Test Album 2," and so on.

You must provide at least one screen shot of your app. You can provide up to five, and if it's possible without being repetitive, you should. Screen shots should be full-screen images.

Using iTunes Connect

You submit and manage apps through iTunes Connect (**itunesconnect.apple.com**). You can also get to iTunes Connect after logging in to the iOS Developer Center (**developer.apple.com/ios**). Figure 26.12 shows the main iTunes Connect page (as of September 2011).

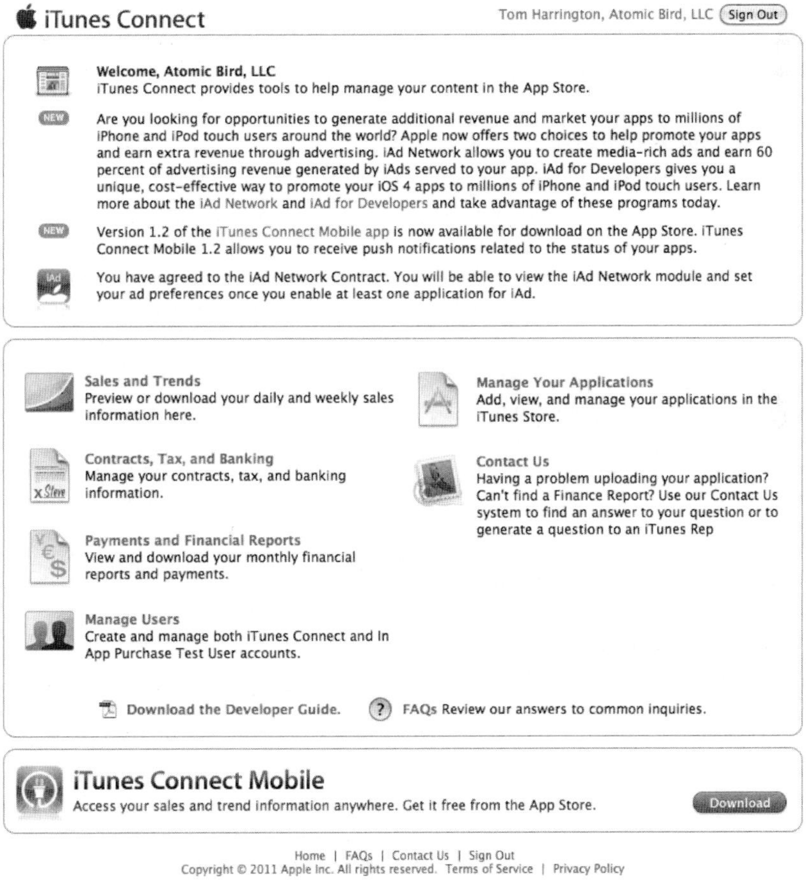

Figure 26.12   iTunes Connect home page

User Roles

Multiple users can have access to the same iTunes Connect account. Different users can be assigned to different roles, depending on what operations they need to perform. You create and manage user accounts in the Manage Users section of the site (see Figure 26.12).

Five roles exist:

- **Admin** users can manage the iTunes Connect account, including creating and deleting users.
- **Legal** users can enter into legal agreements like the iOS Paid Applications contract and can request promotional codes for paid apps.
- **Finance** users can manage financial details, including sales and banking information as well as contracts.
- **Technical** users can upload and manage apps.
- **Sales** users can access sales reports.

Users can be assigned to multiple roles, if it makes sense to do so.

Managing Applications

The Manage Your Applications section is where you'll set up new applications and make changes for new versions of apps. This is where you'll use the app information and assets you gathered for the app. When you're ready to submit the first version of an app, you need to create an entry for the app in iTunes Connect before you'll be able to upload the app archive. Likewise, when updating to a new version of an app, you'll need to create the new version in iTunes Connect before uploading it. Start the process by clicking the **Manage Your Applications** link, and then the **Add New App** button in the window that appears.

iTunes Connect will walk you through the process of entering the app metadata and uploading screen shots, beginning with the App Name, SKU Number, and Bundle ID (Figure 26.13).

The rest of the information and assets will come in later stages, which progress wizard-style until you have finished. At that point you will have created the app in the iTunes Connect database, and the status will be Waiting for Upload.

Submitting the App

It's time! All the preliminaries are complete, and it's time to upload your app. You can upload apps to iTunes Connect directly from Xcode. To start the process, build an App Store archive as described earlier in this chapter. The Organizer window (shown in Figure 26.14) will open, showing the new archive and any previous archives. It's useful to double-click in the Comment column to add a brief descriptive note to the archive, so that later on you'll know why each archive was created.

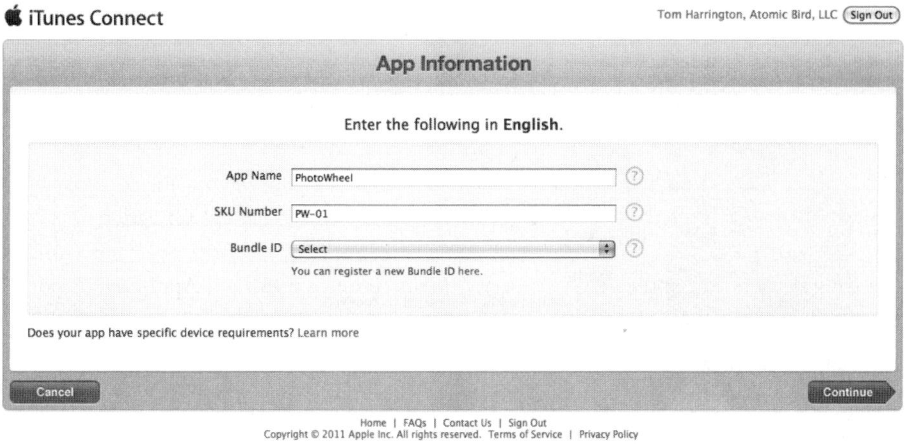

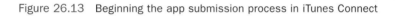

Figure 26.13 Beginning the app submission process in iTunes Connect

Figure 26.14 Xcode Organizer showing an archive ready for the
App Store

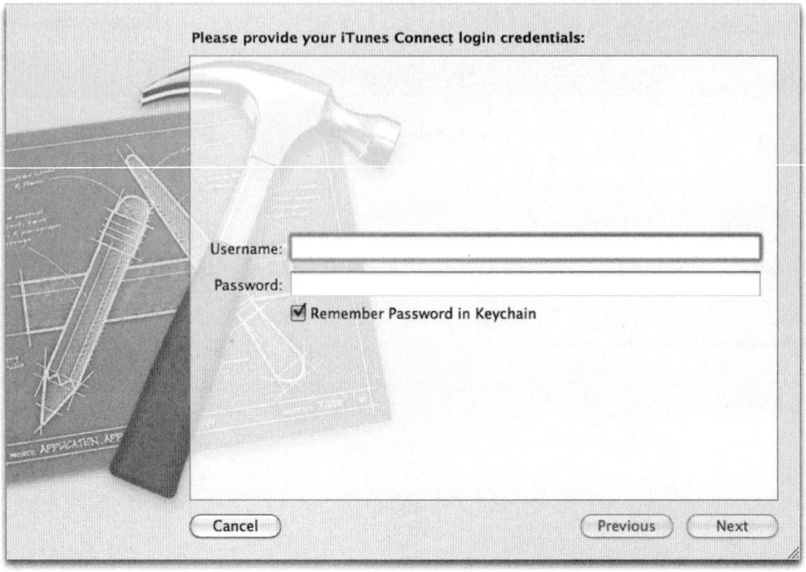

Figure 26.15   Logging in to iTunes Connect from Xcode

When you upload the app, iTunes Connect will perform several automatic checks on the app to verify details like proper code signing and valid icon files. You can run these checks without submitting the app by using the **Validate...** button, shown in Figure 26.14. You can use this button at any time after the app's entry has been created in iTunes Connect, even if you're not ready to submit the app yet.

If the app passes validation, you're ready to go! Click **Submit...** to begin the upload process. Xcode will prompt you to log in to your iTunes Connect account (Figure 26.15).

Once you have logged in to iTunes Connect, Xcode prompts you for your Application ID and code signing information. The Application popup menu is populated based on the apps in your account that are in the Waiting for Upload stage. If you see No Value in the Application popup (as shown in Figure 26.16), make sure that you have completed the process described earlier for creating an app entry in iTunes Connect.

As with the iTunes Connect Web site, Xcode walks you through the rest of the upload process.

Next: Take a well-earned break. Writing apps is hard, and you deserve a rest.

Going Further

Or perhaps not.

One common misconception is that all you need to do to sell an app is get it into the App Store. However, in case you haven't been keeping score, there are over

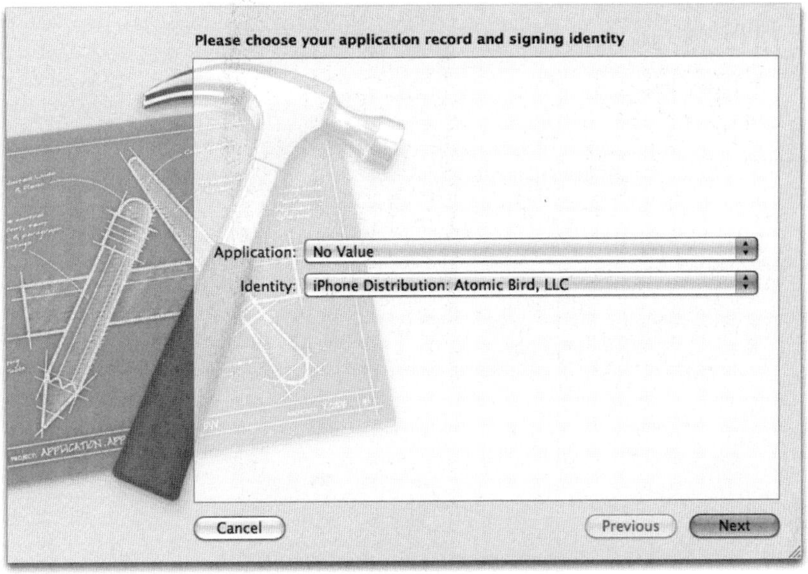

Figure 26.16   Choosing the Application and code signing Identity

500,000 apps in the App Store. Even a great app is going to get lost in that crowd if you don't take some extra steps to get your app noticed.

Marketing and promotion are a major part of what makes some apps more successful than others. Technical aspects are vitally important but are not sufficient to turn a great app idea into a successful app. An app needs a good Web site that provides more information than the App Store, including demo videos when possible. That's just the minimum, though. If you're not experienced in promoting apps, a good start is Dave Wooldridge and Michael Schneider's book *The Business of iPhone App Development* (Apress, 2010). Don't neglect this step, or your app may languish in obscurity regardless of how compelling or well written it may be.

Summary

In this chapter you have gone from having an app that you can run on your own iPad to having one that you can share with testers and release to the world. The steps sometimes seem convoluted, but they're the last steps leading to a real app that people around the world can download and use. Building and releasing an app is a big deal and can be a lot of work. But if it were easy, everyone would do it.

You did it! Congratulations!

The Final Word

Whew! You made it to the end of the book. You can confidently say you are an iPad programmer, but more important, you can say you are an iOS programmer. See, without you knowing it, we have surreptitiously taught you all the key things you'll need to launch your career as an iOS developer. While you have been building Photo-Wheel, you may not have noticed that we have shown you how to

- Effectively use Xcode and Interface Builder (Chapters 2 and 3)
- Master Objective-C (Chapter 4)
- Program with Cocoa Touch (Chapter 5)
- Build user interfaces with a storyboard (Chapter 14)
- Leverage Core Data (Chapter 13) and iCloud syncing (Chapter 22)
- Create multi-touch gestures (Chapter 11)
- Build custom views (Chapters 10 and 16)
- Use view controllers (Chapter 15) and perform custom view transitions (Chapters 15 and 17)
- Make use of scroll views in different ways (Chapters 16 and 17)
- Add print (Chapter 19) and email (Chapter 20) capabilities to your apps
- Incorporate AirPlay into your apps (Chapter 23)
- Apply image filters and effects using Core Image (Chapter 24)
- Diagnose and fix bugs in your apps (Chapter 25)
- Hook into Web services from your apps (Chapter 21)
- Prepare your apps for submission to the App Store (Chapter 26)

You can use this list as a guide for when you're working on projects in the future. For example, if you need to work with Core Data, you can flip to Chapter 13 for a refresher. Need to add multi-touch gesture support for your app? There's a chapter for that, Chapter 11. The best part of all of this is that you have built an app from start to finish, from concept to App Store submission. Congratulations!

What's Next

This book serves as a jump start for you becoming an iOS programmer, but there is so much more to learn, especially if being an iOS programmer is a career choice for you. Here are some things you can do to become an even better iOS programmer:

- Continue reading books. A list of recommended books is available at **learnipadprogramming.com/recommended-books/**.

- Search and participate in online forums such as the Apple Developer Forums (**devforums.apple.com**) and StackOverflow (**stackoverflow.com**).

- Read blog sites such as *Cocoa Is My Girlfriend* (**www.cimgf.com**), *iPhone Development* (**iphonedevelopment.blogspot.com**), and Ray Wenderlich's *Tutorials for iOS Developers* (**raywenderlich.com**).

- Attend conferences such as Apple's WWDC (**developer.apple.com/wwdc/**), 360|iDev (**360idev.com**), Voices That Matter (**voicesthatmatter.com**), and NSConference (**nsconference.com**).

- Attend local meet-ups and developer gatherings such as CocoaHeads (**cocoaheads.org**) and NSCoder Night (**nscodernight.com**).

And, most important, **always keep learning**.

We wish you all the best, and we can't wait to hear about and see the many cool and exciting apps you will build. You can send your questions, comments, and anything else you would like to share with us to Kirby@whitepeaksoftware.com and tph@atomicbird.com.

A

Installing the Developer Tools

Before you can write your first iPad application, you need the developer's tools. The developer tools consist of everything you need to write iOS and Mac OS X applications, including the integrated development environment (IDE) called Xcode; the user interface designer called Interface Builder; the compiler compatible for compiling C, C++, and Objective-C code; the debugger for debugging your code; and Instruments, a tool for tracking memory leaks and profiling your application. A handful of other really useful tools are also included. Collectively the developer tools are called Xcode, with the Xcode IDE being the primary tool in the arsenal.

Xcode is available for free from the Mac App Store. It's also available for download to members of the iOS Developer Program, which costs $99 per year.

Which is the better option for you? If you are curious about iPad and iPhone programming and do not wish to spend any money up front, download Xcode from the Mac App Store. After all, it is free. On the other hand, if you are serious about writing apps for iOS, you need to join the iOS Developer Program. Membership provides benefits that you do not get by simply downloading Xcode from the Mac App Store.

Membership Has Its Privileges

As a member of the iOS Developer Program, not only do you have access to the development tools (Xcode), but you also have access to a slew of resources that are invaluable to iOS developers. These resources include access to sample code, how-to videos, recent WWDC session videos, and Apple's own Developer Forums (**devforums.apple.com**). Members also have access to the latest beta versions of iOS and Xcode. But even more important, only members of the iOS Developer Program can have their apps installed on a real device.

This means that you must be a member of the Developer Program if you wish to run and test your app on an iPad or iPhone. You must also be a member if you wish to distribute your app. This includes Ad Hoc distribution and distribution through the App Store (see Chapter 26, "Distributing Your App," for more information). Without a membership to the iOS Developer Program you will be limited to running and testing your app through the simulator.

> **Note**
>
> iOS Developer Program members should consider downloading Xcode from the Mac App Store as well. Apple frequently has beta versions of Xcode available to members, and you can have multiple versions of Xcode installed at the same time. Download Xcode from the Mac App Store to ensure that you always have the latest official release of Xcode installed in the default location (*/Developer* on your hard drive), and manually install beta versions of Xcode in a separate location, such as */DeveloperBeta*.

Joining the iOS Developer Program

When you join the iOS Developer Program, you choose from three program types: Standard Individual, Standard Company, or Enterprise. Which type you choose depends on your needs and purpose. The differences are listed in Table A.1.

> **Note**
>
> There is a fourth program type, University, which is available only to higher educational institutions looking to include iOS development in their curriculum. The University program type is not covered in this book.

> **Note**
>
> You can register as an Apple Developer for free at **developer.apple.com/programs/register/**. As a registered Apple Developer, you have access to the public releases of Xcode and some resources in the Dev Center, but you still cannot test your apps on devices or distribute your app to others.

Which Program Type Is Right for You?

Choosing the right program type is important because changing program types in the future can be a bit troublesome. Companies wishing to deploy proprietary in-house apps to employees can join the Enterprise Program. A Dun & Bradstreet number is required for this program type. Individuals and companies wishing to sell their applications through the App Store should select either the Standard Individual or Standard Company option. Standard Individual and Standard Company are the two most commonly selected program types, so let's look at them in more detail.

There is one primary difference between Standard Individual and Standard Company. Standard Company allows you to create development teams. You can add team programmers to the account at no additional cost. A team programmer has access to all the same resources as a Standard Individual. You can add and remove team members at any time, which is handy when you are hiring new iOS programmers or rolling off contract programmers after finishing a project.

Table A.1   iOS Developer Program Benefits

	Registered Apple Developer	Standard Individual	Standard Company	Enterprise Program	University Program
Price	Free	$99 per year	$99 per year	$299 per year	Free
Dev Center Resources	Yes (but limited)	Yes	Yes	Yes	Yes
iOS SDK	Yes	Yes	Yes	Yes	Yes
Prerelease Software and Tools		Yes	Yes	Yes	
Ability to Create Development Teams			Yes	Yes	Yes
Access to the Apple Developer Forums		Yes	Yes	Yes	Yes
Technical Support Incidents		2 per membership year	2 per membership year	2 per membership year	
Test on Devices (iPod touch, iPhone, and iPad)		Yes	Yes	Yes	Yes
Ad Hoc Distribution		Yes	Yes	Yes	
In-House Distribution				Yes	
App Store Distribution		Yes	Yes		

> **Note**
>
> An individual can be a team programmer for one or more Standard Company accounts while still having her own account. For instance, I sell my own iPhone and iPad apps, so I enrolled my company under the Standard Company program type. I also do contract programming, which means I am also a Team Member for other companies. When I log in to the iOS Development Center Web site, I am asked to select which team I wish to use for the current session, as seen in Figure A.1.

The general rule of thumb to follow when deciding what program type is right for you is this: If you are an individual with no plans to set up a company, sign up as an individual. If you are already set up as a company, even if you are a one-person company, sign up as a company. If you sign up an individual and decide later to set up a company presence, you can change your program type. It will involve talking with Apple and it may take time to transition program types, but it is possible. And if you represent a company with a D-U-N-S number and you need to distribute apps in-house only, sign up for the Enterprise Program.

What You Need to Register

Collecting the required registration information before beginning the process will help speed up registration. Table A.2 lists the basic information you will need. Free feel to make a copy of this table and use it as a worksheet.

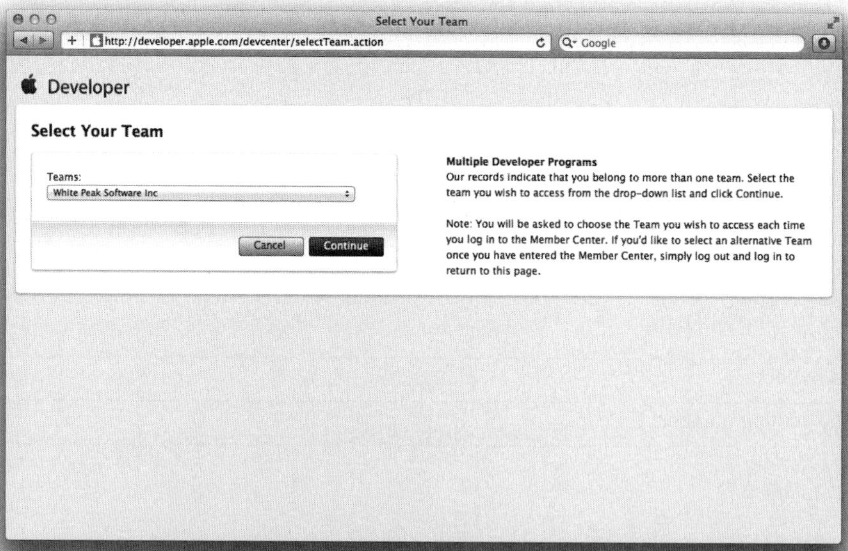

Figure A.1   The Select Your Team prompt is displayed during the login process when you are a member of multiple teams.

> **Note**
>
> The information listed in Table A.2 is based on registration within the United States. Information required may differ in other countries.

Table A.2   **Information Needed to Complete the Apple Developer and iOS Developer Program Registration**

Personal Profile	
Apple ID (Create a new one or use an existing ID.)	
Password	
Birth date	
Security question and answer (for password recovery, etc.)	
Name (account holder's name)	
Email address	
Company or organization name	
Mailing address (street, city, state, ZIP code)	
Telephone number	
If you plan to sell your app and/or use iAds	
Taxpayer identification number (SSN or EIN in the United States)	
Legal entity name (your name, company name, DBA, etc.)	
Address (street, city, state, ZIP code)	
Company contacts (name and contact information for senior management, finance, technical, legal, and promotions; can be the same person)	
Banking Information	
Bank country	
ABA routing number	
Bank name	
Bank account number	
Account holder name	
Bank account type	
Bank account currency	

Create or Use an Existing Apple ID

Apple recommends that you create a new Apple ID if you are enrolling in the iOS Developer Program for business purposes. This is good advice if you are an employee setting up an account for the company you work for. Apple also recommends setting up a different Apple ID if you currently have an iTunes account to avoid potential accounting and reporting issues. As an indie developer, I use my iTunes account as my Apple ID for the iOS Developer Program and I have not experienced any issues. However, your mileage may vary.

Downloading Xcode

There are two options for downloading Xcode. Option 1 is to download it through the Mac App Store. Just search for "Xcode" and download it as you would any other app available in the Mac App Store.

Option 2 is to visit and sign in to the iOS Dev Center (**developer.apple.com/ios/**). From there you can download the latest release of Xcode, including the beta version if available (and only if you are a paid member of the Developer Program).

> **Note**
>
> The Xcode download file tends to be rather large, weighing in at just over 3GB, so the download will likely take more than a few minutes to complete.

Installing Xcode

If you downloaded Xcode through the Mac App Store, launch the installer app by selecting it from Launchpad or from the icon available in the Dock. This performs a default install of Xcode. If you wish to perform a custom install—for example, to select the destination directory—you must download Xcode from the Dev Center.

If you have downloaded Xcode through the Dev Center, you will find the Xcode *.dmg* file in your *Downloads* directory. Open the *Downloads* directory in Finder and double-click the Xcode disk image. This will mount the image on your system. Double-click the Xcode and iOS SDK package found in the disk image to begin the installation process.

The installer guides you through the steps of installing Xcode and the iOS SDK. Generally, you will accept the installer's default settings. The install process needs approximately 8GB of drive space.

> **Note**
>
> I recommend having at least 12GB of available space. I have found that the install process tends to run slower when there is limited available space on the hard drive.

The time it takes for the installer to complete the installation will vary based on machine type, CPU speed, available hard drive space, and available RAM. Approximately 10 to 20 minutes seems to be the norm.

Note

It is perfectly safe, and recommended, to install the latest version of Xcode on top of a previous version of Xcode, assuming you no longer need the previous version. It is, however, possible to have multiple versions of Xcode installed on the same machine.

I tend to install the public release of Xcode in the default directory (*/Developer*) and beta versions of newer Xcode releases in a separate directory (*/DeveloperBeta*). The install location is an option you can change during the install guide, as seen in Figure A.2. Note, however, that the install location cannot be changed in the Mac App Store version.

Congratulations! Xcode is now installed on your system. You can find all of the tools in the *Developer* folder at the root of your hard drive (*/Developer*), and Xcode is found in */Developer/Applications*. You can launch Xcode by clicking the Xcode icon in the Dock or in Launchpad.

Tip

If Xcode is not in your Dock, open Finder, navigate to */Developer/Applications*, and drag the Xcode icon to your Dock.

You are now ready to begin writing your first iOS application.

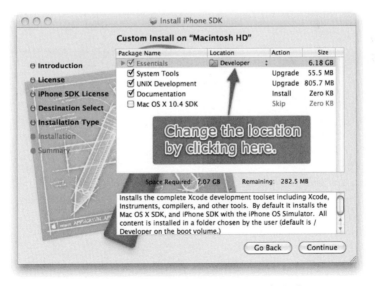

Figure A.2   Xcode is installed in */Developer* by default, but you can change the location during the install guide.

Index

Developer's Library

ESSENTIAL REFERENCES FOR PROGRAMMING PROFESSIONALS

**Objective-C Phrasebook,
Second Edition**

David Chisnall

ISBN-13: 978-0-321-81375-6

**The iOS 5 Developer's
Cookbook, Third Edition**

Erica Sadun

ISBN-13: 978-0-321-75426-4

**Programming in
Objective-C,
Fourth Edition**

Stephen G. Kochan

ISBN-13: 978-0-321-81190-5

Other Developer's Library Titles

TITLE	AUTHOR	ISBN-13
Android™ Wireless Application Development, Second Edition	Lauren Darcey / Shane Conder	978-0-321-74301-5
Cocoa® Programming Developer's Handbook	David Chisnall	978-0-321-63963-9
Cocoa Design Patterns	Erik M. Buck / Donald A. Yacktman	978-0-321-53502-3
PHP and MySQL® Web Development, Fourth Edition	Luke Welling / Laura Thomson	978-0-672-32916-6

Developer's Library books are available at most retail and online bookstores. For more information or to order direct, visit our online bookstore at **informit.com/store**.

Online editions of all Developer's Library titles are available by subscription from Safari Books Online at **safari.informit.com**.

Addison
Wesley

**Developer's
Library**

informit.com/devlibrary

Essential Resources for Mac and iOS Developers

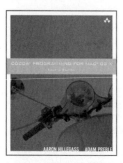

LEARNING iPad
PROGRAMMING
A Hands-On Guide to Building iPad Apps with iOS 5

KIRBY TURNER
TOM HARRINGTON
Foreword by Mark Dalrymple

FREE
Online Edition

Safari
Books Online

Your purchase of *Learning iPad Programming* includes access to a free online edition for 45 days through the **Safari Books Online** subscription service. Nearly every Addison-Wesley Professional book is available online through **Safari Books Online**, along with thousands of books and videos from publishers such as Cisco Press, Exam Cram, IBM Press, O'Reilly Media, Prentice Hall, Que, and Sams.

Safari Books Online is a digital library providing searchable, on-demand access to thousands of technology, digital media, and professional development books and videos from leading publishers. With one monthly or yearly subscription price, you get unlimited access to learning tools and information on topics including mobile app and software development, tips and tricks on using your favorite gadgets, networking, project management, graphic design, and much more.

Activate your FREE Online Edition at
informit.com/safarifree

STEP 1: Enter the coupon code: VASXNGA.

STEP 2: New Safari users, complete the brief registration form.
Safari subscribers, just log in.

If you have difficulty registering on Safari or accessing the online edition,
please e-mail customer-service@safaribooksonline.com

Addison
Wesley   AdobePress   ALPHA   Cisco Press   FT Press   IBM Press.   Microsoft Press   New Riders   O'REILLY

Peachpit Press   PRENTICE HALL   Que   Redbooks   SAMS   SAS Publishing   WILEY   wrox